Fodor's 2002

London

Fodor's Travel Publications • New York, Toronto, London, Sydney, Auckland

CONTENTS

MAPS

Circled letters in text correspond to letters on the photographs. For more information on the sights pictured, turn to the indicated page number Ⓐ⟩ on each photograph.

A hundred movies and *Masterpiece Theater* productions have prepared you for London's quintessentially British brew of history, royalty, dignity, and civility. Even before you arrive, its images are imprinted on your consciousness. The dome of St. Paul's is iconically familiar. So are the Tower Guards, Big Ben, and the Thames. Walk along its light-strung promenade at dusk before an

DESTINATION LONDON

evening of theater, after a day of shopping or palace-hopping, and you'll understand why so many visitors have so loved the city for so long, since before the nursery-rhyme bridge fell down—and why, of all the world's travel destinations, London may be the most revisited.

After the Great Fire of 1666, London's dominant architectural element was the charred beam. But then, upon the city's

ARCHITECTURE

ashes, Sir Christopher Wren fashioned a new city and left a mark that seems indelible, if only because of his Ⓐ**St. Paul's Cathedral,** whose majestic dome humbles all modern buildings nearby. Of late, architecture has become a hot topic among Londoners, who are fortunate heirs to a rich legacy in stone that includes Westminster Cathedral, Ⓒ**Westminster Abbey,** the Ⓔ**Royal Courts of Justice,** and the Houses of Parliament, whose clock tower holds Ⓓ**Big Ben.** Prince Charles is a keen critic, a fervent advocate of the traditional. Members of the architecture establishment sometimes roll their eyes at his pronouncements (and if they *like* the prince, bite their tongues). The modern and postmodern booms sweeping the city have kindled heated

Ⓑ 90

debates. Most Londoners, however, admire buildings such as the Ⓑ**Lloyd's of London** headquarters created by the same Richard Rogers who designed the Millennium Dome in Greenwich and set the French to quarreling over the Pompidou Center. With its complex structure boldly arrayed on the outside, it's a cool

Ⓒ 54

PARLIAMENT
STREET SW1

Toilets

setting for so august an institution. Sir Norman Foster's Millennium Bridge connecting St.
Paul's Cathedral with the new
Tate Modern quite literally
brings together the old and
the new. But that, too, is London for you: traditional and
edgy at the same time.

Ⓔ 82

ROYAL
LONDON

Trappings of royalty set London apart not only from the rest of Britain but from all the cities of the world. Even in places such as Stockholm and Madrid, where kings and queens still make a living embodying their nation's heritage, royals are simply not such a big deal. Almost more than any other people, the English nurture an emotional investment in their sovereigns and the proud legacy they represent—despite the controversy that rages over the viability of the monarchy. Britons still snap up tabloids when royals are in the headlines, congregate for processions of the Royal Livery from the Ⓐ**Royal Mews,** and throng the streets on the Queen's birthday for the parade known as Trooping the Colour. Pilgrimlike, they visit Ⓑ**Kensington Palace,** former home of Diana, Princess of Wales. The royal warrant in the windows of fine shops signals

Ⓑ▷128

Ⓐ▷51

Ⓒ▷41

Ⓓ▷42

wares of the highest quality. The royalty connection and the castles, palaces, and collections of paintings left by royals through the centuries fill the imagination of travelers, as well. Who could fail to gawk at the incomparably regal State Dining Room in ©**Buckingham Palace** or to marvel at the Ⓓ**Changing of the Guard** outside? Everyone wants to inspect the splendid Crown Jewels in the Ⓔ Ⓕ**Tower of London,** once the final stop for unlucky royals, children included, on the outs with their kinsmen on the throne. A chat with one of its Yeoman Warders, who have guarded the Tower for 500 years, yields a fascinating look at British history— and gives you a sense of just how much the Crown has meant through the centuries to the people of Shakespeare's "sceptered isle."

Ⓔ▷95

Ⓕ▷95

Ⓐ 174

In the 1980s any commentary on dining in London might have ended right about *here*. Today restaurants are London's new passion, and newcomers are always bursting onto the scene, often with amazing chefs hanging their toques in the kitchen. In restaurants such as the ©**Sugar Club,** inventive cuisine is the irresistible draw. Sometimes the setting is as original as the food—that's notably true at South Kensington's Ⓐ**Bibendum** and at Notting Hill's

DINING OUT

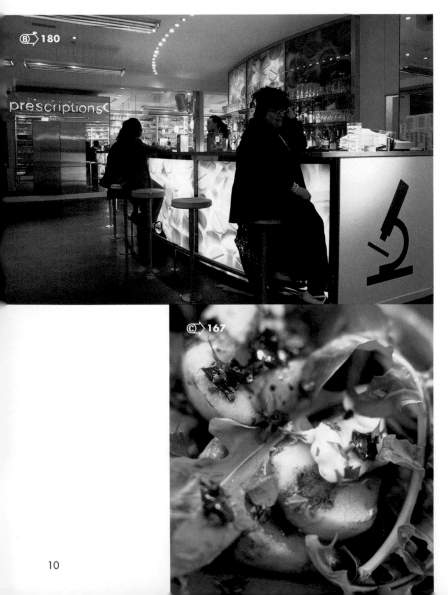

Ⓑ 180

prescriptions

© 167

Ⓓ＞282

Ⓑ**Pharmacy.** Or the glitterati may come for the romance of a stellar panorama like the one at the South Bank's Ⓕ**OXO Tower Brasserie and Restaurant.** Mean-

Ⓔ＞183

while, as gastrodomes serving world cuisines proliferate, local traditions endure. The Savoy Grill remains the power dining room par excellence, Fortnum & Mason's Fountain lives on, endearingly frumpy, and simply excellent fish-and-chips pack 'em in at Ⓔ**Geales,** although it lacks both theme and clever concept. Stylish snacking is everywhere—witness the options at Ⓓ**Leadenhall Market,** a fine Victorian arcade. More than anything else in recent years, London's exuberant food scene has infused the city with excitement and has become one more facet to celebrate.

Ⓕ＞183

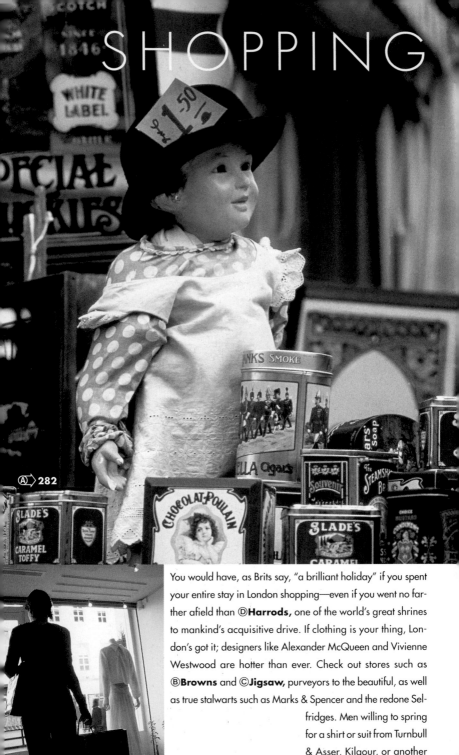

SHOPPING

Ⓐ▷ **282**

Ⓑ▷ **270**

You would have, as Brits say, "a brilliant holiday" if you spent your entire stay in London shopping—even if you went no farther afield than Ⓓ**Harrods,** one of the world's great shrines to mankind's acquisitive drive. If clothing is your thing, London's got it; designers like Alexander McQueen and Vivienne Westwood are hotter than ever. Check out stores such as Ⓑ**Browns** and Ⓒ**Jigsaw,** purveyors to the beautiful, as well as true stalwarts such as Marks & Spencer and the redone Selfridges. Men willing to spring for a shirt or suit from Turnbull & Asser, Kilgour, or another of London's bespoke tailors

Ⓒ▷ **266**

place themselves in the hands of true artists—and are treated like peers from first fitting to last. Elegant enclaves like May-fair's Ⓔ**Burlington Arcade** are good places to commission the best suit you'll ever own.

Ⓔ〉 62

Ⓕ〉 276

Ⓐ**Portobello Market,** for many the best of London's famous bazaars, stretches farther than you can see, overflowing with ephemera, silver, porcelain, and other appurtenances of merry old England. For the loveliest shopping experience of all, stop in at Ⓕ**Floris,** whose perfumes were a favorite of Queen Victoria's. If consumerism is allowed in heaven, this is what it must look like.

MUSEUMS
AND MARVELS

Ⓐ▷81

A blizzard of blue plaques all over town proclaims the historic importance of structures as wide-ranging as Dennis Severs's House, the Geffrye Museum, and the Ⓐ**Dickens House Museum** and turn London itself into something of a museum. High culture and low, it's here. The Ⓑ**National Gallery** holds Bronzino's *An Allegory with Venus and Cupid* and a flurry of masterworks that are instantly familiar. Hertford House showcases the splendid Wallace Collection, stuffed

Ⓑ▷47

ⓒ 59

ⓓ 130

with old masters and fine French furniture. Gracious England lives on here and in wonderful stately homes such as Spencer House and Leighton House. If you had defeated Napoléon, saving Europe in the process, you might have hung your medals in an imposing structure like gilded ©**Apsley House** (where the Duke of Wellington's trophies remain). Farther afield are Chiswick House and Ham House, and Ⓔ**Hampton Court Palace,** where Henry VIII gamely battled gout and a rotation of subsequent monarchs took up residence, having fallen in love with the place. Visit and you will instantly see why: the grounds are beautiful beyond description, the palace is extraordinary, and, in the best English tradition, it is reputedly frequented by a royal ghost. Sightings are free. Then there's the Ⓓ**Natural History Museum,** very much of the 19th century outside but totally 21st within. Many of its ingenious displays are animated and as delightful to grown-ups as to kids.

Ⓔ 154

15

MUSEUMS
AND MARVELS

Of all of London's great museums, the ⒻBritish Museum is preeminent. Think of it as a jumbo time capsule. The full scope of human endeavor is represented here, including the Rosetta Stone and the Sutton Hoo Treasure, as well as such exquisite, if controversial, treasures of antiquity as the Elgin Marbles of ancient Greece. Impressive in its own right is the ⒽVictoria and Albert Museum, whose

Ⓗ ▷ 131

whimsically eclectic collections might someday, conceivably, include a hat from one of the schoolchildren who tour it regularly. At the Tate Gallery's renovated Millbank site, ⒾTate Britain focuses on British artists, displaying art from the past five centuries together in theme galleries. As a break from sheer beauty or just to see what attracts millions every year, make a beeline for ⒼMadame Tussaud's and commune with a forever-young and toothy Dudley Moore and dozens of other celebrities both dead and alive.

A 134

If you spend all your time in central London, you'll go home having seen . . . central London. A stroll in one of the city's many neighborhoods makes a fine break from more purposeful sightseeing. Each has its attitude and style: Knightsbridge and Kens-

CITY OF VILLAGES

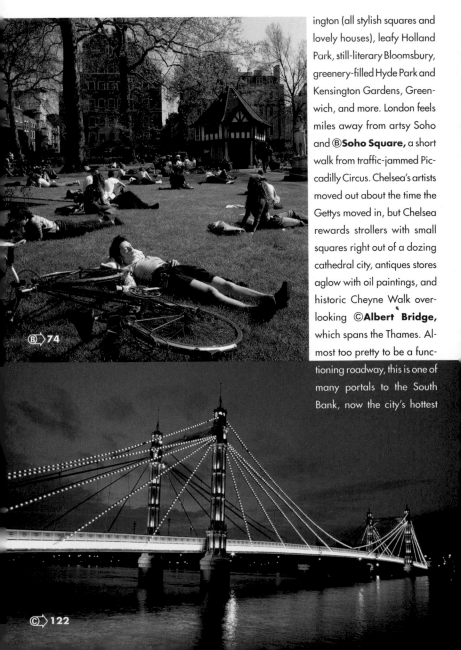

B 74

ington (all stylish squares and lovely houses), leafy Holland Park, still-literary Bloomsbury, greenery-filled Hyde Park and Kensington Gardens, Greenwich, and more. London feels miles away from artsy Soho and B**Soho Square,** a short walk from traffic-jammed Piccadilly Circus. Chelsea's artists moved out about the time the Gettys moved in, but Chelsea rewards strollers with small squares right out of a dozing cathedral city, antiques stores aglow with oil paintings, and historic Cheyne Walk overlooking C**Albert Bridge,** which spans the Thames. Almost too pretty to be a functioning roadway, this is one of many portals to the South Bank, now the city's hottest

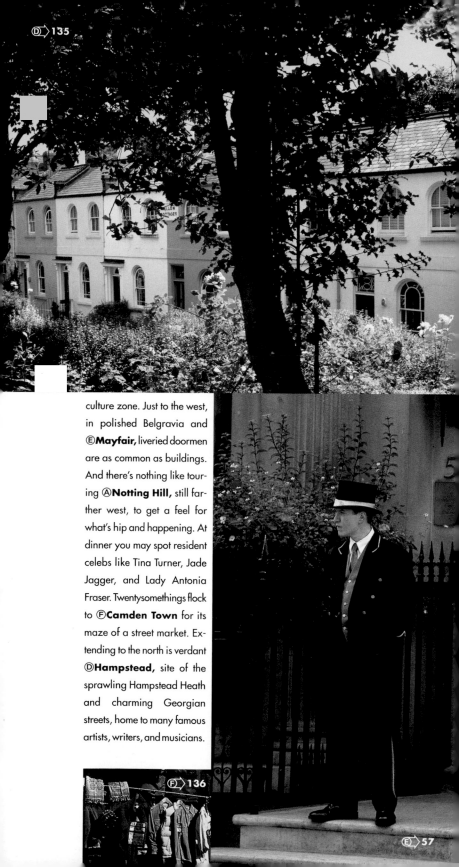

culture zone. Just to the west, in polished Belgravia and ⒺMayfair, liveried doormen are as common as buildings. And there's nothing like touring ⒶNotting Hill, still farther west, to get a feel for what's hip and happening. At dinner you may spot resident celebs like Tina Turner, Jade Jagger, and Lady Antonia Fraser. Twentysomethings flock to ⒻCamden Town for its maze of a street market. Extending to the north is verdant ⒹHampstead, site of the sprawling Hampstead Heath and charming Georgian streets, home to many famous artists, writers, and musicians.

Ⓕ 136

Ⓐ 151

Londoners love greenery and flowers—madly, if you consider the acreage devoted to things horticultural. Parks are said to be a city's lungs; in London they are also the city's heart—abloom, successively, with crocuses, azaleas, rhododendrons, daffodils, tulips, lilacs, roses, water lilies, and heather. In May don't miss the prestigious Chelsea Flower Show. Of all London's green spaces, the best known may be Ⓕ**Hyde Park,** whose famed Speaker's Corner, with its soapbox orators, can bring out the heckler in any-

PARKS AND GARDENS

Ⓑ 51

Ⓒ 51

body. ⒶKew Gardens is a mandatory stop for all those who, back home, enjoy getting soil under their fingernails. Its sprawling Royal Botanic Gardens both dazzle and edify.

By Buckingham Palace, and property of the monarchy, ⒷSt. James's Park is a favorite of bird lovers (some bird lovers become favorites of the birds). You'll even find pelicans here. In adjoining ⒸGreen Park, also part of the Queen's backyard, daffodils rule in spring. On summer days, Londoners love to laze the afternoon away in ⒹRegent's Park. The formal, fountained Italian parterres at ⒺKensington Gardens are perhaps a touch exotic, think Brits, who favor the more natural look of the English garden (after all, they invented it).

Several nations have monarchs. Many nations play cricket (some better than England). But none comes close to matching the most British institution of all: the pub. Sir Arthur Conan Doyle used to unwind from mystery writing at what is now the ®**Sherlock Holmes.** If Charles Dickens had frequented all the pubs claiming him for a patron, he would have died young and unpublished. (The ®**George Inn** is one that can truly call him

PUBS

its own.) Pubs are the seat of England's soul, and in London there's a local on every corner, with names charming enough to inspire pub crawls—the

©➤190

Crown and Goose, Ye Olde Cheshire Cheese, the Ⓐ**Lamb & Flag,** the Ⓒ**Albert,** Jack Straw's Castle. By all means, try meeting the English in a pub. Nowhere else do you get to know them so well. Think of the pub as a common hearthside, where locals, sometimes with kids in tow, come to affirm community. In summer, when some pub keepers set up tables on the sidewalk or in a patio or garden, you may also think of the pub as a community park that serves refreshments. Thick, chocolatey stout or bitter, served warm, may be an acquired taste, even when gently brewed the traditional way, but most travelers acquire it quickly, and pub grub—hearty fare like shepherd's pie and often, lately, more ambitious cuisine—enhances the experience.

Ⓓ➤190

ARTS AND
NIGHTLIFE

If London dazzles you by day, wait till the sun goes down. Many travelers come specifically for theater vacations, cramming into a few days as many shows as they might see in a few years back home. The sheer number of productions in the district known as the ⒶWest End makes this possible. Reasonable ticket prices help, too. And Shakespeare lives: in summer, productions of his plays are a cherished tradition at Ⓑ**Regent's Park Open-Air Theatre** and are becoming so at the reconstructed Globe on the South Bank. Audiences at the Globe experience living history as well as great drama. The theater clones the Elizabethan original, right down to the standing-room pit, and the Bard's work (and his humor) seem all the more topical. Also in summer, between July and September, ticket prices are slashed at Ⓒ**Royal Albert Hall** for its Proms series. Then and during the rest of the year, performances by local and international musicians fill the concert calendar, divas draw sellout crowds, and dancers of the Royal Ballet, English National Ballet, and other stellar companies jeté across a handful of stages. As for nightlife, the scene ranges from casinos to karaoke, comedy to drag cabarets, heavy metal to world-beat clubs, and there's plenty of good jazz. Think of it like this: when you dance all night at clubs like Ⓓ**Sound,** you get an early start on your next London day.

Ⓑ▷**241**

Ⓒ▷**238**

Ⓓ▷**229**

GREAT ITINERARIES

London in 5 Days

In a city with as many richly stocked museums and match-less marvels as London, you risk seeing half of everything or all of nothing. So use the efficient itineraries below to keep you on track as you explore both the famous sights and those off the beaten path. Although you'll need those familiar red double-decker buses and the Underground to cover long distances, you'll soon discover how London rewards those who stroll its streets. So

that you don't show up somewhere and find you've missed the boat, shuffle the itinerary segments with the closing hours, listed below, in mind.

DAY 1

Spend your first day in Royal London, which contains much that is historic and traditional in British life. Beat the crowds and get an early start at magnifi-cent, medieval West-minster Abbey—if Prince Charles becomes king, this is where he will be crowned. After an hour exploring the abbey, make the 15-minute walk (or tube it from Westminster to St. James's Park) to catch the Chang-ing of the Guard at 11:20, outside (A)Buckingham Palace. Don't dawdle—optimally you need to get there by 10:45. In season an alterna-

© 45

tive option is to tour Buck House itself, as the British quippingly call it. Next stroll down the Mall, enjoying the very view the monarch sees when she rides in her gilded coach to open Parliament every year. Passing King George IV's glorious Carlton House Terrace, walk through the Admiralty Arch into Trafalgar Square, the very center of the city. Spend an hour or two in the National Gallery, the finest art museum in the land. If you're interested in history or you'll have time on another day for the National Gallery, go instead to nearby St. Martin's Place and the National Portrait Gallery, a visual who's who of England. From Trafalgar Square, head south to Whitehall, which is lined with grand government buildings, the Baroque-era Banqueting House, outside of which King Charles I was beheaded, and the Horse Guards Parade (Her Majesty's mounted guardsmen make a great photo-op). Head past 10 Downing Street—the Prime

Tuesday or Wednesday. But remember that from August through March, the Changing of the Guard (usually a daily event) occurs only every other day; check schedules before you plan. Buckingham Palace is open daily in season—from late August to early October. When the Houses of Parliament are open to visitors, the House of Lords is closed from Thursday to Sunday, the House of Commons from Friday to Sunday; optimal times are complex, so check the Houses of Parliament schedule in Chapter 1. On Sunday the Banqueting House is closed, and Westminster Abbey (except for the museum) is open only to those attending services.

DAY 2

Think of this day as London 101—a tour of the city's postcard sights. Begin at the ⑧British Museum—home to the Elgin Marbles, Rosetta Stone, and the Sutton Hoo Treasure—and explore the adjacent treasures of bookish Bloomsbury, including the

wark; stop at Tate Modern art gallery or take in a play at Shakespeare's Globe, the most famous theater in the world. At day's end, journey along old Father Thames east to Le Pont de la Tour or west to the OXO Tower to enjoy a riverside dinner with London spectacularly illuminated at your feet.
☺ Don't plan on doing day 2 on Sunday, when both the Dickens House Museum and Sir John Soane's Museum are closed. Note that Shakespeare's Globe stages plays in the open-air theater only from May to September.

DAY 3

Explore St. James's and Mayfair, the core of London's West End, the smartest and most atmospheric central area of the city. From Piccadilly Circus go west on Piccadilly to splurge on breakfast at the Queen's grocers, Fortnum & Mason.
For a brush with royalty,

Fleet St. • St. Paul's Cathedral

Blackfriars

THE CITY

Blackfriars Bridge • River Thames

OXO Tower • Tate Modern • Shakespeare's Globe Theatre

Southwark St.

SOUTHWARK

Tooley St. • Tower Bridge

Le Pont de la Tour

Minister's residence—to the Houses of Parliament. To see them, you have two options: either wait in line for the limited seats available in the Strangers Gallery of either house (use the St. Stephen's Entrance opposite the abbey), or prebook a tour, which shows off all the State Rooms. Eventually you'll hear ©Big Ben signaling the approaching dinner hour, just in time for your reservation at Rules, London's most beautiful restaurant, and a feast in the same salon where Lillie Langtry and the Prince of Wales once dined.
☺ It's best to do this tour on

Dickens House Museum and the British Library (on Euston Road, 10 blocks north), then perhaps track the spirit of Virginia Woolf on verdant Bedford, Russell, and Bloomsbury squares. Now head southeast toward the Thames to visit the Regency delight that is Sir John Soane's Museum at Lincoln's Inn. Continue south to Fleet Street, then east to 17th-century St. Paul's Cathedral, the city's presiding spirit. Wander south through the crooked streets of Blackfriars to Blackfriars Bridge and cross the Thames to South-

maybe even with Wills and Harry, detour several blocks to Prince Charles's Tudor-era home, St. James's Palace near St. James's Square, then continue on to palatial Spencer House, once home to the ancestors of the late Princess of Wales. From Piccadilly travel north for some ritzy window-shopping on Bond Street, in the 19th-century Burlington Arcade, and along Savile Row, continuing on through beautiful Mayfair via Mount Street,

Carlos Place—tea at the Connaught Hotel, anyone?—and Grosvenor Square. From here take Duke Street north to view the Fragonards and Halses at the Wallace Collection on Manchester Square. Keep going south to Park Lane and just before Hyde Park Corner visit Apsley House, flanked by the Wellington Arch and a statue of Achilles pointing to the Duke's time-burnished mansion. To the southwest is the splendidly aristocratic enclave of Belgravia, London at its most *Upstairs, Downstairs.* ☺ *Apsley House is closed on Monday and Spencer House is open only on Sunday.*

DAY 4

London legends populate this itinerary. First take a break from the city and travel up to its most famous "village,"

tube stop to pick up a spine-chilling Jack the Ripper Mystery Walk through the East End.
☺ *Note that the East End Jack the Ripper tours begin at 7 PM.*

Brompton Road for lunch in Knightsbridge and shopping at Harrods or Harvey Nichols. Afterward you can go north or south. To the north, in Kensington Gardens, you can salute the Peter Pan statue, then visit historic Kensington Palace, childhood home of Queen Victoria and repository of the Royal Dress

Hampstead. After taking in the picturesque houses, chic cafés, and Church Row—London's most complete Georgian street—move on to (if you're a Beatlemaniac) Abbey Road, in nearby St. John's Wood. Then tube it down to Baker Street, visit the Sherlock Holmes Museum or Madame Tussaud's (a must for kids), then go north to Regent's Park and its swooningly elegant Cumberland Terrace and Chester Terrace (*101 Dalmatians'* Dearly family, the "pets" of Pongo and Perdita, lived here on the Outer Circle). In the afternoon take the tube to Tower Hill and the legendary Ⓓ Tower of London to see the Crown Jewels and the eight Tower Ravens. At dusk cross the street to the Tower Hill

DAY 5

This segment of your itinerary is all about shopping, history, and priceless art. Begin at the "museum mile" of South Kensington. See either the Victoria and Albert Museum, or, if you have children in tow, opt for the Natural History Museum or the Science Museum. Head up

Collection. Continuing on Kensington High Street to Holland Park you will come to Leighton House, home of the noted 19th-century orientalist painter Lord Leighton. Have dinner in sassy and sophisticated Notting Hill. Alternatively from Knightsbridge you might head south to historic Chelsea to charming Cheyne Walk and the Tate Britain. If you go this route you can

Map labels:
To Hampstead, Church Row
Abbey Road
ST. JOHN'S WOOD
St. John's Wood Tube Station
Abbey Rd.
St. John's Wood Rd.
REGENT'S PARK
Cumberland Terrace
Chester Terrace
York Terrace
Great Portland Street Tube Station
Baker Street Tube Station
Marylebone
Baker St.
Madame Tussaud's Wax Museum
Sherlock Holmes Museum
MARYLEBONE
BAYSWATER
MAYFAIR
ST. JAMES PARK
Notting Hill Gate
Notting Hill
Kensington Palace
Peter Pan Statue
Kensington Gardens
HOLLAND PARK
Holland Park
Kensington High St.
KENSINGTON
Kensington Rd.
KNIGHTSBRIDGE
Harvey Nichols
Harrods
Brompton Rd.
Sloane St.
BELGRAVIA
Leighton House
Science Museum
Victoria and Albert Museum
Natural History Museum
BROMPTON
SOUTH KENSINGTON
Kings Rd.
Chelsea
PIMLICO
Chelsea Embankment
Cheyne Walk

ensure a gala finale for your stay by booking tickets to a play or musical in the West End's Theatreland. But by now you will have learned that London is the most wonderful free show in the world.

🕐 Any day but Tuesday you can tour Leighton House.

If You Have More Time

Spectacular day trips lie upriver and down. Easily reachable by boat along the Thames to the east is Greenwich, with attractions such as the *Cutty Sark*, a 19th-century clipper, and the not-to-be-missed National Maritime Museum. Westward on the Thames from London lie destinations that take you back, not forward, in

tube or a taxi to Hyde Park Circle to see one of London's most spectacular town houses, Apsley House. You're in posh Mayfair now, so stroll to the Burlington Arcade and Bond Street for some world-class shopping, then head north to view the treasures at the Wallace Collection. From Marble Arch take the tube to Kensington High Street and Kensington Palace. After touring the historic palace, repair to its Orangery for tea and a well-deserved time-out. Try the best of contemporary British cuisine in nearby Notting Hill or book an evening in Theatreland.

backtrack to Waterloo Pier; if it's raining, tube it from Tower Hill to Waterloo Station). On the way, watch a film at the BFI London IMAX Cinema, ride British Airways London Eye, the world's largest observation wheel, and tour the London Aquarium. At day's end take the tube back to Piccadilly and have tea at Fortnum & Mason.

A Kid's Day Out

Although children can't fly over the town as Peter Pan and Wendy did so thrillingly, this tour will show them a London packed with wonders. Get an early start with a tube ride to the Tower of London, home to the fabled Beefeater guards (plus its eight resident ravens; be sure to say hello to Thor, who talks). Across the street see the lively presentation about the Thames in the Tower Bridge. Cross to the south bank and hang a left toward Butler's Wharf for lunch. If you have teens, stop on Tooley Street at the goriest museum in town: the London Dungeon, a hoot of a horror waxworks show. Recross the river to catch a ferry at Tower Pier for a thrilling 15-minute cruise to Waterloo Pier (or, as far as Westminster Pier, from which you can walk across Westminster Bridge and then

time: Chiswick House, Kew Gardens, Syon House, and the 17th-century Ⓔ Hampton Court Palace, half rose-red Tudor brick, half serenely classical, still buried deep in parkland.

If You Have 3 Days

Touring the largest city in England in the space of three days sounds difficult, but it's long enough to give you a tempting taste of the city. Follow the itineraries for days 1 and 2 above, then begin your third day at the legend-haunted Tower of London. After a morning tour, take the

Ⓔ 154

FODOR'S
CHOICE

Even with so many special places in London, Fodor's writers and editors have their favorites. Here are a few that stand out.

QUINTESSENTIAL LONDON

Afternoon Performance at Shakespeare's Globe. London at its Wellsian time-machine best, this open-to-the-skies reconstruction of Shakespeare's beloved "Wooden O" transports you back to Elizabethan London. ☞ p. 118

Beatles' Magical Mystery Tour. This wonderful stroll down Memory Lane offered by Original London Walks includes the London Palladium, No. 3 Savile Row—the Fab Four's London headquarters—and Abbey Road. Yeah, yeah, yeah! ☞ p. 140

Ⓓ Changing of the Guard. Adding a dash of red to the gloomiest of London days, the colorful regiments of guards march in front of Buckingham Palace as the band plays. ☞ p. 42

ⓒ Houses of Parliament at Sunset. Cross the Thames to Jubilee Gardens to see this view of London at its storybook best. ☞ p. 45

Ⓖ Sunday Afternoon at Speakers' Corner, Hyde Park. A space especially reserved for anyone with anything to say that *must* be said publicly makes for great entertainment. Speakers seem to be most oratorical on Sunday afternoons. ☞ p. 134

Ⓗ Tower Bridge at Night. A dramatically floodlighted Tower Bridge confronts you as you come out of the Design Museum on a winter's night. Have your camera ready. ☞ p. 95

MAGNIFICENT MUSEUMS

Apsley House. Known as No. 1 London, this was the residence of the Duke of Wellington, fabled conqueror of Napoléon. The house's centerpiece, the Waterloo Gallery, is one of the grandest rooms in Europe. ☞ p. 59

Ⓙ British Museum. You could move into this grand pile and never tire of all that it has to offer, from the Rosetta Stone to the sublime Elgin Marbles from ancient Greece. ☞ p. 78

Ⓑ National Gallery. Da Vincis, Rubenses, and Rembrandts fill the rooms here—the richest trove of old-master paintings in Britain. ☞ p. 47

Sir John Soane's Museum. Eccentric architect of the Bank of England, Sir John left his house to the nation on the condition that nothing be changed. The result is a Regency-era phantasmagoria of colors, unusual perspectives, and objets d'art. ☞ p. 82

Spencer House. The London house to end all London houses, this glamorous Palladian mansion was built by Princess Diana's ancestors and proves that even the 18th-century Spencers were no slouches in the flash department. ☞ p. 66

Tate Britain. Works by British artists from the 16th century to the present are on display here and at the Tate's offspring, Tate Modern. ☞ p. 52

LODGING

The Beaufort. Use this set of Victorian houses, run by an all-female staff, as a home away from home, especially if you plan to spend all your time next door at Harrods. ££££ ☞ p. 209

Ⓕ Claridge's. The same fine qualities that attracted the king of Morocco, among many others, to this world-renowned Mayfair hotel are sure to make you feel right at home, too. ££££ ☞ p. 199

Covent Garden Hotel. Discerning travelers now call this the most stylish hotel in London. ££££ ☞ p. 204

The Savoy. Secure a river suite at this historic, late-Victorian hotel overlooking the Thames, and you'll get one of the best stays—and views—in London. ££££ ☞ p. 206

Ⓘ The Pelham. Designed to capture the essence of English country housedom, this boutique hotel is a tranquil country retreat in South Kensington. £££–££££ ☞ p. 213

Dorset Square Hotel. Tim and Kit Kemp, hoteliers extraordinaire, decanted the English country look into a fine pair of Regency town houses and

then turned up the volume in the first of their four London addresses. ££ ☞ p. 202

Abbey House. Rooms at this popular B&B in a pretty, white-stucco Victorian town house—once home to a bishop and an MP—have both washbasins and color TVs. £ ☞ p. 209

DINING

ⒶⒺ La Tante Claire. Pierre Koffmann may be London's best chef, and he is practicing his seemingly effortless art at the Berkeley Hotel. The service is impeccable and the French wine list impressive, but food is the point. ££££ ☞ p. 177

Oak Room. At this Marco Pierre White creation, expect grand style—foie gras, caviar, and truffles—and truly adventurous preparations. ££££ ☞ p. 163

Rules. Come, escape from the 21st century. London's answer to Maxim's in Paris, Rules enjoys an incomparably delicious 19th-century setting, one that has welcomed everyone from Dickens to the Prince of Wales. £££ ☞ p. 171

Le Caprice. This glamorous place has stood the test of time—the food is great, the ambience even better. The other reason everyone comes here is that everyone else does, which leads to the best people-watching in town. ££–£££ ☞ p. 165

The Cow. Notting Hillbillies and other stylish folk adore this luxe "gastro-pub." A serious chef whips up Tuscan-British specialties, but some diners prefer the half-dozen Irish rock oysters with a pint of Guinness. ££ ☞ p. 182

The Eagle. This superior pub, with wooden floors, a few sofas, and art on the walls, serves amazingly good-value Portuguese/Spanish food. £–££ ☞ p. 186

Quality Chop House. The food at this converted greasy spoon is a glorious parody of "caf" food (bangers and mash, egg and chips); the seats resemble Victorian pews. £–££ ☞ p. 184

1   EXPLORING LONDON

If London contained only its landmarks—Buckingham Palace, Big Ben, the Tower of London—it would still rank as one of the world's top destinations. But England's capital is much more. It is a bevy of British bobbies, an ocean of black umbrellas, and an unconquered continuance of more than 2,000 years of history. A city that loves to be explored, London beckons with great museums, royal pageantry, and historic delights. Visit the Duke of Wellington's house or track Jack the Ripper's shadow in Whitechapel. East End, West End, you'll find London is a dickens of a place.

Updated by
Jacqueline
Brown and
Catherine
Belonogoff

L ONDON IS AN ANCIENT CITY whose history greets you at every turn. To gain a sense of its continuity, stand on Waterloo Bridge at the hour of sunset. To the east, the great globe of St. Paul's Cathedral glows golden in the fading sunlight as it has since the 17th century, still majestic amid the towers of glass and steel that hem it in. To the west stand the mock-medieval ramparts of Westminster, home to the "Mother of Parliaments," which has met here or hereabouts since the 1250s. Past them both snakes the swift, dark Thames, as it flowed past the first Roman settlement here nearly 2,000 years ago.

For much of its history, innumerable epigrams and observations have been coined about London by both her enthusiasts and detractors. The great 18th-century writer and wit Samuel Johnson said that a man who is tired of London is tired of life. Oliver Wendell Holmes said, "No person can be said to know London. The most that anyone can claim is that he knows something of it." Simply stated, London is one of the most interesting places on earth. There is no other place like it in its agglomeration of architectural sins and sudden intervention of almost rural sights, in its medley of styles, in its mixture of the green loveliness of parks and the modern gleam of neon. Thankfully, the old London of Queen Anne and Georgian architecture can still be discovered under the hasty routine of later additions.

Discovering it takes a bit of work, however. Modern-day London still largely reflects its medieval layout, a willfully difficult tangle of streets. This swirl of spaghetti will be totally confusing to anyone brought up on the rigidity of a grid system. Even Londoners, most of whom own a copy of the indispensable A–Z street finder (they come under different names), get lost in their own city. But London's bewildering street pattern will be a plus for the visitor who wants to experience its indefinable historic atmosphere. London is a walker's city and will repay every moment you spend exploring on foot. The visitor to London who wants to penetrate beyond the city's crust is well advised to not only visit St. Paul's Cathedral and the Tower but also set aside some of his or her limited time for random wandering. Walk in the back streets and mews around Park Lane and Kensington. Pass up Buckingham Palace for Kew, the smallest royal palace, beautifully situated in the botanical gardens. Take in the National Gallery, but don't forget London's "time machine" museums, such as the 19th-century homes of Linley Sambourne and Sir John Soane. For out-and-out glamour, pay a call on the palatial Wallace Collection and Apsley House, the historic residence of the Duke of Wellington. Abandon the city's standard-issue chain stores to discover unique shopping emporiums, such as the gentlemen's outfitters of St. James's. Getting off the beaten track will help you visualize the shape, or rather the various shapes, of Old London, a curious city that engulfed its own past for the sake of modernity but still lives and breathes the air of history.

Today, that sense of modernity is stronger than ever. Everyone is talking about swinging-again London. It is still, as *Vanity Fair* proclaimed, "the coolest, hottest city in the world." Millennium fever left its trophies on the capital—a panoply of new buildings—and London is now more than ever the *only* place to be, as *Newsweek* declared. The boom economy of the mid-'90s helped the city's art, style, fashion, and dining scenes make headlines around the world. London's chefs have become superstars; its fashion designers have conquered Paris (John Galliano, Alexander McQueen, and Stella McCartney have made their mark at Dior, Givenchy, and Chloë); avant-garde artists have made waves at the august Royal Academy of Arts; the city's raging after-hours scene is packed with music mavens ready to catch the next big thing; and the theater (including the National Theatre) continues its tradition of radical, shocking productions, which barely seem to turn most hairs. Even Shakespeare embraces cool: the Bard's own, reborn Globe—the fabled "wooden O"—is functioning brilliantly on the bank of the Thames just 200 yards from where it stood in the 16th century; when the troupe here presented *Two Gentlemen of Verona,* cast members were costumed in Ray-Ban sunglasses and sneakers.

On the other hand, while the outward shapes may be altered and the inner spirit may be warmer—the 1997 funeral of Diana, Princess of Wales, was far removed from the conventional picture of a somewhat staid city of people who don't display their emotions—the bedrock of London's character and tradition remains the same. Deep down, Britons have a sense of the continuity of history. Even in the modern metropolis, some things rarely change. The British bobby is alive and well. The tall, red, double-decker buses still lumber from stop to stop, though their aesthetic match at street level, the glossy red telephone booth, is slowly disappearing. And teatime is still a hallowed part of the day, with, if you search hard enough, toasted crumpets still laced with sweet butter. Then, of course, there is that greatest living link with the past—the Royal Family. Don't let the tag "typical tourist" stop you from enjoying the pageantry of the Windsors, one of the greatest free shows in the world. Line up for the Changing of the Guard and poke into the Royal Mews for a look at the Coronation Coach, which will be polished brilliantly for the queen's Golden Jubilee state occasions in 2002. Pomp reaches its zenith in mid-June when the queen celebrates her official birthday with a parade called Trooping the Colour. Royalty-watching is by no means restricted to fascinated foreigners. You only have to open London's tabloid newspapers to read reports of the latest rumors. Then again, more and more people are feeling that what goes on inside Buckingham Palace is no one's affair but the queen's.

In the end, the London you'll discover will surely include some of our enthusiastic recommendations, but be prepared to be taken by surprise as well. The best that a great city has to offer often comes in unexpected ways. Armed with energy and curiosity, and the practical information and helpful hints in the following pages, you can be sure of one thing: to quote Dr. Johnson again, you'll be able to find "in London all that life can afford."

New & Noteworthy

The post-millennium building frenzy continues as museums and galleries strive to become more technological and visitor-friendly. Many national collections have extended opening hours and free admission for kids. At press time (summer 2001), the government was also considering introducing free admission to all national museums in 2002. Classicism spearheaded by innovation is the byword for recent offerings: the glittering Great Court of the British Museum; the latest technological gizmos at the British Library; the state-of-the-art branch of the Tate Gallery—Tate Modern (with a new look at the old Tate, or Tate Britain)—now installed at the futuristic Bankside Power Station; the multimillion-pound makeovers of the Sadler's Wells Theatre and the Royal Opera House; the new face of the National Portrait Gallery; and the scintillating space-age Science Museum. Thanks to these attractions, swinging-again London might be considered Europe's most future-forward spot.

The opening of the surrealist museum Dalí Universe and the BFI London IMAX Cinema, not to mention Tate Modern, have made the South Bank a hot spot. In addition, the British Airways London Eye

Belsize Rd.
Abbey Rd.
Acacia Rd.
St. John's Wood Ter.
Crowndale Rd. Pancras
Eversholt St.
Hampstead Rd.

Regent's Park

Abercorn Pl.
Maida Vale
Randolph Rd.
Clifton Rd.
Bloomfield Rd.
Harrow Rd.

Grove End Rd.
Circus Rd.
Wellington Rd.
St. John's Wood Rd.
Prince Albert Rd.
Park Rd.
Queen Circle
Outer Circle

Euston Station

Inner Circle
Chester Rd.
Albany St.
Euston Rd.

Euston Rd.

Edgware Rd.
Lisson Grove

BLOOM

MARYLEBONE

Dorset Square
Marylebone Rd.
Marylebone Rd.
Gloucester Pl.
Baker St.
Marylebone High St.
Harley St.
Gt. Portland St.
Portland Pl.
Maple St.
Tottenham Court Rd.
Gower

Bishop's Bridge Rd.
Marylebone Flyover
Seymour Pl.

Telecom Tower

Barret St.
St.

Paddington Station

Praed St.
Sussex Gdns.
Edgware Rd.
Manchester Square
Manchester Square
Duke St.
Wigmore St.
Oxford Oxford Circus
Berners St.

BAYSWATER

Craven Hill
Oxford St.
Grosvenor Square
Brook St.
Grosvenor St.
New Bond St.
Bond St.
Regent St.

SOHO

Bayswater Rd.
N. Carriage Dr.
Berkeley Square
Brewer St.
Shaftesb
Queensway

Bayswater Rd.
U.S. Embassy
S. Audley St.

Royal Academy

Piccadilly Circus

Jermyn St.

Hyde Park
Park Lane
MAYFAIR
Curzon St.
St. James's St.
Pall Mall
Regent St.

Kensington Gardens
The Serpentine
Piccadilly
Green Park
St. James's St.
The Mall

Round Pond
W. Carriage
St. James's Park

Kensington Palace

S. Carriage Rd.
Constitution Hill
Birdcage Walk

Kensington Rd.
Kensington Gore
Kensington Rd.
Knightsbridge
Buckingham Palace

Palace Gate
Gloucester Rd.
Royal Albert Hall
Sloane St.
Grosvenor Pl.

Prince Consort Rd.
Victoria and Albert Museum
Belgrave Square
Victoria

Science Museum

BELGRAVIA
Eaton Square
Victoria Station
Horseferry

Exhibition Rd.
Brompton Rd.
Pont St.
Cadogan Pl.
Buckingham Palace Rd.
Wilton Rd.
VICTORIA

Natural History Museum
KNIGHTSBRIDGE

Cromwell Rd.
Queen's Gate

SOUTH KENSINGTON
Old Brompton Rd.
Sloane Ave.
Warwick Way
Belgrave Rd.

Redcliffe Gdns.
Fulham Rd.
CHELSEA
King's Rd.
Pimlico Rd.
Chelsea Br. Rd.
Lupus St.
PIMLICO
Rd.

Finborough Rd.
Old Church St.
Sydney St.
Oakley St.
Royal Hospital Rd.
Chelsea Br.
Grosvenor
Nine Elms

Cheyne Walk
Chelsea Embankment
River Thames
Albert Br.
Battersea Br.

Battersea Park

continues to offer unrivaled views of London and beyond from its see-through, podlike capsules.

At the Victoria & Albert Museum, the Spiral, a dramatic new exhibit space designed by Daniel Libeskind, is now slated to rise in 2004. The British Galleries at the V&A are scheduled to open by the end of 2001; with amazing detail and masses of historical objects, the galleries tell the story of the last 400 years in Britain from art to design to day-to-day life.

The Queen's Golden Jubilee year, 2002, will see much pomp and pageantry: you might even catch a glimpse of the gilt royal carriages streaming out of Buckingham Palace to a grand state occasion. Within the palace, the Queen's Gallery is undergoing a major expansion, to be completed in March 2002; the Royal Collection of old masterpieces is to have twice as much exhibition space, and there will be a new micro gallery where you can see more of the unhung pieces on screen.

Londoners on their way to the Tate Modern, the Docklands developments, and ancient Greenwich with its regenerated "Greenwich Peninsula," have new tube stations on the ultra-modern Jubilee Line, plus extra services on the time-honored mode of transport called Father Thames. Waterloo Millennium Pier, beside the London Eye observation wheel, now connects to the new Millennium Dome Pier. The new Millennium Bridge, purely for pedestrians, opened in June 2000 to great fanfare but closed after a wobbly start. With new stabilizers in place, it was scheduled to reopen by fall 2001.

WESTMINSTER AND ROYAL LONDON

This tour might be called "London for Beginners." If you went no farther than these few acres, you would see many of the most famous sights, from the Houses of Parliament, Big Ben, Westminster Abbey, and Buckingham Palace to two of the world's greatest art collections, housed in the National and Tate Britain galleries. You can truly call this area Royal London, as it is neatly bounded by the triangle of streets that make up the route that the queen usually takes when journeying from Buckingham Palace to the Abbey or to the Houses of Parliament on state occasions. The three points on this royal triangle are Trafalgar Square, Westminster, and Buckingham Palace. If you have time to visit only one part of London, undoubtedly this should be it. There is as much history in these few acres as in many entire cities, as the statues of kings, queens, soldiers, and statesmen that stand guard at every corner attest—this is concentrated sightseeing, so pace yourself. The main drawback to sightseeing here is that half the world is doing it at the same time. So, even if you're tired after a long day on your feet, try to come back in the evening, after the crowds have dispersed, to drink in the serenity and grandeur at your leisure. You'll get to see it in a new light, literally, as much of Royal London is spectacularly floodlighted at night.

Westminster is by far the younger of the capital's two centers, post-dating the City by some 1,000 years. Edward the Confessor put it on the map when he packed up his court from its cramped City quarters and moved it west a couple of miles, founding the abbey church of Westminster—the minster west of the City—in 1050. Subsequent kings continued to hold court here until Henry VIII decamped to Whitehall Palace in 1512, leaving Westminster to the politicians. And here they are still, not in the palace, which burned almost to the ground in 1834, but in the Victorian mock-Gothic Houses of Parliament, whose 320-ft-high Clock Tower (Big Ben) is as much a symbol of London as the Eiffel Tower is of Paris.

*Numbers in the text correspond to numbers in the margin and on the
Westminster and Royal London map.*

A Good Walk

Trafalgar Square ① is the obvious place to start for several reasons. It
is the geographical core of London and home to many political demonstrations, a raucous New Year's Eve party, and the highest concentration of bus stops and pigeons in the capital. After taking in the instantly
identifiable **Nelson's Column** ② in the center (read about the area on
a plaque marking its 150th anniversary), head for the **National Gallery** ③,
on the north side—this is Britain's greatest trove of masterpieces. Detour around the corner to see the **National Portrait Gallery** ④, a parade of the famous that can be very rewarding to anyone interested in
what makes the British tick. East of the National Gallery, still on
Trafalgar Square, see the much-loved church **St. Martin-in-the-Fields** ⑤;
then, stepping through grand **Admiralty Arch** ⑥ down on the southwest corner, enter the royal pink road, the **Mall,** with St. James's Park
on your left. On your right is the **Institute of Contemporary Arts** ⑦,
known as the ICA and housed in the great Regency architect John Nash's
Carlton House Terrace ⑧. At the foot of the Mall is one of London's
most famous sights, **Buckingham Palace** ⑨, home, of course, to the monarch of the land and punctuated by the ornate, white-marble **Queen
Victoria Memorial** ⑩. Turning left and left again, almost doubling
back, follow the southern perimeter of St. James's Park around Birdcage Walk (the **Queen's Gallery** ⑪, with masterpieces from Her Majesty's
vast art collection, is a few steps to the right at the side of the palace;
it's closed until March 2002) passing **Wellington Barracks** ⑫, headquarters of the queen's guards, and, in turn, the hulking Home Office
and **Queen Anne's Gate** ⑬. Cross Horse Guards Road at the eastern
edge of the park and walk down Great George Street, with **St. Margaret's Church** ⑭ on your right. Continue across Parliament Square to
come to another of the great sights of London, the **Houses of Parliament** ⑮, with the famous Clock Tower, known the world over as Big
Ben. A clockwise turn around the square brings you to yet another major
landmark, breathtaking **Westminster Abbey** ⑯. Complete the circuit
and head north up Whitehall, passing the **Cabinet War Rooms** ⑰,
where you'll see a simple monolith in the middle of the street—the Cenotaph designed by Edwin Lutyens in 1920 in commemoration of the 1918
armistice. The gated alley on your left is **Downing Street** ⑱, where England's modest "White House" stands at No. 10. Soon after that, you
pass **Horse Guards Parade** ⑲, the setting for the queen's birthday celebration, Trooping the Colour, with the classical Inigo Jones **Banqueting House** ⑳, scene of Charles I's execution, opposite. It's well worth
it to backtrack a little ways down Whitehall and Abingdon Street, to
Millbank and the **Tate Britain** ㉑, the expanded collection of British art
at the site of the old Tate Gallery.

TIMING
You could achieve this walk of roughly 3 mi in just over an hour, but
you could just as easily spend a week's vacation on this route alone.
Allow as much time as you can for the two great museums—the National Gallery requires at *least* two hours; the National Portrait Gallery
can be whizzed round in less than one. Westminster Abbey can take
half a day—especially in summer, when lines are long—both to get into
and to get around in. In summer, you can get inside Buckingham
Palace, too, a half day's operation increased to a whole day if you see
the Royal Mews and the Queen's Gallery or the Guards Museum. If
the Changing of the Guard is a priority, make sure you time this walk
correctly.

Westminster and Royal London

This is an easy neighborhood to access, especially if you start at Trafalgar Square, where many buses stop. The central neighborhood tube stop, Charing Cross (on the Jubilee, Northern, and Bakerloo lines), exits at the beginning of Northumberland Avenue, on the southeast corner. Practically all buses stop around here, including Buses 3, 9, 11, 12, 16, 24, 29, 53, 88, 139, and 159. Just to the north of Trafalgar Square on Charing Cross Road is the Leicester Square tube stop (on the Northern and Piccadilly lines), which is just behind the galleries. Alternative tube stations on the south side are St. James's Park (on the District and Circle lines), which is the best for Buckingham Palace, or the next stop, Westminster, which deposits you right by the bridge, in the shadow of Big Ben.

Sights to See

6 Admiralty Arch. Gateway to the Mall—no, not an indoor shopping center but one of the very grand avenues of London—this is one of London's stateliest urban set pieces. Situated on the southwest corner of Trafalgar Square, the arch, which was named after the adjacent Royal Navy headquarters, was designed in 1910 by Sir Aston Webb as part of a ceremonial route to Buckingham Palace. As you pass under the enormous triple archway—though not through the central arch, opened only for state occasions—the atmosphere changes along with the color of the road, for you are exiting frenetic Trafalgar Square and entering the Mall (rhymes with shall)—the elegant avenue that leads directly to the palace. ⊠ *The Mall, Cockspur St., Trafalgar Sq., SW1. Tube: Charing Cross.*

20 Banqueting House. This is all that remains today of the Tudor Palace of Whitehall, which was (according to one foreign visitor) "ill-built, and nothing but a heap of houses." James I commissioned Inigo Jones (1573–1652), one of England's great architects, to do a grand remodeling. Influenced during a sojourn in Tuscany by Andrea Palladio's work, Jones brought Palladian sophistication and purity back to London with him. The resulting graceful and disciplined classical style of Banqueting House must have stunned its early occupants. In the quiet vaults beneath, James would escape the stresses of being a sovereign with a glass or two. His son, Charles I, enhanced the interior by employing the Flemish painter Peter Paul Rubens to glorify his father all over the ceiling. As it turned out, these allegorical paintings, depicting a wise monarch being received into heaven, were the last thing Charles saw before he was beheaded by Cromwell's Parliamentarians in 1649. But his son, Charles II, was able to celebrate the restoration of the monarchy in this same setting 20 years later. ⊠ *Whitehall, SW1,* ☎ *020/7930–4179,* WEB *www.hrp.org.uk.* ⊠ *£3.60, includes free audio guide.* ☉ *Mon.–Sat. 10–5; closed on short notice for banquets, so call first. Tube: Charing Cross, Embankment, or Westminster.*

9 Buckingham Palace. Supreme among the symbols of London, indeed of Britain generally and of the Royal Family, Buckingham Palace tops many must-see lists—although the building itself is no masterpiece and has housed the monarch only since Victoria (1819–1901) moved here from Kensington Palace on her accession in 1837. Its great gray bulk sums up the imperious splendor of so much of the city: stately, magnificent, and ponderous. When Victoria moved in, the place was a mess. George IV, on his accession in 1820, had fancied the idea of moving to Buckingham House, his parents' former home, and had employed John Nash, as usual, to remodel it. The government authorized only "repair and improvement"; Nash, that tireless spendthrift, overspent his budget by about half a million pounds. George died, Nash was dismissed, and Edward Blore finished the building, adding the now familiar east front (facing the Mall). Victoria arrived to faulty drains and sticky doors and windows, but they did not mar her affection for the place, nor that of her son, Edward VII. The Portland stone facade dates only from 1913 (the same stone used for the Victoria Memorial outside the Palace and Admiralty Arch at the foot of the Mall), and the interior was renovated and redecorated only after it sustained World War II bomb damage. Indeed, compared to other great London residences, this is very much a Johnny-come-lately affair.

The palace contains 19 state rooms, 52 royal and guest bedrooms, 188 staff bedrooms, 92 offices, and 78 bathrooms—a prerequisite for the 450 people who work there, and the mere 50,000 who are entertained during the year. The state rooms are where much of the business of royalty is played out—investitures, state banquets, and receptions for the great and good. The royal apartments are in the north wing; when the queen is in residence, the royal standard is raised. Until fairly recently all the quarters were off-limits to the public, but funds to pay for the reparations after the 1992 fire at Windsor Castle had to be found. And so the state rooms are on show from August to early October, a period when the Royal Family is away. A visit to the palace's west wing is a fascinating glimpse into another world: the fabulously gilt interiors are not merely museum pieces but pomp and pageantry at work. A tour starts from the Ambassadors' Court entrance, through to the **Entrée**, where portraits of past kings look down. The classical tone is set with Ionic columns in honeyed Bath stone, marble pillars in cool Carrara white, fine French and English furniture, and Chinese vases. Once through the **Grand Hall**, the **Grand Staircase**, and **Guard Room** (too small for the royal bodyguards—Yeoman of the Guard and Gentlemen-at-Arms in their traditional red and gold uniforms), the superlatives for the richness and elegance before your eyes could begin to wane. Prepare to be completely and utterly gilded out as Nash's ornate designs unfold through the numerous drawing rooms—each more jaw-dropping and neck-craning than the last—decorated with awesome ceilings and chandeliers, and magnificent objects brought from the Prince Regent's original palatial home, Carlton House. (Some of the most precious Sèvres porcelain in the world found its way here after the French Revolution.) The **Throne Room** is opulent with gilt Baroque decor and the original 1953 coronation throne chairs. Queen Victoria used to hold balls here, but today it is the backdrop for royal wedding photographs and presentations. By now, when eyes are becoming glazed, the **Picture Gallery** is a restful feast of renowned art. The collection was begun by Charles I, and the works are periodically rearranged. Highlights among the many masterpieces are works by Rubens, Vermeer, Van Dyck, Cuyp, and Canaletto. The state rooms are graced with some of Her Majesty's most famous Old Master paintings, but other artwork is on view in the **Queen's Gallery** (closed for renovation until March 2002), near the south side of the palace. The palace tour continues through more galleries and drawing rooms filled with exquisite paintings and tapestries, culminating with the **State Dining Room** and its overly elaborate Blore ceiling. The table is sadly not set for a banquet with its usual crystal, gold, and silverware, but a solitary pair of ewers stands at attention.

From here there are views across the sweeping gardens. But without an invitation to one of the queen's summer garden parties you won't see more of the magnificent 45-acre grounds. The **Changing of the Guard**, with all the ceremony monarchists and children adore, remains one of London's best free shows and culminates in front of the palace. Marching to live music, the guards proceed up the Mall from St. James's Palace

JUST REMEMBER TO ADDRESS HER AS "YOUR MAJESTY"

YOU'VE SEEN BIG BEN, the Tower, and Westminster Abbey. But somehow you feel something is missing: a close encounter with Britain's most famous attraction—Her actual Majesty. True, you've toured Buckingham Palace, but the Windsors are notorious for never standing at a window (the London *Times* once suggested that the palace mount a full-scale mechanical procession of royal figures to parade in and out of the palace, on the hour, in cuckoo-clock fashion), and the odds are that you won't be bumping into Elizabeth II on the tube. But at a surprisingly wide variety of royal events, you can catch a glimpse of her, along with many other Windsor personages. Fairs and fetes, polo matches and horse races, first nights and banquets galore—her date book is crammed with such events and, on one of them—who knows?—you might even meet her on a royal walkabout.

The Queen and the Royal Family, in fact, attend approximately 400 functions a year, and if you want to know what she and the rest of the Royal Family are doing on any given date, turn to the *Court Circular*, printed in the major London dailies. You might catch Prince Charles launching a ship, Princess Margaret attending a film premiere, or the Queen at a hospital's ribbon-cutting ceremony. But most visitors want to see the royals in all their dazzling pomp and circumstance. For this, the best bet is the second Saturday in June, when the Trooping the Colour is usually held to celebrate the queen's official birthday. This spectacular parade begins when she leaves Buckingham Palace in her carriage and rides down the Mall to arrive at Horse Guards Parade at 11 exactly. (Well, occasionally the clock has been timed to strike as she arrives and not vice versa!) If you wish to obtain one of the 7,000 seats to watch the Trooping the Colour rehearsal or the spectacle itself (no more than two seats per request, distributed by ballot), enclose a letter and stamped, self-addressed envelope or International Reply Coupon—from January to February 28 only—to **Ticket Office** (✉ Headquarters Household Division, Horse Guards, London SW1A 2AX, ☎ 020/7414–2479). Of course, you can also just line up along the Mall with your binoculars!

Another time you can catch the queen in all her regalia is when she and the Duke of Edinburgh ride in state to Westminster to open the Houses of Parliament. The famous gilded coach that became such an icon of fairy-tale glamour at Elizabeth II's coronation parades from Buckingham Palace to Parliament, escorted by the brilliantly uniformed and superbly mounted Household Cavalry—on a clear day, it is to be hoped, for this ceremony takes place in late October or early November, depending on the exigencies of Parliament. As the queen enters the Houses, the air shakes with the booming of heavy guns, and all London knows that the democratic processes that have so long protected England from oppression have once again been renewed with all their age-old ceremony. But perhaps the nicest time to see the Queen is during Royal Ascot, held at the racetrack near Windsor Castle—just a short train ride out of London—usually during the third week of June (Tuesday–Friday). After several races, the queen invariably walks down to the paddock on a special path, greeting race-goers as she proceeds. Americans wishing to reserve a seat in the Royal Enclosure should apply to the **American Embassy** (✉ 24 Grosvenor Square, London W1) before the end of March. But remember: you must be sponsored by two guests who have attended Ascot at least seven times before! (Fashion note: the big party hats come out on Ladies Day, normally the Thursday of the meet.) If you're lucky enough to meet the Queen (contrary to her stodgy public persona, she's actually a great wit), just remember to address her as "Your Majesty."

to Buckingham Palace. Shortly afterward, the new guard approaches from Wellington Barracks via Birdcage Walk. Once the old and new guards are in the forecourt, the old guard symbolically hands over the keys to the palace. The ceremony usually takes place on schedule, but the guards sometimes cancel owing to bad weather; check the signs in the forecourt or phone. Get there by 10:30 AM to grab a spot in the best viewing section at the gate facing the palace, since most of the hoopla takes place behind the railings in the forecourt. Be sure to prebook tour reservations of the palace with a credit card by phone. ✉ *Buckingham Palace Rd., SW1,* ☎ *020/7839–1377; 020/7799–2331 24-hr information; 020/7321–2233 credit-card reservations, subject to 50p booking charge,* WEB *www.royal.gov.uk.* ✉ *£11.* ☉ *Early Aug.–early Oct., daily 9:30–4:15 (confirm dates, which are subject to queen's mandate). Changing of the Guard Apr.–July, daily 11:30 AM; Aug.–Mar., alternating days only 11:30 AM. AE, MC, V. Tube: Victoria or St. James's Park.*

⑰ Cabinet War Rooms. It was from this small maze of 17 bomb-proof underground rooms—in back of the hulking Foreign Office—that Britain's World War II fortunes were directed. During air raids, the Cabinet met here—the Cabinet Room is still arranged as if a meeting were about to convene; in the Map Room, the Allied campaign is charted; the Prime Minister's Room holds the desk from which Winston Churchill (1874–1965) made his morale-boosting broadcasts; and the Telephone Room has his hot line to FDR. The great man only slept here on a number of occasions; he preferred the comfort of Downing Street, even at the height of the German blitz. ✉ *Clive Steps, King Charles St., SW1,* ☎ *020/7930–6961,* WEB *www.iwm.org.uk.* ✉ *£5.* ☉ *Apr.– Sept., daily 9:30–5:15; Oct.–Mar., daily 10–5:15. Tube: Westminster.*

❽ Carlton House Terrace. This is a glorious example of Regency architect John Nash's genius. Between 1812 and 1830, under the patronage of George IV (Prince Regent until George III's death in 1820), Nash was the architect for the grand scheme of Regent Street and the sweep of neoclassical houses encircling Regent's Park. The Prince Regent, who lived at Carlton House, had plans to build a country villa at Primrose Hill (to the north of the park), connected by a grand road—hence Regent Street. Even though it was considered a most extravagant building for its time, Carlton House was demolished after the prince's accession to the throne. Nash's Carlton House Terrace, no less imposing, with white-stucco facades and massive Corinthian columns, was built in its place. It was a smart address, needless to say, and one that Prime Ministers Gladstone (1856) and Palmerston (1857–75) enjoyed. Today Carlton House Terrace is home to the Royal College of Pathologists (No. 2), the Royal Society (No. 6, whose members included Isaac Newton and Charles Darwin), the Turf Club (No. 5), and, at No. 12, the **Institute of Contemporary Arts**, better known as the ICA. ✉ *The Mall, W1. Tube: Charing Cross.*

⑱ Downing Street. Looking like an unassuming alley but barred by iron gates at both its Whitehall and Horse Guards Road approaches, this is location of the famous **No. 10,** London's modest version of the White House. Only three houses remain of the terrace built circa 1680 by Sir George Downing, who spent enough of his youth in America to graduate from Harvard—the second man ever to do so. **No. 11** is traditionally the residence of the chancellor of the exchequer (secretary of the treasury), and **No. 12** is the party whips' office. No. 10 has officially housed the prime minister since 1732. (The gates were former prime minister Margaret Thatcher's brainstorm.) Just south of Downing Street, in the middle of Whitehall, you'll see the **Cenotaph,** a stark white monolith designed in 1920 by Edward Lutyens to commemorate the 1918 armistice. On Remembrance Day (the Sunday nearest November 11) it is strewn with red poppies to honor the dead of both world wars and all British soldiers killed in action since, with the first wreath laid by the queen. ✉ *Whitehall, SW1. Tube: Westminster.*

⑲ Horse Guards Parade. Once the tiltyard of Whitehall Palace, where jousting tournaments were held, the Horse Guards Parade is now notable mainly for the annual Trooping the Colour ceremony, in which the queen takes the Royal Salute, her official birthday gift, on the second Saturday in June. (Like Paddington Bear, the queen has two birthdays; her real one is on April 21.) There is pageantry galore, with marching bands—the occasional guardsman fainting clean away from the heat building up under his weighty busby—and throngs of onlookers. Covering the vast expanse of the square that faces Horse Guards Road, opposite St. James's Park at one end and Whitehall at the other, the ceremony is televised. At the Whitehall facade of Horse Guards, the changing of two mounted sentries known as the **mounted guard** provides what may be London's most frequently exercised photo opportunity. ✉ *Whitehall, SW1.* ⊙ *Queen's mounted guard Ceremony Mon.–Sat. 11 AM, Sun. 10 AM. Tube: Westminster.*

★ **⑮ Houses of Parliament.** Overlooking the Thames, the Houses of Parliament are, arguably, the city's most famous and photogenic sight, with the Clock Tower—which everyone calls Big Ben—keeping watch on the corner and Westminster Abbey ahead of you across Parliament Square. The most romantic view of the complex is from the opposite (south) side of the river, a vista especially dramatic at night when the storybook spires, pinnacles, and towers of the great building are floodlighted green and gold—a fairy-tale vision only missing the presence of Peter Pan and Wendy on their way to Never-Never Land.

The Palace of Westminster, as the complex is still properly called, was established by Edward the Confessor in the 11th century, when he moved his court here from the City. It has served as the seat of English administrative power, on and off, ever since. In 1512, Henry VIII (1491–1547) abandoned it for Whitehall, and it ceased to be an official royal residence after 1547. At the Reformation, the Royal Chapel was secularized and became the first meeting place of the Commons. The Lords settled in the White Chamber. These, along with everything but the **Jewel Tower** and **Westminster Hall,** were destroyed in 1834 when "the sticks"—the arcane elmwood "tally" sticks notched for loans paid out and paid back, beneath the Lords' Chamber, on which the court had kept its accounts until 1826—were incinerated, and the fire got out of hand. Westminster Hall, with its remarkable hammer-beam roof, was the work of William the Conqueror's son, William Rufus. It is one of the largest remaining Norman halls in Europe, and its dramatic interior was the scene of the trial of Charles I.

After the 1834 fire, architects were invited to submit plans for new Houses of Parliament in the grandiose "Gothic or Elizabethan style." Charles Barry's were selected from among 97 entries, partly because Barry had invited the architect and designer Augustus Pugin to add the requisite neo-Gothic curlicues to his own Renaissance-influenced style. As you can see, it was a happy collaboration, with Barry's classical proportions offset by Pugin's ornamental flourishes—although the latter were toned down by Gilbert Scott when he rebuilt the bomb-damaged House of Commons after World War II. The two towers were Pugin's work. The **Clock Tower,** now virtually the symbol of London, was completed in 1858 after long delays due to bickering over the clock's design. (Barry designed the faces himself in the end.) It contains the 13-ton bell known as Big Ben, which chimes the hour (and the quarters). Some say Ben was "Big Ben" Caunt, heavyweight champ; others, Sir Benjamin Hall, the far-from-slim Westminster building works commissioner. At the southwest end of the main Parliament building is the 336-ft-high **Victoria Tower,** agleam from its restoration and cleaning. The rest of the complex was scrubbed down some years ago; the revelation of the honey stone under the dowdy, smog-blackened facades, which seemed almost symbolic at the time, cheered London up no end.

The building itself, which covers 8 acres, is a series of chambers, lobbies, and offices joined by more than 2 mi of passages. There are two Houses, Lords and Commons. The former has undergone a radical reform by Mr. Blair's Labour party. On November 5, 2000 (somewhat symbolically, on the anniversary of Guy Fawkes's attempt to blow up the Houses of Parliament in 1605), more than 100 hereditary peers (earls, lords, viscounts, and other aristocrats) failed to win the right to continue to be elected to their seats in the House of Lords. This much-downsized House of Lords is part of the Labour Party's drive to democratize and modernize the ancient institution. The House of Commons is made up of 659 elected Members of Parliament (MPs). The party with the most MPs forms the government, its leader becoming prime minister; other parties form the Opposition. Since 1642, when Charles I tried to have five MPs arrested, no monarch has been allowed into the House of Commons. The state opening of Parliament in November consequently takes place in the House of Lords. Visitors aren't allowed many places in the Houses of Parliament, though the Visitors' Galleries of the House of Commons do afford a view of the best free show in London, staged in the world's most renowned ego chamber. The opposing banks of green leather benches seat only 437 MPs—not that this is much of a problem, since absentees far outnumber the diligent. When MPs vote, they exit by the "Aye" or the "No" corridor, thus being counted by the party whips. When they speak, it is not directly to each other but through the Speaker, who also decides who will get the floor each day. Elaborate procedures notwithstanding, debate is often drowned out by amazingly raucous and immature jeers and insults.

Other public areas of the 1,100-room labyrinth are rather magnificently got up in high neo-Gothic style and punctuated with stirring frescoes commissioned by Prince Albert. You pass these en route to the Visitors' Galleries—if, that is, you are patient enough to wait in line for hours (the Lords line is shorter) or have applied in advance for the special "line of route" tour (open only to overseas visitors) by writing to the **Parliamentary Education Unit** (✉ House of Commons Information Office, House of Commons, London, SW1A 2TT) at least a month in advance of your visit. The tour takes you through the Queen's Robing Room, Royal Gallery, House of Lords, Central Hall (where MPs meet their constituents—the lucky ones get to accompany their MP to a prestigious tea on the terrace), House of Commons, and out into the spectacular Westminster Hall. Watch for the "VR" (Victoria Regina) monograms in the carpets and carving belying the "medieval" detailing as 19th-century work. Permits for tours of up to 16 people are available Friday afternoon between 3:30 and 5:30 while the House is sitting. The time to catch the action is Question Time—when the prime minister defends himself against the attacks of his "right honorable friends" on Wednesday between 3 and 3:30 PM (it's also live on BBC2). Foreigners are required to secure tickets from their respective embassies. The next best time to visit is either chamber's regular Question Time, held Monday–Thursday 2:30–3:30. The easiest time to get into the Commons is during an evening session—Parliament is still sitting if the top of the Clock Tower is illuminated.

For a special exhibition devoted to the "History of Parliament: Past and Present," head to the **Jewel Tower**, across the street from Victoria Tower, on Abingdon Street (also called Old Palace Yard), just south of Parliament Square. Not to be confused with the other famed jewel tower at the Tower of London, this was the stronghold for Edward III's treasure in 1366. It's also one of the original parts of the old Palace of Westminster and still retains some original beams; part of the moat and medieval quay still remain. (The tower is run by English Heritage, with a small charge for entry.) Be sure to have your name placed in advance on the waiting list for the twice-weekly tours of the **Lord Chancellor's Residence**, a popular attraction since its spectacular renovation. ⊠ *St. Stephen's Entrance, St. Margaret St., SW1,* ☎ *020/7219–3000; 020/7219–4272 Commons information; 020/7219–3107 Lords information; 020/7222– 2219 Jewel Tower; 020/7219–2184 Lord Chancellor's Residence,* WEB *www.parliament.uk.* ☞ *Free.* ☻ *Commons Mon.–Thurs. 2:30–10, Fri. 9:30–3 (although not every Fri.); Lords Mon.–Thurs. 2:30–10; Lord Chancellor's Residence Tues. and Thurs. 10:30–12. Closed Easter wk, July– Oct., and 3 wks at Christmas. Tube: Westminster.*

➐ Institute of Contemporary Arts (ICA). Behind its incongruous white-stucco facade, at No. 12 Carlton House Terrace, the ICA has provided a stage for the avant-garde in performance, theater, dance, visual art, and music since it was established in 1947. There are two cinemas, an underused library of video artists' works, a bookshop, a café and a bar, and a team of adventurous curators. ⊠ *The Mall, W1,* ☎ *020/7930– 3647,* WEB *www.ica.org.uk.* ☞ *1-day, weekday membership £1.50; weekend, £2.50; additional charge for cinema screenings.* ☻ *Daily noon– 9:30, later for some events. Tube: Charing Cross or Piccadilly Circus.*

NEED A BREAK?

The **ICAfé** is windowless but brightly lighted, with a self-service counter offering good hot dishes, salads, quiches, and desserts. The bar upstairs, which serves baguette sandwiches, has a picture window overlooking the Mall. Both are packed before popular performances and are subject to the £1.50 one-day membership fee.

The Mall. This street was laid out around 1660 for the game of *pell mell* (a type of croquet crossed with golf), which also gave Pall Mall its name, and it quickly became the place to be seen. Samuel Pepys, Jonathan Swift, and Alexander Pope all wrote about it, and it continued as the beau monde's social playground into the early 19th century, long after the game it was built for had gone out of vogue. Something of the former style survives on those summer days when the queen is throwing a Buckingham Palace garden party: hundreds of her subjects throng the Mall, from the grand and titled to the humble and hardworking, all of whom have donned hat and frock to take afternoon tea with the monarch—or somewhere near her—on the lawns of Buck House. The old Mall still runs alongside the graceful, pink, 115-ft-wide avenue that replaced it in 1904 for just such occasions. ⊠ *The Mall, SW1. Tube: Charing Cross, Green Park.*

★ **➌ National Gallery.** Jan Van Eyck's *Arnolfini Portrait,* Leonardo da Vinci's *Madonna of the Rocks,* Velázquez's *Rokeby Venus,* Constable's *Hay Wain . . .* you get the picture. There are about 2,200 other paintings in this museum—many of them instantly recognizable and among the most treasured works of art anywhere. The museum's low, gray, colonnaded neoclassic facade fills the north side of Trafalgar Square. The institution was founded in 1824, when George IV and a connoisseur named Sir George Beaumont persuaded a reluctant government to spend £57,000 to acquire part of the recently deceased philanthropist John Julius Angerstein's collection. These 38 paintings, including works by Raphael, Rembrandt, Titian, and Rubens, were augmented by 16 of Sir George's own and exhibited in Angerstein's Pall Mall residence until 1838, when William Wilkins's building was completed. By the end of the century, enthusiastic directors and generous patrons had turned the National Gallery into one of the world's foremost collections, with works from painters of the Italian Renaissance and earlier, from the Flemish and Dutch masters, the Spanish school, and of course the English tradition, including Hogarth, Gainsborough, Stubbs, and Constable.

In 1991, following years of wrangling and the rehanging of the entire collection, the Sainsbury Wing was opened. It had been financed by the eponymous British grocery dynasty to house the early Renaissance collection and designed—eventually—by the American architect Robert Venturi after previous plans were abandoned. (Prince Charles didn't like these modernist designs. "A monstrous carbuncle on the face of a much-loved friend" was his headline-making comment.) Occasionally, this wing hosts noted temporary exhibitions.

The collection is really too overwhelming to absorb in a single viewing. It is wise to acquaint yourself with the layout—easy to negotiate compared with that of other European galleries—and plot a route in advance. The **Micro Gallery,** a computer information center in the Sainsbury Wing, might be the place to start. You can access in-depth information on any work here, choose your favorites, and print out a free personal tour map that marks the paintings you most want to see. Careful, though—you could spend hours in here scrolling through this colorful if pixelized history of art.

The following is a list of 10 of the most familiar works, to jog your memory, whet your appetite, and offer a starting point for your own exploration. The first five are in the Sainsbury Wing. In chronological order: (1) **Van Eyck** (circa 1395–1441), *The Arnolfini Portrait.* A solemn couple holds hands, the fish-eye mirror behind them mysteriously illuminating what can't be seen from the front view. (2) **Uccello** (1397–1475), *The Battle of San Romano.* In a work commissioned by the Medici family, the Florentine commander on a rearing white warhorse leads armored knights into battle against the Sienese. (3) **Bellini** (circa 1430–1516), *The Doge Leonardo Loredan.* The artist captured the Venetian doge's beatific expression (and snail-shell "buttons") at the beginning of his 20 years in office. (4) **Botticelli** (1445–1510), *Venus and Mars.* Mars sleeps, exhausted by the love goddess, oblivious to the lance wielded by mischievous putti and the buzzing of wasps. (5) **Leonardo da Vinci** (1452–1519), *The Virgin and Child.* This haunting black chalk cartoon is partly famous for having been attacked at gunpoint, and it now gets extra protection behind glass and screens. (6) **Caravaggio** (1573–1610), *The Supper at Emmaus.* A cinematically lighted, freshly resurrected Christ blesses bread in an astonishingly domestic vision from the master of chiaroscuro. (7) **Velázquez** (1599–1660), *The Toilet of Venus.* "The Rokeby Venus," named for its previous home in Yorkshire, has the most famously beautiful back in any gallery. She's the only surviving female nude by Velázquez. (8) **Constable** (1776–1837), *The Hay Wain.* Rendered overfamiliar by too many greeting cards, this is the definitive image of golden-age rural England. (9) **Turner** (1775–1851), *The Fighting Téméraire.* Most of the collection's other Turners were moved to the Tate Britain; the final voyage of the great French battleship into a livid, hazy sunset stayed here. (10) **Seurat** (1859–91), *Bathers at Asnières.* This static summer day's idyll is one of the pointillist extraordinaire's best-known works.

Glaring omissions from the above include some of the most popular pictures in the gallery, by Piero della Francesca, Titian, Holbein, Bosch, Brueghel, Rembrandt, Vermeer, Canaletto, Claude, Tiepolo, Gainsborough, Ingres, Monet, Renoir, and van Gogh. You can't miss the two most spectacular works on view—due to their mammoth size—Sebastiano del Piombo's *Sermon on the Mount* and Stubbs's stunning *Whistlejacket*. These great paintings aren't the only thing glowing in the rooms of the National Gallery—thanks to government patronage and lottery monies, salons here now gleam with stunning brocades and opulent silks. Rubens's *Samson and Delilah* has never looked better.

The collection of Dutch 17th-century paintings is one of the greatest in the world, and pieces by Hals, Hooch, Ruisdel, Hobbema, and Cuyp are shown in renewed natural light and gracious decor. There is also a program of temporary themed exhibitions where key works are loaned from other galleries of world renown. If you visit during the school vacations, there are special programs and trails for children that are not to be missed. Neither are the Ten Minute Talks, which illuminate the story behind a key work of art. Check the information desk, or Web site, for details. ✉ *Trafalgar Sq., WC2,* ☎ *020/7747–2885,* WEB *www. nationalgallery.org.uk.* 🎟 *Free; charge for special exhibitions.* ☉ *Daily 10–6, Wed. until 9 (special exhibition in Sainsbury Wing, Wed. until 10); 1-hr free guided tour starts at Sainsbury Wing daily at 11:30 and 2:30 (and additionally 6:30 Wed.). Tube: Charing Cross or Leicester Sq.*

NEED A BREAK? The **Brasserie** in the Sainsbury Wing of the National Gallery offers a fashionable lunch—mussels, gravlax, charcuterie, salads, a hot special—plus baguette sandwiches, pastries, tea, coffee, and wine, in a sophisticated, spacious room on the second floor.

★ ❹ **National Portrait Gallery.** An idiosyncratic collection that presents a potted history of Britain through its people, past and present, this museum is an essential visit for all history and literature buffs. The gallery has also been given a complete rejuvenation by the architects Jeremy Dixon and Edward Jones, who have been responsible for the Royal Opera House renaissance. In May 2000, the previously dark, dingy stairways and rooms were opened to reveal new galleries and spaces that are light, bright, and more easily accessible. The entrance lobby has an escalator directly to a skylit gallery displaying the oldest works in the Tudor Gallery. A rooftop restaurant with classy British cuisine, open beyond gallery hours, will satiate skyline droolers. Here you'll see one of the best landscapes for real: a panoramic view of Nelson's Column and the backdrop along the Mall to the Houses of Parliament. Back in the basement are a lecture theater, computer gallery, bookshop, and café. The National Portrait Gallery has the largest cache of portraits in the world and, with the architectural face-lift, has doubled its exhibition space. Throughout the gallery, the subject, not the artist, is the point; and there are numerous notable works. In the Tudor Gallery—a modern update on a Tudor long hall—is a Holbein cartoon of Henry VIII; Stubbs's self-portrait hangs in the refurbished 17th-century rooms; and Hockney's appears in the modern Balcony Gallery, mixed up with photographs, busts, caricatures, and amateur paintings. (The miniature of Jane Austen by her sister Cassandra, for instance, is the only likeness that exists of the great novelist.) Many of the faces are obscure and will be just as unknown to English visitors because the portraits outlasted their sitters' fame—not so surprising when the portraitists are such greats as Reynolds, Gainsborough, Lawrence, and Romney. But the annotation is comprehensive, the layout is easy to negotiate—chronological, with the oldest at the top—and there is a separate research center for those who get hooked on particular personages. Don't miss the Victorian and early 20th-century portrait galleries or the photography gallery. ⊠ *St. Martin's Pl., WC2,* ☎ *020/7312–2463 recorded information,* WEB *www.npg.org.uk.* 🎟 *Free.* ☉ *Mon.–Wed., weekends 10–6; Thurs.–Fri. 10–9. Tube: Charing Cross or Leicester Sq.*

② Nelson's Column. Trafalgar Square takes its name from the Battle of Trafalgar, Admiral Lord Horatio Nelson's great naval victory over the French, in 1805. Appropriately, the dominant landmark here is this famous column, a 145-ft-high granite perch from which E. H. Baily's 1843 statue of Nelson (1758–1805), one of England's favorite heroes, keeps watch; three bas-reliefs depicting his victories at Cape St. Vincent, the Battle of the Nile, and Copenhagen (and a fourth, his death at Trafalgar itself in 1805) sit around the base. All four bas-reliefs were cast from cannons he captured. The four majestic lions, designed by the Victorian painter Sir Edwin Landseer, were added in 1867. The calling cards of generations of picturesque pigeons have been a corrosive problem for the statue; this may have been finally solved by the statue's new gel coating. ⊠ *Trafalgar Sq., WC2. Tube: Charing Cross or Leicester Sq.*

⑬ Queen Anne's Gate. Standing south of Birdcage Walk, by St. James's Park, are these two pretty 18th-century closes, once separate but now linked by a statue of the last Stuart monarch. (Another statue of Anne, beside St. Paul's, inspired the doggerel "Brandy Nan, Brandy Nan, you're left in the lurch, your face to the gin shop, your back to the church"— proving that her attempts to disguise her habitual tipple in a teapot fooled nobody.) ⊠ *Queen Anne's Gate, SW1. Tube: St James's Park.*

⑩ Queen Victoria Memorial. You can't overlook this monument if you're near Buckingham Palace, which it faces from the traffic island at the west end of the Mall. The monument was conceived by Sir Aston Webb as the nucleus of his ceremonial route down the Mall to the Palace, and it was executed by the sculptor Thomas Brock, who was knighted on the spot when the memorial was revealed to the world in 1911. Many wonder why he was given that honor, since the thing is Victoriana incarnate: the frumpy queen glares down the Mall, with golden-winged Victory overhead and her siblings Truth, Justice, and Charity, plus Manufacture, Progress-and-Peace, War-and-Shipbuilding, and so on—in Osbert Sitwell's words, "tons of allegorical females . . . with whole litters of their cretinous children"—surrounding her. ⊠ *The Mall and Spur Rd. Tube: Victoria or St. James's Park.*

⑪ Queen's Gallery. This is the former chapel at the south side of Buckingham Palace, which has been open to visitors since 1962 for special, temporary exhibitions (focusing on small parts of the collection, such as Her Majesty's Michelangelo drawings). Closed for renovation at press time, the gallery will reopen in March 2002, expanded and technologically updated to improve public access and enjoyment of the collection. The Standing Gallery will display a selection of paintings and the Graphic Art Gallery will exhibit drawings and watercolors, while the original main gallery will shows changing exhibitions including fine furniture, porcelain, and decorative arts. As only a part of the collection is hung at any one time, in the micro gallery you will be able to view other works in her majesty's vast art collection on screen. A splendid new Nash-style entrance, in tune with the grandeur of the collection, replaces the previous nondescript side door. Call for admission fee details. ⊠ *Buckingham Palace Rd., SW1,* ☎ *020/7799–2331,* WEB *www.royal.gov.uk.* ☉ *1st wk in Mar.–3rd wk in Dec., Tues.–Sat. 9:30–4:30, Sun. 2–4:30. Tube: Victoria or St. James's Park.*

🕊 **Royal Mews.** Unmissable children's entertainment, this museum is the home of Her Majesty's Coronation Coach. Standing nearly next door to the Queen's Gallery, the Royal Mews were designed by famed Regency-era architect John Nash. Mews were originally falcons' quarters (the name comes from their "mewing," or feather shedding), but horses gradually eclipsed birds of prey. Now some of the magnificent royal beasts live here alongside the fabulous bejeweled glass and golden coaches they draw on state occasions. ⊠ *Buckingham Palace Rd., SW1,* ☎ *020/7839–1377,* WEB *www.royal.gov.uk.* 🖅 *£4.60.* ◎ *Mon.–Thurs. noon–4, until 4:30 in summer (call for months), last admission 30 mins before closing. Closed royal and state occasions; call ahead. Tube: Victoria or St. James's Park.*

St. James's Park. With three palaces at its borders (the ancient Palace of Westminster, now the Houses of Parliament; the Tudor **St. James's Palace**; and Buckingham Palace), St James's Park is acclaimed as the most royal of the royal parks. It is also London's smallest, most ornamental park, as well as the oldest; it was acquired by Henry VIII in 1532 for a deer park. The land was marshy and took its name from the lepers' hospital dedicated to St. James. Henry VIII built the palace next to the park, which was used for hunting only—duelling and sword fights were forbidden. James I improved the land and installed an aviary and zoo (complete with crocodiles). Charles II (after his exile in France and because of his admiration for Louis XIV's formal Versailles Palace landscapes) had formal gardens laid out, with avenues, fruit orchards, and a canal. Lawns were grazed by goats, sheep, and deer. The Mall, alongside, also became used for the French croquet-type game of *paille-maille,* or pell mell. Its present shape more or less reflects what John Nash designed under George IV, turning the canal into a graceful lake (which was cemented in at a depth of 4 ft in 1855, so don't even think of swimming) and generally naturalizing the gardens. St. James's Park makes a spectacular frame for the towers of Westminster and Victoria—especially at night, when the illuminated fountains play and the skyline beyond the trees looks like a floating fairyland.

About 17 species of birds—including pelicans, geese, ducks, and swans (which belong to the queen)—now breed on and around Duck Island at the east end of the lake, attracting ornithologists at dawn. Later on summer days the deck chairs (which you must pay to use) are crammed with office workers lunching while being serenaded by music from the bandstands. But the best time to stroll the leafy walkways is after dark, with Westminster Abbey and the Houses of Parliament rising above the floodlighted lake. ⊠ *The Mall or Horse Guards approach, or Birdcage Walk, SW1. Tube: St. James's Park or Westminster.*

St. John's, Smith Square. Completed around 1720, St. John's charmingly dominates Smith Square, an elegant enclave of perfectly preserved early 18th-century town houses that still looks like the London of Dr. Johnson. The Smith Square address is much sought after by MPs, especially of the Tory persuasion; No. 32 is the Conservative Party Headquarters. The Baroque church is well known to Londoners as a chamber-music venue; its popular lunchtime concerts are often broadcast on the radio. ⊠ *North of Horseferry St., end of John Islip St., SW1,* ☎ *020/7222–1061.* ◎ *Weekdays 10–5 (may be closed during concert rehearsals), Sat. for concerts only. Tube: Westminster.*

NEED A
BREAK?

In the Crypt of St. John's, Smith Square, is the **Footstool**—about the only place to find refreshments around here. It has an interesting and reasonably priced lunchtime menu and also serves evening meals on concert nights, weekdays 11:30 AM–2:30 PM and 5:50 PM–10 PM. On Saturday, times for pre-concert meals and snacks vary according to the concert program.

⑭ St. Margaret's Church. Dwarfed by its northern neighbor, Westminster Abbey, this church was founded in the 12th century and rebuilt between 1486 and 1523. St. Margaret's is the parish church of the Houses of Parliament and much sought after for weddings: Samuel Pepys married here in 1655, Winston Churchill in 1908. The east Crucifixion window celebrates another union, the marriage of Prince Arthur and Catherine of Aragon. Unfortunately, it arrived so late that Arthur was dead and Catherine had married his brother, Henry VIII. Sir Walter Raleigh is among the notables buried here, only without his head, which had been removed at Old Palace Yard, Westminster, and kept by his wife, who was said to be fond of asking visitors, "Have you met Sir Walter?" as she produced it from a velvet bag. ⊠ *Parliament Sq., SW1. Tube: Westminster.*

⑤ St. Martin-in-the-Fields. The small medieval chapel that once stood here, probably used by the monks of Westminster Abbey, was indeed surrounded by fields. These gave way to a grand rebuilding, completed in 1726, and St. Martin's grew to become one of Britain's best-loved churches. James Gibbs's classical temple-with-spire design became a familiar pattern for churches in early Colonial America. Though it seems dwarfed by the surrounding structures of Trafalgar Square, the spire is actually slightly taller than Nelson's Column, which it overlooks. It is a welcome sight for the homeless, who have sought soup and shelter here since 1914. The church is also a haven for music lovers; the internationally known Academy of St. Martin-in-the-Fields was founded here, and a popular program of lunchtime (free) and evening concerts continues today (tickets are available from the box office in the crypt). The church's musty interior has a wonderful atmosphere for music making—but the wooden benches can make it hard to give your undivided attention to the music. St. Martin's is often called the royal parish church, partly because Charles II was christened here. The crypt is a hive of lively activity, with a café, bookshop, plus the **London Brass-Rubbing Centre,** where you can make your own souvenir knight, lady, or monarch from replica tomb brasses, with metallic waxes, paper, and instructions provided for about £5; and the **St. Martin's Gallery,** showing contemporary work. There is also a crafts market in the courtyard behind the church. ⊠ *Trafalgar Sq., WC2,* ☎ *020/7930–0089 or* ☎ *020/ 7839–8362 for evening-concert credit-card bookings,* WEB *www.stmartin- in-the-fields.org.* ☉ *Church daily 8–8; crypt Mon.–Sat. 10–8, Sun. noon–6; box office Mon.–Wed. 10–6, Thurs.–Sat. 10–7. Tube: Charing Cross or Leicester Sq.*

NEED A BREAK?   St. Martin's **Café-in-the-Crypt** serves full meals, sandwiches, snacks, and even wine by the glass, Monday–Saturday 10–8 and Sunday noon–8.

★ ㉑ Tate Britain. The gallery previously known as the Tate has been given a new name and direction. Although its fabulous new offspring, Tate Modern opened across the river at Bankside in May 2000, the original has not flagged in its wake. The gallery, which first opened in 1897, funded by the sugar magnate Sir Henry Tate, was relaunched with a fresh face—and theme galleries—in March 2000. As the bold new name proclaims, great British artists from the 16th century to the present day are the focus. It's a brilliant celebration, and it's been done in an entirely new way. The galleries, organized around themes (Family and Society, Literature and Fantasy, and Home and Abroad) display key works from different eras alongside one another. This strategy also resques from storage many important pieces that had rarely seen the light of day. The Family and Society section, for instance, charts a sequence from religious art to the popular portraits and scenes of domesticity (works by Van Dyck, Hogarth, and Reynolds rub shoulders with Rossetti, Sickert, and Bacon) and poverty in cities (works by Frith, Lowry, and Gilbert and George). Literature and Fantasy conjures together such artists as Barry, Millais, Stanley Spencer, and Blake, the original mind-blower. The Home and Abroad gallery covers the breadth of country landscape (Stubbs, Gainsborough, Turner, Nash). Other galleries explore themes such as Nudes (Freud, John, and Leighton); Painters in Focus (from Joshua Reynolds to Stanley Spencer); and British Artists in Focus (from Gainsborough to Hockney, with a special Constable section).

The Turner Bequest consists of J. M. W. Turner's personal collection; he left it to the nation on condition that the works be displayed together. The James Stirling–designed Clore Gallery (to the right of the main gallery) has fulfilled his wish since 1987, and it should not be missed. The annual Turner Prize gets artists and non-artists into a frenzy about what art has come to—or where it's going.

You can rent a "Tateinform," a hand-held audio guide, with commentaries by curators, experts, and some of the artists themselves. About a 20-minute walk south of the Houses of Parliament, the Tate is also accessible if you tube it to the Pimlico stop, then take a five-minute, signposted walk. A shuttle bus and boat service link Tate Britain with Tate Modern at Bankside across the river. ⊠ *Millbank, SW1,* ☎ *020/7887–8000; 020/7887–8008 recorded information,* WEB *www.tate.org.uk.* 🖼 *Free; special exhibitions £3–£7.* ☉ *Daily 10–5:50. Tube: Pimlico.*

❶ Trafalgar Square. This is the center of London, by dint of a plaque on the corner of the Strand and Charing Cross Road from which distances on U.K. signposts are measured. It is the home of the **National Gallery** and of one of London's most distinctive landmarks, **Nelson's Column.** Permanently thronged with people—Londoners and tourists alike—and roaring traffic, it remains London's "living room." Great events, such as New Year's Eve, royal weddings, elections, and sporting triumphs will always see the crowds gathering in the city's most famous square.

The square is a commanding open space, built on the grand scale demanded by its central position in the capital of an empire that once reached to the farthest corners of the globe. Long ago, however, the site housed the Royal Mews, where Edward I (1239–1307) kept his royal hawks and lodged his falconers (not the numberless Edward the Confessor of Westminster Abbey fame, who died in 1066; this one, known as "Longshanks," died of dysentery in 1307). Later, all the kings' horses were stabled here, in increasingly smart quarters, until 1830, when John Nash had the buildings torn down as part of his Charing Cross Improvement Scheme. Nash cleverly exploited the square's natural incline—it slopes down from north to south—making it a succession of high points from which to look down the imposing carriageways that run dramatically away from it toward the Thames, the Houses of Parliament, and Buckingham Palace. Upon Nash's death, the design baton was passed to Sir Charles Barry and then to Sir Edwin Lutyens.

There's a pathetic history attached to the **equestrian statue of Charles I,** which stands near Whitehall on the southern slope of the square (on a pedestal *possibly* designed by Sir Christopher Wren and *possibly* carved by Grinling Gibbons). After Charles's High Treasurer ordered it (from Hubert le Sueur), the Puritan Oliver Cromwell tumbled Charles from the throne and commissioned a scrap dealer with the appropriate name of Rivett to melt the king down. Rivett apparently buried the statue in his garden and made a fortune peddling knickknacks wrought, he claimed, from its metal, only to produce the statue miraculously unscathed after the restoration of the monarchy—and to make more cash reselling it to the authorities. In 1767 Charles II had it placed where it stands today, near the spot where his father was executed in 1649. Each year, on January 30, the day of the king's death, the Royal Stuart Society lays a wreath at the foot of the statue.

Today, street performers enhance the square's intermittent atmosphere of celebration, which is strongest in December, first when the lights on the gigantic Christmas tree (an annual gift from Norway to thank the British for harboring its Royal Family during World War II) are turned on, and then, less festively, when thousands see in the New Year. ⊠ *Trafalgar Sq., SW1. Tube: Charing Cross.*

⑫ Wellington Barracks. These are the headquarters of the Guards Division, the queen's five regiments of elite foot guards (Grenadier, Coldstream, Scots, Irish, and Welsh) who protect the sovereign and patrol her palace dressed in tunics of gold-purled scarlet and tall fur "busby" helmets of Canadian brown bearskin. (London fact: the two items together cost more than £4,000.) If you want to learn more about the guards, you can visit the **Guards Museum**; the entrance is next to the Guards Chapel. ⊠ *Wellington Barracks, Birdcage Walk, SW1,* ☎ *020/ 7930–4466, ext. 3430.* 🖾 *£2.* ⊙ *Daily 10–4. Tube: St. James's Park.*

★ **⑯ Westminster Abbey.** Marked by the teeming human contents of tour buses, off the south side of Parliament Square, this is where nearly all of England's monarchs have been crowned amid great heraldic splendor; most are buried here, too. The main nave is packed with atmosphere, crowds, and memories, as it has witnessed many splendid coronation ceremonies, royal weddings, and, more recently, the funeral of Diana, Princess of Wales. As the most ancient of London's great churches, the place is crammed with spectacular medieval architecture. Other than the mysterious gloom of the vast interior, the first thing to strike most people is the fantastic proliferation of statues, tombs, and commemorative tablets: in parts, the building seems more like a stonemason's yard than a place of worship. But it is in its latter capacity that this landmark truly comes into its own. Although attending a service is not something to undertake purely for sightseeing reasons, it provides a glimpse of the abbey in its full majesty, accompanied by music from the Westminster choristers and the organ that Henry Purcell once played. During a service, you won't be bothered by the frequent and jarring loudspeaker announcements made during peak hours, requesting "a minute of silence" from the noisy masses.

The origins of Westminster Abbey are uncertain. The first church on the site may have been built as early as the 7th century by the Saxon king Sebert (who may be buried here, alongside his queen and sister); a Benedictine abbey was established in the 10th century. There were certainly preexisting foundations when Edward the Confessor was crowned in 1040, moved his palace to Westminster, and began building a church. Only traces have been found of that incarnation, which was consecrated eight days before Edward's death in 1065. (It appears in the Bayeaux Tapestry.) Edward's canonization in 1139 gave a succession of kings added incentive to shower the abbey with attention and improvements. Henry III, full of ideas from his travels in France, pulled it down and started again with Amiens and Rheims in mind. In fact, it was the master mason Henry de Reyns ("of Rheims") who, between 1245 and 1254, put up the transepts, north front, and rose win-

Westminster Abbey

dows, as well as part of the cloisters and chapter house; and it was his master plan that, funded by Richard II, was resumed 100 years later. Henry V (reigned 1413–22) and Henry VII (1485–1509) were the chief succeeding benefactors. The abbey was eventually completed in 1532. After that, Sir Christopher Wren had a hand in shaping the place; his west towers were completed in 1745, 22 years after his death, by Nicholas Hawksmoor. The most riotous elements of the interior were, similarly, much later affairs.

There is only one way around the abbey, and as there will almost certainly be a long stream of shuffling visitors at your heels, you'll need to be alert to catch the highlights. Entering by the north door, the first thing you see on your left are the overbearing and extravagant 18th-century monuments of statesmen in the north transept and north-transept chapels. Look up to your right to see the painted-glass rose window, the largest of its kind. At many points the view of the abbey is crowded by the many statues and screens; to your right is the 19th-

(and part 13th-) century choir screen, while to the left is the sacrarium, containing the medieval kings' tombs which screen the **Chapel of St. Edward the Confessor.** Due to its incredibly ancient fragility, the shrine to the pre-Norman king known as Edward the Confessor is closed off, but continuing to the foot of the Henry VII Chapel steps you can still see the hot seat of power, the **Coronation Chair,** which has been briefly graced by nearly every regal posterior. Edward I ordered it around 1300; it used to shelter the Stone of Scone (pronounced "Skoon"), upon which Scottish kings had been crowned since time began, but this precious relic was returned in 1996 to Scotland's Edinburgh Castle. The stone is to be returned to England, however, for the duration of future coronations.

Proceed up the steps into one of the architectural glories of Britain, the **Henry VII Chapel,** passing the huge white marble tomb of Elizabeth I, buried with her half sister, "Bloody" Mary I; then the tomb of Henry VII with his queen, Elizabeth of York, by the Renaissance master Torrigiano (otherwise known for having been banished from Florence after breaking Michelangelo's nose). Close by are monuments to the young daughters of James I; Sophia, who only lived for three days, is remembered by a single alabaster candle. An urn holds the purported remains of the so-called Princes in the Tower—Edward V and Richard. All around are magnificent sculptures of saints, philosophers, and kings, with wild mermaids and monsters carved on the choir-stall misericords (undersides) and with exquisite fan vaulting above—one of the miracles of Western architecture. (Keep an eye open for St. Wilgefort, who was so concerned to protect her chastity that she prayed to God for help and woke up one morning with a full growth of beard.)

The tombs and monuments with which Westminster Abbey is packed (some would say stuffed) began to appear at an accelerated rate starting in the 18th century (newest additions are ten 20th-century figures, including Martin Luther King, over the west door of the nave). One earlier occupant, though, was Geoffrey Chaucer, who in 1400 became the first poet to be buried in **Poets' Corner.** Most of the other honored writers have only their memorials here, not their bones: William Shakespeare and William Blake (who both had a long wait before the dean deemed them holy enough to be here at all), John Milton, Jane Austen, Samuel Taylor Coleridge, and William Wordsworth. Charles Dickens is both celebrated and buried in this crowded corner.

After the elbow battle you are guaranteed in Poets' Corner, you exit the main body of the abbey by a door from the south transept and south choir aisle to the comparative calm of the **cloisters,** where monks once strolled in contemplation and you may do the same. Go nearly all the way round and an archway leads to the quiet green **Dean's Yard,** where you can catch a fine view of the massive flying buttresses above. Also here is the entrance to Westminster School, formerly a monastic college, now one of Britain's finest public (which means the exact opposite to Americans) schools; Christopher Wren and Ben Jonson number among the old boys. Return to the cloisters and the abbey rooms used by monarchs of the middle ages (there's a separate small fee). The **chapter house,** a stunning octagonal room supported by a central column and adorned with 14th-century frescoes, is where the King's Council and, after that, an early version of the Commons, met between 1257 and 1547. Underfoot is one of the finest surviving tiled floors in the country. The **Abbey Museum** is in the undercroft, which survives from Edward the Confessor's original church, and includes a collection of deliciously macabre effigies made from the death masks and actual clothing of Charles II and Admiral Lord Nelson (complete with eye patch) and the battle kit of shield, saddle, and helmet of Henry V at Agincourt, among other fascinating relics. The **Pyx Chamber**, or Chapel of the Pyx, next door, contains the abbey's treasure, just as it did when it was the royal strong room during the 13th century. In fact, the columns date back to the 11th century; the pyx was the name for the monks' box of gold and silver.

Returning to the abbey and the nave, look to the foot of the wall in the north aisle opposite the organ loft. All of Ben Jonson is buried here—upright in accord with his modest demand for a 22-ft grave site (only his memorial is in Poets' Corner). ("O rare Ben Jonson," reads his epitaph, in a modest pun on the Latin *orare*, "to pray for.") James Watt and Michael Faraday are among the scientists with memorials; Sir Isaac Newton has both grave and memorial. There is only one painter: Godfrey Kneller, whose dying words were "By God, I will not be buried in Westminster."

The poignant **Tomb of the Unknown Warrior**, an anonymous World War I martyr, lies buried near the exit in memory of the soldiers fallen in both world wars. Nearby is one of the very few tributes to a foreigner, a plaque to Franklin D. Roosevelt. Note that photography is not permitted anywhere in the abbey. ⊠ *Broad Sanctuary, SW1,* ☏ *020/7222–5152,* WEB *www.westminster-abbey.org.* ☜ *Abbey £6; undercroft museum, Pyx Chamber treasury, and chapter house £2.50, £1 if you have bought a ticket to the abbey.* ☺ *Mon.—Sat. 9–3:45 (last admission Sat. 1:45). undercroft museum, Pyx Chamber treasury, and chapter house daily 10:30–4. Abbey closed weekdays and Sunday to visitors during services. Tube: Westminster.*

Westminster Cathedral. This massive cathedral is hard to miss—once you are almost upon it, that is. It's in a 21-year-old paved square that has fallen on hard times. The cathedral is the seat of the Cardinal of Westminster, head of the Roman Catholic Church in Britain; consequently it is London's principal Roman Catholic church. The asymmetrical redbrick Byzantine hulk, dating only from 1903, is banded with stripes of Portland stone and abutted by a 273-ft-high campanile at the northwest corner, which you can scale by elevator. Faced with the daunting proximity of the heavenly Westminster Abbey, the architect, John Francis Bentley, flew in the face of fashion by rejecting neo-Gothic in favor of the Byzantine idiom, which still provides maximum contrast today—not only with the great church but with just about all of London. The interior is partly unfinished but worth seeing for its atmosphere of brooding mystery, its mosaics, and its noted Eric Gill reliefs depicting the stations of the cross. Just inside the main entrance is the tomb of the much loved Cardinal Basil Hume, who died on June 17, 1999, after holding the seat for more than 25 years. ⊠ *Ashley Pl.,* ☏ *020/7798–9055.* ☜ *Tower £2.* ☺ *Cathedral daily 7–7. Tower Apr.–Sept., daily 9:30–5; Oct.–Mar., Thurs.–Sun. 9:30–5. Tube: Victoria.*

ST. JAMES'S AND MAYFAIR

St. James's and Mayfair form the very core of London's West End, the city's smartest central area. No textbook sights here; rather, these neighborhoods epitomize much of the flavor that is peculiarly London's—the sense of being in a great, rich, (once) powerful city is almost palpable as you wander along its posh and polished streets. Here is the highest concentration of grand hotels, department stores, exclusive shops, glamorous restaurants, commercial art galleries, auction houses, swanky offices—all accoutrements that give this area an unmistakable air of wealth and leisure, even on busy days.

A late-17th-century ghost in the streets of contemporary St. James's would not need to bother walking through walls because practically none have moved since he knew them. Its boundaries, clockwise from the north, are Piccadilly, Haymarket, the Mall, and Green Park: a neat rectangle, with a protruding spur satisfyingly located at Cockspur Street. The rectangle used to describe "gentlemen's London," where Sir was outfitted head and foot (but not in between, since the tailors were, and still are, north of Piccadilly in Savile Row) before repairing to his club. In fact, this has been a fashionable part of town from the first, largely by dint of the eponymous palace, St. James's, which was a royal residence—if not *the* palace—from the time of Henry VIII until the beginning of the Victorian era. In 1996, St. James's once again became a truly royal residence, as Prince Charles took up quarters here, shortly after leaving the Kensington Palace digs he once shared with his then wife.

Mayfair, like St. James's, is precisely delineated—a trapezoid contained by, respectively, Oxford Street and Piccadilly on the north and south, Regent Street and Park Lane on the east and west. Within its boundaries are streets both broad and narrow, but mostly unusually straight and gridlike for London, making it fairly easy to negotiate.

Numbers in the text correspond to numbers in the margin and on the St. James's and Mayfair map.

A Good Walk

Starting in Trafalgar Square, you'll find Cockspur Street off the southwest corner; follow it to the foot of **Haymarket.** On your right is London's oldest shopping arcade, the splendid Regency Royal Opera Arcade, which John Nash finished in 1818. Now you come to **Pall Mall** ①, a showcase of 18th- and 19th-century patrician architecture and home to such famous gentlemen's retreats as the Reform Club, halfway along on the right, from which Phileas Fogg set out to go around the world. At the end of Pall Mall, you collide with the small, Tudor brick **St. James's Palace** ②. Continue along Cleveland Row by the side of the palace to spy on York House, home of the Duke and Duchess of Kent; then turn left into Stable Yard Road to Lancaster House, built for the Duke of York in the 1820s but more notable as the venue for the 1978 conference that led to the end of white rule in Rhodesia (now Zimbabwe); and Clarence House, designed by John Nash and built in 1825 for the Duke of Clarence (who became William IV) and now home to the Queen Mother. Now, head north up along St. James's Street to St. James's Place, where, if you turn left, you can spot, at No. 27, one of London's most spectacular 18th-century mansions, **Spencer House** ③, home of Diana's ancestors; the interior can be viewed on tours given on Sunday only throughout the year (except August and January).

Cross back over St. James's Street to King Street—No. 8 is Christie's, the fine art auctioneers; Duke Street on the left harbors further exclusive little art salons—but straight ahead is **St. James's Square** ④, one of London's oldest squares and home of the London Library. Leave the square by Duke of York Street to the north, and turn left on **Jermyn Street** ⑤, the world center of gentlemen's paraphernalia shops. Set back from the street is the lovely **St. James's Church** ⑥. A right on Duke Street brings you to Piccadilly. Turn right again, and you'll pass the exclusive department store that supplies the queen's groceries, Fortnum & Mason, on the right, and the **Royal Academy of Arts** ⑦, opposite, with famous **Piccadilly Circus** ⑧ ahead. Turn around—Wellington Arch and **Apsley House (Wellington Museum)** ⑨, the gloriously opulent mansion the Duke of Wellington once called home, are ahead in the distance. Cross the street and head north up the shopping mecca of **Bond Street** ⑩, with **Burlington Arcade** ⑪ to the right. You could de-tour by turning right before you reach Oxford Street into Brook Street (the composer Handel lived at No. 25), which leads to Hanover Square. Turning right down St. George Street brings you to the porticoes of St. George's Church, where Percy Bysshe Shelley and George Eliot, among others, had their weddings. A right turn after the church down Mill Street brings you into Savile Row, the fashionable center for custom-made suits and coats since the mid-19th century. No. 3 is a mecca for Beatlemaniacs: the former headquarters of Apple Records and the site of John, Paul, George, and Ringo's legendary rooftop concert (the build-ing now houses a financial institution and is not open to the public). Continuing from Savile Row to behind the Royal Academy is Albany Street, one of the smartest addresses since the turn of the 19th century. You can peer through the railings at the posh Henry Holland apart-ments built for fashionable bachelors, which included Byron, Prime Min-isters Gladstone and Heath, Graham Greene, and latterly actor Terence Stamp. From Savile Row, head west on Grosvenor Street to Duke Street: slightly to the south you'll find a couple of Mayfair's beauty spots—Carlos Place (site of the Connaught) and neighboring Mount Row, both adorned with some veddy, veddy elegant residences. Here, too, is Mount Street, a pedigree-proud shopping avenue; take South Audley Street one block south to discover St. George's Gardens, a fine place for a picnic. Head over to Hyde Park to take in **Speakers' Cor-ner** ⑫ and **Marble Arch** ⑬. Shop-till-you-droppers can then explore Ox-ford Street (**Selfridges** ⑭ and **Marks & Spencer** are here), while art lovers will want to continue north to Manchester Square for the magnificent **Wallace Collection** ⑮. TV aficionados should, instead, make a beeline a few blocks east for the **BBC Experience** ⑯.

TIMING

Although this walk doesn't cover an enormous distance, you'll prob-ably do a lot of doubling back and detouring down beckoning alleys—and into interesting shops. If you want to do more than window-shop, we suggest most emphatically a weekday jaunt, starting in the morn-ing, so you get time for visits to the Royal Academy and the Wallace Collection or perhaps some of the commercial art galleries in and around Cork Street. The walk alone should take less than two hours. Add at least an hour for Apsley House, and another two for the Wal-lace Collection. Any of those could easily consume an afternoon, if you have one to spare. Shopping could take all week.

HOW TO GET THERE

You could start walking around this area from Trafalgar Square, or get the Piccadilly or Bakerloo Line to the Piccadilly Circus tube stop, the Piccadilly to the Hyde Park Corner stop, or the Central Line to any of the stops along Oxford Street—Marble Arch, Bond Street (also Ju-bilee Line), Oxford Circus (also Victoria and Bakerloo lines), or Tot-tenham Court Road (also Northern Line). The Green Park stop on the Piccadilly, Victoria, or Jubilee Line is also central to many of this neighborhood's sights. The best buses are 8, 9, 14, 19, 22, and 38 along Piccadilly, especially the 8, which loops around via New Bond Street to Oxford Street and skims the eastern border of Green Park down Grosvenor Place.

Sights to See

★ ❾ **Apsley House (Wellington Museum).** For Hyde Park Corner read "heroes corner"; even in the subway, beneath the turmoil of traffic, the Duke of Wellington's heroic exploits are retold in murals. The years of war against the French, and the subsequent final defeat of Napoléon at the Battle of Waterloo in 1815 made Wellington—Arthur Welles-

60

St. James's and Mayfair

Apsley House
(Wellington
Museum) 9

BBC Experience . . . 16

Bond Street 10

Burlington
Arcade 11

Jermyn Street 5

Marble Arch 13

Pall Mall 1

Piccadilly Circus 8

Royal Academy
of Arts 7

St. James's
Church 6

St. James's Palace . . 2

St. James's
Square 4

Selfridges 14

Speaker's
Corner 12

Spencer House 3

Wallace
Collection 15

ley—the greatest soldier and statesman in the land. The house is flanked by imposing statues: opposite is the 1828 Decimus Burton **Wellington Arch** with the four-horse chariot of peace as its pinnacle. Cast from captured French guns, the legendary **Achilles** statue points the way with thrusting shield to the ducal mansion from the tip of Hyde Park. Once known, quite simply, as No. 1, London, this was long celebrated as the best address in town. Built by Robert Adam and later refaced and extended, this was home to the Duke of Wellington from 1817 until his death in 1852. As the Wellington Museum, it has been kept as the "Iron Duke" liked it—even the railings outside are painted pale green as the duke once had them—his uniforms and weapons, his porcelain and plate, and his extensive art collection are displayed heroically. Unmissable, in every sense (and considered rather too athletic for the time), is the gigantic Canova statue of a nude (but fig-leafed) Napoléon Bonaparte, Wellington's archenemy, which presides over the grand staircase, leading to the many elegant reception rooms. The most stunning is the Waterloo Gallery, where the annual banquet for officers who fought beside Wellington was held. With its heavily sculpted and gilded ceiling, its feast of old master paintings on red damask walls, and commanding gray candelabra, it is a veritable orgy of opulence. Apsley House installed iron shutters in 1830 after rioters, protesting the duke's opposition (he was briefly prime minister) to the Reform Bill, broke the windows. Yes, the British loved him for defeating Napoléon, but mocked him with the name Iron Duke—referring not only to his military prowess but to his indomitable will. ✉ *149 Piccadilly, W1,* ☎ *020/7499–5676,* 🌐 *www.vam.ac.uk.* ✉ *£4.50; free sound guides.* ☉ *Tues.–Sun. 11–4:30. Tube: Hyde Park Corner.*

⑯ **BBC Experience.** For those who have been weaned on a steady diet of *Masterpiece Théatre* presentations, the BBC is the greatest television producer in the world. These fans, and those of the BBC's countless other programs, will be happy to know that they can get delve into the history of the corporation and its landmark screen and radio clips from the rich archives, going back over 75 years. The emphasis is on interaction and there is ample opportunity to get in on the act, literally—want to try your hand at commentating on a sports game, presenting a weather forecast, or making your own director's cut of a segment of *EastEnders*? Tickets can be purchased at the front door, or you can prebook a tour with a credit card. There's a massive gift shop. ✉ *Broadcasting House, Portland Pl., W1,* ☎ *0870/603–0304,* 🌐 *www.bbc.co.uk/experience.* ✉ *£7.50.* ☉ *Daily 10–4:30. Tube: Oxford Circus.*

Berkeley Square. As anyone who's heard the old song knows, the name rhymes with "starkly." Not many of its original mid-18th-century houses are left, but look at Nos. 42–46 (especially No. 44, which the architectural historian Sir Nikolaus Pevsner thought London's finest terraced house) and Nos. 49–52 to get some idea of why it was once London's top address—not that it's in the least humble now. Snob nightclub Annabels is one current resident. ✉ *Berkeley Sq, W1. Tube: Green Park.*

⑩ **Bond Street.** This world-class shopping haunt is divided into northern "New" (1710) and southern "Old" (1690) halves. New Bond Street boasts **Sotheby's,** the world-famous auction house, at No. 35, but there are other opportunities to flirt with financial ruin on Old Bond Street: the mirror-lined Chanel store, the vainglorious marble acres of Gianni Versace, and the boutique of the more sophisticated Gucci, plus Tiffany's British outpost and art dealers Colnaghi, Léger, Thos. Agnew, and Marlborough Fine Arts. **Cork Street,** which parallels the top half of Old Bond Street, is where London's top dealers in contemporary art have their galleries—you're welcome to browse, but dress appropriately. ⊠ *Tube: Bond Street, Green Park.*

⑪ **Burlington Arcade.** Perhaps the finest of Mayfair's enchanting covered shopping alleys is the second oldest in London, built in 1819 for Lord Cavendish, to stop the hoi polloi from throwing rubbish into his garden at Burlington House, which is behind the arcade. It's still patrolled by top-hatted beadles, who preserve decorum by preventing you from singing, running, or carrying open umbrellas. ⊠ *Piccadilly, W1. Tube: Green Park or Piccadilly Circus.*

Faraday Museum. In the basement of the Royal Institution is a reconstruction of the laboratory where the physicist Michael Faraday discovered electromagnetic induction in 1831—with echoes of Frankenstein. ⊠ *21 Albermarle St., W1,* ☎ *020/7409–2992,* WEB *www.ri.ac.uk.* ⊠ *£1.* ⊙ *Weekdays 10–5. Tube: Green Park.*

Grosvenor Square. This square (pronounced "*Grove*-na") was laid out in 1725–31 and is as desirable an address today as it was then. Americans certainly thought so—from John Adams, the second president, who as ambassador lived at No. 38, to Dwight D. Eisenhower, whose wartime headquarters was at No. 20. Now the ugly '50s block of the U.S. Embassy occupies the entire west side, and a British memorial to Franklin D. Roosevelt stands in the center. The little brick chapel used by Eisenhower's men during World War II, the 1730 Grosvenor Chapel, stands a couple of blocks south of the square on South Audley Street, with the entrance to pretty **St. George's Gardens** to its left. Across the gardens is the headquarters of the English Jesuits as well as the society-wedding favorite, the mid-19th-century Church of the Immaculate Conception, known as Farm Street because that is the name of the street on which it stands. ⊠ *W1. Tube: Bond St.*

❺ **Jermyn Street.** This is where the gentleman purchases his traditional fashion accessories. He buys his shaving sundries and hip flask from Geo. F. Trumper; briar pipe from Astley's; scent from Floris (for women, too—both the Prince of Wales and his mother are Floris customers), whose interiors are exceedingly historic and beautiful, or Czech & Speake; shirts from Turnbull & Asser; and deerstalkers and panamas from Bates the Hatter. Don't forget the regal cheeses from Paxton & Whitfield (founded in 1740 and a legend among dairies). Shop your way east along Jermyn Street, and you're practically in Piccadilly Circus. ⊠ *SW1. Tube: Piccadilly Circus.*

⑬ **Marble Arch.** The name denotes both the traffic whirlpool where Bayswater Road segues into Oxford Street and John Nash's 1827 arch, which moved here from Buckingham Palace in 1851. Search the sidewalk on the traffic island opposite the cinema to find the stone plaque that marks (roughly) the place where the Tyburn Tree stood for four centuries, until 1783. This was London's central gallows, a huge wooden structure with hanging accommodations for 21. Hanging days were holidays, the spectacle supposedly functioning as a crime deterrent for the hoi polloi. It didn't work, alas. Oranges, gingerbread, and gin were sold, alongside "personal favors," to vast, rowdy crowds, and the condemned, dressed in finery for his special moment, was treated more as hero than as villain. Cross over (or under—there are signs to help in the labyrinth) to the northeastern corner of Hyde Park to Speakers' Corner. Believe it or not, there are two tiny apartments in Marble Arch, rented out by the National Trust. ⊠ *Park La., W1. Tube: Marble Arch.*

NEED A
BREAK? Smarter than the usual street café, **Sotheby's Café** (⊠ 34–35 New Bond St., W1) is a cut above, as you would expect of this classy auction house in the chic shopping quarter of Bond Street. Lunches, such as the lobster club sandwich, aren't terribly cheap, but service is included within the tab.

❶ Pall Mall. Like its near-namesake, *the* Mall, Pall Mall rhymes with "shall" and derives its name from the cross between croquet and golf that the Italians, who invented it, called *pallo a maglio* and the French, who made it chic, called *palle-maille*. In England it was taken up with enthusiasm by James I, who called it "pell mell" and passed it down the royal line, until Charles II had a new road laid out for it in 1661. Needless to say, Catherine Street, as Pall Mall was officially named (after Charles's queen, Catherine of Braganza), was *very* fashionable. No. 79 must have been one of its livelier addresses, since Charles's gregarious mistress, Nell Gwynne, lived there. The king gave her the house when she complained about being a mere leaseholder, protesting that she had "always conveyed free under the Crown" (as it were); it remains, to this day, the only privately owned bit of Pall Mall's south side. Stroll slowly, the better to appreciate the creamy facades and perfect proportions along this showcase of 18th- and 19th-century British architecture.

Notable examples are two James Barry–designed buildings, the **Travellers' Club** and the **Reform Club,** both representatives of the upper-class gentleman's retreat that made St. James's the club land of London. The Reform is the most famous club of all, thanks partly to Jules Verne's Phileas Fogg, who accepted the around-the-world-in-80-days bet in its smoking room and was thus soon qualified to join the Travellers'. And— hallelujah—women can join the Reform. The RAC Club (for Royal Automobile Club, but it's never known as that), with its marble swimming pool, and the Oxford and Cambridge Club complete the Pall Mall quota; there are other, even older establishments—Brooks's, the Carlton, Boodles, and White's (founded in 1736, the oldest of all)—in St. James's Street around the corner, alongside *the* gentleman's bespoke (custom) shoemaker, Lobb's, and, at No. 6, *the* hatter, James Lock, which has one of the most historic store facades in the city—you half expect Lord Byron or Anthony Trollope to walk out the door. Waterloo Place, around the corner, is a continuation of this gentleman's quarter. ⊠ *SW1. Tube: Piccadilly Circus.*

❽ Piccadilly Circus. New York has its Times Square, in Venice it's Piazza San Marco, and London has Piccadilly Circus. As natives say, if you stand here long enough, you will meet everyone you know. The name came into use during the early 17th century, when a humble tailor on the Strand named Robert Baker sold an awful lot of picadils—a collar ruff all the rage in courtly circles—and built a house with the proceeds. Snobs dubbed his new-money mansion Piccadilly Hall, and the name stuck. As for "Circus," that refers not to the menagerie of back-packers and camera-clickers clustered around the steps of **Eros** but to the circular junction of five major roads.

Eros, London's favorite statue and symbol of the *Evening Standard* newspaper, is not in fact the Greek god of erotic love at all, but the angel of Christian charity, commissioned in 1893 from the young sculptor Alfred Gilbert as a memorial to the philanthropic Earl of Shaftesbury (the angel's bow and arrow are a sweet allusion to the earl's name). It cost Gilbert £7,000 to cast the statue he called his "missile of kindness" in the novel medium of aluminum, and because he was paid only £3,000, he promptly went bankrupt and fled the country. (Not to worry—he was knighted in the end.) Eros has lately done his best to bankrupt Westminster Council, too, owing to some urgent leg surgery and a new coat of protective microcrystalline synthetic wax. Around Eros, London roars on—this hub is home to a very large branch of Tower Records, the tawdry Trocadero Centre (video arcades, food courts, chain stores, the Guinness World of Records), a SegaWorld, and a perpetual traffic jam. Beneath the blight, however, is beauty: just behind the modern bank of neon advertisements are some of the most elegant Edwardian-era buildings in town. ⊠ *W1. Tube: Piccadilly Circus.*

Portland Place. The elegant throughway to Regent's Park was London's widest street in the 1780s, when brothers Robert and James Adam designed it. The first sight to greet you here, drawing the eye around the awkward corner, is the curvaceous portico and pointy Gothic spire of **All Souls Church,** one part of Nash's Regent Street plan that remains. It is now the venue for innumerable concerts and Anglican services broadcast to the nation by the British Broadcasting Corporation. The 1931 block of Broadcasting House next door is home to the BBC's five radio stations and the **BBC Experience.** It curves, too, if less beautifully, and features an Eric Gill sculpture of Shakespeare's Ariel (aerial—get it?) over the entrance, from which the playful sculptor was obliged to excise a portion of phallus lest it offend public decency—which the modified model did in any case. At No. 66, opposite the Chinese Embassy, the Royal Institute of British Architects has a small exhibitions gallery devoted to shows from its esteemed members. Here, too, if you need a break, is a tasteful branch of a Patisserie Valerie café. ⊠ *W1. Tube: Oxford Circus or Great Portland St.*

Regent Street. This curvaceous thoroughfare was conceived by John Nash and his patron, the Prince Regent—the future George IV—as a kind of ultra-catwalk from the Prince's palace, Carlton House, to Regent's Park (then called Marylebone Park). The section between Piccadilly and Oxford Street was to be called the Quadrant and lined with colonnaded shops purveying "articles of fashion and taste," in a big PR exercise to improve London's image as the provincial cousin of smarter European capitals. The scheme was never fully implemented, and what there was fell into such disrepair that, early this century, Aston Webb (of the Mall route) collaborated on the redesign you see today. It is still a major shopping street. Hamleys, the gigantic toy emporium, is fun; and since 1875 there has been Liberty, which originally imported silks from the East then diversified to other Asian goods, and is now best known for its "Liberty print" cottons, its jewelry department, and—still—its high-class Asian imports. The mock-Tudor interior, with stained glass and beams taken from battleships, is worth a look. ⊠ *W1. Tube: Piccadilly Circus or Oxford Circus.*

❼ Royal Academy of Arts. Burlington House was built in the Palladian style for the Earl of Burlington around 1720, and it is one of the few surviving mansions from that period. The chief occupant today is the Royal Academy of Arts (RA), which mounts major art exhibitions, usually years in the planning. Old Masters are the basic bill of fare, but in 1997 the academy mounted a show of Britain's leading enfants terribles, called "Sensation," which caused just that. One can only imagine what Sir Joshua Reynolds—whose statue is in the academy courtyard—would have made of Damien Hirst's formaldehyde-preserved tiger-shark sculpture. The academy's own fabled collection has unfortunately been dispersed to other museums, notably the Tate Britain and the National Gallery; the latter got the prize—the *Taddeo Tondo* (a sculpted disk) by Michelangelo of the Madonna and Child. But the return is that major exhibitions plunder other collections heavily to pro-

HOW TO USE THIS GUIDE

Great trips begin with great planning, and this guide makes planning easy. It's packed with everything you need—insider advice on hotels and restaurants, cool tools, practical tips, essential maps, and much more.

COOL TOOLS

Fodor's Choice Top picks are marked throughout with a star.

Great Itineraries These tours, planned by Fodor's experts, give you the skinny on what you can see and do in the time you have.

Smart Travel Tips A to Z This special section is packed with important contacts and advice on everything from how to get around to what to pack.

Good Walks You won't miss a thing if you follow the numbered bullets on our maps.

Need a Break? Looking for a quick bite to eat or a spot to rest? These sure bets are along the way.

Off the Beaten Path Some lesser-known sights are worth a detour. We've marked those you should make time for.

POST-IT® FLAGS
Dog-ear no more!

"Post-it" is a registered trademark of 3M.

Favorite restaurants • Essential maps • Frequently used numbers • Walking tours • Can't-miss sights • Smart Travel Tips • Web sites • Top shops • Hot nightclubs • Addresses • Smart contacts • Events • Off-the-beaten-path spots • Favorite restaurants • Essential maps • Frequently used numbers • Walking tours •

ICONS AND SYMBOLS

Watch for these symbols throughout:

★	Our special recommendations
✕	Restaurant
⌂	Lodging establishment
✕⌂	Lodging establishment whose restaurant warrants a special trip
☺	Good for kids
☞	Sends you to another section of the guide for more information
✉	Address
☎	Telephone number
FAX	Fax number
WEB	Web site
🎫	Admission price
☉	Opening hours
$-$$$$	Lodging and dining price categories, keyed to strategically sited price charts. Check the index for locations.
①❶	Numbers in white and black circles on the maps, in the margins, and within tours correspond to one another.

ON THE WEB

Continue your planning with these useful tools found at **www.fodors.com**, the Web's best source for travel information.

"Rich with resources." —*New York Times*

"Navigation is a cinch." —*Forbes* "Best of the Web" list

"Put together by people bursting with know-how."
                              —*Sunday Times* (London)

Create a Miniguide Pinpoint hotels, restaurants, and attractions that have what you want at the price you want to pay.

Rants and Raves Find out what readers say about Fodor's picks—or write your own reviews of hotels and restaurants you've just visited.

Travel Talk Post your questions and get answers from fellow travelers, or share your own experiences.

On-Line Booking Find the best prices on airline tickets, rental cars, cruises, or vacations, and book them on the spot.

About our Books Learn about other Fodor's guides to your destination and many others.

Expert Advice and Trip Ideas From what to tip to how to take great photos, from the national parks to Nepal, Fodors.com has suggestions that'll make your trip a breeze. Log on and get informed and inspired.

Smart Resources Check the weather in your destination or convert your currency. Learn the local language or link to the latest event listings. Or consult hundreds of detailed maps—all in one place.

duce barnstorming exhibitions. The mammoth Monet show in 1998 broke all attendance records and saw the gallery open for 24 hours on the final weekend to squeeze in ticketholders. For 2002, an exhibit on international artists in Paris from 1900 to 1968 is planned. Every June, the RA mounts the **Summer Exhibition,** a mishmash of sculpture and painting, with about 1,000 things crammed into every cranny. Craving art now? Try the shop; it's one of the best museum stores in town. ✉ *Burlington House, Piccadilly, W1,* ☎ *020/7300–8000; 020/7300–5760 recorded information,* WEB *www.royalacademy.org.uk.* ✉ *Admission varies according to exhibition.* ☉ *Sat.–Thurs. 10–6, Fri. 10–8:30. Tube: Piccadilly Circus or Green Park.*

NEED A BREAK?
The **Royal Academy Restaurant** has hot dishes at lunchtime, very good vegetarian options, and an extensive salad selection that is inexpensive for such a swish location. Desserts and cakes are masterpieces. It's a popular place to meet for a bite throughout the day, as you can eat here without paying admission but still drink in the artistic atmosphere. It's open weekdays 10–5:30, with a dinner menu on Friday from 6:15 to 10:30.

6 **St. James's Church.** Recessed from the street behind a courtyard, the church is filled most days with an antiques and crafts market. Completed in 1684, this was the last of Sir Christopher Wren's London churches and his own favorite. It contains one of Grinling Gibbons's finest works, an ornate limewood reredos (the screen behind the altar). The organ is a survivor of Whitehall Palace and was brought here in 1691. A 1940 bomb scored a direct hit here, but the church has been completely restored, albeit with a fiberglass spire. It's a lively place, offering all manner of lectures and concerts. ✉ *Piccadilly, W1,* ☎ *020/7381–0441 for concert program and tickets. Tube: Piccadilly Circus or Green Park.*

2 **St. James's Palace.** With its solitary sentry posted at the gate, this surprisingly small palace of Tudor brick was once home to many British sovereigns, including the first Elizabeth and Charles I, who spent his last night here before his execution. Today it is the residence of another Charles—the future King Charles III (that is, if the current Prince of Wales makes it to Westminster Abbey). His front door actually debouches right onto the street, but he always uses a back entrance. Matters to ponder as you look (you can't go in): the palace was named after a hospital for women lepers, which stood here during the 11th century; Henry VIII had it built; foreign ambassadors to Britain are still accredited to the Court of St. James's even though it has rarely been a primary royal residence; and the present queen made her first speech here. Friary Court out front is a splendid setting for Trooping the Colour, part of the Changing of the Guard ceremony. Everyone loves to take a snap of the scarlet-coated guardsman standing sentinel outside the imposing Tudor gateway. ✉ *Friary Court, SW1. Tube: Green Park.*

4 **St. James's Square.** One of London's oldest and leafiest squares was also the most snobbish address of all when it was laid out around 1670, with 14 resident dukes and earls installed by 1720. Since 1841, No. 14—one of the several 18th-century residences spared by World War II bombs—has housed the **London Library,** founded by Thomas Carlyle (☞ Carlyle's House *in* Chelsea and Belgravia, *below*), and which, with its million or so volumes, is considered the best private humanities library in the land. You can go in and read the famous authors' complaints in the comments book—but not the famous authors' books, unless you join, at £100 a year. ✉ *SW1. Tube: Piccadilly Circus.*

⑭ **Selfridges.** With its row of massive Ionic columns, this huge store was opened three years after Harry Gordon Selfridge came to London from Chicago in 1906. Now British-run, Selfridges rivals Harrods in size and stock, and it is finally rivaling its glamour, too, since investing in major face-lift operations. ⊠ *400 Oxford St., W1,* ☎ *020/ 7629–1234. Tube: Marble Arch or Bond St.*

Shepherd Market. Though it looks like a quaint and villagelike tangle of streetlets, this was anything *but* quaint when Edward Shepherd laid it out in 1735 on the site of the orgiastic, two-week-long May Fair (which gave the whole district its name). Now there are sandwich bars, pubs and restaurants, boutiques and nightclubs, and a (fading) red-light reputation in the narrow lanes. ⊠ *Curzon and Shepherd Sts., W1. Tube: Green Park.*

⑫ **Speakers' Corner.** This corner harbors one of London's most public spectacles. Here, on Sunday afternoons, anyone is welcome to mount a soapbox and declaim upon any topic. It's an irresistible showcase of eccentricity, though sadly diminished since the death in 1994 of the "Protein Man," who thought the eating of meat, cheese, and peanuts led to uncontrollable acts of passion that would destroy Western civilization. The pamphlets he sold for four decades down Oxford Street are now collector's items. ⊠ *Cumberland Gate, Park La., W1. Tube: Marble Arch.*

★ ❸ **Spencer House.** Ancestral abode of the Spencers—Diana, Princess of Wales's family—this great mansion is perhaps the finest example of 18th-century elegance, on a domestic scale, extant in London. Superlatively restored by Lord Rothschild, the house was built in 1766 for the first Earl Spencer, heir to the first Duchess of Marlborough. A gorgeous Doric facade, complete with a pediment adorned with classical statues, announces at once Earl Spencer's passion for the Grand Tour and the classical antiquities of the past. Inside, James "Athenian" Stuart decorated the gilded State Rooms, including the Painted Room, the first completely Neoclassic room in Europe. The most ostentatious part of the house (and the Spencers did not shrink from ostentation—witness the £40,000 diamond shoe buckles the first countess proudly wore) is the florid bow window of the Palm Room: covered with stucco palm trees, it conjures up both ancient Palmyra and modern Miami Beach. ⊠ *27 St. James's Pl., SW1,* ☎ *020/7499–8620,* WEB *www.spencerhouse.co.uk.* 🎫 *£6.* ☉ *Sept.–Dec. and Feb.–July, Sun. 10:45–4:45 (guided tour leaves approx. every 25 mins; tickets on sale Sun. at 10:30). Tube: Green Park.*

★ ⑮ **Wallace Collection.** Assembled by four generations of Marquesses of Hertford and given to the nation by the widow of Sir Richard Wallace, bastard son of the fourth, this collection of art and artifacts is important, exciting, undervisited—and free. As at the Frick Collection in New York, the setting, Hertford House, is part of the show: the fine late-18th-century mansion, built for the Duke of Manchester, contains a basement floor with educational activities, several galleries, and a courtyard, covered by a glass roof, with exhibit space and an upscale restaurant.

The first marquess was a patron of Sir Joshua Reynolds, the second bought Hertford House, the third—a flamboyant socialite—favored Sèvres porcelain and 17th-century Dutch painting; but it was the eccentric fourth marquess who, from his self-imposed exile in Paris, really built the collection, snapping up Bouchers, Fragonards, Watteaus, and Lancrets for a song (the French Revolution having rendered them dangerously unfashionable), augmenting these with furniture and sculpture and sending his son Richard out to do the deals. With 30 years of practice behind him, Richard Wallace continued acquiring treasures after his father's death, scouring Italy for majolica and Renaissance gold, then moving most of it to London. Look for Rembrandt's portrait of his son, the Rubens landscape, Gainsborough and Romney portraits, the Van Dycks and Canalettos, the French rooms, and of course the porcelain. The highlight is Fragonard's *The Swing*, which conjures up the 18th century's let-them-eat-cake frivolity better than any other painting around. Don't forget to smile back at Frans Hals's *Laughing Cavalier* in the Big Gallery or pay your respects to Thomas Sully's enchanting *Queen Victoria*, which resides in a rouge-pink salon (just to the right of the main entrance). There is a fine collection of armor and weaponry in the basement as a break from all the upstairs gentility. ⊠ *Hertford House, Manchester Sq., W1,* ☎ *020/7935–0687,* WEB *www.the-wallace-collection.org.uk.* ⌨ *Free.* ⊙ *Mon.–Sat. 10–5, Sun. noon–5. Tube: Bond St.*

Waterloo Place. This is a long rectangle off Pall Mall, punctuated by the Duke of York Memorial Column atop the Duke of York Steps and littered with statues, among them Florence Nightingale, the "Lady with the Lamp" nurse-heroine of the Crimean War; Captain R. F. Scott, who led a disastrous Antarctic expedition in 1911–12 and is here frozen in a bronze by his wife; Edward VII, mounted; George VI; and, as usual, Victoria, here in terra-cotta. Flanking Waterloo Place and looking onto Pall Mall are two of the gentlemen's clubs for which St. James's came to be known as Clubland: the **Athenaeum** and the former United Service Club, a favorite haunt of the Duke of Wellington, now the **Institute of Directors**. The latter was built by John Nash in 1827–28 but was given a face-lift by Decimus Burton 30 years later to match it up with the Athenaeum across the way, which he had designed. It's fitting that you gaze on the Athenaeum first, since it was—and is—the most elite of all the societies. (It called itself "the Society" until 1830 just to rub it in.) Most prime ministers and cabinet ministers, archbishops, and bishops have belonged; the founder, John Wilson Croker (the first to call the British right-wingers "Conservatives"), decreed it the club for artists and writers, and so literary types (Sir Arthur Conan Doyle, Rudyard Kipling, J. M. Barrie—the posh ones) have graced its lists, too. Women are barred. Most clubs will tolerate female guests these days, but few admit women members, and anyway it's almost impossible to become a member unless you have the connections—which, of course, is the whole point. ⊠ *Regent St., Pall Mall, SW1. Piccadilly Circus.*

SOHO AND COVENT GARDEN

An area delineated by Regent Street, Coventry and Cranbourn streets, Charing Cross Road, and the eastern half of Oxford Street encloses Soho, the most fun part of the West End. This appellation, unlike the New York neighborhood's similar one, is not an elision of anything but a blast from the past—derived (as far as we know) from the shouts of "So-ho!" that royal huntsmen in Whitehall Palace's parklands were once heard to cry. One of Charles II's illegitimate sons, the Duke of Monmouth, was an early resident, his dubious pedigree setting the tone for the future: for many years, Soho was London's center of strip shows, peep shows, clip joints, sex shops, and brothels. The mid-'80s brought legislation that granted expensive licenses to a few such establishments and closed down the rest; most prostitution had already been ousted by the 1959 Street Offences Act. Only a cosmetic smear of red-light activity remains now, plus one or two purveyors of couture fetish wear for trendy club-goers.

These clubs, which cluster around the Soho grid, are the diametric opposite of the St. James's gentlemen's museums—they cater to youth, change soundtracks every month, and post tyrannical fashion police at the door. Another breed of Soho club is the strictly members-only media haunts (the Groucho, the Soho House, Fred's, Brown's, Black's), salons for carefully segregated strata of high-income hipsters. The same crowd populates the astonishing selection of restaurants, but then so do the rest of London and all its visitors—because Soho is gourmet country.

It was after the First World War, when London households relinquished their resident cooks en masse, that Soho's gastronomic reputation was established. It had been a cosmopolitan area since the first immigrant wave of French Huguenots arrived in the 1680s. More French came fleeing the revolution during the late 18th century, then the Paris Commune of 1870, followed by Germans, Russians, Poles, Greeks, and (especially) Italians, and, much later, Chinese. Pedestrianized Gerrard Street, south of Shaftsbury Avenue, is the hub of London's compact Chinatown, which boasts restaurants, dim sum houses, Chinese supermarkets, and Chinese New Year's celebrations, plus a brace of scarlet pagoda-style archways and a pair of phone booths with pictogram dialing instructions.

The former Covent Garden Market became the Covent Garden Piazza, with the Central Market in the middle, in 1980, and it still functions as the center of a neighborhood—one that has always been alluded to as "colorful." It was originally the "convent garden" belonging to the Abbey of St. Peter at Westminster (later Westminster Abbey). The land was given to the first Earl of Bedford by the Crown after the Dissolution of the Monasteries in 1536. The earls—later promoted to dukes—of Bedford held on to the place right up until 1918, when the 11th duke managed to off-load what had by then become a liability. In between, the area enclosed by Long Acre, St. Martin's Lane, Drury Lane, and assorted streets north of the Strand had gone from the height of fashion (until the snobs moved west to brand-new St. James's) to a period of arty-literary bohemia during the 18th century, followed by an era of vice and mayhem, once more to become vegetable provisioner to London when the market building went up in the 1830s, followed by the Flower Market in 1870 (Eliza Dolittle's haunt in Shaw's *Pygmalion* and Lerner and Loewe's musical version, *My Fair Lady*).

Still, it was no Mayfair, what with 1,000-odd market porters spending their 40 shillings a week in the alehouses, brothels, and gambling dens that had never quite disappeared. By the time the Covent Garden Estate Company took over the running of the market from the 11th duke, it seemed as if seediness had set in for good, and when the fruit-and-veg trade moved out to the bigger, better Nine Elms Market in Vauxhall in 1974, it left behind a decrepit wasteland. But this is one of London's success stories: the Greater London Council (now sadly defunct) stepped in with a dream of a rehabilitation plan—not unlike the one that was tried, though less successfully, in the Parisian equivalent, Les Halles. By 1980 the transformation was complete.

Numbers in the text below correspond to numbers in the margin and on the Soho and Covent Garden map.

A Good Walk

Soho, being small, is easy to explore, though it's also easy to mistake one narrow, crowded street for another, and even Londoners go astray here. Enter from the northwest corner, Oxford Circus, and head south for about 200 yards down Regent Street, turn left onto Great Marlborough Street, and head to the top of **Carnaby Street** ①. Turn right off Broadwick Street into Berwick (pronounced "Berrick") Street, famed as central London's best fruit-and-vegetable market. Then step through tiny Walker's Court (ignoring the notorious hookers' bulletin board); cross Brewer Street, named for two extinct 18th-century breweries; and you'll have arrived at Soho's hip (and very gay) hangout, Old Compton Street. From here, Wardour, Dean, Frith, and Greek streets lead north, all of them bursting with restaurants and clubs. Either of the last two leads north to **Soho Square** ②, but head one block south instead, to Shaftesbury Avenue, heart of theaterland, across which you'll find Chinatown's main drag, Gerrard Street. Below Gerrard Street is **Leicester Square** ③, and running along its west side is Charing Cross Road, the bibliophile's dream. You'll find some of the best of the specialist bookshops in little Cecil Court, running east just before Trafalgar Square.

The easiest way to find the **Covent Garden Piazza** ④ and market building is to walk down Cranbourn Street, next to the Leicester Square tube, then down Long Acre, and turn right at James Street. Around here are **St. Paul's Church** ⑤—the actors' church—the **London Transport Museum** ⑥, and the **Theatre Museum** ⑦, as well as plenty of shops and cafés. (If your aim is to shop, Neal Street, Floral Street, the streets around Seven Dials, and the Thomas Neal's mall all reward exploration.) From Seven Dials, veer 45 degrees south onto Mercer Street, turning right on Long Acre, then left onto Garrick Street, past the **Garrick Club** ⑧, left onto Rose Street, and right onto Floral Street. At the other end you'll emerge onto Bow Street, right next to the **Royal Opera House** ⑨ and the **Bow Street Magistrates' Court** ⑩. Continuing on and turning left onto Russell Street, you reach Drury Lane and the **Theatre Royal, Drury Lane** ⑪.

At the end of Drury Lane is the Aldwych, a great big croissant of a potential traffic accident, with a central island on which stand three hulking monoliths: India House, Melbourne House, and the handsome 1935 Neoclassic Bush House, headquarters of the BBC World Service. Stranded on traffic islands to the west are the 1717 St. Mary-le-Strand; James Gibbs's (of St. Martin-in-the-Fields fame) first public building, inspired by the Baroque churches of Rome; and Wren's St. Clement Danes (with a tower appended by Gibbs), whose 10 bells peal the tune of the nursery rhyme "Oranges and lemons, Say the bells of St. Clements . . ." even though the bells in the rhyme belong to the St. Clements in Eastcheap. Inside is a book listing 1,900 American airmen who were killed during World War II. Heading west, perhaps stopping at **Somerset House** ⑫ and the **Courtauld Institute of Art** within, walk the ¾-mi traffic-clogged Strand to the southern end, where you take Villiers Street down to the Thames. See the historic York Watergate, once the gateway leading from the Duke of Buckingham's garden to the river steps, and **Cleopatra's Needle** ⑬ by Victoria Embankment Gardens; cross the gardens northwest to the **Adelphi** ⑭, circumnavigating the Strand by sticking to the embankment walk; and you'll soon reach Waterloo Bridge, where (weather permitting) you can catch some of London's most glamorous views, toward both the City and Westminster around the Thames bend.

TIMING

The distance covered here is around 5 mi if you include the lengthy walk down the Strand and riverside stroll back. Skip that and it's barely a couple of miles, but you will almost certainly get lost, because the streets in both Covent Garden and Soho are winding, chaotic, and not logically disposed. Although getting lost is half the fun, it does make it hard to predict how long this walk will take. You can whiz round both neighborhoods in an hour, but if the area appeals at all, you'll

Soho and Covent Garden

River Thames

KEY

⊖ Tube Station

N

Inner Temple Garden

Royal Courts of Justice

Chancery Ln.

Fleet St.

St. Clement Danes

Embankment

Strand Ln.

Roman Bath

12

Lincoln's Inn Fields

Lincoln's Inn Fields

Aldwych

Lancaster Pl.

Waterloo Br.

Kingsway

Strand

Savoy St.

Victoria Embankment

13

Kemble St.

Gt. Queen St.

Drury Ln.

Wild St.

Russell St.

11

Catherine St.

Wellington St.

Great Queen St.

York Watergate

Parker St.

10

7

6

Savoy Pl.

Bow St.

9

4

Long Acre

5

Endell St.

Bedford St.

William IV St.

14

Macklin St.

Drury Ln.

Betterton St.

Garrick St.

8

St. Martin's Ln.

John Adam St.

Villiers St.

Shelton St.

Neal St.

Monmouth St.

Cecil Ct.

Charing Cross Station

High St.

New Oxford St.

Shaftesbury Ave.

High Holborn

Charing Cross Rd.

Cranbourn

Leicester Sq.

National Gallery

Trafalgar Sq.

Greek St.

Frith St.

Gerrard St.

Lisle St.

3

Whitcomb St.

Soho Sq.

2

Rupert St.

Rupert St.

Coventry St.

Haymarket

Rathbone Pl.

Dean St.

Old Compton St.

Piccadilly Circus

Regent St.

Newman St.

Wardour St.

Walker's Ct.

Denman St.

Berners St.

Berwick St.

Brewer St.

Noel St.

Glasshouse St.

Poland St.

Wells St.

Marshall St.

Golden Sq.

Warwick St.

Jermyn St.

Oxford St.

Carnaby St.

1

Sackville St.

Tichfield St.

Beak St.

Regent St.

Savile Row

Vigo St.

Portland St.

Gt. Marlborough St.

Gt. Portland St.

Old Burlington St.

Cork St.

Conduit St.

Prince's St.

Old Bond St.

Regent St.

Oxford Circus

Hanover Sq.

Hanover St.

Saint George St.

Albemarle St.

Margaret St.

Dover St.

Harewood Pl.

Maddox St.

Wigmore St.

Cavendish Sq.

Holles St.

Brook St.

New Bond St.

Grosvenor St.

Henrietta Pl.

Brook's Mews

Berkeley Sq.

Bruton St.

Davies St.

0   220 yds

0   200 m

Adelphi **14**	St. Paul's Church . . . **5**
Bow Street Magistrates' Court **10**	Soho Square **2**
	Somerset House . . . **12**
Carnaby Street **1**	Theatre Museum . . . **7**
Cleopatra's Needle **13**	Theatre Royal, Drury Lane **11**
Covent Garden Piazza **4**	
Garrick Club **8**	
Leicester Square . . . **3**	
London Transport Museum **6**	
Royal Opera House **9**	

want all day—for shopping, lunch, the Theatre and Transport museums, and the Courtauld Galleries. One way to do it is to start at Leicester Square at 2 PM, when the Half Price Theatre Booth opens; pick up tickets for later; and then walk, shop, and eat in between.

HOW TO GET THERE

A popular way to get to Soho is to hop on the Northern Line to Tottenham Court Road and walk south down Charing Cross Road, then west along Old Compton Street into the district proper, or eastward, by turning left at Shaftesbury Avenue, over to the Covent Garden area. The Covent Garden tube stop is on the Piccadilly Line; Leicester Square—the nearest tube to Soho—is on the Northern and Piccadilly Lines. The best Soho buses are Buses 3, 8, 10, 12, 13, 15, 23, 38, 73, 139, 159, and 176 to Charing Cross Road and Shaftesbury Avenue; for Covent Garden, get those listed above or the ones that stop along the Strand: Buses 9, 11, 13, 15, and 23.

Sights to See

⑭ **Adelphi.** This regal riverfront row of houses was the work of London's Scottish architects—all four of them. John, Robert, James, and William Adam, being brothers, gave rise to the name, from the Greek *adelphoi,* meaning brothers. All the late-18th-century design stars were roped in to beautify the interiors, but the grandeur gradually eroded, and today very few of the 24 houses remain; Nos. 1–4 Robert Street, and No. 7 Adam Street are the best. ⊠ *The Strand, WC2. Tube: Charing Cross, Temple.*

⑩ **Bow Street Magistrates' Court.** This was where the prototype of the modern police force first operated. Known as the Bow Street Runners (because they chased thieves on foot), they were the brainchild of the second Bow Street magistrate—none other than Henry Fielding, the author of *Tom Jones* and *Joseph Andrews.* The late-19th-century edifice on the site went up during one of the market improvement drives. It now houses three courts, including that of the Metropolitan Chief Magistrate, who hears all extradition applications. ⊠ *Bow St., WC2. Tube: Covent Garden.*

❶ **Carnaby Street.** The '60s synonym for swinging London fell into a post-party depression, reemerging sometime during the 1980s as the main drag of a public-relations invention called West Soho. Blank stares would greet anyone asking directions to such a place, but it is geographically logical, and the tangle of streets—Foubert's Place, Broadwick Street, Marshall Street—do cohere, at least in type of merchandise (youth accessories, mostly, with a smattering of up-and-coming, happening designer boutiques and fashionable restaurants). Broadwick Street is also notable as the birthplace, at No. 74, in 1758, of the great visionary poet and painter William Blake. At age 26 he relocated back to this house for a year to sell prints next door, at No. 72 (now an ugly tower block), and then remained a Soho resident on Poland Street. ⊠ *W1. Tube: Oxford Circus.*

⑬ **Cleopatra's Needle.** Off the triangular-handkerchief Victoria Embankment Gardens, where office sandwich-eaters and people who call it home coexist, is London's *very oldest thing,* predating its arbitrary namesake, and London itself, by centuries. The 60-ft pink granite obelisk was erected at Heliopolis, in lower Egypt, in about 1475 BC, then moved to Alexandria, where in 1819 Mohammed Ali, the Turkish viceroy of Egypt, rescued it from its fallen state and presented it to the British. The British, though grateful, had not the faintest idea how to get the 186-ton gift home, so they left it there for years until an expatriate English engineer contrived an iron pontoon to float it to Lon don via Spain. The sphinxes are a later, British addition. Future archaeologists will find an 1878 time capsule underneath, containing the morning papers, several Bibles, a railway timetable, some pins, a razor, and a dozen photos of Victorian pinup girls. ⊠ *Embankment, WC2. Tube: Charing Cross or Embankment.*

Courtauld Institute of Art. One of London's most beloved art collections, the Courtauld reopened in October 1998 in grand 18th-century classical **Somerset House.** Founded in 1931 by the textile magnate Samuel Courtauld, this is London's finest Impressionist and Post-Impressionist collection, ranging from Bonnard to Van Gogh (Manet's *Bar at the Folies-Bergère* is the star), with bonus post-Renaissance works thrown in. Botticelli, Brueghel, Tiepolo, and Rubens are also represented, thanks to the exquisite bequest of Count Antoine Seilern's Princes Gate collection. ⊠ *The Strand, WC2,* ☎ *020/7848–2526,* WEB *www.courtauld.ac.uk.* 🎟 *£4; free Mon. noon–6.* 🕑 *Mon.–Sat. 10–6, Sun. noon–6 (last admission 5:15). Tube: Covent Garden, Holborn, or Temple.*

❹ Covent Garden Piazza. The restored 1840 market building around which Covent Garden pivots is known as the Piazza. Inside, the shops are mostly higher-class clothing chains, plus a couple of cafés and some knickknack stores that are good for gifts. There's a superior crafts market on most days, too. If you turn right, you'll reach the indoor **Jubilee Market,** with stalls selling clothing, army surplus gear, more crafts, and more knickknacks. At yet another market off to the left (on the way back to the tube), the leather goods, antiques, and secondhand clothing stalls are a little more exciting. In summer it may seem that everyone you see around the Piazza (and the crowds are legion) is a fellow tourist, but there is still plenty of office life in the area, and Londoners continue to flock here. By the church in the square, street performers—from global musicians to jugglers and mime artists—play to the crowds. ⊠ *Covent Garden, WC2. Tube: Covent Garden.*

❽ Garrick Club. Named for the 18th-century actor and theater manager David Garrick, this club is, because of its literary-theatrical bent, more louche than its St. James's brothers, and famous actors, from Sir Laurence Olivier down, have always been proud to join—along with Dickens, Thackeray, and Trollope, in their time. Find the **Lamb & Flag** down teeny Rose Street to the left. Dickens drank in this pub, better known in its 17th-century youth as the Bucket of Blood, owing to the bare-knuckle boxing matches held upstairs. (You'll find that many London pubs claim Dickens as an habitué, and it's unclear whether they exaggerate or the author was the city's premier sot.) ⊠ *15 Garrick St., WC2. Tube: Leicester Sq. or Covent Garden.*

❸ Leicester Square. This square (pronounced "Lester") is showing no sign of its great age. Looking at the neon of the major movie houses, the fast-food outlets (plus a useful Häagen-Dazs café), and the disco entrances, you'd never guess it was laid out around 1630. By the 19th century it was already bustling and disreputable, and now it's usually one of the only places crowded after midnight—with suburban teenagers, backpackers, and London's swelling ranks of the homeless. That said, it is not a threatening place, and the liveliness can be quite cheering. In the middle is a statue of a sulking Shakespeare, clearly wishing he were somewhere else and perhaps remembering the days when the cinemas were live theaters—burlesque houses, but live all the same. Here, too, are figures of Hogarth, Reynolds, and Charlie Chaplin, and underneath, but not visible, is a £22 million electrical substation. One landmark certainly worth visiting is the **Society of London Theatre ticket kiosk,** on the southwest corner, which sells half-price tickets for many of that evening's performances. On the northeast corner, in Leicester

Place, stands the church of **Notre Dame de France,** with a wonderful mural by Jean Cocteau in one of its side chapels. ✉ *WC2. Tube: Covent Garden.*

⑥ **London Transport Museum.** Housed in the old Flower Market at the southeast corner of the Covent Garden Piazza, this museum tells the story of mass transportation in the capital, and it is much better than it sounds. It is particularly child-friendly, with lots of touch-screen interactive material; live actors in costume (including a Victorian horse-dung collector, though you should go early to see them); old rolling stock; period smells and sounds; and, best of all, a tube-driving simulator. There's also a café and a shop selling the wonderful old London Transport posters, plus mugs, socks, bow ties, and so on, printed with that elegant London tube map, designed by Harry Beck in 1933 and still in use today. ✉ *Piazza, WC2,* ☎ *020/7379–6344,* WEB *www.lt-museum.co.uk.* ✄ *£5.50.* ☉ *Sat.–Thurs. 10–6, Fri. 11–6. Tube: Covent Garden.*

Neal Street. One of Covent Garden's most intriguing shopping streets begins north of Long Acre, catercorner to the tube station, and is closed to traffic halfway down. Here you can buy everything you never knew you needed—apricot tea, sitars, vintage aviators' jackets, silk kimonos, Alvar Aalto vases, halogen desk lamps, shoes with heel lower than toe, collapsible top hats, and so on. To the left off Neal Street, on Earlham Street, is Thomas Neal's—a new, upmarket, designerish clothing and housewares mall named after the founder (in 1693) of the star-shape cobbled junction of tiny streets just past there, called Seven Dials—a surprisingly residential enclave, with lots going on behind the tenement-style warehouse facades. The small and intimate **Donmar Warehouse Theatre** is part of the complex; it has presents a radical range of theater—such as Nicole Kidman in *The Blue Room.* Turning left onto the next street off Neal Street, Shorts Gardens, you come to Neal's Yard (note the comical, water-operated wooden clock), originally just a whole-foods wholesaler and now an entire holistic village, with therapy rooms, an organic bakery and dairy, a great vegetarian café, and a medical herbalist's shop reminiscent of a medieval apothecary. ✉ *WC2. Tube: Covent Garden.*

Rock Circus. This shamelessly touristy offshoot of Madame Tussaud's waxworks features animatronic and wax pop stars miming to their hits or frozen in time, chronologically displayed to give the impression of a museum of popular music. As some might imagine, this is strictly for younger teens. ✉ *London Pavilion, Piccadilly Circus, W1,* ☎ *020/7734–7203,* WEB *www.rock-circus.com.* ✄ *£8.25.* ☉ *Wed.–Mon. 10–5:30; Tues. 11–5:30. Tube: Piccadilly Circus.*

⑨ **Royal Opera House.** Here, in days of yore, Joan Sutherland brought down the house as Lucia di Lammermoor, and Rudolf Nureyev and Margot Fonteyn became the greatest ballet duo of all time. For such delights, seats were top dollar—nearly £100—or just one-twentieth of that lordly amount. Whatever the price, it was worth it if you loved red-and-gold Victorian decor, which always managed to give a very special feel to the hush that precedes the start of a performance. London's premier opera venue was designed in 1858 by E. M. Barry, son of Sir Charles, the House of Commons architect. This is actually the third theater on the site. The first opened in 1732 and burned down in 1808; the second opened a year later under the aegis of one John Anderson, only to succumb to fire in 1856 (Anderson, who had lost two theaters already, had an appalling record when it came to keeping the limelights apart from the curtains).

The entire building was recently overhauled spectacularly as a modern, practical, technologically streamlined opera house, while keeping the magic of the grand Victorian theater. Without doubt, the glass and steel Floral Hall (so badly damaged by fire in the 1950s it was used only for storing scenery) is the most wonderful jaw-dropping feature, and visitors can wander in and drink in the atmosphere during the day. The same is true of the Amphitheatre Bar and Piazza concourse, which give a splendid panorama across the city. The whole ethos is of a grand opening up of what was perceived as being for the elite (there are free lunchtime chamber concerts and a full educational program for schoolchildren). Behind the scenes, conditions for the two companies sharing the space, the Royal Opera and the Royal Ballet, have been drastically improved—the Royal Ballet has a real home with state-of-the-art rehearsal rooms, and there are practice rooms for the musicians. The signs are looking good for the Opera House to recover its form and shake off the shower of bad publicity that has surrounded it for far too long. ⊠ *Bow St.,* ☎ *020/7240–1200 or 020/7304–4000,* WEB *www.royaloperahouse.org. Tube: Covent Garden.*

❺ St. Paul's Church. If you want to commune with the spirits of Vivien Leigh, Noël Coward, Edith Evans, and Charlie Chaplin, this might be the place. Memorials to them and many other theater greats are found in this 1633 work of the renowned Inigo Jones, which has always been known as "the actors' church" thanks to the neighboring theater district and St. Paul's prominent parishioners (well-known actors often read the lessons at services). Fittingly, its portico was the setting for *Pygmalion*'s opening scene. St. Paul's Church (Wren's mammoth St. Paul's cathedral is eastward in the City) is across the Covent Garden Piazza, often picturesquely punctuated with street entertainers—those who have passed auditions for this most coveted of London's street venues. ⊠ *Bedford St., WC2. Tube: Covent Garden.*

❷ Soho Square. Laid out about 1680, this square was fashionable during the 18th century. Only two of the original houses still stand, plus the 19th-century central garden. It's now a place of peace and offices (among them Paul McCartney's music publishers and Bloomsbury Publishing). That isn't a Tudor landmark in the center but a Tudor-style thatch-and-daub Victorian gardener's hut—an almost fairy-tale sight to enjoy during a take-out lunch in the park. ⊠ *W1. Tube: Tottenham Court Rd.*

NEED A BREAK?   Take any excuse you can think of to visit either of Soho's wonderful rival patisseries: **Maison Bertaux** (⊠ 28 Greek St.) or **Pâtisserie Valerie** (⊠ 44 Old Compton St.). Both serve divine gâteaux, milles-feuilles, croissants, éclairs, and more, the former in an upstairs salon, the latter in a darkish room behind the cake counters.

⓬ Somerset House. An old royal palace once stood on the site, but the 18th-century building that finally replaced it was the work of Sir William Chambers (1726–96) during the reign of George III. It was built to house government offices, principally those of the Navy; for the first time in over one hundred years, these gracious rooms are on view for free, including the Seamen's Waiting Hall and the Nelson Stair. In addition, the Navy Commissioners' Barge has returned to dry dock at the Water Gate. The rooms are on the south side of the building, by the river, while the **Courtauld Institute of Art** occupies most of the north building, facing the busy Strand. Between is the cobbled Italianate courtyard, where Admiral Nelson used to walk, which is the scene of concerts and other cultural events. Cafés and a restored river terrace adjoin the property, and a stone-and-glass footbridge leads across the river.

In the vaults of the house is **The Gilbert Collection**, a museum of intricate works of silver, gold snuff boxes, and Italian mosaics. The micromosaics on tables, portrait miniatures, and jewelry are made in such fine detail that you might think they're painted, so be glad if you're offered a magnifying glass—it's the best way to fully appreciate the fine detail. The **Hermitage Rooms** contain permanent exhibition space for some of the treasures from the State Hermitage Museum in Russia. The opening show consisted of a selection of jewels, antiquities, portraits, and miniatures amassed by Catherine the Great, one of the greatest collectors of all time. ⊠ *The Strand, WC2,* ☎ *020/7845–4600, 020/ 7240–4080 Gilbert Collection, 020/7845–4630 Hermitage,* WEB *www.somerset-house.org.uk.* ⊞ *Somerset House free; Gilbert Collection £4 (combined ticket to Gilbert and Courtauld Institute of Art £7); Hermitage Rooms £6.* ☉ *Mon.–Sat. 10–6, Sun. noon–6 (last admission 5:15). Tube: Charing Cross.*

Strand. Remember Judy Garland doing Burlington Bertie in Chaplin drag, walking down the Strand with gloves in hand, in *A Star Is Born*? William Hargreaves's song was a popular number in the Strand music halls that put the street on the map afresh in the early 1900s. Now its presence on maps is about all that the characterless Strand has to recommend it. ⊠ *WC2. Tube: Charing Cross.*

⊕ ❼ **Theatre Museum.** This mostly below-ground museum aims to re-create the excitement of theater itself. There are usually programs in progress allowing children to get in a mess with makeup or have a giant dressing-up session. Permanent exhibits paint a history of the English stage from the 16th century to Mick Jagger's jumpsuit, with tens of thousands of theater playbills and sections on such topics as Hamlet through the ages and pantomime—the peculiar British theatrical tradition whereby men dress as ugly women (as distinct from RuPaul) and girls wear tights and play princes. There's a little theater in the bowels of the museum and a ticket desk for "real" theaters around town, plus an archive holding video recordings and audiotapes of significant British theatrical productions. ⊠ *7 Russell St., WC2,* ☎ *020/7836– 7891,* WEB *www.theatremuseum.org.* ⊞ *£4.50.* ☉ *Tues.–Sun. 10–6 (last admission 5:30). Tube: Covent Garden.*

⓫ **Theatre Royal, Drury Lane.** This is London's best-known auditorium and almost its largest. Since World War II, its forte has been musicals (past ones have included *The King and I, My Fair Lady, South Pacific, Hello, Dolly!* and *A Chorus Line*)—though David Garrick, who managed it from 1747 to 1776, made its name by reviving the works of the by-then-obscure William Shakespeare. It enjoys all the romantic accessories of a London theater—a history of fires (it burned down three times, once in a Wren-built incarnation), riots (in 1737, when a posse of footmen demanded free admission), attempted regicides (George II in 1716 and his grandson George III in 1800), and even sightings of the most famous phantom of theaterland, the Man in Grey (in the Circle, matinees). The entrance is on Catherine Street. ⊠ *Catherine St., WC2. Tube: Covent Garden.*

BLOOMSBURY AND LEGAL LONDON

The character of an area of London can change visibly from one street to the next. Nowhere is this so clear as in the contrast between fun-loving Soho and intellectual Bloomsbury, a mere 100 yards to the northeast, or between arty, trendy Covent Garden and—on the other side of Kingsway—sober Holborn. Both Bloomsbury and Holborn are almost purely residential and should be seen by day. The first district is best known for its famous flowering of literary-arty bohemia, personified by the clique known as the Bloomsbury Group during this century's first three decades, and for the British Museum and the University of London, which dominate it now. The second sounds as exciting as, say, a center for accountants or dentists, but don't be put off—filled with magnificently ancient buildings, it's more interesting and beautiful than you might suppose.

Let's get the Bloomsbury Group out of the way since you can't visit them and nothing exists to mark its territory beyond a sprinkling of blue plaques. (These government-sponsored tablets commemorate persons who enhanced "human welfare or happiness" and have been dead for at least 20 years.) There's also a plaque in Bloomsbury Square saying nothing about this elite core of writers and artists except that they lived around here. The chief Bloomsburies were Virginia Woolf, E. M. Forster, Vanessa and Clive Bell, Duncan Grant, Dora Carrington, Roger Fry, John Maynard Keynes, and Lytton Strachey, with satellites including Rupert Brooke and Christopher Isherwood. They agreed with G. E. Moore's philosophical notion that "the pleasures of human intercourse and the enjoyment of beautiful objects . . . form the rational ultimate end of social progress." True to their beliefs, when they weren't producing beautiful objects, the friends enjoyed much human intercourse, as has been exhaustively documented, not least in Virginia Woolf's own diaries. All you need do to find out more about them is to read the "Review" supplements of the Sunday broadsheets, which are forever running Bloomsbury exposés as if they were fresh gossip.

More clearly visible than those literary salons is the time-warp territory of interlocking alleys, gardens and cobbled courts, and town houses and halls where London's legal profession grew up. The Great Fire of 1666 razed most of the city but spared the buildings of legal London, and the whole neighborhood oozes history. What is best about the area is that it lacks the commercial veneer of other historic sites, mostly because it still is very much the center of London's legal profession. Barristers, berobed and bewigged, may add an anachronistic frisson to your sightseeing, but they're only on their way to work.

They are headed for one of the four Inns of Court: Gray's Inn, Lincoln's Inn, Middle Temple, and Inner Temple. Those arcane names are simply explained. The inns were just that: lodging houses for the lawyers who, back in the 14th century, clustered together here so everyone knew where to find them and ultimately took over the running of the inns themselves. The temples were built on land owned by the Knights Templar, a chivalric order founded during the First Crusade in the 11th century; their 12th-century Temple Church still stands here. Few barristers (British for trial lawyers) still live in the inns, but nearly all keep chambers (British for barristers' offices) here, and all are still obliged to eat a requisite number of meals in the hall of "their" inn during training—no dinner, no career. They take exams, too.

Numbers in the text correspond to numbers in the margin and on the Bloomsbury and Legal London map.

A Good Walk

From Russell Square tube stop, walk south down Southampton Row and west on Great Russell Street, passing **Bloomsbury Square** on the left, en route to London's biggest and most important collection of antiquities, the **British Museum** ①. Leaving this via the back exit leads you to Montague Place, which you should cross to Malet Street, straight ahead, to reach the **University of London** ②. On the left after you pass the university buildings is the back of the Royal Academy of Dramatic Art, or RADA (its entrance is on Gower Street), where at least half of the most stellar British thespians got their training, with **University College** ③ following at the top of Malet Place. For a delightful detour, head west over to Scala Street (just one block west from the Goodge Street tube stop, then one block north on Charlotte Street) to find the delightful Victorian-era wonders of **Pollock's Toy Museum** ④. The streets around here and Fitzroy Square, built by the Adam brothers, are known as Fitzrovia, so named by literary soaks who drank at the Fitzroy Tavern on Charlotte Street. Back around the university, head over to Gordon Street to reach Gordon Square. For the prettiest little street with picturesque 19th-century shop fronts, divert to Woburn Walk (Irish poet Yeats lived at No. 5). If you're interested in Asian art, stop in at the **Percival David Foundation of Chinese Art** ⑤; if you want to check out the spectacular **British Library** ⑥ or its **National Sound Archive,** head north up to Euston Road. Otherwise, continue south down busy Woburn Place, veering left down Guilford Street to reach Coram's Fields, home of the **Thomas Coram Foundation** (closed until early 2003); then turn left south of there on Guilford Place, then right to Doughty Street and the **Dickens House Museum** ⑦. Two streets west, parallel to Doughty Street, is Lamb's Conduit Street (whose pretty pub, the Lamb, Dickens inevitably frequented).

At the bottom of Lamb's Conduit Street you reach Theobalds Road, where you enter the first of the Inns of Court, **Gray's Inn** ⑧. From here, emerge onto High Holborn (pronounced "Hoe-bun"); heavy with traffic, it is the main route from the City to the West End and Westminster and still the center of London's diamond and jewelry trade. Pass another ghost of former trading, **Staple Inn** ⑨, and turn left down tiny Great Turnstile Row to reach **Lincoln's Inn** ⑩, where you pass the Hall and continue around the west side of New Square to Carey Street, which leads you round into Portugal Street. Here you'll find the Old Curiosity Shop, probably one of the rare places in London Dickens did *not* frequent. Recross to the north side of Lincoln's Inn Fields to **Sir John Soane's Museum** ⑪ or walk the other way on Carey Street to reach the **Royal Courts of Justice** ⑫, which run through to the Strand. Off to the left is Fleet Street and the 1610 **Prince Henry's Room** ⑬. Cross the Strand to **Temple** ⑭, and pass through the elaborate stone arch to Middle Temple Lane, which you follow past **Temple Church** ⑮ to the Thames.

TIMING
This is a substantial walk of 3 to 4 mi, and it has two distinct halves. The first half, around Bloomsbury, is not so interesting on the surface, but it features a major highlight of London, the British Museum, where you could easily add 1 mi to your total and certainly at least two hours. The Dickens House is also worth a stop. The second half, legal London, is a real walker's walk, with most of the highlights in the architecture and atmosphere of the buildings and streets. The exception is Sir John Soane's Museum, which will absorb an extra hour. The walk alone can be done comfortably in two hours and is best on a sunny day.

HOW TO GET THERE
The best tube stops for the Inns of Court are Holborn on the Central and Piccadilly lines (surface and walk east up High Holborn, then south), or Chancery Lane on the Central Line. For the British Museum, Tottenham Court Road (Northern and Central lines) and Russell Square (Piccadilly Line) are equidistant. Bus 7 is the best bus for the BM; for the Inns of Court, get Bus 8, 17, 25, 45, 46, or 243 to High Holborn or Bus 17, 19, 38, 45, 46, 55, or 243 to Theobalds Road.

Sights to See

Bloomsbury Square. This was laid out in 1660, making it the earliest of the Bloomsbury squares, although none of the original houses remain; what is most remarkable about it now is that you can always find a parking spot in the huge underground garage. You'll find it by exiting the tube at Tottenham Court Road—a straight, very ugly street where London buys its electrical appliances, hi-fi equipment, and computer accessories—and taking Great Russell Street east. Bloomsbury is dotted with squares—Gordon, Tavistock, Bedford, and Brunswick are some of the more picturesque ones. ⊠ *WC1. Tube: Tottenham Court Rd.*

❻ British Library. Since 1759, the British Library had always been housed in the British Museum on Gordon Square. But space ran out long ago. The collection of around 18 million volumes now has a home in state-of-the-art surroundings, and if you are a researcher, it's a wonderful place to work (special passes are required). The library's treasures are on view to the general public: Magna Carta, a Gutenberg Bible, Jane Austen's writings, Shakespeare's First Folio, and musical manuscripts by Handel and Sir Paul McCartney are on show in the John Ritblat Gallery. The Workshop of Words, Sound & Images explores the vitality of the living word, and on weekends and during school vacations there are hands-on demonstrations of how a book comes together. Feast your eyes also on the six-story glass tower that holds the 65,000-volume collection of George III, plus a permanent exhibition of rare stamps. And if all that wordiness is just too much, you can relax in the library's piazza or restaurant and take in one of the free concerts in the amphitheater. ⊠ *96 Euston Rd., NW1,* ☏ *020/7412–7332,* WEB *www.bl.uk.* ☐ *Free.* ☉ *Mon. and Wed.–Fri. 9:30–6, Tues. 9:30–8, Sat. 9:30–5; Sun. 11–5. Tube: Euston or King's Cross.*

★ ☝ ❶ British Museum. With a facade like a great temple, this celebrated treasure house—filled with plunder of incalculable value and beauty from around the globe—is housed in a ponderously dignified Greco-Victorian building that makes for a suitably grand impression. Inside you'll find some of the greatest relics of humankind: the Elgin Marbles, the Rosetta Stone, the Sutton Hoo Treasure—everything, it seems, but the Ark of the Covenant. The museum is rapidly shaking off its ponderous dust as a rash of new galleries opens and sections are updated. The focal point is the unmissable Great Court, a brilliant techno-classical design with a vast glass roof, which highlights and reveals the museum's best-kept secret—an inner courtyard—for the first time in 150 years. New galleries and exhibit space will celebrate the museum's 250th birthday in 2003. The revered Reading Room made a welcome comeback in 2000 after careful restoration. The floor space is vast, split into nearly 100 galleries—so arm yourself with a free floor plan directly as you go in or they'll have to send out search parties to rescue you.

The collection began in 1753, when Sir Hans Sloane, physician to Queen Anne and George II, bequeathed his personal collection of curiosities and antiquities to the nation. It then quickly grew, thanks to enthusiastic kleptomaniacs after the Napoleonic Wars—most notoriously the seventh Earl of Elgin, who carried off the marbles from the Parthenon and Erechtheum while on a Greek vacation between 1801 and 1804.

The enormous building, with its classical Greek-style facade featuring figures representing the Progress of Civilization, was finished in 1847, the work of Sir Robert Smirke. Wherever you go, there are marvels, but certain objects and collections are more important, rarer, older, or downright unique, and because you may wish to include these in your wanderings, here follows a highly edited overview (in order of encounter) of the BM's greatest hits:

Bloomsbury and Legal London

Close to the entrance, in the south end of Room 25, is the **Rosetta Stone,** found in 1799 and carved in 196 BC with a decree of Ptolemy V in Egyptian hieroglyphics, demotic, and Greek. It was this multilingual inscription that provided the French Egyptologist Jean-François Champollion with the key to deciphering hieroglyphics.

Perhaps the **Elgin Marbles** ought not to be here, but since they are—and they are, after all, among the most graceful and heartbreakingly beautiful sculptures on earth—you can find them in Room 8, west of the entrance in the Parthenon Galleries. The marbles are displayed along with an in-depth, high-tech exhibit of the sculptures and the Acropolis, and bring to the fore the rumbling debate on whether the Greeks should reclaim their spectacular sculptural heritage. Above the debate are the lofty remains of the Parthenon frieze that girdled the interior of Athena's temple on the Acropolis, carved around 440 BC (the handless, footless Dionysus who used to recline along its east pediment is especially well known). While you're in the west wing, you can see one of the Seven Wonders of the Ancient World—in fragment form, unfortunately—in Room 12: the **Mausoleum of Halikarnassos.** This 4th-century tomb of Mausolus, King of Caria, was the original "mausoleum."

Upstairs are some of the most perennially popular galleries, especially beloved by children: Rooms 62–63, where the **Egyptian mummies** live. With the opening of the Roxie Walker Galleries in May 1999, even more relics from the Egyptian realm of the dead are on view—in addition to more mummies there is a menagerie of animal companions and fascinating items buried alongside the mummies. Scanners have helped reveal further secrets of the mummies, and some displays allow an even closer look beneath the wraps.

Proceeding clockwise, you'll come to Room 49, where the **Mildenhall Treasure** glitters in the refurbished Weston Gallery of Roman Britain. This haul of 4th-century Roman silver tableware was found beneath the sod of a Suffolk field in 1942. Next door, in Room 41, is the equally splendid **Sutton Hoo Treasure,** including swords and helmets, bowls and buckles, all encrusted with jewels—which was buried at sea with (they think) Redwald, King of the Angles, in the 7th century and excavated from a Suffolk field in 1938–39.

In Room 50 lies Pete Marsh, so named by the archaeologists who unearthed the **Lindow Man** from a Cheshire peat marsh. He was ritually slain, probably as a human sacrifice, in the 1st century and lay perfectly pickled in his bog until 1984. In the upper level of the museum is the Money Gallery, which holds ancient coins and medals. Back on the ground floor, in Room 33d, The **Chase Manhattan Gallery of North America** has one of the largest collections of native culture outside the North American continent, going back to the earliest hunters 10,000 years ago. The Korea Foundation Gallery has royal gold crown of Silla (5th–6th century), on loan from the National Museum of Korea, as its centerpiece along with ceramics and rare ancient manuscripts. ✉ *Great Russell St., WC1,* ☎ *020/7636–1555,* WEB *www.thebritishmuseum.ac.uk.* ✉ *Free (suggested donation of £2).* ☺ *Mon.–Sat. 10–5, Sun. noon–6. Tube: Tottenham Court Rd., Holborn, or Russell Sq.*

NEED A BREAK? The British Museum's self-service **restaurant and café** get very crowded, but serve a reasonably tasty menu beneath a plaster cast of a part of the Parthenon frieze that Lord Elgin didn't remove. The restaurant is open Monday–Saturday noon–4:30, Sunday noon–5:30; the café, Monday–Saturday 10–3.

❼ Dickens House Museum. This is the only one of the many London houses Charles Dickens (1812–70) inhabited that's still standing, and it would have had a real claim to his fame in any case because he wrote *Oliver Twist* and *Nicholas Nickleby* and finished *Pickwick Papers* here between 1837 and 1839. The house looks exactly as it would have in Dickens's day, complete with first editions, letters, and a tall clerk's desk (where the master wrote standing up, often while chatting with visiting friends and relatives). There's a treat for Lionel Bart fans—his score of *Oliver!* Down in the basement is a replica of the Dingley Dell kitchen from *Pickwick Papers.* ⊠ *48 Doughty St., WC1,* ☎ *020/ 7405–2127,* ⓦⒺⒷ *www.dickensmuseum.com.* 🎟 *£4.* ☉ *Mon.–Sat. 10– 5. Tube: Chancery La. or Russell Sq.*

❽ Gray's Inn. Although the least architecturally interesting of the four Inns of Court and the one most damaged by German bombs in the 1940s, this still has its romantic associations. In 1594, Shakespeare's *Comedy of Errors* was performed for the first time in its hall—which was lovingly restored after World War II and has a fine Elizabethan screen of carved oak. You must make advance arrangements to view the Tudor-style Gray's Inn's Hall (apply in writing, in advance, to the administrator, the Under Treasurer), but you can stroll around the secluded and spacious gardens, first planted by Francis Bacon in 1606. ⊠ *Gray's Inn Rd., Holborn,* ☎ *020/7458–7800.* ☉ *Weekdays 10–4. Tube: Holborn or Temple.*

★ ❿ Lincoln's Inn. There's plenty to see at one of the oldest, best-preserved, and most comely of the Inns of Court—from the Chancery Lane Tudor brick gatehouse to the wide-open, tree-lined, atmospheric Lincoln's Inn Fields and the 15th-century chapel remodeled by Inigo Jones in 1620. The wisteria-clad New Square, London's only complete 17th-century square, is not the newest part of the complex; in fact, the oldest-looking buildings are the 1845 Hall and Library, which you must obtain the porter's permission to enter. ⊠ *Chancery La., WC2,* ☎ *020/7405– 1393.* ☉ *Gardens weekdays 7–7, Chapel weekdays noon–2:30; public may also attend Sun. service in Chapel at 11:30 during legal terms. Tube: Chancery La.*

National Sound Archive. In this aural outpost of the British Library, you may listen to the voice of the queen who made this neighborhood possible; the million recordings held here include one of Victoria speaking sometime in the 1880s, but you have to book in advance to hear her, or anyone else. There's a small exhibit of early recording equipment and ephemera, too. ⊠ *British Library, 96 Euston Rd., NW1,* ☎ *020/7412–7440,* ⓦⒺⒷ *www.bl.uk.* 🎟 *Free.* ☉ *Mon. 10–8, Tues.–Thurs. 9:30–8, Fri.–Sat. 9:30–5. Tube: Kings Cross.*

❺ Percival David Foundation of Chinese Art. This collection, belonging to the University of London, is dominated by ceramics from the Sung to Qing dynasties—from the 10th to the 19th century, in other words. It's on **Gordon Square,** which Virginia Woolf, the Bells, John Maynard Keynes (all at No. 46), and Lytton Strachey (at No. 51) called home for a while. ⊠ *53 Gordon Sq., WC1,* ☎ *020/7387–3909.* 🎟 *Free.* ☉ *Weekdays 10:30–5. Tube: Russell Sq.*

☝ ❹ Pollock's Toy Museum. For some, this will merit a visit whether they have children or not. A charming treasure trove of a small museum in a warren of rooms in an 18th-century town house, Pollock's is crammed with antique dolls, dollhouses, and teddy bears. Best of all are the fabulous little toy theaters that Pollock made famous during the Victorian era—more than a few of England's most famous actors grew up playing with these cardboard delights. Even better: you can still buy reproductions of these cut-and-paste theater kits in the toy store on the premises. (Bring lots of money if you want to purchase some of the antique kits still for sale.) ✉ *1 Scala St., W1,* ☎ *020/7636–3452.* ▣ *£3.* ◷ *Mon.–Sat. 10–5. Tube: Goodge St.*

⓭ Prince Henry's Room. This is the Jacobean half-timber house built in 1610 to celebrate the investiture of Henry, James I's eldest son, as Prince of Wales; it's marked with his coat of arms and a PH on the ceiling. It's an entrance to the lawyers' sanctum, Temple, where the Strand becomes Fleet Street, and you can go in to visit the small Samuel Pepys exhibition. ✉ *17 Fleet St., EC4,* ☎ *020/7936–2710.* ▣ *Free.* ◷ *Mon.–Sat. 11–2. Tube: Temple.*

⓬ Royal Courts of Justice. Here is the vast Victorian Gothic pile containing the nation's principal law courts, with 1,000-odd rooms running off 3½ mi of corridor. And here are heard the most important civil law cases—that's everything from divorce to fraud, with libel in between— and you can sit in the viewing gallery to watch any trial you like, for a live version of *Court TV.* The more dramatic criminal cases are heard at the Old Bailey. Other sights are the 238-ft-long main hall and the compact exhibition of judges' robes. ✉ *The Strand, WC2,* ☎ *020/7947– 6000,* WEB *www.open.gov.uk.* ▣ *Free.* ◷ *Weekdays 9:30–4:30 (during Aug. there are no sittings and public areas close at 2:30). Tube: Temple.*

★ ⓫ Sir John Soane's Museum. Guaranteed to raise a smile from the most blasé and footsore tourist, this museum hardly deserves the burden of its dry name. Sir John (1753–1837), architect of the Bank of England, bequeathed his house to the nation on condition that nothing be changed. We owe him our thanks because he obviously had enormous fun with his home, having had the means to finance great experiments in perspective and scale and to fill the space with some wonderful pieces. There are also different exhibitions on subjects as broad and as varied as Sir John's interests: from early architecture to more modern art. In the Picture Room, for instance, two of Hogarth's *Rake's Progress* series are among the paintings on panels that swing away to reveal secret gallery pockets with more paintings. Everywhere mirrors and colors play tricks with light and space, and split-level floors worthy of a fairground fun house disorient you. In a basement chamber sits the vast 1300 BC sarcophagus of Seti I, lighted by a domed skylight two stories above. When Sir John acquired this priceless object for £2,000, he celebrated with a three-day party. ✉ *13 Lincoln's Inn Fields, WC2,* ☎ *020/7405–2107,* WEB *www.soane.org.* ▣ *Free.* ◷ *Tues.–Sat. 10–5; also 6–9 on the first Tues. of every month. Tube: Holborn.*

⓽ Staple Inn. Despite its name, this is not an inn of court but the former wool staple, where wool was weighed and traded and its merchants were lodged. It is central London's oldest surviving Elizabethan half-timber building and, thanks to extensive restoration, with its overhanging upper stories, oriel windows, and black gables striping the white walls, looks the same as it must have in 1586 when it was brand-new. ✉ *Holborn, WC1.* ◷ *Courtyard weekdays 9–5. Tube: Chancery La.*

⓮ Temple. The entrance to Temple—the collective name for **Inner Temple** and **Middle Temple,** and the exact point of entry into the City—is marked by a young bronze griffin, the **Temple Bar Memorial** (1880). He is the symbol of the City, having replaced (sadly) a Wren gateway (though you can't deny he makes a splendidly heraldic snapshot). In the buildings opposite is an elaborate stone arch through which you pass into Middle Temple Lane, past a row of 17th-century timber-frame houses, and on into Fountain Court. This lane runs all the way to the Thames,

BLUE PLAQUE ATTACK!

AS YOU WANDER AROUND LONDON, you'll see lots of small, blue, oval-shape plaques on the sides and facades of buildings, describing which famous, semifamous, or obscure but brilliant person once lived there. The first was placed outside Lord Byron's birthplace (now no more) by the Royal Society of Arts. There are around 700 blue plaques, erected by different bodies—you may even find some green ones which originated from Westminster City Council—but English Heritage now maintains the responsibility. Below are some of the highlights:

James Barrie (100 Bayswater Rd., Hyde Park, W2); Hector Berlioz (58 Queen Anne St., Marylebone, W1); Elizabeth Barrett Browning (50 Wimpole St., Marylebone, W1); Robert Browning (17 Warwick Crescent, Hyde Park, W2); Frederic Chopin (4 St. James's Place, St. James's, W1); Captain James Cook (88 Mile End Rd., Mile End, E1); Sir Winston Churchill (28 Hyde Park Gate, Kensington, SW7); T. S. Eliot (3 Kensington Court. Gdns., Kensington); Mahatma Gandhi (20 Baron's Court Rd., West Kensington, W14); George Frederic Handel (25 Brook St., Mayfair, W1); Karl Marx (28 Dean St., Soho, W1); Wolfgang Amadeus Mozart (180 Ebury St., Belgravia, SW1); Sir Isaac Newton (87 Jermyn St., St. James's, SW1); Florence Nightingale (10 South St., Mayfair, W1); George Bernard Shaw (29 Fitzroy Sq., Bloomsbury, W1); Percy Bysshe Shelley (15 Poland St., Soho, W1); Mark Twain (23 Tedworth Sq., Chelsea, SW3); Oscar Wilde (34 Tite St., Chelsea, SW3); William Butler Yeats (23 Fitzroy Rd., Camden, NW1).

more or less separating the two Temples, past the sloping lawns of Middle Temple Gardens, on the east border of which is the Elizabethan **Middle Temple Hall**. If it's open, don't miss that hammer-beam roof, among the finest in the land. ⊠ *Middle Temple La.,* ☎ *020/7427–4800.* ⊙ *Weekdays 10–11:30 and (when not in use) 3–4. Tube: Temple.*

⑮ Temple Church. Featuring "the Round"—a rare circular nave—this church was built by the Knights Templar in the 12th century. The Red Knights (so called after the red crosses they wore—you can see them in effigy around the nave) held their secret initiation rites in the crypt here. Having started poor, holy, and dedicated to the protection of pilgrims, they grew rich from showers of royal gifts, until in the 14th century they were charged with heresy, blasphemy, and sodomy, thrown into the Tower, and stripped of their wealth. You might suppose the church to be thickly atmospheric, but Victorian and postwar restorers have tamed its air of antique mystery. Still, it's a very fine Gothic-Romanesque church, whose 1240 chancel ("the Oblong") has been accused of perfection. ⊠ *The Temple, EC4,* ☎ *020/7353–1736.* ⊙ *Wed.–Sat. 10–4, Sun. 12:30–3. Tube: Temple.*

Thomas Coram Foundation. Capt. Thomas Coram devoted half his life to setting up a sanctuary and hospital, which he called the Foundling Hospital, for London's street orphans. He was a remarkable man, a master mariner and shipbuilder who, having played a major role in the colonization of Massachusetts, returned to London in 1732 to encounter sights he could not endure—babies and children "left to die on dung hills." Petitioning the lunching ladies of his day and their lords, he raised the necessary funds to set up what became the most celebrated good cause around, thanks partly to the sparkling benefactors he attracted. Currently this site is closed; the Foundling Museum is refurbishing the rooms and collection, which should reopen for tours in early 2003. ✉ *40 Brunswick Sq., WC2,* ☎ *020/7841–3600. Currently closed to visitors; call to determine if museum has reopened. Tube: Russell Sq.*

❸ University College. Set in a satisfyingly classical edifice designed by the architect of the National Gallery, William Wilkins, the college has within its portals the **Slade School of Fine Art,** which did for many of Britain's artists what the nearby Royal Academy of Dramatic Art (on Gower Street) did for its actors. On view inside is a fine collection of sculpture by an alumnus, John Flaxman. You can also see more Egyptian artifacts, if you didn't get enough at the neighboring British Museum (☎ 020/7679–2884), in the **Petrie Museum** (☎ 020/7679–2884), accessed from Malet Place, on the first floor of the DMS Watson building. It houses an outstanding, huge collection of fascinating objects of Egyptian archaeology—jewelry, toys, papyri, and some of the world's oldest garments. It has proved so popular with schoolchildren that it is now open Saturday 10–1 in addition to Tuesday–Friday 1–5. The South Cloisters contain one of London's weirder treasures: the clothed skeleton of one of the university's founders, Jeremy Bentham, who bequeathed himself to the college. ✉ *WC1. Tube: Euston Sq. or Goodge St.*

❷ University of London. This relatively youthful institution grew out of the need for a nondenominational center for higher education (Oxford and Cambridge both demanded religious conformity to the Church of England). It was founded by Dissenters in 1826, with its first examinations held 12 years later. Jews and Roman Catholics were not the only people admitted for the first time to an English university—women were, too, though they had to wait 50 years (until 1878) to sit for a degree. ✉ *Russell Sq., WC1. Tube: Russell Sq.*

Wig and Pen Club. The club—another of those St. James's–style affairs, this time for "men of justice, journalists, and businessmen of the City" (plus former U.S. presidents Nixon and Reagan)—has its home in the only Strand building to have survived the Great Fire of 1666. Its Legal Tours allow access to the gorgeous gardens of the Inner and Middle Temples, plus other secret sights, and include meals, refreshments, and honorary membership for the day (and women are most welcome). Tours of the club and inns of court are given by accredited city guide Julian Romain. ✉ *229–230 The Strand, WC2,* ☎ *020/8599–6500 for tour booking details. Tube: Aldwych or Temple.*

THE CITY

You may have assumed you had entered the City of London when your plane touched down at Heathrow, but note that capital letter: the City of London is not the same as the city of London. The "capital-C" City is an autonomous district, separately governed since William the Conqueror's time, and despite its compact size (it's known as the Square Mile), it remains the financial engine of Britain and one of the world's leading centers of trade. The City, however, is more than just London's Wall Street: it is also home to two of London's most notable sights, the Tower of London and St. Paul's, one of the world's greatest cathedrals—truly a case of the money changers' encompassing the temple! Temple Bar marks the western edge of the district, which does cover 677 acres, though not in a remotely straight-sided fashion. The curvy shape described by its boundaries—Smithfield in the north, Aldgate and Tower Hill in the east, and the Thames in the south—resembles nothing so much as an armadillo, with Temple Bar at snout level.

The City is London's most ancient part, although there is little remaining to remind you of that beyond a scattering of Roman stones. It was Aulus Plautius, Roman ruler of Britain under Claudius, who established the Romans' first stronghold on the Thames halfway through the 1st century AD. The name "Londinium," though, probably derives from the Celtic *Lyn-dun,* meaning "fortified town on the lake," which suggests far earlier settlement. It was really only after Edward the Confessor moved his court to Westminster in 1060 that the City gathered momentum. As Westminster took over the administrative role, the City was free to develop the commercial heart that still beats strong.

The Romans had already found Londinium's position handy for trade—the river being navigable yet far enough inland to allow for its defense—but it was the establishment of crafts guilds in the Middle Ages, followed in Tudor and Stuart times by the proliferation of great trading companies (the Honourable East India Company, founded in 1600, was the star), that really started the cash flowing.

Three times the City has faced devastation—and that's not counting the "Black Monday" of 1992, when the pound sterling crashed. The Great Fire of 1666 spared practically none of the labyrinthine medieval streets—a blessing in disguise, actually, because the Great Plague of the year before had wiped (or driven) out most of the population and left a terrible mess in the cramped, downright sordid houses. With the wind in the west, they said, you could smell London from Tilbury. The fire necessitated a total reconstruction, in which Sir Christopher Wren had a big hand, contributing not only his masterpiece, St. Paul's Cathedral, but 49 parish churches as well.

A third wave of destruction, after the plague and the fire, was dealt by German bombers during the Second World War. In 57 nights devoted to the City, they wrought as much havoc as the Great Fire had managed. The ruins were rebuilt, but slowly and with no overall plan, creating an awkward patchwork of old and new, interesting and flagrantly awful. The City's colorful past can be hard to visualize in the midst of today's gray reality, but there are clues. Wander through its maze of streets and you will come across ancient coats of arms and street names redolent of life in the Middle Ages: Ropemaker Street, Pudding Lane, Jewry Street, and Fish Street. During the week, the place is overrun with people—but since a mere 8,000 or so people call it home today, the City is deserted on weekends, with most restaurants shuttered and streets forlorn and windswept. It's this swing from hectic activity to near total silence that accounts for much of the City's unique atmosphere. Where else does the Lord Mayor, clad in ceremonial robes and chain of office, ride in an 18th-century coach—during the installation of a new Lord Mayor—past buildings in which satellite communications have long since become routine?

Numbers in the text correspond to numbers in the margin and on the City map.

A Good Walk

Begin at the gateway to the City—and we mean that literally. Until the 18th century there were eight such gates, of which only one survives; the others exist in name only (Cripplegate, Ludgate, Bishopsgate, Moorgate, and so on). The surviving one is Temple Bar, a bronze griffin on the Strand opposite the Royal Courts of Justice, at which the sovereign has to ask permission to enter the City from the Lord Mayor. Walk east to **Fleet Street** and turn left on Bolt Court to Gough Square and **Dr. Johnson's House** ①, passing **Ye Olde Cheshire Cheese** ② on Wine Office Court en route back to Fleet Street and the journalists' church,

St. Bride's ③. The end of Fleet Street is marked by the messy traffic intersection called Ludgate Circus, which you should cross to Ludgate Hill to reach **Old Bailey** ④ and the Central Criminal Courts.

Continuing along Ludgate Hill, you come to **St. Paul's Cathedral** ⑤, Wren's masterpiece. A modern marvel by Norman Foster, the **Millennium Bridge** ⑥, is in clear view from St. Paul's Churchyard. Then retrace your steps to Newgate Street, to the road called Little Britain, where you'll see the archway to **St. Bartholomew the Great Church** ⑦ on the left and come to London's meat market, Smithfield, at the end. Cross Aldersgate Street and take the right fork to London Wall, named for the Roman rampart that stood along it. It's a dismal street, now dominated by postmodern architect Terry Farrell's late-'80s follies, but about halfway along you can see a section of 2nd- to 4th-century wall at St. Alphege Garden. There's another bit in an appropriate spot back at the start of London Wall, outside the **Museum of London** ⑧; and behind that are the **Barbican Centre** ⑨, an important arts mecca of gray concrete, and **St. Giles Without Cripplegate** ⑩. You can walk all around here without touching the ground (well, ground level).

Back on London Wall, turn south into Coleman Street, then right onto Masons Avenue to reach Basinghall Street and the **Guildhall** ⑪; then follow Milk Street south to Cheapside ("cheap" derives from the Old English via Middle English *chep,* for trade); it was on this street that the bakers of Bread Street, the cobblers of Cordwainers Street, the goldsmiths of Goldsmith Street, and all their brothers gathered to sell their wares. Here is another symbolic center of London, the church of **St. Mary-le-Bow** ⑫. Walk to the east end of Cheapside, where seven roads meet, and you will be facing the **Bank of England** ⑬. Turn your back on the bank, and there's the Lord Mayor's Palladian-style residence, Mansion House. Wren's **St. Stephen Walbrook Church** ⑭ rises behind it and the **Royal Exchange** ⑮ stands between Threadneedle Street and Cornhill. Farther down Cornhill to Lime Street is **Lloyd's of London** ⑯.

Now head down Queen Victoria Street, where you'll pass the remains of the Roman **Temple of Mithras** ⑰; then, after a sharp left turn onto Cannon Street, you'll come upon the **Monument** ⑱, Wren's memorial to the Great Fire of London. Just south of there is **London Bridge** ⑲. Turn left onto Lower Thames Street, for just under a mile's walk—passing Billingsgate, London's principal fish market for 900 years (until 1982), and the Custom House, built early in the last century—to the **Tower of London** ⑳, which may be the single most unmissable of London's sights. **Tower Bridge** ㉑, just outside it, isn't bad either.

TIMING

This is a marathon. Unless you want to be walking all day without a chance to do justice to London's most famous sights, the Tower of London and St. Paul's Cathedral—not to mention the Museum of London, Tower Bridge, and the Barbican Centre—you should consider splitting the walk into segments. Conversely, if you're not planning to go inside, this walk makes for a great day out, with lots of surprising vistas, river views, and history. The City is a wasteland on weekends and after dark, so choose your time. There's a certain romantic charm to the streets when they're deserted, but it's hard to find lunch.

HOW TO GET THERE

This is a big and confusing area, with, however, several tube stops that will deposit you within walking distance of most sights. They are the following: on the Central Line, the Bank and St. Paul's stops; on the District and Circle lines, the Monument, Cannon Street, and Mansion House stops (plus Blackfriars, which is a little off-center). The Moor-

The City

87

KEY
Tube Station

River Thames

Bank of England ... 13
Barbican Centre ... 9
Dr. Johnson's House ... 1
Guildhall ... 11
Lloyd's of London ... 16

London Bridge ... 19
Millennium Bridge ... 6
Monument ... 18
Museum of London ... 8
Old Bailey ... 4

Royal Exchange ... 15
St. Bartholomew the Great Church ... 7
St. Bride's ... 3
St. Giles Without Cripplegate ... 10
St. Mary-le-Bow ... 12

St. Paul's Cathedral ... 5
St. Stephen Walbrook Church ... 14
Temple of Mithras ... 17
Tower Bridge ... 21

Tower of London ... 20
Ye Olde Cheshire Cheese ... 2

gate and Barbican stops (Circle, Metropolitan, Hammersmith, and City lines) are the nearest to the theaters of the Barbican Centre, while the next stop west, Farringdon, is best for exploring Clerkenwell. Finally, the only sensible way to get to the Tower of London is via the District and Circle lines to the Tower Hill stop. As for buses, Nos. 4, 11, 15, 17, 23, 26, 76, and 172 deposit you centrally, by St. Paul's. For the Barbican Centre, Buses 4, 56, 172, 141, 172, and 271 to Moorgate are best.

Sights to See

⑬ Bank of England. Known familiarly for the past couple of centuries as "the Old Lady of Threadneedle Street," after someone's parliamentary quip, the bank, which has been central to the British economy since 1694, manages the national debt and the foreign exchange reserves, issues banknotes, sets interest rates, looks after England's gold, and regulates the country's banking system. Sir John Soane designed the Neoclassic hulk in 1788, wrapping it in windowless walls, which are all that survives of his building. It is ironic that an executive of so sober an institution should have been Kenneth Grahame, author of *The Wind in the Willows*. This and other facets of the bank's history are traced in the Bank of England Museum. ⊠ *Bartholomew La., EC4,* ☎ *020/7601–5545,* WEB *www.bankofengland.co.uk.* ⊡ *Free.* ☉ *Weekdays and Lord Mayor's Show day 10–5. Tube: Bank or Monument.*

⑨ Barbican Centre. Home to two theaters; the London Symphony Orchestra and its auditorium; the Guildhall School of Music and Drama; a major art gallery for touring and its own special exhibitions; two cinemas; a convention center; an upscale restaurant, cafés, and literary bookshops; and apartments for a hapless two-thirds of the City's residents (most part-time), the Barbican is an enormous concrete maze Londoners love to hate. In 2001 the Royal Shakespeare Company announced that it would stage plays in the West End rather than only in th Barbican. The name comes from a defensive fortification of the City, and defensive is what Barbican apologists (including architects Chamberlain, Powell, and Bon) became when the complex was finally revealed in 1982. There ensued an epidemic of jokes about getting lost forever in the Barbican bowels and even though you can follow yellow lines, Oz-like, on the floors, it is still difficult to navigate. Londoners accept the place, because of its imaginative contents. Actors rate the theater acoustics especially high, and the steep rake of the seating makes for a good stage view. The dance and music programs are adventurous without straying too far from core favorites. Try to sample some of the Barbican's annual dance, drama, and music fest between May and October, which attracts top-billing international performers. The exhibitions in the **Barbican Art Gallery** are extremely popular and often showcase modern, populist topics ranging from the Shaker movement to *Star Wars* the movie. Also worth a look are the free displays in the Concourse Gallery.

Negotiating the winding walkways of the residential section, spotting stray sculptures and water gardens, then descending to the lower depths of the Centre (where you find the studio auditorium, aptly named the Pit), all has its charm. Secreted on an upper floor is an enormous, lush conservatory in a towering glass palace, spacious enough for full-grown trees to flourish. Although not often open to the public, you may be able to get into a tour. These are conducted for a minimum of 10 people and must be booked in advance. ⊠ *Silk St., EC2,* ☎ *020/ 7638–8891; 020/7628–3351 RSC backstage tour,* WEB *www.barbican.org.uk.* ⊡ *Barbican Centre free; art gallery £3–£5.* ☉ *Barbican Centre Mon.–Sat. 9 AM–11 PM, Sun. noon–11 PM; gallery Mon.–Sat. 10–7:30, Sun. noon–7:30; conservatory weekends noon–5:30 when not in use for private function (call first). Tube: Moorgate or Barbican.*

The Barbican Centre's **Waterside Café** has salads, sandwiches, and pastries; they're unremarkable but are served in a tranquil, enclosed concrete (naturally) waterside terrace. Sometimes customers are serenaded by practice sessions of the Guildhall School of Music and Drama's orchestra next door.

❶ Dr. Johnson's House. This is where Samuel Johnson lived between 1746 and 1759, while in the worst of health, compiling his famous dictionary in the attic. Like Dickens, he lived all over town, and as Dickens House is the only one of his houses still extant, this is the only one of Johnson's residences remaining today. It is an appropriately 17th-century house, exactly the kind of place you would expect the Great Bear, as Johnson was nicknamed, to live. It is a shrine to the man possibly more attached to London than anyone else ever, and it includes a first edition of his dictionary among the Johnson and Boswell mementos. After soaking up the atmosphere, repair around the corner in Wine Office Court to the famed Ye Olde Cheshire Cheese pub, once Johnson and Boswell's favorite watering hole. ⊠ *17 Gough Sq., EC4,* ☎ *020/7353–3745.* 🖘 *£4.* ☉ *May–Sept., Mon.–Sat. 11–5:30; Oct.–Apr., Mon.–Sat. 11–5. Tube: Blackfriars or Chancery La.*

Fleet Street. This famous street follows the course of, and is named after, one of London's ghost rivers. The Fleet, so called by the Anglo-Saxons, spent most of its centuries above ground as an open sewer, offending local nostrils until banished below in 1766. It still flows underfoot, now a sanctioned section of London's sewer system. The street's sometime nickname, "Street of Shame," has nothing to do with the stench. It refers to the trade that made it famous: the press. Since the end of the 15th century, when Wynkyn de Worde set up England's first printing press here, and especially after 1702, when the first newspaper, the *Daily Courant,* moved in, followed by (literally) all the rest, "Fleet Street" has been synonymous with newspaper journalism. The papers themselves all moved out during the 1980s, but the British press is still collectively known as "Fleet Street." To find a relic from the old days, check out the black-glass-and-chrome art deco *Daily Mirror* building. ⊠ *EC4. Tube: Blackfriars or St. Paul's.*

⑪ Guildhall. In the symbolic nerve center of the City, the Corporation of London ceremonially elects and installs its Lord Mayor as it has for 800 years. The Guildhall was built in 1411, and though it failed to avoid either the 1666 or 1940 flames, its core survived, with a new roof sensitively appended during the 1950s and further cosmetic embellishments added during the '70s. The fabulous hall is a psychedelic patchwork of coats of arms and banners of the City Livery Companies, which inherited the mantle of the medieval trade guilds, to which we owe the invention of the City in the first place. Actually, this honor belongs to two giants, Gog and Magog, the pair of mythical beings who founded ancient Albion and who glower upon the prime minister's annual November banquet from their west-gallery grandstand in 9-ft-high painted lime-wood form.

To the right of Guildhall Yard is the **Guildhall Art Gallery,** the corporation's collection dating from 1885. Consisting mainly of portraits of royals and statesmen, the gallery has a fair sprinkling of weighty battlescapes from the 18th century for good measure. London landscapes give a picture of the old City in days gone by, and there are a couple of surprises in the form of pre-Raphaelite beauties. The 1970s west wing houses the **Guildhall Library**; it has mainly City-related books and documents, plus a collection belonging to one of the Livery Companies, the Worshipful Company of Clockmakers, with more than

600 timepieces on show, including a skull-faced watch that belonged to Mary, Queen of Scots. ⊠ *Gresham St., EC2,* ☎ *020/7606–3030; gallery 020/7332–1632, 020/7332–3700 recorded information,* WEB *www.cityoflondon.gov.uk.* 🖃 *Free; gallery £2.50.* ◷ *Mon.–Sat. 9:30–5; Clockmakers Collection weekdays 9:30–4:45; gallery Mon.–Sat. 10–5, Sun. noon–4. Print room and bookshop closed Sat. Tube: St. Paul's, Moorgate, Bank, or Mansion House.*

🔟 **Lloyd's of London.** Richard Rogers's (of Paris Pompidou Centre fame) fantastical steel-and-glass medium-rise of six towers around a vast atrium, with his trademark inside-out ventilation shafts, stairwells, and gantries, may be the most exciting recent structure erected in London. The building is best seen at night, when cobalt and lime spotlights make it leap out of the deeply boring gray skyline as though it were Carmen Miranda at a wake. The institution that commissioned this fabulous £163 million fun house has been trading in insurance for two centuries and is famous the world over for several reasons: (1) having started in a coffeehouse; (2) insuring Betty Grable's legs; (3) accepting no corporate responsibility for losses, which are carried by its investors; (4) having its "Names"—the rich people who underwrite Lloyd's losses; (5) seeming unassailable for a very long time . . . ; (6) losing £2.9 billion in 1990; (7) causing, with its losses, the financial ruination, and worse, of many Names. ⊠ *1 Lime St., EC3. Tube: Bank, Monument, Liverpool St., or Aldgate.*

🔟 **London Bridge.** Dating from only 1972, this bridge replaced the 1831 Sir John Rennie number that now graces Lake Havasu City, Arizona, the impulse purchase of someone at the McCulloch Oil Corporation, who (rumor has it) was under the impression that he'd bought the far more picturesque Tower Bridge. The version before that one, the first in stone and the most renowned of all, stood for 600 years after it was built in 1176, the focus of many a gathering thanks to the shops and houses crammed along its length, not to mention the boiled and tar-dipped heads of traitors that decorated its gatehouse after being removed in the Tower of London. Before *that* the Saxons had put up a wooden bridge; it collapsed in 1014, which was probably the origin of the refrain "London Bridge is falling down." Nobody is sure of the exact location of the very earliest London Bridge—the Roman version around whose focus London grew—but it was certainly very close to the 100-ft-wide, three-span, prestressed concrete cantilever one that you see today. ⊠ *EC3, SE1. Tube: London Bridge or Monument.*

🔟 **Millennium Bridge.** This is not just another bridge, but the first pedestrian-only bridge to open in central London in more than century, the last being Tower Bridge in 1894. Designed by Norman Foster and sculptor Anthony Caro, it opened in June 2000, and thousands lined up to enjoy the so-called "blaze of light" built of aluminium and steel. A stabilization problem led to the closing of the bridge, but it was scheduled to reopen by fall 2001. The bridge connects the old City—St. Paul's Cathedral area—with the Tate Modern art gallery. On the south bank side, the bridge marks the middle of the Millennium Mile, a newly devised walkway taking in a clutch of popular sights. The views are breathtaking: from the bridge, you can look downriver to the Tower of London, Tower Bridge, and beyond, and up to Somerset House, with the London Eye and Big Ben rising above the river's bend. You'll also have perhaps the best-ever view of St. Paul's Cathedral. ⊠ *Peters Hill, Bankside, EC4, SE1,* ☎ *020/7403–8299. Mansion House, Blackfriars, or Southwark.*

🔟 **Monument.** Commemorating the "dreadful visitation" of the Great Fire of 1666, this is the world's tallest isolated stone column. It is the work of Wren, who was asked to erect it "On or as neere unto the place where the said Fire soe unhappily began as conveniently may be." And so here it is—at 202 ft exactly as tall as the distance it stands from Farriner's baking house in Pudding Lane, where the fire started. Above the viewing gallery (311 steps up—a better workout than any StairMaster) is a flaming bronze urn with a cage around it to prevent suicidal jumps, which were a trend for a while in the 19th century. ⊠ *Monument St., EC3,* ☎ *020/7626–2717.* ⊞ *£1.50; combination ticket with Tower Bridge, £6.75.* ☉ *Daily 10–5:40 (hrs subject to change; phone before visiting). Tube: Monument.*

ⓒ ⑧ **Museum of London.** If there's one place to get the history of London sorted out, it's here—although there's a great deal to sort out: Oliver Cromwell's death mask, Queen Victoria's crinolined gowns, Selfridges's Art Deco elevators, and the Lord Mayor's coach are just some of the goodies here. Various fascinating exhibitions—from London Bodies (magnetically gruesome) to early Briton king Alfred the Great and the life and times of the Rothschilds—regularly entice more crowds. The museum appropriately shelters a section of the 2nd- to 4th-century London wall, which you can view from a window inside, near the Roman monumental arch the museum's archaeologists reconstructed a mere two decades ago. Anyone with the least interest in how this city evolved will adore this museum, especially said reconstructions and the dioramas—like one of the Great Fire (flickering flames! sound effects!), a 1940s air-raid shelter, a Georgian prison cell, a Roman living room, and a Victorian street complete with fully stocked shops—as well as the Catwalk, which guides you interactively through the ages. There are special Sunday and holiday sessions that allow children to handle and discover many objects not on view. Galleries proceed chronologically for easy comprehension right up to the new London Now gallery. All museum tickets allow unlimited return visits for one year. ⊠ *London Wall, EC2,* ☎ *020/7600–0807,* ₩ᴇʙ *www. museumoflondon.org.uk.* ⊞ *£5; free 4:30–5:50.* ☉ *Mon.–Sat. 10–5:50, Sun. noon–5:50. Tube: Barbican.*

❹ **Old Bailey.** This, the present-day **Central Criminal Court,** is where Newgate Prison stood from the 12th century right until the beginning of the 20th century. Few survived for long in the version pulled down in 1770. Those who didn't starve were hanged, or pressed to death in the Press Yard, or they succumbed to the virulent gaol (the archaic British spelling of "jail") fever—any of which must have been preferable to a life in the stinking, subterranean, lightless Stone Hold or to the robberies, beatings, and general victimization endemic in what the novelist Henry Fielding called the "prototype of hell." The next model lasted only a couple of years before being torn down by raving mobs during the anti-Catholic Gordon Riots of 1780, to be replaced by the Newgate that Dickens visited several times (obviously in between pubs) and described in several novels. In fact, Fagin ended up in the Condemned Hold here in *Oliver Twist,* from which he would have been taken to the public scaffold that replaced the Tyburn Tree and stood outside the prison until 1868. The Central Criminal Court replaced Newgate in 1907. The most famous and most interesting feature of the solid Edwardian building is the gilded statue of blind Justice perched on top, scales in her left hand, sword in her right. Ask the doorman which current trial is likely to prove juicy, if you're that kind of ghoul—you may catch the conviction of the next Crippen or Christie (England's most notorious wife-murderers, both tried here). Cameras are not allowed in the court. Check the day's hearings on the sign outside. There are some restrictions on entry (children under 14 are not allowed); call the information line first. ⊠ *Newgate St., EC4,* ☎ *020/7248–3277 in-*

formation. ⊙ *Public Gallery weekdays 9:30–1 and 2–4:30 (line forms at Newgate St. entrance). Tube: Blackfriars.*

⑮ Royal Exchange. Inhabiting the isosceles triangle between Threadneedle Street and Cornhill, this is the third version to have stood here but the first to have been blessed by Queen Victoria—at its 1844 opening. Sir William Tite designed the massive templelike building—its pediment featuring 17 limestone figures (Commerce, plus merchants) supported by eight sizable Corinthian columns—to house the then-thriving futures market. The market has now moved on, leaving the Royal Exchange, which you may no longer enter, as a monument to money. ⊠ *Cornhill and Threadneedle St., EC3. Tube: Bank.*

❼ St. Bartholomew the Great Church. Reached via a perfect half-timber gatehouse atop a 13th-century stone archway, this is one of London's oldest churches. Along with its namesake on the other side of the road, St. Bartholomew's Hospital, the Norman church was founded by Rahere, Henry I's court jester. At the Dissolution of the Monasteries, Henry VIII had most of it torn down; the Romanesque choir loft is all that survives from the 12th century. ⊠ *West Smithfield, EC1,* ☎ *020/7606–5171.* ⊙ *Weekdays 8:30–5, Sat. 10:30–1:30, Sun. 2–6. Tube: Barbican.*

❸ St. Bride's. From afar, study the extraordinary steeple of this church—its uniquely tiered shape gave rise, legend has it, to the traditional wedding cake. This, the first of Wren's city churches, did not escape wartime bomb damage and was reconsecrated only in 1960 after a 17-year-long restoration. As St. Paul's (in Covent Garden) is the actors' church, so St. Bride's belongs to journalists, many of whom have been buried or memorialized here, as reading the wall plaques will tell you. Even before the press moved in, it was a popular place to take the final rest. By 1664 the crypts were so crowded that diarist Samuel Pepys had to bribe the grave digger to "justle together" some bodies to make room for his deceased brother. Now the crypts house a museum of the church's rich history, and a bit of Roman sidewalk. ⊠ *Fleet St., EC4,* ☎ *020/7353–1301.* 🎟 *Free.* ⊙ *Weekdays 8–5, Sat. 9–5, Sun. between services at 11 and 6:30. Tube: Chancery La.*

❿ St. Giles Without Cripplegate. Standing south of the Barbican complex, this is one of the only City churches to have withstood the Great Fire, only to succumb to the Blitz bombs three centuries later. The tower and a few walls survived; the rest was rebuilt to the 16th-century plan during the 1950s, and now the little church struggles hopelessly for attention among the Barbican towers, whose parishioners it tends. Past parishioners include Oliver Cromwell, married here in 1620, and John Milton, buried here in 1674. St. Giles was the patron saint for cripples, hence Cripplegate. ⊠ *Fore St., EC2.* ⊙ *Weekdays 9:30–5:30, Sun. 8–5:30. Tube: Barbican or Moorgate.*

⑫ St. Mary-le-Bow. Wren's 1673 church has one of the most famous sets of bells around—a Londoner must be born within the sound of Bow Bells to be a true cockney. The origin of that idea was probably the curfew rung on the Bow Bells during the 14th century, even though "cockney" only came to mean Londoner three centuries later, and then it was an insult. The Bow takes its name from the bow-shape arches in the Norman crypt. ⊠ *Cheapside, EC2.* ⊙ *Mon.–Thurs. 6:30–5:45, Fri. 6:30–4, weekends special services only. Tube: Mansion House.*

NEED A
BREAK?

The **Place Below** is below the church, in St. Mary-le-Bow's crypt, and gets packed with City workers weekday lunchtime—the self-service soup and quiche are particularly good. Lunches are served from 10:30 until

St. Paul's Cathedral

2:30, weekdays only. It's also open for breakfast (from 7:30) and morning coffee.

★ ☝ ❺ **St. Paul's Cathedral.** The symbolic heart of London, St. Paul's will take your breath away. In fact, its dome—the world's third largest—will already be familiar, since you see it peeping through on the skyline from many an angle, riding high (although now nudged by skyscrapers) over the rooftops of the City, just as it does in Canaletto's 18th-century views of the Thames. The cathedral is, of course, the masterpiece of Sir Christopher Wren (1632–1723), completed in 1710 after 35 years of building and much argument with the Royal Commission, then, much later, miraculously (mostly) spared by the World War II bombs. Wren had originally been commissioned to restore Old St. Paul's, the Norman cathedral that had replaced, in its turn, three earlier versions, but the Great Fire left so little of it standing that a new cathedral was deemed necessary.

Wren's first plan, known as the "New Model," did not make it past the drawing board, while the second, known as the "Great Model," got as far as the 20-ft oak rendering you can see here today before it, too, was rejected, whereupon Wren is said to have burst into tears. The third, however, known as the Warrant Design (because it received the royal warrant), was accepted, with the fortunate coda that the architect be allowed to make changes as he saw fit. Without that, there would be no dome, because the approved design had featured a steeple. Parliament felt that building was proceeding too slowly (in fact, 35 years is lightning speed, as cathedrals go) and withheld half of Wren's pay for the last 13 years of work. He was pushing 80 when Queen Anne finally coughed up the arrears.

When you enter and see the dome from the inside, you may find that it seems smaller than you expected. You aren't imagining things—it *is* smaller, and 60 ft lower, than the lead-covered outer dome. Between the inner and outer domes is a brick cone, which supports the familiar 850-ton lantern, surmounted by its golden ball and cross. Nobody can resist making a beeline for the dome, so we'll start beneath it, standing dead center, on the beautiful sunburst floor, Wren's focal mirror of the magnificent design above.

Now climb the 259 spiral steps to the **Whispering Gallery.** This is the part of the cathedral with which you bribe children, who are fascinated by the acoustic phenomenon: whisper something to the wall on one side, and a second later it transmits clearly to the other side, 107 ft away. The only problem is identifying "your" whisper from the cacophony of everyone else's. Look down onto the nave from here, and up to the frescoes of St. Paul by Sir James Thornhill (who nearly fell off while painting them), before ascending farther to the Stone Gallery, which encircles the outside of the dome and affords a spectacular panorama of London. Up again (careful—you will have tackled 627 steps altogether), and you reach the Golden Gallery, from which you can view the lantern through a circular opening called the oculus.

Back downstairs there are the inevitable monuments and memorials to see, though fewer than one might expect because Wren didn't want his masterpiece cluttered up. The poet John Donne, who had been Dean of St. Paul's for his final 10 years (he died in 1631), lies in the south choir aisle; his is the only monument remaining from Old St. Paul's. There is Wren's own memorial, with an epitaph by his son (who also worked on the building) that reads succinctly: LECTOR, SI MONUMENTUM REQUIRIS, CIRCUMSPICE (READER, IF YOU SEEK HIS MONUMENT, LOOK AROUND YOU). The vivacious choir-stall carvings nearby are the work of Grinling Gibbons, as is the organ, which Wren designed and Handel played. The painters Sir Joshua Reynolds and J. M. W. Turner are commemorated, as is George Washington. The American connection continues behind the high altar in the **American Memorial Chapel,** dedicated in 1958 to the 28,000 GIs stationed here who lost their lives in World War II.

A visit to the **crypt** brings you to Wren's tomb (also with his son's epitaph), the black marble sarcophagus containing Admiral Nelson (who was pickled in alcohol for his final voyage here from Trafalgar), and an equestrian statue of the Duke of Wellington on top of his grandiose tomb. A café and gift shop are also in the crypt. Finally, to catch Wren's facade and dome at its most splendid, remember to make a return trip to see St. Paul's at night. ⊠ *St. Paul's Churchyard, Ludgate Hill, EC4,* ☎ *020/7236–4128,* WEB *www.stpauls.co.uk.* ⊠ *Cathedral, crypt, ambulatory, and gallery £5.* ☉ *Cathedral Mon.–Sat. 8:30–4* *(closed occasionally for special services); ambulatory, crypt, and gallery Mon.–Sat. 9:30–4:15. Tube: St. Paul's.*

⓱ St. Stephen Walbrook Church. This is the parish church many think is Wren's best, by virtue of its practice dome, which predates the big one at St. Paul's by some 30 years. Two inside sights warrant investigation: Henry Moore's 1987 central stone altar, which sits beneath the dome ("like a lump of Camembert," say critics), and, well, a telephone—an eloquent tribute to that genuine savior of souls, Rector Chad Varah, who founded the Samaritans, givers of phone aid to the suicidal, here in 1953. ☒ *Walbrook St., EC4.* ☉ *Mon.–Thurs. 10–4, Fri. 10–3. Tube: Bank or Cannon St.*

⓱ Temple of Mithras. This minor place of pilgrimage in the Roman City was unearthed on a building site in 1954 and was taken, at first, for an early Christian church. In fact, worshipers here favored Christ's chief rival during the 3rd and 4th centuries: Mithras, the Persian god of light. Mithraists aimed for all the big virtues but still were not appreciated by early Christians, from whom their sculptures and treasures had to be concealed. These devotional objects are now on display back at the Museum of London, while here, on Queen Victoria Street, not far from the Bank of England, you can see the foundations of the temple itself. ☒ *Temple Court, Queen Victoria St., EC4. Tube: Bank.*

★ ☙ ㉑ **Tower Bridge.** Despite its venerable, nay, medieval, appearance, this is a Victorian youngster that celebrated its centenary in June 1994. Constructed of steel, then clothed in Portland stone, it was deliberately styled in the Gothic persuasion to complement the Tower next door, and it is famous for its enormous bascules—the "arms," which open to allow large ships through. Nowadays this rarely happens, but when river traffic was dense, the bascules were raised about five times a day.

The bridge's 100th-birthday gift was a new exhibition, **Tower Bridge Experience,** one of London's most imaginative and fun attractions. You are conducted back in time in the company of "Harry Stoner," an animatronic bridge construction worker worthy of Disneyland, to witness the birth of the Thames's last downstream bridge. History and engineering lessons are painlessly absorbed as you meet the ghost of the bridge's architect, Sir Horace Jones; see the bascules work; and wander the walkways with their grand upstream–downstream views annotated by interactive video displays. Be sure to hang on to your ticket and follow the signs to the Engine Rooms for part two; here the original steam-driven hydraulic engines gleam, and a cute rococo theater is the setting for an Edwardian-style music-hall production of the bridge's story. ☏ *020/7403-3761,* 🕸 *www.towerbridge.org.uk.* ☒ *£6.25; combination ticket with Monument, £6.75.* ☉ *Apr.–Oct., daily 10–5:15; Nov.–Mar., daily 9:30–5:15 (last entry at 4). Tube: Tower Hill.*

★ ⓴ **Tower of London.** This has top billing on many tourist itineraries for good reason. Nowhere else does London's history come to life so vividly as in this minicity of melodramatic towers stuffed to bursting with heraldry and treasure, the intimate details of lords and dukes and princes and sovereigns etched in the walls (literally in some places, as you'll see), and quite a few pints of royal blood spilled on the stones. New systems ensure that lines are minimal, so you'll be able to put in place all those grisly torture scenes you saw in the film *Elizabeth*. And thankfully, you need no longer spend all day in line for the prize exhibit, the Crown Jewels, since they have been transplanted to a new home where moving walkways hasten progress at the busiest times.

The reason the Tower holds the royal gems is that it is still one of the royal palaces, although no monarch since Henry VII has called it home. It has also housed the Royal Mint, the Public Records, the Royal Menagerie (which formed the basis of London Zoo), and the Royal Observatory, although its most renowned and titillating function has been, of course, as a jail and place of torture and execution.

A person was mighty privileged to be beheaded in the peace and seclusion of **Tower Green** instead of before the mob at Tower Hill. In fact, only seven people were ever important enough—among them Anne Boleyn and Catherine Howard, wives two and five, respectively, of Henry VIII's six; Elizabeth I's friend Robert Devereux, the Earl of Essex; and the nine-day queen, Lady Jane Grey, aged 17. Tower Green's other function was as a corpse dumping ground when the chapel just got too full. In 1998, the executioner's block—with its bathetic forehead-size dent—and his axe, along with the equally famous rack and the more obscure "scavenger's daughter" (which pressed a body nearly to death), plus assorted thumbscrews, "iron maidens," and so forth, took up temporary residence in the newly opened collection of the Royal Armouries in Leeds, Yorkshire; after an undetermined time, they will return to the Royal Armouries collection of the Tower of London. Fans of this horrifying niche of heavy metal might also want to pay a call on the London Dungeon attraction, just across the Thames.

Before we go any farther, you should know about the excellent free and fact-packed tours that depart every half hour or so from the Middle Tower. They are conducted by the 39 Yeoman Warders, better known as Beefeaters—ex-servicemen dressed in resplendent navy-and-red (scarlet-and-gold on special occasions) Tudor outfits. Beefeaters have been guarding the tower since Henry VII appointed them in 1485. One of them, the Yeoman Ravenmaster, is responsible for making life comfortable for Hardey, George, Hugine, Mumin, Cedric, Odin, Thor (who talks), and Gwylem—the Tower Ravens. This used to be a delicate duty, because if they were to desert the tower (goes the legend), the kingdom would fall. Today, the tower takes no chances: the ravens' wings are clipped.

In prime position stands the oldest part of the tower and the most conspicuous of its buildings, the **White Tower.** This central keep was begun in 1078 by William the Conqueror; by the time it was completed, in 1097, it was the tallest building in London, underlining the might of those victorious Normans. Henry III (1207–72) had it whitewashed, which is where the name comes from, then used it as a barracks and as housing for his menagerie, including the first elephant ever seen in the land.

The spiral staircase—winding clockwise to help the right-handed swordsman defend it—is the only way up, and here you'll find the **Royal Armouries,** Britain's national museum of arms and armor, with about 40,000 pieces on display. One of the tower's original functions was as an arsenal, supplying armor and weapons to the kings and their armies. Henry VIII started the collection in earnest, founding a workshop at Greenwich as a kind of bespoke tailor of armor to the gentry, but the public didn't get to see it until the second half of the 17th century, during Charles II's reign—which makes the Tower Armouries Britain's oldest public museum.

Here you can see weapons and armor from Britain and the Continent, dating from Saxon and Viking times right up to our own. Among the highlights are four suits of armor Henry VIII commissioned to fit his ever-increasing bulk, plus one for his horse. The medieval warhorse was nothing without his *shaffron,* or head protector, and here you'll find a 500-year-old example, one of the oldest pieces of horse armor in the world. Don't miss the tiny armors on the third floor—one belonging to Henry's son (who survived in it to become Edward VI) and another just a bit more than 3 ft tall. The impressive, carved Line of Kings is not to be missed. The **New Armouries** have been renovated into a new restaurant.

Most of the interior of the White Tower has been much altered over the centuries, but the **Chapel of St. John the Evangelist,** downstairs from the armories, is a pure example of 11th-century Norman—very rare, very simple, and very beautiful. The other fortifications and buildings surrounding the White Tower date from the 11th to 19th centuries. Starting from the main entrance, you can't miss the **moat.** Until the Duke of Wellington had it drained in 1843, this was a stinking, stagnant mush, obstinately resisting all attempts to flush it with water from the Thames. Now there's a little raven graveyard in the grassed-over channel, with touching memorials to some of the old birds (who are not known for their kind natures, by the way, and you risk a savage pecking if you try to befriend them).

Across the moat, the **Middle Tower** and the **Byward Tower** form the principal landward entrance, with **Traitors' Gate** a little farther on to the right. This is the London equivalent of Venice's Bridge of Sighs, which led to the cells in the Doge's Palace. Unlike the Venetian monument, Traitors' Gate is not architecturally beautiful but was the last walkway of daylight before condemned prisoners were doomed to darkness and death in the dungeons. During the period when the Thames was London's chief thoroughfare, this was the main entrance to the Tower.

Immediately opposite Traitors' Gate is the former Garden Tower, better known since about 1570 as the **Bloody Tower.** Its name comes from one of the most famous unsolved murders in history, the saga of the "little princes in the Tower." In 1483 the uncrowned boy king Edward

V and his brother Richard were left here by their uncle, Richard of Gloucester, after the death of their father, Edward I. They were never seen again, Gloucester was crowned Richard III, and in 1674 two little skeletons were found under the stairs to the White Tower. The obvious conclusions have always been drawn—and were, in fact, even before the skeletons were discovered.

Another famous inmate was Sir Walter Raleigh, who was kept here from 1603 to 1616. It wasn't such an ordeal, as you'll see when you visit his spacious rooms, where he kept two servants, had his wife and two sons live with him (the younger boy was christened in the Tower chapel), and amused himself by writing his *History of the World.* Unfortunately, he was less lucky on his second visit in 1618, which terminated in his execution at Whitehall.

Next to the Bloody Tower is the circular **Wakefield Tower,** which dates from the 13th century and once contained the king's private apartments. It was the scene of another royal murder in 1471, when Henry VI was killed in mid-prayer. Henry founded Eton College and King's College, Cambridge, and they haven't forgotten: every May 21, envoys from both institutions mark the anniversary of his murder by laying white lilies on the site.

The most dazzling and most famous exhibits in the Tower are, of course, the **Crown Jewels,** now housed in the **Jewel House, Waterloo Block.** In their new settings you get so close to the fabled gems you feel you could polish them (if it weren't for the wafers of bulletproof glass), and they are enhanced by laser lighting, which nearly hurts the eyes with sparkle. Before you meet them in person, you are given a high-definition-film preview, which features scenes from Elizabeth's 1953 coronation.

It's commonplace to call these baubles priceless, but it's impossible not to drop your jaw at the notion of their worth. They were, in fact, stolen once—by Col. Thomas Blood, in 1671—though taken only as far as a nearby wharf. The colonel was given a royal pension instead of a beating, fueling speculation that Charles II, short of ready cash as usual, had had his hand in the escapade somewhere. These days security is as fiendish as you'd expect, since the jewels—even though they would be impossible for thieves to sell—are *so* priceless that they're not insured. However, they are polished every January by the royal jewelers.

A brief résumé of the top jewels: finest of all is the **Royal Sceptre,** containing the earth's largest cut diamond, the 530-carat Star of Africa. This is also known as Cullinan I, having been cut from the South African Cullinan, which weighed 20 ounces when dug up from a De Beers mine at the beginning of the century. Another chip off the block, Cullinan II, lives on the **Imperial State Crown** that Prince Charles is due to wear at his coronation—the same one that Elizabeth II wore in her coronation procession; it was made for Victoria's coronation in 1838. Aside from its 2,800 diamonds, it features the Black Prince's ruby, which Henry V was supposed to have worn at Agincourt and which is actually an imposter—it's no ruby but, rather, a semiprecious spinel. The other most famous gem is the Koh-i-noor, or "Mountain of Light," which adorns the **Queen Mother's crown.** When Victoria was presented with this gift horse in 1850, she looked it in the mouth, found it lacking in glitter, and had it chopped down to almost half its weight.

An addendum to the major jewels in the Martin Tower is accurately called "Crowns and Diamonds." See naked crown frames—the coronation crown of George IV, George I's Imperial State Crown, Victoria's State Crown—surrounded by 12,500 loose diamonds on permanent loan from De Beers. It's a graphic illustration of how the Royals once had to rent the stones that would adorn their headpiece on the big day.

The little chapel of **St. Peter ad Vincula** can be visited only as part of a Yeoman Warder tour. The second church on the site, it conceals the remains of some 2,000 people executed at the Tower, Anne Boleyn and Catherine Howard among them. Being traitors, they were not so much buried as dumped under the flagstones, but the genteel Victorians had the courtesy to rebury their bones during renovations.

One of the more evocative towers is **Beauchamp Tower**, built west of Tower Green by Edward I (1272–1307). It was soon designated as a jail for the higher class of miscreant, including Lady Jane Grey, who is thought to have added her Latin graffiti to the many inscriptions here.

Just south of the Beauchamp Tower is an L-shape row of half-timber Tudor houses, with the **Queen's House** at the center. Built for the governor of the Tower in 1530, this place saw the interrogation or incarceration of several celebrated prisoners, including Anne Boleyn and the Gunpowder Plot conspirators. The Queen's House also played host to the Tower's last-ever prisoner, Rudolph Hess, the Nazi who parachuted over Scotland on a spy mission and was taken prisoner here.

Allow at least three hours to explore, and arrive early in summer to beat the huge crowds. You can buy your ticket at any tube stop to save time, too. Don't forget to stroll along the battlements before you leave; from them, you get a wonderful overview of the whole Tower of London. For tickets to Ceremony of the Keys (locking of main gates, nightly at 10), write well in advance to the Resident Governor and Keeper of the Jewel House (Queen's House, H. M. Tower of London, EC3). Give your name, the dates you wish to attend (including alternate dates), and number of people (up to seven) in your party, and enclose a self-addressed, stamped envelope. Yeoman Warder guides leave daily from Middle Tower, subject to weather and availability, at no charge (but a tip is always appreciated), about every 30 minutes until 3:30 in summer, 2:30 in winter. ⊠ *H. M. Tower of London, Tower Hill, EC3,* ☎ *020/7709–0765 or 020/7680–9004,* ⟨WEB⟩ *www.hrp.org.uk.* ⊠ *£11.* ☉ *Mar.–Oct., Mon.–Sat. 9–5, Sun. 10–5; Nov.–Feb., Tues.–Sat. 9–4, Sun.–Mon. 10–4 (the Tower closes 1 hr after last admission time and all internal buildings close 30 mins after last admission). Tube: Tower Hill.*

➋ **Ye Olde Cheshire Cheese.** This is one of the many places in which that acerbic compiler of the first dictionary, Dr. Johnson, drank (like Dickens, he is claimed by many a pub). This was, in fact, his "local," around the corner from his house. It retains a venerable open-fires-in-tiny-rooms charm when not too packed with tourists. Among 19th-century writers who followed Johnson's footsteps to the bar here were Mark Twain and, yes, Charles Dickens. ⊠ *145 Fleet St., EC4,* ☎ *020/7373–6170.* ☉ *Mon.–Sat. 11–11, Sun. noon–3 and 6–10. Tube: Blackfriars.*

THE EAST END

Made famous by Dickens and infamous by Jack the Ripper, the East End remains one of London's most hauntingly evocative neighborhoods. There is a good argument for considering it the real London, since East Enders are born "within the sound of Bow Bells" and are therefore cockneys through and through (not to mention models for the characters of England's favorite soap opera, *EastEnders*). The district began as separate villages—Whitechapel and Spitalfields, Shoreditch, Mile End, and Bethnal Green—melding together during the population boom of the 19th century, a boom that was shaped by French Huguenot and Jewish refugees, by poverty, and, in the past several decades, by a growing Bengali community. Whitechapel is where the Salvation Army was founded and the original Liberty Bell was forged, but, of course, what everyone remembers about it is that its Victorian slum streets were stalked by the most infamous serial killer of all, Jack the Ripper. Many outfitters offer walking tours of "Jack's London." Two centuries earlier, neighboring Spitalfields provided sanctuary for the French Huguenots. They had fled here after the Edict of Nantes (which had allowed them religious freedom in Catholic France) was revoked in 1685, and had found work in the nascent silk industry, many of them becoming prosperous master weavers. Today, as it turns out, Spitalfields is one of London's most cutting-edge neighborhoods, with stylish boutiques and artists setting up shop. All in all, prosperous is not really the word for the East End of today, but what the area lacks in traditional tourist attractions it makes up for in history and urban romance of a sublime sort.

Numbers in the text correspond to numbers in the margin and on the East End map.

A Good Walk

The easiest way to reach Whitechapel High Street is via the District Line to Aldgate East tube stop. Turn left out of the station. Behind No. 90 Whitechapel High Street once stood George Yard Buildings, where Jack the Ripper's first victim, Martha Turner, was discovered in August 1888. Nowadays you'll come across the **Whitechapel Art Gallery** ① instead. Continue east until you reach Fieldgate Street on the right, where you'll find the **Whitechapel Bell Foundry** ②; then, retracing your steps, turn right onto Osborn Street, which soon becomes **Brick Lane** ③.

Brick Lane itself and the narrow streets running off it offer a paradigm of the East End's development. Its population has always been in flux, with some moving in to find refuge here as others were escaping its poverty. Just before the start of Brick Lane you can take a short detour (turn left, then right) to see the birthplace of one who did just that. Flower and Dean streets, past the ugly 1970s housing project on Thrawl Street and once the most disreputable street in London, was where Abe Sapperstein, founder of the Harlem Globetrotters, was born in 1908. On the west end of **Fournier Street** ④, see Nicholas Hawksmoor's masterpiece, **Christ Church, Spitalfields** ⑤, and some fine early Georgian houses; then follow Wilkes Street north of the church, where you'll find more 1720s Huguenot houses, and turn right onto Princelet Street, once important to the Jewish settlers. Where No. 6 stands now, the first of several thriving Yiddish theaters opened in 1886, playing to packed houses until the following year, when a false fire alarm, rung during a January performance, ended with 17 people being crushed to death and so demoralized the theater's actor-founder, Jacob Adler, that he moved his troupe to New York. Adler played a major role in founding that city's great Yiddish theater tradition—which, in turn, had a significant effect on Hollywood. The Spitalfields Centre occupies and is raising funds to restore and open to the public the house at No. 19 Princelet Street, which harbored French Huguenots (the upper windows are wider than usual so the Huguenot silk weavers had light to work) and, later, Polish Jews (behind its elegant Georgian door, Jacob Davidson, a shoe warehouseman, formed the Loyal United Friendly Society and a tiny synagogue). Spitalfields' grand Georgian houses were crammed with lodgings and workshops for the poor and persecuted. As you walk these quiet streets now, where many of the doors and window shutters have fresh, gleaming paint, there is an air of intellectual restoration and respect for heritage. It's an enclave of mysterious beauty.

Now you reach Brick Lane again and the **Black Eagle Brewery** ⑥. Turn left at Hanbury Street, where, in 1888, behind a seedy lodging house at No. 29, Jack the Ripper left his third mutilated victim, "Dark" Annie Chapman. A double murder followed, and then, after a month's lull, came the death on this street of Marie Kelly, the Ripper's last victim and his most revolting murder of all. He had been able to work indoors this time, and Kelly, a young widow, was found strewn all over the room, charred remains of her clothing in the fire grate. (Of course, Jack the Ripper's identity never has been discovered, although to this day theories are still bandied about—the latest one taken up by historians fingers Francis Twomblety, an American quack doctor.)

Now turn onto Lamb Street and the two northern entrances to **Spitalfields Market** ⑦ or turn left on Commercial Street to Folgate Street and **Dennis Severs's House** ⑧. Elder Street, just off Folgate, is another gem of original 18th-century houses. On the south and east side of Spitalfields Market are yet more time-warp streets that are worth a wander, such as Gun Street, where artist Mark Gertler (1891–1939) lived at No. 32. (If you have kids, they might have fun—and learn something, too—going to **Spitalfields City Farm** ⑨ a few blocks away.) Go back west through Folgate Street to reach Shoreditch High Street, where you can catch Bus 22A, 22B, or 149 north to Kingsland Road, or get there across Bethnal Green Road, left, then right onto Club Row, to **Arnold Circus** ⑩ and then two streets north, to **Columbia Road** ⑪. Cross Hackney Road and slip up Waterson Street—that's about a ½-mi walk. On Kingsland Road, you'll come to the row of early 18th-century almshouses that are the **Geffrye Museum** ⑫. Head east about 500 yards on Hackney Road (Cremer Street, south of the museum, gets you there), to reach **Hackney City Farm** ⑬. Going south down Warner Place (across Hackney Road opposite the farm entrance), you come to Old Bethnal Green Road, at the end of which a right turn brings you to the **Bethnal Green Museum of Childhood** ⑭.

Now you can catch either Bus 106 or 253 or walk south about ½ mi down Cambridge Heath Road as far as the Mile End Road. Turning left, you'll pass several historical landmarks that provide more food for thought than thrills for the senses. On the north side of the street are the former **Trinity Almshouses** ⑮, with the statue of William Booth on the very spot where the first Salvation Army meetings were held. Behind you, on the northwest corner of Cambridge Heath Road is the **Blind Beggar** ⑯ pub, with the **Royal London Hospital** ⑰ a few yards to the left and its Archives behind. The **Ragged School Museum** ⑱ is off our map, but easily walked from Mile End tube stop via Stepney Green and Ben Jonson Road, or from the Trinity Almshouses.

TIMING

This is a long walk, and not for everyone. The East End isn't picturesque, and the sights are anything but world famous. However, those who get pleasure from discovery and an adventurous route will enjoy these hidden corners. If you visit on a Sunday morning, the East End has a festive air: about half the neighborhood sprouts hundreds of market stalls (especially in and around Middlesex Street, Brick Lane, and Columbia Road). After shopping, you could go on to take brunch among cows and sheep on a farm, then play at being Georgians in a restored, candlelit 18th-century town house. You would miss out on a few weekday-only sights, but—as a Victorian peep-show barker might say—yer pays yer money and yer takes yer choice. A weekday focus for your jaunt might well be the excellent Whitechapel Gallery, the Geffrye Museum, or the Bethnal Green Museum of Childhood, any of which will take an hour or two. Aside from visits, the walk alone is a three

The East End

SOUTH HACKNEY

London Fields Station

Haggerston Rd.
Hertford Rd.
Lee St.
More Rd.
Kingsland Rd.
Queensbridge Rd.
Albion Dr.
Shrubland Rd.
Brougham Rd.
Westgate St.
Mare St.
Tudor Rd.
King Edward's Rd.
Victoria Park Rd.
Gore Rd.
Boating Lake
Deer Park

Dunston Rd.
Pownall Rd.
Regents Row
Bush Rd.
Andrew's Rd.
Northiam St.

Grand Union Canal
Laburnum St.
Whiston Rd.
Nuttall St.
Hows St.
Haggerston Park
Pritchards Rd.
Bishop's Way
Sewardstone Rd.

Hoxton St.
Geffrye St.
HAGGERSTON
Dun-Loe St.
Cambridge Heath Station
Russia La.
Approach Rd.
Old Ford Rd.
Roman Rd.

Cremer St.
Hackney Rd.
Columbia Rd.
Warner Pl.
Temple St.
Cambridge Heath Rd.
Cyprus St.
Globe Rd.
Meath Gardens

SHOREDITCH
Curtain Rd.
Old St.
Gosset St.
Barnet Grove
Turin St.
Old Bethnal Green Rd.
Vallance Rd.
BETHNAL GREEN
Sceptre Rd.
Morpeth St.
Bancroft Rd.
Grantley St.

Great Eastern St.
Shoreditch High St.
Swanfield St.
Brick La.
Red Church St.
Bethnal Green Rd.
Bethnal Green Rd.
Weavers Fields
Cephas St.
Colbert Ave.
Globe Rd.
White Horse La.

Cheshire St.
Dunbridge St.
Bethnal Green Station
Cambridge Heath Rd.
Collingwood St.
Mile End Rd.
Stepney Green

Quaker St.
Buxton St.
Burial Ground
Brady St.
Redman's Rd.
Smithy St.
Stepney Green

Appold St.
Commercial St.
Lamb St.
Hanbury St.
Montague St.
Greatorex St.
Whitechapel Rd.
Raven Row
Cavell St.
Sidney St.
Stepney Way
Jamaica St.

Liverpool St. Station
Middlesex St.
Old Montague St.
New Rd.
Settles St.
Myrtle St.
Greenfield Rd.
Whitechapel Rd.
STEPNEY

Bishops Gate
Houndsditch
Whitechapel Rd.
Castle St.
Braham St.
Adler St.
Gowers Wk.
Alie St.
Varden St.
Nelson St.
Commercial Rd.
Cannon St.
Bigland St.

KEY
🚇 Tube Station
0 440 yards
0 400 meters

N

hour marathon, done at a brisk pace. The suggested bus links might be appealing, since the in-between parts aren't going to win tourism awards.

HOW TO GET THERE

The best tube stop to start from is Whitechapel or Aldgate East on the District/Hammersmith and City lines or Aldgate on the Metropolitan and Circle lines. Buses 8, 25, 26, 35, 47, 48, and 78 are useful. To continue up into the northern part of the area, around Shoreditch and Spitalfields, including the Geffrye Museum (get the 22A or B or the 67 for that), get Buses 8, 22A, 22B, 26, 35, 47, 48, 55, 67, 78, and 242 to the junction of Shoreditch High Street and Bishopsgate.

Sights to See

⑩ Arnold Circus. A perfect circle of Arts and Crafts–style houses around a central raised bandstand, this is the core of the Boundary Estate—"model" housing built by Victorian philanthropists and do-gooders for the slum-dwelling locals and completed as the 20th century began. It's of special interest to architecture buffs. ✉ *E2. Tube: Liverpool St. or Old St.*

🐾 ⑭ Bethnal Green Museum of Childhood. This is the East End outpost of the Victoria & Albert Museum—in fact, this entire iron, glass, and brown-brick building was transported here from South Kensington in 1875. Since then, believe it or not, its contents have grown into the biggest toy collection in the world. The central hall is a bit like the Geffrye Museum zapped into miniature: here are dollhouses (some royal) of every period. Each genre of plaything has its own enclosure, so if teddy bears are your weakness, you need waste no time with the train sets. The museum's title is justified upstairs, in the fascinating—and possibly unique—galleries on the social history of childhood. Free art workshops are given Saturdays for children over the age of 3 with ticket from the admission desk. ✉ *Cambridge Heath Rd., E2,* ☎ *020/8983–5200, 020/8980–2415 recorded information.* 🎟 *Free.* ⊘ *Sat.–Thurs. 10–5:50; art workshop Sat. 11, noon, 2, 3. Tube: Bethnal Green.*

❻ Black Eagle Brewery. This is the only one of the former East End breweries still standing. It is a very handsome example of Georgian and 19th-century industrial architecture, too, along with its mirrored 1977 extension. It belonged to Truman, Hanbury, Buxton & Co., which in 1873 was the largest brewery in the world (the English always did like their bitters). The building now houses the East End Tourism Trust offices and the present Truman brewery's administration. You can't go in except to look at the old stables and vat house on the east side. The old brewery canteen used to be the **Brick Lane Music Hall** (✉ 134–146 Curtain Rd., ☎ 020/7739–9996), but this has now moved to larger premises a couple of roads away; there, you'll find East End Jewish fare (latkes—potato pancakes—are a feature on most menus) and an old-fashioned laugh-a-minute cabaret show on tap. ✉ *91 Brick La., E1. Tube: Aldgate East or Shoreditch.*

⑯ The Blind Beggar. This is the Victorian den of iniquity where Salvation Army founder William Booth preached his first sermon. Also, on the south side of the street stands a stone inscribed, HERE WILLIAM BOOTH COMMENCED THE WORK OF THE SALVATION ARMY, JULY 1865, marking the position of the first Sally Army platform, while back by the pub, a statue of William Booth stands where the first meetings were held. Booth didn't supply the pub's main claim to fame, though. The Blind Beggar's real notoriety dates only from March 1966, when Ronnie Kray—one of the Kray twins, the former gangster kings of London's East End underworld—shot dead rival "godfather" George Cornell in the saloon bar. The original Albion Brewery was next door, celebrated home to the first bottled brown ale. ⊠ *337 Whitechapel Rd., E1. Tube: Whitechapel.*

❸ Brick Lane. This street has, in its time, seen the manufacture of bricks (during the 16th century, when it was named), beer, and bagels, but nowadays it is the center of the East End's Bengali community. (You can still get the bagels, though, at No. 159, the 24-hour **Beigel Bake.**) All along here you'll see shops selling psychedelic saris and stacks of sticky Indian sweets, video stores renting Indian movies, and Bengali, Bangladeshi, and Pakistani restaurants, popular among Londoners for the most authentic and least expensive curries in town. On Sunday morning the entire street is packed with stalls in a companion market to the nearby Petticoat Lane. ⊠ *Brick La., E1. Tube: Aldgate East or Shoreditch.*

❺ Christ Church, Spitalfields. This is the 1729 masterpiece of Wren's associate, Nicholas Hawksmoor. Hawksmoor built only six London churches; this one was commissioned as part of Parliament's 1711 "Fifty New Churches Act." The idea was to score points for the Church of England against such nonconformists as the Protestant Huguenots. (It must have worked; in the churchyard, you can still see some of their gravestones, with epitaphs in French.) The Spitalfields district once flourished thanks to the silk-weaving trade of its émigré population, but as the silk industry declined (19th-century machinery had made hand weaving obsolete), the church fell into disrepair and its gardens even acquired a reputation as a tramps' ground (and the sobriquet "Itchy Park"). By 1958 the structure was crumbling to bits and had to be closed. It was saved from demolition—but only just—and reopened in 1987. Restoration work on the exterior is now complete, although the interior work continues. Opening hours are restricted to those listed below, although you can also admire the interior during the Spitalfields Festival in June and December, when there are lunchtime and evening concerts; call ☎ 020/7377–0287 for details. There is always a fine view of the colonnaded portico and tall spire from Brushfield Street to the west. ⊠ *Commercial St., E1,* ☎ *020/7247–7202.* ☜ *Free; charge for concerts.* ☺ *Weekdays noon–2, Sun. services. Tube: Aldgate East.*

⓫ Columbia Road. On Sundays, this narrow street gets buried under forests of potted palms, azaleas, ivy, ficus, freesia, tiger lilies, carnations, roses, and hosts of daffodils in London's main plant and flower market. Prices are ultralow, and lots of the Victorian shop windows around the stalls are filled with horticultural wares—terra-cotta pots, vases, gardening tools, hats, and antiques. ☺ *Sun. 7–2. Tube: Old St., then Bus 55.*

★ ❽ Dennis Severs's House. Ever want to feel what Ebenezer Scrooge felt when the three ghosts visited him? Enter this extraordinary time machine of a house—a Georgian terrace belonging to the eponymous performer-designer-scholar from Escondido, California, who dedicated his life not only to restoring his house but also to raising the ghosts of a fictitious Jervis family that might have inhabited it over the course of two centuries. Severs, who died in December 1999, lived a replica of Georgian life, without electricity but with a butler in full 18th-century livery to light the candles and lay the fires—for the Jervises. His assistant still carries on the tradition. The rooms are shadowy set pieces of rose-laden Victorian wallpapers, Jacobean paneling, Georgian wing chairs, Baroque carved ornaments, "Protestant" colors (upstairs), and "Catholic" shades (downstairs). Once a month there is an open house; reservations are essential on Monday, when the house is viewed by candlelight. Private visits by special arrangement are possible. ⊠ *18 Folgate St., E1,* ☎ *020/7247–4013.* ☜ *£7 for Sun. open house; £10 for* *candlelit Mon. evenings.* ⊘ *1st Sun. of month 2–5, 1st Mon. call for hrs (reservations required). Tube: Liverpool St.*

❹ **Fournier Street.** This contains fine examples of the neighborhood's characteristic Georgian terraced houses, many of them built by the richest of the early 18th-century Huguenot silk weavers (see the enlarged windows on the upper floors). Most of those along the north side of Fournier Street have now been restored by conservationists; others still contain textile sweatshops—only now the workers are Bengali. On the Brick Lane corner is the **Jamme Masjid,** where local Muslims worship. UMBRA SUMMUS (WE ARE SHADOWS) announces the inscription above the entrance, an apt epitaph for the successive communities that have had temporary claim on the building. Built in 1742 as a Huguenot chapel, it converted to Methodism in 1809, only to become the Spitalfields Great Synagogue when the Orthodox Machzikei Hadath sect bought it in 1897. ⊠ *E1. Tube: Liverpool St.*

★ ⑫ **Geffrye Museum.** This is a small and perfectly formed museum that re-creates domestic English interiors of every period from Elizabethan through postwar '50s utility, all in sequence, so that you walk through time. The best thing about the Geffrye (named after the 17th-century Lord Mayor of London whose land this was) is that its rooms are not the grand parlors of the gentry one normally sees in historic houses but copies of real family homes, as if talented movie-set designers had been let loose instead of academic museum curators. There's also a walled, scented herb garden and a full program of accessible lectures, including regular "bring a room to life" talks. A suite of 20th-century rooms opened in November 1998. ⊠ *Kingsland Rd., E2,* ☎ *020/7739–9893,* WEB *www.geffrye-museum.org.uk.* ☜ *Free.* ⊘ *Tues.–Sat. 10–5, Sun. noon–5. Tube: Old St., then Bus 243; Liverpool St., then Bus 149, 242, or 243A.*

☝ ⑬ **Hackney City Farm.** This one is smaller than the city farm at Spitalfields, and so are its animals. Bees and butterflies are the stars here, along with the kinds of wildflowers they like, as well as an ecologically sound pond. If you're walking this route, drop in and buy a pot of London honey. ⊠ *1A Goldsmiths Row, E2,* ☎ *020/7729–6381.* ☜ *Free.* ⊘ *Tues.–Sun. 10–4:30. Tube: Bethnal Green.*

☝ ⑱ **Ragged School Museum.** In its time, this was the largest school in London and a place where impoverished children could escape their deprived homes to get free education and a good meal. The museum recreates the children's experiences with a time-capsule classroom, dating from the 1880s. Even after their short school career, the students were helped to find their first jobs, and hopefully a way out of their poverty trap. At home, they were probably living in one room with the rest of their usually large family, eking out a sad life with little future prospect of improvement. The school was their passport to a better life.

It's an eye-opener for adults, and a fun time-travel experience for kids who get the chance to work with such materials as scratchy slates and chalks—just like Victorian kids did more than 100 years ago, in one of the many organized workshops. There are guided tours, an exhibit on the history of the area, a bookshop, and a café overlooking the canal, where you can take stock of the facilities young students have at their disposal today. ⊠ *46–50 Copperfield Rd., EC3,* ☎ *020/8980–6405,* WEB *www.raggedschoolmuseum.org.uk.* ☜ *Free.* ⊘ *Wed.–Thurs. 10–5, first Sun. of month 2–5.*

⑰ **Royal London Hospital.** Founded in 1740, the Royal London was once as nasty as its then-neighborhood near the Tower of London. Waste was carried out in buckets and dumped in the street; bedbugs and alcoholic nurses were problems; but according to hospital records patients didn't die—they were "relieved." Anyone who lived but refused to give thanks to both the hospital committee and God went on a blacklist, to be banned from further treatment. In 1757, the hospital moved to a new building, the core of the one you see today. By then it had become one of the best hospitals in London, and it was enhanced further by the addition of a small medical school in 1785, and again, 70 years later, an entire state-of-the-art medical college. Thomas John Barnado, who went on to found the famous Dr. Barnado's Homes for Orphans, came to train here in 1866. Ten years later, with the opening of a new wing, the hospital became the largest in the United Kingdom, and now, though mostly rebuilt since World War II, it remains one of London's most capacious. Behind it, in the crypt of St. Augustine with St. Philip's Church, on Newark Street, the **Royal London Hospital Archives** has displays of medical paraphernalia, objects, and documentation to illustrate the 250-year history of this East London institution. ⊠ *Whitechapel Rd., E1,* ☎ *020/7377–7608.* 🎫 *Free.* ⊙ *Hospital and garden daily 9–6, archives weekdays 10–4:30. Tube: Whitechapel.*

☺ ❾ **Spitalfields City Farm.** This is just what it sounds like—a sliver of rural England squashed between housing projects. It's one of about a dozen such places in London, which exist to educate city kids in country matters. A tiny farm shop sells freshly laid eggs and farm recipes. ⊠ *Pedley St., E1,* ☎ *020/7247–8762.* 🎫 *Free.* ⊙ *Tues.–Sun. 10:30–5. Tube: Shoreditch or Liverpool St.*

❼ **Spitalfields Market.** There's been a market here since the mid-17th century, but the current version is overflowing with crafts and design shops and stalls, a sports hall, restaurants and bars (with a pan-world palette, from Spanish tapas to Thai), and different-purpose markets every day of the week. The nearer the weekend, the busier it all gets, culminating in the Sunday arts-and-crafts and green market—the best day to go. There's also a burgeoning events program with arts and concerts. ⊠ *65 Brushfield St., E1,* ☎ *020/7377–1496.* 🎫 *Free.* ⊙ *Daily 10–7; market stalls weekdays 10–3, Sun. 9:30–5. Tube: Liverpool St.*

OFF THE   **SUTTON HOUSE –** Homerton (part of Hackney, east of London) hasn't
BEATEN PATH   much to recommend it, but Sutton House has survived the inroads of modern block estates. When it was built in 1535, it was surrounded by fields and a country village. Now run by the National Trust, the mansion was first owned by Ralph Sadleir, a important courtier to Henry VIII. The Tudor linen-fold paneling in the parlor is some of the finest in London and can only be seen elsewhere in Hampton Court; the carved stone fireplaces are also original. The painted stairwell with its wall friezes has been carefully preserved. The kitchen, which has fascinating cooking implements of the time, leads onto a cobbled Italianate courtyard—you could be a thousand miles from deepest Hackney. There's a café, a gift shop, and exhibitions—including a computer on which you can read a copy of a local Victorian child's diary. It's a special place that transports you light-years away from the thronging traffic and ugly apartment blocks just outside. ⊠ *2 Homerton High St., E9,* ☎ *020/8986–2264, www.nationaltrust.org.uk. Tube: Highbury and Islington, then Bus 377 or 30; Whitechapel, then Bus 106 or 253.*

⓯ **Trinity Almshouses.** This is just a redbrick student hostel, but it has interesting origins, having been built (possibly with Wren's help) in 1695 for "28 decayed Masters and Commanders of Ships or ye widows of such," bombed during World War II, and restored by the London

County Council. Behind, even better concealed, is the oldest Jewish cemetery in Britain, founded by the Sephardic community in 1657 after Cromwell allowed them back into the country. (If you would like to view the cemetery, call the **United Synagogues Cemetery Maintenance Department,** ☏ 020/7790–1445.) ✉ *Mile End Rd., E1. Tube: Whitechapel or Stepney Green.*

❶ **Whitechapel Art Gallery.** Housed in a spacious 1901 Art Nouveau building, this has an international reputation for its shows, which are often on the cutting edge of contemporary art. The American painter Jackson Pollock exhibited here in the 1950s, as did pop artist Robert Rauschenberg in the '60s, and David Hockney had his first solo show here in the '70s. More recently, the Tate Gallery visited the Whitechapel and bought American Bill Viola's powerful video installation, the *Nantes Triptych,* which shows Viola submerged underwater, his wife giving birth on one side, his mother dying in a hospital on the other. Other exhibitions highlight the local community and culture, and there are programs of lectures, too. The Whitechapel Café serves remarkably inexpensive, home-cooked, whole-food hot meals, soups, and cakes. ✉ *Whitechapel High St., E1,* ☏ 020/7522–7888. ⊡ *Free (fee for some exhibitions).* ⊙ *Tues. and Thurs.–Sun. 11–5, Wed. 11–8. Tube: Aldgate East.*

❷ **Whitechapel Bell Foundry.** It may be off the beaten track, but this working foundry was responsible for some of the world's better-known chimes. Before moving to this site in 1738, the foundry cast Westminster Abbey's bells (in the 1580s), but its biggest work, in every sense, was the 13-ton Big Ben, cast in 1858 by George Mears and requiring 16 horses to transport it from here to Westminster. The foundry's other important work was casting the original Liberty Bell (now in Philadelphia) in 1752, and both it and Big Ben can be seen in pictures, along with exhibits about bell making, in a little museum in the shop. Note: the actual foundry is off-limits, for health and safety reasons, but in the small front shop you can buy bell paraphernalia and browse through the historic photos. There are guided tours of the foundry on Saturday morning only, but bookings are usually made months in advance (call for information and fees). ✉ *34 Whitechapel Rd., E1,* ☏ 020/7247–2599. ⊙ *Weekdays 8:30–5:30. Tube: Aldgate East.*

OFF THE
BEATEN PATH

WILLIAM MORRIS GALLERY – An 18th-century house in northeast London where the artistic polymath William Morris (1834–96)—craftsman, painter, and writer—lived for eight years, this gallery contains many examples of his work and that of his fellow artisans in the Arts and Crafts movement. ✉ *Water House, Lloyd Park, Forest Rd.,* ☏ 020/ 8527–3782. ⊙ *Tues.–Sat. 10–1 and 2–5, 1st Sun. of month 10–1 and 2–5. Tube: Walthamstow Central, then 15-min walk down Hoe St., turn left at Forest Rd.*

THE SOUTH BANK

That old, snide North London quip about needing a passport to cross the Thames is no longer heard. For decades, natives never ventured beyond the watery curtain that divides the city in half; tourists, too, rarely troubled with the area unless they were departing from Waterloo Station. But lately, a host of attractions is drawing even the most ardent northerners across the great divide. The adjunct branch of the Tate Gallery is the star; perhaps in keeping with Britain's most renowned new artist Damien Hirst (who often uses utensils and other found objects), Tate Modern takes something functional—a 1930s power station—and makes it a place for inspiration and creativity. At the South Bank Centre, the world's largest observation wheel, officially called the British Airways London Eye, gives visitors a 25-minute flight over the city. Even looked at from a great height, the South Bank—which occupies the riverside stretch between Waterloo Bridge and Hungerford Bridge—still isn't beautiful, but if it's culture you're hunting for, this complex of theaters and museums is fantastic. Today, developers and local authorities have expanded the South Bank's potential farther east with an explosion of attractions that are turning this once-neglected district into one of London's most happening new neighborhoods. The 1980s brought renovations and innovations such as Gabriel's Wharf, London Bridge City, Hay's Galleria, and Butler's Wharf; the '90s arrived, and so did such headline-making sights as the spectacular reconstruction of Shakespeare's Globe—the most famous theater in the world—the OXO Tower, and the London Aquarium. The South Bank has since become a dazzling perch for culture vultures.

Actually, it is fitting that so much of London's artistic life should once again be centered here on the South Bank—back in the days of Ye Olde London Towne, **Southwark** was the city's oldest "suburb": though just across London Bridge, it was conveniently outside the City walls and laws and therefore the ideal location for the theaters, taverns, and cock-fighting arenas that served as after-hours entertainment in the Middle Ages. The Globe Theatre, in which Shakespeare acted and held shares, was one of several established here after theaters were banished from the City in 1574 for encouraging truancy in young apprentices and for being generally rowdy. In truth, the Globe was as likely to stage a few bouts of bearbaiting as the latest interpretations of Shakespeare. Today, at the reconstructed "Wooden O," of course, you can just see the latter.

Numbers in the text correspond to numbers in the margin and on the South Bank map.

A Good Walk

Start scenically at the south end of Tower Bridge, finding the steps on the east (left) side, which descend to the start of a pedestrians-only street, Shad Thames. Now turn your back on the bridge and follow this quaint path between cliffs of the good-as-new warehouses, which are now **Butler's Wharf** ① but were once the seedy, dingy, dangerous shadow lands where Dickens killed off Bill Sikes in *Oliver Twist*. See the foodies' center, the Gastrodrome, and the **Design Museum** ②; then, just before you get back to Tower Bridge, turn away from the river (along Horsleydown Lane), follow Tooley Street, and take either the right turn at Morgan Lane to **HMS Belfast** ③ or continue to **Hay's Galleria** ④, with London Bridge and the **London Dungeon** ⑤ beyond. Next, turn left onto Joiner Street underneath the arches of London's first (1836) railway, then right onto St. Thomas Street, where you'll find the **Old Operating Theatre Museum** ⑥. **Southwark Cathedral** ⑦ is just across Borough High Street, past the organic Saturday Borough Market and past another of the South Bank's office developments, St. Mary Overy's Dock, down Cathedral Street. See the west wall, with a rose-window outline of Winchester House, the palace of the Bishops of Winchester until 1626, built into it, and take a tour of the little **Golden Hinde** ⑧ and the **Clink** ⑨ next door. Continue to the end of Clink Street onto Bankside, detouring left up Rose Alley, where in 1989 the remains of the famous Jacobean Rose Theatre were unearthed (because of office development surrounding the preserved foundations, however, there's not much to see). Just before you reach the place to imbibe culture, you come to **Vinopolis** ⑩, the world's first leisure complex celebrating wine. Then head to the next little alley, New Globe Walk, where there is much to see: the reconstruction of that most famous of Jacobean theaters, **Shakespeare's Globe The-**

atre ⑪. Next along Bankside is the 17th-century Cardinal's Wharf, where, as a plaque explains, Wren lived while St. Paul's Cathedral was being built; then Bankside Power Station, now the **Tate Modern** ⑫ at Bankside and **Bankside Gallery** ⑬. Stretching from the new Tate back across the river to the St. Paul's Cathedral steps in the City is the Millennium Bridge, a pedestrian bridge across the Thames.

Now you reach your fifth bridge on this walk, Blackfriars Bridge, which you pass beneath to join the street called Upper Ground, spending some time in the Coin Street Community Builders' fast-emerging neighborhood, which features the **OXO Tower** ⑭ and Gabriel's Wharf, a marketplace of shops and cafés. Farther along Upper Ground, you reach the South Bank Centre, with the **Royal National Theatre** ⑮ first, followed by the **Museum of the Moving Image (MOMI)** and National Film Theatre (both of which are closed for refurbishment until 2003), the **Royal Festival Hall** ⑯, and the **Hayward Gallery** ⑰. The **BFI London IMAX Cinema** ⑱ sits just down Waterloo road behind the MOMI and the Hayward Gallery. Carry on round the curve of the river and you come to the magnificent **British Airways London Eye** ⑲. You'll find distractions all over this section of the walk, especially in summer—secondhand-book stalls, entertainers, and a series of plaques annotating the buildings opposite. When you've passed the South Bank Centre, look across the river for the quintessential postcard vista of the Houses of Parliament, which continues past Westminster Bridge to St. Thomas's Hospital. Next, you reach the former County Hall, which now houses the **London Aquarium** ⑳ and the surrealist museum **Dalí Universe** ㉑. Farther along the river, beyond the **Florence Nightingale Museum** ㉒, **Lambeth Palace** ㉓ stands by Lambeth Bridge, with the **Museum of Garden History** ㉔ in St. Mary's next door. If you take a detour to the right off Lambeth Road, you could be "doing the Lambeth Walk" down the street of the same name. A cockney tradition ever since the 17th century, when there was a spa here, the Sunday stroll was immortalized in a song from the 1937 musical *Me and My Girl*. A little farther east along Lambeth Road you reach the **Imperial War Museum** ㉕.

TIMING

On a fine day, this 2- to 3-mi walk makes a very scenic wander, since you're following the south bank of the great Thames nearly all the way. Fabulous views across to the north bank take you past St. Paul's and the Houses of Parliament, and you pass—under, over, or around—no fewer than seven bridges. It's bound to take far longer than a couple of hours because there is so much to see. The BFI London IMAX Cinema, Tate Modern, the Imperial War Museum, Shakespeare's Globe, the Hayward Gallery, the Design Museum, and the London Aquarium could each take more than an hour (depending on your interests), while the London Dungeon doesn't take long, unless you have kids in tow—which is why you'd go in at all. The other museums on this route—the Clink, Dalí Universe, Garden History, Old Operating Theatre, Florence Nightingale, the South Bank Centre foyers, and the Bankside Gallery—are compact enough to squeeze together. You can finish this walk with a flourish by going to one of three theatres—the Lytleton, the Cottesloe, or the Olivier—at the National Theatre complex, to the National Film Theatre, or to Shakespeare's Globe, but remember that the theaters stay dark on Sundays. Dinner or a riverside drink at the OXO Tower Brasserie, the Gastrodrome restaurants, or the People's Palace is another idea for a big finish.

HOW TO GET THERE

The tube stop to use is London Bridge on the Jubilee or Northern line, though you could also start at Monument on the District and Circle lines and walk across London Bridge to the beginning of the walk. At the end of the walk you'll end up at Waterloo on the Northern and Bakerloo lines. You could also leave on the Embankment stop (same lines, plus District and Circle) or Charing Cross (the Jubilee and Northern lines) by walking across the Charing Cross pedestrian bridge. Buses that take you into the rather confusing territory behind the South Bank Centre include Buses 1, 68, 76, 168, 171, 176, 178, and 188. For farther downstream, near Shakespeare's Globe, get the 21, 35, 40, 47, or 133 to Tooley Street, or get the tube to Blackfriars and walk across that bridge (offering a particularly scenic walk) to the stunning new Southwark station on the Jubilee line, or to Mansion House and walk across Southwark Bridge. The latter is the best way to the OXO Tower.

Sights to See

⓭ **Bankside Gallery.** Two artistic societies—the Royal Society of Painter-Printmakers-Etchers and the Royal Watercolour Society—have their headquarters here. Together they mount exhibitions of current members' work, usually for sale, alongside artists' materials and books. ⊠ *48 Hopton St., SE1,* ☎ *020/7928–7521.* ⊠ *£3.50.* ☉ *Tues., Thurs., and Sat. 10–8, Sun. 1–5, Wed. and Fri. 10–5. Tube: Blackfriars or Southwark.*

⓲ **BFI London IMAX Cinema.** With the largest screen in London—the height of five doubledecker buses and a width that completely fills your eye—the IMAX Cinema guarantees an eyeful of technological and celluloid innovation. Choose from 2D or 3D films. ⊠ *Waterloo Bridge at Stamford St., SE1,* ☎ *020/7902–1234,* WEB *www.bfi.org.uk.* ⊠ *£6.40.* ☉ *Sun.–Thurs. noon–8:45, Fri.–Sat. noon–10. Tube: Waterloo, Exit 5.*

⓳ **British Airways London Eye.** If you long to see London from a different perspective, this giant ride, the fourth highest structure in London, will give you the chance. At 500 ft, the highest observation wheel in the world towers over the South Bank from the Jubilee Gardens next to County Hall. The fainthearted may want to pass up the 25-minute slow-motion hover over the city. ⊠ *Jubilee Gardens, SE1,* ☎ *0870/ 500–0600,* WEB *www.british-airways.com/londoneye.* ⊠ *£7.95.* ☉ *Apr.–Oct., daily 9–sunset; Nov.–Mar., daily 10–6. Tube: Waterloo.*

❶ **Butler's Wharf.** An '80s development that is maturing gracefully, this wharf is full of deluxe loft-style warehouse conversions and swanky buildings housing restaurants and galleries. People flock here thanks partly to London's saint of the stomach, Sir Terence Conran (also responsible for high-profile central London restaurants Bibendum, Mezzo, and Quaglino's). He has given it his "Gastrodrome" of four restaurants (including the fabulous Pont de la Tour), a vintner's, a deli, and a bakery. ⊠ *SE1. Tube: London Bridge or Tower Hill, then walk across river.*

❾ **The Clink.** Giving rise to the term "clink," which still means jail, this institution was originally the prison attached to Winchester House, palace of the Bishops of Winchester until 1626. One of five Southwark prisons, it was the first to detain women, most of whom were called "Winchester geese"—another euphemism meaning prostitutes. The world's oldest profession was endemic in Southwark, especially around the bishops' area of jurisdiction, which was known as "the Liberty of the Clink." Their graces' sensible solution was to license prostitution rather than ban it, but a Winchester goose who flouted the rules ended up in the Clink. Now there is a museum tracing the history of prostitution in "the Liberty" and showing what the Clink was like during its 16th-century prime. ⊠ *1 Clink St., SE1,* ☎ *020/7403–6515,* WEB *www.clink.co.uk.* ⊠ *£4.* ☉ *Daily 10–6. Tube: London Bridge.*

The South Bank

440 yds
400 m

KEY
Ⓘ Tube Station

Bankside Gallery **13**
BFI London IMAX Cinema **18**
British Airways London Eye . . **19**
Butler's Wharf **1**
The Clink **9**

Dali Universe **21**
Design Museum **2**
Florence Nightingale Museum . . **22**
Golden Hinde **8**
Hay's Galleria **4**

Hayward Gallery **21**
HMS *Belfast* **3**
Imperial War Museum . . **25**
Lambeth Palace **23**
London Aquarium **20**

London Dungeon **5**
Museum of Garden History . . **24**
Old Operating Theatre Museum . . **6**
OXO Tower **14**

Royal Festival Hall **16**
Royal National Theatre **15**
Shakespeare's Globe Theatre . . **11**
Southwark Cathedral **7**

Tate Modern **12**
Vinopolis **10**

㉑ **Dalí Universe.** This truly surrealist museum has the largest collection of Salvador Dalí's sculpture and a great many of his drawings, paintings, and lithographs. Dalí-inspired furniture is even on display. Neatly arranged into three areas, Sensuality and Femininity, Religion and Mythology, and Dreams and Fantasy, the museum reflects Dalí's eclectic work. Hitchcock fans will be mesmerized by the *Spellbound* painting made especially for the eponymous 1945 movie. ✉ *County Hall, Riverside Building, Westminster Bridge Rd., SE1,* ☎ *020/7620–2420,* 🌐 *www.daliuniverse.com.* 💷 *£8.50.* ⏰ *Daily 10–5:30. Tube: Waterloo or Westminster.*

❷ **Design Museum.** This was the first museum in the world (it opened in 1989) to elevate everyday design and design classics to the status of art by placing them in their social and cultural context. On the top floor, the Collection traces the evolution of mass-produced goods, with display cases full of telephones and washing machines, plates and hi-fi equipment, computers and Coke bottles, and plenty of backup material, from ads to films. Alongside the Collection, the regularly revamped Review looks deeply into a particular aspect of the consumer durable. Special exhibitions are held downstairs on the first floor, and there's also a program of lectures and events, as well as the very good Blueprint Café, a funky restaurant with its own river terrace and superb views of London. ✉ *28 Shad Thames, SE1,* ☎ *020/7403–6933,* 🌐 *www.designmuseum.org.* 💷 *£5.50.* ⏰ *Weekdays 11:30–5:50, weekends 10:30–5:50. Tube: London Bridge or Bermondsey.*

OFF THE
BEATEN PATH

DULWICH PICTURE GALLERY – A highly distinguished small gallery, the Dulwich has impressive works by Rembrandt, Van Dyck, Rubens, Poussin, and Gainsborough, among others. Anyone who fell in love with Sir John Soane's house may wish to make the trek out here, since this gallery was also designed by the visionary architect. If you do come all this way, you'll also enjoy wandering around Dulwich Village, with its handsome 18th-century houses strung out along its main street. Most of the land around here belongs to the famous local school, the Dulwich College Estate, founded in the early 17th century by the actor Edward Alleyn, and this keeps strict control of modern development. Opposite the gallery, Dulwich Park is a well-kept municipal park with a particularly fine display of rhododendrons in late May. ✉ *College Rd.,* ☎ *020/8693–8000.* 💷 *£5.* ⏰ *Tues.–Fri. 10–5, weekends 1–5. British Rail: West Dulwich (from Victoria or London Bridge).*

㉒ **Florence Nightingale Museum.** Here you can learn all about the founder of the first school of nursing, that most famous of health-care reformers, "the Lady with the Lamp." See the reconstruction of the barracks ward at Scutari, Turkey, where she tended soldiers during the Crimean War (1854–56) and earned her nickname. Here you also find a Victorian East End slum cottage showing what she did to improve living conditions among the poor—and the famous lamp. The museum is in **St. Thomas's Hospital,** which was built in 1868 to the specifications of Florence Nightingale. Most of it was bombed to bits in the Blitz, then rebuilt to become one of London's teaching hospitals. ✉ *2 Lambeth Palace Rd., SE1,* ☎ *020/7620–0374,* 🌐 *www.florence-nightingale.co.uk.* 💷 *£4.80.* ⏰ *Mon.–Tues., Thurs.–Fri. 10–4, Wed. 11:30–3:30. Tube: Waterloo or Westminster, then walk over bridge.*

❽ ***Golden Hinde.*** Sir Francis Drake circumnavigated the globe in this little galleon, or one just like it. This exact replica made a 23-year round-the-world voyage—much of it spent along U.S. coasts, both Pacific and Atlantic—and has settled here to continue its educational purpose. If you want information along with your visit, book a tour for £3 in advance. ✉ *St. Mary Overy's Dock, Southwark, SE1,* ☎ *020/7403–0123,* WEB *www.goldenhinde.co.uk.* 🎫 *£2.50.* ⊙ *Daily 9:30–5:30. Tube: London Bridge or Mansion House.*

❹ Hay's Galleria. Hay's Wharf was built by Thomas Cubitt in 1857 on the spot where the port of London's oldest wharf had stood since 1651. It was once known as "London's larder" on account of the quantity of edibles that landed here. It then wound down gradually and closed in 1970. In 1987 it was reborn as this Covent Garden–like parade of bars and restaurants, offices, and shops, all weatherproofed by an arched glass atrium roof supported by tall iron columns. The centerpiece is a fanciful kinetic sculpture by David Kemp, *The Navigators,* which looks like the skeleton of a pirate schooner crossed with a dragon and spouts water from various orifices. Needless to say, jugglers, string quartets, and crafts stalls abound. This courtyard hub of the developing London Bridge City needed all the help it could get in its early days, but it has settled in nicely now with its captive crowd of office workers from the adjacent new developments. ✉ *2 Battlebridge La., SE1,* ☎ *020/7940–7770,* WEB *www.haysgalleria.co.uk. Tube: London Bridge.*

⓱ Hayward Gallery. This is one of the city's major art-exhibition spaces, its bias fixed firmly in the 20th century. The stained and windowless bunker tucked behind the South Bank Centre concert halls has been the brunt of most of the criticism of Thames-side buildings, enduring constant threats to flatten it and start again. But it's still here, topped by its multicolor neon tube sculpture, the most familiar feature on the South Bank skyline. ✉ *South Bank Complex, SE1,* ☎ *020/7928–3144,* WEB *www.hayward-gallery.co.uk.* 🎫 *Admission varies according to exhibition.* ⊙ *Thurs.–Mon. 10–6, Tues.–Wed. 10–8. Tube: Waterloo.*

👈 ❸ HMS *Belfast.* At 656 ft., this is one of the largest and most powerful cruisers the Royal Navy has ever had. It played an important role in the D-Day landings off Normandy, left for the Far East after the war, and has been becalmed here since 1971. On board there's an outpost of the **Imperial War Museum,** which tells the Royal Navy's story from 1914 to the present and shows you what life on a World War II battleship was like, from mess decks and bakery to punishment cells and from operations room to engine room and armaments. ✉ *Morgan's La., Tooley St., SE1,* ☎ *020/7940–6434,* WEB *www.iwm.org.uk.* 🎫 *£4.70.* ⊙ *Mid-Mar.–Oct., daily 10–6; Nov.–mid-Mar., daily 10–4:15. Tube: London Bridge.*

OFF THE
BEATEN PATH

HORNIMAN MUSEUM – This educational museum of anthropology, which also manages to be fun, is set in 16 acres of gardens in South London with well-displayed ethnographic and natural history collections. Recent additions include an aquarium stocked with endangered species and the African Worlds section. A new extension is scheduled to open in spring 2002. It will contain galleries for world cultures and temporary exhibitions; the Centre for Understanding, with hands-on displays for younger visitors; and a new café and shop. ✉ *100 London Rd., Forest Hill,* ☎ *020/8699–1872,* WEB *www.horniman.ac.uk.* 🎫 *Free.* ⊙ *Mon.–Sat. 10:30–5:30, Sun. 2–5:30. British Rail: Forest Hill (from London Bridge or Victoria).*

㉕ Imperial War Museum. Despite its title, this museum of 20th-century warfare does not glorify bloodshed but attempts to evoke what it was like to live through the two world wars. Of course, there is hardware for martial-minded children—a Battle of Britain Spitfire, a German V2 rocket, tanks, guns, submarines—but there is an equal amount of war art (David Bomberg, Henry Moore, John Singer Sargent, Graham Sutherland, to name a few), poetry, photography, and documentary film footage. One very affecting exhibit is *The Blitz Experience,* which is just what it sounds like—a 10-minute taste of an air raid in a street of acrid smoke with sirens blaring and searchlights glaring. There is also a permanent Holocaust exhibition, funded from a generous lottery grant. More recent wars attended by British forces are thoughtfully commemorated, too, right up to the Gulf War of 1991.

The museum is housed in an elegant domed and colonnaded building, erected in the early 19th century to house the Bethlehem Hospital for the Insane, better known as the infamous Bedlam. By 1816, when the patients were moved here, they were no longer kept in cages to be taunted by tourists (see the final scene of Hogarth's *Rake's Progress* at Sir John Soane's Museum for some sense of how horrific it was), since reformers—and George III's madness—had effected more humane standards of confinement. Bedlam moved to Surrey in 1930. ⊠ *Lambeth Rd., SE1,* ☎ *020/7416–5320,* WEB *www.iwm.org.uk.* ⊠ *£5.50.* ☼ *Daily 10–6. Tube: Lambeth North.*

㉓ **Lambeth Palace.** For 800 years, this has been the London base of the Archbishop of Canterbury, head of the Church of England. Much of the palace is hidden behind great walls, and even the Tudor gatehouse, visible from the street, is closed to the public, but you can stand here and absorb the historical vibrations echoing from momentous events. These include the 1381 storming of the palace during the Peasants' Revolt against the poll tax and the 1534 clash of wills when Thomas More refused to sign the Oath of Supremacy claiming Henry VIII (and not the pope) as leader of the English Church, for which he was sent to the Tower and executed for treason the following year. Adjacent to this house is the Museum of Garden History. ⊠ *Lambeth Palace Rd., SE1,* WEB *www.archbishopofcanterbury.org. Tube: Waterloo.*

🐾 ⑳ **London Aquarium.** County Hall was the original name of this curved, colonnaded Neoclassic hulk, which, with the interference of two world wars, took 46 years (1912–58) to build. It was once home to London's local government, the Greater London Council (GLC), which mutated out of the London County Council in 1965 and disbanded in 1986. After a £25 million injection, a three-level aquarium (full of sharks and stingrays) was installed. There are also educational exhibits and piscine sights previously unseen on these shores. It is not the biggest aquarium you've ever seen—especially if you've been to SeaWorld—but the exhibit is well arranged on several subterranean levels, with areas for different oceans, water environments, and climate zones, including a stunning coral reef, and the highlight: the rain forest, which is almost like the real thing. ⊠ *County Hall, Riverside Building, Westminster Bridge Rd., SE1,* ☎ *020/7967–8000,* WEB *www.londonaquarium.co.uk.* ⊠ *£8.50.* ☼ *Daily 10–5. Tube: Westminster or Waterloo.*

🐾 ⑤ **London Dungeon.** Here's the goriest, grisliest, gruesomest museum in town, where realistic waxwork people are subjected in graphic detail to all the historical horrors the Tower of London merely tells you about. Tableaux depict famous bloody moments—like Anne Boleyn's decapitation or the martyrdom of St. George—alongside the torture, murder, and ritual slaughter of lesser-known victims, all to a soundtrack of screaming, wailing, and agonized moaning. London's times of deepest terror—the Great Fire and the Great Plague—are brought to life, too, and so are its public hangings. And did you ever wonder what a disembowelment actually looks like? See it here. Naturally, children absolutely adore this place, but be warned—nervous kiddies may find it too truly frightening. Expect long lines. ⊠ *28–34 Tooley St., SE1,*

☎ *020/7403–7221.* ⌨ *£9.50.* ⊙ *Apr.–Sept., daily 10–5:30; Oct.– Mar., daily 10–5. Tube: London Bridge.*

㉔ **Museum of Garden History.** Housed in St. Mary's Church, next to Lambeth Palace, this museum was founded in 1977 (when the church was deconsecrated), by the Tradescant Trust. The trust is named after John Tradescant (circa 1575–1638), botanist extraordinaire, who brought to these shores the lilac, larch, and jasmine, and a spiderwort named *Tradescantia* in his honor. In the nave are changing horticultural exhibitions, supplemented by a reconstructed—or regrown—17th-century knot garden. Tradescant's tomb in the graveyard is carved with scenes from his worldwide plant-discovery tours and surrounded with the plants he discovered. William Bligh, captain of the *Bounty*, is buried nearby—appropriately enough, as the *Bounty* was on a breadfruit-gathering mission when the crew mutinied in 1787. ✉ *Lambeth Palace Rd., SE1,* ☎ *020/7261–1891,* WEB *www.museumgardenhistory.org.* ⌨ *Donations welcome.* ⊙ *Early Mar.–mid-Dec., weekdays 10:30–5, Sun. 10:30–5. Tube: Waterloo.*

Ⓒ **Museum of the Moving Image (MOMI).** It is closed until 2003 for a major expansion, but the MOMI has everything from exhibits on the history of cinema to a program in which you become the star of the show. During 2002 the museum has a touring exhibition; some exhibits may be viewed at the Science Museum and in the foyer of the BFI London IMAX Cinema. The adjacent **National Film Theatre** (NFT) is also being renovated. At press time, it was anticipated that the NFT would move to a temporary location while the brand-new four-screen cinema is built on the South Bank. The NFT has easily the best repertory programming in London, favoring obscure, foreign, silent, forgotten, classic, noir, and short films over blockbusters. For details on British Film Institute activities, you can phone the events line at ☎ 087/0240–4050. ✉ *South Bank Centre, SE1,* ☎ *020/7401–2636,* WEB *www.bfi.org.uk. Tube: Waterloo.*

NEED A BREAK?

There are many options along the South Bank for a quick bite or a gourmet meal. **OXO Tower Brasserie** (✉ OXO Tower Wharf, Bargehouse St., SE1, ☎ 020/7803–3888) is the more low-key and slightly cheaper half of the famous OXO Tower restaurant. Besides a menu of tasty Asian-inspired morsels, it offers through its floor-to-ceiling windows an unbeatable vista of the Thames and its north bank dotted with famous sites like Big Ben, St. Paul's Cathedral, and Westminster Abbey. If OXO Tower is too crowded or too expensive, try the street-level and far more proletariat **People's Palace** (✉ Royal Festival Hall, South Bank Centre, SE1, ☎ 020/7928–9999).

---

❻ **Old Operating Theatre Museum.** All that remains of one of England's oldest hospitals, which stood here from the 12th century until the railway forced it to move in 1862, this was where women went under the knife. The theater was bricked up and forgotten for a century but has now been restored into an exhibition of early 19th-century medical practices: the operating table onto which the gagged and blindfolded patients were roped; the box of sawdust underneath for catching their blood; the knives, pliers, and handsaws the surgeons wielded; and—this was a theater in the round—the spectators' seats. Next door is a sweeter show: the **Herb Garret,** with displays of medicinal herbs used during the same period. ✉ *9A St. Thomas St., SE1,* ☎ *020/7955–4791,* WEB *www.thegarret.org.uk.* ⌨ *£3.25.* ⊙ *Daily 10:30–5:30. Tube: London Bridge.*

❶❹ **OXO Tower.** This might very well turn out to be the 21st-century version of Big Ben—a wonderfully renovated Art Deco–era tower, filled with designers' workshops overlooking the Thames. Long a London landmark to the cognoscenti, the OXO has graduated from its former incarnations as a power-generating station and warehouse into a vibrant community of artists' and designers' workshops, a pair of restaurants and cafés, as well as five floors of the best low-income housing in the city, via a £20 million plan by Coin Street Community Builders. There's a rooftop viewing gallery (a balcony for observation) for the latest river vista in town, and a performance area on the first floor, which comes alive all summer long—as does the entire surrounding neighborhood. All the designers and artisans have been selected by totally nondemocratic methods, meaning the work is of incredibly high standard. They all rely on you to disturb them whenever they're open. Don't be shy—they really mean it; visitors are most welcome, whether buying, commissioning, or just browsing. The biggest draw remains the OXO Tower Restaurant extravaganza for a meal or a martini. ⊠ *Bargehouse St., SE1,* ☎ *020/7401–3610.* ▦ *Free.* ☉ *Studios and shops Tues.–Sun. 11–6. Tube: Blackfriars or Waterloo.*

⑯ Royal Festival Hall. This is the largest auditorium of the South Bank Centre, with superb acoustics and a 3,000-plus capacity. It is the oldest of the riverside blocks, raised as the centerpiece of the 1951 Festival of Britain, a postwar morale-boosting exercise. The London Philharmonic resides here; symphony orchestras from the world over like to visit; and choral works, ballet, serious jazz and pop, and even films with live accompaniment are staged. Also featured are a multiplicity of foyers with free rotating exhibitions; a good, independently run restaurant, the People's Palace; free jazz in the main foyer on Sunday, and a very fine bookstore. The next building you come to also contains concert halls, one medium and one small, the **Queen Elizabeth Hall** and the **Purcell Room**, respectively. Both offer predominantly classical recitals of international caliber, with due respect paid to 20th-century composers and the more established jazz and vocal artists. ⊠ *South Bank Centre, SE1,* ☎ *020/7960–4242,* ▦ *www.rfh.org.uk. Tube: Waterloo.*

⑮ Royal National Theatre. When it opened in 1976, Londoners generally felt the same way about this low-slung, multilayered block the color of heavy storm clouds and designed by Sir Denys Lasdun that they would feel a decade later about the far nastier Barbican Centre. But whatever its merits or demerits as a landscape feature (and architects have subsequently given it an overall thumbs-up, rejecting the derogatory-sounding term "brutalist"), the Royal National Theatre—still abbreviated colloquially to the pre–royal warrant "NT"—has wonderful insides.

There are three auditoriums in the complex. The biggest one, the **Olivier,** is named after Sir Laurence, chairman of the first building commission and first artistic director of the National Theatre Company, formed in 1962. (In between the first proposal of a national theater for Britain and the 1949 formation of that building commission, an entire century had passed.) The **Lyttleton** theater has a traditional proscenium arch, while the little **Cottesloe** mounts studio productions and new work in the round. Interspersed with the theaters is a multilayered foyer with exhibitions, bars, and restaurants, and free entertainment. The whole place is lively six days a week. The Royal National Theatre Company does not rest on its laurels: it attracts many of the nation's top actors (Anthony Hopkins, for one, does time here) in addition to launching future stars. Because it is a repertory company, you'll have several plays from which to choose even if your London sojourn is short, but, tickets or not, wander around and catch the buzz. ⊠ *South Bank, SE1,* ☎ *020/7452–3000 box office,* ▦ *www.nt-online.org.* ▦ *Tour £3.50.* ☉ *1-hr tour of theater backstage Mon.–Sat. at 10:15, 12:30, and 5:30; foyer Mon.–Sat. 10 AM–11 PM. Tube: Waterloo.*

SHAKESPEARE LIVES! REBIRTH OF THE GLOBE THEATRE

AS IT IS SAID about the one true church, Britain's theater is also founded on a rock—the enduring Shakespeare. Stratford-upon-Avon remains the primary shrine, but 1997 welcomed the opening of the cathedral—London's Globe Theatre. More than three centuries ago, the Puritans closed the first "wooden O," for which venue Shakespeare wrote *Hamlet, King Lear,* and *Julius Caesar,* among other peerless dramas. Now, more than 350 years later, the most famous playhouse in the world has been lovingly recreated, down to its Norfolk-reed roof. The theater has been reconstructed just 200 yards from its original site—ground as holy to Shakespeare's followers as Bayreuth's is to Wagner-philes.

For sheer drama—literally—few things can top the memorable jolt of walking into the Globe. Enter, and some Wellsian genie transports you back to Elizabethan England. Step past the entrance into a soaring 45-ft-high arena, made surprisingly intimate by three half-timber galleries picturesquely encircling the stage. Ahead of you is the "pit," or orchestra level, filling up with 500 standees—"groundlings," to use the historic term—massed in front of the high stage. Soaring overhead is a twin-gabled stage canopy—the "heavens"—framed by exquisitely painted trompe-l'oeil marble columns and a "lords' gallery," all fretted with gilded bosses, painted planets, and celestial bodies. Above you is the lowering London sky, which may at any time provide an authentic mid-performance drenching!

Of course, the Globe is not a perfect time capsule. Occasionally, Juliet's wherefores will have to compete with the roar of jets. Ladies no longer proffer oranges or stools, and yesteryear's magpie hats have been superseded by Ray-Bans and baseball caps. Some ground rules have also changed. Most performances begin in the afternoon and, while floodlighting will be used to illuminate the theater at dusk, there will be no spotlights to focus the action on stage. The audience, on view at all times, becomes as much a part of the theatrical proceedings as the actors. Elizabethans made theatergoing almost as blood-and-thunder an experience as a football game of today. You've heard of the Super Bowl: view this as the Shakespeare Bowl—go ahead and boo Iago or hiss at Macbeth; you'll have plenty of company.

The Globe Theatre is but one facet of the entire complex, which includes the 300-seat Inigo Jones indoor theater (to be used year-round, unlike the open-air Globe, open only from May to September), a restaurant, an education center (with wonderful classes and lectures year-round), a library and shop, and the largest Shakespearean exhibition in the world. Happily, even when the Globe is not open for performances, a guided tour will always include its interior—a perfect opportunity to try out your "Friends, Romans, Countrymen!"

⓫ Shakespeare's Globe Theatre. Three decades ago, Sam Wanamaker—then an aspiring actor—pulled up in Southwark in a cab and was amazed to find that the fabled Shakespeare's Globe Playhouse didn't actually exist. Worse, a tiny plaque was the only sign on the former site of the world's most legendary theater. So appalled was he that London lacked a center for the study and worship of the Bard of Bards, Wanamaker worked ceaselessly, until his death in 1993, to raise funds for his dream—a full-scale reconstruction of the theater. The dream was realized in 1996 when an exact replica of Shakespeare's open-roof Globe Playhouse (built in 1599; incinerated in 1613) was created, using authentic Elizabethan materials and craft techniques—green oak timbers joined only with wooden pegs and mortise and tenon joints; plaster made of lime, sand, and goat's hair; and the first thatched roof in London since the Great Fire. In addition, a second, indoor theater has been added, built to a design of the 17th-century architect Inigo Jones. The whole complex stands 200 yards from the original Globe on the appropriate site of the 17th-century Davies Amphitheatre, admittedly more a bull-baiting, prizefighting sort of venue than a temple to the legitimate stage, but at least Samuel Pepys immortalized it in his diaries.

The Globe is a celebration of the great Bard's life (1564–1616) and work, an actual rebirth of his "wooden O" (see *Henry V*), where his plays are presented in natural light (and sometimes rain) to 1,000 people on wooden benches in the "bays," plus 500 "groundlings," who stand on a carpet of filbert shells and clinker, just as they did nearly four centuries ago. For any theater buff, this stunning project is unmissable. Although the open-air Globe Theatre offers performances only during the summer season (generally mid-May to mid-September), it can be viewed year-round if you take the helpful tour offered by the **Shakespeare's Globe Exhibition Centre,** an adjacent museum that provides fascinating background material on both the Elizabethan theater and the actual construction of the new Globe. The **New Shakespeare's Globe Exhibition** is touted as the largest ever to focus on Shakespeare, his work, and his contemporaries; this "all-singing, all-dancing" exhibition is housed in the Underglobe, beneath the Globe site. ⊠ *New Globe Walk, Bankside, SE1,* ☎ *020/7902–1500; 020/7401–9919 box office; 020/7902–1500 New Shakespeare's Globe Exhibition,* FAX *020/ 7401–8261,* WEB *www.shakespeares-globe.org.* ☜ *£6.* ☉ *Museum daily 9–4, plays May–Sept. (call for performance schedule). Tube: Southwark, then walk to Blackfriars bridge and descend the steps; Mansion House, then walk across Southwark Bridge; or Blackfriars, then walk across Blackfriars Bridge.*

➐ Southwark Cathedral. Pronounced "Suth-uck," this is the second-oldest Gothic church in London, after Westminster Abbey, with parts dating back to the 12th century. Although it houses some remarkable memorials, not to mention a program of lunchtime concerts, it is seldom visited. It was promoted to cathedral status only in 1905; before that it was the priory church of St. Mary Overy (as in "over the water"—on the South Bank). Look for the gaudily renovated 1408 tomb of the poet John Gower, friend of Chaucer, and for the Harvard Chapel. Another notable buried here is Edmund Shakespeare, brother of William. ⊠ *Montague Close, SE1,* ☎ *020/7367–6700,* WEB *www.dswark.org.* ☜ *Free.* ☉ *Daily 8–6. Tube: London Bridge.*

⓬ Tate Modern. This much-anticipated new branch of the Tate Gallery opened in May 2000 in the Bankside Power Station. Shuttered for decades, the station has glowered magnificently on its Thames-side site ever since it was built in the 1930s. Now it has been renovated by Swiss architects Herzog & de Meuron to make a dazzling venue for some of the Tate's overflowing treasures. For decades, the old Millbank Gallery of the Tate Britain had been so overstuffed the curators had to resort to a revolving menu of paintings and sculpture. The power station (designed by the same man who created the famous red telephone box) and its 8½-acre site now house the surplus, running from classic works by Matisse, Picasso, Dalí, Moore, Bacon, and Warhol to the most-talked-about British artists of today. ✉ *25 Summer St., SE1,* ☎ *020/7887–8000,* WEB *www.tate.org.uk.* ✈ *Free.* ☉ *Sun.–Thurs. 10–6, Fri.–Sat 10–10. Tube: Blackfriars or Southwark.*

❿ Vinopolis. The Brits are perhaps not the first nation you would expect to erect a monument to wine, but here it is—Vinopolis, City of Wine. Spread over 2 acres between the Globe Theatre and London Bridge, its arched vaults promise multimedia tours of the world's wine cultures, tastings, retail shops, an art gallery, restaurants, and a wine school. You can learn about wine production and history, and then have a chance to put your newfound knowledge to the test in the Tasting Halls. The four restaurants claim to offer more wines by the glass than anywhere else in the city, and you can, of course, buy from an enormous selection of world vintages, many of them available for delivery. Keep in mind that the last entry is two hours before the scheduled closing time. ✉ *1 Bank End St.,* ☎ *087/0444–4777,* WEB *www.vinopolis.co.uk.* ✈ *£11.50.* ☉ *Mon. 11–9, Tues.–Fri. 11–6, Sat. 11–8, Sun 11–6. Tube: London Bridge.*

CHELSEA AND BELGRAVIA

Chelsea is where J. M. W. Turner painted his sunsets and John Singer Sargent his society portraits, where Oscar Wilde wrote *The Importance of Being Earnest,* and where Mary Quant cut her first miniskirt. Today, Chelsea is a neighborhood as handsome as its real estate is costly. Strolling its streets, you will often notice gigantic windows adorning otherwise ordinary houses. They are remnants of Chelsea's 19th-century bohemian days, when they served to bring light into artists' studios; now they are mostly used to hike property values a few notches higher. This is the place—the King's Road in particular—that gave birth to Swinging '60s London, then to '70s punk youth culture. The millennial version of this colorful thoroughfare is not really the center of anything, but it's hard not to like wandering down it.

Chelsea's next-door neighborhood is aristocratic Belgravia, with the King's Road and Knightsbridge as its respective southern and northern borders, Sloane Street and Grosvenor Place its western and eastern ones, and vast Belgrave Square, home to many embassies, in the middle. Diagonally across the square, Belgrave Place will lead past grand mansions (all painted Wedgwood-white to denote that they, like every other house in this district, are the property of England's richest landowners, the Dukes of Westminster) through to Eaton Square, the aptly chosen locale for the TV series *Upstairs, Downstairs.* It is no accident that this whole neighborhood of wealth and splendor is grouped around the back of Buckingham Palace—many titled peers wished to live adjacent to the Court. Belgravia is relatively young: it was built between the 1820s and the 1850s by the builder-developer-entrepreneur Thomas Cubitt (who had as great an influence on the look of London in his day as Wren and Nash had in theirs), under the patronage of Lord Grosvenor, and was intended to rival Mayfair for spectacular snob value and expense. Today it still does.

Numbers in the text correspond to numbers in the margin and on the Chelsea and Belgravia map.

Chelsea and Belgravia

Hyde Park

Rotten Row

South Carriage Dr

Knightsbridge

Knightsbridge

Green Park

Buckingham Palace Gardens

Ennismore Gdns.

Lowndes Sq.

Wilton Pl.

Grosvenor Cres.

Belgrave Sq.

Grosvenor Pl.

Brompton Rd.

Hans Rd.

Basil St.

Hans Pl.

Pavilion Rd.

Sloane St.

Lowndes St.

Chesham Pl.

Upper Belgrave St.

Lower Belgrave St.

7

Beauchamp Pl.

Pont St.

Pont St.

Cadogan Pl.

Lyall

Eaton Pl.

St. Eaton Sq.

King's Rd.

Eaton Sq.

Eccleston St.

Walton St.

Lennox Gdns.

Cadogan Sq.

Cliveden Pl. Eaton

Elizabeth

Ebury

Victoria Station

Cromwell Rd. Thurloe Pl.

Brompton Rd.

Rawlings St.

Cadogan St.

Sloane Sq.

MILITARY MAN

Row

Chester Ter.

Victoria Coach Station

Pelham St.

Draycott Ave.

Draycott Pl.

Bourne St.

Lwr. Sloane St.

Sloane Gdns.

Holbein Pl.

Buckingham Palace Rd.

Ixworth Pl.

Elystan St.

Sloane Ave.

6

Pimlico Rd.

Cale St.

Elystan Pl.

Fulham Rd.

Sydney St.

Smith St.

Cheltenham Ter.

Franklin's Row

Ebury Bridge Rd.

St. Leonard's

Christchurch St.

Burton's Court

Royal Hospital Rd.

Chelsea Bridge Rd.

Chelsea Br.

King's Rd.

Radnor Wk.

Flood St.

Chelsea Manor St.

4

West Rd.

5

Ranelagh Gardens

Old Church St.

Oakley St.

Glebe Pl.

Upr. Cheyne Row

2

Lwr. Cheyne Row

3

Tite St.

Chelsea Embankment

Danvers St.

Cheyne Wk.

Cheyne Wk.

1

Cheyne Wk.

Albert Br.

River Thames

Battersea Br.

Battersea Park

KEY

⊖ Tube Station

0 — 440 yds

0 — 400 m

A Good Walk

Start at **Cheyne Walk** ①, stretching in both directions from Albert Bridge, going all the way west to see the statue of Thomas More, then doubling back for a left turn into Cheyne Row to reach **Carlyle's House** ②. Where the east end of Cheyne Walk runs into Royal Hospital Road, you'll find the **Chelsea Physic Garden** ③, while a right after the garden on Royal Hospital Road brings you to the **National Army Museum** ④. Royal Hospital Road takes its name from the institution next door to the museum, the magnificent **Royal Hospital** ⑤. A left turn from here up Franklin's Row and Cheltenham Terrace brings you to famous **King's Road** ⑥, which you could follow east until you reach the beginning of Belgravia: Sloane Square, named after Sir Hans Sloane, whose collection founded the British Museum and who bought the manor of Chelsea in 1712. Cross the square more or less in a straight line, and follow Cliveden Place for a taste of Belgravia. The grand, white-stucco houses have changed not at all since the mid-19th century, and Eaton Square, which you'll soon come upon, remains such a desirable address that the rare event of one of its houses' coming on the market makes all the property pages. Its most famous residents were fictional, of course, as the enduringly popular period soap *Upstairs, Downstairs* was set here. A left turn on **Belgrave Place** ⑦ brings you to Belgrave Square, dense with embassies, but the best thing to do around here is follow your nose. Other than Palladian-perfect mansions, chic alleys, and magnificent Georgian squares—in addition to Belgrave and Eaton, the smaller Lowndes, Cadogan, Trevor, Brompton, and Montpelier—there are no particular Belgravia sights. After taking in Belgrave Place and the picturesque mews next to Eaton Place, however, you might continue eastward on Belgrave Place, walk south several blocks on Eaton Place, and head for the lovely warren of streets and alleys around Chester Row and Minerva Mews.

TIMING

This may read like a short hop, but the walk above covers a good 2 to 3 mi. If you explore side streets, you could double the figure—and exploring these streets is the best aspect of these neighborhoods, which are primarily residential and expensive. The houses along the way will detain you, and the shops will for longer; even though King's Road isn't what it used to be, it's still fruitful. In summer you'll want to spend time in the Physic Garden or around the Royal Hospital, so make sure you're heading out on one of the opening days. If you're dead set on the Physic Garden, that means Wednesday or Sunday afternoon from April to October.

HOW TO GET THERE

Chelsea is notoriously ill-served by tube stops. To start the walk at Cheyne Walk, take the tube to Earl's Court on the District Line then take Bus 328 on Earl's Court Road to its terminus at World's End on King's Road. From there walk away from the bus on King's Road and take a right on Glebe Place to reach Cheyne Row and Carlyle's House. Alternatively, if you're more interested in shopping than sightseeing you can take the District and Circle lines to Sloane Square, then strike out by foot along King's Road. Or catch a bus (11, 19, 22, 137, or 211). Farther down toward the river, around World's End and Fulham, the 19, 49, 319, and 345 are the buses to look for. The edge of Belgravia farthest from Chelsea is accessible from Hyde Park Corner on the Piccadilly Line. Buses 2, 8, 9, 10, 14, 16, 19, 22, 36, 38, 52, 73, 74, 82, and 137 also stop there. Choose a bus that appears on both lists for travel between the two neighborhoods.

Sights to See

❼ Belgrave Place. One of the main arteries of Belgravia—London's swankiest neighborhood—Belgrave Place is lined with grand, imposing Regency-era mansions (now mostly embassies). Walk down this street toward Eaton Place to pass two of Belgravia's most beautiful mews—Eaton Mews North and Eccleston Mews, both fronted by grand Westminster-white rusticated entrances right out of a 19th-century engraving: there are few other places where London is both so picturesque and elegant.

❷ Carlyle's House. This house hosted a thriving salon of 19th-century authors, attracted by the fame of Thomas Carlyle (1795–1881)—author of a blockbuster history of the French Revolution that is now almost forgotten and the amusing *Sartor Resartus* and by the wit of his wife, the poet Jane Carlyle. Dickens, Thackeray, Tennyson, and Browning were regular visitors, and you can see the second-floor drawing room where they met just as they saw it, complete with leather armchair, decoupage screen, fireplace, and oil lamps, all in ruddy Victorian hues. ⊠ *24 Cheyne Row, SW3,* ☎ *020/7352–7087 or 014/9475–5559.* ⊠ *£3.30.* ☉ *Apr.–Oct., Wed.–Sun. 11–4:30. Tube: Sloane Sq., then walk down King's Rd. or take Bus 11, 19, 22, 49, 219, or 249.*

❸ Chelsea Physic Garden. First planted by the Society of Apothecaries in 1673 for the study of medicinal plants, these gardens are still in use for the same purpose today. The herbs and shrubs and flowers, planted to a strict plan but tumbling over the paths nevertheless, are interspersed with woodland areas, England's first rock garden, and ancient trees, some of which were tragically uprooted in a 1987 storm. In the middle stands a statue of Sir Hans Sloane, physician to Queen Anne and George II, whose collection formed the basis of the British Museum and who saved the garden from closing in 1722, making sure nobody would ever be allowed to build over it. ⊠ *Swan Walk, 66 Royal Hospital Rd., SW3,* ☎ *020/7352–5646,* [WEB] *www.cpgarden.demon.co.uk.* ⊠ *£4.* ☉ *Apr.–Oct., Wed. noon–5 and Sun. 2–6; daily noon–5 during Chelsea Flower Show (3rd wk of May). Tube: Sloane Sq., then walk down King's Rd., or take Bus 11, 19, 22, 319, 211 or 239 (get off at Chelsea Old Town Hall).*

★ ❶ Cheyne Walk. Its name rhyming with "rainy," this street features some beautiful Queen Anne houses (particularly Norman Shaw's ornamental 1876 Cheyne House, to the right off Albert Bridge) and a storm of blue plaques marking famous ex-residents' homes. George Eliot died at No. 4 in 1880; Dante Gabriel Rossetti annoyed the neighbors of No. 16 with his peacock collection (there's still a clause in the lease banning the birds); Henry James died at Carlyle Mansions (after the King's Head and Eight Bells pub), and later residents were T. S. Eliot and Ian Fleming. The western reaches were painters' territory, most notably of James McNeill Whistler, who lived at No. 96 and then No. 101, and J. M. W. Turner, who used No. 119 as a retreat, shielding his identity behind the name Adm. "Puggy" Booth. Also toward the western end, outside the Church of All Saints, is a golden-faced statue of **Thomas More** (who wouldn't sign the Oath of Supremacy at Lambeth Palace in 1534 and was executed as a traitor), looking pensive and beatific on a throne facing the river, a 1969 addition to the Walk.

❻ King's Road. This was where the miniskirt first strutted its stuff in the '60s and where Vivienne Westwood and Malcolm McLaren clothed the Sex Pistols in bondage trousers from their shop, "Sex", in 1975, thus spawning punk rock. Westwood, one of Britain's most innovative fashion stars, still runs her shop at No. 430, where the road, fittingly, kinks. Both boutique and neighborhood are called **World's End,** possibly because Chelsea-ites believe that's what happens here. The Fulham district begins around this stretch, full of yuppie singles and more shopping opportunities. The other end of King's Road, leading into Sloane Square, has various fashion stores (no longer style-setters, on the whole) and some rather good antiques shops and markets along the way. The **Pheasantry,** at No. 152, is recognizable by some over-the-top Grecian statuary in a fancy portico. Named in its mid-19th-century pheasant-breeding days, it had a phase from 1916 to 1934 as a ballet school where Margot Fonteyn and Alicia Markova learned first position. Now it's a branch of the ubiquitous Pizza Express. The Peter Jones department store marks the exit from the north of Chelsea and the beginning of Belgravia: Sloane Square. Conran's trendy restaurant **Bluebird,** at No. 352, is a great place to stop for lunch.

❹ **National Army Museum.** This museum covers the history of British land forces from the Yeoman of the Guard (the first professional army, founded in 1485 and ancestors of the Tower's Beefeaters) to the present. It is best explained in its current exhibit, titled "The Rise of the Redcoat," which takes you from Henry V (1413–22) all the way to George III (1760–1820). A great deal of effort is made to convey the experience of those who lived through the wars, and a visit will enhance anyone's grasp of London's history and its personages. ✉ *Royal Hospital Rd., SW3,* ☎ *020/7730–0717,* WEB *www.national-army-museum.ac.uk.* ▭ *Free.* ☉ *Daily 10–5:30. Tube: Sloane Sq.*

❺ **Royal Hospital.** The hospice for elderly and infirm soldiers was founded by Charles II in 1682—some say after a badgering from his softhearted, high-profile mistress, Nell Gwynne, but more probably as an act of expedience. His troops had hitherto enjoyed not so much as a meager pension and were growing restive after the civil wars of 1642–46 and 1648. Charles wisely appointed the great architect of burned-out City churches, Sir Christopher Wren, to design this small village of brick and Portland stone set in manicured gardens (which you can visit) surrounding the Figure Court —named after the 1692 bronze figure of Charles II dressed up as a Roman soldier—and the Great Hall (dining room) and chapel. The latter is enhanced by the choir stalls of Grinling Gibbons (who did the bronze of Charles, too), the former by a vast oil of Charles on horseback by Antonio Verrio, and both are open to inspection.

No doubt you will run into some of the 400-odd residents. Despite their advancing years, these "Chelsea Pensioners" are no shrinking violets. In summer and for special occasions they sport dandy scarlet frock coats with gold buttons, medals, and natty tricorne hats, and since they are of proven good character (a condition of entry, along with old age and loyal service), they might offer to show you around—in which case you may wish to supplement their daily beer and tobacco allowance with a tip.

May is the important month at the Royal Hospital. The 29th is Oak Apple Day, when the pensioners celebrate Charles II's birthday by draping oak leaves on his statue and parading around it in memory of a hollow oak tree that expedited the king's miraculous escape from the 1651 Battle of Worcester. In the same month, the Chelsea Flower Show, the year's highlight for thousands of garden-obsessed Brits, is also held here. ✉ *Royal Hospital Rd., SW3,* ☎ *020/7730–0161,* WEB *www.chelseapensioners.org.uk.* ▭ *Free.* ☉ *Weekdays 10–noon and 2–4, weekends 10–noon. Tube: Sloane Sq.*

KNIGHTSBRIDGE, KENSINGTON, AND HOLLAND PARK

Even in these supposedly democratic days, you still sometimes hear people say that the *only* place to live in London is in the grand residential area of the Royal Borough of Kensington. True, the district is an endless cavalcade of streets lined with splendid houses with pillared porches, but there are other fetching attractions here as well—some of the most fascinating museums in London, stylish squares, elegant antiques shops, and Kensington Palace (formerly the home of Diana, Princess of Wales, and of Queen Victoria when she was a girl)—which helped to put the district on the map. South and west of this historic edifice, you'll find the stamping grounds of the Sloane Rangers—a quintessentially London type of gilded youth whose upper-class accents make English sound like a foreign language. They tend to haunt salubrious Knightsbridge, east of Belgravia and north of Chelsea, offering as it does about equal doses of elite residential streets and ultra-shopping opportunities. To its east is one of the highest concentrations of important artifacts anywhere, the Museum Mile of South Kensington, with the rest of Kensington offering peaceful strolls and a noisy main street. The Holland Park neighborhood is worth visiting for its big, fancy, tree-shaded houses and its exquisite and unexpected park.

Kensington first became the Royal Borough of Kensington (and Chelsea) by virtue of a king's asthma. William III, who suffered terribly from the Thames mists over Whitehall, decided in 1689 to buy Nottingham House in the rural village of Kensington so that he could breathe more easily; and besides, his wife and co-monarch, Mary II, felt confined by water and wall at Whitehall. Courtiers and functionaries and society folk soon followed where the crowns led, and by the time Queen Anne was on the throne (1702–14), Kensington was overflowing. In a way, it still is, because most of its grand houses, and the Victorian ones of Holland Park, have been divided into apartments or else are serving as foreign embassies.

Numbers in the text correspond to numbers in the margin and on the Knightsbridge, Kensington, and Holland Park map.

A Good Walk

This is an all-weather walk—museums and shops for rainy days, grass and strolls for sunshine. When you surface from the Knightsbridge tube station—one of London's deepest—you are immediately engulfed by the manic drivers, professional shoppers, and ladies-who-lunch who make up the local population. If you're in a shopping mood, start with Harvey Nichols—right at the tube—and its six floors of total fashion. Sloane Street, leading south, is strung with the boutiques of big-name European designers, while **Harrods** ① is found to the west down Brompton Road; continue west down this road, pausing at Beauchamp (pronounced "Bee-chum") Place and Walton Street if shopping is your intention. Presently, at the junction of Brompton and Cromwell roads, you'll come to the pale, Italianate **Brompton Oratory** ②, which marks the beginning of museum territory, with the vast **Victoria & Albert Museum** ③, the **Natural History Museum** ④, and the child-friendly **Science Museum** ⑤ behind it. (The neighborhood's three large museums, incidentally, can also be reached via a long underground passage from the South Kensington tube station.) Turn left to continue north up Exhibition Road, a kind of unfinished cultural main drag that was Prince Albert's conception, toward the road after which British moviemakers named their fake blood, Kensington Gore, to reach the giant, round

Wedgwood china–box of the **Royal Albert Hall** ⑥, the glittering **Albert Memorial** ⑦ opposite, and the **Royal College of Art** ⑧ next door.

Now follow **Kensington Gardens** (which is what this western neighbor of Hyde Park is called) west to its end, and a little farther, perhaps detouring into the park to see **Kensington Palace** ⑨ and, behind it, one of London's rare, private "Millionaires' Row" sanctuaries, **Kensington Palace Gardens** ⑩. Turn off Kensington High Street down little Derry Street, with the offices of London's local paper, the *Evening Standard,* on the left and what was once Derry and Tom's department store—it closed down in the '70s—on the right. (The best feature of the store was its magical roof garden, complete with palm trees, ponds, and flamingos; it's still there, now part of a nightclub owned by Richard Branson, the high-profile London figure also responsible for the Virgin Megastores, Virgin Atlantic Airways, etc.). Take a turn around peaceful **Kensington Square** ⑪; then, returning to High Street, either follow Kensington Church Street up to Notting Hill Gate—with the little 1870 St. Mary Abbots Church on its southwest corner and a cornucopia of expensive antiques in its shops all along the way—or take the longer, scenic route.

To do this, turn left off Kensington Church Street onto Holland Street, admiring the sweet 18th-century houses (Nos. 10, 12–13, and 18–26 remain). As you cross Hornton Street you'll see to your left an orange-brick 1970s building, the Kensington Civic Centre (donor of parking permits, home of the local council); Holland Street becomes the leafy Duchess of Bedford's Walk, with Queen Elizabeth College, part of London University, on the right. Turn left before Holland Park into Phillimore Gardens (perhaps detouring east into Phillimore Place to see No. 44, where Kenneth Grahame, author of *The Wind in the Willows,* lived from 1901 to 1908), then left again into Stafford Terrace to reach **Linley Sambourne House** (closed for repairs during 2002). Step back to High Street and turn right. For a tranquil time-out, head past the gates into **Holland Park** ⑫. Exit the park at the gate by the tennis courts (near the Orangery) onto Ilchester Place, follow Melbury Road a few yards, and turn right onto Holland Park Road to reach **Leighton House** ⑬. Late in the 19th century, Melbury Road was a veritable colony of artists, though the Victorian muse they followed failed to appeal to later sensibilities, and they're now an obscure bunch—except for Dickens's illustrator, Marcus Stone, who had No. 8 built in 1876. From here you could turn right onto Addison Road to see the Technicolor tiles rioting over Sir Ernest Debenham's Peacock House at No. 8 (he founded the eponymous Oxford Street department store). If you continue north, you reach plane tree–lined Holland Park Avenue, main thoroughfare of an expensive residential neighborhood that provides more pleasant strolling territory, if you feel you haven't walked enough.

TIMING

This walk is at least 4 mi long and is almost impossible to achieve without venturing inside somewhere. The best way to approach these neighborhoods is to treat Knightsbridge shopping and the South Kensington museums at one go. The rest of the tour works as a scenic walk on a fine day, because places to see—such as Leighton House and Kensington Palace—are less time-consuming than the V&A and the Natural History, and Science museums. During "term time," these are populated by more or less orderly school parties during the week, while weekends and school vacations see them fill up with more random arrangements of children. The parks are best in the growing seasons—early spring for crocuses and daffodils and summer for roses—and in the fall, when the foliage show easily rivals New England's. Kensington Gardens closes

Knightsbridge, Kensington, and Holland Park

440 yds

400 m

South Carriage Dr.

Sloane St.

Cadogan Sq.

Hans Cres.

Hans Pl.

Pont

Basil St.

Hans Rd.

Lennox Gdns.

The Serpentine

Rotten Row

Knightsbridge

Brompton Rd.

Beauchamp Pl.

Walton St.

Hans St.

Brompton Sq.

Brompton Rd.

Hyde Park

Ennismore Gdns.

Cottage Pl.

Cromwell Gdns.

Thurloe St.

Pelham St.

The Ring

Exhibition Rd.

Imperial College Rd.

Thurloe St.

Harrington Rd.

Kensington Gore

Prince Consort Rd.

Kensington Gardens

The Flower Walk

Kensington Rd.

Queen's Gate

Queen's Gate Ter.

Gloucester

Rd.

Cromwell Rd.

The Broad Walk

Palace Gate

Victoria Rd.

Cornwall Gdns.

Kensington Palace Gardens

Kensington Church St.

Holland St.

Kensington High St.

Kensington Sq.

Marloes

Rd.

Cromwell Rd.

Hornton St.

Rd.

Stafford Ter.

Allen St.

Abingdon Rd.

Earl's Court Rd.

Campden Hill

Phillimore Gdns.

Edwardes Sq.

Warwick Gdns.

Warwick Rd.

Pembroke Rd.

Ilchester Pl.

Melbury Rd.

Holland Pk. Rd.

Holland Park

N

KEY

Ⓘ Tube Station
ⓘ Tourist Information

Albert Memorial **7**	Kensington Palace Gardens . . . **10**
Brompton Oratory **2**	Kensington Square . . **11**
Harrods **1**	Leighton House **13**
Holland Park **12**	Natural History Museum **4**
Kensington Palace **9**	Royal Albert Hall . . . **6**
Royal College of Art **8**	
Science Museum **5**	
Victoria & Albert Museum **3**	

its gates at sundown, though you can get into Holland Park later in summer, thanks to the restaurant and the Open Air Theatre.

HOW TO GET THERE

There are many tubes here, but which you choose will depend on which part you want. Knightsbridge on the Piccadilly Line, Kensington High Street on the District and Circle, and Holland Park on the Central Line are the best ones. The best buses between Kensington High Street and Knightsbridge are Buses 9, 10, and 52. From Kensington to Holland Park, get the 9, 27, 28, or 31.

Sights to See

7 **Albert Memorial.** The Victorian era is epitomized in this neo-Gothic shrine to Prince Albert. The 14-ft bronze statue looks as if it were created yesterday, thanks to its fresh coat of gold leaf (donated by an anonymous benefactor). Albert's grieving widow, Queen Victoria, had this elaborate confection erected on the spot where his Great Exhibition had stood a mere decade before his early death from typhoid fever in 1861. ⊠ *Kensington Gore, opposite Royal Albert Hall, Hyde Park. Tube: Knightsbridge.*

2 **Brompton Oratory.** This is a late product of the mid-19th-century English Roman Catholic revival led by John Henry Cardinal Newman (1801–90), who established the oratory in 1884 and whose statue you see outside. Architect Herbert Gribble, a previously unknown 29-year-old, won the competition to design the place, an honor that you may conclude went to his head when you see the vast, incredibly ornate interior. It is punctuated by treasures far older than the church itself, like the giant *Twelve Apostles* in the nave, carved from Carrara marble by Giuseppe Mazzuoli in the 1680s and brought here from Siena's cathedral. ⊠ *Brompton Rd.,* ☎ *020/7808–0900.* 🎫 *Free.* ☉ *Open 6:30 AM– 8 PM. Services Mon.–Fri. 7, 8, 10, 12:30, and 6, Sat. 7, 8, 10, and 6, Sun. 7, 8:30, 11, 12:30, 4:30 and 7. Tube: South Kensington.*

1 **Harrods.** Just in case you don't notice it, this well-known shopping mecca frames its domed terra-cotta Edwardian outline in thousands of white lights each night. The 15-acre Egyptian-owned store's sales weeks are world class, and the atmosphere is as frenetic as that of a stock market floor; its motto, *Omnia, omnibus, ubique* (Everything, for everyone, everywhere), is not too far from the truth. Visit the pet department, a highlight for children, and don't miss the extravagant Food Hall, with its stunning Art Nouveau tiling in the neighborhood of meat and poultry and continuing on in the fishmongers' territory, where its glory is rivaled by displays of the sea produce itself. This is the place to acquire your green-and-gold souvenir Harrods bag, as food prices are surprisingly competitive. ⊠ *87–135 Brompton Rd., SW1,* ☎ *020/7730–1234,* WEB *www.harrods.com.* ☉ *Mon.–Sat. 10–7. Tube: Knightsbridge.*

NEED A
BREAK?

Pâtisserie Valerie (⊠ 215 Brompton Rd., SW3, ☎ 020/7832–9971), just down the road from Harrods, keeps in tune with your posh day out offering light café meals and splendid pastries and coffee.

12 **Holland Park.** The former grounds of the Jacobean Holland House opened to the public only in 1952. Since then, many treats have been laid on within its 60 acres. Holland House itself was nearly flattened by World War II bombs, but the east wing remains, now incorporated into a youth hostel and providing a fantastical stage for the April–September **Open Air Theatre** (☎ 020/7602–7856 box office). The glass-walled Orangery also survived to host art exhibitions and wedding receptions, while next door, the former Garden Ballroom has become the upmarket Belvedere restaurant; nearby is a lovely café. From the

Belvedere's terrace you see the formal Dutch Garden, planted by Lady Holland in the 1790s with the first English dahlias. North of that are woodland walks; lawns populated by peacocks, guinea fowl, and the odd, awkward emu; a fragrant rose garden; great banks of rhododendrons and azaleas, which bloom profusely in May; a well-supervised children's Adventure Playground; and even a Japanese water garden, legacy of the 1991 London Festival of Japan. If that's not enough, you can watch cricket on the Cricket Lawn on the south side or tennis on the several courts. ☉ *Daily dawn–dusk. Tube: Holland Park or High St. Kensington.*

OFF THE BEATEN PATH

KENSAL GREEN CEMETERY – Heralding itself as "London's first necropolis," this West London cemetery was established in 1832 and beats the more famous Highgate for atmosphere, if only because it is less populated by the living. Within its 77 acres are more freestanding mausoleums than in any other cemetery in Britain, some of them almost the size of small churches and most of them constructed while their future occupants were still alive. Those who balked at burial but couldn't afford a mausoleum of their own could opt for a spot in the catacombs, and these, with their stacks of moldering caskets, are a definite highlight for seekers of the macabre, though they can only be seen as part of a tour. In the cemetery you'll find the final resting places of the novelists Trollope, Thackeray, and Wilkie Collins; of the great 19th-century engineer Isambard Kingdom Brunel; and of Decimus Burton, Victorian architect of the Athenaeum Club, the Wellington Arch, and the Kew Gardens greenhouses. ⊠ *Harrow Rd., W10,* ☎ *020/8969–0152; 020/7402–2749 tours.* 🖃 *Suggested donation £2.* ☉ *Mon.-Sat. 9–4:30, Sun. 10–5; tours Sun. 2 pm (including the catacombs on the 1st and 3rd Sun. of the month). Tube: Kensal Green.*

★ ⑨ **Kensington Palace.** The long history of this palace has been eclipsed in the last few years by its most recent—and some might say its most famous—inhabitant: the late Princess Diana. She resided here, so this was where the crowds flocked when the tragic news of her death was heard. With millions of flowers and tributes laid outside its gates, Kensington Palace was seen on every news bulletin worldwide. Now peace has returned, although arguments sporadically flare as to how the mother of the future king should be remembered. Plans for an immense memorial fountain in the gardens have been shelved, as angry local residents have vociferously claimed that the area is not able to handle the number of visitors this would generate. Of course, Kensington Palace was well known long before Diana brought it new front-page status. Socially speaking, Kensington was put on the map when King William III, "much incommoded by the Smoak of the Coal Fires of London," decided in the 17th century to vacate Whitehall and relocate to a new palace outside the center city in the "village" of Kensington. The new palace did not enjoy a smooth passage as a royal residence. Twelve years of renovation were needed before William and Mary could move in, and it continued to undergo all manner of refurbishment during the succeeding three reigns. By coincidence, these monarchs happened to suffer rather ignominious deaths. William III fell off his horse when it stumbled on a molehill, and succumbed to pleurisy in 1702. Then, in 1714, Queen Anne (who, you may recall, was fond of brandy) suffered an apoplectic fit thought to have been brought on by overeating. Next, George I, the first of the Hanoverian Georges, had a stroke said to have been caused by "a surfeit of melons"—admittedly not at Kensington, but in a coach carrying him to Hanover in 1727. Worst of all, in 1760, poor George II burst a blood vessel while on the toilet.

When you pack your MCI Calling Card, it's like packing your loved ones along too.

Your MCI Calling Card is the easy way to stay in touch when you travel. Use it to call to and from over 125 countries. Plus, every time you call, you can earn frequent flier miles. So wherever your travels take you, call home with your MCI Calling Card. It's even easy to get one. Just visit **www.mci.com/worldphone.**

EASY TO CALL WORLDWIDE

1. Just enter the WorldPhone® access number of the country you're calling from.
2. Enter or give the operator your MCI Calling Card number.
3. Enter or give the number you're calling.

Austria ◆	0800-200-235
Belgium ◆	0800-10012
Czech Republic ◆	00-42-000112
Denmark ◆	8001-0022
Estonia ★	0800-800-1122
Finland ◆	08001-102-80
France ◆	0-800-99-0019
Germany	0800-888-8000
Greece ◆	00-800-1211

Hungary ◆	06▼-800-01411
Ireland	1-800-55-1001
Italy ◆	172-1022
Luxembourg	8002-0112
Netherlands ◆	0800-022-91-22
Norway ◆	800-19912
Poland ÷	00-800-111-21-22
Portugal ÷	800-800-123
Romania ÷	01-800-1800
Russia ◆ ÷	747-3322
Spain	900-99-0014
Sweden ◆	020-795-922
Switzerland ◆	0800-89-0222
Ukraine ÷	8▼10-013
United Kingdom	0800-89-0222
Vatican City	172-1022

◆ Public phones may require deposit of coin or phone card for dial tone. ★ Not available from public pay phones. ▼ Wait for second dial tone. ÷ Limited availability.

EARN FREQUENT FLIER MILES

SEE THE WORLD
IN FULL COLOR

Fodor's Exploring Guides bring all the great sights vividly to life with hundreds of photographs, fascinating historical background, and colorful anecdotes. Detailed maps and practical information keep you headed in the right direction.

Pair a **Fodor's** Exploring Guide with your trusted Gold Guide for a complete planning package.

But the royal curtain here always rang up on a remarkable new cast of characters, no more so than when the 18-year-old Princess Victoria of Kent was called from her bed in June 1837 by the Archbishop of Canterbury and the Lord Chamberlain. She was told that her uncle, William IV, was dead, and she was to be queen. The state rooms where Victoria had her ultrastrict upbringing have recently been renovated, a process that still continues, gradually restoring more of the fabulous Court Dress Collection to our sight. In the meantime, the King's Apartments are the best part of the (compulsory) guided tour. Look out for Tintorettos and Van Dycks among the canvases; see the Mortlake tapestries commissioned by Charles I; and look at the ceiling in the Cupola Room: it appears to be domed but is actually as flat as a pancake. This palace is an essential stop for royalty vultures because it's the only one where you may actually catch a glimpse of the real thing. Princess Margaret, the Duke and Duchess of Gloucester, and Prince and Princess Michael of Kent all have apartments here, as did, of course, Diana, Princess of Wales, until her death. For a consoling (and expensive) cup of tea, repair to the palace's Orangery—surely one of London's most civilized settings and the festive hall where many Windsor birthday parties and weddings were held (a good number of which Princess Diana attended).

Extending back centuries, the **Royal Ceremonial Dress Collection** shows an array of state and occasional dresses, hats, and shoes worn by Britain's Royal Family. Diana-watchers will note the difference between the regal if dowdy garments of Her Majesty the Queen compared to the glittering, contemporary fashions of her daughter-in-law. Other dazzlers of note are the coronation robes of Queen Mary and George V and a regal mantua—a 6-ft-wide court dress. ⊠ *The Broad Walk, Kensington Gardens, W8,* ☎ *020/7937–9561,* WEB *www.hrp.org.uk.* ⊠ *£9.50, including admission to the Dress Collection.* ☉ *Mar.–Oct., daily 10–5; Nov.–Feb., daily 10–4. Tube: High St. Kensington.*

⑩ Kensington Palace Gardens. Starting behind Kensington Palace, this is one of London's rare private roads, guarded and gated both here and at the Notting Hill Gate end. If you walk it, you will see why it earned the nickname "Millionaires' Row"—it is lined with palatial white-stucco houses designed by a selection of the best architects of the mid-19th century. The novelist William Makepeace Thackeray, author of *Vanity Fair,* died in 1863 at No. 2—which now houses the Israeli embassy.

⑪ Kensington Square. Laid out around the time William moved to Kensington Palace up the road, this is one of London's most venerable squares. A few early 18th-century houses remain, with Nos. 11 and 12 the oldest.

NEED A BREAK? | Revel in the regal atmosphere while sipping a cup of tea and daintily nibbling tasty treats at the **Orangery** (⊠ Kensington Palace, W8, ☎ 020/376–0239).

⑬ Leighton House. This was the home of Frederic Leighton (1830–96)—painter, sculptor, and president of the Royal Academy. The prize room here is the incredible Arab Hall. George Aitchison designed this Moorish fantasy in 1879 to show off Leighton's valuable 13th- to 17th-century Islamic tile collection, and, adorned with marble columns, dome, and fountain, it is exotic beyond belief. The rest of the rooms are more conventionally, stuffily Victorian, but they do feature many paintings by Leighton, plus those of Edward Burne-Jones, John Millais, and other leading Pre-Raphaelites. ⊠ *12 Holland Park Rd., W14,* ☎ *020/7602–3316.* ⊠ *Free.* ☉ *Wed.–Mon. 11–5:30. Tube: High St. Kensington.*

Linley Sambourne House. Stuffed with delightful Victorian and Edwardian antiques, fabrics, and paintings, this is one of the most charming 19th-century London houses extant—small wonder that it was used in Merchant and Ivory's *A Room with a View*. In the 1870s it was the home of the political cartoonist Edward Linley Sambourne. Unfortunately, it's closed during 2002 for much-needed repairs. ⊠ *18 Stafford Terr., W8,* ☎ *020/8994–1019.*

❹ **Natural History Museum.** Architect Alfred Waterhouse had relief panels scattered across the outrageously ornate French Romanesque–style terra-cotta facade of this museum, depicting extant creatures to the left of the entrance, extinct ones to the right. Inside, that categorization is sort of continued in reverse, with dinosaurs on the left and the Ecology Gallery on the right. Both of these renovated exhibits (the former with life-size moving dinosaurs, the latter complete with "moonlit rain forest") make essential viewing in a museum that, realizing it was becoming crusty, invested millions overhauling itself in recent years.

The Creepy Crawlies Gallery features a nightmarish, super-enlarged scorpion yet ends up making tarantulas cute (8 out of 10 animal species, one learns here, are arthropods). Other wonderful bits include the Human Biology Hall, which you arrive at through a birth-simulation chamber; the full-size blue whale; and the moving dinosaur diorama. The Earth Galleries are also unmissable, with ambitious exhibits about the structure of our planet: The Power Within with an earthquake simulation, Restless Surface, and Visions of the Earth. Understandably, this place usually resembles a grade-school recess. ⊠ *Cromwell Rd., SW7,* ☎ *020/7942–5000,* WEB *www.nhm.ac.uk.* ⊡ *£7.50; free weekdays 4:30–5:50 and weekends 5–5:50.* ☉ *Mon.–Sat. 10–5:50, Sun. 11–5:50. Tube: South Kensington.*

❻ **Royal Albert Hall.** This domed, circular 8,000-seat auditorium (as well as the Albert Memorial, opposite) was made possible by the Victorian public, who donated funds for it. More money was raised, however, by selling 1,300 future seats at £100 apiece—not for the first night but for every night for 999 years. (Some descendants of purchasers still use the seats.) The Albert Hall is best known for its annual July–September Henry Wood Promenade Concerts (the "Proms"), with bargain-price standing (or promenading, or sitting-on-the-floor) tickets sold on the night of concert. ⊠ *Kensington Gore, SW7,* ☎ *020/7589–8212,* WEB *www.alberthall.co.uk.* ⊡ *Prices vary with event. Tube: South Kensington.*

❽ **Royal College of Art.** Housed in a glass-dominated building designed by Sir Hugh Casson in 1973, the RCA provides great contrast with the Victoriana surrounding it, including the Albert Hall next door. Famous in the 1950s and '60s for processing David Hockney, Peter Blake, and Eduardo Paolozzi, the college is still one of the country's foremost art and design schools, and there's usually an exhibition, lecture, or event going on here that's open to the public. ⊠ *Kensington Gore, SW7,* ☎ *020/7590–4185,* WEB *www.rca.ac.uk.* ⊡ *Free.* ☉ *Weekdays 10–6 (call to check times). Tube: South Kensington.*

❺ **Science Museum.** This, the third of the great South Kensington museums, stands behind the Natural History Museum in a far plainer building. It features loads of hands-on exhibits, with entire schools of children apparently decanted inside to interact with them; but it is, after all, painlessly educational. Highlights include the Launch Pad gallery, which demonstrates basic scientific principles (try the plasma ball, where your hands attract "lightning"—if you can get them on it); *Puffing Billy,* the oldest train in the world; and the actual *Apollo 10* capsule. The newest attraction is the Wellcome Wing, a £45 million addition devoted to contemporary science, medicine, and technology, which also includes a 450-seat IMAX cinema. ✉ *Exhibition Rd., SW7,* ☎ *020/7942–4000,* WEB *www.sciencemuseum.org.uk.* 🎟 *£6.95; free daily 4:30–6.* ⊘ *Daily 10–6. Tube: South Kensington.*

★ ❸ **Victoria & Albert Museum.** Recognizable by the copy of Victoria's imperial crown on the lantern above the central cupola, this institution is always referred to as the V&A. It is a huge museum, showcasing the applied arts of all disciplines, all periods, all nationalities, and all tastes, and it is a wonderful, generous place to get lost in, full of innovation and completely devoid of pretension. The collections are *so* catholic that confusion is a hazard—one minute you're gazing on the Jacobean oak four-poster Great Bed of Ware (one of the V&A's most prized possessions, given that Shakespeare immortalized it in *Twelfth Night*) and the next you're in the 20th-century end of the equally celebrated Dress Collection, coveting a Jean Muir frock you could actually buy at nearby Harrods. The £31 million British Galleries, to open by the end of 2001, are the latest addition to the museum. The galleries showcase 400 years of British art and design from 1500 to 1900. Displays include George Gilbert Scott's model of the Albert Memorial and the first-ever English fork made in 1632. Information about how a 16th-century bed was made and how women got into carriages with hoop skirts is also provided. In 2005 architect Daniel Liebeskind's dynamic and audacious architectural masterpiece, the Spiral, will open, with stunning views of London from the top floor.

Prince Albert, Victoria's adored consort, was responsible for the genesis of this permanent version of the 1851 Great Exhibition, and his queen laid its foundation stone in her final public London appearance, in 1899. From the start, the V&A had an important role as a research institution, and that role continues today, with many resources available to scholars, designers, artists, and conservators. Two such resources are the Textiles and Dress 20th Century Reference Centre, with ingenious space-saving storage systems for thousands of bolts of cloth, and the Textile Study Galleries, which perform the same function for 2,000 years' worth of the past.

Follow your own whims around the enormous gallery space, but try to reach the spectacular Glass Gallery, where a collection spanning four millennia is reflected between room-size mirrors under young designer Danny Lane's breathtaking glass balustrade. Recent additions include the Raphael Galleries, housing seven massive cartoons the painter completed in 1516 for his Sistine Chapel tapestries, and the Silver Galleries, displaying six centuries of English silver. The museum stays open late on Wednesdays and the last Friday of every month for Late View—a kind of museum salon, with lectures (for a fee) and a wine bar. ✉ *Cromwell Rd., SW7,* ☎ *020/7942–2000,* WEB *www.vam.ac.uk.* 🎟 *£5; free daily after 4:30 and during Late View.* ⊘ *Daily 10–5:45; Late View Wed. 6:30–9:30, last Fri. of the month 6–10. Tube: South Kensington.*

| NEED A BREAK? | Indulge in a true national tradition—the English breakfast—at the **New Restaurant at the V&A** (✉ Cromwell Rd., SW7, ☎ 020/7581–2159), served here daily from 11 until 1. There's also a Sunday Roast, from 1 until 2:45, complete with a jazz trio. |

HYDE PARK, KENSINGTON GARDENS, AND NOTTING HILL

The royal parks of Hyde Park and Kensington Gardens are among London's unique features: great swaths of green in the middle of the city, where it really is possible to escape from London's fast pace. Although some of this territory was covered in the Knightsbridge, Kensington, and Holland Park tour, this is another option for visiting the royal parks (without the museums) that also takes in Portobello Road and Notting Hill. The description "royal" is somewhat paradoxical, for today these are the most democratic of places, where Londoners from all walks of life come to relax (and let off steam as soapbox orators). Although it's probably been centuries since any major royal had a casual stroll here, these parks remain the property of the Crown, and it was the Crown that saved them from being devoured by the city's late-18th-century growth spurt. North of the pair of parks—which are separate entities, although the boundary is virtually invisible—lies Bayswater. Farther northwest lies Notting Hill, a trendsetting square mile of multiethnicity, music, and markets, with lots of restaurants to see and be seen in and younger, more egalitarian, and more adventurous versions of Cork Street's commercial modern-art galleries. The style-watching media has dubbed the local residents Notting Hillbillies. The whole area has mushroomed around one of the world's great antiques markets, Portobello Road.

A Good Walk

Where else would you enter Hyde Park but at **Hyde Park Corner**? The most impressive of the many entrances is the Hyde Park Screen by Apsley House, usually called **Decimus Burton's Gateway** because it was he who designed this triple-arched monument in 1828. The next gate along to the north, a gaudy unicorns-and-lions-rampant number, was a 90th-birthday gift to Elizabeth the Queen Mother and is therefore the **Queen Mother's Gate.** Follow the southern perimeter along the sand track called **Rotten Row,** now used by the Household Cavalry, which lives at the **Knightsbridge Barracks** to the left.

Follow Rotten Row west to the **Serpentine.** When you pass its **Bridge** you leave Hyde Park and enter **Kensington Gardens** and its **Serpentine Gallery.** En route to the formal garden at the end of the Long Water, the **Fountains,** you pass statues of **Peter Pan** and the horse and rider called **Physical Energy.** Continuing westward, you reach **Round Pond** and Kensington Palace. Follow the Broad Walk north past the playground on the left and leave the park by Black Lion Gate; you are almost opposite Queensway, a rather peculiar, cosmopolitan street of ethnic confusion, late-night cafés and restaurants, a skating rink, and the Whiteleys shopping-and-movie mall. Turn left at the end into Westbourne Grove, however, and you've entered Notting Hill; you'll reach the famous **Portobello Road** after a few blocks. Turn left for the Saturday antiques market and shops, right to reach the Westway and the flea market. For Notting Hill's grandest houses, stroll over to Lansdowne Road, Lansdowne Crescent, and Lansdowne Square—two blocks west of Kensington Park Row.

TIMING

This is a route that changes vastly on weekends. Saturday is Portobello Road's most fun day, so you may prefer to start at the end and work backward, using the parks for relaxation after your shopping exertions. Do the same on Friday if you're a flea-market fan. Sunday, the Hyde Park and Kensington Gardens railings all along Bayswater Road are hung with very bad art, which may slow your progress; this is also prime perambulation day for locals. Whatever your priorities, this is a long walk if you explore every corner, with the perimeter of the two parks alone covering a good 4 mi and about half as far again around the remainder of the route. You could cut out a lot of park without missing out on essential sights and walk the whole thing in a brisk three hours.

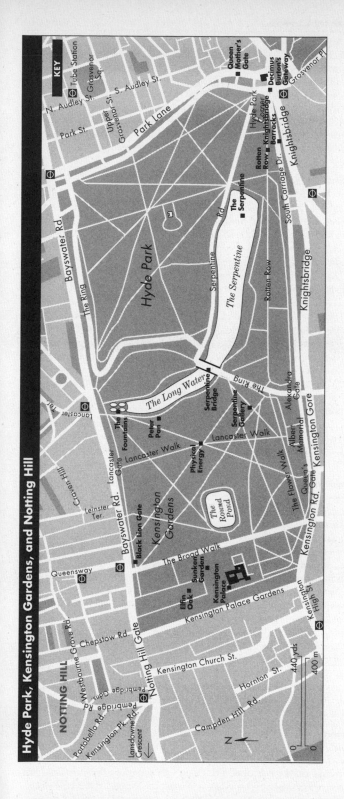

Hyde Park, Kensington Gardens, and Notting Hill

For Hyde Park and Kensington Gardens, get off the Central Line at Queensway or Lancaster Gate, or enter the park from Hyde Park Corner on the Piccadilly Line. If you want Portobello Market and environs, the best tube stop is Ladbroke Grove or Westbourne Park (Hammersmith and City lines), and then ask directions; the Notting Hill stop on the District, Circle, and Central lines is also an option. Buses for the area include Buses 12, 70, and 94 for seeing anything off Bayswater Road or Buses 27, 28, 31, and 52 for penetrating the depths of Notting Hill.

Sights to See

Ⓒ **Hyde Park.** Along with the smaller St. James's and Green parks to the east, Hyde Park started as Henry VIII's hunting grounds. He more or less stole the land for his own personal pleasure from the monks at Westminster in the 1536 Dissolution of the Monasteries. James I was more generous and allowed the public in at the beginning of the 17th century, as long as they were "respectably dressed." Nowadays, as summer visitors can see, you may wear whatever you like—a bathing suit will do. Along its south side runs **Rotten Row.** It was Henry VIII's royal path to the hunt—hence the name, a corruption of *route du roi*. It's still used by the Household Cavalry, who live at the **Knightsbridge Barracks**—a high-rise and a long, low, ugly red block—to the left. This is the brigade that mounts the guard at Buckingham Palace, and you can see them leave to perform this duty in full regalia, plumed helmet and all, at around 10:30, or await the return of the exhausted ex-guard about noon. Sunday's **Speaker's Corner** in the park near Marble Arch is an unmissable spectacle of vehement, sometimes comical, and always entertaining orators. From June to August, Hyde Park is the venue for the Royal Parks Summer Festival with live jazz evenings, opera, and plays all over the park. ☎ *020/7298–2100,* WEB *www.royalparks.co.uk.* ☉ *Daily 5 AM–midnight. Tube: Hyde Park Corner, Lancaster Gate, Marble Arch, or Knighstbridge.*

Ⓒ **Kensington Gardens.** More formal than neighboring Hyde Park, Kensington Gardens was first laid out as palace grounds. The paved Italian garden at the top of the Long Water, the **Fountains,** is a reminder of this, though of course **Kensington Palace** itself is the main clue to the gardens' royal status, with its early 19th-century Sunken Garden north of the palace complex, complete with a living tunnel of lime trees (i.e., linden trees) and golden laburnum. Several statues are worth looking out for: George Frampton's 1912 *Peter Pan* is a bronze of the boy who lived on an island in the Serpentine and never grew up and whose creator, J. M. Barrie, lived at 100 Bayswater Road, not 500 yards from here. Southwest of Peter at the intersection of several paths is George Frederick Watts's 1904 bronze of a muscle-bound horse and rider, entitled *Physical Energy.* By the Princess Diana Memorial Playground, close to the Round Pond, is the remains of a tree carved with scores of tiny woodland creatures, Ivor Innes's *Elfin Oak.* The **Round Pond** acts as a magnet for model-boat enthusiasts and duck feeders. WEB *www.royalparks.co.uk.* ☉ *Daily dawn–dusk. Tube: Lancaster Gate or Queensway.*

Notting Hill. Currently the best place to wear sunglasses, smoke Gauloises, and contemplate the latest issue of *Wallpaper,* "the Hill" now ranks as London's coolest neighborhood (for this week, at least). Centered on the Portobello Road antiques market, this district is bordered to the west by Lansdowne Crescent—lined by the Hill's poshest 19th-century terraced row houses—and to the east by Chepstow Road, with Notting Hill Gate and Westbourne Grove Road marking south and north boundaries. In between, Rastafarians rub elbows with wealthy young Brits (a.k.a. "Trustafarians"), and residents like fashion designer Rifat Ozbek, CNN's Christiane Amanpour, and historian Lady Antonia Fraser can be spotted at the chic shops on Westbourne Grove and in the lively café on Kensington Park Road. There are no historic sites here, so explore just to savor the flavor. *Tube: Notting Hill Gate or Ladbroke Grove.*

Portobello Road. Tempted by tassels, looking for a 19th-century snuff spoon, an ancient print of North Africa, or a dashingly Deco frock (just don't believe the dealer when he says the Vionnet label just fell off), or hunting for a gracefully Georgian silhouette of the Earl of Chesterfield? Head to Portobello Road, world famous for its Saturday antiques market (arrive at about 9 AM to find the real treasures-in-the-trash; after 10, the crowds pack in wall to wall). Actually, the Portobello Market is three markets: antiques, "fruit and veg," and a flea market. The street begins at Notting Hill Gate, though the antiques stalls start a couple of blocks north, around Chepstow Villas. Lining the sloping street are also dozens of antiques shops and indoor markets, open most days—in fact, serious collectors will want to do Portobello on a weekday, when they can explore the 90-some antiques and art stores in relative peace. Where the road levels off, around Elgin Crescent, youth culture and a vibrant neighborhood life kick in, with all manner of interesting small stores and restaurants interspersed with the fruit and vegetable market. This continues to the Westway overpass ("flyover" in British), where London's best flea market (high-class, vintage, antique, and secondhand clothing; jewelry; and junk) happens Fridays and Saturdays, then on up to Goldbourne Road. There's a strong West Indian flavor to Notting Hill, with a Trinidad-style Carnival centered along Portobello Road on the August bank-holiday weekend. *Tube: Notting Hill Gate or Ladbroke Grove.*

Serpentine Gallery. Influential on the trendy art circuit, this gallery hangs several exhibitions of modern work a year, often very avant-garde, indeed, and always worth a look. It overlooks the west bank of the **Serpentine,** a beloved lake, much frequented in summer, when the south-shore Lido resembles a beach and the water is dotted with hired rowboats. Walk the bank, and you will soon reach the picturesque, stone **Serpentine Bridge,** built in 1826 by George Rennie, which marks the boundary between Hyde Park and Kensington Gardens. ⊠ *Kensington Gardens, W2,* ☎ *020/7402–6075,* WEB *www.serpentinegallery.org.* ⌨ *Free.* ⊙ *Daily 10–6; call to check if open. Tube: Lancaster Gate.*

REGENT'S PARK AND HAMPSTEAD

Regent's Park and Hampstead in North London contain some of the prettiest and most rural parts of the city, as well as some of the most aristocratic architecture in the world (thanks to the terraces and town houses of John Nash, 19th-century design whiz) and some important historical sights. For the sheer pleasure of idle exploring, these city districts are hard to beat. All told, this section covers a large area. It starts from the Georgian houses superimposed on medieval Maryburne; continues around John Nash's Regency facades and his park; stretches on into North London's canal-side youth center; climbs up the hill to the city's chicest, most expensive "village"; and finishes, fittingly, at its most famous cemetery.

Marylebone Road (pronounced "Marra-le-bun" after Queen Mary *le bon*) these days is remarkable mostly for its permanent traffic jam, some of it heading to Madame Tussaud's. At the east end is the first part of

John Nash's impressive Regent's Park scheme, the elegantly curvaceous Park Crescent (1812–18), which Nash planned as a full circus at the northern end of his ceremonial route from St. James's. Like most of the other Nash houses around the park, it was wrecked during World War II, reconstructed, and rebuilt behind the repaired facade in the 1960s. Northeast of the park, Camden Town is the neighborhood that houses London's highest concentration of single people in their twenties.

The cliché about Hampstead is that it is just like a pretty little village— albeit one with designer shops, expensive French delicatessens, restaurants, cafés, cinemas, and so on. In fact, like so many other London neighborhoods, Hampstead did start as a separate village, when plague-bedeviled medieval Londoners fled the city to this clean hilltop 4 mi away. By the 18th century, its reputation for cleanliness had spread so far that its water was being bottled and sold to the hoi polloi down the hill as the Perrier of its day. That was the beginning of Hampstead's heyday as an artistic and literary retreat attracting many famous writers, painters, and musicians to its leafy lanes—as it still does. Just strolling around here is rewarding: not only are the streets incredibly picturesque, they also offer some of London's best Georgian buildings.

Numbers in the text correspond to numbers in the margin and on the Regent's Park and Hampstead map.

A Good Walk

Begin at the tube station whose name will thrill the Sherlock Holmes fan: Baker Street—the **Sherlock Holmes Museum** ① is at No. 221B, of course. Turn left and follow the line of tour buses past **Madame Tussaud's** ② and the **London Planetarium**; then go to the end of Harley Street—an English synonym for private (as opposed to state-funded) medicine because it is lined with the consulting rooms of the country's top specialist doctors—to Park Crescent and, across the street, **Regent's Park** ③. Enter along the Outer Circle and turn left on Chester Road. Straight ahead are Queen Mary's Gardens, the lake, and the **Regent's Park Open-Air Theatre** ④.

If you want to take a look at the most elegant street in London, head straight ahead up Chester Road to **Cumberland Terrace** (1827), the porticoed white-stucco structure that overlooks the eastern edge of the park like a Grecian temple. This is one of architect Joseph Nash's most famous Regency-era creations. His most elegant urban stage set, however, is reached by continuing two blocks south, where **Chester Place** (1825) debouches into a cream-colored, magnificent triumphal arch, with its name emblazoned across the top of the arch. Nash aficionados will want to continue eight blocks to the north to see Park Village East and West, two streets that are lined with enchanting "villas" in the 19th-century mode.

If you haven't made this architectural detour outside the park to see Nash's buildings, continue within the park from Regent's Park Open-Air Theatre along Chester Road until the Broad Walk, and then make a left. Look west past the mock-Tudor prefab tearoom for one of London's rare, uninterrupted open vistas toward the London Central Mosque; and then continue on to the **London Zoo** ⑤. From here, you can take a round-trip detour on the water bus and spy on the back gardens along the **Grand Union Canal** (which everyone calls the Regent's Canal) to Little Venice. This canal is flanked with enormous white wedding-cake houses, separated from the banks with willow trees and long gardens, making it a beautiful strolling location. Alternatively you can walk along the whole canal, past the animals in the zoo down to Camden Lock, one of Britain's largest markets.

Regent's Park and Hampstead

North of the zoo, cross Prince Albert Road to the man-made Primrose Hill, a high point (literally, at 206 ft) and the best place to be on the night of November 5, when London's biggest bonfire burns a Guy Fawkes effigy and the council puts on a spectacular fireworks display. Heading east from here (the easiest route is Regent's Park Road, then left down Parkway, past the **Jewish Museum** ⑥), brings you to the center of Camden Town. Turn left at the foot of Parkway, and battle your way north along Camden High Street (actually, the crowds are unbearably dense only on the weekend) to **Camden Lock** ⑦. From here you can keep going east, although it's less scenic, to King's Cross, site of one of London's main train stations, the new British Library building, the city's highest concentration of streetwalkers, and the **London Canal Museum** ⑧.

Back at the Lock, you could walk up Haverstock Hill or travel three stops on the Northern Line from Camden Town tube station (make sure you take the Edgware branch) to Hampstead. Cross High Street to Heath Street and turn right to Church Row, said to be London's most complete Georgian street. At the west end is the 1745 "village" church of St. John's, where the painter John Constable is buried. Just south of the tube station, Flask Walk is another beautiful street, narrow and shop-lined at the High Street end, then widening after you pass the Flask—the pub it is named for. This place has a pretty courtyard and was described by Samuel Richardson in his 18th-century novel *Clarissa* as "a place where second-rate persons are to be found, often in a swinish condition." Nearby Well Walk was where a spring surfaced, its place now marked by a dried-up fountain. John Constable lived here, as well as John Keats (in, of course, **Keats House** ⑨) and, later, D. H. Lawrence. Head some blocks north to regal **Fenton House,** a National Trust treasure trove with some lovely gardens; then amble around the corner and alongside Fenton House to reach Admiral's Walk, where you may gaze at the house with a roof that echoes the quarterdeck of a ship immortalized in *Mary Poppins*. About 15-minutes' walk farther along East Heath Road you'll find the Gothic manse (now owned by Boy George) that inspired Hell Hall in *One Hundred and One Dalmatians*. You now have two choices: if you've had enough fresh air, walk all the way down Fitzjohn's Avenue and visit the **Freud Museum** ⑩, where Sigmund Freud lived and worked, and then continue down Finchley Road to the impressive **Saatchi Collection** ⑪, a huge, cavernous gallery space; Beatles aficionados will head posthaste, instead, to the fabled **Abbey Road Studios** ⑫. If you've been blessed with a clear London day, take advantage and follow the long walk northeast up Spaniards Road, traversing **Hampstead Heath** to Hampstead Lane, to the bucolic oasis of **Kenwood House** ⑬, well worth a visit for its setting alone. To the east of Hampstead, and also topping a hill, is the former village of Highgate, which has some fine houses, especially along its Georgian High Street, and retains a peaceful period atmosphere. But it is most famous for **Highgate Cemetery** ⑭.

TIMING

You may well want to divide this tour into segments, using the (notoriously inefficient) Northern Line of the tube to jump between the Regent's Park and Hampstead neighborhoods. It will take you at least three or even four hours to cover the full length of this walk on foot.

There are several approaches. In summer, with children, you might consider a North London jaunt in Regent's Park, the zoo, Camden Lock, and a canal trip, a day's worth of sightseeing. If you wanted to add Madame Tussaud's and the planetarium, you'd have a frenetic day, especially in summer, because you might be in line for over an hour. You could start a summer's day without children at the other end, with Hampstead Heath, Kenwood House, a stroll around Hampstead, and a pub or two on the agenda. Teenagers and youth might want to spend all day shopping in Camden Town. Both Camden and Hampstead are usually fairly busy during the week as well, for in addition to being shopping havens they are residential neighborhoods. Bear in mind that much of this itinerary may be washed out by rain.

HOW TO GET THERE

For Regent's Park, go to Regent's Park tube station (on the Bakerloo Line), though Camden Town on the Northern Line, with a walk up Parkway, is almost as close. Hampstead is best accessed from the Hampstead tube stop. Make sure you get on the right branch of the Northern Line—you want the Edgware branch. Buses for Regent's Park include Buses 18, 27, and 30 along the Marylebone Road or Buses 13, 82, 113, 139, and 274 to Lord's Cricket Ground. Take the 274 for the zoo. For Hampstead, catch the 268.

Sights to See

★ ⑫ **Abbey Road Studios.** The most famous Beatles site in London, this is the fabled studio where the Fab Four recorded their entire output. The studios themselves are closed to the public, but many travelers journey here to see the famous traffic crossing used by the group on the cover of their *Abbey Road* album. ⊠ *3 Abbey Rd., NW8*, WEB *www.abbeyroad.co.uk. Tube: St. John's Wood.*

☺ ⑦ **Camden Lock.** What was once just a pair of locks on the Grand Union Canal has now developed into London's third-most-visited tourist attraction. It's a vast honeycomb of markets that sell just about everything, but mostly crafts, clothing (vintage, ethnic, and young designer), and antiques. Here, especially on a weekend, the crowds are dense, young, and relentless. You may tire of the identical T-shirts, pants, boots, vintage wear, and cheap leather on their backs and in the shops. Camden does have its charms, though. Gentrification has layered over a once overwhelmingly Irish neighborhood, vestiges of which coexist with the youth culture. Charm is evident in sections of the market itself as well as in other markets, including the bustling fruit-and-vegetable market on Inverness Street. Along the canal are some stylish examples of Nicholas Grimshaw architecture (architect of Waterloo Station), as well as the MTV offices with their designer graffiti. ⊠ *Camden Lock, Camden High St., NW1*, WEB *www.camdenlock.net.* ☉ *Weekends. Tube: Camden Town or Chalk Farm.*

NEED A BREAK? You will not go hungry in Camden Town. Among the countless cafés, bars, pubs, and restaurants, the following stand out for good value and good food: **Marine Ices** (⊠ 8 Haverstock Hill, NW3, ☎ 020/7482–9003) has a window dispensing ice cream to strollers, and pasta, pizza, and sundaes inside. **Bar Gansa** (⊠ 2 Inverness St., NW1, ☎ 020/7267–8909) offers Spanish tapas—small dishes for sharing. **Cottons Rhum Shop, Bar and Restaurant** (⊠ 55 Chalk Farm Rd., NW1, ☎ 020/7482–1096) is a Caribbean island in miniature, with great rum cocktails and jerk chicken.

Fenton House. This is Hampstead's oldest surviving house. Now a National Trust property, it has an interesting collection of antiques and period interiors, along with some 17th century–style gardens. Baroque enthusiasts can join a tour of the large collection of keyboard instruments, given by the curator. ⊠ *Hampstead Grove, NW3*, ☎ *020/7435–3471.* ☚ *£4.10.* ☉ *Mar., weekends 2–5; Apr.–Oct., Wed.–Fri. 2–5, weekends 11–5:30. Tours 1st Thurs. of month. Tube: Hampstead.*

STRAWBERRY BEATLES FOREVER: A TRIP TO ABBEY ROAD

FOR COUNTLESS BEATLEMANIACS and baby boomers, No. 3 Abbey Road is one of the most beloved spots in London. Here, outside the legendary Abbey Road Studios, is the most famous zebra crossing in the world. Immortalized on the Beatles' 1969 *Abbey Road* album, this footpath became a mod monument when, on August 8 of that year, John, Paul, George, and Ringo posed—walking symbolically *away* from the recording facility, incidentally—for photographer Iain Macmillan for the famous album shot.

Today, many fans venture to Abbey Road to leave their signatures on the white-stucco fence that fronts the studio facility. "All You Need Is Beatles!," "God Is a Beatle!," "Imagine—John coming back!," "John Is Gone—What a Price to Pay for Being a Genius!," "Why don't you do it in the road?," and "Strawberry Beatles Forever" are a few of the flourishes left (note that these are whitewashed out every three months, by agreement with the neighborhood community, to make room for new graffiti).

The recording facility's Studio 2 is where the Beatles recorded their entire output, from "Love Me Do" onward, including, most momentously, *Sgt. Pepper's Lonely Hearts Club Band* (early 1967). Since this was, for all intents and purposes, the Beatles' professional home for much of their career, many of their most famous photos were taken here. The most celebrated, of course, was the sleeve jacket photo for the eponymous album. On Friday, August 8, 1969, at 11:35 AM, photographer Macmillan balanced his Hasselblad atop a stepladder before the zebra crossing and photographed the four lads three times crossing west and three times east. Paul's sandals came off only with the third shot. Shot number 5 was the one seen around the world.

Today, tourists like to Beatle-ize themselves by taking the same sort of photo, but be careful: rushing cars make Abbey Road a dangerous intersection. Currently, there are few places in London that commemorate the Fab Four (wouldn't it be wonderful if Abbey Road Studios, now closed to the public, could become a Beatles museum one day?), so the best way Beatle-lovers can enjoy the history of the group is to take one of the smashing walking tours offered by the **Original London Walks** (☎ 020/7624-3978), including **"The Beatles In-My-Life Walk"** (11 AM at the Baker Street underground on Saturday and Tuesday) and **"The Beatles Magical Mystery Tour"** (11 AM at Dominion Theater Exit, Tottenham Court Road, on Sunday and Thursday).

Abbey Road is in the elegant neighborhood of St. John's Wood, just a 10-minute ride on the tube from central London. Take the Jubilee subway line to the St. John's Wood tube stop, head southwest three blocks down Grove End Road, and—especially if you were one of the 63 million people who tuned in to the *Ed Sullivan Show* on February 8, 1964, and grew up with the Beatles—be prepared for a heart-stopping vista right out of Memory Lane.

⑩ **Freud Museum.** The father of psychoanalysis lived here for only a few months, between his escape from Nazi persecution in his native Vienna in 1938 and his death in 1939. Many of his possessions emigrated with him and were set up by his daughter, Anna (herself a pioneer of child psychoanalysis), as a shrine to her father's life and work. Four years after Anna's death in 1982 the house was opened as a museum. It replicates the atmosphere of Freud's famous consulting rooms, particularly through the presence of *the couch.* You'll find Freud-related books, lectures, and study groups here, too. ✉ *20 Maresfield Gardens, NW3,* ☎ *020/7435–2002,* WEB *www.freud.org.uk.* 🖾 *£4.* ☉ *Wed.–Sun. noon–5. Tube: Swiss Cottage or Finchley Rd.*

✋ **Hampstead Heath.** For an escape from the ordered prettiness of Hampstead, head to the heath—a wild park, which spreads for miles to the north and boasts stunning views of London. On the southwest corner stands the rebuilt version of a famous inn, once Dickens's favorite haunt, **Jack Straw's Castle** (✉ North End Way, NW3, ☎ 020/7435–8885). It is named after the Peasants' Revolt leader who hid out and was captured here in 1381 after destroying Sir Robert Hales's residence and priory, the Priory of St. John. Hales was hated for enforcing the poll tax, which led to the uprising—and which, when reintroduced in 1990, proved equally unpopular the second time around. Another historic pub stands off the northwest edge, on Hampstead Lane. The **Spaniards Inn** (✉ Spaniards Rd., NW3, ☎ 020/8731–6571) is little changed since the early 18th century, when (they say) the notorious highwayman Dick Turpin hung out here. Keats also drank here, as did Shelley and Byron.

⑭ **Highgate Cemetery.** The older west side of this sprawling early Victorian graveyard, featuring many an overwrought stone memorial, can be visited only by a tour given by the Friends of Highgate Cemetery—a group of volunteers who virtually saved the place from ruin. The shady streets of the dead, Egyptian Avenue and the Circle of Lebanon, are particularly Poe-like, but the famous graves are mostly on the newer, less atmospheric east side. This side can be wandered freely. Karl Marx's enormous black bust is probably the most-visited site, but George Eliot is also buried here. This is not London's oldest cemetery—that distinction belongs to Kensal Green, with its spine-chilling catacombs and Gothic mausoleums. ✉ *Swains La., Highgate, N6,* ☎ *020/8340–1834,* WEB *www.highgate-cemetery.org.* 🖾 *East side £1, west-side tour £2.* ☉ *Call for opening times and visitor information; hrs vary according to whether a funeral service is scheduled. Tube: Archway.*

⑥ **Jewish Museum.** This museum tells a potted history of the Jews in London from Norman times, though the bulk of the exhibits date from the end of the 17th century (when Cromwell repealed the laws against Jewish settlement) and later. ✉ *Raymond Burton House, 129 Albert St., NW1,* ☎ *020/7284–1997.* 🖾 *£3.* ☉ *Sun. 10–5, Mon.–Thurs. 10–4. Tube: Camden Town.*

⑨ **Keats House.** Here you can see the plum tree under which the young Romantic poet composed "Ode to a Nightingale," many of his original manuscripts, his library, and other possessions he managed to acquire in his short life. It was in February 1820 that Keats coughed blood up into his handkerchief and exclaimed, "I know the color of that blood; it is arterial blood. I cannot be deceived in that color. That drop of blood is my death warrant. I must die." He left this house in September, moved to Rome, and died of consumption there, in early 1821, at age 25. ✉ *Keats House, Wentworth Pl., Keats Grove, NW3,* ☎ *020/7435–2062.* 🖾 *£3.* ☉ *Apr.–Oct., Tues.–Sun. noon–5; Nov.–Mar., Tues.–Sun. noon–4. Tube: Hampstead.*

Hampstead is full of restaurants, including a few that have been here forever. Try the **Coffee Cup** (⌧ 74 Hampstead High St., NW3, ☎ 020/
435–7565), serving English breakfasts all day to a hip crowd of locals,
or the **Hampstead Tea Rooms** (⌧ 9 South End Rd., NW3, ☎ 020/
7435–9563) for its sandwiches, pies, and its great window full of pastries and cream cakes. For a more substantial but still speedy meal, stop
at the **Hampstead Creperie** (⌧ 77 Hampstead High St., NW3, ☎ 020/
7372–0081), which serves authentic sweet and savory French crepes
from a little cart on the street. The quaintest pub in Hampstead, complete
with fireplace and timber frame, is the **Hollybush** (⌧ 22 Holly Mount,
NW3, ☎ 020/7435–2892), which dates back to 1807. Tucked away
on a side street, it is open until 11 each night and serves traditional English lunches and dinners, often to the accompaniment of live Irish music.

⑬ Kenwood House. Perfectly and properly Palladian, this mansion was
first built in 1616 and remodeled by Robert Adam in 1764. Adam refaced
most of the exterior and added the gaudy library, which, with its
curved painted ceiling, rather garish coloring, and gilded detailing, is
the sole highlight of the house for decor buffs. What is unmissable here
is the **Iveagh Bequest**, a collection of paintings that the Earl of Iveagh
gave the nation in 1927, starring a wonderful Rembrandt self-portrait
and works by Reynolds, Van Dyck, Hals, Gainsborough, and Turner.
Top billing goes to Vermeer's *Guitar Player*, one of the most beautiful
paintings in the world. In front of the house, a graceful lawn slopes
down to a little lake crossed by a trompe-l'oeil bridge—all in perfect
18th-century upper-class taste. Nowadays the lake is dominated by its
concert bowl, which stages a summer series of orchestral concerts, including an annual performance of Handel's *Music for the Royal Fireworks*, complete with fireworks. ⌧ *Hampstead La., NW3,* ☎ *020/8348–
1286.* 🎫 *Free.* ⊙ *Easter–Aug., Sat.–Mon., Tues., and Thurs. 10–6, Wed.
and Fri. 10:30–6; Dec.–Easter, Sat.–Mon., Tues., and Thurs. 10–4, Wed.
and Fri. 10:30–5; Sept.–Nov. Sat.–Mon., Tues., and Thurs. 10–4, Wed.
and Fri. 10:30–4. Tube: Golder's Green, then Bus 210.*

❽ London Canal Museum. Here, in a former ice storage house, you can
learn about the rise and fall of London's once extensive canal network.
Outside, on the Battlebridge Basin, float the gaily painted narrow
boats of modern canal dwellers—a few steps and a world away from
King's Cross, which remains one of London's least salubrious neighborhoods. The quirky little museum is accessible from Camden Lock
if you take the towpath. ⌧ *12–13 New Wharf Rd., N1,* ☎ *020/7713–
0836,* WEB *www.canalmuseum.org.uk.* 🎫 *£2.50.* ⊙ *Tues.–Sun. 10–3:45.
Tube: King's Cross.*

☝ London Planetarium. This domed building stands right next to Madame
Tussaud's, but it could hardly provide greater contrast with the waxworks (though you can save a bit of cash by combining them in a single visit). Inside the dome, exact simulations of the night sky are
projected by the Digistar Mark 2 and accompanied by gosh-wow-fancy-
that narration. The shows, which change daily, are good enough to ad-
dict children to astronomy. There are also regular laser shows and rock
music extravaganzas. Beat the crowds by calling in advance for timed
entry tickets to both Madame Tussaud's and the Planetarium. ⌧ *Marylebone Rd., NW1,* ☎ *020/7935–6861 or 087/0400–3000 for timed
entry tickets.* 🎫 *£6.75, combined ticket with Madame Tussaud's
£14.45.* ⊙ *Weekdays 11:30–6, weekends 9:30–6; show every 40 mins
weekdays 12:20–5, weekends 10:20–5. Tube: Baker Street.*

☝ ❺ London Zoo. The zoo opened in 1828 and peaked in popularity during the 1950s, when more than 3 million visitors passed through its

turnstiles every year. But recently it faced the prospect of closing its gates forever. Its problems started when animal-crazy Brits, anxious about the morality of caging wild beasts, simply stopped visiting. But the zoo fought back, pulling heartstrings with a "Save Our Zoo" campaign and tragic predictions of mass euthanasia for homeless polar bears. At the 11th hour it found commercial sponsorship that was generous enough not only to keep the wolves from the door (or, rather, indoors) but also to fund a great big modernization program. So successful has the zoo's revival been that it has now glitteringly expanded to include the Web of Life—a conservation and education center set in a spanking new glass pavilion. And to ensure that the celebration of life does not go unheralded, the zoo has taken on a poet-in-residence, the young but highly acclaimed Tobias Hill. If you get the chance, catch one of his readings or popular children's workshops at the zoo.

Zoo highlights (unchanged over the years) include the Elephant and Rhino Pavilion (which closely resembles the South Bank Arts Complex); the graceful Snowdon Aviary, spacious enough to allow its tenants free flight; and the 1936 Penguin Pool, where feeding time sends small children into raptures. New thrills include a desert swarming with locusts; a rain forest alive with butterflies, bats, and hummingbirds; and a cave lighted by fireflies. This is the headquarters of the Zoological Society of London, and much work is done here in wildlife conservation, education, and the breeding of endangered species. The emphasis has been shifted onto this aspect of the exhibits. The first step along this road was the Children's Zoo, which shows how people and animals live together and features domestic animals from around the world. ⊠ *Regent's Park, NW1,* ☎ *020/7722–3333,* WEB *www.londonzoo.co.uk.* ⊠ *£8.50.* ☉ *Mar.–Oct., daily 10–5:30; Nov.–Feb., daily 10–4; pig feed daily 12:30; pelican feed daily 1; aquarium feed daily 2:30. Tube: Camden Town, then Bus 74.*

🐣 ➋ **Madame Tussaud's.** This—one of London's busiest sights—is nothing more and nothing less than the world's premier exhibition of lifelike waxwork models of celebrities. Madame T. learned her craft while making death masks of French Revolution victims, and in 1835 set up her first show of the famous ones near this spot. Nowadays, Super Stars of entertainment, in their own hall of the same name, outrank any aristo in popularity, along with the newest segment, The Spirit of London, and a Time Taxi Ride that visits every notable Londoner from Shakespeare to Benny Hill. But top billing still goes to the murderers in the Chamber of Horrors, who stare glassy-eyed at visitors—one from an electric chair, one sitting next to the tin bath where he dissolved several wives in quicklime. What, aside from ghoulish prurience, makes people stand in line to invest in London's most expensive museum ticket? It is the thrill of rubbing shoulders with Shakespeare, Martin Luther King Jr., the Queen, and the Beatles—most of them dressed in their very own outfits—in a single day. Beat the crowds by calling in advance for timed entry tickets. ⊠ *Marylebone Rd., NW1,* ☎ *020/7935–6861 or 087/0400–3000 for timed entry tickets,* WEB *www.madame-tussauds.com.* ⊠ *£11.95, combined ticket with planetarium £14.45.* ☉ *Sept.–June, weekdays 10–5:30, weekends 9:30–5:30; July–Aug., daily 9:30–5:30. Tube: Baker St..*

★ ➌ **Regent's Park.** The youngest of London's great parks, Regent's Park was laid out in 1812 by John Nash, who worked for his patron, the Prince Regent (hence the name), who was crowned George IV in 1820. The idea was to re-create the feel of a grand country residence close to the center of town, with all those magnificent white-stucco terraces facing in on the park. As you walk the Outer Circle, you'll see how

successfully Nash's plans were carried out, although the focus of it all—
a palace for the prince—was never actually built (George was too
busy fiddling with the one he already had, Buckingham Palace). The
most famous and impressive of Nash's terraces would have been in the
prince's line of vision from the planned palace. **Cumberland Terrace**
has a central block of Ionic columns surmounted by a triangular Wedg-
wood-blue pediment that is like a giant cameo. Snow-white statuary
personifying Britannia and her empire (the work of the on-site architect, James Thomson) single it out from the pack. The noted architectural
historian Sir John Summerson described it thus: "the backcloth as it
were to Act III, and easily the most breathtaking architectural panorama
in London."

As in all London parks, planting here is planned with the aim of having something in bloom in all seasons, but if you hit the park in May,
June, or July, head first to the Inner Circle. Your nostrils should lead
you to **Queen Mary's Gardens,** a fragrant 17-acre circle that riots with
roses in summer and heather, azaleas, and evergreens in other seasons.
The **Broad Walk** is a good vantage point from which to glimpse the
minaret and golden dome of the **London Central Mosque** on the far
west side of the park. If it's a summer evening or a Sunday afternoon,
witness a remarkable recent phenomenon. Wherever you look, the sport
being enthusiastically played is not cricket but softball, now Britain's
fastest-growing participant sport (bring your mitt). You're likely to see
cricket, too, plus a lot of dog walkers—not for nothing did Dodie Smith
set her novel *A Hundred and One Dalmations* in an Outer Circle
house. ☎ 020/7486–7905, WEB *www.royalparks.co.uk.*

④ Regent's Park Open-Air Theatre. They have mounted Shakespeare
productions here every summer since 1932; everyone from Vivien
Leigh to Jeremy Irons has performed here. *A Midsummer Night's
Dream* is the one to catch—never is that enchanted Greek wood more
lifelike than it is here, augmented by genuine bird squawks and a rising moon. The park can get chilly, so bring a blanket; rain stops the
play only when heavy. ⊠ *Open-Air Theatre, Regent's Park, NW1,* ☎
020/7486–2431. ☉ *June–Aug., evening performances 7:30, matinees
2:30. Tube: Baker St. or Regent's Park.*

⑪ Saatchi Collection. This blinding white space is all crisp angles and
quietness, the better to contemplate the front lines of contemporary painting, installations, and sculpture—by the likes of Lucian Freud, Paula
Rego, Damian Hirst, Rachel Whiteread, Janine Antoni—collected by
the advertising mogul. ⊠ *98A Boundary Rd., NW8,* ☎ *020/7624–8299.*
▭ *£5.* ☉ *Thurs.–Sun. noon–6. Tube: Swiss Cottage or St. John's Wood.*

❶ Sherlock Holmes Museum. You know you've reached this museum when
you see the actor dressed as a Victorian policeman outside and the sign
that claims this as 221B Baker Street, the address of Arthur Conan
Doyle's fictional detective. Inside, "Holmes's housekeeper" conducts
you into a series of Victorian rooms full of Sherlock-abilia. It's all so
realistic, you may actually begin to believe in Holmes' existence. ⊠
221B Baker St., NW1, ☎ *020/7935–8866,* WEB *www.sherlock-
homes.co.uk.* ▭ *£6.* ☉ *Daily 9:30–6. Tube: Baker St.*

2 Willow Road. Modern movement master Ernö Goldfinger put this
house up in the 1930s, and the National Trust has now kindly restored
it and filled it with important (and currently very trendy) modernist
furniture and art. Note that there are limited visitor hours with timed
tickets because the house is small. ⊠ *2 Willow Rd., NW1,* ☎ *020/7435–
6166.* ▭ *£4.* ☉ *Mar.–Oct., Thurs.–Sat. noon–5; Nov.–Dec., Sat. noon–
5. Tube: Hampstead.*

GREENWICH

About 8 mi downstream from central London—which means seaward, to the east—lies a neighborhood that has recently had front-page fame thrust upon it. Once a sleepy, charming self-contained village with elegant, perfectly proportioned buildings and tall ships anchored at the river bank, Greenwich became the site of the Millennium Dome and, consequently, synonymous with the millennium. The Dome—either a spectacular monument to mankind or, according to some British critics, a dazzling waste of £758 million of public money—is now closed to the public and has been on offer to several companies; its future remained unclear at press time. Greenwich really scored on transportation when it became the center of the millennium universe. Now there are more roads leading to it than to Rome—but don't try driving there, as all new routes are strictly public transportation. Take the new Jubilee Line extensions, and if you're an architecture buff, get out at every stop—each one was designed by a different cutting-edge architect.

Greenwich has many attractions. Spreading both grandly and elegantly beside the river are the colonnades and pediments of Sir Christopher Wren's Royal Naval College and Inigo Jones's Queen's House, both of which seem to be part of a complex of Grecian temples transported to the Thames. Here, too, is the Old Royal Observatory, which measures time for our entire planet, and the Greenwich Meridian, which divides the world in two—you can stand astride it with one foot in either hemisphere. This is also where the millennium officially started (when this clock said so). The National Maritime Museum and the proud clipper ship *Cutty Sark* thrill seafaring types, and landlubbers can stroll the green acres of parkland that surround the buildings, the quaint 19th-century houses, and the weekend crafts and antiques markets.

Numbers in the text correspond to numbers in the margin and on the Greenwich map.

A Good Walk

To start your walk, take the Docklands Light Railway (DLR) or a ferry to Cutty Sark station and begin your tour with the **Cutty Sark** ①. Follow King William Walk and then take a right on College Approach towards Wren's majestic **Royal Naval College** ②. The **Queen's House** ③, followed by the **National Maritime Museum** ④ sit just down King William Walk on Romney Road. Now head up the hill in Greenwich Park, overlooking the Naval College and Maritime Museum, to the **Old Royal Observatory** ⑤ and the **Ranger's House** ⑥. Walking back through the park toward the river, you'll enter the pretty streets of Greenwich Village to the west. There are plenty of bookstores and antiques shops for browsing and, at the foot of Crooms Hill, the modern Greenwich Theatre—a West End theater, despite its location, that mounts well-regarded, often star-spangled productions—and the **Fan Museum** ⑦ opposite. Finish up at the excellent **Greenwich Market** ⑧ and the Victorian **Royal Charter Market** ⑨ by the *Cutty Sark,* on College Approach. If you've still energy and time, a visit to the Thames Barrier Visitors' Centre is a nice way to explore the banks of the Thames.

TIMING

The boat trip takes about an hour from Westminster Pier (next to Big Ben), or 25 minutes from the Tower of London, so figure in enough time for the round-trip. Beyond the main new attractions, there are such riches here, especially if the maritime theme is your thing, that whatever time you allow will seem halved. If the weather's good, you'll be tempted to stroll aimlessly around the quaint village streets, too, and maybe take a turn in the park. If you want to take in the markets, you'll need to come on a weekend.

HOW TO GET THERE

Once, Greenwich was thought of as remote by Londoners, with only the river as a direct route. Now, with new transport links in the form of the Docklands Light Railway and the tube's Jubilee Line, getting here is both easy and inexpensive. The quickest route to Greenwich is the tube to Canary Wharf and the Docklands Light Rail (or DLR, the driverless elevated train with good views of the Docklands) to the *Cutty Sark*. You can also exit the DLR at Island Gardens and walk under the Thames to Greenwich for a thrill.

The river connections to Greenwich mean that the journey to Greenwich is fun in itself, for you will then get the best possible vista of the Royal Naval College, with the Queen's House behind. On the way, the boat glides past famous sights on the London skyline (there's a guaranteed spine chill on passing the Tower) and the ever-changing docklands, and there's always a cockney navigator enhancing the views with wise-guy commentary. **Ferries** from central London to Greenwich take 30–55 minutes and leave from various piers: from Charing Cross and Tower piers (☎ 020/7987–1185), from Westminster Pier (☎ 020/7930–4097), and from the Thames Barrier Pier (☎ 020/8305–0300).

Sights to See

① *Cutty Sark.* This romantic clipper was built in 1869, one of fleets and fleets of similar wooden tall-masted clippers that plied the seven seas in the 19th century, trading in exotic commodities—tea, in this case. The *Cutty Sark*, the last to survive, was also the fastest, sailing the China–London route in 1871 in only 107 days. Now the photogenic vessel lies in dry dock, a museum of one kind of seafaring life—and not a comfortable kind for the 28-strong crew, as you'll see. The collection of figureheads is amusing, too. The *Cutty Sark* gardens were remodeled for Greenwich's moment of fame in 2000. ⊠ *King William Walk, SE10,* ☎ *020/8858–3445,* WEB *www.cuttysark.org.uk.* ⊠ *£3.50.* ⊘ *Daily 10–5 (last admission 4:30). DLR: Cutty Sark.*

⑦ **Fan Museum.** In two newly restored houses dating from the 1820s, opposite the Greenwich Theatre, is this highly unusual museum. The 2,000 fans here, which date from the 17th century onward, compose the world's only such collection, and the history and purpose of these often exquisitely crafted objects are satisfyingly explained. It was the personal vision—and fan collection—of Helene Alexander that brought it into being in 1991, and the workshop and conservation and study center that she has also set up ensure that this anachronistic art has a future. ⊠ *12 Croom's Hill, SE10,* ☎ *020/8858–7879,* WEB *www.fan-museum.org.* ⊠ *£3.50.* ⊘ *Tues.–Sat. 11–5, Sun. noon–5. DLR: Greenwich.*

⑧ **Greenwich Market.** If you're visiting on the weekend, this market on Burney Street near the Fan Museum and Greenwich Theatre is open for business. It has a lot of bric-a-brac and books, too, and it's well known among the cognoscenti as a good source for vintage clothing. ⊠ *Burney St., SE10.* ⊘ *Weekends 9–5. DLR: Cutty Sark.*

④ **National Maritime Museum.** One of Greenwich's star attractions contains everything to do with the British at sea, in the form of paintings, models, maps, globes, sextants, uniforms (including the one Nelson died in at Trafalgar, complete with bloodstained bullet hole), and—best of all—actual boats, including a collection of ornate, gilded royal barges. There is an immense glazed roof, creating an indoor courtyard. ⊠ *Romney Rd., SE10,* ☎ *020/8858–4422.* ⊠ *£5, including Queen's House and Old Royal Observatory.* ⊘ *Mon.–Sat. 10–6, Sun. noon–6. DLR: Greenwich.*

⑤ **Old Royal Observatory.** Founded in 1675 by Charles II, this imposing institution was designed the same year by Christopher Wren for John

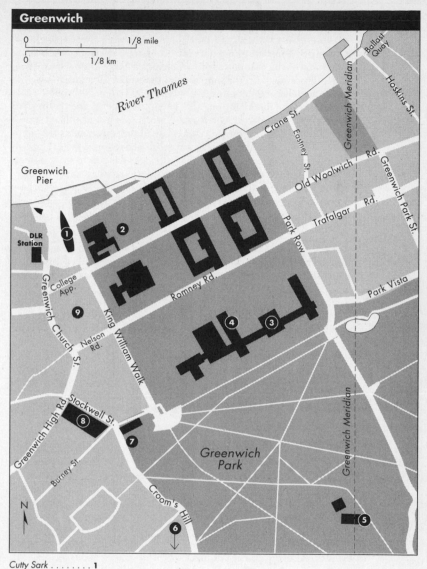

Greenwich

0 ——————— 1/8 mile
0 ——————— 1/8 km

River Thames

Greenwich Pier

DLR Station

Crane St.

Eastney St.

Old Woolwich Rd.

Greenwich Meridian

Ballast Quay

Hoskins St.

New Greenwich Park St.

Trafalgar Rd.

Park Row

College App.

Greenwich Church St.

King William Walk

Nelson Rd.

Romney Rd.

Park Vista

Greenwich High Rd.

Stockwell St.

Burney St.

Croom's Hill

Greenwich Park

Greenwich Meridian

N

1 2 9 3 4 5 6 7 8

Flamsteed, the first Astronomer Royal. The red ball you see on its roof has been there only since 1833. It drops every day at 1 PM, and you can set your watch by it, as the sailors on the Thames always have. This Greenwich Timeball, along with the Gate Clock inside the observatory, is the most visible manifestation of Greenwich Mean Time—since 1884, the ultimate standard for time around the world. Greenwich is on the **prime meridian** at 0° longitude. A brass line laid among the cobblestones here marks the meridian, one side being the eastern, one the western hemisphere. In 1948 the Old Royal Observatory lost its official status: London's glow had grown too intense, and the astronomers moved to Sussex, while the Astronomer Royal decamped to Cambridge. They left various telescopes, chronometers, and clocks for you to view in their absence. An excellent exhibition on the solution to the problem of measuring longitude includes John Harrison's famous clocks, H1–H4, now in working order ⊠ *Greenwich Park, SE10,* ☎ *020/8858–4422,* WEB *www.rog.nmm.ac.uk.* ⊠ *£5, including Queen's House and National Maritime Museum.* ☉ *Daily 10–5. DLR: Greenwich.*

★ ❸ **Queen's House.** The queen for whom Inigo Jones began designing the house in 1616 was James I's Anne of Denmark, but she died three years later, and it was Charles I's French wife, Henrietta Maria, who inherited the building when it was completed in 1635. It is no less than Britain's first classical building—the first, that is, to use the lessons of Italian Renaissance architecture—and is therefore of enormous importance in the history of English architecture. Inside, the Tulip Stair, named for the fleur de lys–style pattern on the balustrade, is especially fine, spiraling up, without a central support, to the Great Hall. The Great Hall itself is a perfect cube, exactly 40 ft in all three directions, decorated with paintings of the Muses, the Virtues, and the Liberal Arts. ⊠ *Romney Rd., SE10,* ☎ *020/8293–9618.* ⊠ *£5, including National Maritime Museum and Old Royal Observatory.* ☉ *Daily 10–5. DLR: Cutty Sark.*

NEED A   After a long walk, the historic **Trafalgar Tavern** (⊠ Park Row, SE10,
BREAK?   ☎ 020/8858–2437), with excellent views of the Thames, is a grand
                place to have a pint and some upmarket pub grub. In warm weather,
                the riverside terrace offers outdoor seating overlooking the Millennium
                Dome. At **Goddard's Ye Olde Pie House** (⊠ 45 Greenwich Church St.,
                SE10), pie and mash are the only things on the menu.

❻ **Ranger's House.** This handsome, early 18th-century mansion, which was the Greenwich Park Ranger's official residence during the 19th century, now houses collections of Jacobean portraits. Concerts are regularly given here, too. It stands just outside the park boundaries, on the southwest side of **Greenwich Park,** one of London's oldest royal parks. It had been in existence for more than 200 years before Charles II commissioned the French landscape artist Le Nôtre (who was responsible for Versailles and for St. James's Park) to redesign it in what was, in the 1660s, the latest French fashion. Look also for Queen Elizabeth's Oak on the east side, around which Henry VIII and his second queen, Anne Boleyn, Elizabeth I's mother, are said to have danced. ⊠ *Chesterfield Walk, Blackheath, SE10,* ☎ *020/8853–0035.* ⊠ *Free.* ☉ *Apr.–Sept., daily 10–1 and 2–6; Oct.–Mar., daily 10–1 and 2–4. DLR: Cutty Sark.*

❾ **Royal Charter Market.** You'll find this Victorian covered crafts market by the *Cutty Sark,* on College Approach. Established as a fruit and vegetable market in 1700, the glass-roofed market now offers arts and crafts everyday except Thursday, when it becomes one of London's premier antiques and collectibles markets. Shopping for crafts is a pleasure, as in most cases you're buying directly from the artist. ✉ *Nelson Rd., SE10,* ☎ *020/7515–7153.* ⊙ *Wed.–Sun. 9:30–5:30, Thurs. 9–5. DLR: Cutty Sark.*

★ ❷ **Royal Naval College.** Begun by Christopher Wren in 1694 as a home, or hospital (as in the Chelsea Royal Hospital, not Charing Cross Hospital), for ancient mariners, it became instead a school for young ones in 1873. Today the University of Greenwich has classes here. You'll notice how the structures part to reveal the Queen's House across the central lawns. Wren, with the help of his assistant, Nicholas Hawksmoor, was at pains to preserve the river vista from the house, and there are few more majestic views in London than the awe-inspiring symmetry he achieved. Behind the college are two buildings you can visit. The **Painted Hall,** the college's dining hall, derives its name from the Baroque murals of William and Mary (reigned 1689–95; William alone 1695–1702) and assorted allegorical figures, the whole supported by trompe-l'oeil pillars that Sir James Thornhill (who decorated the inside of St. Paul's dome, too) painted between 1707 and 1717. In the opposite building stands the **College Chapel,** which was rebuilt after a fire in 1779 and is altogether lighter, in a more restrained, neo-Grecian style. At Christmas 1805, Admiral Nelson's body was brought from the Battle of Trafalgar to lie in state here. ✉ *Royal Naval College, King William Walk, SE10,* ☎ *020/8858–2154,* ⓦᴇʙ *www.greenwichfoundation.org.uk.* ✆ *Free.* ⊙ *Daily 2:30–4:45. DLR: Cutty Sark.*

OFF THE BEATEN PATH
THAMES BARRIER VISITORS' CENTRE – Learn what comes between London and its famous river—a futuristic-looking metal barrier that has been described as the eighth wonder of the world. Multimedia presentations, a film on the Thames' history, working models, and views of the barrier itself put the importance of the relationship between London and its river in perspective. ✉ *Unity Way, Eastmoor St., SE18,* ☎ *020/8854–1373.* ✆ *£3.40.* ⊙ *Weekdays 10–5, weekends 10:30–5:30. British Rail: Charlton (from London Bridge).*

UPSTREAM FROM LONDON

The Thames is Britain's longest river. It winds its way through the Cotswolds, beyond Oxford and past majestic Windsor Castle—here far more the lazy, leafy country river than the dark-gray urban waterway you see in London. Once you leave the city center, going west, or upstream, you reach a series of former villages—Chiswick, Kew, Richmond, Putney—that, apart from the roar of aircraft coming in to land at Heathrow a few miles farther west, still retain a peaceful, almost rural atmosphere, especially in places where parkland rolls down to the riverbank. In fact, it was really only at the beginning of the 20th century that London proper expanded to encompass these villages. The royal palaces and grand houses that dot the area were built as country residences with easy access to London by river.

TIMING
Each of the places we list here could easily absorb a whole day of your time, and Hampton Court is especially huge.

HOW TO GET THERE
Access is fairly easy: the District Line of the underground runs out to Kew and Richmond, as does Network SouthEast from Waterloo, which also serves Twickenham and Hampton Court. For Chiswick House or Hogarth's House, take British Rail to Chiswick station or take the District Line to Turnham Green. Both options require walking to reach the destination, but Chiswick station is a bit closer to the houses.

British Rail also runs trains to Kew Bridge, which is convenient to Strand-on-the-Green. For Kew Gardens, take the District Line heading towards Richmond and get off at Kew Gardens. British Rail also stops nearby; from the station it's a pleasant walk down a tree-lined residential avenue to the gardens.

A pleasant if slow way to go is by river. Boats depart from Westminster Pier, just by Big Ben (☎ 020/7930–4097) for Kew (1½ hours), Richmond (2–3 hours), and Hampton Court (4 hours) several times a day in summer, less frequently from October through March. As you can tell from those sailing times, the boat trip is worth taking only if you make it an integral part of your day out, and even then, be aware that it can get very breezy on the water and that the scenery going upstream is by no means constantly fascinating.

Chiswick and Kew

Chiswick is the nearest Thames-side destination to London, with Kew just a mile or so beyond it. Much of Chiswick, developed at the beginning of this century, is today a nondescript suburb. Incongruously stranded among the terraced houses, however, a number of fine 18th-century houses and a charming little village survive. The village atmosphere of Kew is still distinct, making this one of the most desirable areas of outer London. What makes Kew famous, though, are the Royal Botanic Gardens.

A Good Walk

Start your walk at the Italianate **Chiswick House** on Burlington Lane. Then follow Burlington Lane and take a left onto Hogarth Lane, which is anything but a lane, to reach **Hogarth's House.** Chiswick's Church Street (reached by an underpass from Hogarth's House) is the nearest thing to a sleepy country village street in all of London, despite its proximity to the Great West Road. Follow it down to the Thames and turn left at its foot to reach the sturdy 18th-century riverfront houses of Chiswick Mall. The ½-mi walk along here takes you far away from mainstream London and into a world of elegance and calm. You will pass several riverside pubs as you head along this stretch of the Thames toward Hammersmith Bridge. The Dove is the prettiest, if the most crowded, with its terrace hanging over the water. The food is better at the Blue Anchor, which you'll reach first.

There's a similarly peaceful walk to be had about 1 mi to the west along the 18th-century river frontage of Strand-on-the-Green, whose houses look over the narrow towpath to the river, their tidy brick facades covered with wisteria and roses in summer. Right before you reach Kew Bridge, you may be ready for a break at the Bell & Crown, where crowds congregate on summer days to watch the Thames roll by. Strand-on-the-Green ends at Kew Bridge, opposite which is Kew Green, where local teams play cricket on summer Sundays. All around it are fine 18th-century houses, and, in the center, a church in which the painters Thomas Gainsborough and John Zoffany (1733–1810) are buried. **Kew Gardens** and **Kew Palace** are just a short walk away over the Kew Bridge.

Sights to See

★ **Chiswick House.** Built circa 1725 by the Earl of Burlington (the Lord Burlington of Burlington House, Piccadilly, home of the Royal Academy, and, of course, the Burlington Arcade) as a country residence in which to entertain friends, and as a kind of temple to the arts, this is the very model of a Palladian villa, inspired by the Villa Capra near Vicenza in northeastern Italy. The house fans out from a central octagonal room in perfect symmetry, guarded by statues of Burlington's heroes, Palladio himself and his disciple Inigo Jones. Burlington's friends—Pope, Swift, Gay, and Handel among them—were well qualified to adorn a temple to the arts. Burlington was a great connoisseur and an important patron of the arts, but he was also an accomplished architect in his own right, fascinated by—obsessed with, even—the architecture and art of the Italian Renaissance and ancient Rome, with which he'd fallen in love during his Italian grand tour. Along with William Kent (1685–1748), who designed the interiors and the rambling gardens here, Burlington did a great deal toward the dissemination of Palladian ideals around Britain: Chiswick House sparked enormous interest, and you'll see these forms reflected in hundreds of later English stately homes both small and large. ✉ *Burlington La., W4,* ☎ *020/8995–0508.* ✉ *£3.50.* ☉ *Apr.–Sept., daily 10–6; Oct.–Mar., Wed.–Sun. 10–6. Tube: Turnham Green.*

Hogarth's House. This is where the painter lived from 1749 until his death in 1764. Unprotected from the six-lane Great West Road, which remains a main route to the West Country, the poor house is besieged by the surrounding traffic, but it's worth visiting for its little museum consisting mostly of the amusingly moralistic engravings for which Hogarth is best known, including the most famous of all, the *Rake's Progress* series of 1735. ✉ *Hogarth La., W4,* ☎ *020/8994–6757.* ✉ *Free.* ☉ *Apr.–Sept., Tues.–Fri. 1–5, weekends 1–6; Oct.–Mar., Tues.–Fri. 1–4, weekends 1–5. Tube: Turnham Green.*

NEED A BREAK? Pubs are the name of the game here at Chiswick's portion of the Thames. Many pubs sit on the bank of the river, offering watery vistas to accompany stout pints of brew. Among the best are the **Bell & Crown** (✉ 72 Strand-on-the-Green, W4, ☎ 020/8994–4164), the **Blue Anchor** (✉ 13 Lower Mall, W6, ☎ 020/8748–2639), and the **Dove** (✉ 19 Upper Mall, W6, ☎ 020/8748–5405).

★ **Kew Gardens.** The Royal Botanic Gardens at Kew are a spectacular 300 acres of public gardens, containing more than 60,000 species of plants. In addition, this is the country's leading botanical institute, with strong royal associations. Until 1840, when Kew Gardens was handed over to the nation, it had been the grounds of two royal residences: the White House (formerly Kew House) and Richmond Lodge, or the Dutch House. George II and Queen Caroline lived at Richmond Lodge in the 1720s, while their eldest son, Frederick, Prince of Wales, and his wife, Princess Augusta, came to the White House during the 1730s. The royal wives were keen gardeners. Queen Caroline got to work on her grounds, while next door Frederick's pleasure garden was developed as a botanical garden by his widow after his death. She introduced all kinds of "exotics," foreign plants brought back to England by botanists. Caroline was aided by a skilled head gardener and by the architect Sir William Chambers, who built a series of temples and follies, of which the crazy 10-story **Pagoda** (1762), visible for miles around, is the star turn. The celebrated botanist Sir Joseph Banks (1743–1820) then took charge of Kew, which developed rapidly in both its roles—as a landscaped garden and as a center of study and research.

The highlights of a visit to Kew are the two great 19th-century greenhouses filled with tropical plants, many of which have been there as long as their housing. Both the **Palm House** and the **Temperate House** were designed by Sir Decimus Burton, the first opening in 1848, the second in 1899; the latter was the biggest greenhouse in the world, and today contains the largest greenhouse plant in the world, a Chilean wine palm rooted in 1846. You can climb the spiral staircase almost to the roof and look down on this and the dense tropical profusion from the walkway. The **Princess of Wales Conservatory,** the latest and the largest plant house at Kew, was opened in 1987 by Princess Diana. Under its bold glass roofs, designed to maximize energy conservation, there are no fewer than 10 climatic zones.

The **Centre for Economic Botany** is housed in the Joseph Banks Building, the majority of which is devoted to Kew's research collection on economic botany and to its library. But the public can enjoy exhibitions here on the theme of plants in everyday life. (There is no admission charge, and the center is open Monday–Saturday 9:10–4:30 and Sunday 9:30–5:30.) The plant houses make Kew worth visiting even in the depths of winter, but in spring and summer the gardens come into their own. In late spring the woodland nature reserve of Queen Charlotte's Cottage Gardens is carpeted in bluebells; a little later, the Rhododendron Dell and the Azalea Garden become swathed in brilliant color. High summer features glorious displays of roses and water lilies, while fall is the time to see the heather garden, near the pagoda. Whatever time of year you visit, something is in bloom, and your journey is never wasted. The main entrance is between Richmond Circus and the traffic circle at Mortlake Road. ⊠ *Kew Rd.,* ☎ *020/8940– 1171,* WEB *www.kew.org.* 🎟 *£5.* ☉ *Gardens Apr.–Oct., weekdays 10– 6, weekends, 9:30–7:30; greenhouse Apr.–Oct., daily 9:30–5:30; Nov.– Mar., daily 10–4. Tube: Kew Gardens.*

Kew Palace. To this day quietly domestic, Kew Palace remains the smallest royal palace in the land. The palace house and gardens offer a glimpse into the 17th century. ⊠ *Kew Gardens.*

NEED A
BREAK?
Maids of Honour (⊠ 288 Kew Rd.), the most traditional of Old English tearooms, is named for the famous tarts invented here and still baked by hand on the premises. Tea is served in the afternoon, Tuesday–Saturday 2:45–5:30.

Richmond

Named after the palace Henry VII built here in 1500, Richmond is still a welcoming and extremely pretty riverside "village," with many handsome (and expensive) houses, antiques shops, a Victorian theater, London's grandest stately home, and, best of all, the largest of London's royal parks.

Sights to See

★ **Ham House.** Ham House stands to the west of Richmond Park, overlooking the Thames and nearly opposite the oddly named Eel Pie Island. The house was built in 1610 by Sir Thomas Vavasour, knight marshal to James I, then refurbished later the same century by the Duke and Duchess of Lauderdale, who, although not particularly nice (a contemporary called the duchess "the coldest friend and the most violent enemy that ever was known"), managed to produce one of the finest houses in Britain at the time. Now that £2 million has been sunk into restoring Ham House—a project overseen by the National Trust—its splendor can be appreciated afresh. The formerly empty library has been filled with 17th- and 18th-century volumes; the original decorations in the Great Hall, Round Gallery, and Great Staircase have been replicated; and all the furniture and fittings, on permanent loan from the V&A, have been cleaned and restored. The 17th-century gardens merit a visit in their own right. You can reach Ham from Richmond on Bus 65 or 371, or by one of Greater London's most pleasant rural walks, lasting half an hour or so, along the eastern riverbank south from Richmond Bridge. ⊠ *Ham St.,* ☎ *020/8940–1950,* WEB *www.guidetorich-*

mond.co.uk. ✉ *House £5, gardens free.* ⊙ *House Mar.–Oct., Sat.–Wed. 1–5; gardens daily 10:30–dusk. Tube: Richmond.*

Marble Hill House. On the northern bank of the Thames, almost opposite Ham House, stands another mansion, this one a near-perfect example of a Palladian villa. Marble Hill House was built in the 1720s by George II for his mistress, the "exceedingly respectable and respected" Henrietta Howard. Later the house was occupied by Mrs. Fitzherbert, who was secretly married to the Prince Regent (later George IV) in 1785. Marble Hill House was restored in 1901 and opened to the public two years later, looking very much like it did in Georgian times. A ferry service operates during the summer from Ham House across the river; access by foot is a half-hour walk south along the west bank from Richmond Bridge. ⊠ *Richmond Rd., Twickenham,* ☎ *020/8892–5115.* ✉ *£3.30.* ⊙ *Apr.–Sept., daily 10–6; Oct.–Mar., Wed.–Sun. 10–4. Tube: Richmond.*

⟲ **Richmond Park.** Charles I enclosed this one in 1637 for hunting purposes, as with practically all the other parks. Unlike the others, however, Richmond Park still has wild red and fallow deer roaming its 2,470 acres of grassland and heath and the oldest oaks you're likely to see—vestiges of the forests that encroached on London from all sides in medieval times. White Lodge, inside the park, was built for George II in 1729. Edward VIII was born here; now it houses the Royal Ballet School. You can walk from the park past the fine 18th-century houses in and around Richmond Hill to the river, admiring first the view from the top. At the Thames, you may notice Quinlan Terry's recent Richmond Riverside development, which met with the approval of England's architectural adviser, Prince Charles, for its classical facades and was vilified by many others for playing it safe. *Tube: Richmond.*

NEED A BREAK? | The **Cricketers** (⊠ Maids of Honour Row, Richmond Green, ☎ 020/8940–4372) serves a good pub lunch. The modern, partially glass-roofed **Caffé Mamma** (⊠ 24 Hill St., ☎ 020/8940–1625) is a good spot for inexpensive Italian food.

★ **Syon House.** Home to Their Graces the Duke and Duchess of Northumberland, this is one of England's most sumptuous stately houses; it has recently been renovated, and it is certainly the only one that's reachable by the London Underground. Several tube stops away from the center city on the District Line, the house is set in a 55-acre park landscaped by Capability Brown. The core of the house is Tudor—two of Henry VIII's queens, Catherine Howard and Lady Jane Grey, made pit stops here before they were sent to the Tower—but the house was redone in the Georgian style in 1761 by famed decorator Robert Adam. He had just returned from studying the sites of classical antiquity in Italy and created two rooms here worthy of any Caesar: the entryway is an amazing study in black and white, pairing neoclassic marbles with antique bronzes, while the Ante-Room contains 12 enormous verdantique columns surmounted by statues of gold—this, no less, was meant to be a waiting room for the duke's servants and retainers. The Red Drawing Room is covered with crimson Spitalfields silk, while the Long Gallery is one of Adam's noblest creations (it was used by Cary Grant and Robert Mitchum for a duel in the 1958 film *The Grass is Greener*). Elsewhere on the grounds are a nature center, a butterfly house, and a Victorian glass conservatory that is famous among connoisseurs for its Victorian charm. ⊠ *Syon Park, Brentford,* ☎ *020/8560–0881,* WEB *www.guidetorichmond.co.uk.* ✉ *£6.25.* ⊙ *House early Apr.–late Oct., Wed.–Thurs. and Sun. 11–5; gardens daily 10–dusk. Tube: Gunnersbury, then take Bus 237 or 267 to Brentlea stop.*

Hampton Court Palace

★ Some 20 mi from central London, on a loop of the Thames upstream from Richmond, stands one of London's oldest royal palaces, more like a small town in size and requiring a day of your time to do it justice. The magnificent Tudor brick house was begun in 1514 by Cardinal Wolsey, the ambitious and worldly lord chancellor (roughly, prime minister) of England and archbishop of York. He wanted it to be the absolute best palace in the land, and in this he succeeded so effectively that Henry VIII grew deeply envious, whereupon Wolsey felt obliged to give Hampton Court to the king. Henry moved in in 1525, adding a great hall and chapel, and proceeded to live much of his rambunctious life here. James I made further improvements at the beginning of the 17th century, but by the end of the century the palace was getting rather run-down. Plans were drawn up by the joint monarchs William III and Mary II to demolish the building and replace it with a still larger and more splendid structure, in conscious emulation of the great palace of Versailles outside Paris. However, the royal purse wouldn't stretch quite that far. It was decided to keep the original buildings but add a new complex adjoining them at the rear, for which Wren was commissioned, and his graceful south wing is one of the highlights of the whole palace. (A serious fire badly damaged some of Wren's chambers in 1986, but they were restored and opened again in 1992, with some of the Tudor features he had covered up uncovered again.) William and, especially, Mary loved Hampton Court and left their mark on the place—see their fine collections of Delftware and other porcelain.

The site beside the slow-moving Thames is perfect. The palace itself—steeped in history, hung with priceless paintings, full of echoing, cobbled courtyards and cavernous Tudor kitchens (complete with deer pies and cooking pots), not to mention the ghost of Catherine Howard screaming her innocence of adultery to an unheeding Henry VIII—is set in a fantastic array of ornamental gardens, lakes, and ponds. Among the horticultural highlights are an Elizabethan knot garden, Henry VIII's Pond Garden, the enormous conical yews around the Fountain Garden, and the Great Vine near the Banqueting House, planted in 1768 and still producing black Hamburg grapes, which you can buy in season. Best of all is the celebrated maze, which you enter to the north of the palace. It was planted in 1714 and is truly fiendish.

Royalty ceased living here with George III; poor George preferred the seclusion of Kew, where he was finally confined in his madness. The private apartments that range down one side of the palace are now occupied by pensioners of the Crown. Known as "grace and favor" apartments, they are among the most coveted homes in the country, with a surfeit of peace and history on their doorsteps. ⊠ *East Molesey,* ☎ *020/8977-8441,* WEB *www.hrp.org.uk.* ✆ *Apartments and maze £10.50, maze alone £2.30, grounds free.* ☉ *State apartments Apr.–Oct., Tues.–Sun. 9:30–6, Mon. 10:15–6; Nov.–Mar., Tues.–Sun. 9:30–4:30, Mon. 10:15–4:30; grounds daily 7–dusk. British Rail: Hampton Court Station from Waterloo or Tube: Richmond, then bus R68.*

2 DINING

No longer would Somerset Maugham be justified in warning, "If you want to eat well in England, have breakfast three times a day." Cool Britannia is now one of the hottest places around for restaurants of every cultural flavor, with London at its hip epicenter. Nearly everyone is passionate about food—even Lord Lloyd Webber, composer of *Cats* and *Phantom of the Opera*, has added restaurant critic to his expanding repertoire of roles. After feasting on modern British cuisine, visit one (or two or three) of London's fabulous pubs for a nightcap. Hit the right one on the right night and watch that legendary British reserve melt away.

AS ANYONE WHO READS the Sunday papers knows, London has had a restaurant boom or, rather, a restaurant atomic explosion. Natives are wondering: How far can this thing go? How many new, trendy, talked-out, flavor-of-the-month gastrodomes can the city support? Even the recent economic tightening of belts hasn't slowed the onslaught. More than ever, London loves its restaurants— all 9,000 of them—from its be-there, wow-factor eateries to its tiny neighborhood joints, from pubs where young foodniks find their feet to swank trendsetters where celebrity chefs launch their ego flights. You, too, will be smitten, since you will be spending, on average, 25% of your travel budget on eating out.

Updated by
Alex Wijeratna

To appreciate London's rise in the culinary firmament, it helps to recall that at one time it was understood that the British ate to live while the French lived to eat. Change was slow in coming after the Second World War, when steamed puddings and overboiled sprouts were still consumed on a daily basis by tweed-and-flannel-wrapped Brits. When people thought of British cuisine, fish-and-chips came to mind. The latter was a grab-and-gulp dish that tasted best wrapped in newspaper (a spoilsport bureaucracy decreed that this wasn't sanitary, so the days of peeping at the latest murder news through a film of oil came to an end). Then there was always shepherd's pie, ubiquitously available in pubs—though not made, according to the song from *Sweeney Todd,* "with real shepherd in it." Visitors used to arrive in London and joke that the most compelling reason Britain conquered half the world was that its residents probably wanted some decent food. Didn't Britain invade Rajasthan just for a good curry?

Today, everything on the culinary front has been transformed. London has caught up as a major food city. New menus evolve every five minutes as chefs outdo each other in creating hot spots that are all about the buzz of "being there." London's restaurant renaissance is credited to innovative chefs and inspired entrepreneurs. Sir Terence Conran began it all with Quaglino's, the first of the megarestaurants. His 480-seater Mezzo became the biggest restaurant in Europe when it opened in 1995, though he has since topped that with Bluebird, complete with grocery store, fishmonger, florist, and food market. His shiny Aurora and elegant Sartoria in Savile Row are the latest additions to the string.

The greatest ambition, though, probably belonged to Marco Pierre White; unfortunately for genius hunters, he has hung up his pans for good, although his empire is everywhere: the Criterion, Mirabelle, Titanic, Quo Vadis, the Oak Room, and the MPW brasserie in Hampstead, are all his creations. Another empire builder who has been going the other way is super-chef Jean-Christophe Novelli. He's downsized; pulling back from running three establishments to concentrate on just one, Maison Novelli, in Clerkenwell.

There are moves on the haute cuisine scene, too. La Tante Claire made a successful transition to the Berkeley Hotel in Knightsbridge, and its old premises have been taken over by master chef Gordon Ramsay. There are, of course, many more stars of this new celebrity category (restaurateurs and chefs); you can read about all of them when you get here by picking up any newspaper. To keep up with the changes, each has reviewers aplenty. Read up on the newest places in the food supplements of the newspapers, especially the Saturday and Sunday editions.

Fortunately, London also does a good job of catering to people interested more in satisfying their appetites without breaking the bank than in following the latest food trends. We have tried to strike a balance in our listings between these extremes, and we've included hip and happening places, neighborhood spots, ethnic alternatives, and old favorites. There are about 80 cuisines on offer in London, and ethnic restaurants have always been a good bet here, especially the thousands of Indian restaurants, since Londoners see a good curry as their birthright. Londoners are busy enlarging their purview to encompass Malaysian, Spanish, and Turkish places, a drove of Thai and Vietnamese restaurants, a new North African pack, and a wave of Japanese and Jewish places. With all this going on, traditional British food, when you track it down, appears as one more exotic cuisine in the pantheon.

As for cost, the democratization of restaurants does not necessarily mean smaller checks, and London is not an inexpensive city. A modest meal for two can cost £100 ($145). Damage-control strategies include making lunch your main meal—the top places have bargain lunch menus, halving the price of evening à la carte—and ordering a second appetizer instead of an entrée, to which few places object. (Note that an appetizer, usually known as a "starter" or "first course," is sometimes called an "entrée," as it is in France, and an entrée in England is dubbed the "main course" or simply "mains.") Seek out fixed-price menus, and watch for hidden extras on the check: cover, bread, or vegetables charged separately, and service. Many restaurants exclude service charges from the menu (which the law obliges them to display outside), then add 10%–15% to the check, or else stamp SERVICE NOT INCLUDED along the bottom, in which case you should add the 10%–15% yourself. Don't pay twice for service—unscrupulous restaurateurs may add service, then leave the total on the credit-card slip blank, hoping for more.

Two final caveats: First, although the chance of contracting so-called Mad Cow Disease is small, you may wish to avoid eating beef or to select beef with a reduced risk of contamination. For more information, *see* Health *in* Smart Travel Tips A to Z. Second, beware of Sundays. Many restaurants are closed, especially in the evening; likewise public holidays. Over the Christmas period, London virtually shuts down—only hotels will be prepared to feed you. When in doubt, call ahead. It's a good idea to book a table at all times, but you'll have gotten the idea by now.

For approximate costs, *see* the dining price chart *in* Smart Travel Tips A to Z.

Mayfair

AMERICAN/CASUAL

££–£££ ✗ **Smollensky's on the Strand.** This American-style bar-restaurant is useful for those with children in tow, especially at lunch on weekends, when the young are fed burgers, fish sticks, and "Kids' Koktails" and are taken off your hands by sundry clowns and magicians. The grownups' menu favors (fresh, additive-free) red meat, with several cuts of steak, the specialty, all served with fries and a choice of sauces. There are potato skins, salads, sandwiches, and fish—from everywhere from New England to New Mexico—and a couple of vegetarian choices. ⊠ *105 The Strand, W1,* ☎ *020/7497–2101. AE, DC, MC, V. Tube: Charing Cross.*

£ ✗ **Condotti.** In a neighborhood not known for its casual dining options, this elegant pizzeria is like a breath of fresh air. Anyone familiar with Pizza Express will know the menu already—because this also belongs to the founder of that chain. The Veneziana (with onions, pine nuts, sultanas, and capers) is everyone's fave, and a donation goes to the Venice in Peril Fund when you order it. Or try the King Edward, with a

London Dining *(Boxes Refer to Detail Maps)*

Hampstead and Camden Town

Regent's Park

Maida Vale

Abbey Rd.

Abercorn Pl.

Grove End Rd.

Hall Rd.

Wellington Rd.

Circus Rd.

St. John's Wood Rd.

Prince Albert Rd.

Outer Circle

Inner Circle

Chester Rd.

Albany St.

Hampstead Rd.

Eus... Sta...

Euston Rd.

Clifton Rd.

Bloomfield Rd.

Lisson Grove

Edgware Rd.

Park Rd.

Marylebone Rd.

Baker St.

Gloucester St.

Harley St.

Portland Pl.

Gt. Portland St.

Tottenham...

Harrow Rd.

Marylebone Flyover

Seymour Pl.

Edgware Rd.

Paddington Station

Sussex Gdns.

Bishop's Br. Rd.

Bayswater Rd.

Mayfair, St. James's, Soho, Covent Garden, and Bloomsbury

Oxford St.

Oxford Circus

Oxfor...

Oxford St.

Grosvenor Square

Brook St.

Bond St.

Grosvenor St.

Regent St.

Kensington and Notting Hill Gate

Berkeley Square

Jermyn St...

Hyde Park

Kensington Gardens

The Serpentine

Park Lane

Piccadilly

Green Park

Constitution Hill

W. Carriage

S. Carriage Rd.

Kensington Rd.

Kensington Gore

Kensington Rd.

Knightsbridge

Grosvenor Pl.

Royal Albert Hall

Prince Consort Rd.

Sloane St.

Belgrave Square

Buckingham Palace Rd.

Victoria Station

Vi...

Gloucester Rd.

Queen's Gate

Exhibition Rd.

Brompton Rd.

Pont St.

Cadogan Pl.

Eaton Square

Wilton Rd.

Cromwell Rd.

Old Brompton Rd.

Sloane Ave.

Sloane Sq.

Pimlico Rd.

Warwick Way

Fulham Rd.

Sydney St.

King's Rd.

Royal Hospital Rd.

Chelsea Br. Rd.

Lupus...

Old Church St.

Oakley St.

Cheyne Walk

Chelsea Embankment

Grosvenor

Albert Br.

River Thames

Battersea Park

South Kensington, Knightsbridge, and Chelsea

King's Cross Station

St. Pancras Station

Pentonville Rd.

City Rd.

King's Cross Rd.

Gray's Inn Rd.

Rosebery Ave.

St. John's St.

Goswell Rd.

East Road

Hoxton St.

Old Gt. Eastern St.

Old St.

Coram's Fields

Judd St.

Woburn Pl.

Southampton Row

Guilford St.

Theobald's Rd.

Clerkenwell Rd.

The City and the South Bank

Liverpool St. Station

London Wall

Moorgate

City Rd.

Bishopsgate

Gower St.

Gt. Russell

Court Rd.

New Oxford St.

High Holborn

Kingsway

Drury Ln.

Charing Cross Rd.

Shaftesbury Ave.

Holborn Viaduct

Newgate St.

Old Bailey

Fleet St.

Law Courts

Adwych

Strand

Victoria

Embankment

Cheapside

Cornhill

Leadenhall St.

Gracechurch St.

Fenchurch St.

Queen Victoria St.

Cannon St.

Cannon St. Station

Blackfriars Station

Blackfriars Br.

Southwark Br.

London Br.

Lower Thames St.

River Thames

market

Regent St.

Piccadilly Circus

Hay

Mall

The Mall

Whitehall

St. James's Park

Waterloo Br.

Charing Cross Stn.

South Bank Arts Complex

Stamford St.

Southwark St.

Tooley St.

London Bridge Station

ge Walk

Westminster Br.

York Rd.

The Cut

Waterloo Station

Blackfriars Rd.

Union St.

Borough High St.

Westminster Br. Rd.

Borough Rd.

London Rd.

New Kent Rd.

St.

Horseferry Rd.

Millbank

Lambeth Br.

Lambeth Palace Rd.

Lambeth Rd.

Kennington Rd.

Imperial War Museum

Walworth Rd.

Regency St.

Tate Gallery

hall Br.

Rd.

Vauxhall Br.

Albert Embankment

Kennington Ln.

Kennington Park Rd.

Vauxhall Station

Kennington Oval

ne Elms Ln.

Rd.

N

0   1 mile

0   1 km

Dining in Mayfair, St. James's, Soho, Covent Garden, and Bloomsbury

potato base instead of bread, and check out the Paolozzis on the walls. ⊠ *4 Mill St., W1,* ☎ *020/7499–1308. AE, DC, MC, V. Tube: Oxford Circus.*

CONTEMPORARY

££–£££   ✕ **Greenhouse.** Tucked away behind the Mayfair mansions in a cute, cobbled mews is this elegant salon for people who like their food big and strong. You sit among extravagant topiary and men in black—with chauffeurs to match—to partake of modern British cuisine wider in influence than that of the now-departed, famous-from-TV chef Gary Rhodes: sea bass sag aloo, onion bhargee, and mushroom risotto. ⊠ *27A Hay's Mews, W1,* ☎ *020/7499–3331. Reservations essential. AE, DC, MC, V. No lunch Sat. Tube: Green Park.*

ENGLISH

£–££   ✕ **Browns.** Unpretentious, crowd-pleasing, child-friendly English feeding is accomplished at the former establishment of the bespoke tailors Messrs. Cooling and Wells, now converted to Edwardian style by the group behind the very successful regional Browns eateries (the Oxford and Cambridge ones are student standbys). The classic Browns steak and Guinness pie is still on the menu, but king prawns, lamb shanks, roasted peppers, salads, and pastas now predominate. ⊠ *47 Maddox St., W1,* ☎ *020/7491–4565. AE, DC, MC, V. Tube: Oxford Circus.*

FRENCH

££££   ✕ **Claridge's Restaurant.** This restaurant is emerging as a tower of quality in the fickle-fashion London dining scene. Go for the OTT Art Deco dining room with its Hercule Poirot/Dame Barbara Cartland ambience: pistol pinks, gaudy gilts, palms, and mirrors. (Dame Barbara dined at the table by the door for 50 years.) The service, from another age, is impeccable. If you can, sit in the "Royal Box"—a lucky alcove for kings and presidents. The sophisticated French menu includes dishes such as meaty canard with Morello cherries, squab with fig, and foie gras. Arrive early for dinner and grab a drink at the Art Deco bar—it's the coolest cocktail lounge in London. Afternoon tea is taken daily and a Hungarian quartet plays in the foyer. ⊠ *Claridge Hotel, Brook St., W1,* ☎ *020/7629–8860. Reservations essential. Jacket and tie. AE, DC, MC, V. Tube: Bond Street.*

££££   ✕ **The Connaught.** This charming and grand mahogany-paneled, vel-
★   vet-upholstered, and crystal-chandeliered dining room belongs to the absolutely exclusive eponymous hotel. Waiters wear tails, tables must be booked far in advance, and prices are fearsome; but the restaurant remains London's most-respected traditional dining room, with famed French chef Michel Bourdin still in charge of the kitchens after more than a quarter of a century. There is nothing wild here, only the mushrooms and fabulous game—venison, guinea fowl, pigeon (not local birds)—presented with traditional trimmings. "Luncheon dishes" from the trolley follow a pattern according to the day of the week (if this is Wednesday, it must be beef) and are not as exorbitant as they seem at first, because the price includes a starter and dessert. The table d'hôte changes daily. The Connaught is by no means a fashionable place, but it is never out of fashion. ⊠ *Carlos Pl., W1,* ☎ *020/7499–7070. Reservations essential. Jacket and tie. AE, DC, MC, V. Tube: Green Park.*

££££   ✕ **Le Gavroche.** Albert Roux's son, Michel, retains many of his father's
★   "capital C" Classical dishes and has added his own style to this place, once considered London's finest restaurant. The basement dining room is comfortable and sedate, pleasing only if your idea of riveting decor is low-ceilinged and accented with potted plants and bland modern paintings. The set lunch is relatively affordable at £38.50 (for canapés and three courses, plus mineral water, a half-bottle of wine, coffee, and pe-

tits fours). In fact, it's the only way to eat here if you don't have an expense account at your disposal—which most patrons do. You must reserve at least one week in advance. ✉ *43 Upper Brook St., W1,* ☎ *020/7408–0881. Reservations essential. Jacket and tie. AE, DC, MC, V. Closed weekends and 10 days at Christmas. Tube: Marble Arch.*

££££ ✕ **Oak Room.** Marco Pierre White used to enjoy Jaggeresque fame from
★ his TV appearances and gossip-column reports of his complicated love life, feuds, and eruptions of fury. Sadly, MPW no longer cooks here at the restaurant of Le Meridien Piccadilly, which enjoys one of London's most spectacular settings—all Belle Epoque soaring ceilings and gilded bits—and palms, not to mention the crisp napery and batteries of flatware. ✉ *Le Meridien, 21 Piccadilly, W1,* ☎ *020/7437–0202. Reservations essential. AE, DC, MC, V. Tube: Piccadilly Circus.*

££££ ✕ **The Square.** Philip Howard's sophisticated set menus are in the
★ French haute tradition, with ideas from all over grafted on. Among the starters you'll find such dishes as roast foie gras with caramelized endive and late-picked muscat grapes or crab lasagne with shellfish and basil, followed perhaps by an herb-crusted saddle of lamb with shallot puree, or a steamed turbot with langoustine and champagne sauce. All are arranged carefully and symmetrically, much like the high-ceiling, marble-effect room. The grown-up clientele is heavy on business types who appreciate impeccable service, complete with a friendly (and necessary—the wine list has the heft of a novel) sommelier. ✉ *6–10 Bruton St., W1,* ☎ *020/7495–7100. Reservations essential. AE, DC, MC, V. No lunch weekends. Tube: Green Park.*

£££ ✕ **Chez Nico at Ninety Park Lane.** Those with refined palates and deep pockets would be well advised not to miss Nico Ladenis's exquisite cuisine, served in this suitably hushed, plush Louis XV dining room next to the Grosvenor House Hotel. Autodidact Nico is one of the world's great chefs, and he's famous for knowing it. The menu is stately, with heavenly light touches. There is no salt on the tables—ask for some at your peril. It's all more affordable in daylight, when you can choose from set lunch menus (£25 for three courses). ✉ *90 Park La., W1,* ☎ *020/7409–1290. Reservations essential. Jacket and tie. AE, DC, MC, V. Closed Sun., no lunch Sat. Tube: Marble Arch.*

££–£££ ✕ **L'Odéon.** This contribution to London's mania for giant restaurants is in a former airline office, its long, low dimensions peculiarly reminiscent of an aircraft, despite the gauzy partitions throughout. Food is elevated French bistro–style with the usual modish Italian additions—grilled fish and meats, wild mushrooms on brioche toast—and is far more affordable in set-menu form, available for lunch and before 7 PM. Tables by the huge arched windows are fun for people-watching. ✉ *65 Regent St., W1,* ☎ *020/7287–1400. AE, DC, MC, V. Tube: Piccadilly Circus.*

££–£££ ✕ **Mirabelle.** This is Marco Pierre White doing what he does best—
★ taking over an age-old establishment, licking it into shape, and turning its fortunes around. The decor is in-your-face lavish, while the food is an excellent interpretation of French with a hint of Italian, with fewer frills on the price. Magical seafood abounds, and some meat creations are remarkable (steak with snails). The range of chocolate desserts is absolutely gutsy. ✉ *56 Curzon St., W1,* ☎ *020/7499–4636. Reservations essential. AE, DC, MC, V. Tube: Green Park.*

££ ✕ **Criterion.** This spectacular, neo-Byzantine mirrored marble hall, which first opened in 1874, is heavy on the awe factor, with dishes to match, and Marco Pierre White's team scores highly. He doesn't cook here, but some of his well-known and often-copied dishes appear on a menu whose divisions include one headed "Farinaceous Dishes"— where you'll find his ballotine of salmon with herbs and *fromage blanc,* for instance. The glamour of the soaring golden ceiling, peacock-blue theater-size drapes, oil paintings, and attentive Gallic service adds up to an elegant night out. ⊠ *Piccadilly Circus, W1,* ☎ *020/7930–0488. AE, DC, MC, V. Tube: Piccadilly Circus.*

INDIAN

££££ ✗ **Tamarind.** Tamarind led the new wave of '90s Indian restaurants and seems to be keeping up the pace. The ambience in this Emily Todhunter–designed Mayfair basement is best described as sumptuous. This is a chic curry spot, with golden arches, framed textiles, gilded staircases, and copper plates. It's exorbitantly expensive, but dishes like *hare maselaeki machchi* (salmon with wispy deep-fried spinach) and creamy *dal bukhari* (black lentils from the northwest frontier) are executed with precision. Try the puddings—they're sweet and good (which doesn't always apply to service). Many say Tamarind does some of the best curry in London, and lots of posh Indians eat here. ⊠ *20 Queen St., W1,* ☎ *020/7629–3561. AE, DC, MC, V. Tube: Green Park.*

IRISH

££ ✗ **Mulligans.** Mulligans is straight out of Dublin, down to the draught Guinness. Downstairs, in the upscale restaurant, order traditional dishes such as roasted partridge and chestnuts or Irish stew with homey accompaniments like "champ and colcannon" (buttery mashed potatoes with cabbage), then a big rice pudding brûlée with whiskey-soused prunes. ⊠ *13–14 Cork St., W1,* ☎ *020/7409–1370. AE, DC, MC, V. Closed Sun., no lunch Sat. Tube: Green Park.*

JAPANESE

£££–££££ ✗ **Nobu.** Nobuyaki Matsuhisa already has New York, Tokyo, Malibu, Milan, Aspen, and Los Angeles, and now he's taken London—and with the same formula of new-style sashimi with a Peruvian influence (such as salmon, ever so slightly seared in sesame oil), plus the famous *omakase* (chef's choice) meals. Nobu is in the Metropolitan, one of London's hippest hotels, with staff, attitude, clientele, and prices to match, and a minimalissimo decor. Ubon, a sister restaurant, (backwards for "Nobu") has opened in Canary Wharf. ⊠ *Metropolitan Hotel, 19 Old Park La., W1,* ☎ *020/7447–4747. Reservations essential. AE, DC, MC, V. No lunch weekends. Tube: Hyde Park.*

LATIN

££ ✗ **Down Mexico Way.** London is warming up to Latin American food, and here among the usual tortillas are a few (somewhat overpriced) adventurous numbers, such as tuna with peach salsa or chicken with cocoa and chili. Look for the beautiful Spanish ceramic tiles. Avoid evenings here if you want a quiet night out—the place is often taken over by party animals. ⊠ *25 Swallow St., W1,* ☎ *020/7437–9895. AE, DC, MC, V. Tube: Piccadilly Circus.*

St. James's

CONTEMPORARY

£££ ✗ **The Avenue.** Huge, loud, and swanky, especially since it got permission to ply its City-glitzy clientele with beverages way beyond its bedtime (here that's until 1 AM Monday–Saturday), this was London's first restaurant to be owned by committee. Unlike the horse designed by committee (a camel), it has worked out fairly well, emulating New York singles-heavy, dining-as-theater glamour, with a long, rose-pink uplighted glass bar. The food is pretty good, generic Euro-Brit with the usual rash of Mediterranean-vegetarian starters and sides. Set menus are competitively priced, but the content does not always deliver, although the service is friendly. ⊠ *7–9 St. James's St., SW1,* ☎ *020/7321–2111. AE, DC, MC, V. Tube: Green Park.*

£££ ✗ **Quaglino's.** Now well into its first decade, Sir Terence Conran's original huge restaurant, "Quags," is *the* out-of-towners' posttheater or celebration destination, while Londoners like its late hours. To the cognoscenti it's *history*, but the aura never fails to impress first-timers. The gigantic sunken restaurant boasts a glamorous staircase, "Crustacea Altar," large bar, and live jazz music. The food is fashionably pan-European with some Asian trimmings—crab with mirin and soy; grilled tuna with black bean and lime; and scallops with bacon, chorizo, and onion cream. Desserts come from somewhere between the Paris bistro and the English nursery, and wine from the Old World and the New, some bottles at modest prices. ✉ *16 Bury St., SW1,* ☎ *020/7930–6767. Reservations essential. AE, DC, MC, V. Tube: Green Park.*

££–£££ ✗ **Le Caprice.** Secreted in a small street behind the Ritz, Le Caprice may
★ command the deepest loyalty of any restaurant in London because it gets everything right: the glamorous, glossy black Eva Jiricna interior; the perfect pitch of the informal but respectful service; the menu, halfway between Euro-peasant and fashion plate. This food—crispy duck and watercress salad; seared scallops with bacon and sorrel; risotto *nero* (with squid); calves' liver with caramelized shallots, mash, and sage; grilled rabbit with black-olive polenta; and divine desserts, too—has no business being so good, because the other reason everyone comes here is that everyone else does, which leads to the best people-watching in town (apart from at its sister restaurant, the Ivy). ✉ *Arlington House, Arlington St., SW1,* ☎ *020/7629–2239. Reservations essential. AE, DC, MC, V. Tube: Green Park.*

CONTINENTAL

££££ ✗ **The Ritz.** Constantly accused of being one of London's prettiest dining rooms, this Belle Epoque palace of marble, gilt, and trompe l'oeil would moisten even Marie Antoinette's eye; add the view over Green Park and the Ritz's secret sunken garden, and it seems beside the point to consider eating. But the British-French cuisine stands up to the visual onslaught, with costly morsels (foie gras, lobster, truffles, caviar, etc.) that are superrich, all served with a flourish. Old retainers still take great pride in this smooth operation and are still here despite the hotel's change of ownership. Englishness is wrested from Louis XVI by a daily roast "from the trolley." A three-course luncheon menu at £35 and a four-course dinner at £51 make the check more bearable, but the wine list is pricey. Friday and Saturday dinner-dances sweetly maintain a dying tradition. ✉ *150 Piccadilly, W1,* ☎ *020/7493–8181. Reservations essential. Jacket and tie. AE, DC, MC, V. Tube: Green Park.*

ENGLISH

£–£££ ✗ **The Fountain.** At the back of Fortnum & Mason is this old-fash-
★ ioned restaurant, as frumpy and popular as a boarding-school matron, serving delicious light meals, toasted snacks, and ice-cream sodas. During the day, go for the Welsh rarebit or Fortnum's steak-and-ale pie; in the evening, a no-frills rump steak is a typical option. It's just the place for afternoon tea and ice-cream sundaes after the Royal Academy or Bond Street shopping, and for pretheater meals. ✉ *181 Piccadilly, W1,* ☎ *020/7734–8040. AE, DC, MC, V. Closed Sun. Tube: Green Park.*

FRENCH

£££–££££ ✗ **L'Oranger.** This offshoot of Aubergine in Chelsea follows a similar
★ route of French-Mediterranean cuisine. The dishes can reach gobsmacking precision and perfection: a ravioli of lamb and tomato consommé; monkfish tail wrapped in crushed black pepper, spinach, and *antiboise* (tomato, olive oil, and basil) sauce; roast fig tartelette with spiced pear and cinnamon ice cream. The conservatory room with its

train of tables up the middle is romantic, plus there's a little courtyard where the last duel in London was fought. The all-French waiters are courteous and not snobby. ⊠ *5 St. James's St., SW1,* ☎ *020/7839-3774. Reservations essential. AE, DC, MC, V. Closed Sun., no lunch Sat. Tube: Green Park.*

£££ ✗ **Morton's.** If you're near Mayfair's clubland of Berkeley Square and require an elegant meal, try Morton's. On the north side of this beautiful square, the first-floor dining room is considered one of the most serene in London, and the classic cooking proves worthy of the setting. It's not cheap, mind you, not for a starter of escalope of foie gras with muscat grapes, walnuts, and dandelion; a simple entrée of risotto of wild mushrooms; or the tournedos Rossini (excellent though it may be). Downstairs is a raucous members-only bar. Watch out for foxy Mayfair ladies of a certain age, roué business brokers, and cufflinked wise guys. ⊠ *28 Berkeley Sq., W1,* ☎ *020/7493-7171. Reservations essential. AE, DC, MC, V. Tube: Green Park.*

LATIN

££ ✗ **Gaucho Grill.** Some say these are the best steaks in London, but that's probably overstating it. Nevertheless, this chain of four Argentinian chophouses (the other locations are Canary Wharf, Hampstead, and the City) are reasonably priced and unreconstructed in their reverence for meat. The steaks are flown vacuum packed from Buenos Aires, and are cut to order. The biggest they've grilled is 1.8 kg (4 lbs!), but standard sizes are 225 g and 300 g (8 oz and 10½ oz). There is not much for vegetarians, but it's great for a beef fix. ⊠ *19 Swallow St., W1,* ☎ *020/7734-4040. AE, DC, MC, V. Tube: Piccadilly Circus.*

NORTH AFRICAN

££ ✗ **Momo.** Momo is one of the hottest tickets in town. If you can book a table, go. Algerian-born Mourad Mazouz—Momo to his friends—has stormed beau London with his casbah-like, Moroccan-inspired North African restaurant, set in a cul-de-sac behind Regent Street. Going Momo is a real experience. The seats are low and placed close together, there's a resident DJ and often live music. North African music troupes sometimes work their way among the awestruck diners. Downstairs is the hot and souk-like members-only Kemia Bar, and next door is Mô—a Moroccan tearoom, open to all. The restaurant menu, which is based on pastilla, tagine, and couscous, doesn't quite match the excitement of the place; lamb merguez is recommended. Luckily, the restaurant CD, *Arabesque,* is now on sale. ⊠ *25 Heddon St., W1,* ☎ *020/7434-4040. Reservations essential. AE, DC, MC, V. Tube: Piccadilly Circus.*

SEAFOOD

££ ✗ **Zinc Bar & Grill.** This brasserie-rotisserie, off Regent Street, is fun
★ and underrated. It has an open (zinc) bar that heaves with music and PR girls. Try a dozen rock oysters, a juicy *plateau de fruit de mer* (seafood platter), or calves' liver with bacon and gravy. Or sip a "Pink Zinc"—champagne and raspberry liqueur. There are good pretheater and prix-fixe deals. ⊠ *21 Heddon St., W1,* ☎ *020/7255-8899. AE, DC, MC, V. Tube: Piccadilly Circus.*

Soho

CAFÉS

£ ✗ **Maison Bertaux.** On two floors in central Soho, this French patisserie is not in the least dainty, but it is the kind of place to refuel after a shopping trek, with a savory pastry at lunchtime, a Danish mid-morning, or even an early supper (it closes at 8 PM). The ancient rivalry with Valerie, around the corner, continues. ⊠ *28 Greek St., W1,* ☎ *020/7437-6007. No credit cards. Tube: Leicester Sq.*

£ ✕ **Patisserie Valerie.** Beloved of film-biz people, students, shoppers, and just about everyone else, this dark and antique pastry shop and café is cherished because nothing has changed in years. The cakes are wondrous creations; just to drool at the window is to enter a chocoholic's paradise. Valerie has also taken over the historic eatery called the Sagne, at 105 Marylebone High Street—the interior there has retained a French-*sud* time warp—and at the Royal Institute of British Architects, 66 Portland Place, which remains a favored spot for lunch. ⊠ *44 Old Compton St., W1,* ☎ *020/7437–3466. AE, DC, MC, V. Tube: Leicester Sq.*

CHINESE

££ ✕ **Fung Shing.** This comfortable, cool-green restaurant is a cut above ★ the Lisle–Wardour Street crowd in both service and ambience, as well as food. The usual Chinatown options are supplemented by some exciting dishes. Salt-baked chicken, served on or off the bone with an accompanying bowl of intense broth, is essential. Reserve a table in the conservatory-style back room. ⊠ *15 Lisle St., WC2,* ☎ *020/7437–1539. AE, DC, MC, V. Tube: Leicester Sq.*

CONTEMPORARY

£££ ✕ **Alastair Little.** Little is one of London's most original—and most imitated—chefs, drawing inspiration from practically everywhere (Thailand, Japan, Scandinavia, France, and North Africa, but chiefly Italy) and sometimes bringing things off brilliantly. His restaurant is provocatively stark and sparse, so all attention focuses on the menu, which changes not once but twice daily to take advantage of the best ingredients. There will certainly be fish, but beyond that it's hard to predict. Look for Little's smaller, cheaper restaurant—with the same name—next to the Ladbroke Grove Tube stop. ⊠ *49 Frith St., W1,* ☎ *020/7734–5183. AE, DC, MC, V. Closed Sun., no lunch Sat. Tube: Leicester Sq.*

££–£££ ✕ **Quo Vadis.** Here, Andy Warhols occupy the former house of Karl Marx. Downstairs in the restaurant, the kitchen is serious and good, and highlights include lobster with garlic bulbs, seafood selections, and a champagne jelly with passion fruit. Artistry does not come cheap, but there are fine fixed-price lunches for £14.50–£17.50. ⊠ *26–29 Dean St., W1,* ☎ *020/7439–4809. Reservations essential. AE, DC, MC, V. Tube: Leicester Sq., Tottenham Court Rd.*

££–£££ ✕ **Sugar Club.** David Selex is picking up well from Peter Gordon, who made his name here and introduced Londoners to Australasian fusion cooking. The fusion is still here, with dishes like buffalo *bocconcini* (mozzarella balls) and tamarillo, or lamb shanks with parsnip puree and *grimolata* (parsley, garlic, and lemon zest). It's one of those places so loved by the native chatterati that you have to reserve way ahead—two weeks in advance is recommended. ⊠ *21 Warwick St., W1,* ☎ *020/7437–7776. Reservations essential. AE, DC, MC, V. Tube: Oxford Circus, Piccadilly Circus.*

££–£££ ✕ **Titanic.** Titanic initially rode high on the crest of a media wave, yet Marco Pierre White, the noted chef who opened this—the splashiest in the tide of trend-driven dining spots—claims it was not inspired by the blockbuster film. But like the movie, this place has pulled in the crowds, plus a clientele of the young, loud, and fashionable including Peter O'Toole, the Marquess of Londonderry. Decor is Art Deco ocean liner. Dinner is fun and casual, ranging from fish-and-chips to squid-ink risotto to sticky toffee pudding; prices are lower than you'd expect for this corner of town; and there's a DJ and dancing until 3 AM on Friday and Saturday. ⊠ *81 Brewer St., W1,* ☎ *020/7437–1912. Reservations essential. AE, DC, MC, V. Tube: Piccadilly Circus.*

CONTINENTAL

££ ✗ **L'Escargot.** This ever-popular media haunt serves Anglo-French food in a ground-floor brasserie and a more formal upstairs restaurant. Reasonably priced wine from a comprehensive list sets off leg of duck and braised red cabbage, or simple poached or grilled fish. With its new face-lift, this place is relaxed and reliable. ✉ *48 Greek St., W1,* ☎ *020/7437–2679. AE, DC, MC, V. Closed Sun. Tube: Leicester Sq.*

ECLECTIC

££ ✗ **Andrew Edmunds.** You wish this always-busy, snug, softly lighted eatery were larger and the seats more forgiving. Tucked away behind Oxford and Carnaby streets, it's a favorite with the film and media bunch, who lunch on the daily-changing set menu. The place is always jammed, thanks to its talent for consistently good food at realistic prices. Starters and main courses range from a taste of Ireland through the Mediterranean to the Middle East. ✉ *46 Lexington St., W1,* ☎ *020/ 7437–5708. AE, MC, V. Tube: Oxford Circus, Piccadilly Circus.*

££ ✗ **Mezzo.** Sir Terence Conran's gargantuan 480-seater rolls on, much maligned and beloved by turns. It's not as polished as his Sartoria in Savile Row or as efficient as Zinc on Heddon Street, but young office and evening crowds still like to hang out here. Downstairs is the restaurant proper, with its huge glass-walled kitchen, Allen Jones murals, grand piano and dance floor, and its contemporary menu that includes goodies like sea bass, rabbit, and chocolate-and-ginger truffle tart. The upstairs bar overlooks an informal Southeast Asian operation called Mezzonine, where wasabi-seared tuna and bean sprouts, coconut-chicken laksa, and deep-fried bream are the order of the day. A late-night café-patisserie is next door. ✉ *100 Wardour St., W1,* ☎ *020/ 7314–4000. AE, DC, MC, V. Tube: Leicester Sq.*

FRENCH

££££ ✗ **Spoon.** London's current top groovy destination has disco vibe to it. Set in Ian Schrager's Sanderson Hotel and designed in that Salvador Dalí way by Philippe Starck, the great Frenchman Alain Ducasse's first London foray has become the place to see and be seen—if you dig that kind of thing. Diners pick 'n' mix the ingredients; ask for help, or (if money is no object) go for the chef-decides "Sexy Spoon" option (£95 a head, with wine.) The soups are sublime—frogs' leg, or potato and white truffle—and the meats are sweet, juicy, and tender. The adjacent 80-ft Long Bar is the place for wacky cocktails and checking out the stars. ✉ *Sanderson Hotel, 50 Berners St., W1,* ☎ *020/7300–1444. Reservations essential. AE, DC, MC, V. Tube: Oxford Circus.*

££–£££ ✗ **Villandry.** Heaven for food lovers, Villandry occupies a food hall lined with Italian-French dark-wood shelves. This cave of wonders positively heaves with quality—French pâtés, Continental cheeses, fruit tarts, biscuits, and breads galore are just some of the tempting offerings. If you must indulge but can't wait to take a bite, there's a tearoom café, a bar, and a fashionable dining room in which to enjoy some exquisite offerings; breakfast, lunch, and dinner are served daily. ✉ *170 Great Portland St., W1,* ☎ *020/7631–3131. AE, DC, MC, V. Tube: Great Portland St.*

ITALIAN

£ ✗ **Bar Italia.** A beloved Frith Street landmark, this caffeine and stand-up snack stop is a favorite oasis for photographers and admen, young Soho-ites, theatergoers, and clubbers—both early and late. Strong cappuccino or espresso is the order of the day, and it comes swift and sure from waiters who have seen the tides of London life come and go for years. ✉ *22 Frith St., W1,* ☎ *020/7437–4520. AE, DC, MC, V. Tube: Leicester Sq.*

£ ✕ **Pollo.** A homey, boisterous, Italian café that's been here forever, and through which all Londoners pass during their student and/or clubbing days, it's good for a quick feed with a bottle of house plonk pretheater or for an afternoon spaghetti carbonara. Watch the crowds in the evenings, though—it's no fun unless you're 18 and in art school. ⊠ *20 Old Compton St., W1,* ☎ *020/7734–5917. No credit cards. Tube: Leicester Sq.*

MALAYSIAN

£ ✕ **Melati.** What amounts to a Malaysian café with wooden tables and, usually, lines at the door is a very useful place when you don't want to spend too much but are looking for a taste thrill. Whole stuffed squid and a tofu omelet, stir-fried vegetables, and the inevitable *nasi goreng* (spicy fried rice with tiny shrimp, onions, garlic, etc.) are among the dishes. ⊠ *21 Great Windmill St., W1,* ☎ *020/7437–2745. AE, MC, V. Tube: Leicester Sq.*

MEDITERRANEAN

££ ✕ **Soho Soho.** The ground floor is a lively café-bar with a (no reservations) rotisserie, while upstairs is a more formal and expensive restaurant. Inspiration comes from Provence, both in the olive-oil cooking style and the decor, with its murals and primary colors. The rotisserie serves omelets, salads, charcuterie, and cheeses, plus a handful of such bistro dishes as suckling pig with Provinçal potatoes; fillet of silver mullet; and vanilla custard tart and berry compote. Or you can stay in the café-bar and just have a kir or a beer. ⊠ *11–13 Frith St., W1,* ☎ *020/7494–3491. AE, DC, MC, V. Tube: Leicester Sq.*

PAN-ASIAN

£ ✕ **Wok Wok.** A bright primary-color decor, friendly service, and a menu of fresh soups, noodles, stir-fries, and rice dishes from all over Asia— Thailand, Vietnam, Malaysia, China, Japan, and Indonesia—ensure that this central branch of a small chain should run on and on, especially given the reasonable cost. ⊠ *10 Frith St., W1,* ☎ *020/7437–7080. AE, DC, MC, V. Tube: Leicester Sq.*

SEAFOOD

££–£££ ✕ **Randall & Aubin.** Consultant chef Ed Baines is shredding up town
★ as London's sexiest TV chef. The former public-school boy, ex-Armani model, and small-screen gastro-hero now has two bodyguards with him when he does celebrity demonstrations. His converted French butcher's shop (with white tiles, meat hooks, and slab-marble table tops) is one of London's buzziest champagne-oyster bars—bang in the middle of Soho's sexland. Go for the Loch Fyne oysters or half a lobster with chips. Peak time, it can take 20 minutes at the bar waiting for a seat. Watch out Thursday to Saturday for the impromptu transvestite cabaret. ⊠ *16 Brewer St., W1,* ☎ *020/7287–4447. Reservations not accepted. AE, DC, MC, V. Tube: Piccadilly Circus.*

££ ✕ **Café Fish.** This cheerful, bustling restaurant has an encyclopedic selection of fish—shark and turbot join the trout, halibut, salmon, and monkfish, arranged on the menu according to cooking method (chargrilled, steamed), plus a chalkboard full of daily specials. The Mediterranean and Asian accents usually delight. Try the bar and canteen on the ground floor for a cornucopia of shellfish, while in the upstairs restaurant you can linger longer over the likes of cod and shrimp. This spot is great for pretheater. ⊠ *36–40 Rupert St., W1,* ☎ *020/7287–8989. AE, DC, MC, V. Tube: Piccadilly Circus.*

THAI

£ ✕ **busabe eathai.** This is one of the best cheap spots in Soho. It was designed as a superior Thai canteen: all around are deep bronzes, rattans, wooden benches, hardwood tables, low lights, and watercolor-paper lampshades. Diners sit at communal tables, but somehow it's still seductive. The menu overflows with noodles, curries, stir-fries, rice, and sides. Try the stir-fry chicken with butternut squash, green curry chicken with pea aubergine, or seafood vermicelli (with prawns, squid, scallops and spicy sour soup). The juices are cool too. One of busabe eathai's mantras is *gan gin gan yuu*, which means "as you eat, so you are." There's no smoking. ⊠ *106–110 Wardour St., W1,* ☎ *020/7255–8686. Reservations not accepted. AE, MC, V. Tube: Leicester Sq.*

VEGETARIAN

£   ✕ **Cranks.** This is a popular vegetarian chain—there are other branches at Great Newport Street, Adelaide Street, Canary Wharf, and Barrett Street—still serving meatless meals similar to those that put the chain on the map back in the hippie, back-to-earth 1960s. It is always crowded and, irritatingly, insists on closing at 8. Food can sometimes be hit or miss. ⊠ *9–11 Tottenham St., W1,* ☎ *020/7631–3912. Reservations not accepted. No credit cards. Closed Sun. Tube: Leicester Sq.*

Covent Garden

AMERICAN

££ ✕ **Joe Allen.** Long hours (thespians flock here after the curtains fall in
★   theaterland) and a welcoming, if loud, brick-walled interior mean New York Joe's London branch is still swinging after more than two decades. The fun, contemporary menu helps: roasted and stuffed poblano chilies and black bean soup are typical starters; entrées include barbecue ribs with black-eyed peas and London's only available corn muffins, or roast monkfish with sun-dried-tomato salsa. There are the perennial egg dishes and huge salads, too, and Yankee desserts such as grilled banana bread with ice cream and hot caramel sauce. ⊠ *13 Exeter St., WC2,,* ☎ *020/7836–0651. Reservations essential. AE, MC, V. Tube: Covent Garden.*

£   ✕ **Maxwell's.** London's first-ever burger joint, now more than a quarter-century old, cloned itself and then grew up. Here's the result, a happy place under the Royal Opera House serving the kind of food you're homesick for: quesadillas and nachos, Buffalo chicken wings, barbecued ribs, Cajun chicken, chef's salad, and a burger to die for. ⊠ *8–9 James St., WC2,* ☎ *020/7836–0303. AE, DC, MC, V. Tube: Covent Garden.*

BELGIAN

££ ✕ **Belgo Centraal.** The wackiest dining concept in town started in Camden at Belgo Noord and was so adored it was cloned uptown in a big basement space you have to enter by elevator. Have mussels and *frites* (fries) in vast quantities, served with your choice of 101 Belgian beers (fruit-flavored, Trappist-brewed, white, or light) by people dressed as monks in a hall like a refectory in a Martian monastery. Also eat *stoemp* (mashed potatoes and cabbage) with steak; Chimay–beer sausages; lobster; or roast chicken. The luxury index is low, but so is the check. ⊠ *50 Earlham St., WC2,* ☎ *020/7813–2233. AE, DC, MC, V. Tube: Covent Garden.*

CAFÉS

£   ✕ **Pret a Manger.** You'll fall over this sandwich chain's cafés wherever you go—even in Selfridge's food hall—and you'll be grateful because the quality and freshness of the chicken breast and avocado on granary bread, the Peking duck wrap, lemon cake, banana bread, almond croissant, and so on, are tops. There's even sushi. ⊠ *78 St. Martin's La., WC2,* ☎ *020/7379–5335. No credit cards. Tube: Covent Garden.*

CONTEMPORARY

£££ ✗ **The Ivy.** It's everybody's favorite restaurant—everybody who works
★ in the media or the arts, that is. In a deco dining room with blinding-
white tablecloths, and Hodgkins and Paolozzis on the walls, the celebrated and the wannabes eat Caesar salad, roast grouse, Thai baked
sea bass, braised oxtail, and rice pudding with Armagnac prunes or
sticky toffee pudding. For star-trekking ("Don't look now, dear, but
there's Ralph Fiennes") this is without a doubt the top place in London. The weekday three-course lunch is a bonus at £15.50. ✉ *1 West
St., WC2, ☎ 020/7836–4751. Reservations essential. AE, DC, MC,
V. Tube: Covent Garden.*

££ ✗ **Bank.** Since Bank's successful opening in 1997, its credit rating has
★ continued to soar. City and fashionable folk flock to this vast eatery
with its spectacular chandelier and equally dazzling menu. Seared fish
and paillard of pheasant; spinach and puy lentils; mousses, brûlées, and
nursery puddings are just small examples of its fast-changing world
palette, which has a definitive mod-Brit touch. Although not a steal
price-wise, the dishes never fail to please. ✉ *1 Kingsway, WC2, ☎ 020/
7379–9797. Reservations essential. AE, DC, MC, V. Tube: Holborn.*

CONTINENTAL

£££ ✗ **Savoy Grill.** The grill continues in the first rank of power-dining locations. Politicians, newspaper barons, and tycoons like the comfort-
ing food and impeccably discreet, attentive service in the low-key,
rather dull, yew-paneled salon. On the menu, an omelet Arnold Bennett (with cheese and smoked haddock) is perennial, and such standards as beef Wellington and saddle of lamb are joined by pak choi
and cèpe risotto. Diners can give their dancing shoes a workout at the
weekly "Stompin' at the Savoy." ✉ *Strand, WC2, ☎ 020/7836–4343.
Reservations essential. Jacket and tie. AE, DC, MC, V. Closed Sun.,
no lunch Sat. Tube: Covent Garden.*

ENGLISH

£££ ✗ **Rules.** Come, escape from the 21st century. More than 200 years
★ old (circa 1798), this gorgeous London institution has welcomed everyone from Dickens to Charlie Chaplin to Lillie Langtry and the Prince
of Wales. The menu is historic and good, even if some food critics feel
it's "theme park-y"; try the noted steak and kidney and mushroom pudding for a virtual taste of the 18th century. Happily, the decor is truly
delicious: with plush red banquettes and lacquered Regency yellow walls
crammed with oil paintings and framed engravings, this is probably
the single most beautiful dining salon in all of London. For a main dish,
try something from the list of daily specials, which will, in season, include game from Rules's own Teesdale estate (venison is disconcert-
ingly called "deer"). Rules is more than a little touristy, but that's because
it's so quaint. ✉ *35 Maiden La., WC2, ☎ 020/7836–5314. AE, DC,
MC, V. Tube: Covent Garden.*

FRENCH

£ ✗ **Café Flo.** This useful brasserie serves unpretentious chicken-liver terrine, baguette sandwiches, steak frites or *poisson-frites* (fish and fries),
tarts, espresso, fresh orange juice, simple set-price weekend menus—
everything for the Francophile on a budget. There are branches in Hampstead, Islington, Ludgate Hill, St. Paul's, Fulham, Richmond, and
Kensington. ✉ *50–51 St. Martin's La., WC2, ☎ 020/7836–8289. AE,
MC, V. Tube: Covent Garden.*

INDIAN

£ ✗ **India Club.** This cheap Indian canteen defies all conventions—but
it's still going strong after 50 years. It has been described as "strange
to the point of weird," but idiosyncratic is more generous. You'll find

it up the non-descript stairs, on the second floor of the Strand Continental Hotel. It's not pretty—Formica tables, linoleum floor, faded pictures of Indian notables—but it's a favorite with local London University students, BBC World Service workers, and people from the Indian High Commission. The menu is split vegetarian/non-vegetarian. You have to be a member of the hotel drinking club (£1) to get a beer from the bar (down two flights), so just stick with the lassies and the *masala dosai* (South Indian pancakes filled with onion and potato). ⊠ *143 Strand, WC2,* ☎ *020/7836–0650. Reservations not accepted. No credit cards. Tube: Charing Cross.*

ITALIAN

££ ✕ **Orso.** The Italian sister of Joe Allen, this basement restaurant has the same snappy staff and a glitzy clientele of showbiz types and hacks. The Tuscan-style menu changes every day, but it always includes excellent pizza and pasta dishes—plus entrées based, perhaps, on grilled rabbit or roast sea bass and first courses of arugula with shaved Parmesan or deep-fried zucchini flowers stuffed with ricotta. Food here is never boring, much like the place itself. Orsino, at 119 Portland Road, W11, is a stylish offshoot, serving much the same fare. ⊠ *27 Wellington St., WC2,* ☎ *020/7240–5269. Reservations essential. AE, MC, V. Tube: Covent Garden.*

£–££ ✕ **Bertorelli's.** Right across from the stage door of the Royal Opera House, Bertorelli's is quietly chic; the food is tempting; and the menu is just innovative enough: sea bass with walnut pesto and monkfish ragout with fennel, wonder beans, Swiss chard, and lime butter are two typical dishes. There is a big café-bar downstairs and a restaurant upstairs. Even more decorous and delicious is the branch at 19–23 Charlotte Street (and do check out its amazing marble-clad rest rooms). ⊠ *44A Floral St., WC2,* ☎ *020/7836–3969. AE, DC, MC, V. Closed Sun. Tube: Covent Garden.*

PAN-ASIAN

£££ ✕ **Asia de Cuba.** It's one of the trendiest restaurants, in the trendiest hotel, in the trendiest city in the world, allegedly. Maybe it's ironic, but it takes an American, Ian Schrager, and his Philippe Starck–designed hotel to bring Cool Britannia to its apogee. Asia de Cuba is the lead restaurant at Schrager's St. Martins Lane Hotel. Walk in at night and it feels like a dreamscape. It's sexy and it's loud; Calvin Klein–clad waiters bop and sit by your side. There are also Asia de Cubas at Morgans in New York and the Mondrian in L.A. The food is fusion and you're supposed to share. The Thai beef salad with Asian greens and roasted coconut is delicious, as is the lobster Mai Tai with rum and red curry. Ian Schrager is right: hotels (and their restaurants) are the new discos. ⊠ *St. Martins Lane Hotel, 45 St. Martin's La., WC2,* ☎ *020/7300– 5588. AE, DC, MC, V. Tube: Leicester Sq.*

SEAFOOD

££–£££ ✕ **J Sheekey.** J Sheekey completes the golden hat trick from the team behind Le Caprice and the Ivy. This is where the stars (you know, Cate Blanchett, George Michael, Johnny Depp) go when the rubbernecking at the Ivy becomes tedious. Sleek, discreet, and clublike, and slap in the heart of theaterland, this revived former fish restaurant is once again a seafood haven. The walls are crammed with talent: Peter O'-Toole, Ollie Reed, Chaplin, Coward, Olivier, Sellers. The decor charms; cracked glazed tiles, lava-rock bar tops, American oak paneling. Sample the wonderful jellied eels, pickled herrings, roll mops, Dover sole, and fish pie. To save money, try the weekend set lunch. ⊠ *28–32 St. Martin's Ct., WC2,* ☎ *020/7240–2565. AE, DC, MC, V. Tube: Leicester Sq.*

£ ✕ **Rock & Sole Plaice.** The appalling pun announces central London's only fish-and-chips joint, complete with inside seating (i.e., it's not only takeout). In addition to salmon, sole, and plaice, there's the usual cod and haddock, battered, deep-fried, and served with fries, ready for the salt and vinegar shakers. ⊠ *47 Endell St., WC2,* ☎ *020/7836–3785. AE, DC, MC, V. Tube: Covent Garden.*

VEGETARIAN

£ ✕ **Food for Thought.** This simple basement restaurant (no liquor license) seats only 50 and is extremely popular, so you'll almost always find a line of people down the stairs. The menu—stir-fries, casseroles, salads, and desserts—changes every day, and each dish is freshly made; there's no microwave. ⊠ *31 Neal St., WC2,* ☎ *020/7836–0239. Reservations not accepted. No credit cards. Closed 1 wk at Christmas. Tube: Covent Garden.*

Bloomsbury

CONTEMPORARY

£ ✕ **Truckles of Pied Bull Yard.** Wine bars were the hit of '70s London, though hardly any survive to tell the tale. This one's fantastic for a post–British Museum glass of something—and Truckles purportedly serves London's least-expensive glass of bubbly. The Olde English ham salad has gone upscale, and southern Europe (ciabatta sandwich with goat cheese) is more often than not on the menu. The nicest area is the courtyard, with tables galore in summer. ⊠ *Off Bury Pl., WC1,* ☎ *020/7404–5338. AE, DC, MC, V. Closed Sun., no dinner Sat. Tube: Holborn.*

FRENCH

££–£££ ✕ **Chez Gérard.** One of an excellent chain of steak-frites restaurants (there are 10 across London), this one has widened the choice on the utterly Gallic menu to include more for non–red meat eaters: smoked salmon and cream-cheese roulade and poached eggs, for instance, plus fish dishes and even something for vegetarians, such as sauté of wild mushrooms with cashew nuts and couscous. Steak, served with shoestring fries and béarnaise sauce, remains the reason to visit, though. ⊠ *8 Charlotte St., W1,* ☎ *020/7636–4975. AE, DC, MC, V. Tube: Goodge St.*

££–£££ ✕ **Elena's L'Etoile.** Elena Salvoni presided for years over L'Escargot in
★ Soho, where she made so many friends among happy customers she was rewarded with her name in lights. This understated century-old place, whose only concession to trendiness of decor is a row of bent-wood chairs unaccountably roped to the top of one wall, is one of London's few remaining unreconstructed French-bistro restaurants. The traditional dishes of duck braised with red cabbage, salmon fish cakes, and *poulet rôti* (roast chicken), crème brûlée, and lemon tart have now been joined by some newer treats, and most diners are guaranteed a warm smile from Elena, even if you're not one of the politician-journalist-actor regulars. ⊠ *30 Charlotte St., W1,* ☎ *020/7636–7189. AE, DC, MC, V. Closed Sun., no lunch Sat. Tube: Goodge St.*

JAPANESE

£ ✕ **Wagamama.** London is wild for Japanese noodles in this big base-
★ ment. It's high-tech, high volume—there are always crowds, with which you share wooden refectory tables—and high turnover, with a fast-moving line at the door. You can choose ramen in or out of soup (topped with sliced meats) or "raw energy" dishes and juices. So successful has this formula proved that there is now a range of clothing, so that grateful diners can *wear* Wagamama. Other branches are at 10A Lexington Street (☎ 020/7292–0990), near Piccadilly Circus, and 101A Wigmore Street (☎ 020/7409–0111). ⊠ *4A Streatham St., WC1,*

☎ 020/7323–9223. *Reservations not accepted. AE, DC, MC, V. Tube: Tottenham Court Rd.*

SEAFOOD

£ ✗ **North Sea Fish Restaurant.** This is the place for the British national
★ dish of fish-and-chips—battered and deep-fried whitefish with thick fries shaken with salt and vinegar. It's a bit tricky to find—three blocks south of St. Pancras station, down Judd Street. Only freshly caught fish is served, and you can order it grilled—though that would defeat the purpose. You can take out or eat in. ⊠ *7–8 Leigh St., WC1,* ☎ *020/7387–5892. AE, DC, MC, V. Closed Sun. Tube: Russell Sq.*

South Kensington

CONTEMPORARY

££–£££ ✗ **Bibendum.** This converted Michelin showroom, adorned with art
★ deco decorations and brilliant stained glass, remains one of London's dining showplaces, even though the great original chef, Simon Hopkinson, is long gone. Hopkinson championed simple dishes prepared perfectly, and current chef Matthew Harris continues in a similar vein, with the same Euro-Brit flair. Try herring with sour cream, any of the risottos, baked artichoke, steak au poivre, or sea bass and salsa verde. Here, too, are brains and tripe as they ought to be cooked. The £28.50 set-price menu at lunchtime is money well spent. ⊠ *Michelin House, 81 Fulham Rd., SW3,* ☎ *020/7581–5817. Reservations essential. AE, DC, MC, V. Tube: South Kensington.*

FRENCH

££ ✗ **Lou Pescadou.** This place is like a little slice of the South of France,
★ with a sea-theme decor and emphatically French staff. The menu changes often and is based on fish—don't miss the *soupe de poisson* (fish soup) with croutons and *rouille* (rose-color, garlicky mayonnaise) if it's featured. The wine list can be on the pricey side. ⊠ *241 Old Brompton Rd., SW5,* ☎ *020/7370–1057. Reservations essential. AE, DC, MC, V. Tube: Earl's Court.*

INDIAN

££ ✗ **Zaika.** Zaika has zoomed in from nowhere to become one of London's finest Indian restaurants. The chef/patron, Vineet Bhatia, mixes age-old flavors with modern sensibilities and is pushing the boundaries of Indian cuisine. The restaurant itself is dark (muds and browns), refined, sensual, and subtle. Indian artifacts hide in holes in the wall. You can't top the signature starter of *dhungar machli tikka* (tandoor home-smoked salmon with drips of mustard and dill), nor can you better the poached scallops in coconut milk drizzled with chili oil and served with masala mashed potato. Request the *gilafi dum biryani* (flaky, crusted lamb biryanyi, served with raita) and sign off with cheeky chocolate samosas ("chocomosas") and Indian ice cream. ⊠ *257–259 Fulham Rd., SW3,* ☎ *020/7351–7823. Reservations essential. AE, MC, V. Tube: South Kensington.*

MEDITERRANEAN

££ ✗ **Brompton Bay.** If you are shopping at Brompton Cross—Voyage,
★ Joseph, Divertimenti—Brompton Bay is good for lunch or dinner. With its clean decor and gold-leaf wall, BB attracts the "Chelsea Set" and local It(ish) Girls. The calm atmosphere is good for a chat *à deux*. The chef, David Massey, is on the rise and his light, contemporary cooking is well suited for those ladies who lunch. He does great char-grilled squid with chili jam and wild rocket and wonderful halibut in pancetta and Jerusalem artichokes. It's sweet with jazz on a balmy summers' evening. ⊠ *96 Draycott Ave., SW3,* ☎ *020/7225–2500. AE, DC, MC, V. Tube: South Kensington.*

Dining in South Kensington, Knightsbridge, and Chelsea

££   ✕ **The Collection.** Enter this former Katharine Hamnett shop through the spotlighted tunnel over the glass drawbridge, and you're immediately engulfed in one of the most fashionable crowds in London—so be careful about your outfit. A huge warehouse setting, adorned with industrial wood beams and steel cables, a vast bar, and a suspended gallery, makes a great theater for people-watching. The loud music makes conversation impossible anyway. Well-dressed wannabes peck at Mediterranean food seasoned with Japanese and Thai accents, all hoping that Mogens Tholstrup, the director-doré, will table-hop on over. The Belgo Group has now taken over, although Tholstrup stays on to preserve the restaurant's signature style. ✉ 264 Brompton Rd., SW3, ☎ 020/7225–1212. AE, DC, MC, V. Tube: South Kensington.

MOROCCAN

££   ✕ **Pasha.** Not quite a taste of old Tangiers, Pasha delivers modern Morocco and due east in a very à la mode manner. Waiters in traditional dress drift between piles of silken cushions and flickering candlelight to bring delicacies such as chicken *pastilla* (pie) and stylish cross-cuisine desserts (brûlée with Turkish delight). The two-hour seating policy grates, however. ✉ 1 Gloucester Rd., SW7, ☎ 020/7589–7969. Reservations essential. AE, DC, MC, V. Tube: Gloucester Rd.

POLISH

£   ✕ **Daquise.** This venerable and well-loved Polish café by the tube station is incongruous in this neighborhood, as it is neither style-conscious nor expensive. Fill your stomach without emptying your pocketbook (or, it must be said, overstimulating your taste buds) on *bigos* (sauerkraut with garlic sausage and mushrooms), stuffed cabbage, cucumber salad, or just coffee and cake. ✉ 20 Thurloe St., SW7, ☎ 020/7589–6117. MC, V. Tube: South Kensington.

Knightsbridge

CONTEMPORARY

£–££   ✕ **The Enterprise.** One of the new breed of gastro-pubs, this is a hot spot for hooray Henrys and brash bucks—near Harrods and Brompton Cross, it's filled with decorative types who complement the decor: paisley-striped wallpaper, Edwardian side tables covered with baskets and farmhouse fruit, vintage books piled up in the windows, white linen and fresh flowers on the tables. The menu isn't overly pretty—seared tuna and char-grilled asparagus, timbale of aubergine, salmon with artichoke hearts—but the ambience certainly is. ✉ 35 Walton St., SW3, ☎ 020/7584–3148. AE, MC, V. Tube: South Kensington.

CONTINENTAL

£   ✕ **Stockpot.** You'll find speedy service at this chain of large, jolly restaurants, often packed to the brim with young people and shoppers. The food is sometimes unstartling but filling and wholesome: try the Lancashire hot pot, for example, and the apple crumble. ✉ 6 Basil St., SW3, ☎ 020/7589–8627. No credit cards. Tube: Knightsbridge; ✉ 38 Panton St., off Leicester Sq., SW1, ☎ 020/7839–5142. Tube: Leicester Square; ✉ 273 King's Rd., Chelsea, SW3, ☎ 020/7823–3175. Tube: Sloane Square.

FRENCH

££££   ✕ **The Capital.** This elegant, clublike dining room has greige rag-rolled walls, a grown-up atmosphere, and formal service. Chef Eric Chavot pursues traditional French cooking, and most of his fine dishes never fail to astonish. These include a saddle of rabbit with sweet onion pastille and thyme jus or sea bass with Alsace bacon and fried calamari. Desserts follow the same exciting route. Set-price menus at lunch

(£24.50) make it somewhat more affordable. ⊠ *22–24 Basil St., SW3,* ☎ *020/7589–5171. Reservations essential. AE, DC, MC, V. Tube: Knightsbridge.*

££££ ✕ **La Tante Claire.** Due to the demand for its tables, one of the best restau-
★ rants in London upped its sticks, pots, and pans and moved to the more
spacious Berkeley Hotel. Chef Pierre Koffmann still reigns over La
Tante Claire, so you can expect the same blindingly brilliant standards
of haute cuisine. From the *carte,* you might choose langostine tails, cit-
rus jus, and celeriac mousse; oxtail with truffle sauce on foie gras; or
Koffmann's signature dish of pigs' feet with sweetbreads and wild
mushrooms. As every expense-accounter knows, the set lunch menu (£28)
is a genuine bargain. Lunch reservations must be made three to four
days in advance, dinner reservations three to four weeks. ⊠ *Berkeley
Hotel, Wilton Pl., SW1,* ☎ *020/7823–2003. Reservations essential. Jacket
and tie. AE, DC, MC, V. Closed Sun., no lunch Sat. Tube: Knightsbridge.*

££–£££ ✕ **Brasserie St. Quentin.** A very popular slice of Paris, this restaurant
is frequented by French expatriates and locals alike. Every inch of the
Gallic menu is explored—queen scallops, escargots, fillet of beef
brioche, tart Tatin—in the bourgeois provincial comfort so many London chains (the Dômes, the Cafés Rouges) try for yet fail to achieve.
⊠ *243 Brompton Rd., SW3,* ☎ *020/7589–8005. AE, DC, MC, V. Tube:
South Kensington.*

ITALIAN

££££ ✕ **Stefano Cavallini.** Showbiz and banking gurus flock to this spot at
the Halkin Hotel—the sister to the more upscale Metropolitan—because there are no paparazzi and no showing off. Goldman Sachs hon-
chos and fashionistas like Donna Karan come to devour what Cavallini
calls *la cucina essenziale*—old Italian recipes reinterpreted for modern
times (less cream, less fat, and more broth and olive oil). It is deeply
expensive, and service is by Armani-clad staff ("pretentious, *moi*?").
Nevertheless, taste sensations include squid-ink risotto with grilled scallops and gray mullet roe, and mallard with celeriac, onion, and green
beans. ⊠ *Halkin Hotel, 5–6 Halkin St., SW1,* ☎ *020/7333–1234. AE,
DC, MC, V. Tube: Hyde Park Corner.*

££££ ✕ **Zafferano.** Princess Margaret, Eric Clapton, Joan Collins (she asked
that the lights be turned down), and any number of other Cartier
brooch–wearing neighborhood Belgravians have flocked to this place,
which, since 1995, has been London's best exponent of *cucina nuova.*
The fireworks are in the kitchen, not in the brick-wall-and-saffron-hued
decor, but *what* fireworks: pheasant with rosemary and black truffle,
venison medallions with mash, and roast cod, lentils and parsley sauce.
The desserts are also *delizioso,* especially the Sardinian pecorino pastries served with undersweetened vanilla ice cream and the panettone
bread-and-butter pudding. Be sure to book early. ⊠ *15 Lowndes St.,
SW1,* ☎ *020/7235–5800. Reservations essential. AE, DC, MC, V.
Tube: Knightsbridge.*

£££ ✕ **Isola.** This guns to be the coolest restaurant in London, so don't be
surprised to see Joseph Fiennes mooching in a corner. The brainchild
of Oliver Peyton (Atlantic Bar & Grill, Mash), Isola is grown-up oste-
ria and Italian fine dining cooked by a Frenchman, Bruno Loubet. Upstairs is banquette-and-booth power dining; downstairs is more larky
and glam—diners sit at off-white leather "compromise sofas" amid the
sparkle of chrome and mirrors, parquet walls, and molecular lighting.
Head for the *zuppa di fagiano e farro* (pheasant soup with cabbage and
faro) and the *faraona al forno* (wood-roasted guinea fowl with liver and
mascarpone). ⊠ *145 Knightsbridge, SW1,* ☎ *020/7838–1044. Reservations essential. AE, DC, MC, V. Tube: Knightsbridge.*

££   ✗ **San Lorenzo.** This well-established, well-heeled trattoria has unexceptional decor and is nothing special food-wise—to say the least, according to some food critics—but it may be just the ticket if you're keen to spot the occasional celebrity or to gaze into the world of ladies who lunch. The usual Italian dishes are here, but they often make a nod to fashion—try wood pigeon with polenta, or any of the veal dishes. ⊠ *22 Beauchamp Pl., SW3,* ☎ *020/7584–1074. No credit cards. Closed Sun. Tube: South Kensington.*

PORTUGUESE

££   ✗ **Caravela.** This narrow, lower-ground-floor place is one of London's few Portuguese restaurants. You can get *caldo verde* (cabbage soup), *bacalhau* (salt-cured cod), and other typical dishes while listening (Wednesday through Saturday) to the national music, fado—desperately sad songs belted out at thrash-metal volume. ⊠ *39 Beauchamp Pl., SW3,* ☎ *020/7581–2366. AE, DC, MC, V. Tube: South Kensington.*

Chelsea

AMERICAN/CASUAL

££   ✗ **Cactus Blue.** Go for dinner or go for a weekend brunch, but go—American southwestern food is hot and happening in London these days, and this is one of the new Tex-Mex places with attitude. You can find the buzz on split levels bathed in ochre hues, with a gamut of cacti on the stairs. On offer are tequilas, beers, and Baja wines, which help slide down yummy crab stacks and quesadillas. ⊠ *86 Fulham Rd., SW3,* ☎ *020/7823–7858. AE, DC, MC, V. Tube: South Kensington.*

££   ✗ **PJ's Grill.** The decor here evokes the Polo Joe lifestyle (hence the name), with wooden floors and stained glass; a vast, slowly revolving propeller from a 1940s Vickers-Viny flying boat; and polo memorabilia. A menu of all-American staples (soft-shell crab, chowder, gumbo, steaks, smoked ribs), big salads, pecan pie, and brownies should please all but vegetarians, and portions are big. This place is more remarkable, though, for ambience than for food—it's open late; it's relaxed, friendly, and efficient; and its bartenders can mix anything. ⊠ *52 Fulham Rd., SW3,* ☎ *020/7581–0025. AE, DC, MC, V. Tube: South Kensington.*

£   ✗ **Chelsea Bun Diner.** Get fed heaps of food for very little money at this hybrid of an American diner and an English greasy spoon. A huge menu of huge portions—burgers, salads, potato skins, many breakfasts, pastas, and pies—is what you get. ⊠ *9A Limerston St., SW10,* ☎ *020/ 7352–3635. Reservations not accepted. V. Tube: Sloane Sq., then Bus 11, 19, 22, or 31.*

CONTEMPORARY

££–£££   ✗ **Bluebird.** From Sir Terence Conran, the man who gave England the wok, the Habitat catalog ("one of the 10 books that changed our life," according to the *Sunday Telegraph*), and several of London's largest restaurants, comes a full-blown gastrodome—foodmarket, florist, fruit stand, butcher shop, kitchen shop, and café-restaurant, all housed in a mammoth former King's Road garage. The place is pale blue and white, very light, and not in the least cozy (read "noisy"), and the food is slightly formulaic: wood-roasted mussels, coriander, lime leaf; or roasted leg of partridge, Savoy cabbage, chips; then warm chocolate cake and espresso ice cream. The menu has more than a nod in the Asia-Pacific direction. Go for the synergy and visual excitement—Conran's chefs share a tendency to promise more than they deliver. ⊠ *350 King's Rd., SW3,* ☎ *020/7559–1000. Reservations essential. AE, DC, MC, V. Tube: Sloane Sq.*

FRENCH

££££ ✗ **Aubergine.** A table at Aubergine (there are only 14) was London's
★ toughest reservation when soccer-pro-turned-cooking-star Gordon
Ramsay was at the stove. Cumbrian chef William Drabble has taken
over and is building his own reputation. His signature dishes are firm
and meaty—boudin of wood pigeon with foie gras, turnip, and jus truffle; best-end Mansergh lamb with onions, garlic, and rosemary. The
decor is alluring and bathed in the hues of impressionist Provence. Lunch
is a thrifty option. ✉ *11 Park Walk, SW10,* ☎ *020/7352–3449. Reservations essential. AE, DC, MC, V. Closed Sun., no lunch Sat. Tube:
South Kensington.*

££££ ✗ **Gordon Ramsay.** When the celebrated La Tante Claire moved out
★ of its old Chelsea abode, Gordon Ramsay—considered to be London's greatest chef—lost no time in getting his feet under its tables. Unfortunately, his new place is on the small side, so it still takes weeks to
book a seat, though not as long as at his former, even tinier Aubergine.
Here, Ramsay is whipping up a storm with white beans, girolles, foie
gras, scallops, and truffles, and by the time you read this he will probably have earned another five awards. For £75, blow out on the seven-
course option, for £60 you can wallow in three dinner courses, or plump
for lunch (£30 for three courses) for a gentler check. ✉ *68–69 Royal
Hospital Rd., SW3,* ☎ *020/7352–4441. Reservations essential. AE, DC,
MC, V. Closed weekends. Tube: Sloane Sq.*

££–£££ ✗ **La Poule au Pot.** One of London's most romantic restaurants, La
★ Poule au Pot is superb for proposals (or assignations). Gallic and rustic, this is a corner of France in darkest Belgravia. The "Chelsea Set"
loves it; Americans too. It is candlelit at night—you could be in a rambling French country house. The country cooking is good, not spectacular. The *poule au pot* (stewed chicken) with uncut vegetables and
lapin à la moutarde (rabbit with mustard) are strong and hearty. There
are fine classics such as beef bourguignonne and French onion soup.
The service comes with bonhomie. ✉ *231 Ebury St., SW1,* ☎ *020/
7730–7763. Reservations essential. AE, DC, MC, V. Tube: Sloane Sq.*

££ ✗ **La Brasserie.** This is a convenient spot for South Kensington museum visits; it has flexible and long opening hours, a menu of entirely
French dishes—from fish soup to tarte Tatin—and a good buzz on Sunday mornings, when the entire well-heeled neighborhood sits around
reading the papers and sipping cappuccino. You can't do that at peak
times, when you must eat, but the food's reliable, if a little overpriced.
✉ *272 Brompton Rd., SW3,* ☎ *020/7584–1668. AE, DC, MC, V. Tube:
South Kensington.*

INDIAN

££ ✗ **Chutney Mary.** London's stalwart Indian restaurant provides a fantasy version of the British Raj, all giant wicker armchairs and palms.
Dishes like masala roast lamb (practically a whole leg, marinated and
spiced) and Malabar chicken curry (with coconut, red chili, and cinnamon) alternate with the more familiar North Indian dishes such as
dum ka murgh (chicken, poppy seed, green chili, and onion). The best
choices are certainly the dishes re-created from the kitchens of Indian
chefs cooking for English palates back in the old Raj days. Servers are
deferential, and desserts, unheard of in tandoori places, are usually worth
leaving room for. The three-course Sunday brunch is a good value at
£15. ✉ *535 King's Rd., SW10,* ☎ *020/7351–3113. Reservations essential. AE, DC, MC, V. Tube: Fulham Broadway.*

Kensington and Notting Hill Gate

AMERICAN/CASUAL

£   ✕ **Tootsies.** A superior burger place, Tootsies is dark but cheerful. Rock music is in the background, usually accompanied by a neighborhood buzz. Alternatives to the burgers, which come with great fries, are big salads, steaks, BLTs, and chicken divertissements. The usual ice creams and pies will do for dessert. There are branches in Fulham, Chiswick, Wimbledon, Kew Barnes, Hampstead, and Richmond. ✉ *120 Holland Park Ave., W11,* ☎ *020/7229–8567. Reservations not accepted. AE, MC, V. Tube: Holland Park.*

CONTEMPORARY

££££ ✕ **Clarke's.** There's no choice on the evening menu at Sally Clarke's restaurant; her four-course dinners feature ultrafresh ingredients, plainly but perfectly cooked, accompanied by home-baked breads. The flower-and-art-speckled room is similarly home-style, if home is one of the big white Kensington houses you see around here. ✉ *124 Kensington Church St., W8,* ☎ *020/7221–9225. Reservations essential. AE, DC, MC, V. Closed Sun. and 2 wks in Aug., no lunch Sat. Tube: Notting Hill Gate.*

££–£££ ✕ **Pharmacy.** The Pharmacy is one of those trendy places where the bar is larger than the restaurant. In this case, the bar seats 120 and is shaped like a gigantic aspirin. Yes, this spot looks like its namesake, and even the menu looks fab—but then, Damien Hirst, artist extraordinaire, was involved in setting up the place. The menu highlights "comfort food" and ranges from carpaccio of whitefish with ginger and sesame to roast Dorset lamb with puy lentils and baked quince with suckling pig. If you can't snag a table, just have fun at the bar and order the drink called "Blood Transfusion." ✉ *150 Notting Hill Gate, W11,* ☎ *020/7221–2442. AE, DC, MC, V. Tube: Notting Hill Gate.*

££   ✕ **Wiz.** Tricky to find in the backwash of Notting Hill, Wiz is worth it when you do. A neighborhood restaurant run by TV guy Antony Worrall Thompson, it operates on tapas principles. The global menu (50 dishes) is grouped geographically (the Americas, Spice Trail, Europe, United Kingdom, North Africa, and the Middle East) and diners choose from a mini-menu under each heading. Some say it's a mishmash, others that the portions are small. Nevertheless, when it works, it works. The cumin dal and tamarind chicken and coconut curry are popular, as are the Szechuan duck and seared scallops with smoked aubergine salad. Locals return time and again. ✉ *123A Clarendon Rd., W11,* ☎ *020/7229–1500. AE, DC, MC, V. Tube: Holland Park.*

CONTINENTAL

££   ✕ **The Belvedere.** There can be no finer setting for a summer supper or a sunny Sunday brunch than a window table—or a balcony one if you luck out—at this stunning restaurant in the middle of Holland Park. The menu has good rib-eye Aberdeen Angus beef with snails and pommes frites, which suits the conservatorylike room. ✉ *Holland Park off Abbotsbury Rd., W8,* ☎ *020/7602–1238. Reservations essential. AE, DC, MC, V. No dinner Sun. Tube: Holland Park.*

ENGLISH

££   ✕ **Julie's.** This sweet 1960s throwback (with a pop-star past) has two parts: an upstairs wine bar and a basement restaurant, both decorated with Victorian ecclesiastical furniture. Jean Shrimpton and Terence Stamp, Bryan Ferry and Jerry Hall, even Sean Connery and Michael Caine used to come in the early days (now it's their children who turn up). The cooking is sound, old-fashioned English (salmon-and-halibut terrine, roast pheasant with chestnut stuffing and wild rowan jelly).

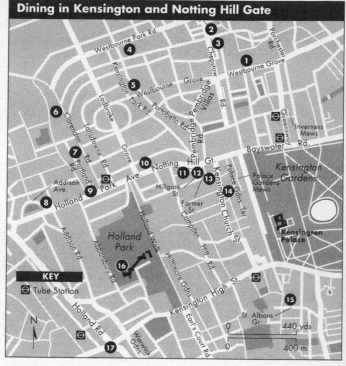

The traditional Sunday lunches are very popular, and in summer there's a garden room for open-air eating. ✉ *137 Portland Rd., W11,* ☎ *020/ 7727–7985. AE, MC, V. No lunch Sat. Tube: Holland Park.*

FRENCH

££ ✗ **Chez Moi.** Sophisticated French food is served in a dark red and black dining room, which, with the tables widely spaced and the lighting low, demands romantic behavior. There are dishes the menu admits are "traditional" that Chez Moi's fans have depended on for more than a quarter-century—like rack of lamb with Dijon mustard and bread crumbs, and filet mignon with port sauce—as well as more novel dishes such as Thai chicken and seared seafood, which take their cue from Asia. The desserts are hit-or-miss, but ample chocolates are brought with the coffee. ✉ *1 Addison Ave., W11,* ☎ *020/7603–8267. Reservations essential. AE, DC, MC, V. Closed Sun., no lunch Sat. Tube: Holland Park.*

GREEK

£ ✗ **Costa's Fish Restaurant.** Come for good value and such down-to-earth Greek food as grilled fish and *kleftiko* (roast lamb on the bone). The atmosphere is homey and happy, and there's a tiny garden open in summer. ✉ *18 Hillgate St., W8,* ☎ *020/7727–4310. No credit cards. Closed Sun. and 3 wks in summer. Tube: Notting Hill Gate.*

MIDDLE EASTERN

£ ✗ **Alounak.** This place has a confusing and raffish air to it, but the Iranian food is decent and tried and tested. Middle Eastern locals come here and the Arab music adds to the flavor. The hot bread and kebabs that emerge from the clay oven by the door are superior quality. Try the *joojeh* kebab or the *zereshk polo* (chicken with rice and Iranian forest berries). Take the Iranian black tea and the Persian sweets, but don't bother with the sour yogurty drinks—they're not to everyone's liking. ⊠ *44 Westbourne Grove, W2,* ☎ *020/7229–0416. MC, V. Tube: Queensway.*

£ ✗ **Yas.** Directly opposite Olympia Exhibition Centre, this friendly Per-
★ sian restaurant with terra-cotta-color walls has a beehive-shape oven by the door, from which lavish bread is brought steaming to your table. Eat this with *panir o sabzi* (soft white cheese with fresh herbs), hum-mus, *borani-e esfena* (yogurt and spinach), *adasi* (lentils), or any of the 15 dips and salads; then have a simple grilled chicken or lamb dish or the daily special—like Sunday's *baghali polow* (lamb shank, broad beans, dill, and rice). It's open until 5 AM every day. ⊠ *7 Hammersmith Rd., W14,* ☎ *020/7603–9148. AE, DC, MC, V. Tube: Olympia.*

CONTEMPORARY

££ ✗ **The Cow.** Not *another* Conran? This place belongs to Tom, son of Sir Terence, although it's a million miles from Quag's and Mezzo. A tiny, chic gastro-pub, it comprises a faux-Dublin back-room bar that serves oysters, salmon cakes, and baked brill. Upstairs a serious chef whips up Tuscan-British specialties—skate poached in minestrone is one temptation. Notting Hillbillies and other stylish folk adore the house special—a half-dozen Irish rock oysters with a pint of Guinness—as well as the mixed grills and steaks that often figure on the menu. ⊠ *89 Westbourne Park Rd., W2,* ☎ *020/7221–5400. Reservations es-sential. AE, MC, V. Tube: Westbourne Park.*

££ ✗ **First Floor.** This place is for well-off but artsy locals, popular for its inventive food and its ambience—it looks like a bombed church inhabited by distressed nobility. There's a great brunch on weekends; otherwise go for Thai fish cakes, monkfish and celeriac, or pecan-encrusted lamb rump with sweet-potato gratin. Sides—*petit dauphinoise* (sliced pota-toes baked in cream) or Asian greens—often hit the heights, as do desserts like hazelnut and Bailey's cheesecake. ⊠ *186 Portobello Rd., W11,* ☎ *020/7243–0072. Reservations essential. AE, DC, MC, V. Tube: Not-ting Hill Gate.*

££ ✗ **Kensington Place.** Being a favorite among the local glitterati keeps
★ this place packed and noisy. A huge plate-glass window and mural are backdrops to fashionable food—grilled foie gras with sweet-corn pan-cake and baked tamarillo with vanilla ice cream are perennials—but it's the fun buzz that draws the crowds. ⊠ *201 Kensington Church St., W8,* ☎ *020/7727–3184. AE, DC, MC, V. Tube: Notting Hill Gate.*

££ ✗ **192.** A noisy, buzzy wine bar–restaurant just off Portobello Road,
★ this is as much a social hangout for the local media mafia as a restau-rant, especially on weekends, when you'll feel like you've gate-crashed a party—if you manage to get a table, that is. The chef likes to keep ahead of fashion and is best on the appetizer list—many people order two of these instead of an entrée. Try the pastas, the seasonal salad (perhaps romanesco, broccoli, anchovy, and gremolata), the fish (sea bass with fennel, lemon, and rosemary; cod, clams, chorizo, and saf-fron broth), or whatever sounds unusual. ⊠ *192 Kensington Park Rd., W11,* ☎ *020/7229–0482. Reservations essential. AE, DC, MC, V. Tube: Notting Hill Gate.*

£ ✗ **Prince Bonaparte.** This is one of the new foodie pubs that draw in the crowds. Forget bangers and mash; here you'll get blackened salmon with refried beans, a yummy toffee pudding, and a wide range of in-teresting beers. Singles take over during the week; young families move in on the weekends. As the night wears on, the place—accented with large windows, church pews, and farmhouse tables—becomes a lively preclub stop (complete with thumping music on weekends). ⊠ *80 Chepstow Rd., W2,* ☎ *020/7313–9491. AE, MC, V. Tube: Notting Hill Gate, Westbourne Park.*

POLISH

££   ✕ **Wódka.** This smart, modern Polish restaurant is the only one in the
★   world, as far as we know, to serve smart, modern Polish food. It is popular with elegant locals and a sprinkling of celebs and often has the
atmosphere of a dinner party. Alongside the smoked salmon, herring,
caviar, and eggplant blinis you might also find venison sausages or roast
duck with *krupnik* (honey-lemon vodka). From the separate menu, order
a carafe of the purest vodka in London (and watch the check inflate);
it's encased in a block of ice and is hand-flavored (with bison grass,
cherries, and rowanberries) by the owner, who, being a Polish prince,
is uniquely qualified to do this. ✉ *12 St. Alban's Grove, W8,* ☎ *020/
7937–6513. Reservations essential. AE, DC, MC, V. No lunch weekends. Tube: High Street Kensington.*

SEAFOOD

£   ✕ **Geales.** This is a cut above your typical fish-and-chips joint, and it
★   is reflected in the prices. The decor is stark, but the fish will have been
swimming just hours beforehand, even the ones from the Caribbean
(grilled swordfish is a specialty). Geales is popular with the rich and
famous, not just loyal locals. ✉ *2 Farmer St., W8,* ☎ *020/7727–7969.
Reservations not accepted. AE, MC, V. Closed 2 wks at Christmas. Tube:
Notting Hill Gate.*

The City and the South Bank

AMERICAN/CASUAL

£   ✕ **Fatboy's Diner.** One for the kids, this is a 1941 chrome trailer transplanted from the banks of the Susquehanna in Pennsylvania and now
secreted, unexpectedly, in a back street, complete with an Astroturf "garden." A '50s jukebox accompanies the dogs, burgers, and fries. ✉ *23
Horner Sq., Spitalfields Market, E1,* ☎ *020/7375–2763. Reservations
not accepted. No credit cards. Tube: Liverpool St.*

CONTEMPORARY

££–£££   ✕ **Maison Novelli.** Jean-Christophe Novelli is one of the heroes of the
★   Mod Brit movement, and his restaurant has drawn foodies from the day
it opened in up-and-buzzing Clerkenwell, near stylish Islington. These
days, gladly, Novelli has downsized and is back running the kitchen after
almost burning out, expanding his empire across London and sharing
his cooking secrets in the *Times.* Favorites include glazed goat cheese,
celeriac, and mozzarella terrine; roast fillet of beef; Beaufort cheese, garlic, and tomatoes; and the famed pig's trotter stuffed "following the mood
of the day." All is not offally, however—you can also come by an elegant sea bass with chorizo or truffle oil, or pan-fried halibut with mus-
sel sauce. Finish it all off with a tarte Tatin with rum-raisin ice cream or
hot-and-cold chocolate cake. ✉ *29–31 Clerkenwell Green, EC1,* ☎ *020/
7251–6606. Reservations essential. AE, DC, MC, V. Tube: Farringdon.*

££–£££   ✕ **OXO Tower Brasserie and Restaurant.** How delightful it is for London to get a room with a view—and *such* a view. On the eighth floor
of the beautifully revived OXO Tower Wharf building near the South
Bank Centre is this elegant space, run by the same people who put the
chic Fifth Floor at Harvey Nichols on the map and featuring Euro-Asia
food with the latest trendy ingredients (acorn-fed black-pig charcuterie
with tomato and pear chutney; Dover sole with sea urchin butter). The
ceiling slats turn and change from white to midnight blue, but who on
earth notices, with the London Eye wheel and St. Paul's dazzling you
across the water? The Brasserie is slightly less expensive than the restaurant, but both have great river views. The terrace tables in summertime
are probably the best places in London. ✉ *Barge House St., Southbank,
SE1,* ☎ *020/7803–3888. AE, DC, MC, V. Tube: Waterloo.*

££ ✕ **St. John.** This former smokehouse (pork, not cigars), converted by
★   erstwhile architect owner-chef Fergus Henderson, has soaring white walls,
    schoolroom lamps, stone floors, iron railings, and plain wooden chairs.
    Some find Henderson's chutzpah scary: one infamous appetizer is rolled
    pig spleen (on a skewer), although the imaginativeness of others—roast
    bone marrow and parsley salad; smoked eel, beetroot, and horseradish—
    excuses this austerity. Entrées (roast lamb and parsnip; smoked had-
    dock and fennel; deviled crab) can appear shockingly nude on the plate,
    but they always have style. An all-French wine list has plenty of affordable
    bottles, plus lots of Malmseys and ports. Service is efficiently friendly,
    and the pastry chef's chocolate slice belongs in the brownie hall of fame.
    ✉ *26 St. John St., EC1,* ☎ *020/7251–0848. Reservations essential. AE,*
    DC, MC, V. Closed Sun. Tube: Farringdon.

ENGLISH

££ ✕ **People's Palace.** Thank goodness for this place—now you can have
    a civilized meal during your South Bank arts encounter. Run inde-
    pendently from the Royal Festival Hall et al., it has remarkably low
    prices considering it has the greatest river view in town (apart from
    OXO). There are occasional mistakes here, but the more British the
    dish, the more reliable it proves to be: roast beef, potted duck, Cor-
    nish crab and red pepper, marmalade sponge, pecan and banana pud-
    ding—all these are fine. Service is a bit flaky, but the soaring space with
    its giant windows makes up for everything. ✉ *Royal Festival Hall, Level*
    3, South Bank, SE1, ☎ *020/7928–9999. AE, DC, MC, V. Tube: Wa-*
    terloo.

£-££ ✕ **Quality Chop House.** This was converted from one of the most gor-
    ★   geous "greasy spoon" cafs in town, retaining the solid Victorian fit-
    tings (including pewlike seats, which you often have to share). It is not
    luxurious, but the food is a glorious parody of cafeteria food—bangers
    and mash turns out to be homemade herbed Toulouse sausage with
    rich veal gravy and light, fluffy potatoes; egg and chips (fries) are not
    remotely greasy. There are also such posh things as salmon cakes and
    steak as well as desserts that change with the seasons. An extension
    has added more fish to the menu including scallops, clams, and jellied
    eels. ✉ *94 Farringdon Rd., EC1,* ☎ *020/7837–5093. Reservations es-*
    sential. MC, V. No lunch Sat. Tube: Farringdon.

£   ✕ **Konditor & Cook.** Very useful for theatrical forays over the river, this
    cafeteria in the Young Vic theater serves full meals a cut above the tired
    quiche and curly sandwiches you might expect. Black ravioli stuffed
    with crab as well as Toulouse sausages with creamed mash are the kind
    of dishes to expect, but the pies and cakes—from the eponymous bak-
    ery around the corner, which supplies half of London—are the stand-
    outs. ✉ *Young Vic Theatre, 66 The Cut, SE1,* ☎ *020/7620–2700. MC,*
    V. Closed Sun. Tube: Waterloo or Southwark.

£   ✕ **Simpson's Tavern.** A bastion of English tradition and male-domi-
    nated custom, this back-alley chophouse was founded in 1759 and has
    admitted women only since 1916. It's popular with pinstripes and stock-
    brokers who come for the traditional fare: steak and kidney pie, liver
    and bacon, chops from the grill, Simpson's salmon cakes, or the house
    speciality of melted Cheddar cheese with Worcester sauce spread on
    toast. It's always full at lunch, so wander in early. ✉ *38½ Castle Ct.,*
    at Ball Ct., EC3, ☎ *020/7626–9985. Reservations not accepted. AE,*
    DC, MC, V. No dinner. Closed Sat.–Sun.

FRENCH

££ ✕ **Le Pont de la Tour.** Sir Terence Conran's place across the river, over-
    ★   looking the bridge that gives it its name, comes into its own in sum-
    mer, when the outside tables are heaven. Inside are a wine merchant,
    bakery and deli; a seafood bar; a brasserie; and this '30s diner–style

Dining in the City and the South Bank

restaurant, smart as the captain's table. Fish and seafood (lobster salad, steamed halibut and hollandaise, sea bream with herb risotto) and meat and game (Denham-estate venison with parsnip-and-bitter-chocolate sauce, Gressingham duck with orange and thyme) feature heavily—vegetarians are out of luck. Prune-and-Armagnac tart or nut fondant could finish a glamorous—and expensive—meal. ⊠ *36D Shad Thames, Butler's Wharf, SE1,* ☎ *020/7403–8403. Reservations essential. AE, DC, MC, V. Tube: Tower Hill.*

JAPANESE

£ ✕ **Moshi Moshi Sushi.** London is taking to sushi like New Yorkers did more than a decade back, and this glass-walled joint above Platform One in Liverpool Street Station set the ball rolling—or the fish train chugging, since the shtick here is that you pick *tekka* or *kappa maki* (tuna or cucumber seaweed rolls, respectively) or *maguro* (tuna), *sake* (salmon), *saba* (mackerel), etc.—in pairs off a conveyor belt that snakes around the counter. At the end, you count up your color-coded plates to pay. The sushi's okay, but this is not the place to go for a sophisticated evening. ⊠ *Unit 24 Liverpool St. Station, EC2,* ☎ *020/7247–3227. Reservations not accepted. MC, V. Closed weekends. Tube: Liverpool St.*

MEDITERRANEAN

££ ✕ **Moro.** Just up the road from the City at the cusp of Clerkenwell and
★ Sadler's Wells Islington borders is Exmouth Market—a cluster of shops, an Italian church with accompanying Italian deli, and Moro, an oasis of a restaurant that has become an award-winning outpost since it opened in 1997. The menu here provides a fashionable mélange of Spanish and North African flavors. Slow-cooked spiced meats, cured serrano hams, salt cod with chickpeas, and other delicacies flavored with fresh herbs are the secret to Moro's success. The only

downside is the persistent noise, but then, that's part of the buzz. ⊠ *34–36 Exmouth Market, EC1,* ☎ *020/7833–8336. Reservations essential. AE, DC, MC, V. No dinner Sun. Tube: Farringdon.*

£–££ ✕ **The Eagle.** If the name makes it sound like a pub, that's because it
★ is a pub, albeit a superior one, with wood floors, a few sofas, and art on the walls. It does, however, belong in the "Restaurants" section by virtue of the amazingly good-value Portuguese-Spanish food, which you choose from the blackboard menu (or by pointing) at the bar. There are about nine dishes, a pasta, three vegetarians, and/or risotto always among them. There are currently quite a few places in London charging four times the price for remarkably similar food; there's also a welcome trend toward pubs serving good meals—one that the Eagle all but started. ⊠ *159 Farringdon Rd., EC1,* ☎ *020/7837–1353. Reservations not accepted. No credit cards. Tube: Farringdon.*

SEAFOOD

££–£££ ✕ **Bill Bentley's.** You can see from the bare walls and the arched ceiling that this once housed a wine merchant's vaults. There are another four City-based branches in London, all equally old-fashioned in feel and all serving classic boarding school–like fish dishes and seafood platters. ⊠ *Swedeland Ct., 202 Bishopsgate, EC2,* ☎ *020/7283–1763. Reservations essential. Jacket and tie. AE, DC, MC, V. Closed weekends; last orders 8:30 PM. Tube: Liverpool St.*

££ ✕ **fish!** This is one of the sensations to hit the London scene. A re-
★ markable diner—designed, sleek and modern, by Julyan Wickham— it sits in the shadow of Southwark Cathedral, looking for the life of it like the glass-covered innards of a giant whale. But, no, it's the Victorian conversion of a section of Borough Market, which still operates across the road. The fish at fish! is excellent, and PC. The langoustine are creel-caught, the salmon organic, and the scallops landed by divers. There are always at least eight types on the menu, from swordfish to brill, skate, and turbot. The splish-splosh in-and-out formula has struck a chord; six new fish! are coming on-stream. ⊠ *Cathedral St., SE1,* ☎ *020/7234–3333. AE, DC, MC, V. Tube: London Bridge.*

££ ✕ **Livebait.** Perhaps no longer as truly fantastic as when it was independently run, this expanded, plain-looking fish restaurant is still packing them in, serving English seafood with a range of British ales by the pint (cockles and mussels alive-alive-o!), home-baked breads (beetroot, garlic, or turmeric, as well as olive and walnut), and all sorts of fish: broiled, in pies, baked, stewed, and generally combined in ways that are never boring. There are also branches in Covent Garden, Wandsworth, the City, Fulham, and Notting Hill. ⊠ *41–43 The Cut, SE1,* ☎ *020/7928–7211. Reservations essential. AE, DC, MC, V. Closed Sun. Tube: Southwark.*

££ ✕ **Sweetings.** Sweetings is uniquely English—a time warp from the old City of London (established circa 1886). There are many things Sweetings doesn't do: dinner, reservations, weekends, credit cards, or coffee. It does, however, do seafood. It's not far from St. Paul's Cathedral, and City gents come for "luncheon." They like the tankards of "Black Velvet" (Guinness and champagne) and they're reassured by the potted shrimps, fried whitebait, smoked haddock and poached eggs, Welsh rarebit, and roe on toast. The West Mersey oysters are jolly good, and the puddings are old nursery-school favorites—spotted dick and steamed syrup pudding. ⊠ *39 Queen Victoria St., EC4,* ☎ *020/7248–3062. Reservations not accepted. No credit cards. Closed weekends, no dinner. Tube: Mansion House.*

Camden Town and Hampstead

CAFÉS

£ ✕ **Coffee Cup.** A Hampstead landmark for just about as long as anyone can remember, this smoky, dingy, uncomfortable café is lovable, very cheap, and therefore always packed. You can get anything (beans, eggs, kippers, mushrooms) on toast, grills, sandwiches, cakes, fry-ups, etc.—nothing healthy or fashionable whatsoever. There are tables outside in summer but no liquor license. ⊠ *74 Hampstead High St., NW3,* ☎ *020/7435–7565. Reservations not accepted. No credit cards. Tube: Hampstead.*

GREEK

££ ✕ **Lemonia.** On a very pleasant street near Regent's Park is this supe-
★ rior version of London Greek—large and light, friendly, and packed every evening. Besides the usual *mezedes* (appetizers), *souvlaki* (kebabs), *stifado* (beef stewed in wine), and so on, there are interesting specials: quail, perhaps, or *gemista* (stuffed vegetables). ⊠ *89 Regent's Park Rd., NW1,* ☎ *020/7586–7454. Reservations essential. MC, V. No lunch Sat., no dinner Sun. Tube: Chalk Farm.*

TURKISH

£ ✕ **Gallipoli II.** This restaurant's charms are well known to local Islingtonians (hence the crowds)—it's a fun-packed palace with top service and bags of style. Things are crammed, however, and the rule is very much "room for one more." The riot of a *meze* (a spread of small dishes) is the best first act: it's bursting with flavor, texture, and color (the *kisir,* crushed wheat with walnut and onion, and falafel are particularly good). Keep the breads coming and you won't need much more. The lamb *incik* is tender and the baklava is appropriately sweet. ⊠ *120 Upper St., N1,* ☎ *020/7359–1578. Reservations essential. MC, V.*

Hammersmith

ITALIAN

££££ ✕ **River Café.** Often touted as having the best Italian food in Europe
★ outside Italy (some think, gasp, in all Europe), this superstar restaurant started a trend with its single-estate olive oils and deliriously simple roasts and pastas. Chefs Rose Gray and Ruth Rogers (wife of famed architect Richard Rogers, who created the minimalist decor) believe in snappingly fresh ingredients, so you get your seared salmon with imported Sicilian lemons, Tuscan bread soup with *cavolo nero* (black leaf cabbage) and Swiss chard, and one of London's highest checks. No matter to the food-obsessed (who swear by the famous Rogers/Gray cookbooks) and off-duty movie stars who flock here. But remember, if you're lucky enough to snag a reservation: this is in distant Hammersmith (way off our maps) and you can be stranded here if you haven't booked a taxi. Note: last food orders are taken at 9:30 PM. ⊠ *Thames Wharf Studios, Rainville Rd., W6,* ☎ *020/7381–8824. Reservations essential. AE, DC, MC, V. Tube: Hammersmith.*

Brunch and Afternoon Tea

It is sometimes suggested that among Londoners brunch is catching on, while the afternoon ritual (often mistakenly referred to as "high tea") is dying out. Tea, the drink, however, is so ingrained in the national character that tea, the meal, will always have a place in the capital, if only as an occasional celebration, a children's treat, or something you do when your American friends are in town. Reserve for all these, unless otherwise noted.

Brunch

Butlers Wharf Chop House. At this—another Terence Conran (Quaglino's, Le Pont de la Tour, Bibendum . . .) venture—brunch (£17 for three courses) is as British as brunch ever gets, with lobster mayonnaise, Stilton and celery soup and such, and a fabulous Thames-side setting. ⊠ *36E Shad Thames, SE1,* ☎ *020/7403–3403. AE, DC, MC, V.* ☺ *Brunch served Sun. noon–3. Tube: Tower Hill.*

Christopher's. Imagine you're in Manhattan at this superior Covent Garden purveyor of American food—it has everything from pancakes, steak, eggs, and fries to salmon cakes and Caesar salad. ⊠ *18 Wellington St., WC2,* ☎ *020/7240–4222. AE, DC, MC, V.* ☺ *Brunch served Sun. 11:30–4:30. Tube: Covent Garden.*

★ **Joe Allen.** This famed hangout is where to take refuge from the lovely British weather and down some Bloody Marys, and maybe a grilled chicken sandwich with Swiss chard, or a salad of spicy sausage, shrimp, and new potatoes. ⊠ *13 Exeter St., WC2,* ☎ *020/7836–0651. Reservations essential. AE, MC, V.* ☺ *Brunch served Sun. noon–4. Tube: Covent Garden.*

Veeraswamy. This restaurant has been here for years, but it's been taken over by the trendy Chutney Mary group from Chelsea and given a modern makeover. The result is great, and what better way to try the delights here than the special Sunday brunch menu (£15 for three courses). You'll be so taken with the fresh aromatic fish and chicken dishes followed by mod-Euro/trad-Indian desserts, you'll be coming back for dinner. ⊠ *Victory House, 101 Regent St., W1,* ☎ *020/7734–1401. AE, DC, MC, V.* ☺ *Brunch served Sun. 12:30–3. Tube: Regent Street.*

Afternoon Tea

Note that Claridge's and the Savoy require jacket and tie.

Brown's Hotel. Brown's does rest on its laurels somewhat, with a packaged aura and nobody around but fellow tourists who believe this to be the most famous. Still, everyone swears by the divine armchairs here. For £20.95 you get sandwiches, a scone with cream and jam, tart, fruitcake, and shortbread. Champagne tea is £28. ⊠ *33 Albermarle St., W1,* ☎ *020/7518–4108. AE, DC, MC, V.* ☺ *Tea served daily 3–6. Tube: Green Park.*

Claridge's. This is the real McCoy, with liveried footmen proffering sandwiches, scones, and superior patisseries (£19 or £22) in the palatial yet genteel Foyer, to the sound of the resident "Hungarian orchestra" (actually a string quartet). ⊠ *Brook St., W1,* ☎ *020/7629–8860. AE, DC, MC, V.* ☺ *Tea served daily 3–5:30. Tube: Bond Street.*

Fortnum & Mason. Upstairs at the Queen's grocers, three set teas are ceremoniously offered: standard afternoon tea (sandwiches, scone, cakes, £17.50), old-fashioned high tea (the traditional nursery meal, adding something more robust and savory, £19.50), and champagne tea (£23). ⊠ *St. James's Restaurant, 4th floor, 181 Piccadilly, W1,* ☎ *020/7734–8040. AE, DC, MC, V.* ☺ *Tea served Mon.–Sat. 3–5:15. Tube: Green Park.*

Harrods. For sweet-toothed people, the Georgian Restaurant Room at this ridiculously well known department store has a high tea that will give you a sugar rush for a week. ⊠ *Brompton Rd., SW3,* ☎ *020/7730–1234. AE, DC, MC, V.* ☺ *Tea served Mon.–Sat. 3:30–5:45. Tube: Knightsbridge.*

The Orangery at Kensington Palace. This Georgian, gorgeous, sunlight-flooded (assuming the sun is out), yes, orangery is the perfect setting for a light lunch or for tea, serving homemade soups and quiche, cakes, shortbread, pastries, and pots of Earl Grey. ⊠ *Kensington Gardens, W8,* ☎ *020/7376–0239. AE, MC, V. Closes at 5, Oct.–Easter; at 6, Easter–Sept. Tube: High Street Kensington or Queensway.*

The Ritz. The Ritz's huge, stagey, and sometimes cold and overly formal Palm Court offers tiered cake stands, silver pots, a harpist, and Louis XVI chaises, plus a great deal of rococo gilt and glitz, all for £27. Reserve at least four weeks ahead, more for weekends. ⊠ *150 Piccadilly, W1,* ☎ *020/7493–8181. AE, DC, MC, V.* ☉ *Tea served daily 2–6. Tube: Green Park.*

The Savoy. The glamorous Thames-side hotel does one of the most pleasant teas (£21.50 or £26); its triple-tiered cake stands are packed with goodies and its tailcoated waiters are thrillingly polite. ⊠ *The Strand, WC2,* ☎ *020/7836–4343. AE, DC, MC, V.* ☉ *Tea served daily 3–5:30. Tube: Charing Cross.*

Pubs

Even today, when television keeps so many people glued to their own hearth and home, the pub, or public house, or "local"—it has many aliases—is still a vital part of British life. It also should be a part of the tourist experience, as there are few better places to meet the natives in their local habitat. Sit at a table if you want privacy; better, help prop up the bar, where no introductions are needed, and watch that legendary British reserve fade away. There are hundreds of pubs in London, but the best—ever fewer of which still feature original Victorian etched glass, Edwardian panels, and Art Nouveau carvings—are listed below.

As we write, "gastro-pub" fever is still sweeping London. At many places, char-grills are being installed in the kitchen out back, while up front the faded wallpapers and the dear ol' Mums are being replaced by abstract paintings and food mavens galore (in fact, the best of these new luxe pubs are dealt with in the restaurant reviews above). Some of the following also feature nouveau pub grub, but whether you have Moroccan chicken or the usually dismal ploughman's special, you'll want to order a pint. What Americans call beer Brits call lager. However, the main Brit pub drink is "bitter"—usually warm. Today, there is a flourishing movement to bring back the traditionally prepared ale that is much less gassy. There's also a vast range of other potations—stouts like Guinness and Murphy's are thick, pitch-black brews you'll either love or hate; ciders, made from apples, are an alcoholic drink in Britain (Bulmer's and Strongbow are the names to remember); shandies are a mix of lager and lemonade or orange sodas; while black and tans are a blend of lager and stout named for the distinctive uniforms worn by early 20th-century British troops. Discuss your choices and other arcane details of drink with the barman, turn to your neighbor, raise the glass, and utter that most pleasant of toasts, "Cheers." Note that in some circles women are expected to drink out of half-pint, not full-pint, glasses. Be warned if you order a drink that would normally be served with ice in the United States—ice cubes are about as common in pubs as they are in Hades.

Arcane licensing laws forbid the serving of alcohol after 11 PM (10:30 on Sunday; different rules for restaurants) and have created, some argue, a nation of alcoholics, driven to down more pints than is decent in a limited time—a circumstance you see in action at 10 minutes to 11, when the "last orders" bell signals a stampede to the bar. That noted, "lock-ins" are an old tradition—pubs that lock the front door after hours and ask remaining customers to leave by the side door—

that bobbies tend to overlook. The list below offers a few pubs selected for central location, historical interest, a pleasant garden, music, or good food, but you might just as happily adopt your own temporary local.

The Albert. Positively heaving with ambience, the Albert must have been designed to be the complete and authentic London pub, with its burnished wood, walls adorned with Victorian prints about the evils of drinking, and a "division bell" (which calls back members of Parliament in time for a vote). The food in the restaurant upstairs is so good reservations are usually required. ⊠ *52 Victoria St., SW1,* ☎ *020/7222–5577. Tube: St. James's Park.*

Black Friar. A step from the Blackfriars tube stop, this spectacular pub has an Arts and Crafts interior that is entertainingly, satirically ecclesiastical, with inlaid mother-of-pearl, wood carvings, stained glass, and marble pillars all over the place. In spite of the finely lettered temperance tracts on view just below the reliefs of monks, fairies, and friars, there are, needless to say, a nice group of beers on tap from independent brewers. ⊠ *174 Queen Victoria St., EC4,* ☎ *020/7236–5474. Tube: Blackfriars.*

Crown and Goose. This is an art-bedecked Camden Town local, where armchairs augment the tables and coffee and herb tea the beers, and good food (steak in baguettes, smoked chicken salad with honey vinaigrette, baked and stuffed mushrooms) is served to the crowds. ⊠ *100 Arlington Rd., NW1,* ☎ *020/7485–8008. Tube: Camden Town.*

Dove Inn. Read the list of famous ex-regulars, from Charles II and Nell Gwyn (mere rumor, but a likely one) to Ernest Hemingway as you wait for a beer at this very popular, very comely 16th-century riverside pub by Hammersmith Bridge. If it's too full, stroll upstream to the Old Ship or the Blue Anchor. ⊠ *19 Upper Mall, W6,* ☎ *020/8748–5405. Tube: Hammersmith.*

French House. In the pub where the French Resistance convened during World War II, Soho hipsters and eccentrics rub shoulders now— more than shoulders, actually, because this tiny, tricolor-waving, photograph-lined pub is always filled to bursting with theater luvvies and literary bods. ⊠ *49 Dean St., W1,* ☎ *020/7437–2799. Tube: Piccadilly Circus.*

George Inn. The inn sits in a courtyard where Shakespeare's plays were once performed. The present building dates from the late 17th century and is central London's last remaining galleried inn. Dickens was a regular—the inn is featured in *Little Dorrit*. Entertainments include Shakespeare performances, medieval jousts, and morris dancing. ⊠ *77 Borough High St., SE1,* ☎ *020/7407–2056. Tube: London Bridge.*

Island Queen. Gigantic caricature pirates leer down at you from the ceiling in this sociable Islington pub, which offers home-cooked food, a busy pool table, and a fab jukebox. The playwright Joe Orton frequented the place; he lived—and died, murdered by his lover—next door. ⊠ *87 Noel Rd., N1,* ☎ *020/7704–7631. Tube: Angel.*

Jack Straw's Castle. Straw was one of the leaders of the Peasants Revolt of 1381, and he was hanged nearby. In Tudor times this was a favorite hangout for highwaymen, but by the 19th century it had become picturesque and respectable; artists painted charming views from it, and Dickens (inevitably) stayed here. Sadly, it was blitzed during World War II, but was rebuilt in 1963. You can admire the views over Hampstead Heath and drink (weather permitting) in the large and lovely outside courtyard. ⊠ *North End Way, NW3,* ☎ *020/7435–8885. Tube: Hampstead.*

The Lamb. Another of Dickens's locals is now a picturesque place for a pint in summer, when you can drink on the patio. ⊠ *94 Lamb's Conduit St., WC1,* ☎ *020/7405–0713. Tube: Farringdon.*

Lamb & Flag. This 17th-century pub was once known as "The Bucket of Blood" because the upstairs room was used as a ring for bare-knuckle boxing. Now, it's a trendy, friendly, and entirely bloodless pub, serving food (at lunchtime only) and real ale. It's on the edge of Covent Garden, off Garrick Street. ⊠ *33 Rose St., WC2,* ☎ *020/7497–9504. Tube: Covent Garden.*

Mayflower. An atmospheric 17th-century riverside inn, with exposed beams and a terrace, this is practically the very place from which the Pilgrims set sail for Plymouth Rock. The inn is licensed to sell American postage stamps. ⊠ *117 Rotherhithe St., SE16,* ☎ *020/7237–4088. Tube: Rotherhithe.*

Museum Tavern. Across the street from the British Museum, this gloriously Victorian pub (although a pub has been here for centuries, and the book behind the bar details it) makes an ideal resting place after the rigors of the culture trail. With lots of fancy glass—etched mirrors and stained-glass panels—gilded pillars, and carvings, the heavily restored hostelry once helped Karl Marx to unwind after a hard day in the Library. He could have spent his *Kapital* on any one of six beers available on tap. ⊠ *49 Great Russell St., WC1,* ☎ *020/7242–8987. Tube: Tottenham Court Road.*

Princess Louise. This fine, popular pub has an over-the-top Victorian interior—glazed terra-cotta, stained and frosted glass, and a glorious painted ceiling. It's not all show, either; the food is a cut above normal pub grub, and there's a good selection of real ales. ⊠ *208 High Holborn, WC1,* ☎ *020/7405–8816. Tube: Holborn.*

Prospect of Whitby. Named after a ship, this is London's oldest riverside pub, dating from 1520. Once upon a time it was called "The Devil's Tavern" because of the low-life criminals—thieves and smugglers—who congregated here. It's ornamented with pewter ware and nautical objects. ⊠ *57 Wapping Wall, E1,* ☎ *020/7481–1095. Tube: Wapping.*

St. James Tavern. This pretty pub is steps from Piccadilly Circus and five major West End theaters; another plus is that it also stays open until 1 AM Tuesday through Saturday. The decor includes lovely hand-painted Doulton tiles depicting Shakespearean scenes. The kitchen is proud of its fish-and-chips. ⊠ *45 Great Windmill St., W1,* ☎ *020/7437–5009. Tube: Piccadilly Circus.*

Sherlock Holmes. This pub used to be known as "The Northumberland Arms," and Arthur Conan Doyle popped in regularly for a pint. It figures in *The Hound of the Baskervilles,* and you can see the hound's head and plaster casts of its huge paws among other Holmes memorabilia in the bar. ⊠ *10 Northumberland St., WC2,* ☎ *020/7930–2644. Tube: Charing Cross.*

Spaniards Inn. This is another historic, oak-beamed pub on Hampstead Heath, boasting a gorgeous rose garden, scene of the tea party in Dickens's *Pickwick Papers.* Dick Turpin, the highwayman, used to frequent the inn; you can see his pistols on display. Romantic poets—Shelley, Keats, Byron—hung out here, and so, of course, did Dickens. It's extremely popular, especially on Sundays, when Londoners take to the heath in search of fresh air. ⊠ *Spaniards Rd., NW3,* ☎ *020/8731–6571. Tube: Hampstead.*

Star Tavern. In the heart of elegant Belgravia, this pub has a postcard-perfect Georgian-era facade. The inside is charming too; Victorian decor and two roaring fireplaces make this a popular spot. ⊠ *6 Belgrave Mews West, SW1,* ☎ *020/7235-3019. Tube: Victoria.*

Windsor Castle. This is one to rest at on a Kensington jaunt, saving a large appetite for the food, especially on Sunday, when they do a traditional roast; other days there are oysters and salads, fish cakes and steak sandwiches. In winter there are blazing fires; in summer, an exquisite walled patio garden. ⊠ *114 Campden Hill Rd., W8,* ☎ *020/7727-8491. Tube: Notting Hill Gate Park.*

Ye Bunch of Grapes. A traditional (which means smoky, noisy, and anti-chic) pub, popular since Victoria was on the throne, in the heart of Shepherd Market, the village-within-Mayfair, this place is still home-away-from-home for a full deck of London characters. ⊠ *16 Shepherd Market, W1,* ☎ *020/7499-1563. Tube: Green Park.*

Ye Olde Cheshire Cheese. Yes, it is a tourist trap, but this most historic of all London pubs (it dates from 1667) deserves a visit anyway, for its sawdust-covered floors, low wood-beam ceilings, and the 14th-century crypt of Whitefriars' monastery under the cellar bar. But if you want to see the set of 17th-century pornographic tiles that once adorned upstairs, you'll have to get special permission from the brewery to see them at the British Museum. This was the most regular of Dr. Johnson's and Dickens's *many* locals. ⊠ *145 Fleet St., EC4,* ☎ *020/7353-6170. Tube: Chancery Lane.*

3 LODGING

Queen Elizabeth hasn't invited you this time?
No matter. Staying at one of London's
grande-dame hotels is the next best thing to
being a guest at the palace—some say even
better. Royally resplendent decor abounds,
and armies of staff are stuck in the pampering
mode—the Windsors should have it so good.
Even in more affordable choices, inimitable
British style brings you a taste of home,
with tea makers and Queen Mum pastel
wallpaper. Still not cozy enough? Borrow
some keys and be a B&B guest.

Updated by
Roland
Chambers

STANDING IN THE PARLORLIKE atmosphere of your lobby—burnished oak paneling, time-stained antiques, chintz-softened sofas, the distant tinkle of teacups in the air—a century seems to slip away. The concierge whispers that Queen Victoria used to visit—she, too, probably got willingly lost in the corridors and crannies. In the grand salon sit ancient Chippendale desks that once bore the concentrated energy of the empire's Kiplings and Hardys. Set near a crackling fire, a roomy leather Chesterfield beckons one to approach its quilted field. Yes, our Olde London Towne fantasies may be fading fast in the light of Blair's Britain, but when it comes time to rest your head, the old-fashioned clichés remain very enticing. Who wouldn't want to lounge in a brocade armchair while cream tea is served by a frock-coated retainer? Or to breakfast on coffee, toast, and croissants in a handmade bed in your powder-blue and white Syrie Maugham–esque boudoir as the Thames flows lazily past your French windows? Choose one of London's heritage-rich hotels—Brown's and Claridge's supply perfect parlors; the Savoy has that river view—and these fantasies can, and always will, be fulfilled.

On the other hand, faster times are bringing more changes to the London hotel scene than there have been in years. Hotels are springing up in places not previously considered "touristy," meaning your stay need not be confined to the bustle and noise of the West End or the exclusive nabes (so exclusive you will find few Brits native to these areas) of Kensington or Knightsbridge. And the variety is not limited to location. In terms of price, the growth is at the top and bottom ends of the market. Immaculately designed, entirely contemporary hotels now are challenging luxurious, old, chintzy favorites while nationwide budget chains take on the B&B scene, offering clean and functional accommodations at friendly prices. Chain hotels with cookie-cutter decor, and—as they used to say—all mod cons (modern conveniences), tended to avoid London's center, but they're moving in now, attracted by the big increase in Chunnel travelers and other inter-Europe wayfarers. It adds another option to your vacation planning: you no longer need to blow your entire budget on your bed.

Still, if you want to do just that, London is the place. Prices can soar into the empyrean here, but many of the best hotels are worth it. Take the Connaught, a landmark whose guests wouldn't *dream* of staying anywhere else. Its Edwardian lobby, created in 1897, is unadulterated by things modern; grand and faded, it is filled with oil paintings and antiques in a way interior designers envy but can't really duplicate. In contrast to this dowager-aunt type are hotels such as the Pelham and Covent Garden—most of them renovated town houses, aglitter with sensationally atmospheric Regency-style interiors and richly appointed with stunning furnishings and guests. Designed to be the very epitome of English country-housedom, these newer boutique hotels appeal to clientele bent on revisiting the landed gentry culture. Waving the banner SMALL IS BEAUTIFUL, they have stolen a march on the genteel sleeping beauties—the Claridges, the Savoys, and the Dorchesters—who, recently awakened, have launched a broad counterattack. The Sultan of Brunei sank tens of millions into refurbishing the Dorchester; a Hunt heiress sponsored a complete makeover of the Lanesborough; and the Connaught, Savoy, and Claridge's have each been renovated to the tune of a mint. Paying top dollar, of course, does not always mean you'll get stately grandeur—several places have moved away from Regency flounces and Laura Ashley–isms into neo-Bauhaus minimalism. The Halkin was the first frill-free grand hotel; now add the Metropolitan and the ultrafashionable Hempel. Look forward also to the Great Eastern, which offers all the advantages of an exorbitant modernity and is the first hotel in its league to be opened in London's financial nerve center—the City. At the other end of the scale, things can be almost as trendy. In design-crazy London, even hostels have become stylish—just look into the future at the Generator.

As the city is the opposite of compact, where you stay can affect your experience significantly. For instance, the West End is equivalent to downtown, but it covers a lot of ground. There's a great deal of difference between, say, posh Park Lane and bustling, touristy Leicester Square, yet both are in the West End. Hotels in Mayfair and St. James's are central and yet distant in both mileage and atmosphere from funky, youthful neighborhoods like Notting Hill and Camden Town and from major tourist sights like the Tower of London, St. Paul's Cathedral, and the large Kensington museums. On the edges of the West End, Soho and Covent Garden have countless restaurants and late-opening bars and clubs.

South Kensington, Kensington, Chelsea, and Knightsbridge are all patrician and peaceful, which will give you a more homey feeling than anything in the West End, while Belgravia is superelegant, geographically and atmospherically about halfway between the extremes. From Bloomsbury it's a short stroll to the shops and restaurants of Covent Garden, to Theatreland, and to the British Museum. Once the preserve of family-run B&Bs, Bloomsbury now features that Terence Conran hotel on leafy Dorset Square, making the area a more fashionable place to stay than in past years. From here, it's a short bus ride to Camden and Regent's Park, too, and Hampstead and Islington are close enough to explore easily. Bayswater is a particularly affordable haven. It's barely considered a real neighborhood by Londoners, but everything is accessible from there, and Hyde Park is your backyard. Notting Hill and Holland Park are worth considering as bases if you want something more down-home plus the antiques of Portobello Road and its surrounding cutting-edge shops and restaurants on your doorstep.

The general custom these days in all but the bottom end of the scale is for rates to be quoted for the room alone (which unless otherwise noted is with bath); breakfast, whether Continental or "full English," usually comes at extra cost. We've noted at the end of each review if breakfast is included in the rate (CP for Continental breakfast daily and BP for full breakfast daily). Note: while some establishments may offer a hearty breakfast, others may offer little more than coffee and rolls; check ahead about what's offered if breakfast is important to you. VAT and service charges are usually included. All hotels listed here are graded according to their weekday, high-season rates from spring 2001. Remember there may be significant discounts at the weekend or off-season. Like those in most other European countries, British hotels are obliged by law to display a tariff at the reception desk. If you have not booked ahead, you are strongly advised to study this carefully.

Be sure to make reservations well in advance. For approximate costs, *see* the lodging price chart, *in* Smart Travel Tips A to Z.

Mayfair to Regent's Park

££££ ▣ **The Athenaeum.** The welcome in this independently run baby grand opposite Green Park is in the details: from Donald, the superconcierge at his door-side desk, to the disposable camera in the minibar to the compact health spa. 34 of the rooms here are actually one-bedroom apartments with a key to fit the hotel's front door. Furniture is distinctive,

London Lodging *(Boxes Refer to Detail Maps)*

Regent's Park

Maida Vale

Abercorn Pl.

Abbey Rd.

Grove End Rd.

Hall Rd.

Clifton Rd.

Wellington Rd.

Prince Albert Rd.

St. John's Wood Rd.

Lisson Grove

Outer Circle

Inner Circle

Park Rd.

Chester Rd.

Albany St.

Outer Circle

Balcombe St.

Bayswater and Notting Hill Gate

Clifton Rd.

Bloomfield Rd.

Edgware Rd.

Dorset Square

Gloucester Pl.

Marylebone Rd.

Portland Pl.

Harley St.

Westway

Harrow Rd.

Harrow Rd.

Marylebone Flyover

Baker St.

Bishop's Bridge Rd.

Westbourne Gr.

Praed St.

Paddington Station

Sussex Gdns.

Mayfair, St. James's, Soho, and Covent Garden

Wigmore St.

Queensway

Craven Hill

Oxford St.

Duke St.

Brook St.

Bond St.

Grosvenor St.

Notting Hill Gate

Bayswater Rd.

Grosvenor Square

U.S. Embassy

S. Audley St.

Berkele Squar

Kensington Gardens

Hyde Park

Park Lane

Curzon St.

The Serpentine

Gre Consti

Kensington Rd.

Kensington Gore

Kensington Rd.

Knightsbridge

Grosvenor

Kensington High St.

Palace Gate

Gloucester Rd.

Prince Consort Rd.

Royal Albert Hall

Sloane St.

Belgrave Square

Exhibition Rd.

Queen's Gate

Brompton Rd.

Pont St.

Cadogan Pl.

Eaton Square

Buckingham Pal

Cromwell Rd.

Sloane Ave.

Sloane Sq.

Kensington, Knightsbridge, Chelsea, Belgravia, and Westminster

Pimlico Rd.

Redcliffe Gdns.

Finborough Rd.

Fulham Rd.

Old Church St.

King's

Rd.

Royal Hospital Rd.

Beaufort St.

Oakley St.

Cheyne Walk

Albert Br.

Chelsea Embankment

Chelsea Br.

River Thames

Battersea Park

Hampstead

King's Cross
Station

Pentonville Rd.

City Rd.

Eversholt St.

St. Pancras
Station

King's Cross Rd.

St. John's St.

Goswell Rd.

East Road

City Rd.

Euston
Station

Judd St.

Gray's Inn Rd.

Rosebery Ave.

Hampstead Rd.

Euston Rd.

Coram's
Fields

Farringdon Rd.

Clerkenwell Rd.

London Wall

Moorgate

Gower St.

Woburn Pl.

Guilford St.

Theobald's Rd.

Bloomsbury
and Beyond

Tottenham Court Rd.

Southampton Row

High Holborn

Holborn
Viaduct

Newgate
St.

Cheapside

N Portland St.

Oxford
Circus

Oxford

St.

Drury Ln.

Kingsway

Adwych

Law
Courts

Old Bailey

Fleet St.

Queen Victoria St.

Cannon St.

Cannon St.
Station

Regent St.

Brewer St.

Shaftesbury

Charing Cross Rd.

Strand

Victoria Embankment

Blackfriars Br.

Southwark Br.

Piccadilly
Circus

Haymarket

St. Regent St.

Charing
Cross Stn.

Waterloo Br.

Stamford St.

Blackfriars Rd.

Docklands

iccadilly

Jermyn

Pall Mall

The Mall

Whitehall

South
Bank
Arts
Complex

York Rd.

Waterloo

The Cut

Southwark St.

Union St.

Borough High St.

Park

on Hill

St. James's
Park

Birdcage Walk

Westminster Br.

Waterloo
Station

Westminster Br. Rd.

Borough Rd.

London Rd.

Borough High St.

Victoria
Station

Victoria St.

Millbank

Lambeth Palace Rd.

Lambeth Rd.

Imperial
War
Museum

Kennington Rd.

New Kent Rd.

Wilton Rd.

Horseferry Rd.

Lambeth Br.

Walworth Rd.

rwick Way

Vauxhall Br.

Tate
Gallery

Rd.

Belgrave Rd.

Albert Embankment

Kennington Park Rd.

Lupus St.

Vauxhall Br.

Kennington Ln.

N

Grosvenor

Rd.

Vauxhall
Station

Kennington
Oval

Nine Elms Ln.

0   1 mile

0   1 km

198

Lodging in Mayfair, St. James's, Soho, and Covent Garden

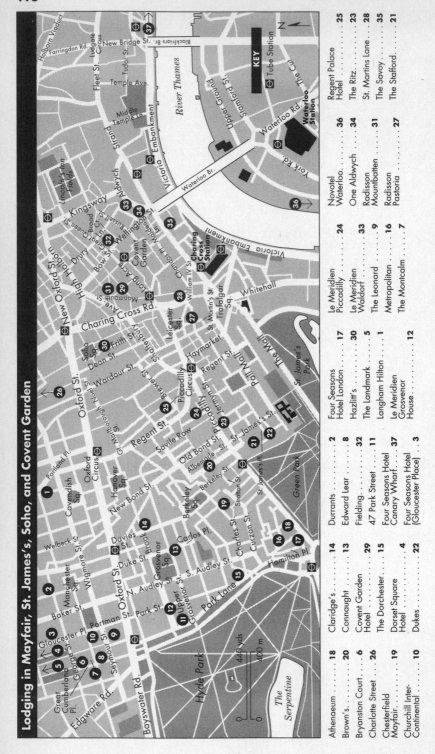

River Thames

New Bridge St.
Blackfriars Br.
The Cut
Holborn Viaduct
Farringdon Rd.
Ludgate Hill
Fleet St.
Tudor St.
Temple Ave.
Middle Temple Ln.
Strand
Aldwych
Kingsway
Lincoln's Inn Fields
New Oxford St.
High Holborn
Drury Ln.
Bow St.
Long Acre
Covent Garden
Charing Cross Rd.
Monmouth St.
Oxford St.
Wardour St.
Dean St.
Frith St.
Soho Sq.
Shaftesbury Ave.
Leicester Sq.
St. Martin's Ln.
Charing Cross Station
Haymarket
Regent St.
Piccadilly Circus
Savile Row
Jermyn St.
Old Bond St.
Piccadilly
St. James's St.
Albemarle St.
Berkeley St.
Green Park
Portland Pl.
Cavendish Sq.
Oxford Circus
Hanover Sq.
New Bond St.
Davies St.
Berkeley Sq.
Carlos Pl.
Grosvenor Sq.
S. Audley St.
Charles St.
Curzon St.
Hamilton Pl.
Welbeck St.
Wigmore St.
Manchester Sq.
Baker St.
Portman Sq.
Gloucester Pl.
George St.
Seymour St.
Edgware Rd.
Great Cumberland Pl.
Oxford St.
Duke St.
N. Audley St.
Upper Grosvenor St.
Park Ln.
Park St.
Hyde Park
Bayswater Rd.
The Serpentine
Victoria Embankment
Waterloo Rd.
York Rd.
Waterloo Station
The Mall
St. James's Park
Whitehall
Trafalgar Sq.
William IV St.
Upper Ground
Stamford St.
Waterloo Br.
Victoria Embankment

Whitehall

440 yds
400 m

N

custom-made leather-top mahogany and yew, set against navy-and-cream drapes, Wedgwood-green walls, and ultrathick cream carpets. Without getting out of bed, you can control lighting and temperature, order free videos and CDs, and listen to your voice mail from your two phone lines. In glittering gray-marble bathrooms are power showers, mirrors angled to get the back of your head; old-fashioned Bronnley toiletries; and hair dryers. Downstairs, there's the cozy Whisky Bar and the not-too-formal Bullochs restaurant. Rooms 201–205 face Green Park; others have a bay window that affords a partial, angled view. ⊠ *116 Piccadilly, W1V 0BJ,* ☎ *020/7499–3464,* FAX *020/7493–1860,* WEB *www.athenaeumhotel.com. 111 rooms, 34 apartments. Restaurant, bar, in-room VCRs, health club. AE, DC, MC, V. Tube: Green Park.*

££££ 🖀 **Brown's.** Founded in 1837 by Lord Byron's "gentleman's gentleman," James Brown, this Victorian country house in central Mayfair comprises 11 Georgian houses and is patronized by many Anglophilic Americans—a habit that was established by the two Roosevelts (Teddy while on honeymoon). Bedrooms feature thick carpets, soft armchairs, brass chandeliers, and brocade wallpapers, as well as air-conditioning, while the public rooms retain their cozy oak-paneled, chintz-laden, grand-father-clock-ticking-in-the-parlor ambience. The restaurant, named 1837 for the year Brown's opened, has a chef who believes in classical French cuisine complete with an encyclopedic wine list. Right outside the door are the boutiques and art galleries of Bond and Cork streets, while in the lounge, one of London's best-known afternoon teas is served from 3 to 5:45. ⊠ *34 Albemarle St., W1X 4BT,* ☎ *020/7493–6020,* FAX *020/7493–9381,* WEB *www.brownshotel.com. 118 rooms. Restaurant, bar. AE, DC, MC, V. Tube: Green Park.*

££££ 🖀 **Churchill Inter-Continental London.** Modern Park Avenue luxury came to London when the Tisch family opened this homage to Winston Churchill in the 1970s. The lobby is opulent and Robert Adams–esque with a gilded ceiling and black marble columns, and the Regency-style grace notes continue throughout. Clementine's—named after the great man's wife—is the main restaurant, while the Churchill Bar and Cigar Divan, a gleaming maple-wood nook, proffers private-label smokes, 75 varieties of whiskeys, and grand-piano entertainment. Business travelers and visiting VIPs love this place and its Portman Square location, just two blocks from Marble Arch, the shops of Oxford Street, and the Wallace Collection. ⊠ *30 Portman Sq., W1A,* ☎ *020/7486–5800,* FAX *020/7486–1255,* WEB *www.interconti.com. 395 rooms, 40 suites. 2 restaurants, bar, meeting room. AE, DC, MC, V. Tube: Marble Arch.*

££££ 🖀 **Claridge's.** Stay here, and you're staying at a hotel legend (founded
★   in 1812), with one of the world's classiest guest lists. The liveried staff is friendly and not in the least condescending, and the rooms are never less than luxurious. Enjoy tea or coffee in the Foyer lounge (24 hours a day) with its Hungarian mini-orchestra or retreat to the stylish Claridge's bar for cocktails and canapés. The bathrooms are spacious (with enormous showerheads), as are the bedrooms, with bells (which still work) to summon either maid or valet from their station on each floor. Beds are handmade and supremely comfortable—the King of Morocco once brought his own, couldn't sleep, and ended up ordering 30 from Claridge's to take home. The grand staircase and magnificent elevator are equally impressive. ⊠ *Brook St., W1A 2JQ,* ☎ *020/7629–8860 or 800/223–6800,* FAX *020/7499–2210,* WEB *www.savoy-group.co.uk. 200 rooms. Restaurant, bar, beauty salon, health club. AE, DC, MC, V. Tube: Bond St.*

££££ 🖀 **The Connaught.** Make reservations well in advance for this very ex-
★   clusive small hotel just off Grosvenor Square—the most understated of any of London's grand hostelries, and the London home-away-

from-home for guests who inherited the Connaught habit from their great-grandfathers. The bar and lounges have the air of an ambassadorial residence, an impression reinforced by the imposing oak staircase and dignified staff. Each bedroom has a foyer, antique furniture (if you don't like the desk, they'll change it), and fresh flowers. If you value privacy, discretion, and the kind of luxury that eschews labels, then this is the place for you. Recent innovations include a fitness studio and drawing room. ⊠ *Carlos Pl., W1Y 6AL,* ☎ *020/7499–7070,* ⅻ⅄ *020/7495– 3262,* ᵂᴱᴮ *www.savoy-group.co.uk. 90 rooms. Restaurant, bar. MC. Tube: Bond St.*

££££   ⊡ **The Dorchester.** Probably no other hotel this opulent manages to be
★   this charming. A London institution since its 1931 inception, the Dorchester appears on every "world's best" list. The glamour level is off the scale: 1,500 square yards of gold leaf and 1,100 square yards of marble. Bedrooms (some not as spacious as you might imagine) have Irish linen sheets on canopied beds, brocades and velvets, individual climate control, dual-voltage outlets, and Italian marble and etched-glass bathrooms with Floris goodies. Decor throughout is in opulent English country-house style, with more than a hint of art deco, in keeping with the original 1930s building. There's a beauty spa, a nightclub, a special theater-ticket concierge, the Oriental Restaurant, and the power-dining Grill Room. Taking afternoon tea, drinking, lounging, and posing are all accomplished in the catwalk-shape Promenade lounge, where you may spot one of the film-star types who will stay nowhere else. ⊠ *Park La., W1A 2HJ,* ☎ *020/7629–8888,* ⅻ⅄ *020/7409– 0114,* ᵂᴱᴮ *www.dorchesterhotel.com. 195 rooms, 53 suites. 2 restaurants, bar, health club, nightclub, business services, meeting room. AE, DC, MC, V. Tube: Marble Arch.*

££££   ⊡ **47 Park Street.** Back to back with the grand hotels of Park Lane, this dear (in every sense) little all-suite hotel has the best room service in town, with 24-hr food direct from the kitchen of Le Gavroche. Business services range from three personal phone lines to in-house translation facilities. Bathrooms are on the small side, but no other drawbacks are apparent in this fabulously discreet, conventionally decorated, quiet, relaxed, and homey haven—as long as you can afford it. ⊠ *47 Park St., W1Y 4EB,* ☎ *020/7491–7282,* ⅻ⅄ *020/7491–7281,* ᵂᴱᴮ *www. 47parkstreet.com. 52 suites. Dining room, bar, baby-sitting, business services. AE, DC, MC, V. Tube: Marble Arch.*

££££   ⊡ **Four Seasons Hotel London.** Business travelers, of course, swear by Four Seasons' standards of luxury and comfort. This hotel opened in the 1970s as Inn on the Park, so if wedding-cake Victorian architecture is your thing, go elsewhere. Still, the discretion and élan of this place (situated opposite Hyde Park, off the end of Piccadilly, and on the cusp of beautiful Mayfair) inspire greater-than-average loyalty in its guests. Every effort is made inside to keep up with the times—new features are constantly being added, the latest being the Lanes restaurant, which offers a sparkling menu and a view of Hyde Park to match. ⊠ *Hamilton Pl., Park La., W1A 1AZ,* ☎ *020/7499–0888 or 800/223– 6800,* ⅻ⅄ *020/7493–6629,* ᵂᴱᴮ *www.fourseasons.com. 228 rooms. Restaurant, health club. AE, DC, MC, V. Tube: Hyde Park Corner.*

££££   ⊡ **The Landmark.** In honor of its 100th anniversary, the one-time Great Central Hotel and former British Rail headquarters was renovated to within a glitzy inch of its life. A palm-filled, eight-story glazed atrium Winter Garden forms the core, and odd-numbered rooms overlook this. If size matters to you, note that even standard rooms here are among the largest in London and have glamorous bathrooms in marble and chrome outfitted with robes and hair dryers. Despite appearances, this is one of the only London grand hotels that doesn't force you to dress up; even jeans are okay, except in the new John Burton-Race restaurant. But eating manna from heaven in jeans is like smoking in church. Slacks, on the other hand, will do. The Landmark is very near Regent's Park; the West End is a 15-min walk away. ✉ *222 Marylebone Rd., NW1 6JQ,* ☎ *020/7631–8000,* FAX *020/7631–8080,* WEB *www. landmarklondon.co.uk. 297 rooms. 3 restaurants, 2 bars, pool, health club, business services. AE, DC, MC, V. Tube: Marylebone.*

££££ 🏨 **Langham Hilton.** Opened in 1865 by the Prince of Wales and once London's center of Victorian chic, the Langham has recently undergone a major face-lift. There's a new floor that caters specifically to the business crowd, and a health club over three floors with swimming pool, gym, hot tub, sauna and Elizabeth Arden treatment rooms. Otherwise, things haven't changed much since Mark Twain used to visit. The exterior is solid Empire stuff, especially at night, when floodlighting lends the pillars and porticos a massive chiaroscuro. Inside, the lobby soars to Castle Howard heights—here you find the Chukka Bar, a stately-house salon glowing with daffodil-yellow walls, for years a fave watering spot for the BBC brass across the way. Guest rooms are done in soothing Queen Mother pastels, and many have marble-bedecked bathrooms. You're just a few blocks from the Oxford Circus tube stop and many of the big Regent Street stores. ✉ *1C Portland Pl., W1B 1JA,* ☎ *020/7636–1000,* FAX *020/7323–2340,* WEB *www.langham.hilton. com. 429 rooms. 2 restaurants, bar, pool, sauna, gym. AE, DC, MC, V. Tube: Oxford Circus.*

££££ 🏨 **Le Meridien Grosvenor House.** "The old lady of Park Lane" is not the kind of place that encourages hushed whispers or that frowns on trendy Alexander McQueen outfits, despite the marble floors and wood-paneled library, open fires, oils, and fine antiques, all inspired by the Earl of Grosvenor's residence, which occupied the site during the 18th century. The hotel health club is one of the best around, thanks to its good-sized pool. Bedrooms are spacious, and most of the marble bathrooms have natural light. ✉ *Park La., W1A 3AA,* ☎ *020/ 7499–6363,* FAX *020/7493–3341,* WEB *www.grosvenorhouse.co.uk. 380 rooms, 70 suites, 136 apartments. 2 restaurants, bar, pool, health club. AE, DC, MC, V. Tube: Marble Arch.*

££££ 🏨 **Le Meridien Piccadilly.** The massive early-20th-century building is fin-de-siècle elegant, if slightly antiseptic in its white-marble-and-plush-carpet public areas. The vast Oak Room restaurant, however, is exquisite in limed oak paneling and gilt, and it is one of the best hotel restaurants in London. The hotel's second restaurant, far less formal, is a miniature Kew Gardens of arched glass, ferns, and palms. Bedrooms vary in size; a few seventh-floor ones have balconies overlooking Piccadilly. Decor is Edwardian gent's club with frills. The health club is both luxurious and exclusive. You can't be more central than here. ✉ *21 Piccadilly, W1V 0BH,* ☎ *020/7734–8000,* FAX *020/7437–3574,* WEB *www.grosvenorhouse.co.uk. 284 rooms. 3 restaurants, bar, pool, sauna, health club, squash, billiards, library, business services. AE, DC, MC, V. Tube: Piccadilly Circus.*

££££ 🏨 **The Metropolitan.** Supertrendy from the moment the DKNY-clad doormen opened the gates, this Park Lane grand is one of the only addresses for fashion folk, the music biz, and Hollywood youth, just as its bar is the hangout of choice (the barman even has his own column in a Sunday newspaper), and its restaurant, leased by Nobu Matsuhisa, of Nobu New York City "new-style sashimi" fame, is among the swankiest in town. The lobby is sleek and postmodern (psst . . . didn't the Royalton and other N.Y.C. hotels do this long ago?). The best rooms overlook Hyde Park, but all have identical minimalist beige-and-white decor, with climate control, bedside panel-operated lighting, U.S./U.K. modem points, ISDN lines, three telephone lines, and satellite and cable TV. The minibar contains the latest alcoholic and health-boosting beverages, and the bathroom's stocked with Kiehl's goodies. Be here, and pose. ⊠ *Old Park La., W1Y 4LB,* ☎ *020/7447–1000,* FAX *020/7447–1100,* WEB *www.metropolitan.co.uk. 137 rooms, 18 suites. Restaurant, bar, in-room data ports, massage, exercise room, business services, meeting room. AE, DC, MC, V. Tube: Hyde Park Corner.*

££££   ⊡ **The Montcalm.** Secreted behind Marble Arch in a peaceful Georgian crescent, the Montcalm has kept a low profile since its rock-star days, but it is now back up there with the best of them, thanks to the Japanese owners, Nikko, who have made it an especially efficient, spotless, and calm hotel with some unusual features. Here is London's only low-allergen bedroom, its only canopied water bed (not in the same room), and one of its few Japanese breakfasts; bathrooms have hair dryers and bidets, and, by the conservatorylike Crescent restaurant, a CD-operated player piano serenades lunchers with a little Brahms. The duplex suites, with their cast-iron spiral staircases, are especially winning. ⊠ *Great Cumberland Pl., W1A 2LF,* ☎ *020/7402–4288,* FAX *020/7724–9180,* WEB *www.montcalm.co.uk. 120 rooms. Restaurant, bar, meeting room. AE, DC, MC, V. Tube: Marble Arch.*

£££–££££   ⊡ **Chesterfield Mayfair.** This former town house of the Earl of Chesterfield is popular with American visitors, many of whom are repeat guests or have links with the English Speaking Union, which has its headquarters next door. It is deep in the heart of Mayfair and has welcoming wood-and-leather public rooms. ⊠ *35 Charles St., W12 SEB,* ☎ *020/7491–2622,* FAX *020/7491–4793,* WEB *www.redcarnationhotels. com. 110 rooms. Restaurant. AE, DC, MC, V. Tube: Green Park.*

£££–££££   ⊡ **The Leonard.** Four 17th-century buildings were combined in 1996 to create this property. Shoppers will particularly appreciate the Mayfair location, just around the corner from Oxford Street. If you stay in a two-bedroom superior suite, you can swing by Marks & Spencer's food halls for provisions, then whip up a dinner in your private kitchen—a plus for families and visitors on longer trips. All suites have a remarkably residential feel, with sitting and bedroom areas set off by small foyers and complemented by a judicious mix of lived-in antiques and comfortable reproductions. For more elbow room, try one of the aptly named grand suites, with their palatial sitting rooms and tall windows. The welcoming lobby area is stocked with complimentary newspapers to read by the fire. ⊠ *15 Seymour St., W1H 5AA,* ☎ *020/7935–2010,* FAX *020/7935–6700,* WEB *www.theleonard.com. 20 suites, 9 rooms. Bar, dining room, room service, exercise room, business services. AE, DC, MC, V. Tube: Marble Arch.*

££   ⊡ **Bryanston Court.** Three Georgian houses have been converted into a hotel in a historic conservation area, a couple of blocks north of Hyde Park and Park Lane. The style is traditional English—open fireplaces, comfortable leather armchairs, oil portraits—though the bedrooms are small and modern, with pink furnishings, creaky floors, and minute bathrooms. Rooms at the back are quieter and face east, so they're bright in the mornings; Room 77 is as big as a suite, but, typical of rooms in London houses, it's dark. This family-run hotel is an excellent value for the area. ⊠ *56–60 Great Cumberland Pl., W1H 7FD,* ☎ *020/7262–3141,* FAX *020/7262–7248,* WEB *www.bryanstonhotel.com. 56 rooms. Breakfast room, bar. AE, DC, MC, V. BP. Tube: Marble Arch.*

££   ⊡ **Dorset Square Hotel.** This special small hotel off Baker Street was
★   the first of five London addresses for husband and wife Tim and Kit Kemp, hoteliers extraordinaire. What they did was decant the English country look into a fine pair of Regency town houses. Everywhere you look are covetable antiques, rich colors, and ideas *House & Garden* subscribers will steal. Naturally, every room is different: the first-floor balconied "Coronet" rooms are the largest, and a virtue is made of the smallness of the small rooms. The marble-and-mahogany bathrooms

have power showers; glossy magazines, a half bottle of claret, and boxes of vitamin C are complimentary. There's a reason for the ubiquitous cricket memorabilia: Dorset Square was the first Lord's grounds. If you want a car rental here, you get a Bentley. ⊠ *39–40 Dorset Sq., NW1 6QN,* ☎ *020/7723–7874,* FAX *020/7724–3328,* WEB *www.firmdale.com. 38 rooms. Restaurant, bar. AE, MC, V. Tube: Baker St.*

££ 🖫 **Durrants.** A hotel since the late 18th century, Durrants occupies a quiet corner almost next to the Wallace Collection, a stone's throw from Oxford Street and the smaller, posher shops of Marylebone High Street. It's a good value for the area, and if you like ye wood-panel, leather-armchair, dark-red patterned carpet style of olde Englishness, this will suit you. ⊠ *George St., W1H 6BH,* ☎ *020/7935–8131,* FAX *020/7487–3510,* WEB *www.durrantshotel.co.uk. 92 rooms, 85 with bath. Restaurant, bar, dining room. AE, MC, V. Tube: Bond St.*

££ 🖫 **Four Seasons Hotel.** This has nothing to do with the Four Seasons opposite Hyde Park or the Four Seasons Hotel Canary Wharf; there are no stunning views over the Thames, Phillipe Starck basins, or soundless elevators here. The rooms are clean, however, and come with a hair dryer in one of the drawers and a digital television by your bed. There's a breakfast room that sports a glass roof. This is bare bones stuff, but the hotel is close to Regent's Park and is reasonably priced. ⊠ *173 Gloucester Pl., NW1 6DX,* ☎ *020/7724–3461,* FAX *020/7402–5594,* WEB *www.4seasonshotel.co.uk. 28 rooms. Breakfast room, lounge. AE, DC, MC, V. CP. Tube: Baker St.*

££ 🖫 **Novotel Waterloo.** Looking otherwise precisely like 280 other hotels in 44 countries, this French-owned, inexpensive, reliable chain hotel offers a fitness center, brasserie, and conference facilities, plus in-room satellite TV, tea/coffeemaker, direct-dial phone, and hair dryer. Views vary, but basically you're looking at Lambeth Palace, the Houses of Parliament, or Big Ben. Mind you, the romance rating does plummet when you can't fling open the window to catch the Thames breeze on account of the guest-room climate-control system. ⊠ *113–127 Lambeth Rd., SE1 7LS,* ☎ *020/7793–1010. 187 rooms. Restaurant, bar, health club, meeting room. AE, DC, MC, V. Tube: Waterloo or Lambeth North.*

£ 🖫 **Edward Lear.** This family-run guest house, just a minute's walk from Oxford Street, is in a Georgian town house that was formerly the home of the master of nonsense verse, Edward Lear. The location is the biggest selling point for this place, as rooms tend to be small and the decor outdated. There are no hotel-type facilities, although if you want a jacket pressed you're welcome to borrow the iron. The management is very proud of the English breakfasts—it uses the same butcher as the Queen. ⊠ *28–30 Seymour St., W1H 5WD,* ☎ *020/7402–5401,* FAX *020/7706–3766,* WEB *www.edlear.com. 31 rooms, 15 with shower (no toilet), 4 with full bath. Breakfast room. MC, V. BP. Tube: Marble Arch.*

St. James's

££££ 🖫 **Dukes.** This small, exclusive, Edwardian-style hotel, with its lantern-lighted entrance, is central but still quiet, as it is set in its own discreet cul-de-sac, where the Stafford also lies. A small hotel of character, it's suitably filled with squashy sofas, oil paintings of assorted dukes, and muted, rich colors, and is the home of the finest dry martinis in town. Its trump cards are that, for such a central location, it offers immense peace and quiet and very reasonable rates, personal service (they greet you by name every time), and an especially sweet suite or two, on the top floor, with views over St. James's Park. ⊠ *35 St. James's Pl., SW1A 1NY,* ☎ *020/7491–4840,* FAX *020/7493–1264,* WEB *www.*

dukeshotel.co.uk. 80 rooms. Restaurant, dining room. AE, DC, MC, V. Tube: Green Park.

££££ ⚃ **The Stafford.** This hotel is most famous for its utterly amazing American Bar, where a million ties, baseball caps, and toy planes hang from a ceiling modeled, presumably, on New York's "21" Club, but it is also prized for its 12 carriage-house rooms, installed in the 18th-century stable block. Relative bargains, each of these cute and private accommodations has its own cobbled mews entrance and features gas-log fires, black-stained exposed beams, CD players, CNN, and safes. The main hotel has navy-and-gold hallways, rooms with china in cabinets or French doors to the bathrooms, and air-conditioning throughout, but the gorgeous mews remains the Stafford's best profile. Guests have complimentary access to Champney's Piccadilly, one of London's top health clubs. ✉ *St. James's Pl., SW1A 1NJ,* ☎ *020/7493–0111,* FAX *020/7493–7121,* WEB *www.thestaffordhotel.co.uk. 81 rooms. Restaurant, bar, dining room. AE, DC, MC, V. Tube: Green Park.*

Soho and Covent Garden

££££ ⚃ **Charlotte Street.** Taking inspiration from the Bloomsbury period, this hotel is the newest of Tim and Kit Kemp's five hotels and it doesn't disappoint. Set in a quiet street in North Soho, it fuses the modern and traditional. Bathrooms are lined with gleaming granite and oak, and there are walk-in showers and deep baths; and, since each bathroom has a mini flat-screen TV, you can catch up on the news while you soak. All rooms are unique: Kit Kemp is a maestro, and you will want to come back to the same room, your room, again and again. The restaurant, Oscar, is excellent. There is a screening room with Ferrari leather chairs if you feel like watching a movie. If not, you might just want to read a paper by the fire. ✉ *15 Charlotte St., W1P 1HB,* ☎ *020/7907–4000,* FAX *020/7806–2002,* WEB *www.charlottestreethotel.com. 52 rooms. Restaurant, gym, cinema. AE, DC, MC, V. Tube: Goodge St.*

££££ ⚃ **Covent Garden Hotel.** A former 1880s hospital in the midst of artsy
★ and boisterous Covent Garden, this hotel is now the London home-away-from-home for a mélange of off-duty celebrities, actors, and style mavens. The public salons will keep even the most picky atmosphere-hunter happy: wallowing in painted silks, style *anglais* ottomans, and 19th-century Romantic oils, they are perfect places to decompress over a glass of sherry. Guest rooms are *World of Interiors* stylish, each showcasing matching-but-mixed couture fabrics to stunning effect. ✉ *10 Monmouth St., WC2H 9HB,* ☎ *020/7806–1000,* FAX *020/7806–1100,* WEB *www.firmdale.com. 58 rooms, 3 suites. Restaurant, minibars, room service, exercise room, laundry service. AE, MC, V. Tube: Covent Garden.*

££££ ⚃ **Four Seasons Hotel Canary Wharf.** Magnificent, copper-roofed, reminding one faintly of George Orwell's Ministry of Truth, the Four Seasons sits on a vast pedestal above a wriggling mass of thruways, tunnels, and overpasses. The astonishing thing about this hotel is the calm. Glass doors swish open; islands of armchairs float on cool gray marble; elevators pass up and down without a murmur. The rooms are identical, but only the more expensive ones have the breathtaking views over the river. The beds are large and unfussy; the windows are plate-glass rectangles, letting in light and the view. Earthly amenities, such as data ports, TVs with Internet access, and outlets with American voltage, are concealed. The northern Italian restaurant has a mouthwatering menu, which does not include pizza. Come here if you are bound to the nearby City and do not love Andrew Lloyd Webber, who is far away in the West End. ✉ *46 Westferry Circus, E14 8R,* ☎ *020/7510–1999,* FAX *020/7510–1990,* WEB *www.fourseasons.com. 142* rooms. *Restaurant, bar, in-room data ports, in-room safes, room service, massage, exercise room, baby-sitting, laundry service, dry cleaning, business services. AE, D, DC, MC, V. Tube: Canary Wharf.*

££££ 🏨 **Le Meridien Waldorf.** Close to the Aldwych theaters and Covent Garden, the Waldorf gleams in luscious Edwardiana, with polished marble floors, chandeliers, and cozily comfortable period bedrooms. This is a booking challenge for the wealthy theatergoer (Waldorf or Savoy?) and a suitably glamorous setting for the famous Palm Court tea dances, still going strong every weekend after nearly 90 years. ✉ *Aldwych, WC2B 4DD,* ☎ *020/7836–2400,* FAX *020/7836–7244,* WEB *www. hotelsengland.com. 292 rooms. Restaurant, 2 bars, brasserie, beauty salon. AE, DC, MC, V. Tube: Aldwych.*

££££ 🏨 **One Aldwych.** If stuffy Victoriana and chintz are not your scene, then One Aldwych's understated blend of contemporary and classic might offer the modern luxe you seek. Set in a grand Edwardian-period pile, this flawlessly designed hotel with its coolly eclectic lobby, feather duvets, Italian linen sheets, and quirky touches—a TV in every bathroom—is the ultimate in twenty-first century style. Poised between the City and the West End (and overlooking a major traffic intersection), the hotel comes complete with stylish restaurants and bars, a swimming pool, and holistic fitness trainers. There's even a high-energy espresso bar, if all this leaves you flat. But like all good things, it comes at a price—and not a cheap one either. ✉ *1 Aldwych, WC2 4BZ,* ☎ *020/7300–1000,* FAX *020/7300–1001,* WEB *www.onealdwych.co.uk. 105 rooms. 2 restaurants, 2 bars, pool, business services, health club. AE, MC, V. Tube: Charing Cross, Covent Garden.*

££££ 🏨 **Radisson Mountbatten.** Naming the hotel after the late Lord Mountbatten, last viceroy of India and favorite uncle of Prince Charles, is probably just an excuse to go overboard with the old British Raj theme. The decor reflects Mountbatten's life: photos of the estate where he lived, Indian furnishings, silks, inlaid tables, and screens. It has a good standard of service; bedrooms in various shades of red, with chintz drapes; and bathrooms of Italian marble. A pianist performs in the comfortable bar, and there are posttheater cabarets at the Ad Lib restaurant twice a week. Two executive floors are being built as part of a major overhaul. On a somewhat lackluster street, the hotel is a minute's walk from the Covent Garden Piazza. ✉ *20 Monmouth St., WC2H 9HD,* ☎ *020/7836–4300,* FAX *020/7340–3540,* WEB *www.radissonedwardian.com. 128 rooms. Restaurant, bar. AE, DC, MC, V. Tube: Covent Garden.*

££££ 🏨 **Radisson Pastoria.** A slightly less exorbitant choice for the theatergoer than the Waldorf and the rest, the Pastoria is handily situated just off Leicester Square. The building is about 70 years old, with a suitably modern decor, the bedrooms done in limed oak with light pink walls and navy-blue carpets. There's a brasserie-style restaurant to dine in, but Soho, which is restaurant central, is only a few hundred yards away. ✉ *3–6 St. Martin's St., WC2H 7HL,* ☎ *020/7930–8641,* FAX *020/ 7925–0551,* WEB *www.radissonedwardian.com. 58 rooms. Restaurant, bar, coffee shop. AE, DC, MC, V. Tube: Leicester Sq.*

££££ 🏨 **The Ritz.** The name conjures the kind of luxury associated with thick swagged curtains, handwoven carpets, the smell of cigars, polish, and fresh lilies; it signifies a magical Edwardian opulence. Although the hotel was not itself in recent decades, a 1995 renovation by the Barclay brothers made it a by-word for blue-chip luxury once more. The only thing that has been lost is a certain vein of moneyed naughtiness that someone like F. Scott Fitzgerald, at least, would have banked on. ✉ *150 Piccadilly, W1J 9BR,* ☎ *020/7493–8181,* FAX *020/7493–2687,* WEB *www.theritzhotel.co.uk. 133 rooms. Restaurant, bar, gym, hair salon, meeting rooms. AE, DC, MC, V. Tube: Piccadilly Circus.*

££££ 🖭 **St. Martins Lane.** Philippe Starck designed Ian Schrager's hip new hotel to be theatrical, and he has succeeded. In the foyer are a Victorian chaise lounge, a row of golden molars doubling as tables, some life-size chess pieces, and the odd bowler hat. The guests are actors here, as is the staff, on display as they sit at the ice trough in the fish bar, wield their chopsticks in Asia de Cuba, or lounge on leather armchairs in the brasserie. Guest rooms are small, expensive, cluttered, and homogeneous, but fans of Schrager's hotels (of which the Sanderson is another London effort) will likely be pleased. ⊠ *45 St. Martins La., WC2N 4HX,* ☎ *020/7300–5500,* ℻ *020/7300–5501. 204 rooms. Restaurant, bar, brasserie, in-room data ports, in-room VCRs, minibars, no-smoking room, room service, massage, sauna, exercise room, dry cleaning, laundry service, concierge, business services, meeting room, parking (fee). AE, MC, V. Tube: Leicester Sq.*

££££ 🖭 **The Savoy.** This historic, grand late-Victorian hotel is beloved by wield-
★   ers of international influence, now as ever. Its celebrated Grill has the premier power-lunch tables; it hosted Elizabeth Taylor's first honeymoon in one of its famous river-view rooms; and it poured one of Europe's first dry martinis in its equally famous American Bar—haunted by Hemingway, Fitzgerald, Gershwin, et al. And does it measure up to this high profile? Absolutely. The impeccably maintained, spacious, elegant, bright, and comfortable rooms are furnished with antiques and serviced by valets. A room facing the Thames costs an arm and a leg and requires an early booking, but no other hotel betters that view. Bathrooms have original fittings, with the same sunflower-size showerheads as at Claridge's. Though the Savoy is as grand as they come, the air is tinged with a certain naughtiness, which goes down well with Hollywood types. Others may enjoy the tea and dancing on Sundays. ⊠ *Strand, WC2R 0EU,* ☎ *020/7836–4343,* ℻ *020/7240–6040,* 🕸 *www. savoy-group.co.uk. 224 rooms. 3 restaurants, 2 bars, pool, beauty salon, health club. AE, DC, MC, V. Tube: Aldwych.*

£££ 🖭 **Hazlitt's.** The solo Soho hotel is in three connected, early 18th-cen-
★   tury houses, one of which was the last home of essayist William Hazlitt (1778–1830). It's a disarmingly friendly place, full of personality, but devoid of elevators, owing to its status as a listed building. Robust antiques are everywhere, assorted prints crowd every wall, plants and stone sculptures appear in odd corners, and every room has a Victorian claw-foot tub in its bathroom. There are tiny sitting rooms, wooden staircases, and more restaurants within strolling distance than you could patronize in a year. Book way ahead—this is the London address of media people, literary types, and antiques dealers. ⊠ *6 Frith St., W1V 5TZ,* ☎ *020/7434–1771,* ℻ *020/7439–1524. 23 rooms. AE, DC, MC, V. Tube: Piccadilly.*

££ 🖭 **The Fielding.** Tucked away in a quiet pedestrian alley by the world's first police station (now Bow St. Magistrates' Court), this small hotel is popular with people visiting London to take in an opera—the Royal Opera House Covent Garden is just down the street. This is the cheapest place to stay in Covent Garden, but for the money you could get you a lot more comfort elsewhere. Bedrooms tend toward the shabby and there are no amenities. ⊠ *4 Broad Ct., Bow St., WC2B 5QZ,* ☎ *020/7836–8305,* ℻ *020/7497–0064. 24 rooms. Bar, breakfast room. AE, DC, MC, V. Tube: Covent Garden.*

££ 🖭 **Regent Palace Hotel.** There are 920 rooms in this warren just off Piccadilly Circus. The foyer is reminiscent of a small airport terminal. In general, the whole place, including the rooms, is in need of an overhaul. However, service is friendly and efficient, and there is a concierge that can help with theater tickets and tours. If you're on a tight budget, are not too fussy, and need to be in the thick of it, this is the place for you. Some rooms have a toilet and shower. ⊠ *Glass House St., W1A 4BZ,*

☎ 020/8400–8703, FAX 020/7734–6435, WEB *www.forte-hotels.co.uk. 920 rooms. Bar, breakfast room, concierge. AE, DC, MC, V. Tube: Piccadilly Circus.*

Kensington

££££   ⛱ **Blakes.** Blakes is another world. It was designed by owner Anouska
★   Hempel (also known as Lady Weinberg), and each room is a fantasy
       packed with precious Biedermeier, Murano glass, and modern pieces
       inside walls of red lacquer and black, or dove-gray moiré, or per-
       haps—like Room 007, the movie stars' favorite suite—blood red and
       lily white. Cinematic mood lighting, featuring recessed halogen spots,
       compounds the impression that you, too, are a movie star living in a
       big-budget biopic. The foyer sets the tone with its piles of cushions,
       Phileas Fogg valises and trunks, black walls, rattan and bamboo, and
       a couple of love birds under a gigantic Asian parasol. Downstairs is
       an equally dramatic, exotic black-and-white restaurant. Stay away if
       you don't like Hollywood or the music biz. ✉ *33 Roland Gardens,
       SW7 3PF,* ☎ *020/7370–6701,* FAX *020/7373–0442. 52 rooms. Restau-
       rant. AE, DC, MC, V. Tube: South Kensington.*

£££–££££ ⛱ **The Cranley.** New owners have refurbished this small Georgian
       town-house hotel in South Ken, bringing together traditional standards
       of service and the latest technology. So it's out with the heavy, swagged
       floral curtains and in with the cool neutrality of our modern age—though
       Auntie Dorris will be delighted to learn that afternoon tea is compli-
       mentary. Many of the bedrooms have high ceilings and huge win-
       dows. ✉ *10–12 Bina Gardens, SW5 0LA,* ☎ *020/7373–0123,* FAX
       020/7373–9497, WEB *www.thecranley.co.uk. 33 rooms, 2 suites, 1
       apartment. AE, DC, MC, V. Tube: Gloucester Rd.*

£££–££££ ⛱ **The Gore.** Just down the road from the Albert Hall, this very friendly
★   hotel is run by the same people who run Hazlitt's and has a similarly
       eclectic selection of prints, etchings, and antiques—the lobby looks like
       a set from a Luchino Visconti film. Upstairs are spectacular follylike
       rooms—Room 101 is a Tudor fantasy with minstrel gallery, stained
       glass, and four-poster bed, and Room 211, done in over-the-top Hol-
       lywood style, has a tiled mural of Greek goddesses in the bathroom.
       The hotel gets a fun, chic, partying crowd. ✉ *189 Queensgate, SW7
       5EX,* ☎ *020/7584–6601,* FAX *020/7589–8127,* WEB *www.gorehotel.com.
       54 rooms. Restaurant. AE, DC, MC, V. Tube: Gloucester Rd.*

£££–££££ ⛱ **Number Sixteen.** A luxury bed-and-breakfast close to South Kens-
       ington tube and three blocks or so from the great museums, Number
       Sixteen stands in a white-portico row of Victorian houses, with no sign
       outside to identify it. There's no uniformity to the bedrooms except
       for their similar spaciousness and refitted bathrooms, but the decor is
       not so much interior-designed as understated—new furniture and mod-
       ern prints are juxtaposed with yellowed oils and antiques. There's an
       elevator and an enticing garden complete with conservatory and foun-
       tainette. ✉ *16 Sumner Pl., SW7 3EG,* ☎ *020/7589–5232; 800/592–
       5387 in U.S.,* FAX *020/7584–8615,* WEB *www.numbersixteenhotel.co.uk.
       36 rooms. Bar. AE, DC, MC, V. BP. Tube: South Kensington.*

££   ⛱ **Forte Posthouse Kensington.** This mammoth, fairly utilitarian hotel
       feels like a smaller one and boasts a few extras you wouldn't expect
       for the rates, at the low end of this category, and a convenient loca-
       tion on a quiet lane off Kensington High Street. The main attraction
       is the health club, with a sizable pool, two squash courts, a steam room,
       and a beauty salon; there's also a secluded little water garden. Stan-
       dard rooms are on the small side, with plain chain-hotel built-in fur-
       niture. Some "executive" rooms are twice the size and are a particularly
       good value. ✉ *Wrights La., W8 5SP,* ☎ *020/8400–9000,* FAX *020/7937–*

Lodging in Kensington, Knightsbridge, Chelsea, Belgravia and Westminster

Abbey House **2**
Basil Street **19**
Beaufort **15**
Berkeley **21**
Blakes **9**
Capital **20**
The Cranley **7**

Crowne Plaza London
St. James Hotel
& Suites **33**
The Diplomat **24**
Eden Plaza **6**
Egerton House **14**
Eleven Cadogan
Gardens **26**

Elizabeth Hotel **28**
Forte Posthouse
Kensington **3**
41 . . . . **32**
The Franklin **13**
The Gallery **5**
The Gore **4**

Goring **30**
The Halkin **22**
Hotel 167 . . . . **8**
Knightsbridge
Green **18**
Knightsbridge
Hotel **16**
La Reserve **10**

The
Lanesborough **23**
L'Hôtel **17**
London County Hall
Travel Inn Capital . . **36**
London
Marriott Hotel,
County Hall **35**

London Tower
Bridge Travel
Inn Capital **37**
Melita House
Hotel **29**
Morgan House **27**
Number Sixteen **12**
The Pelham **11**

The Rubens **31**
The Sloane **25**
St. Ermin's Hotel . . . **34**
Vicarage **1**

8289. 543 rooms. 3 restaurants, 2 bars, pool, health club, squash, baby-sitting. AE, DC, MC, V. Tube: High Street Kensington.

££ ▣ **The Gallery.** This hotel is a stone's throw from the Natural History Museum, the shops of South Kensington and Chelsea, and the once racy but now merely trendy King's Road. There are lush carpets, cozy fires, and sturdy furniture. The rooms are a good size with solid comfortable beds. The bathrooms have London's ubiquitous polished granite. Included in the price is a full English breakfast—which will make lunching something of a challenge. ⊠ *10 Queensberry Pl., SW7 2E8,* ☎ *020/7915–0000,* FAX *020/7915–4400,* WEB *www.eeh.co.uk. 36 rooms. Breakfast room. AE, DC, MC, V. Tube: South Kensington. BP.*

£ ▣ **Abbey House.** Next door to the Vicarage, Abbey House has been
★ voted "Best Value, Best Quality B&B in London" in several surveys, so you'll have to book well in advance for the doubles. In a pretty, white-stucco 1860 Victorian town house—once home to a bishop and an M.P. before World War II—the hotel is in an excellent location close to trendy Notting Hill. Rooms are spacious and have color TVs and washbasins, but every room shares a bath with another. An English breakfast is included in the rates, and a cuppa (cup of tea) is complimentary. ⊠ *11 Vicarage Gate, W8 4AG,* ☎ *020/7727–2594,* WEB *www.abbeyhouse-kensington.com. 16 rooms without bath. No credit cards. BP. Tube: High Street Kensington.*

£ ▣ **Eden Plaza.** It isn't very idyllic at all, but it is across the street from the Natural History Museum in swanky South Kensington. The reasonably priced rooms are extremely compact—there's about one foot of space around the bed, and the walls have been painted in bright neon colors. Despite their small size, the rooms do have closets, mirrors, satellite TV, tea/coffeemakers, and hair dryers cleverly concealed. ⊠ *68–69 Queensgate, SW7 5JT,* ☎ *020/7370–6111,* FAX *020/7370–0932. 62 rooms. Bar. AE, MC, V. CP. Tube: Gloucester Rd.*

£ ▣ **Hotel 167.** Just a two-minute walk from the V&A is this white-stucco Victorian corner house. Rooms are pleasantly decorated with pine furniture and muted tones and each has cable TV and a minibar. The hallways and stairwells have seen better days. ⊠ *167 Old Brompton Rd., SW5 0AN,* ☎ *020/7373–0672,* FAX *020/7373–3360,* WEB *www. hotel167.com. 18 rooms. Breakfast room. AE, DC, MC, V. CP. Tube: Gloucester Rd.*

£ ▣ **The Vicarage.** Spend the cash you save here in the surrounding Kensington antiques shops. This has long been a favorite for the budget-minded. Family-owned and set on a leaf-shaded street just off Kensington Church Street, the Vicarage occupies a large white Victorian house. The decor is sweetly anachronistic, full of heavy and dark-stained wood furniture, patterned carpets, and brass pendant lights, and there's a little conservatory. Many of the bedrooms now have TVs. All in all, this still remains a charmer—but it is beginning to fray around the edges. All rooms share the bathroom, but a few doubles have their own showers. ⊠ *10 Vicarage Gate, W8 4AG,* ☎ *020/7229–4030,* FAX *020/7792–5989,* WEB *www.londonvicaragehotel.com. 18 rooms without bath. No credit cards. BP. Tube: High Street Kensington.*

Knightsbridge, Chelsea, Belgravia, Victoria, and Westminster

££££ ▣ **The Beaufort.** You can practically hear the jingle of Harrods' cash
★ registers from a room at the Beaufort, the brainchild of ex–TV announcer Diana Wallis, who employs an all-woman team to run the hotel. Actually, "hotel" is a misnomer for this elegant pair of Victorian houses. There's a sitting room instead of reception; guests have a front door key, the run of the drinks cabinet, and even their own phone number.

The high-ceilinged, generously proportioned rooms are decorated in muted, sophisticated shades to suit the muted, sophisticated atmosphere—but don't worry, you're encouraged by the incredibly sweet staff to feel at home. The rates are high but include unlimited drinks (Grand Cru champagne if you fancy), English cream tea, breakfast, and membership at a local health club. ⊠ *33 Beaufort Gardens, SW3 1PP,* ☎ *020/7584–5252,* FAX *020/7589–2834,* WEB *www.thebeaufort.co.uk. 28 rooms. AE, DC, MC, V. CP. Tube: Knightsbridge.*

££££ 🔟 **The Berkeley.** The Berkeley is a successful mixture of the old and
★ the new—a luxurious, air-conditioned, double-glazed modern building with a splendid penthouse swimming pool that opens to the sky when the weather's good. The bedrooms have swags of William Morris prints or are plain and masculine with little balconies overlooking the street. All have sitting areas and big, tiled bathrooms with bidets. For the ridiculously rich, there are spectacular suites, one with its own conservatory terrace, another with a sauna, but—such is the elegance of this place—you'd feel almost as spoiled in a normal room. La Tante Claire, one of London's finest restaurants, is designed on a camellia theme, the flower that was the favorite of French fashion guru Coco Chanel. The other restaurant is just as glittering: Vong, the Thai-French hybrid cloned from New York, whose expensive decor, work-of-art dishes, and exorbitant prices are going down very well with London's big spenders. ⊠ *Wilton Pl., SW1X 7RL,* ☎ *020/7235–6000,* FAX *020/7235–4330,* WEB *www.savoy-group.co.uk. 160 rooms. 2 restaurants, beauty salon, health club, pool, cinema. AE, DC, MC, V. Tube: Knightsbridge.*

££££ 🔟 **The Capital.** Reserve well ahead if you want a room here—as you must for a table in the hotel's superb restaurant. This grand hotel decanted into a private house is the work of the Levin family, who also own L'Hôtel, and it exudes their irreproachable taste, with fine-grained woods, original prints, and shelves of books. The 6 rooms of the Edwardian Wing, with its carved-wood staircase, were already the height of fashion in the 1920s when this was the Squires Hotel. Today, the stylish interiors enjoy the attentions of superstar designer Nina Campbell and master joiner David Linley. ⊠ *22–24 Basil St., SW3 1AT,* ☎ *020/7589–5171,* FAX *020/7225–0011,* WEB *www.capitalhotel.co.uk. 48 rooms. Restaurant, bar, dining room, meeting rooms. AE, DC, MC, V. Tube: Knightsbridge.*

££££ 🔟 **Crowne Plaza London St. James Hotel & Suites.** You enter this Edwardian pile through a pair of enormous wrought-iron gates, which used to admit carriages into what is now the towering reception. From here, you pass ranks of green-leather sofas to reach the pièce de résistance: the landscaped courtyard with its fountain and ceramic frieze of scenes from Shakespeare. Some bedrooms are disproportionately large but cost the same as standards—the reverse is also true, so beware the expensive shoe boxes—and all are plainly decorated in pallid shades with a smattering of antiques and the odd (and some are *very* odd) painting. There are two good restaurants and a business center, and many apartments offer good deals for weekly and longer stays, but unless you have business at Buckingham Palace or around Victoria, the location isn't central enough to warrant the rates. ⊠ *45–51 Buckingham Gate, SW1E 6AF,* ☎ *020/7834–6655,* FAX *020/7630–7587,* WEB *www.london.crowneplaza. com. 356 rooms. 2 restaurants, coffee shop, health club, business services. AE, DC, MC, V. Tube: St. James's Park.*

££££ 🔟 **41.** Elegance doesn't always mean chintz and brocade, a point proven by the simply named "41." The black-and-white decor, with art deco touches, lends an air of subtle sophistication. The rooms are filled with high-tech gadgets—the television is also a personal computer with high-speed Internet access. A printer, scanner, and fax are at your fingertips. You'll even find business cards with your name on them. When you're finished with work, relax on the buttery-soft leather sofa in front of the fireplace, recline on the exquisite bed linens and feather duvets, or luxuriate in the marble bath overflowing with Penhaligon toiletries. Gourmet meals are included in the rate, so feel free to dine in your room or in the mahogany-panel executive lounge. Feeling peckish at half past three? Your butler will be glad to bring something up. ✉ *41 Buckingham Palace Rd., SW1W OPS,* ☎ *020/7300–0041,* FAX *020/7300–0141,* WEB *www.redcarnationhotels.com. 16 rooms, 4 suites. Lounge, in-room data ports, in-room fax, in-room safe, minibars, room service, dry cleaning, laundry service, business services, meeting rooms. AE, DC, MC, V. Tube: Victoria.*

££££ 🏨 **The Goring.** Readers love this hotel—after all, where else does the concierge offer to pack up some bread crumbs for the ducks if you're heading for a stroll in Hyde Park? This hotel is useful if you have to drop in at Buckingham Palace, just around the corner. In fact, visiting VIPs use it regularly as a conveniently close, and suitably dignified, base for royal occasions. The hotel was built by Mr. Goring in 1910 and is now run by third-generation Gorings. The atmosphere remains Edwardian: bathrooms are marble-fitted, and some of the bedrooms have brass bedsteads and the original built-in closets; many have been opulently redecorated. The newly revamped bar and terrace look onto a well-tended garden. ✉ *15 Beeston Pl., Grosvenor Gardens, SW1W 0JW,* ☎ *020/7396–9000,* FAX *020/7834–4393,* WEB *www.goringhotel.co.uk. 74 rooms. Restaurant, bar. AE, DC, MC, V. Tube: Victoria.*

££££ 🏨 **The Halkin.** If you can't take any more Regency stripes, English-country florals, or Louis XV chaises, this luxurious little place is the antidote. Chill out to the Milanese design: the clean-cut white-marble lobby with its royal-blue-leather bucket chairs; the arresting, curved, charcoal-gray corridors; the "diseased mahogany" veneers; and the gray-on-gray bedrooms that light up when you insert your electronic key. Wealthy business and media types frequent the Halkin, so rooms feature fax machines and two phone lines with conference-call capacities, along with two touch-control pads for all the gadgets, cable TV, and VCR. The bathrooms are palaces of shiny chrome. Staying here might be like living in the Design Museum, except that this place employs some of the friendliest staff around—who look pretty good in their blue or black Armani uniforms. ✉ *5 Halkin St., SW1X 7DJ,* ☎ *020/7333–1000,* FAX *020/7333–1100,* WEB *www.halkin.co.uk. 41 rooms. Restaurant, business services. AE, DC, MC, V. Tube: Hyde Park Corner.*

££££ 🏨 **The Lanesborough.** This very grand hotel acts for all the world as though
★   the Prince Regent took a ride through time and is about to resume residence. Royally proportioned public rooms (not lounges but "the Library" and "the Withdrawing Room") lead one off the other like an exquisite giant Chinese box in this multimillion-pound, American-run conversion of the old St. George's Hospital opposite Wellington's house. Everything undulates with richness—brocades and Regency stripes; moiré silks and fleurs-de-lys in the colors of precious stones; magnificent antiques and oil paintings; reproductions of more gilded splendor than the originals; handwoven £250-per-square-yard carpet—as if Liberace and Laura Ashley had collaborated on the design. All you do to register is sign the visitor's book, then retire to your room, where you are waited on by a personal butler. Full-size Lanesborough toiletries, umbrellas (take them home), robes (don't), a drinks tray (pay by the inch), and even business cards with your temporary fax (in every room) and phone numbers (two lines) are waiting. If you yearn for a bygone age and are very rich, this is certainly for you. ✉ *Hyde Park Corner, SW1X 7TA,* ☎ *020/7259–5599,* FAX *020/7259–5606,* WEB *www.lanesborough.com. 95 rooms. 2 restaurants, bar. AE, DC, MC, V. Tube: Hyde Park Corner.*

££££ 🏨 **London Marriott Hotel, County Hall.** This exceptionally grand hotel has what visitors to London most often request and which up until now has not been available—a view of the Houses of Parliament across the Thames (which means, of course, that the hotel is not in Westminster but on the south side of the river). It's in the former home of the long-defunct local governing body—a mammoth, spectacular, pedimented and columned affair—and uses the old Members' entrance, with its bronze doors and marble lobby leading into the former Council Chamber. A Marriott is a reliable thing, and this one has all the expected deluxe accoutrements—from modern, businesslike decor to almost instantly arriving elevators, and from conference facilities to the use of the fantastic 24-hour Health & Fitness Spa on the top floors. ✉ *County Hall, SE1 7PB,* ☎ *020/7928–5200,* FAX *020/7928–5300,* WEB *www.marriott.com. 200 rooms. Bar, lounge, pool, health club. AE, DC, MC, V. Tube: Westminster.*

££££ 🏨 **The Rubens.** This hotel likes to say it treats you like royalty—after all, you're only a stone's throw from the real thing, with Buckingham Palace just across the road. And if this is how Her Majesty lives, then we've all got reason to be jealous. This elegant hotel, looking out over the Royal Mews, provides the sort of deep comfort needed to soothe away a hard day's sightseeing, with armchairs just crying out for you to sink into them with a cup of Earl Grey. With decent-size, well-appointed rooms—not quite furnished like the ones at the palace, it must be said—and a location that could not be more truly central, this hotel remains a favorite for many travelers. ✉ *39 Buckingham Palace Rd., SW1W OPS,* ☎ *020/7834–6600,* FAX *020/7233–6037,* WEB *www.redcarnationhotels. com. 180 rooms. Restaurant, bar. AE, DC, MC, V. Tube: Victoria.*

£££ ££££ 🏨 **Basil Street.** This gracious Edwardian hotel is on a quiet street behind busy Brompton Road and off (rich) shoppers' heaven, Sloane Street. It has been family-run for nearly a century, and it has always been popular with lone women travelers, who, during their stay, get automatic membership at the Parrot Club—an enormous lounge, with copies of *The Lady* and *Country Life* among the coffee cups. All the bedrooms are different; many are like Grandma's guest room, with fluffy duvets and a random selection of furniture. You can write letters home in the peaceful gallery, which has polished wood floors and fine Turkish carpets underneath a higgledy-piggledy wealth of antiques. Americans with a taste for period charm favor this place; some come back often enough to merit the title "Basilite"—a privileged regular offered a 15% discount. ✉ *Basil St., SW3 1AH,* ☎ *020/7581–3311,* FAX *020/7581– 3693,* WEB *www.thebasil.com. 80 rooms. Restaurant. AE, DC, MC, V. Tube: Knightsbridge.*

£££–££££ 🏨 **Egerton House.** This absolutely peaceful, private house–style small hotel was the first in the stable that includes the Franklin and Dukes, and it remains many people's favorite, appealing especially, for some reason, to bankers. Many chintzy, floral, or Regency-stripe bedrooms overlook the gorgeous gardens in back; some have quirky shapes, others have four-poster beds, still others are extra-well appointed with closet space—in other words, all are different. The staff here is especially personable—and the manager would love to know what you think of the selections in his handwritten local restaurant guide. ✉ *17–19 Egerton Terr., SW3 2BX,* ☎ *020/7589–2412,* FAX *020/7584–6540,* WEB *www.egertonhousehotel.co.uk. 30 rooms. AE, DC, MC, V. Tube: Knightsbridge.*

£££–££££ 🏨 **Eleven Cadogan Gardens.** This aristocratic, late-Victorian gabled town house is the perfect spot for a pampered honeymoon, but it's very difficult to get into—and we're not referring to the lack of sign or reception desk. Fine period furniture and antiques, books and magazines on the tables, landscape paintings and portraits, coupled with some of that solid, no-nonsense furniture that *real* English country houses have in unaesthetic abundance make for a family-home ambience; you might be borrowing the house and servants of some wealthy friends while they're away. Take the elevator or walk up the fine oak staircase to your room, which will have mahogany furniture, a restful color scheme, and pretty bedspreads and drapes. The best rooms are at the back, overlooking a private garden. If you wish to hire a chauffeur-driven car, there is one on standby. ⊠ *11 Cadogan Gardens, Sloane Sq., SW3 2RJ,* ☎ *020/7730–3426,* FAX *020/7730–5217,* WEB *www.number-eleven.co.uk. 62 rooms. AE, MC, V. Tube: Sloane Sq.*

£££–££££   🏠 **The Franklin.** It's hard to imagine, while taking tea in this pretty hotel overlooking a quiet, grassy square, that you're an amble away from busy Brompton and Cromwell roads and the splendors of the V&A. A few of the rooms are small, but the marble bathrooms—in which Floris toiletries and heated towel racks are standard issue—are not; the large garden rooms and suites (which fall into the ££££ category) are romantic indeed. Tea is served daily in the lounge, and there's also a self-service bar. The staff is friendly and accommodating. ⊠ *28 Egerton Gardens, SW3 2DB,* ☎ *020/7584–5533,* FAX *020/7584–5449,* WEB *www.franklinhotel.co.uk. 47 rooms. Bar, parking (fee). AE, DC, MC, V. Tube: South Kensington.*

£££–££££   🏠 **The Pelham.** The second of Tim and Kit Kemp's gorgeous hotels, this
★   place opened in 1989 and is run along exactly the same lines as the Dorset Square, except that this one looks more like the country house to end all country houses. There's 18th-century pine paneling in the drawing room—one of the most ravishingly elegant hotel salons anywhere—flowers galore, quite a bit of glazed chintz and antique-lace bed linen, and the odd four-poster and bedroom fireplace. The first-floor (American second-floor) suites are extra spacious with their high ceilings and chandeliers, while some of the top-floor rooms under the eaves have sloping ceilings and casement windows. The Pelham stands opposite the South Kensington tube stop, by the big museums, and close to the shops of Brompton Cross and Knightsbridge. ⊠ *15 Cromwell Pl., SW7 2LA,* ☎ *020/7589–8288,* FAX *020/7584–8444,* WEB *www.firmdale.com. 50 rooms. Restaurant. AE, MC, V. Tube: South Kensington.*

£££   🏠 **L'Hôtel.** An upscale bed-and-breakfast run by the same Levins who
★   own the Capital next door, L'Hôtel is a plainer alternative—less pampering, unfussy decor. There's an air of provincial France, with white wrought-iron bedsteads, pine furniture, and delicious breakfast croissants and baguettes (included in the room rate) served in the Le Metro cellar wine bar (open to nonguests). Le Metro also serves light meals at lunchtime and in the evenings. This really is like a house—you're given your own front-door key, there's no elevator, and the staff leaves in the evening. Reserve ahead—it's very popular. ⊠ *28 Basil St., SW3 1AT,* ☎ *020/7589–6286,* FAX *020/7225–0011. 12 rooms. Restaurant, bar. AE, V. CP. Tube: Knightsbridge.*

£££   🏠 **St. Ermin's Hotel.** Smack-dab in the middle of Westminster, this hotel is just a short stroll from Westminster Abbey and minutes from Buckingham Palace and the Houses of Parliament. An Edwardian anomaly in the shadow of modern skyscrapers, the hotel is set on a tiny cul-de-sac courtyard fronted with beasts-rampant gates. The lobby is an extravaganza of Victorian Baroque—all cake-frosting stucco work in shades of baby blue and creamy white. The Cloisters restaurant features one of the most magnificent (and overlooked) dining decors in London: a 19th-century Jacobean-style salon. Guest rooms are tastefully decorated; some have snug dimensions. ⊠ *Caxton St., SW1H 0QW,* ☎ *020/ 7222–7888,* FAX *020/7222–6914,* WEB *www.london-uk-hotels.net. 290 rooms, 8 suites. Restaurant, bar, minibars, room service, laundry service. AE, DC, MC, V. CP. Tube: St. James's Park.*

££–£££ ⊞ **The Sloane.** Many hotels use the word "unique" to describe their identical canopied beds or garden views, but the tiny Sloane really *is* unique. It is the only hotel we know of in which you can lie in your canopied bed, pick up the phone, and buy the bed. You could buy the phone, too, but it's the covetable, tasteful antiques that you might actually be tempted to take home, and these are also for sale. Nothing so tacky as a price tag besmirches the gorgeous decor—which doesn't stint on strong hues to show off the ever-changing collection of Regency armoires and occasional tables, Victorian desk lamps and crystal decanters—instead, the sweet, young Euro staff maintains a book of price lists at the desk. Room service is not 24-hour, but there's an aerie of a secret roof terrace, with upholstered garden furniture and a panorama over Chelsea, where lunch and dinner are served to guests. ✉ *29 Draycott Pl., SW3 2SH,* ☎ *020/7581–5757,* FAX *020/7584–1348,* WEB *www. premierhotels.com. 12 rooms. AE, DC, MC, V. Tube: Sloane Sq.*

££ ⊞ **The Diplomat.** From its aristocratically elegant exterior, this hotel looks like a Cecil Beaton stage set: a Wedgwood-white "palazzo" terrace house built by the 19th-century architect Thomas Cubitt, flatiron-shape (it stands at the confluence of two streets), and often decked out with hanging flowerpots of geraniums, it is the very picture of Belgravian chic. Inside, the reception area gives way to a circular staircase lighted by a Regency-era chandelier and topped by a winter-garden dome. Rooms are pleasantly decorated, some with Victorian touches; in the basement is a breakfast nook (a buffet is included in the daily rates). This hotel truly comes into its own once you step out the doorway and find yourself in the heart of Belgravia's beautiful 19th-century mansions (Baroness Thatcher is a block away) and mews. ✉ *2 Chesham St., SW1X 8DT,* ☎ *020/7235–1544,* FAX *020/7259–6153. 27 rooms. Business services. AE, DC, MC, V. BP. Tube: Sloane Sq. or Knightsbridge.*

££ ⊞ **Knightsbridge Green.** This Georgian hotel is only a two-minute walk from Harrods, if that is where you wish to shop. One floor is French style, with white furniture; another English, in beech. Costing only £25 more than a double room, the suites are not overpriced, and all rooms have trouser presses and tea/coffeemakers. There's no restaurant, but there are plenty in the area; or if you ask, they'll send the porter out to find you a sandwich. Coffee and cake are left out in the lounge—a detail that exemplifies the friendliness of this place. ✉ *159 Knightsbridge, SW1X 7PD,* ☎ *020/7584–6274,* FAX *020/7225–1635. 17 rooms, 11 suites. AE, MC, V. Closed 3 days at Christmas. Tube: Knightsbridge.*

££ ⊞ **Knightsbridge Hotel.** When it comes to measuring location versus value, this could be considered an ideal stopping place. On a tree-lined, quiet, stately square, the Knightsbridge is just a moment from Harrods and a few blocks from the chic boutiques and restaurants of Beauchamp Place. A family-run hotel, it's set in a town house built in the early 1800s. Guest rooms are unassuming yet well furnished. ✉ *12 Beaufort Gardens, SW3 1PT,* ☎ *020/7589–9271,* FAX *020/7823–9672,* WEB *www. knightsbridgehotel.co.uk. 40 rooms. Exercise room. AE, MC, V. BP. Tube: Knightsbridge.*

£–££ ⊞ **La Reserve.** You'll find this unusual small hotel, at the top of its price category, in the lively, classy residential neighborhood of Fulham. The varnished floorboards, black Venetian blinds, works of art (for sale), and primary-color upholstery in the public areas are contemporary. Bedrooms have minibars, hair dryers, trouser presses, and tea/coffeemakers. Fulham is not within walking distance of central London, but it is two minutes from the Fulham Broadway tube, near Chelsea Football (soccer) Grounds and plenty of restaurants; there's also an in-house brasserie. ✉ *422–428 Fulham Rd., SW6 1DU,* ☎ *020/7385–8561,* FAX *020/7385–7662. 43 rooms. Restaurant, bar, free parking. AE, DC, MC, V. BP. Tube: Fulham Broadway.*

£ 🏠 **Elizabeth Hotel.** Near Victoria Station, this hotel once served as the private home of aristocrats (including relatives of Edward VII). These days it offers standard rooms near an attractive garden square. Rooms come with a bath and/or shower, TV, and English breakfast. Shared-bath single and double are also available. ⊠ *37 Eccleston Sq., SW1V 1PB,* ☎ *020/7828–6812,* FAX *020/7828–6814,* WEB *www.elizabeth-hotel. com. 38 rooms. Lounge. No credit cards. BP. Tube: Victoria.*

£ 🏠 **London County Hall Travel Inn Capital.** Don't get too excited—this neighbor of the fancy Marriott lacks the river view (it's at the back of the grand former seat of local government). Still, you get an incredible value, with the standard facilities of the cookie-cutter rooms of this chain: TV, tea/coffeemaker, en suite bath/shower and—best of all for families on a budget—fold-out beds that let you accommodate two kids at no extra charge. *That's* a bargain. ⊠ *Belvedere Rd., SE1 7PB,* ☎ *020/7902–1600 (central reservation line),* FAX *020/7902–1619,* WEB *www.travelinn.co.uk. 312 rooms. Restaurant. AE, DC, MC, V. Tube: Westminster.*

£ 🏠 **London Tower Bridge Travel Inn Capital.** The name may not be snappy, but the price certainly is—practically unbeatable, especially for families. Not exactly central, this hotel is based in the Tower Hill area, which has good tube connections. Despite having been around for centuries, this is now one of London's most up-and-coming neighborhoods. ⊠ *Tower Bridge Rd., SE1,* ☎ *020/7940–3700,* FAX *020/7940–3719,* WEB *www.travelinn.co.uk. 196 rooms. Restaurant, bar. AE, MC, V. Tube: Tower Bridge.*

£ 🏠 **Melita House Hotel.** Run by the Gabriele family for 30 years, this small hotel is a short walk from the Tate Britain and Victoria Station. Each room is kitted out with fridge, hair dryer, safe, and direct phone line. Full English breakfast is included in the rate. ⊠ *35 Charlwood St., SW1V 2DU,* ☎ *020/7828–0471,* FAX *020/7932–0988,* WEB *www.melita. com. 22 rooms. Breakfast room. AE, MC, V. BP. Tube: Victoria.*

£ 🏠 **Morgan House.** Near Victoria Station in classy Belgravia, this charming Georgian B&B has flowery rooms with orthopedic mattresses, TVs, hair dryers, beautiful ornamental fireplaces, and tea- and coffee-making facilities. The house has one family room with bunk beds and a double bed. Ask for a room in the back if you're sensitive to street noise. ⊠ *120 Ebury St., SW1W 9QQ,* ☎ *020/7730–2384,* FAX *020/7730–8442,* WEB *www.morganhouse.co.uk. 11 rooms, 8 without bath. Breakfast room. No credit cards. BP. Tube: Victoria.*

Bayswater and Notting Hill Gate

££££ 🏠 **The Halcyon.** Discretion, decadent decor, and disco divas (everyone ★ from RuPaul to Snoop Doggy Dogg) make this expensive, enormous, wedding-cake Edwardian on Holland Park Avenue desperately desirable. You want film stars? They've got Johnny Depp, William Hurt, and Julia Roberts, and there are usually local residents like Sting, John Cleese, and *Absolutely Fabulous*'s Joanna Lumley haunting the absolutely excellent restaurant. But it's for perfect service and gorgeous rooms you'd follow them here. The Blue Room has moons and stars, the Egyptian Suite is canopied like a bedouin tent, one room has heraldic motifs, and the Halcyon Suite has its own conservatory. All rooms are very large, with the high ceilings and big windows typical of the grand houses here—a 10-min tube ride from the West End and steps from London's most exquisite park. ⊠ *81 Holland Park, W11 3RZ,* ☎ *020/7727–7288,* FAX *020/7229–8516,* WEB *www.halcyon-hotel.co.uk. 42 rooms. Restaurant. AE, DC, MC, V. Tube: Holland Park.*

££££ 🏠 **The Hempel.** This is a prime contender for the "most glamorous hostelry in London" prize. Anouska Hempel did the lush and lavish Blakes,

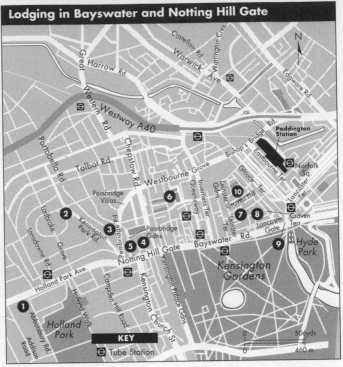

Lodging in Bayswater and Notting Hill Gate

KEY

⊖ Tube Station

then did a 180-degree turn into these stunning, crisp, clean, white-on-white-on-white-on-white spaces—and we do mean spaces. There's nothing jarring, nothing extraneous, and no visible means of support beneath the furniture. Of course, the Hempel appeals greatly to showbizzy style hounds. Elton John (remember when he went Zen and sold all his gewgaws?) was one of the first party-throwers in the restaurant here. But beware: the minimalist decor is not for everyone. ✉ *31–35 Craven Hill Gardens, W2 3EA,* ☎ *020/7298–9000,* ℻ *020/7472–4666. 43 rooms. Restaurant, bar. AE, DC, MC, V. Tube: Lancaster Gate.*

£££ 🏠 **The Portobello.** This small, eccentric place has long been a favorite of high-style mavens in the music and design worlds, and it must be said that a tinge of the groovy early '70s still adheres to the corners, and also to the Victorian-Chinoiserie decor (which has turned a bit shabby in a few rooms, enhancing the louche and laid-back effect). The hotel consists of two adjoining Victorian houses that (as is common around here) back onto a beautiful large garden shared with the neighbors. The "Cabin Rooms" are minute: everything you need is accessible by reaching out your hand from the bed. Many bigger rooms have freestanding Victorian claw-foot bathtubs, though the famous round-bed suite has the pièce de résistance of the bath world—an Edwardian "bathing machine," all knobs and shiny brass pipes. Rates include breakfast, and there's a 24-hour bar-restaurant in the basement, though there are a hundred other options in this very happening area. ✉ *22 Stanley Gardens, W11 2NG,* ☎ *020/7727–2777,* ℻ *020/7792–9641,* 🌐 *www.portobello-hotel.co.uk. 22 rooms. Restaurant, bar. AE, DC, MC, V. CP. Closed 10 days at Christmas. Tube: Notting Hill.*

££–£££ 🏠 **Pembridge Court.** In a colonnaded white-stucco Victorian row house, this sweet home away from home of a hotel is cozy with scatter cushions and books, quirky Victoriana, two resident cats, and framed fans from the neighboring Portobello Market. Bedrooms have a great deal of swagged floral drapery, direct-dial phones, and satellite TV, and there's an elevator to the upper floors. Rates include English breakfast—take that into account when doing your sums, since only the half-size small twin rooms fall into the ££ category; larger ones are £10–£30 more. ✉ *34 Pembridge Gardens, W2 4DX,* ☎ 020/7229–9977, FAX 020/7727–4982 or 800/709–9882, WEB *www.pemct.co.uk. 20 rooms. Restaurant. AE, DC, MC, V. BP. Tube: Notting Hill.*

££ ⊞ **Abbey Court.** This is a very elegant little hotel that is more like a private home—albeit one with a resident designer. It's in a gracious white Victorian mansion in a quiet streetlet off Notting Hill Gate, which gives easy access to most of London. Inside, the era of Victoria is reflected in deep-red wallpapers (downstairs), Murano glass and gilt-framed mirrors, framed prints, mahogany, and plenty of antiques. Bathrooms look the part but are entirely modern in gray Italian marble, with brass fittings and whirlpool baths. There's 24-hour room service instead of a restaurant (there are plenty around here, though), and guests can relax in the sitting room or the pretty conservatory. ✉ *20 Pembridge Gardens, W2 4DU,* ☎ 020/7221–7518, FAX 020/7792–0858, WEB *www.abbeycourthotel.co.uk. 22 rooms. AE, DC, MC, V. CP. Tube: Notting Hill.*

££ ⊞ **The Commodore.** This peaceful hotel made up of three converted Victorians is close to the Columbia but deeper in the big leafy square known as Lancaster Gate. It's a find of a very different stripe, as you'll notice on entering the cozy, carpeted lounge. Try your best to get one of the amazing rooms—as superior to the regular ones as Harrods is to Kmart but priced the same. Three of these are split-level rooms, with sleeping gallery, all large, all different, all with something special—like a walk-in closet with its own stained-glass window. One (No. 11) is a duplex, entered through a secret mirrored door off a lemon-yellow hallway with palms and Greek statuary; a thick-carpeted, *very* quiet bedroom is upstairs and its toilet below. This place is increasingly popular, so book ahead. ✉ *50 Lancaster Gate, W2 3NA,* ☎ 020/7402–5291, FAX 020/7262–1088, WEB *www.commodore-hotel.com. 90 rooms. Bar, business services. AE, MC, V. CP. Tube: Lancaster Gate.*

££ ⊞ **London Elizabeth.** Steps from Hyde Park and the Lancaster Gate tube
★ (and from rows of depressing, cheap hotels) is this family-owned gem. The facade is one of the most charming in London, and the charm continues inside—foyer and lounge are crammed with coffee tables and chintz drapery, lace antimacassars, and little chandeliers. This country sensibility persists through the bedrooms done up in palest blue-striped walls, wooden picture rails and Welsh wool bedspreads, or in pink cabbage-rose prints and mahogany furniture. Although rooms vary in size, there's a tendency here to make sure that what you lose on the swings (small wedge-shape room) you gain on the roundabouts (bigger bathroom, or a small balcony), and all have TV, direct-dial phone, and hair dryer. The Anglo-Irish staff is on call around the clock, and there's a restaurant, the Rose Garden, handy in this culinary wasteland. ✉ *Lancaster Terr., W2 3PF,* ☎ 020/7402–6641, FAX 020/7224–8900, WEB *www.londonelizabethhotel.co.uk. 55 rooms. Restaurant, bar. AE, DC, MC, V. CP. Tube: Lancaster Gate.*

£ ⊞ **The Columbia.** The public rooms in these five joined-up Victorians are as big as museum halls. The clean, high-ceiling bedrooms, some of which are very large (three to four beds) and have park views and balconies, also offer TVs, hair dryers, tea/coffeemakers, direct-dial phones, and safes. Decor tends to teak veneer, khaki-beige-brown color schemes, and avocado bathroom suites, but who expects Regency Revival at these prices? It's popular with tour groups. ✉ *95–99 Lancaster Gate, W2 3NS,* ☎ 020/7402–0021, FAX 020/7706–4691, WEB *www.columbiahotel.co.uk. 103 rooms. Restaurant, bar, meeting room. AE, MC, V. BP. Tube: Lancaster Gate.*

£   🖼 **Garden Court Hotel.** Built in 1870, the hotel consists of two 19th-century townhouses in a quiet Victorian garden square. Each of the comfortable rooms has a character of its own, complete with some original Victorian fittings. Rooms with toilet and shower cost £30 more. The paved garden is relaxing in good weather and the owners are eager to please. ⊠ *30–31 Kensington Gardens Sq., W2 4BG,* ☎ *020/7229-2553,* FAX *020/7727-2749,* WEB *www.gardencourthotel.co.uk. 32 rooms, some without bath. MC, V. BP. Tube: Bayswater or Queensway.*

£   🖼 **The Gate.** It's absolutely teeny—just a house at the very top of Portobello Road, off Notting Hill Gate. The plain bedrooms have refrigerators, TVs, direct-dial phones, and tea/coffee facilities, plus bath (unless you opt for a smaller, £10-cheaper, shower-only room), and you can have the inclusive Continental breakfast brought up to you, or take it in the first-floor lounge. ⊠ *6 Portobello Rd., W11 3DG,* ☎ *020/ 7221-0707,* FAX *020/7221-9128,* WEB *www.gatehotel.com. 6 rooms, some with shower. AE, MC, V. CP. Tube: Notting Hill Gate.*

Bloomsbury, Holborn, Euston, and the City

££££   🖼 **Great Eastern.** The word on the street is that the Great Eastern used to be a house of ill repute—but it isn't any longer. Reopened in 2000 under the Terence Conran flag, it's a sturdy pillar of the modern establishment. There are four restaurants—offering sushi, fish, brasserie, and haute cuisine—two bars, a gym, private dining and function rooms, a florist, and a place called Ren that sells bath products. Some of the rooms look out over Liverpool Street and Bishopsgate. Others look inward to the stained-glass dome of the Aurora restaurant or the Gallery. Unsurprisingly, suits of all kinds flock to this first-rate hotel. ⊠ *Liverpool St. at Bishopsgate, E2M 7QN,* ☎ *020/7618-5000,* FAX *020/7618-5001,* WEB *www.great-eastern-hotel.co.uk. 246 rooms, 21 suites. 4 restaurants, 2 bars, 12 dining rooms, gym, cinema. AE, DC, MC, V. Tube: Liverpool St.*

£££–££££   🖼 **Myhotel.** A hotel where tipping is discouraged and where guests brief the management on their likes and dislikes? Where you have a member of staff assigned to you personally, to see to all your needs? Where a public room is dedicated to inner karma? Yes, here it is, the work of owner Andrew Thrasyvoulou and the frighteningly omniscient Terence Conran with the help of a feng shui designer to check the building for negative energy. Myhotel, Conran's first hotel venture, is aimed at the young, hip traveler who expects his or her hotel to be an experience in itself. Within easy walking distance of the British Museum, Soho, Covent Garden, and the West End, Myhotel is finding its niche among an upmarket but open-minded breed of tourists. ⊠ *11–13 Bayley St., Bedford Sq., WC1 B3HD,* ☎ *020/7667-6000,* FAX *020/7667-6001,* WEB *www.myhotels.co.uk. 76 rooms. Bar, exercise room, library, business services. AE, DC, MC, V. Tube: Tottenham Court Rd.*

£££–££££   🖼 **The Rookery.** From the bijoux-size but beautiful rooms in this little hotel you see some of the most ancient parts of London. Set in the City district, the Rookery is just a step away from the Jerusalem Tavern, from which it is said the Knights of St. John left to fight the Crusades. From the magnificent Rook's Nest, the hotel's tower that is a complete duplex suite, you can see both St. Paul's and Old Bailey, London's famous criminal court. If you look closely, some of Dickens's characters still seem to linger around this district, if they haven't been ousted by the fashionable and wealthy young crowd now busy colonizing the area. Each double has an antique four-poster bed and period pictures, with all the modern appliances tastefully hidden away. ⊠ *Peter's La. at Cowcross St., EC1M 6DS,* ☎ *020/7336-0931,* FAX *020/7336-0932. 33 rooms. Bar, business services. AE, MC, V. Tube: Farringdon.*

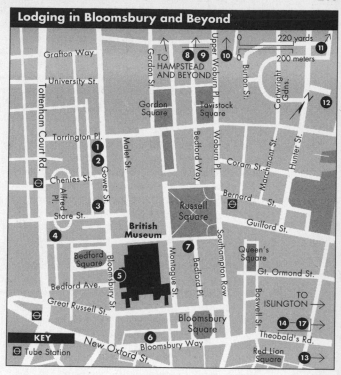

Lodging in Bloomsbury and Beyond

£££ 🏨 **Academy Town House.** These three joined-up Georgian houses, boasting a little patio garden and a fashion-conscious mirrored and wood-floor basement restaurant, Alchemy, supply the most sophisticated and hotel-like facilities in the Gower Street "hotel row." The comfortable bedrooms have a TV, direct-dial phones, and tea/coffeemakers. Like most of the hotels in this section, the Academy neighbors the British Museum and University of London, a feature that appeals to culture vultures on a budget and affluent students. ✉ *21 Gower St., WC1E 6HG,* ☎ *020/7631–4115,* 𝔽𝔸𝕏 *020/7636–3442,* WEB *www.etontownhouse. com. 48 rooms. Restaurant, bar. AE, DC, MC, V. BP. Tube: Tottenham Court Rd.*

£££ 🏨 **Thistle Bloomsbury.** On the main street, steps from the British Museum, this is one Edwardian-style hotel that really does feel sweetly old-fashioned, while avoiding shabbiness or stuffiness—especially since the £6 million refurbishment of this former temperance house (tea/coffeemakers and free in-house movies are now among the facilities). The rooms in the turret on the southwest corner, with their curved, six-window wall, are worth asking for, while executive suites have four-posters and Jacuzzis at a rate that falls in the middle of the £££ category. ✉ *Bloomsbury Way, WC1A 2SD,* ☎ *020/7242–5881,* 𝔽𝔸𝕏 *020/7831–0225,* WEB *www.thistlehotels.com. 138 rooms. Restaurant, bar, meeting room. AE, DC, MC, V. Tube: Holborn.*

£ 🏨 **Alhambra Hotel.** One of the best bargains in Bloomsbury, this family-run hotel has singles as low as £32 and doubles as low as £45. Rooms tend to be small with dated decor, but are clean and a good value. Some rooms have a shower; some have a shower and toilet. The hotel is spread across several properties on the street, some of which are newer than others. ✉ *17–19 Argyle St., WC1H 8EJ,* ☎ *020/7837–9575,* 𝔽𝔸𝕏 *020/ 7916–2476,* WEB *www.alhambrahotel.com. 52 rooms. AE, DC, MC, V. BP. Tube: King's Cross.*

£   🖭 **Arosfa Hotel.** The friendly owners, Mr. and Mrs. Dorta, mark this
    B&B directly opposite Dillons bookstore apart from the Gower Street
    hotel pack—that, and the fact that this was once the home of Pre-
    Raphaelite painter Sir John Everett Millais. Rooms are simple and spot-
    less, and they're equipped with TVs and sinks, but not necessarily with
    their own shower. Those at the back are far quieter, though newly in-
    stalled double glazing somewhat tames the Gower Street din. ⊠ *83
    Gower St., WC1E 6HJ,* ☎ *020/7636–2115,* FAX *020/7636–2115,* WEB
    *www.arosfahotel.freeserve.co.uk. 16 rooms, 2 with shower. MC, V. BP.
    Tube: Goodge St.*

£   🖭 **The Generator.** Easily the grooviest youth hostel in town, this for-
    mer police barracks has a friendly, funky, and international vibe. Talk-
    ing Heads, the Internet café, provides handy maps and leaflets, plus a
    chance to get on-line. The Generator Bar has cheap drinks and a
    rowdy, young clientele, and the Fuel Stop cafeteria provides inexpen-
    sive meals. Rooms—designed on a prison-cell theme complete with bunk
    beds and dim views—are simple but clean. Singles run about £40, twins
    (there are no doubles) about £27 per person, with prices dropping down
    to just over £20 for dormitory rooms. This is an excellent choice for
    the youthful and adventurous traveler. ⊠ *MacNaghten House, Comp-
    ton Pl. off Tavistock Pl., WC1H 9SD,* ☎ *020/7388–7666,* FAX *020/7388–
    7644,* WEB *www.the-generator.co.uk. 217 rooms without bath. Restau-
    rant, bar. MC, V. BP. Tube: Russell Sq.*

£   🖭 **The Morgan.** This is a Georgian row-house hotel, family run with
★   charm and panache. Rooms are small and functionally furnished yet
    friendly and cheerful overall, with phones and TVs. The five newish
    apartments are particularly pleasing: three times the size of normal rooms
    (and an extra £15 per night), complete with kitchens and private
    phone lines. The tiny, paneled breakfast room is straight out of an 18th-
    century doll's house. The back rooms overlook the British Museum.
    ⊠ *24 Bloomsbury St., WC1B 3QJ,* ☎ *020/7636–3735,* FAX *020/7636–
    3045. 15 rooms with shower, 5 apartments. MC, V. BP. Tube: Tottenham
    Court Rd. or Russell Sq.*

£   🖭 **The Ridgemount.** The kindly British owners, Mr. and Mrs. Rees, make
    you feel at home. Rooms tend to have a 1970s decor, but offer a cheap
    sleep in a reasonable neighborhood. The public areas, especially the
    family-style breakfast room, have a friendly, cluttered Victorian feel.
    Some rooms overlook a leafy garden, and 14 have an en-suite bath-
    room, for about £15 extra per night. ⊠ *65 Gower St., WC1E 6HJ,* ☎
    020/7636–1141, FAX *0207/636–2558. 33 rooms, 14 with bath. MC, V.
    BP. Tube: Goodge St.*

£   🖭 **St. Margaret's.** A popular hotel near the British Museum, St. Mar-
    garet's offers well-lit rooms with high ceilings, telephones, and TVs in
    a Georgian-era building. The friendly Italian family that runs the hotel
    is sure to welcome you by name if you stay long enough. Beware that
    prices are higher for one-night stays. Back rooms have a garden view.
    ⊠ *26 Bedford Pl., WC1B 5JL,* ☎ *020/7636–4277,* FAX *020/7323–
    3066. 64 rooms, 12 with bath. No credit cards. BP. Tube: Russell Sq.
    or Holborn.*

Hampstead and Islington

£££ 🖭 **Hilton London Islington.** This purpose-built hotel next door to the
    Islington Business Design Centre has a madly colored, soaring lobby
    and its own neighborhood to explore, as well as easy access to central
    London via the tube stop a minute's walk away. One of a reliable, small
    Scottish chain, the hotel has ultramodern rooms with climate control,
    satellite TV, and trouser presses, plus, in many of them, panoramic sky-
    line views. ⊠ *53 Upper St., N1 0UY,* ☎ *020/7354–7700,* FAX *020/7354–*

7711, WEB *www.stakis.co.uk. 178 rooms, 6 suites. Restaurant, bar, exercise room, meeting room. AE, DC, MC, V. Tube: Angel.*

££ 🖭 **Great Northern.** Walk out the back door of King's Cross Station and you'll smack straight into the Great Northern, built in 1854. It is no beauty. Claret carpets, Regency stripes, boxlike rooms, and a smoke-filled bar do not necessarily appeal to the delicate palate. But there is solid Northern sense in constructing corridors wide enough for 19th-century ladies to sweep their skirts through. Each room has a television and a trouser press; drinks are available 24 hours a day from the night porter's secret hoard. Brutally convenient, without a taint of whimsy, the Great Northern is triumphantly rooted in the age of steam. ⊠ *Cheney Rd., N1 9AN,* ☎ *020/7837–5454,* FAX *0207/278–5270,* WEB *www.compasshotels.co.uk. 82 rooms. Restaurant, bar, meeting room. AE, DC, MC, V. BP. Tube: King's Cross.*

££ 🖭 **Swiss Cottage Hotel.** It's a little out of the way on a peaceful street behind the Swiss Cottage tube stop, but this charming hotel will suit those who like to stay in a residential district, save a little on the check, and still have their home comforts. The lounge and reception area are stuffed with antiques and reproductions and are smilingly staffed. In summer, French windows open from the bar and the breakfast room. Bedrooms are in Victorian style, most are good-sized, and all come with full English breakfast. ⊠ *4 Adamson Rd., NW3 3HP,* ☎ *020/7722–2281,* FAX *020/7483–4588,* WEB *www.swisscottagehotel.co.uk. 54 rooms. Bar, breakfast room. AE, DC, MC, V. BP. Tube: Swiss Cottage.*

£–££ 🖭 **La Gaffe.** A short walk up one of Hampstead's magnificent hills, La Gaffe is run by Italian Bernardo Stella, who has been welcoming the same guests back to these early 18th-century shepherds' cottages for more than 20 years, and his restaurant has been going for nearly 40. Make no mistake, rooms are tiny, with showers only, and the predominantly peach-and-green decor isn't luxurious, but the popular wine bar and restaurant, which (naturally) serve Italian food, are yours to lounge around in at all hours. Between the two "wings" is a raised patio for summer, and each room has TV and phone. ⊠ *107–111 Heath St., NW3 6SS,* ☎ *020/7435–8965,* FAX *020/7794–7592,* WEB *www.la-gaffe.co.uk. 18 rooms with shower. Restaurant, café, bar. AE, MC, V. CP. Tube: Hampstead.*

£ 🖭 **Florence Street B&B.** Technically, this place doesn't have a name, but that doesn't make it anonymous. Lady Valerie Rossmore is a master of that thespian virtue of making everyone feel special. The London kitchen would bring tears to the eyes of any Beatrix Potter fan. The house is full of light, and in the evenings there is a lovely little conservatory reserved exclusively for guests. ⊠ *Florence St.,* ☎ FAX *020/7359–5293. 2 rooms. No credit cards. Tube: Highbury Islington or Angel.*

£ 🖭 **Hampstead Village Guest House.** This eccentric Victorian guesthouse offers distinctive and comfortable rooms cluttered with antiques and curiosities. The Blue Room has its own free-standing tub, and the Yellow Room has a roof terrace and a canopy bed. Guests are encouraged to relax in the garden or play with the resident dog, Marley. Families will appreciate the separate garden studio, which houses up to five people and has its own kitchenette. Book ahead for this hot property. Breakfast costs £7 extra. ⊠ *2 Kemplay Rd., NW3 1SY,* ☎ *020/7435–8679,* FAX *020/7794–0254,* WEB *www.hampsteadguesthouse.com. 8 rooms. No credit cards. Tube: Hampstead.*

Bed-and-Breakfast and Apartment Agencies

££ 🖭 **Bulldog Club.** It promises luxe, chic, and delightful accommodations. In days of yore, you actually got to book rooms in some of London's poshest houses, where grown-up children's rooms were converted for guests. A three-year membership is around £25, with most properties available for around £100 a night. A full British breakfast as well as other goodies are often provided. Accommodations are generally available in Knightsbridge, Kensington, and Chelsea. ⊠ *14 Dewhurst Rd., W14 0ET,* ☎ *020/7371–3202,* 🖷 *020/7371–2015,* 🆆🅴🅱 *www. bulldogclub.com. AE, MC, V.*

££ 🔝 **Uptown Reservations.** As the name implies, this B&B booking service accepts only the tonier addresses and specializes in finding hosted homes or short-term apartments for Americans, often executives of small corporations. Nearly all the 85 homes on its register are in Knightsbridge, Belgravia, Kensington, and Chelsea, with a few lying farther west in Holland Park or to the north in Hampstead. The private homes vary, of course, but all are good-looking and have private bathrooms for guests, plus full Continental breakfast. ⊠ *50 Christchurch St., SW3 4AR,* ☎ *020/7351–3445,* 🖷 *020/7351–9383. Facilities vary. Payment by bank transfer or U.S. check or credit card; 20% deposit required. AE, MC, V.*

£–££ 🔝 **London B&B.** This long-established family-run agency has some truly spectacular—and some more modest—London homes that host guests, in practically all neighborhoods of the city. Check many of them out via its Web site before making a commitment. The staff here is most personable and helpful. ⊠ *Box 124859, San Diego, CA 92112,* ☎ *800/ 872–2632,* 🆆🅴🅱 *www.londonbandb.com. 30% deposit required.*

£ 🔝 **Primrose Hill B&B.** This is a small, friendly bed-and-breakfast agency genuinely "committed to the idea that traveling shouldn't be a rip-off." Expatriate American Gail O'Farrell has family homes (to which guests get their own latchkeys) in or near villagey Hampstead, and all are comfortable or more than comfortable. So far this has been one of those word-of-mouth secrets, but now that everyone knows, book well ahead. ⊠ *14 Edis St., NW1 8LG,* ☎ *020/7722–6869. No credit cards.*

4 NIGHTLIFE AND THE ARTS

"Ladies and gentlemen, the curtain is about to rise" on London's artful pleasures: Bussell at the ballet, Domingo at the Royal Albert Hall, and the best theater in the world—perhaps Ralph Fiennes and Vanessa Redgrave doing star turns, *Oliver!* in a West End revival, and unparalleled servings of Shakespeare. You can see, say, *The Winter's Tale* at the reconstructed Globe Theatre, where the interaction between player and audience often goes beyond polite applause. Finish off the night at a club sizzling with comedy, cabaret, or all that jazz.

Updated by
Tim Perry

A FTER DARK, LONDON is a wonderful place to play. Shakespearean theater and Handel oratorios, chart-friendly discos and post-industrial techno-rock raves, Andrew Lloyd Webber–ish extravaganzas, the roof-rattling Proms concerts, magnificent opera and ballet—if you're into the arts and after-hours scenes, you'll be quickly whirling to a pounding beat. The arts scene has definitely stabilized. After a period of being shunted, gypsylike, from place to place in London, the performing Muses look to be settling back into revamped, revitalized homes. The world-renowned Royal Opera House, after years of executive shuffling and counterblasts, reopened in time for the new millennium. And inside the Opera House, the Royal Ballet has a permanent home. It seemed likely for a while that the English National Opera—or ENO, as it is called—might abandon the Coliseum, its home since 1968, but it is now sure to stay put. Other good news is that the excellent Old Vic theater is alive and well and continuing with a great, and often challenging, mixed calendar of programs. This coming year, the state of after-hours London looks fine indeed.

NIGHTLIFE

Nighttime London has rejuvenated itself, with a tangible spirit of fun abroad on the streets, and new hangouts opening at an unprecedented rate. Whatever your pleasure, there's somewhere to go. Are you a club animal? London's boîtes are famously hip, hot, and happening. Music? From indie bands (short for "independent" and referring to their record label more than their state of mind) to resident orchestras, free jazz to opera, it's everywhere. Cabaret of the traditional torch-song sort is undergoing a little revival, while comedy, which never slowed down in the first place, remains one of the city's favorite ways to wind down. The gay listing is small but gives you all you need to find the scene, and there is a fabulous scene. Just remember when you hit the town at night that regular bars (those without special extended licenses) stop serving alcohol at 11 PM (10:30 on Sunday) and the tubes stop running around midnight, although the city is reasonably well served by night buses.

Such details can inhibit the free flow of enjoyment, it has to be said. Although there's been a lot of hype about swinging London in recent years, it is no less depressing than it ever was to be thrown out of your warm and fuzzy pub corner at the sound of the bell to try to find a bar with a late license. It is worth remembering that these rather archaic licensing laws (which were made in World War I to keep working men out of the pubs) are currently under review by the Labour government, and it looks more likely than ever that they will be amended in the near future. If they are, Londoners will be denied their favorite opportunity (save the weather) to grumble, and Britain will finally be set to catch up with the rest of Europe. An optimistic start to this process was made at the beginning of the millennium when a 220-year-old law that banned dancing on Sunday was rescinded, meaning that nightclubs will now be allowed to open on that day. On the whole, the club scene is for under-30s. If you don't have your ear to the ground in the youth culture department, you will feel out of place in nearly all venues listed under "Clubs" in *Time Out*, the weekly magazine that updates everything to do in London. But if you must put on the glad rags and boogie, we do list a couple of places for swingers nostalgic for that action. The jazz and world-music scenes are a different matter. Live music makes for a popular night out for all ages and types. A general rule of thumb: if you like the music, you'll like the crowd.

The Britpop fad of the mid-90s is pretty much dead, and the demise of the jangly guitar band has opened up the scene, with punk and metal enjoying particular success at the box office. Live music in the city is now more eclectic than ever and one of the joys of the current London music scene is discovering your own bands and catching the latest hype before it's hyped. Again, read between the lines in the listings magazines to find your niche. Another, completely weird trend you may choose to follow has been imitation, or "tribute," bands—Utter Madness, Björn Again, Abba Gold, Ludwig Beatles, YMCA Village People, Below Average White Band, and so on—that perform to party-animal crowds. On the opposite end of the authenticity scale, Latin and flamenco sounds are growing, and you can sometimes learn the dances in a free class before the band comes on.

Bars

With a couple of exceptions (Freedom Brewing Company, The Maple Leaf), the places below are stylish and perfect for sipping martinis and munching hors d'oeuvres. Londoners, however, truly come into their own at their neighborhood pubs.

American Bar. Festooned with a chin-dropping array of collegiate ties, bric-a-brac, and antique toys, this is one of London's most sensational funhouse interiors. Even if you're not feeling homesick for the other side of the pond, be sure to check out this dazzler. ⊠ *Stafford Hotel, 16–18 St. James's Pl., SW1A,* ☎ *020/7493–0111.* ⊘ *Weekdays 11:30 AM–midnight, Sat. 11:30 AM–3 PM and 5:30–midnight, Sun. noon–2:30 PM and 6:30–10:30. Tube: Green Park.*

Atlantic Bar and Grill. This vast, glamorous, wood-floor basement caused a revolution when, in early 1994, it became the first central London bar to be granted a late-late alcohol license. Although there are now others, it's still popular, so that the only way to get a table on a weekend night is to book it for dinner—luckily, the food's fine. ⊠ *20 Glasshouse St., W1,* ☎ *020/7734–4888.* ⊘ *Mon.–Sat. noon–3 AM, Sun. 6 PM–10:30 PM. Tube: Piccadilly Circus.*

Beach Blanket Babylon. In Notting Hill, close to Portobello Market, this always-packed singles bar is distinguishable by its fanciful decor—like a fairy-tale grotto or a medieval dungeon, visited by the gargoyles of Notre-Dame. ⊠ *45 Ledbury Rd., W11,* ☎ *020/7229–2907.* ⊘ *Daily noon–11 PM. Tube: Notting Hill Gate.*

Bug Bar. Slightly out of the way if you are staying in Central London, but well worth a visit if you are in the area, this mellow bar, attached to a restaurant called Bar Humbug that serves decent food, is in the crypt of a church and offers an off-the-beaten-track opportunity to hang with some funky Londoners. An added bonus for music lovers is that various DJs often spin here for free, although there is a cover charge of around £5 on Friday and Saturday. ⊠ *Brixton Hill (under St. Matthew's Church), SW2,* ☎ *020/7738–3184.* ⊘ *Wed. 7 PM–1 AM, Thurs. 7 PM–2 AM, Fri. and Sat. 7 PM–3 AM, Sun. 7 PM–2 AM. Tube: Brixton.*

Cadogan Hotel Bar. One step beyond the door here and you're back in the Edwardian era. You half-expect Lillie Langtry, the famed actress and mistress of King Edward VII, to waltz in the door—but then, she used to live upstairs at this stylish hotel. If you feel like toasting Oscar Wilde with his favorite drink, a hock and seltzer, you'd better do it elsewhere—poor Oscar was arrested in this very bar that fateful day. ⊠ *Cadogan Hotel, 75 Sloane St., SW1,* ☎ *020/7235–7141.* ⊘ *Daily 11–11. Tube: Sloane Sq.*

Café de Paris. Open since 1914 and known as the "Bower of Love," this is one of London's most glamour-puss settings. Once a haunt of royals and consorts, the boîte brought in such stars as Noel Coward,

Marlene Dietrich, Fred Astaire, and Frank Sinatra. Spot the VIP table, where diners are presented with a minimum bill of £1,000. ☒ *3–4 Coventry St., W1V 7FL,* ☎ *020/7734–7700,* FAX *020/7434–0347.* ☉ *Weekdays 5 PM–4 AM.* ☒ *£10–£15. Tube: Piccadilly Circus.*

Freedom Brewing Company. Brewpubs haven't yet stamped their mark on London, but until they do this subterranean space with a big metal bar and wooden benches is your best bet. Attracting a mix of media workers, trendy shoppers, and tourists, it has home-brewed ales and modern British food. ☒ *41 Earlham St., WC2,* ☎ *020/7240–0606.* ☉ *Mon.–Sat. 11–11, Sun. noon–10:30 PM. Tube: Covent Garden.*

Library. In this very comfortable but self-consciously "period" bar at the swanky Lanesborough Hotel, bar manager Salvatore Calabrese offers his completely eccentric collection of ancient cognacs, made in years when something important happened. A shot of this liquid history can set you back £500. Enjoy the luxe surroundings and don't ask for a brandy Alexander. ☒ *1 Lanesborough Pl., Hyde Park Corner, SW1,* ☎ *020/7259–5599.* ☉ *Mon.–Sat. 11–11, Sun. noon–10:30. Tube: Hyde Park Corner.*

Maple Leaf. Probably the only West End bar serving Molson on tap, this spacious pub-bar is Canada's cultural ambassador in London. As such, it attracts mostly sports fans and party people who come for hockey games, a wide range of beers, and decent burgers. ☒ *41 Maiden La., WC2,* ☎ *020/7240–2843.* ☉ *Mon.–Sat. 11-11, Sun. noon–10:30. Tube: Covent Garden.*

Mybar. A haven of trendiness amidst the rather workaday drag that is Tottenham Court Road, this small but bright and tastefully mirror-laden bar within the Myhotel bustles with those who want to get away from the dismal pubs in the area. Good cocktails, an attentive barstaff, and a range of barsnacks, including sushi, make this a decent place for a short stop in the area. ☒ *11–13 Bayley St., WC1,* ☎ *020/7667–6000.* ☉ *Daily 11–11. Tube: Tottenham Court Rd.*

Pool. Continuing an upward trend of industrial-style hip bars in Shoreditch—one of London's latest up-and-coming areas—this bar derives its name from three American pool tables that are usually in use. The interior is elegant, with striking lighting and colors. Drinks are fairly pricey, but the food is better than most other pub grub. ☒ *104–108 Curtain Rd., EC2,* ☎ *020/7739–9608.* ☉ *Weekdays noon–11 PM, Sat. 5 PM–11 PM, Sun. noon–10:30 PM. Tube: Old St.*

Twentyfour. One of the very few high-rise bars in London, this has a charming, living room feel. Expensive wines and inventive cocktails are the order of the day here and bar food is also available. ☒ *Level 24, Tower 42, 25 Old Broad St., EC2,* ☎ *020/7877–2424.* ☉ *Weekdays noon–11 PM. Tube: Bank or Liverpool St.*

Vibe Bar. This eastside bar occupies a big square room in a former brewery. The Internet and Playstation terminals are usually busy and in the evening there's loud dance music courtesy of DJs. In summer the patio provides respite from the chaos. ☒ *The Brewery, 91–95 Brick La., E1,* ☎ *020/7377–2899.* ☉ *Weekdays 8:30 AM–11 PM, Sat. 8:30 AM–midnight, Sun. 8:30 AM–11 PM. Tube: Aldgate.*

Cabaret

Banana Cabaret. A big-name headliner, Mark Thomas, and lots of variety on the undercard is the recipe of this very popular nightclub. It's quite a bit south but is only a hundred yards from Balham station and there's a reliable minicab office close by for those tempted to make a long night of it. ☒ *Bedford Pub, 77 Bedford Hill, SW12,* ☎ *020/8673–8904.* ☒ *£10.* ☉ *Sat. 7 PM–2 AM. Tube: Balham.*

Canal Café Theatre. Sketch-based comedy cabaret, which provides a witty take on current affairs, is the staple of this canalside venue in the smart Little Venice area. There are two shows Monday through Sat-

urday at 7:30 and 9:30 PM; Sundays they kick off half an hour earlier.
⊠ *Bridge House, Delamere Terr., W2,* ☎ *020/7289–6054.* ⊠ *£5–£10.*
⊙ *Mon.–Sat. 7 PM–11 PM, Sun. 6:30 PM–10:30 PM. Tube: Warwick Ave.*
Comedy Café. In addition to a wide range of stand-up comedy, this popular dive in the City has a talent night on Wednesdays and late-night
dancing weekends. Admission charges are occasionally waived. Food
is available in the evening and there's usually a late license (for alcohol). ⊠ *66 Rivington St., EC2,* ☎ *020/7739–5706.* ⊠ *Free–£12.* ⊙
Wed.–Thurs. 7 PM–midnight, Fri.–Sat. 7 PM–2 AM. Tube: Old St.
Comedy Store. Now firmly at home in a bigger and better space, this
is the improv factory where the United Kingdom's funniest stand-ups
cut their teeth. The name performers and new talent you'll see may be
strangers to you, but you're guaranteed to laugh. ⊠ *1A Oxendon St.,*
SW1, ☎ *020/7344–4444 or 020/7344–0234.* ⊠ *£12–£15.* ⊙ *Shows*
Tues.–Thurs. and Sun. at 8, Fri.–Sat. at 8 and midnight. Tube: Piccadilly
Circus or Leicester Square.
Hackney Empire. Black comics and adherents of political radicalism
do their thing at this great old community theater in a dog-eared part
of town. Call for show schedules. ⊠ *291 Mare St., E8 1EJ,* ☎ *020/*
8985–2424. ⊠ *£4–£25. Rail: Hackney Central.*
Jongleurs Camden Lock. Jongleurs was the first chain of comedy clubs
in the country and this flagship venue is popular because of its late-
night bars. The billing, sometimes featuring North American comics,
is strong but not quite as tasty as at the Comedy Store. ⊠ *Dingwalls*
Building, Camden Lock, off Camden High St., NW1, ☎ *0870/787–*
0707. ⊙ *Fri. 8:15 PM–2 AM, Sat. 7:15 PM–10 PM and 10:30 PM–3 AM.*
⊠ *£12. Tube: Camden Town.*
Lee Hurst's Backyard Comedy Club. Owned by comic and TV performer
Lee Hurst (who is the regular MC here), this 400-seat club in a scruffy
part of the East End hosts stand-ups until 11:30 PM. There's a DJ and
bar service until 2 AM. ⊠ *231 Cambridge Heath Rd., E2,* ☎ *020/7739–*
3122. ⊙ *Fri. and Sat. 8:30 PM–2 AM.* ⊠ *£11. Tube: Bethnal Green.*

Casinos

Unfortunately for those who like a bit of spontaneity, the 1968 Gaming Act states that any person wishing to gamble must make a decla-
ration of intent to gamble at the gaming house in question and must
apply for membership in person. Membership now takes 24 hours to
process. In many cases, clubs prefer that the applicant's membership
be proposed by an existing member. Personal guests of existing members are, however, allowed to participate.

Crockford's. This is a civilized club, established more than 150 years
ago, with none of the jostling for tables that mars many of the flashier
clubs. It has attracted a large international clientele since its move from
St. James's to Mayfair. The club offers American roulette, Punto Banco,
and blackjack. ⊠ *30 Curzon St., W1,* ☎ *020/7493–7771.* ⊠ *Membership*
£300 yearly. ⊙ *Daily noon–4 AM. Jacket required. Tube: Green Park.*
Golden Nugget. This large casino just off Piccadilly has blackjack,
roulette, and Punto Banco. ⊠ *22–32 Shaftesbury Ave., W1,* ☎ *020/*
7439–0099. ⊠ *Life membership £10.* ⊙ *Daily 2 PM–4 AM. Tube: Pic-*
cadilly Circus.
Palm Beach Casino. In what used to be the old ballroom of the Mayfair Hotel, this is a fast-moving and exciting club attracting a large international membership. It has a red-and-gold interior, with a plush
restaurant and bar. You can choose from American roulette, blackjack,
casino stub poker, and Punto Banco. ⊠ *30 Berkeley St., W1,* ☎ *020/*
7493–6585. ⊠ *Life membership £25.* ⊙ *Daily 2 PM–4 AM. Jacket and*
tie. Tube: Green Park.

Sportsman Club. This one has a dice table as well as Punto Banco, American roulette, and blackjack. There is no membership charge. ✉ *40 Bryanston St., W1,* ☎ *020/7414–0061.* ⊙ *Daily 12:30 PM–4 AM. Jacket required. Tube: Marble Arch.*

Dance Clubs

A mini-revolution in the London club world in the late '90s saw the opening of two several-story, multi-dance-floor-equipped clubs called Home and Fabric, which can accommodate hundreds of clubbers at a time. In addition to these places, there are clubs that specialize in everything from techno to garage to disco. Always call ahead, especially to the dance and youth-oriented places, because the club scene is constantly changing. One-nighters (theme nights that take place at particular clubs on the same night every week, or move around from club to club) are very popular but tend to confuse matters with erratic opening and closing times—always check the daily listings in *Time Out* for current information.

Bagley's Studio. This used to be the largest club in town. Bagley's is notable for getting in the big DJs for one-night blitzes. It doesn't come cheap, though. After surfacing at King's Cross, walk north on York Way, and turn left on Goods Way. ✉ *King's Cross Freight Depot, N1,* ☎ *020/7278–2777.* 🎟 *£12–£15.* ⊙ *Sat. 10 PM–7 AM, with other raves usually scheduled for Thurs. and Fri. Tube: King's Cross.*

Bar Rumba. This steamy, sweaty dance club is almost always crammed full and hosts a different style of music each night. Saturday night is garage music; Thursday is drum and base; Tuesday night pulsates to the rhythm of salsa music; and Monday there are world-beat sessions. Dress in layers, because it gets very hot. *36 Shaftesbury Ave., W1,* ☎ *020/7287–2715.* 🎟 *£3–£12.* ⊙ *Weeknights 9 PM–3 AM, Sat. 9 PM–6 AM, Sun. 9 PM–1:30 AM. Tube: Piccadilly Circus.*

Camden Palace. It would be difficult to find a facial wrinkle in this huge place, even if you could see through the laser lights. Try to find your way around the three floors of bars. There is live music on indie-rock Tuesday, anthemic house every Friday, and harder-edged house on Saturday. ✉ *1A Camden High St., NW1,* ☎ *020/7387–0428.* 🎟 *£5–£20.* ⊙ *Tues.–Thurs. 10 PM–2 AM, Fri.–Sat. 10 PM–6 AM. Tube: Mornington Crescent or Camden Town.*

Dogstar. This popular South London hangout is inside a spacious and atmospheric pub that is usually populated by funky locals. The club plays host to a variety of DJs throughout the week and is sometimes free. Dress down because the atmosphere is usually quite gritty. Follow or precede your visit with a drink at the nearby Bug Bar and your sampling of local Brixton life will be complete. ✉ *389 Coldharbour La., SW9,* ☎ *020/7733–7515.* 🎟 *Free–£6.* ⊙ *Mon.–Thurs. noon–2:30 AM, Fri.–Sat. noon–4:30 AM. Tube: Brixton.*

Elbow Room. A pool hall and restaurant by day, it has DJs spinning a variety of tunes from rock crossover to hard house by night. The club, owned by U.S. dance producer Arthur Baker, has eleven tables, leather-booth seating, and a neon-lit bar. One of the best deals is the Sunday Jam when some very good rock bands play here for free and Baker himself spends some time on the decks. ✉ *89–91 Chapel Market, N1,* ☎ *020/7278–3244.* 🎟 *Free–£5.* ⊙ *Mon.–Wed. noon–2 AM, Thurs.–Sat. noon–3 AM, Sun. noon–1 AM. Tube: Angel.*

The End. After five years, one of London's best clubs got even better in 2001 when it knocked through to the adjoining bar and created a cool space with three dance floors, four bars, and a lounge area. In essence, The End is a club run by clubbers (noted DJ Mr. C owns the joint), and the air-conditioning is a bonus. Expect big names on weekends including Carl Cox and Fatboy Slim. ⊠ *16A West Central St., WC1,* ☎ *020/7419–9199.* ☜ *£5–£15.* ☾ *Mon., Wed.–Thurs. 9 PM–3:30 AM, Fri. and Sat. 10 PM–6 AM. Tube: Tottenham Court Rd.*

Fabric. This, along with Home, really was the name on every clubbers lips when it opened in 1999. Huge and trendy, it manages to cater to vast numbers of people (with three dance floors, five sound systems, three bars, a roof terrace, etc.) while at the same time remaining cutting-edge and hip. It has hip-hop crews and other live acts playing every Friday; in general, weekends are a hive of DJ activity, while weeknights at Fabric are usually reserved for high-profile launches and special parties. Drinks are reasonably priced. Perhaps its main selling point is a 24-hour music and dancing license that lasts from Thursday to Sunday. Another is that it is in the heart of the burgeoning East London community that is *the* place to be right now. ⊠ *77A Charterhouse St., EC1,* ☎ *020/7490–0444.* ☜ *£10–£15.* ☾ *Weekdays vary, Fri.–Sat. 9 PM–7 AM. Tube: Farringdon.*

Gardening Club. Next door to the Rock Garden, but far hipper than that ancient dive, this club has different music, ambience, and groovers on alternating nights. ⊠ *4 The Piazza, WC2,* ☎ *020/7497–3154.* ☜ *£5–£13.* ☾ *Mon.–Thurs. 10 PM–3 AM, Fri.–Sat. 11 PM–4 AM, Sun. 8 PM–midnight. Tube: Covent Garden.*

Hanover Grand. A swank and opulent big West End club, the Hanover attracts TV stars and footballers whose exploits here you can later read about in the tabloids. Funky U.S. garage takes over on Friday, while Saturday's glam disco and house pull in all those who want to be seen. The lines outside get long, so dress up to impress the bouncers. ⊠ *6 Hanover St., W1,* ☎ *020/7499–7977.* ☜ *£5–£15.* ☾ *Wed. 10:30 PM–3:30 AM, Thurs.–Fri. 10:30 PM–4 AM, Sat. 10:30 PM–5 AM. Tube: Oxford Circus.*

Home. Originally an import from Sydney, Home is another supertrendy, cutting-edge London development. Housed in an ultramodern seven-story building in the heart of London, Home offers everything a clubber could yearn for, from an impressive list of DJs, to the multimedia café and the restaurant with a bird's-eye view of the city, to the chill-out zone. Sunday is gay night. ⊠ *1 Leicester Sq., WC2,* ☎ *020/7909–0000.* ☜ *£5–£15.* ☾ *Thurs.–Fri. 10 PM–3 AM, Sat. 9 PM–3 AM, Sun. 5 PM–midnight. Tube: Piccadilly Circus or Leicester Sq.*

Ministry of Sound. This is more of an industry than a club, with its own record label, magazine, line of apparel, and, of course, DJs. Inside, there are chill-out rooms, dance floors, promotional Sony Playstations, Absolut shot bars—all the club kid's favorite things. If you are one, and you only have time for one night out, make it here. ⊠ *103 Gaunt St., SE1,* ☎ *020/7378–6528.* ☜ *£10–£15.* ☾ *Fri. 10:30 PM–6 AM, Sat. midnight–9 AM. Tube: Elephant and Castle.*

Notting Hill Arts Club. In one of London's trendiest neighborhoods, this is an innovative club-bar with a high-profile reputation. Saturdays showcase Outcaste, devoted to Asian underground music; other nights include Brazilian Love Affair or French house beats. Radio 4 is an indie disco that attracts rock stars like Liam Gallagher and Courtney Love; it's run by Oasis's former label boss. Art exhibitions are sometimes held here, too. ⊠ *21 Notting Hill Gate, W11,* ☎ *020/7460–4459.* ☜ *£3–£5.* ☾ *Mon.–Wed. 6 PM–1 AM, Sat. 6 PM–2 AM, Sun. 4 PM–1 AM. Tube: Notting Hill Gate.*

Sound. Right in the heart of the West End, this big-bucks restaurant and venue hasn't captured the imagination of Londoners just yet. Bliss, a U.K. garage night on Thursdays, is one of the best ways to experience the high-tech, futuristic, but cramped, palace. ⊠ *Swiss Center, Leicester Sq., WC2,* ☎ *020/7287–1010.* ☜ *Thurs.–Tues. £12–£15; Wed. £5.* ☾ *Wed. 7:30 PM–midnight, Fri. 10:30 PM–4:30 AM, Sat. 10 PM–4 AM. Tube: Leicester Sq.*

Subterania. This is the place to go to hang out with London's real party people. Intimidatingly cool at times, and usually populated by the hard-core clubbing crowd, this West London club hosts nights that range from serious roots reggae and hip-hop to animated disco and garage. Expect a good fallout from the nearby Portobello–Notting Hill crowd, and dress down rather than up if you want to blend. ⊠ *12 Acklam Rd. (under Westway), W10,* ☎ *020/8960–4590.* ⌨ *£5–£10.* ☉ *Mon.–Thurs. 8 PM–2 AM, Fri.–Sun. 10 PM–3 AM. Tube: Ladbroke Grove.*

Wag. This tenacious representative of Soho's club circuit takes on a different character according to the night and the DJ spinning. One extremely loud, sweaty level houses bars and dance spaces, and on a quieter, cooler floor there's a restaurant serving dinner and breakfast. ⊠ *33–35 Wardour St., W1,* ☎ *020/7437–5534.* ⌨ *£5–£10.* ☉ *Tues.–Thurs. 10 PM–3 AM, Fri. 10 PM–4 AM, Sat. 10 PM–5 AM. Tube: Piccadilly Circus.*

Eclectic Music

The Borderline. This extremely central venue, with faux southwestern decor and a sound system that could be better, has built its reputation on booking some of the best Americana, blues, and singer-songwriter acts from around the world. At times the atmosphere can be a mite precious, to say the least. ⊠ *Orange Yard off Manette St., W1,* ☎ *020/7734–2095.* ⌨ *£6–£15.* ☉ *Mon.–Sat. 8 PM–11 PM. Tube: Tottenham Court Rd.*

Roadhouse. True to its name, Roadhouse pays homage to the American dream of the open road, with a Harley behind the bar and much memorabilia. Music fits into the feel-good-but-middle-of-the-road end of the R&B-blues-rock-soul spectrum. ⊠ *Jubilee Hall, Covent Garden, WC2,* ☎ *020/7240–6001.* ⌨ *Free–£10.* ☉ *Mon.–Sat. 5:30 PM–3 AM, Sun. 5:30 PM–10:30 PM. Tube: Covent Garden.*

Shepherd's Bush Empire. Converted from the BBC TV theater, where Terry Wogan, the United Kingdom's Johnny Carson, recorded his show for years and years, this place hosts a variety of rock, soul, and country acts. Check listings for open hours. ⊠ *Shepherd's Bush Green, W12,* ☎ *020/7771–2000.* ⌨ *£12–£15. Tube: Shepherd's Bush.*

Spitz. In charming Spitalfields Market, where the City interfaces with the East End, this two-level venue has an eclectic range of music that includes world-beat, folk, Americana, and electronic sounds. The downstairs bar, which has DJs and art exhibits, attracts a friendly crowd. ⊠ *109 Commercial St., E1,* ☎ *020/7392–9032.* ⌨ *£4–£8.* ☉ *Mon. 5:30 PM–11 PM; Tues.–Sun. 11 AM–midnight. Tube: Liverpool St.*

12 Bar Club. An array of notable soul, blues, Americana, and acoustic acts perform in this intimate setting. If it's crammed downstairs there might just be room on the tiny balcony upstairs. Although there's a late bar, it may close early on a quiet night. ⊠ *22–23 Denmark St., WC2,* ☎ *020/7916–6989.* ⌨ *£5–£10.* ☉ *Mon.–Sat. 8 PM–2 AM, Sun. 8 PM–midnight. Tube: Tottenham Court Rd.*

Jazz and Blues

Jazz is alive and kicking in London: more and more restaurants and bars are bringing in jazz musicians to entertain their clientele, though you may encounter rather dull traditional stuff or Miles Davis wannabes. Central locations as well as established neighborhood venues (such as those below) are bringing in the best names and charge accordingly. The city hosts two major festivals: the Soho Jazz Festival, held in October, tends to stick to the traditional and Dixieland mold, while the more innovative London Jazz Festival, which takes place every November, promotes experimental jazz as well as an array of top world-beat names. These festivals are held at venues throughout the capital.

Ain't Nothin' but Blues. The name sums up this bar that whips up a sweaty and smoky atmosphere. Local musicians, as well as some notable names, squeeze onto the tiny stage. There's good bar food of the chili and gumbo variety. Most weekday nights there is no cover. ✉ *20 Kingly St., W1,* ☎ *020/7287–0514.* 🎫 *Free–£10. Tube: Oxford Circus.*

Bull's Head. Its pleasant setting—in the well-heeled neighborhood of Barnes, right on the River Thames—and big names who jam here regularly make Bull's Head well worth the excursion out beyond Hammersmith. It's open normal pub hours, and shows start nightly at 8:30 PM. ✉ *373 Lonsdale Rd., Barnes, SW13,* ☎ *020/8876–5241.* 🎫 *£4–£10. Tube: Hammersmith then Bus 209 to Barnes Bridge.*

Jazz Café. This palace of high-tech cool in a converted bank in bohemian Camden remains an essential hangout for fans of both the mainstream end of the repertoire and younger crossover performers. It's steps from Camden Town tube. ✉ *3–5 Parkway, NW1,* ☎ *020/7916–6060.* 🎫 *£6–£20.* ⊙ *Mon.–Thurs. 7 PM–1 AM, Fri.–Sat. 7 PM–2 AM, Sun. 7 PM–midnight. Tube: Camden Town.*

100 Club. The best for blues and Dixie, plus the occasional rock or indie band, this Oxford Street subterranean has the correct paint-peeling, smoke-choked, dance-inducing atmosphere. There's a food counter on weekends. ✉ *100 Oxford St., W1,* ☎ *020/7636–0933.* 🎫 *£6–£10.* ⊙ *Mon.–Thurs. 7:30–midnight, Fri.–Sat. 7:30 PM–2 AM, Sun. 7:30 PM–11:30 PM. Tube: Oxford Circus or Tottenham Court Rd.*

Pizza Express. It may seem strange, since Pizza Express is the capital's best-loved chain of pizza houses, but this is also one of London's principal jazz venues, with music every night except Monday in the basement restaurant. The interior is darkly lit; the lineups (often featuring visiting U.S. performers) are interesting; and the Italian-style thin-crust pizzas are great. Eight other branches also have live music; check the listings for details. ✉ *10 Dean St., W1,* ☎ *020/7437–9595 or 020/7439–8722.* 🎫 *£8–£20.* ⊙ *From 11:30 AM for food; music nightly 9 PM–midnight. Tube: Tottenham Court Rd.*

Ronnie Scott's. Since opening in the '60s, this legendary Soho jazz club has attracted all the big names. It's usually packed and hot, the food isn't great, and service is slow—the staff can't move through the crowds, either; the atmosphere, however, can't be beat, and it's probably still one of London's best jazz clubs, even since the sad departure of its eponymous founder and saxophonist. Reservations are recommended. ✉ *47 Frith St., W1,* ☎ *020/7439–0747.* 🎫 *£15–£20 non-members, £5–£9 members, annual membership £50.* ⊙ *Mon.–Sat. 8:30 PM–3 AM, Sun. 7:30 PM–11:30 PM. Tube: Leicester Sq.*

606 Club. Way out to the west, in deepest Fulham, this is a civilized sit-down club with late hours, showcasing mainstream and contemporary jazz—basically, well-known British artists. You must eat a meal in order to consume alcohol, so allow for an extra £20 per head on top of the cover charge. ✉ *90 Lots Rd., SW10,* ☎ *020/7352–5953.* 🎫 *£5–£6.* ⊙ *Mon.–Wed. 7:30 PM–1:15 AM, Thurs.–Sat. 8 PM–2 AM, Sun. 8 PM–11:30 PM. Tube: Fulham Broadway.*

Rock

Since the '60s, London has had one of the best live music scene in the world: everyone of note (with the exception of one Elvis Presley) has played here, and the city is an essential stop on any band's world tour. Quite often it is possible to catch arena-circuit American bands playing at small clubs or theaters. Add the vibrancy of emerging artists and styles to a varied collection of venues, and you have the recipe for a great time.

There are a couple of drawbacks: most shows are over by 11 PM and some even earlier than that, especially at the Astoria, where the support band often trudges on as early as 7:30 PM and headliners kick off at 9 PM. It's simply just not enough rock and roll. The other big problem is that many shows sell out very quickly, leaving fans at the mercy of scalpers who are at their worst outside the venues in question. It's a good idea to buy tickets in advance for acts that you really must see. The "Gigs" page at www.nme.com is one of the most comprehensive search engines and allows you to book tickets on-line.

The Astoria. Very central and quite hip, this place holds 2,000 people and hosts the hottest bands. Shows can start very early, as the building is often cleared immediately following gigs for club events. Check listings for open hours. ⊠ *157 Charing Cross Rd., W1,* ☎ *020/7434–9592.* ⌨ *£8–£15. Tube: Tottenham Court Rd.*

Barfly Club. Formerly known as the Splash Club (the people who gave Skunk Anansie, Kula Shaker, and Oasis their big breaks), this is one of the finest small clubs in the capital. There are three bands nightly, with events regularly scheduled by some of the top rocker magazines and radio stations, plus indie discos on Friday and Saturday. ⊠ *The Monarch, 49 Chalk Farm Rd., NW1,* ☎ *020/7916–1049.* ⌨ *£6.* ☉ *Daily 7:30 PM–11 PM. Tube: Camden Town or Chalk Farm.*

Brixton Academy. Despite a capacity of 4,000 people, the Academy retains a clublike charm and has interesting Art Deco architecture, plenty of bars, and upstairs seating. The sloping floor can be a bit scary, especially when slicked up by a night of beer, but it provides good views of the stage. There are occasional late shows on Saturdays. Check listings for open hours. ⊠ *211 Stockwell Rd., SW9,* ☎ *020/7771–2000.* ⌨ *£10–£20. Tube: Brixton.*

Dingwalls. Once a comedy club, Dingwalls now hosts a variety of established and breaking rock acts as well as country and folk crossover contenders several nights a week. It's in the cutesy Camden Lock warehouses, and while it's a nicely groomed place, the long lines at the bar can be irksome. ⊠ *Camden Lock off Camden High St., NW1,* ☎ *020/7267–1577.* ⌨ *£7–£15.* ☉ *7:30 PM–midnight. Tube: Camden Town.*

Forum. This ex-ballroom with a balcony and dance floor packs in the customers, and it consistently attracts the best medium-to-big-name performers, too. ⊠ *9–17 Highgate Rd., NW5,* ☎ *020/7344–0044.* ⌨ *£10–£15.* ☉ *Most nights 7–11. Tube: Kentish Town.*

Ocean. A new name on the scene in 2001, this tastefully renovated spot contains two cozy halls plus a main space that holds 2,000 standing or 1,000 seated cabaret style. Booked by people who have established a reputation for getting cult American bands, it's a welcome addition to the city's live scene even if it isn't close to a tube. Check listings for open hours. ⊠ *270 Mare St., E8,* ☎ *020/8533–0111. British Rail: Hackney Central.*

Water Rats. There are gigs most nights of the week in the tiny back room of this pub. The usual fare is a hot new band (plus two usually unknown support bands) that's less raucous and sometimes more rootsy than those at Camden indie venues. ⊠ *328 Gray's Inn Rd., WC1,* ☎ *020/7284–0077.* ⌨ *£5–£7.* ☉ *Mon.–Sat. 8 PM–11 PM. Tube: King's Cross.*

The Gay Scene

Since February 1994, with the long-overdue lowering of the age of consent from 21, 18-year-old gay men in Britain have had the blessing of the law in doing what they've always done. The change did not extend to lesbians, nor did it need to, because there has never been any legislation that so much as mentions gay women—a circumstance that, believe it or not, dates from Queen Victoria's point-blank refusal to believe that women paired off with women.

The whole of London has benefited hugely from the blossoming of gay nightlife. Soho, especially Old Compton Street, has something of a pre-AIDS Christopher Street atmosphere, with gay shops, bars, restaurants, and even beauty salons (get your chest waxed here) jostling for space, and it has now settled into happy coexistence with club kids, restaurant patrons, and tourists. Though lesbians are included in the gay clubbing scene (as are anyone's straight friends), it's predominantly men-for-men. Lesbian chic is as trendy in London as it is in New York or Los Angeles, but it has a lower profile, generally, than the male equivalent, and it also tends to be more politically strident. Any women-only event in London attracts a large proportion of gay women.

Check the listings in *Time Out*, the weekly *MetroXtra (MX)*, and the monthly *Gay Times* for events.

Bars, Cafés, and Pubs

Unless otherwise stated, hours for pubs and bars in this section are the same as for all London pubs, with drinks available up to 11 PM.

Box. Modern, and *très* chic, the Box has different DJs spinning every night. For peckish punters there is food before 5 PM every day. ⊠ *Seven Dials, 32–34 Monmouth St., WC2,* ☏ *020/7240–5828.* ⊘ *Mon.–Sat. 5:30–11 PM, Sun. 6:30–10:30 PM. Tube: Leicester Sq.*

Candy Bar. This lesbian bar plays fun, trendy tunes and has seating outdoors. Men are welcome as guests. ⊠ *23–24 Bateman St., W1,* ☏ *020/ 7494–4041.* ⊞ *£5 after 9 PM, Fri.–Sat..* ⊘ *Mon.–Thurs. noon–1 AM, Fri. and Sat. noon–3 AM, Sun. noon–11 PM. Tube: Tottenham Court Rd.*

Edge. Poseurs are welcome at this hip Soho hangout, where straight groovers mix and mingle with gay men over the four floors. Get more for your money in summer, when sidewalk tables offer an enviable view of Soho's daily street theater. Risk the vodkas infused with candy. ⊠ *11 Soho Sq., W1,* ☏ *020/7439–1313.* ⊘ *Mon.–Sat. noon–1 AM, Sun. 1–10:30 PM. Tube: Oxford Circus.*

Freedom. This is a popular café-bar central to the Soho scene. It has late-night music and DJs on the lower floor, and is licensed to serve alcohol until 3 AM. There is a rigid and sometimes frigid door policy, enforced by bouncers after 11 PM. ⊠ *60–66 Wardour St., W1,* ☏ *020/ 7734–0071.* ⊞ *£3–£5 after 11 PM.* ⊘ *Mon.–Sat. 11 AM–3 AM, Sun. 11 AM–midnight. Tube: Piccadilly Circus.*

Yard. This is Soho's best-looking and biggest café-bar, centered on the eponymous courtyard and getting very full and smoky at night. Upstairs is a little more genteel, with sofas. Get a bottomless coffee or a club sandwich. ⊠ *57 Rupert St., W1,* ☏ *020/7437–2652.* ⊘ *Mon.–Sat. noon–11 PM. Tube: Piccadilly Circus.*

Clubs

Some of the best gay dance clubs are held once a week in mixed clubs. The following are well established and likely still to be going strong, but it's best to call first.

Atelier. This bustling Thursday-night mixed-gay session, in a stylish club, attracts those from the media, movies, music, and fashion worlds. ⊠ *The End, 18 West Central St., WC1,* ☏ *020/7419–9199.* ⊞ *£5.* ⊘ *Thurs. 9 PM–3:30 AM. Tube: Tottenham Court Rd.*

Heaven. Aptly named, it has by far the best light show on any London dance floor, and it's unpretentious, loud, and huge, with a labyrinth of quiet rooms, bars, and live-music parlors. If you go to just one club, this is the one to choose. Friday is straight night. ⊠ *The Arches, Vil-*

liers St., WC2, ☎ 020/7930–2020. 🖾 £1–£10. ☯ Weekdays 10:30 PM–
3:30 AM, Sat. 11:30 PM–6 AM. Tube: Charing Cross.

Love Muscle. A steaming, mixed-gender Saturday-night party, this blast
offers eight hours of dance classics at a big Brixton club. ⊠ The Fridge,
Town Hall Parade, Brixton Hill, SW2, ☎ 020/7326–5100. 🖾 £13. ☯
Sat. 10 PM–7 AM. Tube: Brixton.

Original Sunday Tea Dance. A longtime fave with the girls, this is a
very camp and very fun Sunday ballroom, line-dance, time-warp disco.
Tea and sandwiches served up until 7 PM. ⊠ BJ's White Swan, 556 Commercial Rd., E14, ☎ 020/7780–9870. 🖾 £2. ☯ Sun. 5:30–midnight.
Tube: Limehouse.

Trade. This London institution among the hedonistic muscle boys is
now over a decade old and begins when many clubs are closing. ⊠
Turnmills, 63 Clerkenwell Rd., EC1, ☎ 020/7250–3409. 🖾 £15. ☯
4 AM–1 PM. Tube: Farringdon.

THE ARTS

There isn't *a* London arts scene—there are lots of them. As long as there
are audiences for Feydeau revivals, drag queens, obscure teenage rock
bands, hit musicals, body-painted Parisian dancers, and improvised stand-
up comedy, someone will stage them in London. Commercial sponsorship
of the arts is in its infancy here compared to what it is in the United
States, and most major arts companies, as well as those smaller ones
lucky enough to be grant-aided, are dependent, to some extent, on (in-
adequate) government subsidy. This ought to mean low ticket prices,
but it doesn't necessarily work that way. Even so, when you consider
how much a London hotel room costs, the city's arts are a bargain.

We've attempted a representative selection in the following listings, but
to find out what's showing now, the weekly magazine *Time Out*
(£2.20, issued every Wednesday) is invaluable. The *Evening Standard*
also carries listings, especially in the supplement "Hot Tickets," which
comes with the Thursday edition, as do the "quality" Sunday papers
and the Saturday *Independent, Guardian,* and *Times*. You'll find
leaflets and flyers in most cinema and theater foyers, too, and you can
pick up the free fortnightly *London Theatre Guide* leaflet from hotels
and tourist information centers.

Ballet

The Royal Opera House is once again the traditional home of the world-
famous Royal Ballet. After 20 years of planning and a two-year clo-
sure for renovation, the stage doors reopened just in time for the new
millennium. A new pricing structure means that tickets are more affordable, although bookings should be made well in advance.

The English National Ballet and visiting international companies perform at the Coliseum. The City Ballet of London performs at the Peacock Theatre. Sadler's Wells Theatre hosts various other ballet companies
and regional and international modern dance troupes. Modern and experimental work is best viewed at the Place.

Ballet Box Offices

Coliseum. ⊠ St. Martin's La., WC2N 4ES, ☎ 020/7632–8300. Tube:
Leicester Sq.

Peacock Theatre. ⊠ Portugal St., WC2, ☎ 020/7863–8222. Tube: Holborn.

The Place. ⊠ 17 Duke's Rd., WC1, ☎ 020/7380–1268. Tube: Euston.

Royal Festival Hall. ⊠ South Bank Arts Centre, SE1 8XX, ☎ 020/7960–
4242. Tube: Waterloo or Embankment Station.

Theaters and Concert Halls

Adelphi	42
Albery	28
Aldwych	36
Apollo	12
Apollo Victoria	46
Arts Theatre	23
Barbican Centre	53
Cambridge	29
Coliseum	27
Comedy	8
Criterion	9
Donmar Warehouse	30
Drury Lane (Theatre Royal)	33
Duchess	38
Duke of York's	26
Fortune	32
Garrick	24
Gielgud	14
Globe (Shakespeare's Globe)	51
Haymarket Theatre Royal	7
Her Majesty's	6
London Palladium	4
Lyceum	39
Lyric	11
Mermaid	52
New Ambassadors	22
New London	31
Old Vic	48
Palace	17
Peacock Theatre	35
Phoenix	18
Piccadilly	10
Players	43
Playhouse	44
Prince Edward	16
Prince of Wales	13
Queens	15
Regent's Park Open-Air Theatre	3
Royal Albert Hall	1
Royal Court Theatre	5
Royal National Theatre	50
Royal Opera House	34
St. Martin-in-the-Fields	25
St. Martin's	21
Savoy	40
Shaftesbury	20
South Bank Arts Complex (Royal Festival Hall)	49
St. John's Smith Square	45
Strand	37
Vaudeville	41
Whitehall	47
Wigmore Hall	2
Wyndhams	19

Royal Opera House. ⊠ *Covent Garden, WC2E 9DD,* ☎ *020/7304–4000. Tube: Covent Garden.*
Sadler's Wells. ⊠ *Rosebery Ave., EC1R 4TN,* ☎ *020/7863–8000. Tube: Angel.*

Concerts

The ticket prices to symphony-size orchestral concerts are fortunately still relatively moderately priced, usually ranging from £5 to £35. If you can't book in advance, then arrive at the hall an hour before the performance for a chance at returns.

The London Symphony Orchestra is in residence at the Barbican Centre, although other top orchestras—including the Philharmonia and the Royal Philharmonic—also perform here. The Barbican also hosts chamber music concerts with such celebrated orchestras as the City of London Sinfonia. The South Bank Centre, which includes the Royal Festival Hall, the Queen Elizabeth Hall, and the small Purcell Room, is a major venue; the Royal Festival Hall is one of the finest concert halls in Europe.

For a different concert-going experience, as well as the chance to take part in a great British tradition, try the Royal Albert Hall during the Promenade Concert season: eight weeks lasting from July to September. The usual chestnuts are featured, along with some novelties, but the capper is the last night, a madly jingoistic display of singing "Land of Hope and Glory," Union Jack waving, and general madness. Demand for tickets is so high that you must enter a lottery. For regular Proms, tickets run £3–£30; special "promenade" (standing) tickets usually cost half the price of normal tickets and are available at the hall on the night of the concert. Note, too, that the concerts have begun to be jumbo-screen broadcast in Hyde Park, but even here a seat on the grass requires a paid ticket.

During the summer, there is an outdoor concert series by the lake at Kenwood. Concerts are part of the program at the open-air theater in Holland Park. Check the listings for details.

You should look for the lunchtime concerts that take place all over the city in smaller concert halls, the big arts-center foyers, and churches; they usually cost less than £5 or are free and will feature string quartets, singers, jazz ensembles, or gospel choirs. St. John's, Smith Square and St. Martin-in-the-Fields are two of the more popular locations. Performances usually begin about 1 PM and last an hour.

Concert Hall Box Offices

Barbican Centre. ⊠ *Barbican, EC2Y 8DS,* ☎ *020/7638–8891 or 020/7638–4141. Tube: Barbican.*
Holland Park. ☎ *020/7602–7856.*
Kenwood. ⊠ *Hampstead Heath,* ☎ *020/7973–3427.*
Royal Albert Hall. ⊠ *Kensington Gore, SW7,* ☎ *020/7589–8212 or 020/7589–8212 for information about Proms concerts. Tube: South Kensington.*
St. John's, Smith Square. ⊠ *SW1P 3HA,* ☎ *020/7222–1061. Tube: Westminster.*
St. Martin-in-the-Fields. ⊠ *Trafalgar Sq., WC2N 4JJ,* ☎ *020/7839–1930. Tube: Charing Cross.*
South Bank Centre. ⊠ *South Bank, SE1 8XX,* ☎ *020/7960–4242. Tube: Waterloo.*
Wigmore Hall. ⊠ *36 Wigmore St., W1H 0BP,* ☎ *020/7935–2141. Tube: Bond St.*

Modern Dance

Contemporary dance thrives in London, with innovative young chore-
ographers and companies constantly emerging (and then, it often
seems, moving to New York). Michael Clark was one of the first of
the new wave; Yolanda Snaith, Bunty Matthias, and choreographer Lea
Anderson's troupe, the Cholmondeleys (pronounced "Chumleys"),
are more examples of home-grown talent. In addition to the many fringe
theaters that produce the odd dance performance, the following theaters showcase contemporary dance:

Chisenhale Dance Space. For avant-garde dance by promising new
dancers from around the world, this is the spot. Sadly, its program has
been reduced in recent years, with just a handful of events taking place
in spring and fall. ✉ *64–84 Chisenhale Rd., E3,* ☎ *020/8961–6617.
Tube: Mile End.*

Peacock Theatre. This compact theatre near the University of London
offers a wide range of contemporary dance as well as ballet. ✉ *Portugal St., WC2,* ☎ *020/7863–8222. Tube: Holborn.*

The Place. It's a dance school by day, a small cutting-edge space by night.
✉ *17 Duke's Rd., WC1,* ☎ *020/7380–1268. Tube: Euston.*

Riverside Studios. This West Side space and sometime television studio is noted for its experimental offerings. ✉ *Crisp Rd., W6 9RL,* ☎
020/8237–1111. Tube: Hammersmith.

Sadler's Wells. The capital's premier venue for dance has a reputation
for unconventional productions, often incorporating multimedia elements. ✉ *Rosebery Ave., EC1R 4TN,* ☎ *020/7863–8000. Tube: Angel.*

Movies

Despite the video invasion, West End movie theaters continue to do
good business. Most of the major houses (Odeon, ABC, etc.) are in
the Leicester Square–Piccadilly Circus area, where tickets average £8.
Mondays and matinees are often cheaper, at around £5, and there are
also fewer crowds. Some theaters offer student discounts, and prices
drop to around £5 as you get out of the West End, becoming even lower
in the suburbs, but unless you're staying there, any savings could be
eaten up by transportation costs.

The few movie clubs and repertory cinemas that still exist screen a wider
range of movies, including classic, Continental, and underground, as
well as rare or underrated masterpieces. Some charge a membership
fee of less than £1.

Everyman. Billing itself as "London's oldest repertory," this cozy theater shows an excellent selection of classic, foreign, avant-garde, and
almost-new Hollywood titles. Many shows are double (even triple) features at no extra cost. ✉ *5 Hollybush Vale, N3,* ☎ *020/7431–1777.
Tube: Hampstead.*

Lux. In the trendy Hoxton district, characterized by club-bars and galleries, this spot has a wild mix of movies (including foreign titles), music
features, and the usual art flicks. ✉ *2–4 Hoxton Sq., N1,* ☎ *020/7864–
0201. Tube: Old St.*

National Film Theatre. The NFT's three cinemas show over 2,000 titles each year, including foreign-language titles, documentaries, cult Hollywood features, and animation. The London Film Festival is based
here each fall, and throughout the year there are mini-festivals, semi-
nars, and guest speakers. Members (£16) get priority on bookings
(useful for special events) and get £1 off each screening. ✉ *South
Bank Centre, South Bank, SE1,* ☎ *020/7928–3232. Tube: Waterloo.*

Rio. This grand old Art Deco cinema has a bar and continues to pro-

vide good mixed programming, with arty double bills as well as matinees for kids. Note: the neighborhood is a bit shabby. ⊠ *107 Kingsland High St., E8,* ☎ *020/7241–9410. British Rail: Dalston.*
Riverside Studios Cinemas. The selection at this converted movie studio changes almost daily. Admission fees are very reasonable. ⊠ *Crisp Rd., W6,* ☎ *020/8237–1111. Tube: Hammersmith.*

Opera

The Royal Opera presides over the main venue for opera in London, the fabled Royal Opera House, which ranks with the Metropolitan Opera House in New York—in every way, except, surprisingly, expense. Long castigated in Britain for its outrageous ticket prices, the Opera House pledged to lower its them following its reopening in 1999. Indeed, now the doors really are open to the masses, since the cheapest tickets are just £2 (for a ballet matinee), although prices escalate to £150 for a top-price opera. Conditions of purchase vary—call for information.

English-language productions are staged at the Coliseum on St. Martin's Lane, home of the English National Opera Company. Prices are generally lower than for the Royal Opera, ranging from £5 to £55, and productions are often innovative and exciting. The ENO sells same-day seats for as little as £2.50.

Opera Box Offices
Royal Albert Hall. ⊠ *Kensington Gore, SW7,* ☎ *020/7589–8212. Tube: South Kensington.*
Barbican Centre. ⊠ *Barbican, EC2Y 8DS,* ☎ *020/7638–8891 or 020/ 7638–4141. Tube: Barbican.*
Coliseum. ⊠ *St. Martin's La., WC2N 4ES,* ☎ *020/7632–8300. Tube: Leicester Sq.*
Royal Festival Hall. ⊠ *South Bank Arts Centre, SE1 8XX,* ☎ *020/7960– 4242. Tube: Waterloo or Embankment Station.*
Royal Opera House. ⊠ *Covent Garden, WC2E 9DD,* ☎ *020/7304– 4000. Tube: Covent Garden.*

Theater

Although the price of a seat rarely falls below a tenner, London's West End theaters still pull in enough punters to cause a mini traffic jam each night before the house lights dim and the curtain rises. From Shakespeare's time to the umpteenth year of *Les Misérables* (or *The Glums,* as it's affectionately known), the West End has what visitors think of as London theater. But there's more to see in London than the offerings of Theatreland and the national companies.

Of the 100 or so legitimate theaters in the capital, 50 are officially "West End," while the remainder go under the blanket title of "fringe." Much like New York's off- and off-off-Broadway, fringe theater encompasses everything from off-the-wall "physical theater" pieces to first runs of new plays and revivals of old ones. A recent typical selection of fringe offerings had one Dickens, an Ibsen, a Kafka, and a couple of Molière productions, as well as several contemporary plays—all in competition. Indeed, even Hollywood's A-team now loves the fringe. At the 300-seat Almedia in Islington, big stars famously play for small bucks. The last few years have seen Kevin Spacey in Eugene O'Neill's *The Iceman Cometh,* Liam Neeson in David Hare's *Judas Kiss,* and Juliette Binoche in Pirandello's *Naked.* No star, in fact, has been too big for a small theater. Nicole Kidman wowed them in Schnitzler's *The Blue Room* at the 250-seat Donmar Warehouse; Ewan McGregor received £250 a week to star in *Little Malcolm and His Struggle Against the Eunuchs* at Hampstead's 174-seater. That's just *non*–West End.

For serious theatergoers, the top of the line is still the Royal Shakespeare Company and the Royal National Theatre Company. During 2001 the Royal Shakespeare Company announced plans to change the company's structure and to mount plays in the West End rather than only at the Barbican Centre, one of the city's primary arts venues. The Royal National Theatre Company performs at another of London's main arts complexes, the Royal National Theatre. Both groups mount consistently excellent productions.

From mid-May through mid-September, you can see the Bard served up in his most spectacular manifestation—at the open-air reconstruction of Shakespeare's Globe Theatre, which opened in June 1997. In addition, Shakespeare under the stars is provided from the last week in May to the third week in September by the New Shakespeare Company at the lovely Regent's Park Open-Air Theatre. Two Shakespeare plays are presented every season, along with a modern musical. Check *Time Out* for details. The renovated Royal Court Theatre, which has produced gritty British and international drama since the middle of the 20th century, reopened in 2000 with a continued dedication to new playwrights and new plays.

Most theaters have matinees twice a week (Wednesday or Thursday, and Saturday) and evening performances that begin at 7:30 or 8; performances on Sunday are rare but not unknown. Prices vary, but in the West End you should expect to pay from £10 for a seat in the upper balcony to at least £25 for a good one in the stalls (orchestra) or dress circle (mezzanine). Tickets may be booked at the individual theater box offices or over the phone by credit card (some box offices or agents have special numbers for these, marked "cc" in the phone book); most theaters still don't charge a fee for the latter. You can also book through ticket agents, such as **First Call** (☎ 020/7420–0000) or **Ticketmaster** (☎ 020/7344–0055; 800/775–2525 in the U.S.), although these usually do charge a booking fee. **Keith Prowse** has a New York office (✉ 234 W. 44th St., Suite 1000, New York, NY 10036, ☎ 212/398–1430 or 800/669–8687), as does **Edwards & Edwards** (✉ 1 Times Sq. Plaza, 12th floor, New York, NY 10036, ☎ 800/223–6108). If you're a theater junkie and want to put together a West End package, *The Complete Guide to London's West End Theatres* has seating plans and booking information for all the houses. It costs £9.95 (plus postage) from the **Society of London Theatres** (☎ 020/7557–6700). Alternatively, the SOLT Half Price Ticket Booth (no phone) on the southwest corner of Leicester Square sells up to four half-price tickets per purchaser on the day of performance for about 25 theaters, subject to availability. It's open Monday–Saturday 2–6:30, Sunday noon–3, and from noon for matinees; there is a £2 service charge, and only cash is accepted. Note that these half-price tickets are invariably for orchestra seats; for more reasonably priced seats, it may be better to go to the actual theater box office. All the larger hotels offer theater bookings, but as they tack on a hefty service charge, you would do better visiting the box offices yourself. You might, however, consider using one particular booking line that doubles the price of tickets: **West End Cares** (☎ 020/7833–3939) donates half of what it charges to AIDS charities.

Warning: Be *very* careful of scalpers outside theaters and working the line at the Half Price Ticket Booth; you might be charged £200 or more for a sought-after ticket (and you'll pay a stiff fine if caught buying a scalped ticket). In recent years, there has been another problem: unscrupulous ticket agents, who sell tickets at four or five times their price from the ticket box offices. Although a service charge is legitimate, this type of scalping certainly isn't, especially because the vast majority of theaters have some tickets (returns and house seats) available on the night of performance.

Theater Directory
The following is a list of West End theaters:

Adelphi. ⊠ *Strand, WC2E 7NA,* ☎ *020/7344–0055. Tube: Charing Cross.*

Albery. ⊠ *St. Martin's La., WC2N 4AH,* ☎ *020/7369–1730. Tube: Leicester Sq.*

Aldwych. ⊠ *Aldwych, WC2B 4DF,* ☎ *020/7416–6003. Tube: Covent Garden.*

Apollo. ⊠ *Shaftesbury Ave., W1V 7HD,* ☎ *020/7494–5070. Tube: Piccadilly Circus.*

Apollo Victoria. ⊠ *Wilton Rd., SW1V ILL,* ☎ *020/7416–6070. Tube: Victoria.*

Arts Theatre. ⊠ *6–7 Great Newport St., WC2H 7JB,* ☎ *020/7836–3334. Tube: Leicester Sq.*

Barbican Centre. ⊠ *Barbican, EC2Y 8DS,* ☎ *020/7638–8891. Tube: Moorgate.*

Cambridge. ⊠ *Earlham St., WC2A 9HH,* ☎ *020/7494–5080. Tube: Covent Garden.*

Comedy. ⊠ *Panton St., SW1Y 4DN,* ☎ *020/7369–1731. Tube: Piccadilly Circus.*

Criterion. ⊠ *Piccadilly Circus, WC2,* ☎ *020/7369–1747. Tube: Piccadilly Circus.*

Dominion. ⊠ *Tottenham Court Rd., W1 0AG,* ☎ *0870/607–7470. Tube: Tottenham Court Rd.*

Donmar Warehouse. ⊠ *41 Earlham St., WC2H 9LD,* ☎ *020/7369–1732. Tube: Covent Garden.*

Drury Lane (Theatre Royal). ⊠ *Catherine St., WC2B 5JF,* ☎ *020/7494–5000. Tube: Covent Garden.*

Duchess. ⊠ *Catherine St., WC2B 5LA,* ☎ *020/7494–5076. Tube: Covent Garden.*

Duke of York's. ⊠ *St. Martin's La., WC2,* ☎ *020/7836–5122. Tube: Leicester Sq.*

Fortune. ⊠ *Russell St., WC2B 5HH,* ☎ *020/7836–2238. Tube: Covent Garden.*

Garrick. ⊠ *Charing Cross Rd., WC2H 0HH,* ☎ *020/7494–5085. Tube: Leicester Sq.*

Gielgud. ⊠ *Shaftesbury Ave., W1V 8AR,* ☎ *020/7494–5065. Tube: Piccadilly Circus.*

Globe (Shakespeare's Globe). ⊠ *New Globe Walk, Bankside, SE1,* ☎ *020/7401–9919. Tube: Mansion House, then walk across Southwark Bridge, or Blackfriars, then walk across Blackfriars Bridge.*

Haymarket Theatre Royal. ⊠ *Haymarket, SW1Y 4HT,* ☎ *020/7930–8800. Tube: Piccadilly Circus.*

Her Majesty's. ⊠ *Haymarket, SW1Y 4QR,* ☎ *020/7494–5400. Tube: Piccadilly Circus.*

London Palladium. ⊠ *8 Argyll St., W1V 1AD,* ☎ *020/7494–5020. Tube: Oxford Circus.*

Lyceum. ⊠ *Wellington St., WC2,* ☎ *0870/243–9000. Tube: Charing Cross.*

Lyric. ⊠ *Shaftesbury Ave., W1V 7HA,* ☎ *020/7494–5045. Tube: Piccadilly Circus.*

Lyric Hammersmith. ⊠ *King St., W6 0QL,* ☎ *020/8741–2311. Tube: Hammersmith.*

Mermaid. ⊠ *Puddle Dock, EC4 3DB,* ☎ *020/7236–1919. Tube: Blackfriars.*

New Ambassadors. ⊠ *West St., WC2,* ☎ *020/7369–1761. Tube: Leicester Sq.*

New London. ⊠ *Drury La., WC2B 5PW,* ☎ *020/7405–0072. Tube: Covent Garden.*

Old Vic. ⊠ *Waterloo Rd., SE1 8NB,* ☎ *020/7369–1762. Tube: Waterloo.*

Palace. ⊠ *Shaftesbury Ave., W1V 8AY,* ☎ *020/7434–0909. Tube: Leicester Sq.*

Phoenix. ⊠ *Charing Cross Rd., WC2H 0JP,* ☎ *020/7369–1733. Tube: Leicester Sq.*

Piccadilly. ⊠ *Denman St., W1V 8DY,* ☎ *020/7369–1734. Tube: Piccadilly Circus.*

Players. ⊠ *The Arches, Villiers St., WC2N 6NQ,* ☎ *020/7839–1134 or 020/7976–1307. Tube: Charing Cross.*

Playhouse. ⊠ *Northumberland Ave., WC2N 6NN,* ☎ *020/7316–4747. Tube: Embankment.*

Prince Edward. ⊠ *Old Compton St., W1V 6HS,* ☎ *020/7447–5400. Tube: Leicester Sq.*

Prince of Wales. ⊠ *31 Coventry St., W1V 8AS,* ☎ *020/7839–5972. Tube: Leicester Sq.*

Queens. ⊠ *51 Shaftesbury Ave., W1V 8AS,* ☎ *020/7494–5040. Tube: Leicester Sq.*

Regent's Park Open-Air Theatre. ⊠ *Inner Circle, Regent's Park., NW1,* ☎ *020/7486–2431. Tube: Baker St., Regent's Park.*

Royal Court Theatre. ⊠ *Sloane Sq., SW1,* ☎ *020/7565–5000. Tube: Sloane Sq.*

Royal National Theatre (Cottesloe, Lyttelton, and Olivier). ⊠ *South Bank Arts Centre, SE1 9PX,* ☎ *020/7452–3000. Tube: Waterloo.*

St. Martin's. ⊠ *West St., WC2H 9NH,* ☎ *020/7836–1443. Tube: Leicester Sq.*

Savoy. ⊠ *Strand, WC2R 0ET,* ☎ *020/7836–8888. Tube: Charing Cross.*

Shaftesbury. ⊠ *Shaftesbury Ave., WC2H 8DP,* ☎ *020/7379–5399. Tube: Holborn.*

Strand. ⊠ *Aldwych, WC2B 5LD,* ☎ *020/7930–8800. Tube: Covent Garden.*

Vaudeville. ⊠ *Strand, WC2R 0NH,* ☎ *020/7836–9987. Tube: Charing Cross.*

Victoria Palace. ⊠ *Victoria St., SW1E 5EA,* ☎ *020/7834–1317. Tube: Victoria.*

Whitehall. ⊠ *14 Whitehall, SW1A 2DY,* ☎ *020/7369–1735. Tube: Charing Cross.*

Wyndhams. ⊠ *Charing Cross Rd., WC2H 0DA,* ☎ *020/7369–1736. Tube: Leicester Sq.*

Fringe

Shows can be straight plays, circus, comedy, musicals, readings, or productions every bit as polished and impressive as those in the West End—except for their location and the price of the seat. Fringe tickets are always considerably less expensive than tickets for West End productions. The following theaters are among the better-known fringe venues:

Almeida. ⊠ *Almeida St., N1 1AT,* ☎ *020/7359–4404. Tube: Angel or Highbury & Islington.*

BAC. ⊠ *176 Lavender Hill, Battersea, SW11 1JX,* ☎ *020/7223–2223. British Rail: Clapham Junction.*

Bush. ⊠ *Shepherds Bush Green, W12 8QD,* ☎ *020/7610–4224. Tube: Goldhawk Rd.*

Donmar Warehouse. ⊠ *Earlham St., WC2,* ☎ *020/7369–1732. Tube: Covent Garden.*

Drill Hall. ⊠ *16 Chenies St., WC1E 7EX,* ☎ *020/7303–5060. Tube: Goodge St.*

The Gate. ⊠ *The Prince Albert, 11 Pembridge Rd., W11 3HQ,* ☎ *020/7229–0706. Tube: Notting Hill Gate.*

Grace Theatre at the Latchmere. ✉ *503 Battersea Park Rd., SW11 3BW,* ☎ *020/7794–0022. Rail: Clapham Junction.*

Hampstead. ✉ *Avenue Rd., NW3 3EX,* ☎ *020/7722–9301. Tube: Swiss Cottage.*

ICA Theatre. ✉ *The Mall, SW1Y 5AH,* ☎ *020/7930–3647. Tube: Charing Cross.*

King's Head. ✉ *115 Upper St., N1 1QN,* ☎ *020/7226–1916. Tube: Highbury & Islington.*

Lyric Studio. ✉ *Lyric Theatre, King St., W6 OQL,* ☎ *020/8741–2311. Tube: Hammersmith.*

New End Theatre. ✉ *27 New End, NW3 1JD,* ☎ *020/7794–0022. Tube: Hampstead.*

Orange Tree. ✉ *1 Clarence St., Richmond, TW9 1SA,* ☎ *020/8940–3633. Tube: Richmond.*

Riverside Studios. ✉ *Crisp Rd., W6 9RL,* ☎ *020/8237–1111. Tube: Hammersmith.*

Soho. ✉ *21 Dean St., W1,* ☎ *020/7478–0100. Tube: Tottenham Court Rd.*

Theatre Royal. ✉ *Stratford East, E15 1BN,* ☎ *020/8534–0310. Tube: Stratford.*

Tricycle Theatre. ✉ *269 Kilburn High Rd., NW6 7JR,* ☎ *020/7328–1000. Tube: Kilburn.*

Young Vic. ✉ *66 The Cut, SE1 8LZ,* ☎ *020/7928–6363. Tube: Waterloo.*

5 OUTDOOR ACTIVITIES AND SPORTS

Some days you win, some days you lose, and some days you get rained out. But that seldom dampens one of the liveliest sports calendars around. Tennis, of course, means Wimbledon (if the show courts are sold out, try for the outside courts). In summer, Her Majesty makes an appearance at Ascot, while the world series of cricket, the Test Matches, is played on the manicured grass of Lord's and the Oval. In cooler weather, football (which means soccer) takes over, and in any season you can enjoy anything from yoga to squash indoors and let it rain, rain, rain.

Updated by
Julius Honnor

THERE ARE THE WIMBLEDON TENNIS CHAMPIONSHIPS, and there's
cricket, and then there's football (soccer in the United States), and
that's about it for the sports fan in London, right? Wrong. London is a great city for the weekend player of almost anything. It really comes into its own in summer, when the parks sprout nets and goals and painted white lines, outdoor swimming pools open, and a season of spectator events gets under way. The listings below concentrate on facilities available to the casual visitor in a whole range of sports and on the more accessible or well-known spectator events. Bring your gear, and branch out from that hotel gym.

PARTICIPANT SPORTS AND FITNESS

If your sport is missing from those listed below, or if you need additional information, **Sportsline** (☎ 020/7222–8000), staffed weekdays 10–6, supplies details about London's clubs, events, and facilities. It's only the price of a local call, but is often busy.

Aerobics

You don't need to buy a membership at any of the following studios, which offer a range of classes for all levels of fitness and are open daily. The average cost for an hour of sweating is £7–£8.

Jubilee Hall. Many are addicted to the "Fatbuster" workouts here, but there are also classes in everything from body sculpting, spinning, and step to kick boxing and jazz dance. ✉ *30 The Piazza, Covent Garden, WC2,* ☎ *020/7379–0008. Tube: Covent Garden.*

Porchester Centre has about eight daily classes graded from beginner to pro, with step, yoga, circuit training, and aquaerobics included in the mix. ✉ *Porchester Centre, Queensway, W2,* ☎ *020/7792–2919. Tube: Bayswater.*

Portobello Green Fitness Club is under the Westway overpass, and you'll have to battle through flea-market shoppers on weekends to reach these popular classes. ✉ *3–5 Thorpe Close, W10,* ☎ *020/8960–2221. Tube: Ladbroke Grove.*

Baseball and Softball

Join in a game on summer afternoons and evenings in Regent's Park or on the south edge of Hyde Park. If you're serious about joining a team contact **BaseballSoftballUK** (☎ 020/7453–7055).

Bicycling

London is becoming more cycle-friendly, with special lanes marked for bicycles on some major roads, but it isn't safe to ride without a helmet. If you plan to cycle much in the city, invest in the excellent *On Your Bike,* which includes a route map and information on bike-friendly trains should you want to get out into the country. It's available in bookshops for £4.95 or directly from the offices of **London Cycling Campaign** (☎ 020/7928–7220).

You can rent anything you want at **Bikepark**—mountain, hybrid, or road bike—from £12 for a day, £30 for two days, or by the week, plus a deposit of £200. All machines are new models and are issued with locks; accessories are available, too. Reserve ahead in summer. ✉ *11–13 Macklin St., WC2,* ☎ *020/7430–0083. Tube: Holborn.* ✉ *63 New Kings Rd., W6,* ☎ *020/7731–7012. Tube: Parsons Green.*

London Bicycle Tour Company offers three-hour bike tours of various London neighborhoods from £11.95. Reserve in advance. You can also go it alone: bikes can be rented for £2.50 an hour or £12 per day (£6 for each subsequent day). You can also rent tandems and hire rickshaws. ✉ *1A Gabriel's Wharf, SE1,* ☎ *0020/7928–6838. Tube: Waterloo.*

Boating

If you feel inspired by the crews at the Henley Royal Regatta or the Oxford and Cambridge Boat Race, you can try your hand at the oars in London's parks. A vigorous afternoon can be had rowing about the large scenic lake in Regent's Park. **Regent's Park Boating Lake** (☎ 020/ 7486–4759) rents rowboats that hold up to five adults at £4 per hour. For those wishing to splash along the Serpentine, Hyde Park has pedalos (paddleboats), canoes, and rowboats holding up to seven people for £5 per hour. Both parks have boats available March through September, daily from 9 to 6:30 PM or dusk, weather permitting.

Gyms

As you'd expect from the Y, **Central YMCA** has every facility and sport, including a great 25-meter pool and a well-equipped gym. Weekly membership is £37.50, a "one-day taster" £15. ✉ *112 Great Russell St., WC1,* ☎ *020/7637–8131. Tube: Tottenham Court Rd.*

The day rate is £6.90 and the monthly rate £51 at **Jubilee Hall,** a very crowded but happening and super-well-equipped central gym. ✉ *30 The Piazza, Covent Garden, WC2,* ☎ *020/7379–0008. Tube: Covent Garden.*

The Peak is expensive (£1,875 per year plus £1,200 joining fee) but has top equipment, a pool, great ninth-floor views over Knightsbridge, and a sauna—with TV—in the full beauty spa. Day memberships are no longer available, but the 20-visit pass for £862 is fully transferable, so a family can share one—as long as they use up the visits within a six-month period. ✉ *Hyatt Carlton Tower Hotel, 2 Cadogan Pl., SW1,* ☎ *020/7858–7008. Tube: Sloane Sq.*

Horseback Riding

Hyde Park Riding Stables keeps a range of horses for hacking the sand tracks. Rates are £30 per person per hour. ✉ *63 Bathurst Mews, W2,* ☎ *020/7723–2813. Tube: Lancaster Gate.*

Ice-Skating

London's most central ice-skating rink is the **Leisure Box,** where skating will cost you £6.50 per session, including skate rental. ✉ *17 Queensway, W2,* ☎ *020/7229–0172. Tube: Queensway.*

Broadgate Ice Arena is the United Kingdom's only outdoor rink. Available to skaters of all abilities, it's usually open between October and early April, and costs £5 a session, plus £2 for skate rental. Call for opening times. ✉ *Broadgate Arena, Eldon St., EC2,* ☎ *020/7505–4068. Tube: Liverpool St.*

Running

London is perfect for joggers. If you don't mind a crowd, more popular spots include Green Park, which gets a stream of runners armed with maps from Piccadilly hotels, and—to a lesser extent—adjacent St. James's Park. Both can get perilous with deck chairs on summer days. You can run a 4-mi perimeter route around Hyde Park and Kensington Gardens or a 2½-mi route in Hyde Park alone if you start at Hyde Park Corner or Marble Arch and encircle the Serpentine. Most Park Lane hotels offer jogging maps for this, their local green space. Regent's Park has the most populated track because it's a sporting kind of place; the Outer Circle loop measures about 2½ mi.

Away from the center, there are longer, scenic runs over more varied terrain at Hampstead Heath, Kenwood, and Parliament Hill, London's highest point, where you'll get a fabulous panoramic sweep over the entire city. Richmond Park is the biggest green space of all, but watch for deer during rutting season (October and November). Back in town, there's a rather traffic-heavy 1½-mi riverside run along Victoria Embankment from Westminster Bridge to the Embankment at Blackfriars Bridge, or a beautiful mile among the rowing clubs and ducks along the Malls—Upper, Lower, and Chiswick—from Hammersmith Bridge.

GROUP RUNS

If you don't want to run alone, call the **London Hash House Harriers** (☎ 020/8995–7879). They organize noncompetitive hour-long runs around interesting bits of town, with loops and checkpoints built in. The cost is £1.

Squash

There are four squash courts at **Finsbury Leisure Centre,** a popular sports center in the City frequented by execs who work nearby. You can book by phone without a membership, and you're more likely to get a court if you show up to play during Londoners' regular office hours, or possibly on weekends, when courts are less busy. A court costs £7.40 for non-members (£5 off-peak) and £5.90 for members (£4 off-peak). Annual membership is between £29 and £39. ⊠ *Norman St., EC1,* ☎ *020/7253–2346. Tube: Old St.*

Swimming

INDOOR POOLS

Chelsea Sports Centre, with a renovated, turn-of-the-century 32- by 12-meter pool, is just off King's Road, so it's usually busy. It's packed with kids on weekends. Each swim costs £2.70. ⊠ *Chelsea Manor St., SW3,* ☎ *020/7352–6985. Tube: South Kensington.*

INDOOR/OUTDOOR POOLS

Oasis has a heated pool (open year-round) and a 32- by 12-meter pool indoors. Needless to say, both pools are packed in summer. ⊠ *32 Endell St., WC2,* ☎ *020/7831–1804. Tube: Covent Garden.*

PARKS

Hampstead Ponds, two Elysian little lakes, are surrounded by grassy lounging areas. The women's one is particularly secluded (though crowded in summer) and is open all year. Opening times vary with sunrise and sunset. The Mixed Pond is open May through September. Both have murky-looking but clean, fresh water. *Coed:* ⊠ *E. Heath Rd., NW3,* ☎ *020/7485–4491. Women only:* ⊠ *Millfield La., N6,* ☎ *020/7485–4491. Tube or British Rail: Hampstead Heath.*

Serpentine Lido is technically a beach on a lake, but a hot day in Hyde Park is surreally reminiscent of the seaside. There are changing facilities, and the swimming section is chlorinated. It's open July through September. ⊠ *Hyde Park, W2,* ☎ *020/7706–3422. Tube: Knightsbridge.*

A suntrap (near Brixton), **Brockwell Lido** has a younger and more modern feel than its Hyde Park and Hampstead Heath alternatives. The easiest way to get here is to take British Rail to Herne Hill. ⊠ *Brockwell Park, SE24,* ☎ *020/7274–3088. Tube: Brixton.*

SPA POOLS

There's a 36- by 14-meter pool for serious lap swimmers at **Porchester Baths,** costing £2.50 a swim, plus a 1920s Turkish bath, sauna, and spa of gorgeous (though slightly faded) grandeur that is more expensive, at £18.70. It has separate sessions for men and women. ⊠ *Queensway, W2,* ☎ *020/7792–2919. Tube: Queensway.*

Tennis

Many London parks have courts that are often cheap or even free, but **Holland Park** is probably the prettiest place to play, with six hard courts available all year. The cost is £9.70 for annual membership and £4.80 per game. ⊠ *Kensington High St., W8,* ☏ *020/7602–2226. Tube: Holland Park.*

Islington Tennis Centre is about the only place where you don't need membership to play indoors year-round, but you need it to reserve by phone. There are two outdoor courts, too, and coaching is available. Prices range from £15 for the indoor courts to £6 for outdoors. ⊠ *Market Rd., N7,* ☏ *020/7700–1370. Tube: Caledonian Rd.*

A surprisingly large and busy green space, **Paddington Sports Club** has a set of 10 courts as well as squash courts and a multi-gym. Annual membership at this members-only club is £380 with a £100 joining fee, but there are no per-game charges. ⊠ *Castellain Rd., W9,* ☏ *020/7286–4515. Tube: Maida Vale.*

Walking

There are plenty of possibilities for rambling in the countryside around the city. Generally well-signposted footpaths offer attractive routes through rural southern England. The Chiltern Hills to the northwest, the South Downs to the south, and Kent to the southeast are probably the best areas to try, and are all reasonably well served by local trains. If you want to walk in a group, the Saturday Walkers' Club, based around the *Time Out Book of Country Walks* (£9.99, available from most bookshops), leaves from a London station every Saturday of the year.

Yoga

Life Centre, London's best yoga school, specializes in the dynamic, energetic Ashtanga Vinyasa technique. Beautiful premises enhance the experience. A huge range of holistic health therapies is available upstairs. Classes cost from £8–£10 and run all day every day. ⊠ *15 Edge St., W8,* ☏ *020/7221–4602. Tube: Notting Hill Gate.*

SPECTATOR SPORTS

Boating

One of London's most beloved sporting events (since 1845) is also the easiest to see, and it's free. The only problem with the late-March Oxford and Cambridge Boat Race is securing a position among the crowds that line the Putney-to-Mortlake route (mostly at pubs along the Hammersmith Lower and Upper Malls, or on Putney Bridge). The Saturday start time varies from year to year according to the tides but is usually around 2:30 PM. The Head of the River Race is the professional version, only this time up to 420 crews of eight row the university course in the other direction. It usually happens the Saturday before the university race, beginning at 10 AM; the best view is from above Chiswick Bridge.

Cricket

Lord's has been hallowed turf for worshipers of England's summer game since 1811. The world series of cricket, the five-day Test Matches, is played here, but tickets are hard to procure. The first stage of the process is to obtain an application form and enter the ballot (lottery) to purchase tickets. If any tickets remain, they are sold over the phone in April. Standard Test Match tickets cost between £18 and £38. One-day internationals can usually be seen by lining up on the day, and top-class county matches are similarly accessible—whether the rules are is quite another matter. ⊠ *St. John's Wood Rd., NW8,* ☎ *020/7432–1066. Tube: St John's Wood.*

The **Oval** is an easier place than Lord's to witness the *thwack* of leather on willow. Though slightly less venerated than its illustrious cousin, the standard of international cricket here is certainly no lower, and you can also see county games of a high standard. ⊠ *Kennington Oval, SE11,* ☎ *020/7582–6660. Tube: Oval.*

Equestrian Events

RACING

The main events of "the Season," as much social as sporting, occur just outside the city. Her Majesty attends **Royal Ascot** (⊠ Grand Stand, Ascot, Berkshire, ☎ 01344/622211) in mid-June, driving from Windsor in an open carriage and processing before the plebs daily at 2. You'll need to book good seats far in advance for this event, although some tickets—far away from the Royal Enclosure and winning post—can be bought on the day of the race for £8. Grandstand tickets, which must be bought well in advance, cost £37–£45. There are also Ascot Heath tickets available for a mere £2, but these only admit you to a picnic area in the middle of the race course. You'll be able to see the horses, of course, but that's not why people come to Ascot. The real spectacle is the crowd itself: enormous headgear is de rigueur on Ladies Day—usually the Thursday of the meet—and those who arrive dressed inappropriately (jeans, shorts, tank tops) will be turned away from their grandstand seats.

Derby Day (⊠ The Grandstand, Epsom Downs, Surrey, ☎ 01372/ 470047), usually held on the first Saturday in June, is, after Ascot, the second biggest social event of the racing calendar; it's also one of the world's greatest races for three-year-olds.

SHOW JUMPING

The late September **Horse of the Year Show** is the top international competition, with fun events held alongside the serious. Best of all are the Pony Club Games, where children perform gymnastics on horseback. ⊠ *Wembley Arena, Wembley, Middlesex,* ☎ *020/8900–9282. Tube: Wembley Park.*

Marathon

Starting at 9:30 AM on a Sunday in April, some 30,000 runners in the huge **Flora London Marathon** (☎ 020/7620–4117) race from Blackheath or Greenwich to Westminster Bridge or the Mall. Entry forms for the following year are available between August and October.

Rugby

This is somewhat similar to American football, but team members play unpadded. It raises the British and (especially) Welsh blood pressure enormously, and has recently undergone a revolution, with Rugby Union joining Rugby League as a professional sport. To find out about top clubs playing Rugby Union in and around the capital during the September to May season, peruse the magazine *Time Out.*

Twickenham hosts the Rugby Union Six–Nations tournament, where newcomer Italy joins old-timers England, France, Scotland, Wales, and Ireland. During this competition, held January through March, rugby can rival even football for the nation's sporting attentions, and tickets for these matches are more precious than gold. The domestic Pilkington Cup Final is fought out at Twickenham in early May. Harlequins and London Scottish are club teams that both play their rugby here. ⊠ *Twickenham Rugby Football Ground, Whitton Rd., Twickenham TW2,* ☎ *020/8892–2000.*

Rugby League is played much more in the north of England than in the south, but for the Challenge Cup Final the teams traditionally come south to London on the last Saturday in April or the first one in May. Until the new Wembley National Stadium opens in 2003 or 2004, the competition will have to find a new venue. You can, however, catch the local Super League (Rugby League) team, the London Broncos, at **Stoop Memorial Ground** (✉ Langhorn Dr., Twickenham TW2, ☎ 020/8410–5000).

Soccer (Football)

To refer to the national sport as "soccer" is to blaspheme. It is football, and its importance to the people and the culture of the country seems to grow inexorably. British football has had massive injections of money from television and sponsorship in recent years, creating millionare players and high-profile foreign stars in the domestic game, but little international success for the English side. The domestic season culminates in the FA Cup Final, traditionally the biggest day in the sporting calendar, for which tickets are about as easy to get as they are for the Super Bowl. International matches during the August through May season are marginally easier to attend. Normally held at Wembley, these games are to be held at the country's other top grounds until the rebuilding of the National Stadium is complete in 2003 or 2004.

For a real taste of this British obsession, nothing beats a match at the home ground of one of the London clubs competing in the Premier League. More than likely you won't see a hint of the infamous hooliganism, but you will be quite carried away by the electric atmosphere only a vast football crowd can generate. Try to book tickets in advance. You might also check out London's lower division games: though the standard of football in Division 3 may not match that of the Premiership, tickets are much cheaper and easier to get hold of, and the atmosphere can be just as fervent. For more information on teams and games, look in *Time Out*.

PREMIER LEAGUE TEAMS

Arsenal is London's most successful team and won the F.A. Cup and Premier League in 1998. ✉ *Avenell Rd., Highbury, N5.* ☎ *020/7413–3366. Tube: Arsenal.*

Charlton Athletic has more passion than money, and its main goal is to prolong its stay in the top division as long as possible. You can get here by taking British Rail to Charlton. ✉ *The Valley, Floyd Rd., SE7,* ☎ *020/8333–4010.*

Chelsea, adored by the slightly more genteel west London fan, has become famous for its showy continental players and style of play. ✉ *Stamford Bridge , Fulham Rd., SW6,* ☎ *020/7386–7799. Tube: Fulham Broadway.*

Fulham has relatively new hopes of joining the big-time, but certainly possess the money and the self-confidence to join the big boys. ✉ *Craven Cottage, Stevenage Rd., SW6,* ☎ *020/7736–6561. Tube: Putney Bridge.*

Tottenham Hotspur, or "Spurs", traditionally an exponent of attractive, positive football, has underperformed in recent years. Take British Rail to White Hart Lane to get here. ✉ *White Hart Lane, 748 High Rd., N17,* ☎ *0870/840–2468.*

West Ham United, historically the high achiever of east London, finds it harder these days to match the salaries or the results of Arsenal or Chelsea. ✉ *Boleyn Ground, Green St., E13,* ☎ *020/8548–2700. Tube: Upton Park.*

Tennis

The **Wimbledon Lawn Tennis Championships**—Wimbledon is famous among fans for the green, green grass of Centre Court; for Pimms and strawberries and cream; and for rain, which always falls, despite the last-week-of-June/first-week-of-July high-summer timing. This event is, of course, one of the four Grand Slam events of the tennis year. Whether you can get tickets is literally down to the luck of the draw, because there's a ballot system (lottery) for advance purchase. To apply, send a self-addressed, stamped envelope between September 1 and December 31 to the All England Lawn Tennis & Croquet Club (✉ Box 98, Church Rd., Wimbledon SW19 5AE, ☎ 020/8946–2244), fill in the application form, and hope for the best.

There are other ways to see the tennis. A block of Centre and Number 1 Court tickets is kept back to sell each day; fanatics line up all night for these, especially in the first week. Each afternoon tickets collected from early-departing spectators are resold (profits go to charity). These may be grandstand seats (with plenty to see—play continues til dusk), because those who can afford to care so little about tennis are often on expensive business freebies or company season tickets. You can also buy entry to the grounds to roam matches on the outside courts, where even the top-seeded players compete early in the fortnight. Get to Southfields or Wimbledon tube station as early as possible and start queuing to be sure of getting one of these. For up-to-date information, the London Tourist Board operates a Wimbledon Information Line (☎ 0839/123417), at a cost of 49p per minute.

If you don't fancy the crowds and snaking queues of Wimbledon, you might watch many of the top names in men's tennis play in the pre-Wimbledon **Stella Artois Tournament.** Ticketmaster (☎ 020/7413–1444) sells tickets for this increasingly popular event. ✉ *Queen's Club, Palliser Rd., W14, ☎ 020/7385–3421. Tube: Barons Court.*

6 SHOPPING

Napoléon must have known what he was talking about when he called Britain a nation of shopkeepers. The finest emporiums are in London, still. You can shop like royalty at Her Majesty's glove maker, run down a leather-bound copy of *Wuthering Heights* at a Charing Cross bookseller, find antique Toby jugs on Portobello Road, or drop in on clothier Paul Smith—a fave of Sir Paul McCartney. Whether you're out for fun or for fashion, London can be the most rewarding of hunting grounds.

Updated by
Jacqueline
Brown

WHEN IT COMES TO LONDON, shopping can be a transforming experience. It's an open secret that Cary Grant was virtually "created" by a bespoke suit from Kilgour, French, Stanbury (the tailors extended the shoulders of his jackets 6½ inches to improve his form and draped the material to slim his hips). Then there was that other fashion plate, the Duchess of Windsor—for at-home style, she couldn't be beat, thanks in part to the soigné accessories she bought at Colefax & Fowler, still purveying the "country-house look" from its shop on Brook Street. Today, London's stores continue to create icons and make styles—as you can see from a visit to Harvey Nichols, shrine of the *Absolutely Fabulous* crowd.

As befits one of the great trading capitals of the world, London's shops have been known to boast, "You name it, we sell it." If you have a yen to keep up with the Windsors, look for the BY APPOINTMENT logo, which means that this particular emporium supplies Her Majesty the Queen, the Queen Mother, Prince Philip, or the Prince of Wales—check the small print and the insignia to find out which. More fashionable types will prefer to check out the ever-expanding Browns of South Molton Street—a label hunter's heaven—while the surrounding small stores there and along quaint St. Christopher's Place aren't bad either. The most ardent fashion victims will shoot to Notting Hill, London's prime fashion location and scene of *that* movie. London's emporiums have gifts in every price range. Head to Bond Street or Knightsbridge if you're looking for the sort of thing you would find in every Rockefeller's Christmas stocking; if you're bargain-hunting, try one of the street-scene antiques fairs (it wasn't so long ago that an original Wordsworth manuscript of "When Severn's Sweeping flood" was discovered in Brick Lane Market for less than $50).

If you have only limited time, zoom in on one or two of the West End's grand department stores, where you'll find enough booty for your entire gift list. Marks & Spencer is one of Britain's largest, and most beloved, chain stores, legendary primarily for its women's lingerie, its men's knitwear, and its range of food, good enough to pass off as home-cooked. Selfridges, London's answer to Macy's in New York, is a splendid pile of '20s architecture that dominates the whole of one block toward Marble Arch and is increasingly fashion-conscious and up to date. Liberty is famous for its prints—multitudes of floral designs, which you can buy as fabric or have made into everything from book covers to dresses. It may be hokey, but Harrods is not to be missed; apart from anything else, it's one of the best free shows in the city. And though Harrods trumpets that it can supply anything to anyone anywhere in the world (once, a baby elephant to Ronald Reagan) and boasts that the Queen sometimes does her Christmas shopping here, you can just pick up one of its distinctive green-and-gold-logo totes—a perfect touch of class for your marketing back home.

Credit cards are accepted virtually everywhere, but to make sure that your Cirrus or Plus card (to cite just two of the leading names) works in European ATMs, have your bank reset it to use a four-digit PIN number before your departure. Apart from bankrupting yourself, the only problem you'll encounter is exhaustion, since London is a town of many far-flung shopping areas. The farthest—in fact on the outskirts of London, at Greenhithe in the county of Kent just by the Thames—is Europe's largest gift to shopaholics, the 240-acre Bluewater. The mega glass-and-steel pleasure palace (with cute Kentish oasthouse roofs) by the water was designed by American architect Eric Kuhne and contains every up-market, high-street, brand-name store, department store, and chain store (more than 320) a shopper could desire. Even though there is space for 13,000 cars, clever shoppers jump the jams and lines going in by taking the train, which departs frequently from Charing Cross. Shuttle buses go directly to the center from the local rail station.

Quick Tours

These itineraries are organized by special interest; full addresses are given in the listings below.

SUPER SHOPPING TOUR

For those who can make their way across the map faster than Napoléon and only have a few hours to spare, here's a suggested plan of action. Just keep in mind that you will return to your hotel room weary and wiped out, and your bathroom scale will show you've become 3 pounds lighter! Let's start with a great London trademark: **Harrods**. Be there when the doors open—this is one-stop shopping at its best (and one of the city's great sights). If you're chic to the cuticles, then make a beeline for **Harvey Nichols**, just a block away. Harvey Nicks always has the best in modern Brit style, be it couture, menswear, or home furnishings. Want a more traditional gift that would please any Lord and Lady Fitzuppity? Head to the nearby **General Trading Co.** on Sloane Street for that lovely Staffordshire spaniel, or run down to Pimlico to see the objets d'art and furniture of **David Linley**, the most talented royal around. For still more decorative goodies, tube or cab it over to Regent Street—one of London's main consumer heavens—and **Liberty** (which actually helped create the Arts and Crafts style of the Edwardian era). High rollers should walk east several blocks to Bond Street, Old and New. Of course, there's nothing like a visit to **Asprey & Garrard** or the other upper-crust stores here to make you acutely aware of how poor you are. Fashionistas should then stroll up through Mayfair several blocks to the northwest and South Molton Street to find **Browns**, flooded with Kate Moss lookalikes, then head down Davies Street to the couture salon of **Vivienne Westwood**. On Davies Street you'll also find **Grays Antique Market** and **Grays in the Mews**—just the places to find a Charles II silver spoon. For gifts with gentler price tags, tube or cab it south to Piccadilly and **Hatchards**—bookseller to the royals, which still retains a trad atmosphere—or nearby **Fortnum & Mason**, the Queen's grocers, to buy some tea. Speaking of which, head upstairs and collapse for the high tea here, or make a last stop at **Floris**, a few blocks south on Jermyn Street—it's one of London's prettiest perfumeries. Opt for a scent once favored by Queen Victoria or— at almost pocket-money prices—a natural-bristle toothbrush. Oh, yes: if you want to add the very latest stores to this list, check out the suggestions in the monthly glossies, such as *Tatler* magazine's "I Can't Get Through the Month Without . . . " shopping pages or the *World of Interiors* "Antennae" section, or the glossy shopping sections in the Sunday newspapers. Whew! As you can see, for out-of-the-ordinary shopping, London can't be beat.

ANTIQUES

Start early morning around 8 AM (Saturday or Wednesday, when the dealers haggle) and head to **Camden Passage** in Islington, where you can browse through silverware, porcelain, prints, and old books. For under £30 you can often find pretty silver spoons. Take the tube from Highbury and Islington to Oxford Circus and the **Liberty** Antiques Department, whose top floor has top-scale antiques, the refurbished chairs with the distinctive Liberty print. If you fancy your chances at auction, just a few blocks south is **Sotheby's**, which has some classy pieces, from Impressionist paintings to country-house furnishings. You can stop for lunch at the Sotheby's Café, or stride on to **Grays Antiques**

Market on Davies Street for smaller, more affordable pieces such as old jewelry, prints, and ceramics.

BARGAINS

In January and July, stores slash prices and armor-plating is a must-have when negotiating London's premier shopping mile, Oxford Street. Shifting street fashion fast is **Top Shop**'s speciality, but for higher quality and over-twenties, **John Lewis** professes to be never knowingly undersold. Whisk into the branch of **Accessorize** at 293 Oxford Street for the latest discount beads and baubles. **Debenhams** department store, a block west, has sale events throughout the year and runs the Jasper Conran diffusion line. Designer shoppers look sharp at **Browns**; check out Browns Labels for Less at No. 50 on nearby Molton Street for big labels at low prices. **Marks & Spencer** in Marble Arch has the largest selection of budget separates, year-round.

Shopping Districts

Camden Town
Crafts and vintage-clothing markets and shops clustered in and around picturesque but over-renovated canalside buildings have filled up every available space all the way up to the Roundhouse, Chalk Farm, in this frenetic mecca for the world's youth. It's a good place for boots, T-shirts, inexpensive leather jackets, ethnic crafts, antiques, and recycled trendy wear. Things are quieter midweek.

Chelsea
Chelsea centers on King's Road, which is no longer synonymous with ultra fashion but still harbors some designer boutiques, plus antiques and home-furnishings emporiums. The fashionable section is more off-road Chelsea, toward Belgravia, where the hot young stars of fashion are creating a haven: Lulu Guinness, Erickson Beamon, and Philip Treacy line up on Elizabeth Street.

Covent Garden
The restored 19th-century market building—in a something-for-everyone neighborhood named for the market itself—features mainly high-class clothing chains, plus good-quality crafts stalls. Neal Street and the surrounding alleys offer amazing gifts of every type—bikes, kites, tea, herbs, beads, hats . . . you name it. Floral Street and Long Acre have designer and chain-store fashion in equal measure, while Monmouth Street, Shorts Gardens, and the Thomas Neal's mall on Earlham Street offer trendy clothes for club kids. The whole area is good for people-watching, too.

Hampstead
For picturesque peace and quiet with your shopping, stroll around here midweek. Upscale clothing stores and representatives of the better chains share the half-dozen streets with cozy boutique-size shops catering to the home and stomach.

Kensington
Kensington Church Street features expensive antiques, plus a little fashion. The main drag, Kensington High Street, is a smaller, less crowded, and classier version of Oxford Street, with a selection of clothing chains and larger stores at the eastern end.

Knightsbridge
Harrods dominates Brompton Road, but there's plenty more, especially for the well-heeled and fashion-conscious. Harvey Nichols is the top clothes stop, with many expensive designers' showcases along Sloane Street. Walton Street and narrow Beauchamp (pronounced "Beecham")

Place offer more of the same, plus home furnishings and knickknacks; and Brompton Cross, at the start of Fulham Road, is the most design-conscious corner of London, with the Conran Shop and Joseph Ettudgui's store leading the field.

Marylebone

Behind the masses of Oxford Street lies this quiet backwater with Marylebone High Street as its main artery. Restaurants once coexisted peacefully along with delis and practical stores until the new Conran Shop and Orrery restaurant sprang up in 1997, bringing with them a retinue of smart new designer furniture stores. Satellite streets now have understated designer women's wear and menswear. Stride along a block or two to Great Portland Street and you'll arrive at the smart Villandry food emporium and the gateway to fashionable Fitzrovia.

Mayfair

Here is Bond Street, Old and New, with desirable dress designers, jewelers, plus fine art (old and new) on Old Bond Street and Cork Street. South Molton Street has high-priced, high-style fashion—especially at Browns—and the tailors of Savile Row are of worldwide renown.

Notting Hill

Branching off from the famous Portobello Road market are various enclaves of boutiques selling young designers' wares, antiques, and things for the home—now favored stops for trendsetters. Go westward and explore the Ledbury Road–Westbourne Grove axis, Clarendon Cross, and Kensington Park Road, for an eclectic mix of antiques and up-to-the-minute must-haves for body and lifestyle. Toward the more bohemian foot of Portobello are Ladbroke Grove and Golborne Road, where, in among the tatty stores, Portuguese cafés, and patisseries, you can bag a bargain. This is one of London's latest treasure-trove areas.

Oxford Street

Overcrowded Oxford Street is past its prime and is lined with tawdry discount shops at the Tottenham Court Road end, but many still flock here for some of London's great department stores in the run up to Marble Arch—particularly Selfridges, John Lewis, and Marks & Spencer—and the interesting boutiques secreted in little St. Christopher's Place and Gees Court.

Piccadilly

Though the actual number of shops is small for a street of its length (Green Park takes up a lot of space), Piccadilly manages to fit in several quintessential British emporiums. Fortnum & Mason is its star, and the historic Burlington Arcade is an elegant experience even for shop-phobics.

Regent Street

At right angles to Oxford Street, this wider, curvier version has several department stores, including legendary Liberty. Hamleys is the capital's toy center; other shops tend to be stylish men's chain stores or airline offices, though there are also shops selling china and bolts of English tweed. "West Soho," around Carnaby Street, stocks designer youth paraphernalia, which these days is becoming more grown-up and desirable.

St. James's

Where the English gentleman shops, this district has some of the most elegant emporiums for hats, handmade shirts and shoes, and silver shaving kits and flasks. Doorways often bear royal warrants, and shops along Jermyn Street, like Floris, have museum-quality interiors and facades. Nothing is cheap, in any sense.

Shopping (Map A): Mayfair, Soho, and Covent Garden

KEY
🚇 Tube Station

Shopping (Map B): Kensington, Knightsbridge, and Chelsea

KEY
Φ Tube Station

Agnès B 8
Antiquarius 22
Erickson Beamon 42
Bonhams 27
Bridgewater 11
Brora 15
Browns 29

Butler and Wilson 12
Children's Book Centre 2
Christie's 7
Christopher Gibbs 41
Connolly 34

Conran Shop 9
Crafts Council Gallery Shop/Victoria & Albert Museum Shop 5
Daisy & Tom 17
David Linley Furniture 40
David Mellor 38

Designer's Guild 13
Egg 33
Elspeth Gibson 16
Emma Hope 37
Gallery of Antique Costumes and Textiles 1
General Trading Co. 36

Hackett 44
Harrods 39
Harvey Nichols 23
Margaret Howell 24
Megan Mathers 14
Philip Treacy 43
Portmeirion 3
Rigby & Peller 25

Les Senteurs 35
Lulu Guiness 28
The Map House 31
Janet Reger 26
Jimmy Choo 32
Judy Greenwood Antiques 10
Kensington Market 4

Rococo 21
Rupert Cavendish 19
Science Museum Gift Shop 6
Scotch House 30
The Singing Tree 20
Steinberg & Tolkien 18

Shopping (Map C): Notting Hill

KEY

⊖ Tube Station

Department Stores

London's department stores range from Harrods—which every tourist is obliged to visit—through many serviceable middle-range stores devoted to the middle-of-the-road tastes of the middle class, to a few cheapjack ones that sell merchandise you would find at a better price back home. Most of the best and biggest department stores are grouped in the West End around Regent Street and Oxford Street, with two notable exceptions out in Knightsbridge.

Harrods. The only English department store classed among monuments and museums on every visitor's list, it hardly needs an introduction. It is swanky and plush and as deep-carpeted as ever; its spectacular food halls are alone worth the trip; and it stands out from the pack for fashion, too. You can forgive the store its immodest motto, *Omnia, omnibus, ubique* ("Everything, for everyone, everywhere"), because there are more than 230 departments, including a pet shop rumored to supply you with anything from aardvarks to zebras on request and a toy department—sorry, "kingdom"—which does the same with plush versions. During the pre-Christmas period and sales—the legendary one is during the last three weeks of January, but another storewide event, usually only one week, is held in mid-July—the entire store is a menagerie. ⊠ *87 Brompton Rd., SW1,* ☎ *020/7730–1234. Tube: Knightsbridge.* (☞ Map B)

Harvey Nichols. It's just a block away from Harrods, but it's not competing on the same turf, because its passion is fashion, all the way. There are nearly six floors of it, including departments for dressing homes and men, but the woman who invests in her wardrobe is the main target. Accessories are strong suits, especially jewelry, scarves, and makeup—England's first MAC counter here was 10 deep for months. The fourth floor now has a chic home-design department, featuring such names as Nina Campbell, Mulberry, Ralph Lauren, and Designer's Guild. A reservation at the Fifth Floor restaurant is coveted. ⊠ *109 Knightsbridge, SW1,* ☎ *020/7235–5000. Tube: Knightsbridge.* (☞ Map B)

John Lewis. This store's motto is "Never knowingly undersold," and for an increasingly wide range of goods at sensible prices, John Lewis is hard to beat. The brother store, Peter Jones, in Sloane Square, has a place in Sloane Ranger history, and you will probably encounter more Barbour jackets, velvet hair bands, and pearls here than anywhere else in town—and that's just on the customers. For the visitor to London who's handy with the needle, John Lewis has a wonderful selection of dress and furnishing fabrics. Many's the American home with John Lewis drapes. ✉ *278 Oxford St., W1,* ☎ *020/7629–7711. Tube: Oxford Circus.* (☞ Map A)

Liberty. With a wonderful black-and-white mock-Tudor facade, it's a peacock among pigeons in humdrum Regent Street. Inside, it is a labyrinthine building, full of nooks and crannies stuffed with goodies, like a dream of an Eastern bazaar. Famous principally for its fabrics, it also has an Oriental department, rich with color; menswear that tends toward the traditional; and women's wear that has lately been spiced up with extra designer ranges. It is a hard store to resist, as you may well find an original gift—especially one made from those classic Liberty prints. ✉ *200 Regent St., W1,* ☎ *020/7734–1234. Tube: Oxford Circus* (☞ Map A)

Selfridges. It's near the Marble Arch end of Oxford Street, where blocks are crowded in the middle of the day and at sale time. This giant, bustling store was started early in the 20th century by an American, though it's now British-owned. If this all-rounder has one outstanding department it has to be its Food Hall, or else its frenetic cosmetics department—one of the largest in Europe—which seems to perfume the air the whole length of Oxford Street. In recent years, Selfridges has made a specialty of high-profile popular designer fashions and has spent a lot of money sprucing up. There's a theater-ticket counter and British Airways travel shop in the basement. ✉ *400 Oxford St., W1,* ☎ *020/7629–1234. Tube: Bond St.* (☞ Map A)

Specialty Stores

Antiques

Investment quality or lovable junk, London has lots. Try markets first—even for pedigree silver, the dealers at these places often have the best wares and the knowledge to match. Camden Passage and Bermondsey are the best; the Portobello market has become a bit of a tourist trap, but its side streets are filled with interesting shops that are open outside market hours (Westbourne Grove is fast becoming the most stylish section of this part of town). Kensington Church Street is *the* antiques-shopping street, with prices and quality both high. If you know your stuff (and your price limit) head out to Tower Bridge Road, south of the river, where there are mammoth antiques warehouses, some of which are open on Sunday. The Furniture Cave, at the corner of Lots Road, Chelsea, has one of the largest stocks around. Or you could try your luck at auction against the dealers. Summer is usually a quiet period, but at any other time, there are plenty of bargains to be had. Of the hundreds of stores, we list a selection to whet your appetite. Opening times vary: many places that are open on Saturday and Sunday will close Monday or Tuesday.

Alfie's Antique Market. A huge and exciting labyrinth on several floors, it has dealers specializing in anything and everything but particularly in textiles, Arts and Crafts furniture, and theater memorabilia. You won't be deliberately stiffed, but it's a caveat emptor kind of place, thanks to the wide range of merchandise. ✉ *13–25 Church St., NW8,* ☎ *020/7723–6066. Closed Sun.–Mon. Tube: Edgware Rd.* (☞ Map A)

Antiquarius. At the Sloane Square end of King's Road is an indoor antiques market with more than 200 stalls offering a wide variety of collectibles, including things that won't bust your baggage allowance: Art Deco brooches, meerschaum pipes, silver salt cellars, and so on. ✉ *131–145 King's Rd., SW3,* ☎ *020/7351–5353. Closed Sun. Tube: Sloane Sq.* (☞ Map B)

Christopher Gibbs. This shop attracts such leading London tastemakers as J. Paul Getty Jr. and Mick Jagger, who, the society columns note, will hardly make a move without the judgment of Mr. Gibbs's legendary eye. If you're in the market for large decorative items, such as marble busts, priceless Elizabethan embroidery, and truly one-of-a-kind antiques from all ages, this is the place to go and dream. ⊠ *3 Dove Walk, Pimlico Rd., SW1,* ☎ *020/7730–8200. Closed weekends. Tube: Sloane Sq.* (☞ Map B)

Coach House. It is one reason why Westbourne Grove is one of the chicest addresses around. A 19th-century garage has been restored by four antiques dealers, and behind a modest street facade extends a vast showroom, with neo-Gothic armoires, Arts and Crafts chairs, and lovely objets d'art. ⊠ *189 Westbourne Grove, W11,* ☎ *020/7229–8306 Closed Sun. Tube: Notting Hill Gate.* (☞ Map C)

Colefax & Fowler. The virtual birthplace of the English country-house look, this is one of the most beautiful interior decorating shops in London. John Fowler, Lady Colefax, and, most importantly, Virginia-born Nancy Lancaster together created that cozy yet grand style, and their legacy is preserved here in wonderful wallpapers, pretty painted-wood flower holders, and assorted antique accents. If you want to make your apartment back home a mini-Chatsworth, be sure to stop in here, if only to soak up the style. ⊠ *39 Brook St., W1,* ☎ *020/7493–2231. Closed weekends. Tube: Bond St.* (☞ Map A)

Facade. It has one of the largest eclectic collections of French and Italian chandeliers, sconces, and table lamps. Most of them aren't wired and cleaned to shining bright, and this is reflected in the reasonable prices, particularly for such an up-and-coming area. ⊠ *196 Westbourne Grove, W11,* ☎ *020/7727–2159. Closed Sun.–Mon. Tube: Notting Hill Gate.* (☞ Map C)

Gallery of Antique Costume and Textiles. Numerous movie directors come here to get the period just right, because everything on the premises, from bedspreads to bloomers, was stitched before 1930—except for the copycat brocade vests. Models and Hollywood actors find incredible (and expensive) clothes here, too. It lies off our maps, but it is easily found three blocks north of the Edgware Road tube stop. ⊠ *2 Church St., NW8,* ☎ *020/7723–9981. Closed Sun. Tube: Edgware Rd.*

Grays Antique Market. Dealers specializing in everything from Sheffield plates to Chippendale furniture assemble here under one roof. Bargains are not impossible, and proper pedigrees are guaranteed. Also try Grays in the Mews (⊠ *1–7 Davies Mews, W1,* ☎ *020/7629–7034*) around the corner, which has more inexpensive, downscale merchandise. ⊠ *58 Davies St., W1,* ☎ *020/7629–7034. Closed Sun.; closed Sat. Jan.–Nov. Tube: Bond St.* (☞ Map A)

Hope and Glory. This is one of the many specialty stores in Kensington with commemorative china and glass from 1887 to the present; there are also affordable lesser pieces. The entrance is on Peel St. ⊠ *131A Kensington Church St., W8,* ☎ *020/7727–8424 Closed Sun. Tube: Notting Hill Gate.* (☞ Map C)

Judy Greenwood Antiques. It beckons with its glowing red walls and a delightful selection of high-style antiques: Miss Havisham-y settees, vintage fabrics and textiles, gilded mirrors, and side tables. ⊠ *657 Fulham Rd., SW6,* ☎ *020/7736–6037. Closed Sun. Tube: Fulham Broadway.* (☞ Map B)

London Silver Vaults. A basement conglomeration of around 40 dealers, it's a treasure trove for the average Joe. Some pieces are spectacular, of course, but you can also pick up a set of Victorian cake forks or a dented candelabrum for around £50. ⊠ *Chancery House, 53–64 Chancery La., WC2,* ☎ *020/7242–3844. Closed Sun. Tube: Chancery Lane.* (☞ Map A)

Megan Mathers. It has one of London's most delectable assortments of stylish antiques: decoupaged 19th-century table obelisks, mini Nelson's Columns, Venetian blackamoor figures—perfect *touches finales* for any high-style room. ✉ *571 King's Rd., SW6,* ☎ *020/7371–7837. Closed Sun. Tube: Sloane Sq.* (☞ Map B)

Rupert Cavendish. This most elevated of dealers has the Biedermeier market cornered, with Empire and Deco bringing up the rear. The shop is a museum experience. ✉ *610 King's Rd., SW6,* ☎ *020/7731–7041. Closed Sun. Tube: Sloane Sq.* (☞ Map B)

Auction Houses

The pointers on going to auction: you don't need bags of money; the catalog prices aren't written in stone; and if you are sure of what you want when you view the presale, then bid with confidence. Below, we list the main houses, which all deal in fine art and furniture. And if you find these are out of your budget, snoop around Lots Road in Chelsea, where you can find more budget-priced contemporary furniture that compares favorably with the price of new.

Bonhams. One of the more buyer-friendly places, it has many interesting collections. Graham Greene's widow recently sold her exquisite dollhouses here. Along with antiques, Bonhams specializes in 20th-century design. There is a branch in Chelsea (Montpelier Galleries, 65–69 Lots Road, SW10). ✉ *Montpelier St., SW7,* ☎ *020/7393–3900. Tube: Knightsbridge.* (☞ Map B)

Christie's. You'll find some great English country-house furniture in varying states of repair, paintings, prints, carpets, lighting, plus all manner of bona fide treasures. It's amazing what can be classed as infinitely desirable: the blue door from the film *Notting Hill* and the blue pinafore dress worn by Judy Garland in *Wizard of Oz* went for a record £5,750 and £199,500 respectively in a recent sale of film memorabilia. ✉ *85 Old Brompton Rd., SW7,* ☎ *020/7581–7611. Tube: South Kensington.* (☞ Map B)

Phillips. It conducts many specialist sales and occasionally has an Old Master painting sale that nearly rivals Christie's. ✉ *101 New Bond St., W1,* ☎ *020/7629–6602. Tube: Bond St.* (☞ Map A)

Sotheby's. There's a well-publicized calendar of regular auctions for the more well heeled. But if you just want to look, ponder on possible purchases and break for lunch in the superb café. ✉ *34–35 New Bond St., W1,* ☎ *020/7293–5000. Tube: Bond St.* (☞ Map A)

Books

Charing Cross Road is London's booksville, with a couple of dozen stores here or hereabout. The many antiquarian booksellers tend to look daunting (deceptively, as Helene Hanff found by correspondence with No. 84), but there are many new bookshops, too.

GENERAL

Borders. It has taken over the Books Etc. here and has a wide range of CDs, videos, author signings and talks, children's storytime and music sessions on Sundays, and a café, not forgetting the vast selection of books (an equally large branch is on Oxford Street). ✉ *120 Charing Cross Rd., WC2,* ☎ *020/7379–6838. Tube: Tottenham Court Rd.* (☞ Map A)

Foyles. This store is especially large—so enormous it can be confusing—but it is the place to come to find almost anything. ✉ *113–119 Charing Cross Rd., WC2,* ☎ *020/7437–5660. Tottenham Court Rd.* (☞ Map A)

Hatchards. This is one of London's well-established bookshops that hasn't been swallowed up by the big players. You can revel in its its old-fashioned charm while perusing the well-stocked shelves lining the winding stairs. The staff have retained old-fashioned helpfulness, too. ✉ *187 Piccadilly, W1,* ☎ *020/7439–9921. Tube: Piccadilly Circus* (☞ Map A)

Waterstone's. Part of an admirable, and expanding chain, it is open late (until 8 PM Mon.–Sat.) and has a program of author readings and signings. The latest monster outlet is the Waterstone's at the revamped old Simpsons store on Piccadilly. ✉ *121–125 Charing Cross Rd., WC2,* ☎ *020/7434–4291. Tube: Tottenham Court Rd.* (☞ Map A)

SPECIALTY

Bell, Book and Radmall. It has quality antiquarian volumes and specializes in modern first editions. ✉ *4 Cecil Ct., WC2,* ☎ *020/7240–2161. Tube: Tottenham Court Rd.* (☞ Map A)

Books for Cooks. With just about every cuisine from around the globe between covers, as well as the complete line-up of celebrity chef editions, it's quite simply the last word in food and cooking. Occasional cookery demonstrations (call for details) offer tempting samples. ✉ *4 Blenheim Crescent, W11,* ☎ *020/7221–1992. Tube: Notting Hill Gate.* (☞ Map C)

Children's Book Centre. In addition to children's books, it carries cards and a mass of multi-media. And if that doesn't spark the imagination, there are toys in the basement. ✉ *237 Kensington High St., W8,* ☎ *020/7937–7497. Tube: High Street Kensington.* (☞ Map B)

Cinema Bookshop. It has the subject taped with a comprehensive selection of old and new books on film from every angle. ✉ *13 Great Russell St., WC1,* ☎ *020/7637–0206. Tube: Tottenham Court Rd.* (☞ Map A)

Compendium. This store has built up a following with its frequent readings and helpful and knowledgeable staff. It has an alternative bent, with books by cult writers, and carries books on a range of topics, including music and ecology. ✉ *234 Camden High St., NW1,* ☎ *020/7485–8944. Tube: Camden Town.* (☞ Map A)

Dance Books. You'll find—yes—dance books, including how-to ballet books and books with trivia about the stars of the dance world—from flamenco to line dancing. ✉ *15 Cecil Ct., WC2,* ☎ *020/7836–2314. Tube: Tottenham Court Rd.* (☞ Map A)

Fisher & Sperr. It has a treasure trove of secondhand books that time forgot. ✉ *46 Highgate High St., N6,* ☎ *020/8340–7244. Tube: Highgate.*

Forbidden Planet. Sci-fi, fantasy, horror, and comic books are for sale here. ✉ *71 New Oxford St., WC1,* ☎ *020/7836–4179. Tube: Tottenham Court Rd.* (☞ Map A)

Gay's the Word. In the heart of London's gay community is this hot spot for literary and leisure interests, with a good selection of new and old books, magazines, and videos. ✉ *66 Marchmont St., WC1,* ☎ *020/7278–7654. Tube: Leicester Sq.* (☞ Map A)

Marchpane. It stocks covetable rare and antique illustrated children's books. ✉ *16 Cecil Ct., WC2,* ☎ *020/7836–8661. Tube: Tottenham Court Rd.* (☞ Map A)

Murder One. This is a must for fans of traditional Agatha Christie novels and techno sci-fi stories; it has everything from crimes of passion to fiendish horror. ✉ *71–73 Charing Cross Rd., WC2,* ☎ *020/7734–3485. Tube: Tottenham Court Rd.* (☞ Map A)

Pleasures of Past Times. You can indulge your nostalgia for Victoriana here. ✉ *11 Cecil Ct., WC2,* ☎ *020/7836–1142. Tube: Tottenham Court Rd..* (☞ Map A)

Silver Moon. This is an accessible and friendly women's bookshop, with modern and classic fiction by women, along with factual books on women's health and political issues. ✉ *64 Charing Cross Rd., WC2,* ☎ *020/7836–7906. Tube: Tottenham Court Rd.* (☞ Map A)

Sportspages. It's an excellent place to start your cricket library. ✉ *Caxton Walk, 94–96 Charing Cross Rd., WC2,* ☎ *020/7240–9604. Tube: Tottenham Court Rd.* (☞ Map A)

Stanfords. Travel books and maps are this shop's specialty. ⊠ *12 Long Acre, WC2,* ☏ *020/7836–1321. Covent Garden.* (☞ Map A)

Talking Bookshop. Just behind Oxford Street, it has the listening scene taped up, with a large selection of fiction for adults and children. ⊠ *11 Wigmore St., W1,* ☏ *020/7491–4117. Tube: Oxford Circus.* (☞ Map A)

Travel Bookshop. A short journey from foodies' paradise, this store covers the world on its shelves. It's great for globetrotters and armchair travelers alike. ⊠ *13 Blenheim Crescent, W11,* ☏ *020/7229–5260 Tube: Notting Hill Gate.* (☞ Map C)

Zwemmer. Just off Charing Cross Road, it sells books on cinema, photography, and design. ⊠ *24 Litchfield St., WC2,* ☏ *020/7240–4158. Tube: Tottenham Court Rd.* (☞ Map A)

CDs and Records

London created the great megastores that have taken over the globe, but for cutting-edge music from the clubs, there are specialty stores galore.

Black Market. Indie, house, garage, world—you'll find the hottest club music around. ⊠ *25 D'Arblay St., W1,* ☏ *020/7437–0478. Tube: Tottenham Court Rd.* (☞ Map A)

MDC Classic Music. The helpful staff will guide you without a blink to the best deals, from Callas to Sutherland, and tell you whether the diva was in form. There's some jazz, too. ⊠ *437 Strand, WC2,* ☏ *020/7240–2157. Tube: Charing Cross.* (☞ Map A)

HMV. Make a special trip to the HMV flagship store for the widest selection. There are lots of autograph sessions and free shows, too. ⊠ *150 Oxford St., W1,* ☏ *020/7631–3423. Tube: Oxford Circus.* (☞ Map A)

Mr. CD. This tiny shop stocks a wide selection for all possible tastes. You must delve to find the bargains, but your discovery will likely be worthwhile. ⊠ *80 Berwick St., W1,* ☏ *020/7439–1097. Tube: Oxford Circus.* (☞ Map A)

Music & Video Exchange. It's fast becoming a mecca for seekers of unusual and mainstream chart music. Young aspiring DJs are to be seen rifling among the used discs and 12-in selection. ⊠ *95 Berwick St., W1,* ☏ *020/7434–2939.* (☞ Map A)

Tower Records. Despite the fact that it doesn't carry records, its specialty departments are some of the best in London. ⊠ *1 Piccadilly Circus, W1,* ☏ *020/7439–2500. Tube: Piccadilly Circus.* (☞ Map A)

Virgin Megastore. This is Richard Branson's pride and joy (though his New York City store is even bigger). It's nice to have it all under one roof, but be prepared for an ear-blasting experience on the massive ground floor which is stacked with current chart music. Other areas, with jazz and classics, have a slightly more relaxed atmosphere. Computer games are in vast supply. ⊠ *14–16 Oxford St., W1,* ☏ *020/7631–1234. Tube: Tottenham Court Rd.* (☞ Map A)

China and Glass

English Wedgwood and Minton china are as collectible as they ever were, and most large department stores carry a selection, alongside lesser varieties with smaller price tags. Regent Street has several off-price purveyors, and, if you're in search of a bargain, Harrods' sale (usually held during the last three weeks of January) can't be beat—but sharpen your elbows first. And for the latest in sleek Italian, French, and Scandinavian china and glassware, check out the modern kitchenware shops, which stock the latest in young designer trends—such as Conran shops, Bluebird, Habitat, and Heal's. For handmade, signature glassware, try the Glass Art Gallery.

Bridgewater. This is the home of all those fruit bowls, cream jugs, and cheese platters that grace every country-style designer kitchen in London and the fashionable burbs. In the neighboring Bridgewater Pottery Café, you can create some of your own designs to take home. ✉ *739 Fulham Rd., SW6,* ☎ *020/7371–5264. Tube: Fulham Broadway.* (☞ Map B)

David Mellor. It has practical Dartington crystal along with more unusual porcelain and pottery pieces by British craftspeople. ✉ *4 Sloane Sq., SW1,* ☎ *020/7730–4259. Tube: Sloane Sq.* (☞ Map B)

Divertimenti. Beautiful kitchenware, unusual culinary gifts such as spoons made from polished horn, and very desirable French pottery from Provence are all sold here. ✉ *45–47 Wigmore St., W1,* ☎ *020/7935–0689. Tube: Oxford Circus* (☞ Map A)

Portmeirion. It's been around for 40 years in its tabletop form (the design inspiration for the signature china is the famed town in North Wales). If you want to delve further into your re-creation of a country kitchen, this is the place. ✉ *13 Kensington Church St., W8,* ☎ *020/7938–1891. Tube: Notting Hill Gate.* (☞ Map B)

Summerhill & Bishop. A little piece of French country kitchen right down to the ancient black bicycle with basket (which probably contains garlic strings), it supplies French embroidered linen, Portuguese and Tuscan stoneware, natural candles and soaps, and all manner of authentic designer culinary ware that gives ambience to sleek city kitchens. ✉ *100 Portland Rd., W11,* ☎ *020/7221–4566. Tube: Notting Hill Gate.* (☞ Map C)

Thomas Goode. One of the world's top shops for formal china and leaded crystal has on display dinner plates designed and made for Dame Nellie Melba, Edward VII, Queen Victoria, and the last viceroy of India. ✉ *19 S. Audley St., W1,* ☎ *020/7499–2823. Tube: Notting Hill Gate.* (☞ Map A)

Clothing

London is one of the world's four fashion capitals (along with Paris, Milan, and New York), and every designer you've ever heard of is sold here somewhere. As well as hosting the top names, though, London retains a reputation for quirky street style, and many an exciting young designer has cut his or her teeth selling early collections at a London street market or on the borders of the central shopping streets—Notting Hill, Islington, East End. Don't just go by the label, and you could be the first to wear clothes by a future star. Traditional British men's outfitters are rather well known. From the Savile Row suit, handmade shirt, and custom shoes to the Harris-tweeds-and-Oxford-brogues English country look that Ralph Lauren purloined, England's indigenous garments make for real investment dressing.

GENERAL

Aquascutum. Known for its classic raincoats, it also stocks the garments to wear underneath, for both men and women. Style keeps up with the times but is firmly on the safe side, making this a good bet for solvent professionals with an anti-fashion-victim attitude. ✉ *100 Regent St., W1,* ☎ *020/7675–9050. Tube: Piccadilly Circus.* (☞ Map A)

Burberry. It tries to evoke an English Heritage ambience, with mahogany closets and stacks of neatly folded merchandise adorned with the trademark "Burberry Check" tartan. In addition to being seen on those famous raincoat linings, the tartan graces scarves, umbrellas, and even pots of passion-fruit curd and tins of shortbread. ✉ *165 Regent St., W1,* ☎ *020/7734–4060;* ✉ *18–22 The Haymarket, SW1,* ☎ *020/7730–3343. Tube: Piccadilly Circus.* (☞ Map A)

Connolly. The leather made by this elite company is the essence of Rolls-Royce elegance and the flash of Ferrari. Drivers leave their vehicles to be made over inside, but you can content yourself with the accessories: a pair of leather driving gloves or a leather driving helmet and goggles. Prices are on a prestige basis—high—although you could settle for a smaller-statement souvenir belt or cuff links. ✉ *32 Grosvenor Mews, SW1,* ☎ *020/7235–3883. Tube: Hyde Park Corner.* (☞ Map B)

Debenhams. This is one of the large department stores lining Oxford Street that has moved up the fashion stakes. Years ago it wasn't on the hip shoppers' map, but with the arrival of the pretty, affordable, Jasper Conran collection, wise buying gals soon homed in, and the latest big name to join the store is Pearce Fionda (other creations, by in-house design, are becoming more desirable, too). Designer candles are still hot purchases, and top interiors creator Kelly Hoppen has her version here. ✉ *334–348 Oxford St., W1,* ☎ *020/7408–4444. Tube: Oxford Circus.* (☞ Map A)

Favourbrook. It tailors exquisite handmade vests, jackets, and dresses, all crafted from silks and brocades, velvets and satins, embroidered linens and chenilles. For ties and cummerbunds as well, men should kit out at 55 Jermyn Street, but from both branches you can order your own *Four Weddings and a Funeral* outfit. ✉ *18 Piccadilly Arcade, W1,* ☎ *020/7491–2337. Tube: Piccadilly Circus.* (☞ Map A)

Herbert Johnson. This store is one of a handful of gentlemen's hatters who still know how to construct deerstalkers, bowlers, flat caps, and panamas—all the classic headgear, with some Ascot-worthy hats for women, too. ✉ *54 St James's St., W1,* ☎ *020/7408–1174. Tube: Piccadilly Circus.* (☞ Map A)

Holland & Holland. At this place for the hunting-and-shooting fraternity, bespoke is the byword. It has everything from guns (by appointment to the Duke of Edinburgh and the Prince of Wales) to clothing requirements for hunting, all with the Holland & Holland brand label. Tailor-made travel wear (especially of the adventure variety) is also available. The company has been in business since 1830 (rifles have been made by the same London factory since 1835) but was bought out by Chanel—a reason for the brighter, trendy yet practical separates aimed at the younger country set. "Sloane rangers" have their own branch at 171–172 Sloane Street. ✉ *31–33 Bruton St., W1,* ☎ *020/7499–4411. Tube: Bond St.* (☞ Map A)

Jigsaw. It's popular for its separates, which don't sacrifice quality to fashion, are reasonably priced, and suit women from their twenties to forties. There's a men's branch on Bruton Street, W1, and other branches are found across town. Juniors get in on the act, too, with their own line, Jigsaw Junior. ✉ *126–127 New Bond St., W1,* ☎ *020/ 7491–4484. Tube: Bond St.* (☞ Map A)

Kensington Market. The diametric opposite of British stiff-upper-lip anti-fashion, it has been a principal purveyor of the constantly changing, frivolous, hip London street style for more than two decades. Hundreds of stalls—some shop-size, others tiny—are crammed into this building; you can get lost for hours trying to find the good bits. ✉ *49– 53 Kensington High St., W8,* ☎ *020/7938–4343. Tube: High Street Kensington.* (☞ Map B)

Marks & Spencer. A major chain of stores that's an integral part of the British way of life, it sells sturdy practical clothes and basic accessories, all at moderate, though not bargain-basement, prices. "Marks and Sparks," as it is popularly known, has never been renowned for its high style, though that is changing as it continues to bring in (anonymously) big-name designers to spice up its lines. What it *is* renowned for is underwear; the English all buy theirs here. This holds true for knitwear as well. This Marble Arch branch has the highest stock turnover of any shop in the land. ✉ *458 Oxford St. (main store), W1,* ☎ *020/7935– 7954. Tube: Marble Arch.* (☞ Map A)

Muji. This exponent of no-frills lifestyle has functional white cotton T-shirts, simply cut underwear, pants in neutral and plain colors, and navy and black sweaters that are all so popular they walk out of the shop. The merchandise is in complete harmony: white earthenware tableware on minimal steel shelving; cream duvets on understated maple beds; gray towels and skin-care products in white recyclable containers—it's a lifestyle dream that defies the cumulative heaps in most mortals' homes. Branches are as follows: 187 Oxford St., W1; 135 Long Acre, Covent Garden, WC2; 157 Kensington High St., W8; 77 King's Rd., Chelsea, SW3. ⊠ *Unit 5, 6–17 Tottenham Court Rd., W1,* ☎ *020/7436-1779. Tube: Tottenham Court Rd.* (☞ Map A)

Mulberry. It outdoes Ralph Lauren in packaging the English look. This quintessentially British company makes covetable, top-quality leather bags, belts, wallets, and cases for all sorts of things (even a mobile phone case and a travel case for laptop or computer organizer). Separates in fine wools, fine cotton shirts, and silk scarves and ties have widened the range. Although it is still considered traditional, Mulberry has increasingly been pursuing a quietly modern, international style niche. ⊠ *11–12 Gees Ct., St. Christopher's Pl., W1,* ☎ *020/7493-2546. Tube: Bond St.* (☞ Map A)

Next. This store carries clothing for men, women, and children that gives Gap a run for its money. In general, the styles are a little wilder and more fashionable, yet are reasonably priced. ⊠ *325–327 Oxford St., W1,* ☎ *020/7409-2746. Tube: Bond St.* (☞ Map A)

Paul Smith. He's your man if you don't want to look outlandish but you're bored with plain pants and sober jackets. Smith's well-tailored suits have a subtle quirkiness (like an outrageous, witty flash of colorful lining); his shirts and ties feature a sense of humor; and his jeans and sweats boast a good cut, Customers include Paul McCartney, Harrison Ford, and David Hockney. The boutique itself is worth seeing: it's re-created from a Victorian chemist's shop, and Smith's own collection of toiletries and jewelry (women are also catered to here) adorns the shelves. The sale shop for discontinued lines is at 23 Avery Row (W1), and the minimalist-style women's store is at 84–86 Sloane Avenue (SW3). But the latest Smith buzz is Westbourne House (122 Kensington Park Rd., W11): a shop in a house designed to feel like an actual London home where women's, men's, and children's clothes and accessories are arranged in homelike settings. ⊠ *40–44 Floral St., WC2,* ☎ *020/7379-7133. Tube: Covent Garden.* (☞ Map A)

Scotch House. As you'd guess, this is the place to buy your kilts, tartan scarves, and argyle socks without going to Edinburgh. It's also well stocked with cashmere and accessories. ⊠ *2 Brompton Rd., SW1,* ☎ *020/7581-2151. Tube: Knightsbridge.* (☞ Map B)

Swaine Adeney. It's been supplying practical supplies for country pursuits since 1750. Not just for the horsey set, it has golf umbrellas, walking sticks, and hip flasks, all beautifully crafted and ingenious. One shouldn't be without the umbrella, with slim tipple-holder flask secreted inside the stick, on a frosty morning. Herbert Johnson, hatter, is housed downstairs. ⊠ *54 St. James's St., SW1,* ☎ *020/7409-7277. Tube: Piccadilly Circus.* (☞ Map A)

Top Shop. One of London's niftiest megachains for young men and women, it's also the largest fashion store in the world. If you can circumnavigate round it and still keep your hearing intact, head for the faux-vintage "souled-out" section—the prices are as reasonable as at any market stall. Top-notch trendsetting designers are keeping the store one step ahead: Clements Ribeiro has produced a line for TS Design. ⊠ *214 Oxford St., W1,* ☎ *020/7636-7700. Tube: Oxford Circus.* (☞ Map A)

Zara. It has swept across Europe and the East (the price tags carry 25 flags and related prices) and has won a firm position in London. It's not hard to see why. The style is young and snappy; colors are great, with clothes sorted into color groupings for work and play; and the prices are unbelievably low. However, don't expect durability. These are fun, fashion pieces with a few basics. The whole spectrum is covered, including accessories: beady bags, wacky shoes and boots, moleskin mule slippers, jewelry. Menswear and a terrific line for kids each has its own floor. ⊠ *118 Regent St., W1,* ☎ *020/7534–9500. Tube: Piccadilly Circus.* (☞ Map A)

CHILDREN'S WEAR

Kids are making it big in retail fashion. While the chain stores, such as Marks & Spencer and Debenhams, produce sensible and fun collections, the fashion chains offer hipper versions and greater selection. Check out H&M, Jigsaw Junior, Next, and Zara, which rival Gap for variety. For ultra-expensive label gear, Harrods and Selfridges give plenty of choice. If you're on the lookout for lesser-known kidswear designers, check out one of the growing number of small boutiques especially for kids, such as those below; kids' clothes are increasingly found in shops for mom, too, such as Cath Kidston.

Daisy & Tom. This shop is for cool kids and smart parents, who know that a happy child is an entertained child. Sadly there is no designer gear for mom to try on while her child is busy on the carousel, cuddling soft toys, or having a haircut. On one dedicated floor there are high-fashion junior clothes (Kenzo, IKKS, and Polo), shoes aplenty (for newborns to 10-year-olds), a bookshop, and a soda fountain–café. What's more, it's all open on Sunday. ⊠ *181–183 King's Rd., SW3,* ☎ *020/7352–5000. Tube: Sloane Sq.* (☞ Map B)

Humla. It brought a colorful taste of Sweden to London before superstore IKEA steamrolled in. Mrs. Harris has been stocking beautifully made, quality children's clothes for 25 years and not so long ago used to make her own stripey handknits at the back of the shop. That originality is there still, although not her own work. Another branch is at 9 Flask Walk, Hampstead, where there is also a collection of nursery furniture and timeless wooden toys. ⊠ *23 St. Christopher's Pl., W1,* ☎ *020/7224–1773. Tube: Bond St.* (☞ Map A)

Lego Kidswear. Part of the Legoland empire, this store sells clothes that, like the timeless building bricks, come in bright, primary colors. Happily, clothes fasten with big zips (not pushed together); are practical and well-made; and range from age 3 months to 10 years. You might think there should be a few boxes of the eponymous bricks to keep kids amused, but none are to be found. Another branch is at 137 Regent St. ⊠ *West One Shopping Centre, 383 Oxford St., W1,* ☎ *020/7629–3929. Tube: Bond St.* (☞ Map A)

MEN'S WEAR

Most stores we list above under General Clothing stock excellent menswear. Try Aquascutum, Burberry, and Paul Smith. All the large department stores, too, carry a wide range of men's clothing, Selfridges and Harrods especially. There is a stealthy revolt away from the bastion of traditional made-to-order suits as young careerists break away from fatherly City-gent tailors. Sharp suiters, such as Ozwald Boateng, are noticeably un–Savile Row in style and demeanor. Those with more flash than cash will hot foot to the trend-setting fashion chains: Top Man at Top Shop and Zara.

Blazer. It stocks medium-price semiformal wear and separates in a more sportive vein. Clothes tend toward the classic, but with style-conscious details and rich colors. There is another branch on Oxford Street, and others are found across town. ✉ *117B Long Acre, WC2,* ☎ *020/7379–0456. Tube: Covent Garden.* (☞ Map A)

Duffer of St. George. In addition to having fashions by hip designers of street style, it sells its own label of sporty and dress-up lines for clubbing and posing with attitude. ✉ *29 Shorts Gardens, WC2,* ☎ *020/7379–4660. Tube: Covent Garden.* (☞ Map A)

Hackett. Started as a posh thrift shop, it once recycled cricket flannels, hunting pinks, Oxford brogues, and similar British wear. Now it makes its own attire, and it has become a genuine—and very good—gentlemen's outfitter, though polo shirts and faux sports gear are a strong theme. ✉ *137 Sloane St. (main store), SW3,* ☎ *020/7730–3331. Tube: Knightsbridge.* (☞ Map B)

Kilgour, French & Stanbury. This classic and highly expensive tailor makes custom-cut suits and shirts (but note the cutters all go to lunch between 1:30 and 2:30 every afternoon). The 11th commandment here: you know a man looks like an English gentleman only when you do not notice that he is well dressed. ✉ *8 Savile Row, W1,* ☎ *020/7734–6905. Tube: Piccadilly Circus.* (☞ Map A)

Malcolm Levene. It's been quietly cutting a dash in increasingly trendy Marylebone district. Before he got the top job, Tony Blair used to buy here, but he is more likely to be seen now in British tailored suits. Levene's is filled with softly constructed menswear (casual weekend wear, trendy business suits, and a hint of formal evening attire) in more unusual fabrics sourced and made in Italy. The range of soft tones and styles doesn't scream fashion but shows a quiet cut of confidence. The staff is delightfully helpful. ✉ *13–15 Chiltern St., W1,* ☎ *020/7487–4383. Tube: Baker St.* (☞ Map A)

Nick Ashley. This boutique in one of the coolest areas of shops and restaurants in London, just west of Portobello, is in the new mold of big-outdoors-goes-urban-cool. Ashley calls it performance wear—whether you're streaking about on a motorbike, loafing about looking cool in the city, or just keeping warm in Egyptian cotton vests and thermal long johns. The laid-back formula of chunky boots, polar fleece, and leather lookalike fabrics brings in the pop stars and young politicos. ✉ *57 Ledbury Rd., W11,* ☎ *020/7221–1221. Tube: Notting Hill Gate.* (☞ Map C)

Ozwald Boateng. It's one of the new breed of bespoke tailors, not on Savile Row but on the fringe. Boateng's made-to-measure suits are sought after (by rock luminaries George Michael, Mick Jagger and Bill Wyman, and even Lisa Stansfield) for their exclusive fabrics, fashionable detail, and shock-color lining as well as great classic cut. If custom tailoring is out of financial reach (around £1,000–£2,000), there is a ready-to-wear collection (from under £1,000), or the zappiest ties to be had in town (from £60). ✉ *9 Vigo St., W1,* ☎ *020/7734–6868. Tube: Piccadilly Circus.* (☞ Map A)

Tom Gilbey. The exciting part of this custom-tailor shop is the Waistcoat Gallery: its exquisite vests—in silk or brocade or hand-embroidered, others marginally plainer—are essential accessories. ✉ *2 New Burlington Pl., W1,* ☎ *020/7734–4877. Tube: Piccadilly Circus.* (☞ Map A)

Turnbull & Asser. This is *the* custom shirtmaker. Unfortunately for those of average means, the first order must be for a minimum of six shirts, from around £100 each. But there's a range of less expensive, though still exquisite, ready-to-wear shirts, too. ✉ *71–72 Jermyn St., W1,* ☎ *020/7808–3000. Tube: Piccadilly Circus.* (☞ Map A)

WOMEN'S WEAR

Accessorize. Shrewd shoppers head here for the latest high-fashion items at low prices. Beady bags, feathery jewels, devoré scarves—clever copies of each season's catwalk versions reach these stores fast. There are branches across town. ✉ *Unit 22, The Market, Covent Garden, WC2,* ☎ *020/7240–2107. Tube: Covent Garden.* (☞ Map A)

Agnès B. It has pretty, understated French clothing: many items are timelessly perfect, like fine knitwear and feminine cotton tops. Prices are mid-range and worthy for the quality—Ms. B has been a stalwart of the fashion press for years. There are branches at 41 Marylebone High Street (W1), 58–62 Heath Street (NW3), and in Hampstead (NW3); 35–36 Floral Street (WC2) has elegant men's suits. ✉ *111 Fulham Rd., SW3,* ☎ *020/7225–3477. Tube: South Kensington.* (☞ Map B)

Brora. You'll find the very latest in cashmere and *those* shawls (pashminas, of course) here. There are prettily dressed-up camisoles, jumpers and cardigans, practical pants, and non-cashmere items as well (picnic blankets and wash bags). Prices are surprisingly mid-range for such high-fashion products. It's surprising that those little cashmere goats haven't become an endangered species—such is the appetite for their delicate wool. ✉ *344 King's Rd., SW3,* ☎ *020/7352–3697. Tube: Sloane Sq.* (☞ Map B)

Browns. It was the first notable store to populate the South Molton Street pedestrian mall, and it seems to sprout more offshoots every time you visit it. Well-established, collectible designers (Donna Karan, Romeo Gigli, Jasper Conran, Jil Sander, Yohji Yamamoto) rub shoulder pads here with younger, funkier names (Dries Van Noten, Clements Ribeiro, Anne Demeulemeester, Hussein Chalayan), and Browns also has its own label. Its July and January sales are famed. Menswear gets a corner, too. Bargain hunters should hotfoot it down to Browns Labels for Less at No. 50. ✉ *23–27 S. Molton St., W1,* ☎ *020/7491–7833. Tube: Bond St.;* ✉ *6C Sloane St., SW1,* ☎ *020/7493–4232. Tube: Knightsbridge.* (☞ Maps A and B)

Cath Kidston. This store brings charming ginghams and flower-sprig cotton prints to housecoats (with matching bed linens, cushions, wallpaper, and bath wear) and nightshirts. In fact, Kidston has everything you could want for a girl's bedroom in an English country cottage. The sweaters are practical, cozy handknits; the Anonymous line includes skimpy lace-edged vest tops and cardigans, and skirts in flouncy wools. There is a delightful children's wear line in the same nostalgic vein. ✉ *8 Clarendon Cross, W11,* ☎ *020/7221–4000. Tube: Notting Hill Gate.* (☞ Map C)

Droopie & Browns. Beautifully constructed, extravagantly theatrical frocks and suits, made up in raw silks, fine linens, brocades, and velvets are to be found here. Colors are strong, tailoring is impeccable, and salespeople don't turn up their noses at larger ladies. ✉ *99 St. Martin's La., WC2,* ☎ *020/7379–4514. Tube: Leicester Sq.* (☞ Map A)

Egg. The loosely ethnic work wear in limited colors with minimal, almost-no-fashion details is a winner. Maureen Doherty (co-founder) worked for Issey Miyake, so you get the idea. The off-street address and locale add to the shop's interest factor: a former Victorian dairy tucked away in a Knightsbridge mews. ✉ *36 Kinnerton St., SW1,* ☎ *020/7235–9315. Tube: Knightsbridge.* (☞ Map B)

Elspeth Gibson. It has been building up a steady following as the firm favorite of models and personalities in the glossy mags and Sunday supplements: these clothes are for the flaunty girlie in you. There are delicate beads on soft cardies; swirly, flirty, embroidered Tyrol-type skirts; and simply herds of cashmere. ✉ *7 Pont St., SW1,* ☎ *020/7235–0601. Tube: Knightsbridge.* (☞ Map B)

Fenwick. Around for years in a prime fashion spot, this shop manages to be very competitive. At sale time, it's a bargain one-stop shop, with a vast selection of bags, gloves, scarves, and shoes, and with a good selection of designers on the upper floors: Ben de Lisi, Jean Muir,

Christian Lacroix, and Katherine Hamnett to name a few. ⊠ *63 New Bond St., W1,* ☎ *020/7629–9161. Tube: Bond St.* (☞ Map A)

Georgina von Etzdorf. Made with finely woven metallic threads and delicate clusters of trapped fibers, Etzdorf's scarves and stoles give any outfit a million-dollar shimmer through the night. Too way-out? Then drool over sumptuous deep-colored devoré velvets and crushed silks (there are irresistible silk ties for men, but they're very expensive). Phosphorescent designs stretch to bags, shoes, and the most gorgeous jackets. A branch is at 1–2 Burlington Arcade, Piccadilly, W1. ⊠ *61 Ledbury Rd., W11,* ☎ *020/7235–0601. Tube: Notting Hill Gate.* (☞ Map C)

Ghost. This store can be found with regularity in the fashion press. The design team, led by Tania Sarne, has the feel of the moment, producing willowy dresses and skirts in silks, velvets, and the ubiquitous viscose, which sculpts into wonderful crinkly textures. Indispensible little cardigans in silky weaves have been the wardrobe essential for quite some time and show no signs of fading. Pretty puff-sleeve blouses are also a strong feature. It's also at 14 Hinde St., W1. ⊠ *36 Ledbury Rd., W1,* ☎ *020/7229–1057. Tube: Notting Hill Gate.* (☞ Map C)

Janet Reger. It's queen of the silk teddy, having become synonymous with the ultimate in luxurious negligees and lingerie many years ago. ⊠ *10 Beauchamp Pl., SW3,* ☎ *020/7584–9360. Tube: Knightsbridge.* (☞ Map B)

Karen Millen. Striking a clever balance between functional working clothes with subtle fashion detailing (muted pastels and soft colors in separates), fun urban weekend wear (leather biker jackets and black-and-white ponyskin coats), and glam for evenings (little dresses with Japanese almond-sprig detail), Millen appeals to all from grown-up teens through women in their forties. Mid-range prices are also a draw. ⊠ *262–264 Regent St., W1,* ☎ *020/7287–6158. Tube: Oxford Circus.* (☞ Map A)

Koh Samui. It stocks the clothing and accessories—some still steaming off the catwalk—of around 40 young designers, most of them British, some exclusive to this store, and all on the cutting edge. There are small items for under a tenner (eclectic hair clips by Japanese designer Heesoo) and drop-dead dresses for thousands of pounds (an exquisite hand-beaded dress by Berardi for £4,500). KS is the place to discover the next wave before *Vogue* gets the story. ⊠ *65 Monmouth St., WC2,* ☎ *020/7240–4280. Tube: Covent Garden.* (☞ Map A)

Laura Ashley. The country dresses, blouses, and skirts, plus wallpapers and fabrics in dateless patterns that rely heavily on flowers, fruit, leaves, or just plain stripes have captured the nostalgic imagination of the world. ⊠ *256–258 Regent St. (main store), W1,* ☎ *020/7437–9760. Tube: Oxford Circus.* (☞ Map A)

Lulu Guinness. This shop struck a death blow to the industrial black nylon bag by bringing in bags of beads, colored silks, and the loveliest designs. Guinness's new store is equally girlish and fun (*Vogue* covers adorn a see-through floor), with a downstairs salon where you can take tea while selecting. ⊠ *3 Ellis St., SW1,* ☎ *020/7823–4828. Tube: Sloane Sq.* (☞ Map B)

Margaret Howell. Along with Paul Smith, Margaret Howell is the top exponent of Britishness in the Far East. Think classic fabrics—wools, silks—and perfect detail. It's the ultimate in investment, one-stop shopping. ⊠ *29 Beauchamp Pl., SW3,* ☎ *020/7584–2462. Tube: Knightsbridge.* (☞ Map B)

Nicole Farhi. This is the place for the career woman who requires quality, cut, *and* style in a suit, plus weekend wear in summer linens and silks, or winter hand-knit woolens. Prices are on the high side, but there is some affordable wear as well, especially the sporty, casual Diversion label. Farhi offers an equally desirable men's line. The downstairs in-store restaurant, Nicole's, is not just somewhere to resuscitate between purchases; Ms. Farhi designed the space and the menu to her own taste, and it is an extension of the fashion statement, a hot spot for lunching fashionistas who like to be seen. It's wise to reserve ahead (☎ 020/7499–8408). Main stores: ✉ *158 Bond St., W1,* ☎ *020/ 7499–8368. Bond St.;* ✉ *25–26 St. Christopher's Pl., W1,* ☎ *020/7486– 3416. Bond St.;* ✉ *27 Hampstead High St., NW3,* ☎ *020/7435–0866. Tube: Hampstead.* (☞ Map A)

Oasis. Good interpretations of designer trends are the stock in trade here. The latest colors and fabrics—from neutrals and brights to heavy jacquards and microfibres, in fact, whatever's hot on the catwalk— are translated into pared-down versions that suit all pockets. ✉ *13 James St., WC2,* ☎ *020/7240–7445. Tube: Covent Garden.* (☞ Map A)

Philip Treacy. This name tops every fashion maven's Santa Claus list. Treacy's magnificent hats regularly grace the pages of *Harper's Bazaar;* one-half Mad Hatter, one-half Cecil Beaton, Treacy's creations always guarantee Making an Entrance. Only the most serious fashion plates need apply, truly: the atelier is open by appointment only. Cheapskates can shoot along to Debenhams department store on Oxford Street, where Treacy has a diffusion line. ✉ *69 Elizabeth St., SW1,* ☎ *020/ 7259–9605. Tube: Sloane Sq.* (☞ Map B)

Rigby & Peller. It's for those who love pretty lingerie. Many of the luxurious makes are here: La Perla and Gottex, as well the corsetières' own line. But if the right fit eludes, have one made to measure. Most of the young royal and aristo ladies buy here, not just because the store holds the royal appointment but because the quality and service are excellent, and much friendlier than you might expect. There is also a branch at 22A Conduit Street, off New Bond Street, W1. ✉ *2 Hans Rd., SW3,* ☎ *020/7584–9360. Tube: Knightsbridge.* (☞ Map B)

Shirtsmith. Custom-made and ready-made shirts, suits, and jackets for women, using fine cottons and Indian silks are the staple here. Some designs are classic and fitted; others are slightly outrageous. ✉ *38B Ledbury Rd., W11,* ☎ *020/7229–3090. Tube: Notting Hill Gate.* (☞ Map C)

Vivienne Westwood. If you want to see where it all started, the Pompadour-punk ball gowns, Lady Hamilton vest coats, and foppish landmark getups are the core of Westwood's first boutique at 430 King's Road. The designer still represents the apex of high-style British couture, and the Davies Street boutique sells the Gold Label line of intoxicatingly glamorous creations: ready-to-wear or made-to-measure. At 44 Conduit Street, the story is the sharper Red Line: hot, pared-down catwalk versions; menswear is also on offer here—the Westwood influence is far-reaching. ✉ *6 Davies St., W1,* ☎ *020/7629–3757. Tube: Bond St.* (☞ Map A)

Warehouse. It has practical, stylish, reasonably priced separates in easy fabrics and lots of fun colors. The finishing isn't so hot, but style, not substance, counts here, and the shop's youthful fans don't seem to mind. The stock changes very quickly, so it always presents a new face to the world. ✉ *19 Argyll St. (main store), W1,* ☎ *020/7437–7101. Tube: Oxford Circus.* (☞ Map A)

Whistles. This small chain stocks its own high-fashion, mid-price label, plus several selected eclectic designers. Clothes are hung in color-coordinated groupings in shops that resemble designers' ateliers. ✉ *The Market (main store), Covent Garden, WC2,* ☎ *020/7379–7401. Tube: Covent Garden;* ✉ *Heath St., NW3,* ☎ *020/7431–2395. Tube: Hampstead.* (☞ Map A)

Design

There's been a tremendous resurgence of interest in objects not mass-produced. The burgeoning market areas such as Spitalfields, the state-of-the-art OXO Tower, and Lesley Craze have become the new, eclectic fashion suppliers of jewelry, clothes, and housewares, and often to personal order. These sites are not in a central place. If you can't stretch out to these areas, then a good starting point is the Crafts Council Gallery Shop within the Victoria & Albert Museum. But forget the outmoded word "crafts"—this work is often more modern than modems.

Contemporary Applied Arts. It recently celebrated its 50th anniversary and has lost none of its edge in showing a huge range of work by designers and craftspeople. Regular shows and exhibitions display anything from glassware and jewelry to furniture and lighting. ⊠ *2 Percy St., W1,* ☎ *020/7436–2344. Tube: Tottenham Court Rd.* (☞ Map A)

Contemporary Ceramics. Formed by some of the best British potters as a cooperative venture to market their wares, this modernized store carries a wide spectrum of pottery, from thoroughly practical pitchers, plates, and bowls to ceramic sculptures. It's possibly the best selection of ceramics to be found in central London (just behind Oxford Street), with each piece carrying its own potted biography. There is a large range of books on the art as well. Prices range from the reasonable to way up. ⊠ *7 Marshall St., W1,* ☎ *020/7437–7605. Tube: Oxford Circus.* (☞ Map A)

Crafts Council Gallery Shop/Victoria & Albert Museum Shop. This is where you'll find a microcosmic selection of the wide range of British craftspeople's work (jewelry, glass, ceramics, toys). Accompanying the exhibitions in the museum are more focused displays, such as the Summer Show showcase. The Crafts Council has a smaller shop at its base in Islington (⊠ 44A Pentonville Rd., N1, ☎ 020/7806–2559), where you can source information on craftspeople and browse in the showcase gallery. ⊠ *Cromwell Rd., SW7,* ☎ *020/7589–5070. Tube: South Kensington.* (☞ Map B)

David Linley Furniture. This outpost for Viscount Linley—the only gentleman in the kingdom who can call the queen "Auntie" and, more importantly, one of the finest furniture designers of today—has heirlooms of the future; the desks and chairs have one foot in the 18th century, another in the 21st. The large pieces are suitably expensive, but small desk accessories and objets d'art are also available. ⊠ *60 Pimlico Rd., SW1,* ☎ *020/7730–7300. Tube: Sloane Sq.* (☞ Map B)

Designers Guild. Tricia Guild shows her fabrics and accessories of fabulous, saturated colors here. Inspirational, many designers vouch; and she has now incorporated furniture, objets d'art, and linens. ⊠ *267–271 and 275–277 King's Rd., SW3,* ☎ *020/7351–5775. Tube: Sloane Sq.* (☞ Map B)

Glass Art Gallery/London Glassblowing Workshop. Glassblowers and designers make decorative and practical pieces on site. The artists are British-based and display their work in the gallery. If you visit on weekdays, you can see them at work, and buy or commission your own variation. Prices can go into the thousands, but there are Saturday sales in April, July, and November-December, when many pieces go for less than £30. In the Leathermarket, which is off our map, you can find other craftspeople as well, most notably a silversmith and papermaker. ⊠ *7 The Leathermarket, Weston St., SE1,* ☎ *020/7403–2800. Tube: London Bridge.* (☞ Map A)

Lesley Craze Gallery. This gallery is making quite a name for itself. Craze has cornered a design market in what is now a fashionable area. You'll find the most exquisite jewelry to drool over, by some 100 young British designers (fashion editors source new talent here for their glossy spreads.) The adjacent Craze 2 and C2+ specialize in nonprecious metals and sumptuous scarves and textiles. ⊠ *33–35 Clerkenwell Green, EC1,* ☎ *020/7608–0393. Tube: Farringdon.* (☞ Map A)

OXO Tower. Many and varied artisans have to pass rigorous selection procedures to set up in the prime riverside workshops and make, display, and sell their work. The workshops are glass-walled, and you're invited in, even if you're just browsing. You can commission, too—anything from a cushion cover to custom-made jewelry, furniture, and sculpture. There are 23 studios in all, and a quick browse on the first floor reveals some very inviting items: hand-painted silk dresses by Nana Agyeman, handwoven textiles by Archipelago, multidiscipline design by Hive. The second floor has more of the same, including lamps, clothing, and jewelry. The very swish Harvey Nick's restaurant is on the eighth—top—floor, which has a fantastic view across the river to St. Paul's and Somerset House. You don't need to pay for the view, as there is a public terrace, but beware of the wind whipping along the Thames. You'll find more craftspeople at Gabriel's Wharf, next door. ⊠ *Bargehouse St., SE1,* ☎ *020/7401–2225. Tube: Southwark.* (☞ Map A)

Space. It has contemporary handmade furniture and other home-style designs, from beanbags and hand-embellished bed linens to sculpted candles. Owner Emma Oldham's theme focuses on mixing the affordable with the aspirational, and she has instigated an exhibition-selling space for individual artists. ⊠ *214 Westbourne Grove, W11,* ☎ *020/7229–6533. Tube: Notting Hill Gate.* (☞ Map C)

Walter Castellazzo Design. Castellazzo has been getting lots of notice in the glossy interiors press with his very individual designs of modern-Gothic painted furniture. His signature style is the tall bookcase (which you'll love or hate) with its gently curving pointed apex. A similar theme is used for wall and corner cabinets and mirrors. Castellazzo's shelves are filled with other craft designers' work: silk purses, metallic cushions, jewelry. His latest direction (commissions undertaken) is toward space-capsule bunk beds in brushed silver with rocket chests of drawers—a must for young space cadets. The store is off our map, in the center of Georgian Highgate Village close to the Gothic Highgate Cemetery. ⊠ *84 Highgate High St., N6,* ☎ *020/8340–3001. Tube: Archway or Highgate, then bus.*

Food Halls & Stores

London excels at posh nosh, and the place with the widest selection of all is Harrods' Food Halls. Even if you don't actually buy one of the beautifully packaged teas, chocolates, or biscuits (though it is hard to resist), you can salivate at the gorgeous displays, from freshly caught fish to furry and feathered game, which are as much akin to art as food. Selfridges is the other department store that comes in a close second; it's not as daunting, instead specializing in more streamlined self-service, with shelves filled with enough gourmet goodies to make a five-star dinner party—to which any of the following places would provide a delicious contribution.

Fortnum & Mason. Although it's the Queen's grocer, this store is, paradoxically, the most egalitarian of gift shops; it has plenty of irresistibly packaged luxury foods, stamped with the gold BY APPOINTMENT crest, for less than £5. Try the teas, preserves, blocks of chocolate, tins of pâté, or a box of Duchy Originals oatcakes—like Paul Newman, the Prince of Wales has gone into the retail food business. ⊠ *181 Piccadilly, W1,* ☎ *020/7734–8040. Tube: Piccadilly Circus.* (☞ Map A)

Paxton & Whitfield. This is the most venerable of London's cheese shops, in business for over 200 years. The fabulous aromas come from some of the world's greatest cheeses stacked on the shelves—in rounds, in boxes, and on straw, but always ready to be tasted. Whichever cheese is in season and ripe for eating is on display for sampling, and the staff is ready to help you pick the best wine to serve with it. ⊠ *93 Jermyn St., SW1,* ☎ *020/7930–0259. Tube: Piccadilly Circus.* (☞ Map A)

BY ROYAL APPOINTMENT

From soft drinks (Coca–Cola) and champagne (Moët & Chandon) to breakfast cereal (Weetabix) and household cleaning fluid (Jeyes), the royal family chooses the products it likes and hands their makers a warrant, a seal of satisfaction that honors the maker. Warrant holders can then adorn their packaging with a regal coat of arms, as well as the words "By Royal Appointment."

Only four royals can bestow warrants: the Queen, the Duke of Edinburgh, Prince Charles, and the Queen Mother. The warrants appear proudly on the facades of many an old and established London specialist shop; you'll find the stores are within a short carriage ride from the royal palaces. Fortnum & Mason is the royal grocer, but for British and Continental cheeses, Paxton & Whitfield holds the seal of approval. The glass cases at Floris, which have displayed classic perfumes since 1730, could be out of a Jane Austen novel. Penhaligon's is similarly well perfumed, and has products for the well-groomed gentleman and his lady.

All members of the royal family pursue sports with a passion. The outfitter for bridling is WH Gidden (15 Clifford St., tel. 020/7495–3670). Farlow's (5 Pall Mall, tel. 020/7839–2423) tackles other hardware (including fishing rods, reels, and shotguns), while Swaine Adeney has riding whips, saddles, and breeches in the best possible taste.

Rococo. It's run by Chantal Coady, who writes, eats, and lives for chocolate. Vegetable fats are forbidden words in this cocoa paradise, and there are interesting and off-beat additions to the main chocolate recipe, such as essence of Earl Grey. ⊠ *321 King's Rd., SW3,* ☎ *020/7352–5857. Tube: Sloane Sq.* (☞ Map B)

Thorntons. It may not be the classiest chocolatier, but that doesn't make one of Britain's most popular chocolate makers any the less desirable. Filled chocolates, chocolate bars, fudge, and toffee are their mainstays, but the truffles are to die for (and there's an extensive selection). Come at Easter-time, and the gift-wrapped eggs are rushing out the door. At this branch you can enjoy tea, coffee, and pastries—in addition to chocolate, of course. ⊠ *254 Regent St., W1,* ☎ *020/ 7434–2483. Tube: Oxford Circus.* (☞ Map A)

Villandry. Step inside the characterless building to a Provençal-style food store. Dark-wood shelves from floor to ceiling are laden with French and Belgian pâtés, French and Italian cheeses, pretty colored pastas, jars of gourmet sauces, and other goodies galore. Bread baskets filled with rolls and pastries sit on heavy wood trestle tables. Behind the rustic calm of the food store are a café and dining room where you can indulge in some of the products. ⊠ *170 Great Portland St., W1,* ☎ *020/7631–3131. Tube: Great Portland St.* (☞ Map A)

Gifts

Of course, virtually anything from any shop in this chapter has gift potential, but these selections lean toward stores with a lot of choice, both in merchandise and price. Chances are you'll be wanting the recipients of your generous bounty to know how far you traveled to procure it for them, so our suggestions tend toward identifiable Britishness.

You should also investigate the possibilities in the shops attached to the major museums, most of which offer far more than racks of souvenir postcards these days. Some of the best are at the British Museum and the V&A. For specialized gifts, the Royal Academy has great prints and cards and art paraphernalia; the London Transport Museum has transport models; the Natural History Museum has the largest selection of toy dinosaurs and real gemstones; and the London Aquarium is top-scale for all things undersea.

GENERAL

British Museum Gift Shop. Here you'll find stacks of Egyptiana, particularly cute scarabs in ceramic. You can be an archaeologist for an afternoon and buy your own ancient pottery pieces. The bookshop has a huge selection and is a mine of historical information for adults and children. ✉ *Great Russell St., WC1,* ☎ *020/7323–8175. Tube: Tottenham Court Rd.* (☞ Map A)

Cross. It's an ultrachic cornucopia with something to suit everyone—even your pet pooch. The idea has been around in other London shops for years, but the Cross succeeds with its ambience (bleached beach house) and hedonistic, beautiful things (silk scarves, brocade bags, embroidered chinoiserie, check housecoats, and fragrant candles and butterflies by Jade Jagger). Finally, the location: the Cross is right in the middle of Portobello–cum–Holland Park, London's trendy area. ✉ *141 Portland Rd., W11,* ☎ *020/7727–6760. Tube: Notting Hill Gate.* (☞ Map C)

General Trading Co. This place has just about every upper-class wedding gift list but also caters to slimmer pockets with merchandise shipped from farther shores (as the name suggests). ✉ *144 Sloane St., SW1,* ☎ *020/7730–0411. Tube: Sloane Sq.* (☞ Map B)

Neal Street East. While it isn't big on British, this importer of Asian everything does carry stock with universal appeal. There are several floors of what you'd expect in the way of woks, chopsticks, bowls, books, kimonos, and toys, but there are also glorious lacquered boxes, woven baskets, amber and silver jewelry, silk flowers, Japanese kites, and loads of fun gifts for less than a fiver. ✉ *5 Neal St., WC2,* ☎ *020/7240–0135. Tube: Covent Garden.* (☞ Map A)

Soccer Scene. At this mammoth temple to the world's most popular sport you can grab any replica kit you care to mention. Beware of some high prices. ✉ *56–57 Carnaby St., W1,* ☎ *020/7439–0778. Tube: Oxford Circus.* (☞ Map A)

Tea House. It purveys everything to do with the British national drink; you can dispatch your entire gift list here. Alongside every variety of tea (including strange or rare brews like orchid, banana, Japanese Rice, and Russian Caravan) are teapots in the shape of a British bobby or a London taxi, plus books, and what the shop terms "teaphernalia"—strainers, trivets, and infusers, plus some gadgets that need explaining. ✉ *15A Neal St., WC2,* ☎ *020/7240–7539. Tube: Covent Garden.* (☞ Map A)

PERFUMES AND COSMETICS

Floris. One of the most beautiful shops in London, it has gleaming glass and Spanish mahogany showcases (acquired from the Great Exhibition of 1851). Gift possibilities include swan's-down powder puffs, cut-glass bottles, and the elegant ivory and faux tortoiseshell combs that the shop has sold since the place opened in 1730. Queen Victoria used to daub her favorite Floris fragrance on her lace handkerchief. ✉ *89 Jermyn St., W1,* ☎ *020/7930–2885. Tube: Piccadilly Circus.* (☞ Map A)

Lush. It's crammed with fresh, pure, very wacky, handmade cosmetics. 13 Rabbit is chocolate and spice soap for the shower; Angels on Bare Skin is divine lavender cleansing mush; Banana Moon, Dirty Boy, and Pineapple Grunt are soaps sliced off huge slabs like cheese and paper-wrapped as in an old-fashioned grocer's; Bath Bombs fizz furiously, then leave the water scattered with rosebuds or scented with honey and vanilla. It's all too irresistible. ⊠ *Unit 11, The Piazza, Covent Garden, WC2, ☎ 020/7240–4570. Tube: Covent Garden. (☞ Map A)*

Neal's Yard Remedies. This place has exquisitely fragranced bath oils, shampoos, massage lotions, soaps, and so on, plus some of the purest essential oils money can buy, complete with burners for scenting the air back home; all are packaged in the company's distinctive cobalt-blue apothecary bottles. ⊠ *15 Neal's Yard, WC2, ☎ 020/7379–7222. Tube: Covent Garden. (☞ Map A)*

Penhaligon's. William Penhaligon, court barber at the end of Queen Victoria's lengthy reign, established this shop. He blended perfumes and toilet waters and often created private blends for such customers as Lord Rothschild and Winston Churchill, using essential oils and natural, sometimes exotic ingredients. You can buy the very same formulations today, along with soaps, talcs, bath oils, and accessories, with the strong whiff of Victoriana both inside and outside the pretty bottles and boxes. Although constructed only a decade ago, the shop is sumptuously outfitted with 19th-century perfumer furnishings. Main branches: ⊠ *41 Wellington St., WC2, ☎ 020/7836–2150. Tube: Covent Garden; ⊠ 16 Burlington Arcade, W1, ☎ 020/7629–1416. Tube: Piccadilly Circus. (☞ Map A)*

Les Senteurs. An intimate, unglossy perfumery run by a French family, it sells some of the lesser-known yet wonderfully timeless fragrances in town. Sample Creed, worn by Eugénie, wife of Emperor Napoléon III. ⊠ *71 Elizabeth St., SW1, ☎ 020/7730–2322. Tube: Sloane Sq. (☞ Map B)*

Space NK Apothecary. This shop is rapidly acquiring cult status as the cutting-edge purveyor of makeup and cosmetics. The makeup artists' lines (MAC, Bobbi Brown, and Stila) lead the alternative trend to the giant names, and new niche lines here always have the newest, hottest colors. You'll also find everything else to complete your body pampering. ⊠ *37 Earlham St., WC2, ☎ 020/7379–7030. Tube: Covent Garden. (☞ Map A)*

STATIONERY

Ordning & Reda. It has the hottest colors of the moment for cool, sleek Swedish stationery and useful pieces to dress up the drabbest of desks. There are high-style rucksacks, too. ⊠ *22 New Row, WC2, ☎ 020/ 7240–8090. Tube: Covent Garden. (☞ Map A)*

Paperchase. The stationery superstore of London, it offers sheets of writing paper in every conceivable shade made of a dozen different mediums, as well as beautiful cards, artists' materials, notebooks, diaries and all types of paperware. The three-floor store includes a bookstore and café. ⊠ *213 Tottenham Court Rd., W1, ☎ 020/7580–8496. Tube: Goodge St. (☞ Map A)*

TOYS AND MODELS

Armoury of St. James's. This shop stocks perfect playthings for kids of all ages in the form of some of the world's finest antique and newly painted lead soldiers (most wars with British involvement can be fought in miniature), plus medals, brass buttons, uniforms, painted drums, and military prints. ⊠ *17 Piccadilly Arcade, SW1, ☎ 020/7493–5082. Tube: Piccadilly Circus. (☞ Map A)*

Hamleys. The huge stock, including six floors of toys and games for children and adults, ranges from traditional teddy bears to computer games and all the latest technological gimmickry. Try to avoid it at Christmas, when police have to rope off a section of Regent Street for customers. ⊠ *188–196 Regent St., W1,* ☎ *020/7494–2000. Tube: Oxford Circus.* (☞ Map A)

Science Museum Gift Shop. It's best for imaginative toys and models, such as those darling little balsa-wood planes. The books and puzzles are extensive and will satisfy the most inquiring minds. ⊠ *Exhibition Rd., SW7,* ☎ *020/7942–4455. Tube: South Kensington.* (☞ Map B)

Singing Tree. A fantastic display of classic English dollhouses and accessories makes this store the leader in its field. The houses themselves might not fit in your hand baggage, but you can still treat yourself to one or two of the exquisite extras. ⊠ *69 New King's Rd., SW6,* ☎ *020/7736–4527. Tube: Fulham Broadway.* (☞ Map B)

Housewares

London's main department stores, such as John Lewis, Harrods, and Selfridges have just about everything you would need in a home from day to night, but if you are looking for something that is a little more cutting edge, then stroll along Tottenham Court Road to the grandfather of them all—Heal's—which is now the grandee among a crop of modern imitators and innovators, including the first Terence Conran baby of the 60s, Habitat. Muji takes home style a step further by embracing clothes to match the furnishings. For handmade, eclectic designer pieces, you should explore farther afield to David Mellor, David Linley Furniture in Chelsea, and the wacky Walter Castellazo Design in Highgate, North London.

Cargo Homeshop. It makes a virtue of light, bright, and funky: you'll find functional tables, chairs, and inexpensive sofas in the latest earthy and vibrant shades—many can be made to order in a tempting range of fabrics from Italy and Spain. If you want to carry away a little something for under £10, try the colorful Indian rag rugs. There is another branch at 245–249 Brompton Rd., SW3. ⊠ *209 Tottenham Court Rd., W1,* ☎ *020/7580–2895. Tube: Goodge St.* (☞ Map A)

Conran Shop. This is the domain of Sir Terence Conran, who has been informing British middle-class taste since he opened Habitat in the '60s. Home enhancers from furniture to stemware, both handmade and mass-produced, famous-name and young-designer, are displayed in a suitably gorgeous building. The household articles are almost objets d'art in their own right. Bluebird on King's Road and the Conran Shop on Marylebone High Street are the latest offspring, with similarly beautiful wares. ⊠ *Michelin House, 81 Fulham Rd., SW3,* ☎ *020/7589–7401. Tube: South Kensington.* (☞ Map B)

Habitat. It has all the cool furnishings from global sources, colorful and shiny kitchen stuff, and linens in the latest ethnic and traditional themes by the store's own designers. Although most items are affordable, the workmanship is such that they may only last until the next decade's trend. The other central branch is in Chelsea (206 King's Rd., SW3). ⊠ *196 Tottenham Court Rd., W1,* ☎ *020/7631–3880. Tube: Goodge St.* (☞ Map A)

Heal's. The king of the furniture shops lining Tottenham Court Road, it has designs that combine modern style with classicism and are well made, particularly beds and seating. Prices are high, but the store makes for delightful browsing, and the kitchenware and decorative pieces are more affordable while still retaining good looks. At Christmas time, Heal's decorative baubles are gorgeous. There is another store at 234 King's Rd., SW3. ⊠ *196 Tottenham Court Rd., W1,* ☎ *020/7636–1666. Tube: Goodge St.* (☞ Map A)

Purves & Purves. It's a great place whether you've over £500 or only a £5 note to spend. Classic modern furniture and kitchenware designs by Phillipe Starck and cool Italian trendsetters are definitely upscale, but almost investment pieces. Inexpensive, colorful, and witty gift items, such as bubbly plastic napkin rings, toothbrushes, or silly soap dishes, abound. The store features many British designs. ⊠ *80–81 and 83 Tottenham Court Rd., W1,* ☎ *020/7580–8223. Tube: Goodge St.* (☞ Map A)

Jewelry

Jewelry—precious, semiprecious, and totally fake—can be had by just rubbing an Aladdin's lamp in London's West End. Of the department stores, Liberty and Harvey Nichols are particularly known for their fashion jewelry, but, in addition to viewing the more traditional baubles, bangles, and beads, check out the exceptionally creative kids on the jewelry block, such as Slim Barrett, whose designs are worn by supermodels, young aristos, and TV personalities. Seek out also the talent in the crafts and jewelry galleries, such as OXO Tower and Lesley Craze.

Asprey & Garrard. It offers a range of exquisite jewelry and gifts, both antique and modern, and has been described as the "classiest and most luxurious shop in the world." If you're in the market for a six-branched Georgian candelabrum or a six-carat emerald-and-diamond brooch, you won't be disappointed. Garrard is the royal jeweler, in charge of the upkeep of the Crown Jewels. ⊠ *167 New Bond St., W1,* ☎ *020/ 7493–6767. Tube: Bond St.* (☞ Map A)

Butler & Wilson. Designed to set off its irresistible costume jewelry to the very best advantage—against a dramatic black background—this shop has some of the best displays in town; it keeps very busy marketing silver, diamanté, French gilt, and pearls by the truckload. ⊠ *20 South Molton St., W1,* ☎ *020/7409–2955. Tube: Bond St.;* ⊠ *189 Fulham Rd., SW3,* ☎ *020/7352–8255. Tube: South Kensington.* (☞ Maps A and B)

Cartier. It exudes an exclusivity that captures the very essence of Bond Street, combining royal connections—Cartier was granted its first royal warrant in 1902—with the last word in luxurious good taste. The store also sells glassware, leather goods, and stationery. ⊠ *175 New Bond St., W1,* ☎ *020/7493–6962. Tube: Bond St.* (☞ Map A)

Dinny Hall. This store has a very simple collection of designs in mainly gold and silver. Pared-down necklaces with a single drop feature, delicate gold spot-diamond earrings, and a simple choker with delicate curls are indicative of the styles on offer—a relief from the many other highly decorative jewels and baubles in fashion at the moment. There is another branch at 54 Fulham Road, SW3. ⊠ *200 Westbourne Gr., W11,* ☎ *020/7792–3913. Tube: Notting Hill Gate.* (☞ Map C)

Erickson Beamon. It's the feather in the British cap. Beamon's highly individual style of chokers, hair decorations, and brooches calls for plenty of colored fronds along with wool and other nonmetallic material woven intricately among the jewels. Designers Alexander McQueen and John Galliano have shown Beamon's bold work to his great advantage, and his dramatic Gothic style has spawned many imitators. Costume pieces start from around £40. ⊠ *38 Elizabeth St., SW1,* ☎ *020/ 7259–0202. Tube: Sloane Sq.* (☞ Map B)

Janet Fitch. Her name regularly hits the glossy fashion pages. This comes as no surprise, as the shop is a showcase for contemporary British designers. From cuff links to tiaras (from the above-mentioned Slim Barrett) at a great price range, you'll find a bauble or two to tempt you. Other branches are at 25A Old Compton Street and 188A King's Road. ⊠ *37A Neal St., WC2,* ☎ *020/7240–6332. Tube: Covent Garden.* (☞ Map A)

Steinberg & Tolkien. This shop has the last word in costume jewelry from the 1920s and onward. Chanel and Schiaparelli are just two of the famous designers that you might leap on here. And if you're lucky, you may find a piece that has been signed by its creator. These pieces are sometimes cheaper than those of the top-notch jewelers, and they may be of extra interest because you know who made them. ✉ *193 King's Rd., SW3,* ☎ *020/7376–3660. Tube: Sloane Sq.* (☞ Map B)

Prints

London harbors loads of prints, and they make great gifts—for yourself, perhaps. We list some West End stores, but also try street markets (Camden Passage in Islington, particularly) and Cecil Court, just north of Trafalgar Square; the intriguing shops close to the British Museum; and the Royal Academy museum shop, which has a small selection. Auction houses, such as Christie's, South Kensington, and Phillips, New Bond Street, can often prove fun hunting grounds.

Grosvenor Prints. Antiquarian prints and 18th- and 19th-century portraits, with an emphasis on views and architecture of London—and dogs!—are for sale. It's an eccentric collection, and the prices range widely, but the stock is so odd that you are bound to find something interesting and unusual to meet both your budget and your taste. ✉ *28 Shelton St., WC2,* ☎ *020/7836–1979. Tube: Covent Garden.* (☞ Map A)

Map House. It has antique maps (that run from a few pounds to several thousand) and excellent reproductions of maps and prints, especially of botanical subjects, cityscapes, and *Punch* cartoons and prints. ✉ *54 Beauchamp Pl., SW3,* ☎ *020/7589–4325. Tube: Knightsbridge.* (☞ Map B)

New Academy Gallery. You can browse through prints (including originals) with a traditional bent: landscapes and scenes of London. The partner gallery—the Curwen, at No. 4, (☎ 020/7636–1459)—has a wider selection of modern art prints. ✉ *34 Windmill St., W1,* ☎ *020/7323–4700. Tube: Tottenham Court Rd.* (☞ Map A)

Shoes

Buckle My Shoe. A place for children who like to be well shod, this store has some of the most expensive makes and exciting styles in every shade imaginable. The little wellie-boots (galoshes) are delightful. ✉ *19 St. Christopher's Place, W1,* ☎ *020/7935–5589. Tube: Bond St.* (☞ Map A)

Emma Hope. This shop with handmade shoes first opened in Amwell St., Islington—handy if you are mooching around Islington and Camden Passage antiques stalls. But since custom footwear has had a mini-meteoric upturn, and the designer's pretty pumps in brocades and satins have been gliding down the catwalks of Nicole Farhi and Betty Jackson, Hope has opened a more upscale central branch in Sloane Square, Chelsea. ✉ *53 Sloane Sq., SW1,* ☎ *020/7259–9566. Tube: Sloane Sq.* (☞ Map B)

Jimmy Choo. It's the name on every supermodel's and fashion editor's feet. Choo's exquisite, elegant designs are fantasy itself, and he's become a contender for Manolo Blahnik's crown. Obviously, these designs aren't cheap—nothing under £100—but the workmanship is out of this world. ✉ *20 Motcomb St., SW1,* ☎ *020/7235–6008. Tube: Knightsbridge.* (☞ Map B)

John Lobb. If you are planning to visit for your first pair of handmade shoes (after which your wooden "last," or foot mold, is kept), take note: this shop has a waiting list of six months plus. As well as plenty of time, you will need to have plenty of money: around £1,500. But this buys a world of choice—from finest calf to exotic elk—and they will be your finest pair of shoes ever. ✉ *9 St. James's St., SW1,* ☎ *020/7930–3664. Tube: Piccadilly Circus.* (☞ Map A)

Shellys. It sells shoes for men and women, from city slickers to shoes for clubbing, at all prices and even at unimaginable platform heights.

Also available are the de rigueur Dr. Marten shoes—Britain's answer to Timberland. ✉ *266–270 Regent St., W1,* ☎ *020/7287–0939. Tube: Oxford Circus.* (☞ Map A)

Swear. This was the shoemaker for the movie *Star Wars,* which is an indicator of the style you can expect to encounter here: wild and wacky, larger-than-life platforms for daring wearers who have a head for the heights of fashion—around 4 inches and up. ✉ *61 Neal St., WC2,* ☎ *020/7240–7673. Tube: Covent Garden.* (☞ Map A)

Street Markets

London is as rich in street markets as it is in parks, and they contribute as much to the city's thriving culture. Practically every neighborhood has its own cluster of fruit-and-vegetable stalls, but we list here the bigger, specialist sort of market, which provides not only a bargain (if you luck out) but also a great day out. A Sunday morning strolling the stalls of Brick Lane and breakfasting on the native bagels (smaller than New York's, but just as good) or a Saturday antiquing on Portobello Road, is a Londoners' pastime as much as it is a tourist activity, and markets are a great way to see the city from the inside out.

Bermondsey. Also known as the New Caledonian Market, it's London's best antiques market, one of the largest, and the one the dealers frequent. The Fridays-only market starts at the unearthly hour of 5 AM, and it's then that the really great buys will be snapped up. You should still be able to find a bargain or two if you turn up a bit later. ✉ *Tower Bridge Rd., SE1.* ☉ *Fri. 5 AM–noon. Bus 15 or 25 to Aldgate, then Bus 42 over Tower Bridge to Bermondsey Sq. Tube: London Bridge or Borough.*

Berwick Street. It's a relief from the frenzy of Oxford Street and its chain and department stores. The hub of the market is in Berwick Street, but there is an overspill through backstreet Soho, past Raymond's Revue Bar, and onto Rupert Street. Behind the bustling stalls there are pleasures galore: cafés, from greasy spoon to chic bar; fresh meat and game; Camembert on the edge of over-ripeness; giant slabs of chocolate; fresh fruits and vegetables; natty custom tailors; Borovik's fabrics; classy, risqué underwear to be found at Agent Provocateur (from Vivienne Westwood's son)—all provide a cosmopolitan, lively, delightfully brassy backdrop. ✉ *W1.* ☉ *Tues. 8–6, Sat. 9–4. Tube: Oxford Circus or Piccadilly Circus.*

Brick Lane. Not a showcase but more a collection of bric-a-brac, it's worth a visit for the bagels from the all-night bakery and a host of bargain Bengali curry houses. The old Truman Brewery (Black Eagle Brewery) has also become a trendy retail focus, with the Vibe Bar, a cybercafé, at its hub. Arty types hang out at the Atlantis Art Shop—and Whitechapel Art Gallery is just a block away. From here it is a stone's throw to Spitalfields, the burgeoning designer market, and the Columbia Road flower market, where the whole of London converges in late spring to buy trays of cheap flowers for window boxes and gardens. ✉ *E1.* ☉ *Sun. 8–1. Bus 25 to Whitechapel Rd., or Bus 8 to Bethnal Green Rd. Tube: Aldgate East or Shoreditch.*

Camden Lock Market. This is the place to visit on a sunny August Sunday if you want your concept of a crowd redefined. Camden is actually several markets gathered around a pair of locks in the Regent's Canal, and it was once very pretty. Now that more stalls and a faux warehouse have been inserted into the surrounding brick railway buildings, the haphazard charm of the place is largely lost, although the variety of merchandise is mind-blowing: vintage and new clothes (design stars have been discovered here), antiques and junk, jewelry and scarves, candlesticks, ceramics, mirrors, and toys. Underneath it's really a date spot for hip teens. The neighborhood is bursting with shops, cafés, and other markets, and it's a whole lot calmer, if stall-free, at midweek. ⊠ *NW1.* ⊗ *Shops Tues.–Sun. 9:30–5:30, stalls weekends 8–6. Bus 24 or 29 to Camden Town. Tube: Camden Town.*

Camden Passage. Despite the name, it's not in Camden but a couple of miles away in Islington, a neighborhood first gentrified by media hippies in the '60s. Around 350 antiques dealers set up stalls here Saturdays and Wednesdays, with the surrounding antiques shops open Tuesday to Saturday 10–5 PM; even in the shops you can try your hand at price negotiation, although prices are generally fair. All in all, this remains a fruitful and picturesque hunting ground. ⊠ *Islington, N1.* ⊗ *Wed. and Sat. 8:30–3. Bus 19 or 38 to Angel. Tube: Angel.*

Greenwich Antiques Market. If you're planning to visit Greenwich, then combine your trip with a wander around this open-air market near St. Alfege Church. You'll find one of the best selections of secondhand and antique clothes in London—quality tweeds and overcoats can be had at amazing prices. ⊠ *Greenwich High Rd., SE10.* ⊗ *Antiques, crafts, and clothes weekends 9–5; fruit and vegetables weekdays 9–5. British Rail to New Gate Cross, then Bus 117; or bus direct to Greenwich.*

Leadenhall Market. The draw here is not so much what you can buy—plants and posh food, mainly—as the building itself. It's a handsome late-Victorian structure, ornate and elaborate, with plenty of atmosphere. ⊠ *Whittington Ave., EC3.* ⊗ *Weekdays 7–4. Tube to Bank or Monument.*

Petticoat Lane. Actually, Petticoat Lane doesn't exist; this Sunday clothing and fashion market, one of London's most entertaining diversions, centers on Middlesex Street, then sprawls in several directions, including northeast to Brick Lane and Spitalfields. Between them, the crammed streets turn up items of dubious parentage (CD players, bikes, car radios), alongside clothes (vintage, new, and just plain tired), jewelry, books, underwear, antiques, woodworking tools, bed linens, jars of pickles, and outright junk. ⊠ *Middlesex St., E1.* ⊗ *Sun. 9–2. Tube to Liverpool St., Aldgate, or Aldgate East.*

Portobello Market. London's most famous market still wins the prize for the all-round best. It sits in a most lively and multicultural part of town; the 1,500-odd antiques dealers don't rip you off (although you should haggle where you can); and it stretches over a mile, changing character completely as it goes. The top end (Notting Hill Gate) is antiquesland and more tourist-bound (with shops mid-week; don't miss antiquers David and Charles Wainwright [No. 251] and Trude Weaver [No. 71]); the middle is where locals buy fruit and vegetables and hang out in trendy restaurants; the section under the elevated highway called the Westway boasts the best flea market in town and then it tails off into a giant rummage sale among record stores, vintage-clothing boutiques, and art galleries. The bargains are to be found, here, in Golborne Road (W10) at the Ladbroke Grove end of Portobello. For original French country furniture and other pretty pieces, the market is hard to beat. For refreshment, pop into one of the many Portuguese patisseries and cafés. The western section of Portobello around the Westbourne Grove end is also worthy of exploration. ⊠ *Portobello Rd., W11.* ⊗ *Fruit and vegetables Mon.–Wed. and Fri. 8–5, Thurs. 8–1; antiques Fri. 8–3; both food market and antiques Sat. 6–5. Bus 52 or Tube to Ladbroke Grove or Notting Hill Gate.*

Spitalfields. Trendsville has arrived in the form of creative crafts and design shops. The scene at this old 3-acre indoor fruit market, near Petticoat Lane, is now reminiscent of a more chic Camden Town, before the student crowds descended. Spitalfields is home to food, crafts, and clothes stalls; cafés; and performance and sports areas. On Sunday the place really comes alive, with stalls selling beautiful paper lampshades, antique clothing, handmade rugs, soap filled with flowers and fruits, homemade cakes, Portuguese deli foods, and cookware. The resident stores have more beautiful things for body and home (particularly Redhouse). In the center, racks of easels are filled with the cheapest (around £10) original artwork from the Alternative Art Market. For refreshment it's possible to eat from West to East, with Spanish tapas or Thai among the bars and food stalls. Some of the oldest wine in London was recently excavated from the huge earthworks next to the market. The three-centuries-old flagons of Madeira were found in the remains of the Master Gunner's House cellar, destroyed in 1682. What's more, they were declared still lively and well balanced. ⊠ *Brushfield St., E1.* ⊙ *Organic market Fri. and Sun. 10–5; general market weekdays 11–3, Sun. 10–5. Tube to Liverpool St., Aldgate, or Aldgate East.*

7 SIDE TRIPS FROM LONDON

Sometimes you just need to get away from Old Smoke, and even if time is limited, a trip to the countryside is well worth your while. A train ride past rolling hills dotted with sheep, a stroll through a preserved medieval town, or a history lesson at one of England's great castles will make you feel as though you added another week to your vacation—such is the change of pace you'll experience.

Updated by
Stephanie
Adler

LONDONERS ARE UNDENIABLY LUCKY. Few urban populations enjoy such glorious—and easily accessible—options for day-tripping. This chapter presents six of the most popular destinations: Bath, Brighton, Cambridge, Oxford, Stratford-upon-Avon, and Windsor Castle. Each can easily be done as a day trip but is also well worth considering for an overnight.

Pleasures and Pastimes

DINING

London is full, nowadays, of restaurants with new-fangled menus that sometimes dazzle and sometimes don't. Beyond the capital, though, the "modern British" revolution seems to have eluded much of the country. Best bets for dining outside London typically include sticking to what each area does best: seafood in Brighton, for example. Look for menus that take cues from local produce, and remember that one of the best ways to experience local culture is to pop into a good old-fashioned pub. For approximate costs, *see* the dining price chart, *in* Smart Travel Tips A to Z.

BATH

"I really believe I shall always be talking of Bath. . . . I do like it so very much. Oh! who can ever be tired of Bath," wrote Jane Austen in *Northanger Abbey*, and, today, thousands of visitors heartily agree with her. A remarkably unsullied Georgian city, Bath looks as if John Wood, its chief architect, "Beau" Nash, its principal dandy, and Jane Austen (1775–1817) might still be seen strolling on the promenade. Stepping out of the train station plumps you right in the center, and Bath is compact enough to explore on foot. A single day is sufficient for you to take in the glorious yellow-stone buildings, tour the Roman baths, and stop for tea, though it will give only a brief hint of the cultural life that continues to thrive in this vibrant town.

Exploring Bath

The Romans set about building the **Pump Room and Roman Baths** around the healing spring of the English goddess Aquae Sulis in AD 60, after wars with the Brits had laid the city to waste. The site became famous as a temple to Minerva, Roman goddess of wisdom. Legend has it that the first taker of these sacred waters was King Lear's leprous father, Prince Bladud, in the 9th century BC. (Yes, it's claimed he was cured.) The waters can still be taken, and they gush at a constant temperature of 46.5°C (116°F). Below the beautifully restored 18th-century Pump Room (as oft-described in Austen's works) is a museum of quirky objects found during excavations. Last admission is 30 minutes before closing, but allow at least 75 mins for the museum. ⊠ *Abbey Churchyard,* ☎ *01225/477784,* WEB *www.romanbaths.co.uk.* ⊡ *£6.90, combined ticket with Assembly Rooms £8.90.* ☉ *Apr.–July, Sept., daily 9–5:30; Aug., daily 9–9; Oct.–Mar., daily 9:30–5.*

Bath Abbey was commissioned by God. Really. The design came to Bishop Oliver King in a dream, and was built during the 15th century. In the **Heritage Vaults** is a museum of archaeological finds, with a scale model of 13th-century Bath. Look up at the fan-vaulted ceilings in the nave and the carved angels on the restored West Front. *Abbey Churchyard,* ☎ *01225/422462,* WEB *www.bathabbey.org.* ⊡ *Abbey free (suggested donation £2), Heritage Vaults £2.* ☉ *Abbey mid-Apr.–Oct., Mon.–Sat. 9–6; Nov.–mid-Apr., Mon.–Sat. 9–4:30. Heritage Vaults Mon.–Sat. 10–4. Call ahead for Sun. hrs.*

A thorough turn around Bath Abbey's many nooks, crannies, and secret passageways will leave you ready to take succor in **Sally Lunn's Refreshment House & Museum** (⊠ North Parade Passage, ☎ 01225/461634). In Bath's oldest house (dating from 1482), this may be the world's only tearoom-museum. Try the eponymous Sally Lunn, invented here in the 17th century: these buns measure a foot across, and are served toasted and piled with sweet or savory toppings. The tearoom is open 10 to 10 Monday through Saturday and 11 to 6 on Sunday; the museum opens at the same time as the tearoom and closes daily at 6. Admission to the museum is free if you're eating, 30p if you're not.

One of the most famous landmarks of the city, **Pulteney Bridge** (⊠ Off Bridge St. at the Grand Parade) was the great Georgian architect Robert Adam's sole contribution to Bath and is, in its way, as fine as the only other bridge in the world with shops lining either side: the Ponte Vecchio in Florence.

Among Bath's remarkable architectural achievements is **The Circus** (⊠ Intersection of Brock, Gay, and Bennett Sts.), a perfectly circular ring of three-story stone houses designed by John Wood. The painter Thomas Gainsborough lived at number 17 from 1760 to 1774.

On the east side of Bath's Circus are more thrills for Austen readers: her much-mentioned **Assembly Rooms**, which now contain the self-explanatory **Museum of Costume,** displaying fashions from the 17th through 20th centuries. Last admission is 30 minutes before closing, but allow one hour to tour the museum. ⊠ *Bennett St.,* ☎ *01225/477789,* WEB *www.museumofcostume.co.uk.* ☜ *£4, combined ticket with Roman Baths £8.90.* ☉ *Daily 10–5.*

The **Royal Crescent** is the most famous site in Bath, and you can't help but see why. Designed by John Wood the Younger, it's perfectly pro-portioned and beautifully sited, with sweeping views over parkland. A marvelous museum at **Number 1 Royal Crescent** shows life as Beau Nash would have lived it circa 1765. ⊠ *1 Royal Crescent,* ☎ *01225/428126,* WEB *www.bath-preservation-trust.org.uk.* ☜ *£4.* ☉ *Mid-Feb.–Oct., Tues.–Sun. 10:30–5; Nov., Tues.–Sun. 10:30–4.*

Dining

£££   ✕ **Number Five.** Just over the Pulteney Bridge from the center of town, this airy bistro, with its plants, framed posters, and cane-back chairs, is an ideal spot for a light lunch. The regularly changing menu includes tasty homemade soups and such dishes as roast quail on wild rice and char-grilled loin of lamb. ⊠ *5 Argyle St.,* ☎ *01225/444499. AE, DC, MC, V. Closed Sun. No lunch Mon.*

££   ✕ **Rascals.** This is a good spot for a meal on a sightseeing day. You can choose the set menu (£10.95–£13.95) or the daily specials. The dishes change regularly: try the marinated goat cheese for starters, then the Andalusian char-grilled pork tenderloin in cranberry–white wine sauce, and the yummy chocolate mousse as a finale. There's a very good wine list. ⊠ *4 Savile Row,* ☎ *01225/330201. MC, V.*

BRIGHTON

Ever since the Prince Regent first visited in 1783, Brighton has been England's most exciting seaside city, and today it's as eccentric and cos-mopolitan as ever. With its rich cultural mix—Regency architecture, pleasure pier, specialist shops, pavement cafés, lively arts, and, of course, the odd and exotic Royal Pavilion—Brighton is a truly ex-traordinary city by the sea. For most of the 20th century the city was known for its tarnished allure, its faded glamor, but recently a young, bustling spirit has breathed new life into this ever-popular destination.

Exploring Brighton

In the 1840s, Brighton featured the very first example of that peculiarly British institution, the amusement pier. The restored **Brighton Pier** follows the great tradition, with a crowded maze of arcade games, amusement-park rides, and chip shops. The decaying ghost of a structure down the beach from Palace Pier is **West Pier** (☎ 01273/321499), which was damaged in World War II and has been closed since 1975. At press time, an extensive renovation program was underway to restore the pier to its former glory, complete with museum, performance area, and restaurants. In the meantime, supremely fascinating tours are given of the rusting Victorian relic. These are not for the faint of heart; participants don hard hats and walk on scaffolding. The tours cost £10 and are given daily mid-April through October, weekends October through mid-April; call for times. ✉ *Waterfront along Madeira Dr.,* ☎ *01273/ 609361,* WEB *www.brightonpier.co.uk.* ✆ *Free, costs of rides vary.* ☉ *June–Aug. daily 9 AM–2 AM; Sept.–May daily 10 AM–midnight.*

The heart of Brighton is the **Steine** (pronounced *steen*), a large open area close to the seafront. This was a river mouth until the Prince of Wales had it drained in 1793.

The most remarkable building on the Steine, perhaps in all Britain, is unquestionably the extravagant, fairy-tale **Royal Pavilion.** Built in 1787 as a simple seaside villa, the Pavilion was transformed between 1815 and 1822 for the Prince Regent (later George IV), who favored an exotic, eastern design with opulent Chinese interiors. When Queen Victoria came to the throne in 1837, she so disapproved of the palace that she planned to demolish it. Fortunately, the local government bought it from her, and after a lengthy process of restoration, the Pavilion looks much as it did in its Regency heyday. The interior is filled with period furniture and ornaments. Take particular note of the Music Room, styled as an Oriental pavilion, and the Banqueting Room, with its enormous flying-dragon "gasolier," or gaslight chandelier, a revolutionary invention in the early 19th century. The gardens, too, have been restored to Regency splendor, following John Nash's design of 1826. ✉ *Old Steine,* ☎ *01273/290900,* WEB *www.brighton.co.uk.* ✆ *£4.90.* ☉ *Oct.–May, daily 10–5; June–Sept., daily 10–6.*

The grounds of the Royal Pavilion contain the **Brighton Museum and Art Gallery,** whose buildings were designed as a stable block for the Price Regent's horses. It has especially interesting Art Nouveau and Art Deco collections. Look out for Salvador Dalí's famous sofa in the shape of Mae West's lips, and have a pause at the Balcony Café for its bird's-eye view over the 20th Century Art and Design Gallery. ✉ *Church St.,* ☎ *01273/290900.* ✆ *Free.* ☉ *Mon., Tues., and Thurs.– Sat. 10–5, Sun. 2–5.*

The Lanes (✉ Bordered by West, North, East, and Prince Albert Sts.) a pedestrian-only maze of alleys and passageways, was once home to legions of fishermen and their families. Now closed to vehicular traffic, the area's cobbled streets are filled with interesting restaurants, boutiques, and antiques shops. The heart of the Lanes is Market Street and Square, lined with fish and seafood restaurants.

Volk's Electric Railway, built by inventor Magnus Volk in 1883, was the first public electric railroad in Britain. It's among Brighton's quirkier delights; you might like to take the 1¼-mi trip along Marine Parade. ✉ *Marine Parade,* ☎ *01273/292718.* ✆ *£1.20 one way, £2.20 round trip.* ☉ *Mid-Apr.–Sept., weekdays 10:30–5, weekends 10:30–6.*

Below the boardwalk near Palace Pier is one of Brighton's most enchanting diversions, the **National Museum of Penny Slot Machines.** This "museum" is just a tiny room crammed with Victorian-era Nickelodeons and fortune-telling machines. Buy a few Victorian pennies, drop them in the slots, and you'll agree: there's nothing like good, old-fashioned fun. ⊠ *250C King's Road Arches, Lower Esplanade (opposite the end of East St.),* ☎ *01273/608620.* 🖻 *Free.* ☺ *Mid-Apr.–June, weekends 11–6; July–Sept., daily 11–6; Oct.–mid-Apr., Sun. 11–6.*

Dining

£££–££££   ✕ **Terre à Terre.** This inspiring vegetarian restaurant is popular, so come early for a light lunch or a more sophisticated evening meal. The butternut-squash risotto, saltimbocca with mushrooms, and eclectic choice of salads should satisfy most palates. ⊠ *71 East St.,* ☎ *01273/729051. AE, DC, MC, V. No lunch Mon.*

££–£££   ✕ **English's Oyster Bar.** Buried in the Lanes, this is one of the few old-
★   fashioned seafood havens left in England. It has been a restaurant for more than 150 years and a family business for more than 50. You can eat succulent oysters and other seafood at the counter or have a table in the dining room. It's reasonably priced and ideal for a relaxing lunch. ⊠ *29–31 East St.,* ☎ *01273/327980. AE, DC, MC, V.*

CAMBRIDGE

Having trouble distinguishing between Oxford and Cambridge? That's not surprising, because in the United Kingdom, the names of these two important educational institutions are often elided into the term "Oxbridge." Their histories, too, are inextricable: Cambridge was founded by Oxford students after a bloody 13th-century clash with Oxford townspeople. Today, a healthy sibling rivalry exists between the two schools.

This university town may be one of the most beautiful cities in Britain, but it is no museum. The first college was founded in 1284; the last only in 1977. Even if the students are on vacation, there's a strong pulse here. It's a preserved medieval city of some 100,000 souls and growing, dominated culturally and architecturally by its famous university and beautified by parks and gardens and the quietly flowing River Cam. Punting on the Cam is a quintessential Cambridge pursuit, followed by a stroll along the Backs, the quaintly named left bank of the Cam to which St. John's, Trinity, Clare, King's, and Queens' colleges, and Trinity Hall show their idyllic backsides.

VISITING THE COLLEGES

College visits are certainly a highlight of a Cambridge tour, but you must remember that the colleges are private homes and workplaces, even out of term. Each an independent entity within the university, some are closed to the public, and access to others is restricted to the chapels and dining rooms (called halls) and sometimes the libraries, too. Some colleges charge a small fee for the privilege of nosing around. All are closed during exams, usually from mid-April to late June. For details about visiting specific colleges not listed here, you can contact **Cambridge University** (☎ 01223/337733, WEB www.cam.ac.uk).

By far the best way to gain access without annoying anyone is to join a walking tour led by an official Blue Badge guide—in fact, many areas are off-limits unless you do. The two-hour tours leave daily from the Tourist Information Centre.

Exploring Cambridge
Pembroke College (1347) has delightful gardens and bowling greens. It is also the site of Christopher Wren's chapel, Wren's first major com-

mission, completed in 1665. ✉ *Pembroke St.,* ☎ *01223/338100,* WEB *www.pem.cam.ac.uk.* ▣ *Free.* ⊙ *Daily dawn–dusk.*

Emmanuel College (1584) is the alma mater of one John Harvard, who gave his books and his name to the New World university. A number of the Pilgrims were Emmanuel alumni, and they remembered their alma mater in naming Cambridge, Massachusetts. ✉ *Emmanuel and St. Andrew's Sts.,* ☎ *01223/334200,* WEB *www.emma.cam.ac.uk.* ▣ *Free.* ⊙ *Daily 9–6.*

East Anglia's finest art gallery, the **Fitzwilliam Museum** contains outstanding collections of art, including several Constable paintings, oil sketches by Rubens, and antiquities from ancient Egypt and elsewhere. ✉ *Trumpington St.,* ☎ *01223/332900,* WEB *www.fitz.cam.ac.uk.* ▣ *Free.* ⊙ *Tues.–Sat. 10–5, Sun. 2:15–5.*

King's College (1441) is notable as the site of the world-famous Gothic-style **King's College Chapel** (built 1446–1547), which, with its great fan-vaulted roof supported by a delicate tracery of columns, has been deemed by some the most glorious flowering of Perpendicular Gothic in Britain. It's the home of the famous choristers, and, to cap it all, Rubens's *Adoration of the Magi* is secreted behind the altar. ✉ *Kings Parade,* ☎ *01223/331155,* WEB *www.kings.cam.ac.uk.* ▣ *£3.50.* ⊙ *Daily 9:30–3:30 (hrs vary with services; call to confirm before visiting).*

NEED A
BREAK?

Stop in at the hole-in-the-wall **Indigo Coffeehouse** (✉ St. Edward's Passage, between King's Parade and Peas Hill, ☎ no phone) for a quick bite to eat before or after a visit to the nearby Tourist Information Centre; it's as familiar as any college-town café. The chalkboard menu lists coffees and teas, light snacks, and made-to-order sandwiches (£2–£3); the brie and cranberry sauce baguette is a good choice.

Peterhouse College is Cambridge's smallest and oldest college, founded in 1284 by the Bishop of Ely. Take a tranquil walk through its former deer park, by the river side of its ivy-clad buildings. ✉ *Trumpington St.,* ☎ *01223/338200,* WEB *www.pet.cam.ac.uk.* ▣ *Free.* ⊙ *Daily 1–5.*

Reached along the Backs, **Queens' College** (after Margaret, queen of Henry VI, and Elizabeth, queen of Edward IV) was built around 1448 and is one of Cambridge's most eye-catching colleges. Enter over the **Mathematical Bridge,** said to have been built by Isaac Newton without any binding save gravity, then dismantled by curious scholars anxious to learn Sir Isaac's secret. The college maintains, however, that the bridge wasn't actually put together until 1749, 22 years after Newton's death, thus debunking the popular myth. Be sure to take in the half-timber President's Lodge. ✉ *Queen's La.,* ☎ *01223/335511,* WEB *www.quns.cam.ac.uk.* ▣ *£1.20 Apr.–Sept., free Oct.–Mar.* ⊙ *Apr.–Sept., daily 10–4:30; Oct.–Mar., daily 1:30–3:30. Closed late May–late June.*

Along King's Parade is **Corpus Christi College.** If you see only one quadrangle, make it the 14th-century Old Court here; it's the longest continuously inhabited college quadrangle in Cambridge. ✉ *King's Parade,* ☎ *01223/338000,* WEB *www.corpus.cam.ac.uk.* ▣ *Free.* ⊙ *Daily dawn–dusk.*

St. John's College (1511), the university's second largest, has noted alumni (Wordsworth had his rooms here) and two of the finest sights in town: the School of Pythagoras, the oldest house in Cambridge; and the Bridge of Sighs, whose only resemblance to its Venetian counterpart is actually its covering. The bridge reaches across the Cam to the mock-Gothic New Court (1825–1831), whose white crenellations have earned it the nickname "the wedding cake." ✉ *St. John's and Bridge*

Sts., ☎ 01223/338600, WEB *www.joh.cam.ac.uk.* 🖃 *£1.75 Mar.–Oct.,
free Nov.–Feb.* ⊙ *Mar.–Oct., daily 10–5; Nov.–Feb., daily dawn–dusk.*

Trinity College was founded by Henry VIII in 1546 and has the largest
student population of all the colleges. Many of Trinity's features match
its size, not least its 17th-century "great court" and the massive gatehouse that houses Great Tom, a giant clock that strikes each hour with
high and low notes. Don't miss the wonderful library by Christopher
Wren. Alumni include Newton, Byron, Tennyson, Wittgenstein, Milne,
and the King Charles III. 🖂 *Trinity St.,* ☎ *01223/338400,* WEB *www.
trin.cam.ac.uk.* 🖃 *£1.75 Mar.–Oct., free Nov.–Feb.* ⊙ *Mar.–Oct.,
daily 10–5; Nov.–Feb., daily 10–dusk.*

Dining

££££   ✕ **Midsummer House.** A classy restaurant set beside the River Cam,
★   across Midsummer Common, the gray-brick Midsummer House is particularly lovely in summer: it has a comfortable conservatory. Set
menus offer a selection of sophisticated European and Mediterranean
dishes. Choices might include tenderly cooked local lamb or the best
from the fish market, adorned with inventively presented vegetables.
🖂 *Midsummer Common,* ☎ *01223/369299. Reservations essential.
AE, MC, V. Closed Mon. No lunch Sat., no dinner Sun.*

£££–££££ ✕ **Brown's.** This huge, airy, French American-style brasserie-diner
was converted from the outpatient department of the old Adden-
brooke's Hospital. The bountiful menu ranges from toasted sandwiches and steak, mushroom, and Guinness pie on up to venison or
gigot of lamb. Check the daily specials, too—fresh fish and pasta are
usually available. It's very busy on weekends, when you may have to
wait in line. 🖂 *23 Trumpington St.,* ☎ *01223/461655. Reservations
not accepted. AE, MC, V.*

OXFORD

To get Oxford fixed in your mind's eye, say the phrase "Dreaming Spires"
over and over—all the tour guides do—and think *Brideshead Revisited,* Sebastian Flyte, and Evelyn Waugh, in general. Think Rhodes scholars—President Clinton was one—and think J. R. R. Tolkien, Percy
Bysshe Shelley, Oscar Wilde, W. H. Auden, and C. S. Lewis.

Oxford University is older than its sibling to the east, dating from the
12th century, but the city is bigger and more cosmopolitan than Cambridge. Of course, here, too, there's no shortage of hushed quadrangles, chapels, and gardens. Bikes are propped against wrought-iron
railings, and punting is popular along the Cherwell (rent a punt yourself from the foot of Magdalen Bridge), but Oxford is also a major industrial center, with large car and steel plants based in its suburbs.

VISITING THE COLLEGES

The same concerns for people's work and privacy hold here as in
Cambridge. Guided city walking tours leave the Oxford Information
Centre several times a day. If you have limited time, get a detailed map
from the tourist office and focus on selected sights. The Oxford University Web site (www.ox.ac.uk) is a great source of information if you're
planning to go it alone.

Note that many of the colleges and university buildings are closed around
Christmas (sometimes Easter, too) and on certain days from April to
June for exams and degree ceremonies.

Exploring Oxford

Any Oxford visit should begin at its very center—a pleasant walk of
10 minutes or so east of the train station—with the splendid univer-

sity church of **St. Mary the Virgin** (1280). Climb 127 steps to the top of its 14th-century tower, and you can get a panoramic view of the entire city. The church's interior is crowded with 700 years' worth of funeral monuments. ⊠ *High St.,* ☎ *01865/279111.* 🎟 *Church free, tower £1.50.* ⊙ *Mon.–Sat. 9–5, Sun., 11:30–5.*

Among Oxford's most famous sights, the **Radcliffe Camera** (1737–1749) is one of the buildings that holds the august **Bodleian Library.** Not many of the two-million-plus volumes are on view to non-dons, but you can see part of the collection on a tour. ⊠ *Broad St.,* ☎ *01865/277224,* WEB *www.bodley.ox.ac.uk.* 🎟 *£3.50, extended tour £7 (call to pre-book).* ⊙ *Tours Mar.–Oct., weekdays 10:30, 11:30, 2, 3 and Sat. 10:30, 11:30; Nov.–Feb., weekdays 2, 3 and Sat. 10:30, 11:30.*

The **Sheldonian Theatre,** built between 1664 and 1668, was Sir Christopher Wren's first major work, and he modeled it on a Roman amphitheater. It was built as a venue for the University's public ceremonies, and graduations are still held here, entirely in Latin, as befits the building's spirit. Outside is one of Oxford's most striking sights—a metal fence topped with stone busts of 18 Roman emperors (modern reproductions of the originals, which were eaten away by pollution). ⊠ *Broad St.,* ☎ *01865/277299,* WEB *www.sheldon.ox.ac.uk.* 🎟 *£1.50.* ⊙ *Apr.–mid-Nov., Mon.–Sat. 10–12:30, 2–4:30; mid-Nov.–Mar., Mon.–Sat. 10–12:30, 2–3:30.*

You can brush up on local history at the **Oxford Story.** Take your place at a medieval student's desk as it trundles, Disney-style, through 800 years of Oxford history—in just 20 minutes! See Edmund Halley discover his comet! Watch the Scholastica's Day Riot of 1355! There's commentary tailored for kids, too. ⊠ *6 Broad St.,* ☎ *01865/790055,* WEB *www.heritageattractions.co.uk.* 🎟 *£5.70.* ⊙ *Apr.–June and Sept.–Oct., daily 9:30–5; July–Aug., daily 9:30–5:30; Nov.–Mar., weekdays 10–4:30, weekends 10–5.*

The **Oxford Union** is home to the university debating society and where many politicians-to-be gave their earliest tirades. You can have a pint and admire the Pre-Raphaelite (Morris, Rossetti, Burne-Jones) murals depicting Arthurian legends. ⊠ *St. Michael's St.,* ☎ *no phone,* WEB *www.oxford-union.org.* 🎟 *Free.* ⊙ *Mon.–Sat. 10 AM–11 PM, Sun. noon–10:30.*

Outside the new (Victorian) college gates of prestigious **Balliol College** (1263) is a cross in the sidewalk made in cobblestones, marking the place where Archbishop Cranmer and Bishops Latimer and Ridley were burnt for their Protestant beliefs in 1555, during the reign of Mary I. The original college gates (rumored to have witnessed the scorching) hang in the library passage, between the inner and outer quadrangles. Today Balliol is among the most left-wing of Oxford's colleges. ⊠ *St. Giles St.,* ☎ *01865/277777,* WEB *www.balliol.ox.ac.uk.* 🎟 *£1.* ⊙ *Daily 2–5 (or dusk, if earlier).*

The **chapel** of **Trinity College** (1555) is an architectural gem, with some superb wood carvings by Grinling Gibbons, a 17th-century master whose work can be found in many an English stately home. ⊠ *Broad St.,* ☎ *01865/279900,* WEB *www.trinity.ox.ac.uk.* 🎟 *£2.* ⊙ *Daily 10:30–noon, 2–5 (or dusk, if earlier).*

The **Ashmolean Museum,** founded in 1683, is Britain's oldest public museum, and here some of the world's most precious things are stashed, all property of the university. See Egyptian, Greek, and Roman artifacts; drawings by Michelangelo and Raphael; European silverware and ceramics; Asian paintings; a world-class numismatic collection; and more.

✉ *Beaumont St.,* ☎ *01865/278000,* WEB *www.ashmol.ox.ac.uk.* ✉ *Free.* ⊙ *Tues.–Sat. 10–5, Sun. 2–5. Closed Mon.*

St. John's College, founded in 1555, is worth visiting for its very large and lovely gardens. ✉ *St. Giles St.,* ☎ *01865/277300,* WEB *www.sjc. ox.ac.uk.* ✉ *Free.* ⊙ *Daily 1–5 (or dusk, if earlier).*

Tom Tower, designed by Christopher Wren, marks the entrance to the leading college of the southern half of Oxford: **Christ Church College.** Called "the House" by its modest members, Christ Church boasts the largest quadrangle in town, named Tom Quad, after the over-6-ton bell in the tower. Christ Church is where Charles Dodgson, better known as Lewis Carroll, was a math don; a shop opposite the meadows in St. Aldate's was the inspiration for the shop in *Through the Looking Glass.* Don't miss the 800-year-old chapel, or the medieval dining hall, with its portraits of former students—John Wesley, William Penn, and 14 prime ministers. Also visit Canterbury Quadrangle, whose **picture gallery** contains works by da Vinci, Michelangelo, and Rubens. ✉ *St. Aldate's,* ☎ *01865/276150,* WEB *www.chch.ox.ac.uk.* ✉ *£3.* ⊙ *Mon.– Sat. 9:30–5:30, Sun. 1–5:30.*

Dining

££££ ✗ **Restaurant Elizabeth.** These small, elegant dining rooms, in a 15th-century building across from Christ Church College, impress upon you their history as a 16th-century bishop's palace. Salmon rolls, roast lamb, and crème brûlée are among the Spanish chef's Continental specialties. ✉ *82 St. Aldate's,* ☎ *01865/242230. Reservations essential. AE, DC, MC, V. Closed Mon.*

STRATFORD-UPON-AVON

Stratford-upon-Avon has become very adept at accommodating the hordes of visitors who come hoping for a glimpse of William Shakespeare's world. Stratford is a handsome town, punctuated with distinctive Tudor half-timber buildings that have survived from its 16th-century heyday as a crafts and trading center. But it can feel at times like a literary amusement park, and if you're not a fan of Bill, you'd probably do better to explore some other quaint English village.

That said, how best to maximize your immersion in the Bard's works? It's difficult to avoid feeling like a herd animal as you board the Shakespeare bus, but packaged tours like **Stratford and the Shakespeare Story** (14 Rother St., ☎ 01789/294466, ✉ £10), with a hop-on/hop-off route around the five Shakespeare Birthplace Trust properties—two of which are out of town—can make life infinitely easier for visitors without cars. And if you can manage an overnight stay, taking in a Royal Shakespeare Company (RSC) production will enrich your Stratford experience.

Exploring Stratford-upon-Avon

Most Stratford visitors begin at **Shakespeare's Birthplace Museum.** The half-timber building in which William grew up has been a national memorial since 1847, and it is now split in half: one part is a re-creation of a typical home of the time, while the other contains an intelligent biographical exhibit about Shakespeare, plus a history of the house itself. ✉ *Henley St.,* ☎ *01789/204016,* WEB *www.shakespeare.org.uk.* ✉ *£6, combined ticket with Shakespeare Birthplace Trust properties (Nash's House; Hall's Croft; Anne Hathaway's Cottage; Mary Arden's House; allow at least 4 hrs, but ticket is valid for one year) £12, 3 in-town properties (not including Anne Hathaway's Cottage and Mary Arden's House) £8.50.* ⊙ *Late Mar.–late Oct., Mon.–Sat. 9–5, Sun. 9:30–5; late Oct.–late Mar., Mon.–Sat. 9:30–4, Sun. 10–4.*

Nash's House, which belonged to Thomas Nash, first husband of Shakespeare's granddaughter Elizabeth Hall, now houses an exhibit charting the history of Stratford against a backdrop of period furniture and tapestries. On the grounds of Nash's House is **New Place,** the home where the Bard spent his last years and died in 1616. An Elizabethan knot garden is set around the remaining foundation of the house, which was destroyed in 1759 by its last owner, Reverend Francis Gastrell, in an attempt to stop the tide of visitors. ✉ *Chapel St.,* ☎ *01789/292325,* WEB *www.shakespeare.org.uk.* ⬚ *£3.50, combined ticket with Shakespeare's Birthplace Trust properties £12.* ◷ *Late Mar.–late Oct., Mon.–Sat. 9:30–5, Sun. 10–5; late Oct.–late Mar., Mon.–Sat. 10–4, Sun. 10:30–4.*

Hall's Croft is Stratford's most beautiful Tudor town house. This was—almost definitely—the home of Shakespeare's daughter, Susanna, and her husband, Dr. John Hall. It's outfitted with furniture of the period and the doctor's dispensary, and the walled garden is delightful. ✉ *Old Town St.,* ☎ *01789/292107,* WEB *www.shakespeare.org.uk.* ⬚ *£3.50, combined ticket with Shakespeare's Birthplace Trust properties £12.* ◷ *Late Mar.–late Oct., Mon.–Sat. 9:30–5, Sun. 10–5; late Oct.–late Mar., Mon.–Sat. 10–4, Sun. 10:30–4.*

"Shakespeare's church," the 13th-century **Holy Trinity,** is fronted by a beautiful avenue of lime trees. Here, in the chancel, the Bard is buried. The bust of Shakespeare is thought to be an authentic likeness, executed a few years after his death. Last admission is 20 minutes before closing. ✉ *Trinity St.,* ☎ *01789/266316.* ⬚ *Church free, chancel £1.* ◷ *Mar.–Oct., Mon.–Sat. 8:30–6, Sun. 2–5; Nov.–Feb., Mon.–Sat. 9–4, Sun. 2–5.*

Perfectly positioned on the bank of the Avon is the **Royal Shakespeare Theatre,** where the Royal Shakespeare Company performs in Stratford, mounting several productions each season. The design of the smaller **Swan Theatre,** in the same building, is based on the original Elizabethan Globe. It's best to book well in advance, but day-of-performance tickets are nearly always available. Backstage tours take place around performances, so call ahead. ✉ *Waterside,* ☎ *01789/403403 box office; 01789/403405 tours,* WEB *www.rsc.org.uk.* ⬚ *Tours £4.* ◷ *Tours weekdays 1:30, 5:30; Sun. hourly noon–3; matinee days (usually Thurs., Sat.) 11:30, 5:30.*

STRATFORD ENVIRONS

The two remaining stops on the Shakespeare trail are just outside Stratford. **Anne Hathaway's Cottage,** the early home of the playwright's wife, is possibly the most picturesque abode in Britain—a rather substantial thatched cottage, it has been restored to reflect the comfortable middle-class Hathaway life. You can walk—it's just over a mile from downtown Stratford. ✉ *Cottage Lane, Shottery,* ☎ *01789/292100,* WEB *www.shakespeare.org.uk.* ⬚ *£4.20, combined ticket with Shakespeare's Birthplace Trust properties £12.* ◷ *Late Mar.–late Oct., Mon.–Sat. 9–5, Sun. 9:30–5; late Oct.–late Mar., Mon.–Sat. 9:30–4, Sun. 10–4.*

The **Shakespeare Countryside Museum,** whose displays illustrate life in the English countryside from Shakespeare's time to the present day, is the main attraction at **Palmer's Farm,** the site of a recent and radical Shakespearean revelation. In October 2000, research findings based on recently discovered real-estate records revealed that the property, which had been referred to since the 18th century as Mary Arden's House, was not in fact the house in which the Bard's mother grew up. The real **Mary Arden's House,** hitherto known as Glebe Farm, was actually nearby and (thankfully, along with the other Shakespeare-related properties around Stratford) already owned by the Shakespeare Birthplace Trust. ✉ *Wilmcote,* ☎ *01789/293455,* WEB *www.shakespeare. org.uk.* 🎫 *£5, combined ticket with Shakespeare's Birthplace Trust properties £12.* ⊙ *Late Mar.–late Oct., Mon.–Sat. 9:30–5, Sun. 10–5; late Oct.–late Mar., Mon.–Sat. 10–4, Sun. 10:30–4.*

Some 8 mi out of Stratford in the medieval town of Warwick, **Warwick Castle** fulfills anyone's most clichéd Camelot daydreams, being a medieval, fortified, much-restored, castellated, moated, landscaped (by Capability Brown) castle. Now managed by the "living-wax" experts at Madame Tussaud's, the castle is a true period museum, complete with dungeons and a torture chamber, state rooms, and the occasional battle reenactment. ✉ *Off Mill St., Warwick,* ☎ *01926/495421; 01926/ 406600 24-hr information line,* WEB *www.warwick-castle.co.uk.* 🎫 *£9.75.* ⊙ *Apr.–Oct., daily 10–6; Nov.–Mar., daily 10–5.*

Dining

££££ ✕ **Box Tree Restaurant.** Overlooking the River Avon and its resident
★   swans, this attractive spot is in the Royal Shakespeare Theatre and serves some of the best food in town. You can dine here either before or after a play, but it's worth a meal even if you're not attending a performance. The set menu offers three courses and coffee; specialties have an Italian slant and include wild boar casserole, breast of duck, and vegetarian pasta dishes. ✉ *Waterside,* ☎ *01789/403415. Reservations essential. AE, MC, V. Closed when theater is closed.*

£–££ ✕ **Black Swan.** Locally called the Dirty Duck, this is one of Stratford's most celebrated pubs, attracting actors since Garrick's days. It has a little veranda overlooking the theaters and the river. Along with a pint of bitter, enjoy English grill specialties, as well as braised oxtail and honey-roasted duck, plus an assortment of bar meals. ✉ *Waterside,* ☎ *01789/297312. AE, DC, MC, V. No dinner Sun.*

WINDSOR CASTLE

The star sight of Windsor, a quiet Berkshire town, is, without doubt, the largest inhabited castle in the world—Windsor Castle. Windsor Great Park, however, shouldn't be forgotten; Eton College, England's most famous public school, with its Old Village, is also a lovely walk across the Thames; and there's the kid's paradise of Legoland.

Windsor is the only royal residence to have been in continuous royal use since the days of William the Conqueror, who chose this site to build a timber stockade soon after his conquest of Britain in 1066. It was Edward III in the 1300s who really founded the castle, building the Norman gateway, the great round tower, and new State Apartments. Charles II restored the State Apartments during the 1600s and, during the 1820s, George IV—that most extravagant of kings with a mania for building—converted what was still essentially a medieval castle into the royal palace you see today. The Queen uses Windsor a lot, spending most weekends here, often joined by family and friends. She's here when the Royal Standard is flown above the Round Tower but not when you see the Union Jack. Be sure to arrive early at the main entrance, as lines can be long.

Exploring Windsor Castle

The massive citadel occupies 13 acres, but the first part you notice on entering is the **Round Tower,** on top of which the standard is flown and at the base of which is the 11th-century Moat Garden. Passing under the portcullis at the Norman Gate, you reach the **Upper Ward,** the quadrangle containing the State Apartments—which you may tour when the Queen is out—and the sovereign's Private Apartments. Processions for foreign heads of state and other ceremonies take place here, as does the Changing of the Guard when the Queen is in. A short walk takes you to the Lower Ward, where the high point is the magnificent **St. George's Chapel,** symbolic and actual guardian of the Order of the Garter, the highest chivalric order in the land, founded in 1348 by Edward III. Ten sovereigns are buried in the chapel—a fantastic Perpendicular Gothic vision 230 ft long, complete with gargoyles, buttresses, banners, swords, and choir stalls. This is also where royal weddings usually take place, the most recent having been that of Prince Edward and Sophie Rhys-Jones in June 1999.

The **State Apartments** are grander than Buckingham Palace's and have the added attraction of a few gems from the Queen's vast art collection: choice canvases by Rubens, Rembrandt, Van Dyck, Gainsborough, Canaletto, and Holbein; da Vinci drawings; Gobelin tapestries; and limewood carvings by Grinling Gibbons. The entrance is through a grand hall holding cases crammed with precious china—some still used for royal banquets. Don't miss the outsize suit of armor in the armory, made for Henry VIII. The views across to Windsor Great Park, the remains of a former royal hunting forest, are magnificent, too. One unmissable treat—and not only for children—is **Queen Mary's Dolls' House,** a 12:1 scale, seven-story palace complete with electricity, running water, and working elevators, designed in 1924 by Sir Edwin Lutyens. The detail is incredible—for example, some of the miniature books in the library are by Kipling, Conan Doyle, Thomas Hardy, and G. K. Chesterton, written by the great authors in their own hand. The diminutive wine bottles hold the real thing, too.

A 1992 fire that started in the Queen's private chapel totally gutted some of the State Apartments. A swift rescue effort meant that, miraculously, hardly any works of art were lost, and a £37 million effort has restored the Grand Reception Room, the Green and Crimson drawing rooms, and the State and Octagonal dining rooms to their former, if not greater, glory. ⊠ *Windsor Castle,* ☎ *01753/868286; 01753/ 831118 recorded information,* WEB *www.royalresidences.com/windsor. html.* 🖾 *£10.50, £8.50 Sun.* ☉ *Mar.–Oct., daily 10–5:30 (last admission at 4); Nov.–Feb., daily 9:45–4:15 (last admission at 3). St. George's Chapel closed Sun..*

SIDE TRIPS A TO Z

To research prices, get advice from other travelers, and book travel arrangements, visit www.fodors.com.

BUS TRAVEL

National Express coach lines runs buses from Victoria Coach Station to five of the towns in this chapter. Coaches depart for Bath (3 hrs) every three hours; for Brighton (2 hrs, 15 min) hourly; for Cambridge (about 2 hrs) hourly; for Oxford (1 hr, 40 mins) about every half hour; and for Stratford-upon-Avon (3 hrs) about five times daily.

Take the Green Line bus to Windsor. It leaves from Stop 1 in front of the Colonnades Shopping Centre on Buckingham Palace Road, *not* from Victoria Coach Station. The fast direct service takes around 1 hour and runs hourly; the stopping services take up to 1 hour, 30 minutes or more. A day-return ticket costs £7.

FARES AND SCHEDULES

➤ BUS INFORMATION: **Green Line** (☎ 020/7668–7261, WEB www.greenline.co.uk). **National Express** (☎ 0870/5808080, WEB www.nationalexpress.co.uk). **Victoria Coach Station** (⊠ Buckingham Palace Rd., SW1).

TRAIN TRAVEL

Trains run from Paddington Station to Bath (75 mins, hourly departures), Oxford (55 mins, hourly departures), and Windsor (45 mins, departures twice hourly). Direct trains leave Paddington for Stratford-upon-Avon (2 hrs, 25 mins) each morning; all other routes require a change at Leamington Spa. Trains depart King's Cross and Liverpool Street stations hourly for Cambridge (1 hr). Victoria Station is the point of departure for rail service to Brighton (45 mins, hourly). Trains depart hourly from Waterloo Station for Windsor (50 mins, departs every 30 mins) and Eton Riverside.

FARES AND SCHEDULES

➤ TRAIN INFORMATION: **Railtrack** (☎ 0870/5808080, WEB www.railtrack.co.uk).

TRANSPORTATION AROUND THE COUNTRYSIDE

Normally, the six towns covered in this chapter are best reached by train. Bus travel costs less, but can take twice as long. However, at press time, passengers on most train routes throughout Britain were experiencing constant and infuriating delays as a result of essential work being carried out on the national rail system. You're best off planning ahead for any day trip: be sure to check the latest timetables before you set off, and try to get an early start, whether you're traveling by train or bus.

VISITOR INFORMATION

➤ TOURIST INFORMATION: **Bath Tourist Information Centre** (✉ Bath St., ☎ 01225/477101, WEB www.visitbath.co.uk). **Brighton Tourist Information Centre** (✉ 10 Bartholomew Sq., ☎ 09067/112255, WEB www.tourism.brighton.co.uk). **Cambridge Tourist Information Centre** (✉ The Old Library, Wheeler St., ☎ 01223/322640, WEB www.cambridge.gov.uk/leisure/tourism.htm). **Oxford Information Centre** (✉ The Old School, Gloucester Green, ☎ 01865/726871, WEB www.oxford.gov.uk/tourism). The **Royal Windsor Information Centre** (✉ 24 High St., ☎ 01753/743900, WEB www.windsor.gov.uk). **Stratford Tourist Information Centre** (✉ Bridgefoot, ☎ 01789/293127, WEB www.shakespeare-country.co.uk).

8 BACKGROUND AND ESSENTIALS

Portrait of London

Books and Videos

Chronology

Map of London Postal Districts

Smart Travel Tips A to Z

THE CITY OF VILLAGES: WHAT'S WHERE

London is an enormous city—600 square mi—on a tiny island, accommodating about 7 million inhabitants, one-eighth of the entire population of England, Scotland, and Wales, but to many travelers it never *really* feels big. It is fashioned on a different scale from other capital cities, as if, given the English penchant for modesty and understatement, it felt embarrassed by its size. Each of the 32 boroughs that compose the whole has its own character, lore, and rhythm. There is the heraldic splendor of Westminster, the chic of artistic Chelsea, the architectural elegance of Belgravia and Mayfair, the cosmopolitan charm of Soho, and the East End, home base of the Cockney—to name just a few. You begin to wonder if there actually is such a person as a generic Londoner. Stay here long enough and Professor Higgins's feat of deducing Eliza Dolittle's very street of birth from the shape of her vowels will seem like nothing special. It's a cliché, but London really is a city of villages.

London's contrasts can best be savored by strolling from one district to another. First pick a starting point such as Piccadilly Circus, which the British think of as the hub of the universe. Keeping your wits about you—the Circus is a swirl of traffic surrounded by grand Edwardian-era buildings—face in the direction of the area of central London you want to explore, and start moving. To the north runs Regent Street, curving up one side of ritzy, mostly residential Mayfair. To the south is Lower Regent Street, leading toward Whitehall, the parks, and the palaces. To the east are Shaftesbury Avenue and Leicester Square, for theaters and Soho; to the west is Piccadilly itself, heading out to Hyde Park and Knightsbridge. This is also a great place to board a double-decker sightseeing bus—just remember to have some sort of protective wrap handy: atop these buses it's *always* windy.

Westminster and Royal London

No matter how you first approach London—historically, geographically, emotionally—all things start at Westminster, one of the truly ancient centers of the city. There is as much history in these few acres as there is in many complete cities. The best show staged for free is in the world's most renowned ego chamber, the House of Commons. Then there is Westminster Abbey, crammed with memorials and monuments to the great, the famous, and the totally forgotten (do not allow your search for noted names to blind you to the spectacular Gothic splendor surrounding you). Whitehall is both an avenue and the heartbeat of the British government; here is the prime minister's official residence, No. 10 Downing Street, and the Horse Guards, where two mounted sentries of the queen's guard provide a memorable image. Whitehall leads to Trafalgar Square and the incomparable National Gallery (art treasures of a more modern ilk lie in the Tate Galleries, Tate Britain, and Tate Modern). From the grand Admiralty Arch, the Mall leads straight to Buckingham Palace, as unprepossessing on the outside as it is sumptuous inside (as summer tours now let you see). Naturally, in a district that regularly witnesses the pomp and pageantry of royal occasions, the streets are wide and the vistas are long. With beautifully kept St. James's Park at its center, the Westminster area exudes dignity and offers frequent glimpses of pinnacles and towers over treetops and, of course, the deep tones of Big Ben counting off the quarter hours.

Belgravia

Just a short carriage ride from Buckingham Palace is London's most splendidly aristocratic enclave: Belgravia, a grande-dame neighborhood of block after block of grand, porticoed mansions. Built in the mid-1800s, it is untouched by neon, with an authentic vintage patina. Most of its streets are lined with terraced row houses, all painted Wedgwood-china white (to signify they remain the property of the Duke of Westminster). Pedigree-proud locations include Belgrave Square, Grosvenor Crescent, and Belgrave Place, but also check out the chic alleyways, called "mews" from the time when they housed Milord's horse and carriage. Although Belgravia remains exclusively residential, and therefore off the usual tourist path, no other spot in London will make you feel so much like warbling "On the Street Where You Live," just as Freddy Eynsford-Hill sang it in *My Fair Lady*.

Bloomsbury

The literary set that made the name Bloomsbury world famous has left hardly a trace, but this remains the heart of learned London. The University of London is here; so are the Law Courts and the British Museum. With the British Library parked just north at St. Pancras, a greater number of books can probably be found in Bloomsbury than in all the rest of London. Virginia Woolf and T. S. Eliot would be pleased to note that some of London's most beautiful domestic architecture, elegant houses that would have been familiar to Dr. Johnson, still line the area's prim squares. At one, Charles Dickens worked on *Oliver Twist* at a tall upright clerk's desk.

Bloomsbury is really part of Holborn, the core of Legal London. The Inns of Court are the finest group of historic buildings in the city, in an almost unspoiled setting—the closest thing to the spirit of Oxford that London has to offer. In Holborn, you'll also find Sir John Soane's Museum, a mansion that whisks you back to the mid-1800s.

Chelsea

Chelsea has always beckoned to free-thinkers and fashion-fringers—from Sir Thomas More to Isadora Duncan (she couldn't find a place to stay her first night, so she decamped to the graveyard at Chelsea Old Church, which natives *still* insist is a lovely place to stay). Major sights include Christopher Wren's magisterial Royal Hospital—now the site of the Chelsea Flower Show—and Cheyne Walk, where Henry James and Dante Gabriel Rossetti once lived. Now an extremely expensive place to live (through parted curtains you may glimpse rooms of exquisite taste), the area on Saturdays continues to draw an army of trendaholics to King's Road, whose boutiques gave birth to the paisleyed '60s and the pink-headed-punk '70s.

The City

Known as "the Square Mile," the City is to London what Wall Street is to Manhattan. As the site of the Celtic settlement the Romans called Londinium, this is the oldest part of London. Unfortunately, thanks to blocks of high-rise apartments and steel skyscrapers, it looks like the newest part. Yet within and around the capital-C City are some of London's most memorable attractions—St. Paul's Cathedral and storybook Tower Bridge. Charles and Diana tied the knot at St. Paul's but they could have found other equally beautiful options here, including St. Bride's (its distinctive multitiered spire gave rise to today's wedding cakes), St. Giles Without Cripplegate, and St. Mary-le-Bow. At the east border of the City is the legendary Tower of London, England's most perfectly preserved medieval fortress, where Sir Thomas More, Anne Boleyn, and the young princes Edward V and his brother Richard, nephews of Richard III, met untimely ends.

Covent Garden

In not much more than a decade, Covent Garden—which lies just to the east of Soho—has gone from a down-at-the-heels district to one of the busiest, most raffishly enjoyable parts of the city. Continental-style open-air cafés create a very un-English atmosphere. Warehouses, once cavernous and grim, now accommodate fashion boutiques and a huge variety of shops favored by the "trendoisie." A network of narrow streets, arcades, and pedestrian malls, the area is dominated by the Piazza—scene of a food market in the 1830s and a flower market in the 1870s. Today the indoor-outdoor complex overflows with clothing shops and crafts stalls, and the updated entrance to the Royal Opera House opens onto the Piazza.

The East End

In the East End, you'll find sights and sounds that are as much a part of the real London as a November fog. Its 19th-century slums—immortalized by Charles Dickens and the evocative etchings of Gustave Doré—are a relic of the past. Today the area possesses a haunting beauty and a warm spirit of humor and friendliness. Sundays you'll find 21st-century versions of the medieval fair: Spitalfields Market and Petticoat Lane. Other fascinating sights include the Geffrye Museum— an overlooked cluster of wonderful historic interiors—Hawksmoor's Christ Church, and the Blind Beggar, the Victorian den of iniquity where Salvation Army founder William Booth was moved to preach his first sermon. Off the main thoroughfare, tap into the true pulse of East End life by exploring the lanes and alleys that still make up one of the world's most fascinating melting pots. If you can fit it in, take one of the evening walking tours that trace the footsteps of the infamous Jack the Ripper; at night, these mean streets still seem shrouded in a Dickensian aura. Down by the river, sprawling eastward from Tower Bridge, the old docks have been regenerated into a modern landscape of glittering office developments. Most notable is Canary Wharf with its towering One Canada Square, the tallest building in Britain. The bright quayside building blocks are the new heart of modern Docklands, with the state-of-the-art elevated electric railway as its artery.

Greenwich

A quick 8-mi jaunt down the Thames will bring you past the National Maritime Museum and the *Cutty Sark* to Greenwich's Royal Observatory, where, if time stood still, all the world's timepieces would be off. When you tire of straddling the hemispheres at the Greenwich Meridian, take a stroll through the acres of parkland that cover the area or, on weekends, the crafts and antiques markets. Sir Christopher Wren's Royal Naval College and Inigo Jones's Queen House both scale architectural heights, while Richard Rogers's now-closed Millennium Dome encapsulates modern style, for better or worse. The pretty streets of Greenwich house numerous bookstores and antiques shops.

Hampstead

One of the great glories of England is the English village, and on the northern outskirts of London you'll find one of the most fetching: Hampstead. Today its classic Georgian houses, its picturesque tidiness, and its expensive French delicatessens attract personages from the arts and wealthy entrepreneurs. For sheer pleasure, exploring Hampstead is hard to top, as an amble along Church Row—possibly the finest (and certainly the prettiest) row of 18th-century houses in London—will prove. London's most beautiful painting by Vermeer is on view at Kenwood House (whose park hosts grand concerts and fireworks in the summer), and the latest Mod Brit artistic scandals are to be often seen at the Saatchi Collection. Here, too, are the Freud Museum and the Keats House; why not visit the garden where the poet penned his immortal "Ode to a Nightingale"? You can go bird-watching in the 800-plus emerald acres of Hampstead Heath. In the nearby neighborhood of St. John's Wood you can visit Abbey Road to snap the famed crossing outside the studios where John, Paul, George, and Ringo recorded nearly all their music.

Hyde Park, Kensington Gardens

When in need of elbow room, Londoners head for Hyde Park and Kensington Gardens. They form an open swath across central London; together with St. James's Park and Green Park, they make up almost 600 beauty-filled acres that offer a taste of serene remoteness from the great city. The handsome trees and quiet walks will refresh you as thoroughly as, centuries ago, these grounds refreshed Henry VIII after a hard day's shenanigans. In the Regency era, splendid horseflesh and equipages were the grand attraction; today, the soapbox orators at Hyde Park Corner (most oratorical on Sunday mornings) remain grand entertainment. Sooner or later everyone heads to the Long Water in Kensington Gardens for one of London's most beloved sights: the Peter Pan statue. Then circumnavigate the Round Pond, or swim in the Serpentine, or try to catch a glimpse of the Household Cavalry on Rotten Row.

Knightsbridge and Kensington

Within the district's cavalcade of streets lined with decorous houses are tucked-away corners—small squares that would not be out of place in a sleepy cathedral town; delightful pubs nestled away in back lanes; and antiques shops, their windows aglow with the luminous colors of oil paintings. Not surprisingly, the capital's snazziest department stores are also here, Harrods and Harvey Nichols. Head first for the area's main attraction, the great museum complex of South Kensington. Raphael and Constable canvases, Ossie Clark couture, and William Morris chairs all beckon at the Victoria and Albert Museum, whose forte is the decorative arts and whose predominant audience is an especially decorative crowd. Next to the V&A come two museums devoted to science, including the Natural History Museum. Most delightful are two historic homes: Leighton House, Lord Leighton's stunning Persian extravaganza, and the Linley Sambourne House, whose elegant Edwardian interiors were featured in *A Room with a View*. Regroup at Kensington Palace—its state rooms and royal dress collection are open to view—then repair to its elegant Orangery for a pot of Earl Grey.

Notting Hill and Holland Park

These are two of London's most fashionable, coveted residential areas. Notting Hill, around Portobello Road, is a trendsetting square mile of multiethnicity, galleries, small and exciting shops, and see-and-be-seen-in restaurants. The style-watching media dubbed the natives—musicians, novelists, and fashion plates—"Notting Hillbillies." If Notting Hill is for the young, neighboring Holland Park is entirely the opposite—the area's leafy streets are full of expensive white-stucco Victorians and lead to bucolic Holland Park itself.

Regent's Park

Helping to frame the northern border of the city, Regent's Park is home to the much-loved zoo and the much-loved Regent's Park Open-Air Theatre. A walk around the perimeter of the park is a must for devotees of classical architecture; the payoff is a view of John Nash's Terraces, a grandiose series of white-stucco terraced houses, built around 1810 for the "People of Quality" who demanded London homes as nearly as possible resembling their grand country estates. In summer, be sure to take in the rose-bedecked Queen Mary's Gardens. Next, head over to the open-air theater for, perhaps, a picture-perfect performance of *A Midsummer Night's Dream*. Year-round, the park is a favorite spot for mothers with strollers, joggers, and hand-holding senior citizens enjoying the fresh air. Watch out for airborne objects—softballs, footballs, and cricket balls.

St. James's and Mayfair

St. James's and Mayfair form the core of the West End, the city's smartest and most desirable central area—St. James's to the south of Piccadilly and north of the Mall, Mayfair to the north of Piccadilly and south of Oxford Street. Neither is stuffed with must-sees, though there is no shortage of history and gorgeous architecture, but they *are* custom-built for window-shopping, expansive strolling, and ogling the lifestyles of London's rich and famous—18th- *and* 21st-century versions. Although many will say Mayfair is only a state of mind, the heart of Mayfair has shifted from the 19th-century's Park Lane to Carlos Place and Mount Street. Of course, the shops of New and Old Bond streets lure the wealthy, but the window-shopping is next best to the real thing and is free. Mayfair is primarily residential, so its homes are off-limits except for two satisfyingly grand houses: Apsley House, the Duke of Wellington's home, built by Robert Adam in 1771 and once known as No. 1, London, and, on gorgeous Manchester Square, the Wallace Collection, situated in a palatial town house filled with Old Master paintings and fine French furniture. The district of St. James's—named after the centuries-old palace that lies at its center—remains the ultimate enclave of the old-fashioned gentleman's London. Here you'll find Pall Mall, with its many noted clubs, including the Reform Club—where Jules Verne's Phileas Fogg wagered he could go around the world in 80 days—and Jermyn Street, where you can follow in the Duke of Windsor's sartorial footsteps by purchasing a half-dozen shirts at Turnbull & Asser.

Soho and Theatreland

Once the setting for London's red-light district, Soho these days is more stylish than seedy, and it is now home to film and record bigwigs (Sir Paul McCartney's offices are here). The area is not especially rich architecturally, but it is nonetheless intriguing. The density of Continental residents around quaint Soho Square means some of London's best restaurants—whether pricey Italian, budget Chinese, or the latest opening—are in the vicinity. Shaftesbury Avenue cuts through the southern part of Soho; this is Theatreland—home to almost 50 West End theaters and beloved of those who love Shakespeare, Maggie Smith, and *Phantom*. To the south lie Leicester Square, London's answer to Times Square, and Charing Cross Road, the bibliophile's dream.

The South Bank

You won't say "How very British" in this section of town across the Thames from London Bridge, which was totally rebuilt after the bombs of World War II flattened the remains of medieval Southwark (only a few stones of the Bishop of Winchester's Palace still stand). If William Shakespeare returned today, however, he would be delighted to find a complete reconstruction of his Globe Theatre, which was inaugurated in 1996, not far from where the original closed in 1642. In fact, this side of the Thames—walk along the riverside embankment for great views of the city—has become a perch for diehard culture vultures: the Design Museum is here, and the gigantic Bankside Power Station building (hard by the Globe) has been refurbished as the Tate Modern. From here, the Millennium Bridge links new regeneration with the Old City at St. Paul's Cathedral. Also here is the South Bank Arts Complex—the country's chief arts center—with its Royal National Theatre, Royal Festival Hall, and London's culinary hot spot, the OXO Tower Restaurant and Brasserie. And who could resist the London Dungeon—a waxwork extravaganza full of scenes featuring plenty of blood 'n' guts—where "a perfectly horrible experience" is guaranteed. Now towering over all is the British Airways London Eye, the tallest observation wheel in Europe. Under its shadow in Jubilee Gardens is Waterloo Pier, where you can catch ferries that ply the Thames.

The Thames Upstream

London has been Britain's power center for centuries, so it is only natural that many visitable places associated with royalty and the ruling establishment—among them, Chiswick, Kew Gardens, Osterley Park, Richmond, and Putney—should be close to the capital. The link between London and these idyllic retreats is Father Thames—who offers a river cruise as a particularly nice way to escape the city on a sweltering summer day. These palaces and country houses are enveloped with serenity and rolling greenery, which explains the astronomical prices that some of the local real estate commands. Stroll around and just enjoy the rural air or find your way out of the famous maze at Hampton Court Palace, England's version of Versailles.

WHAT TO READ AND WATCH BEFORE YOU GO

London has been the focus of countless books and essays. For sonorous eloquence, you still must reach back more than half a century to Henry James's *English Hours* and Virginia Woolf's *The London Scene*. Today, most suggested reading lists begin with V. S. Pritchett's *London Perceived* and H. V. Morton's *In Search of London,* both decades old. Two more up-to-date books with a general compass are: John Russell's *London,* a sumptuously illustrated art book, and Christopher Hibbert's *In London: The Biography of a City.* Piet Schreuders's *The Beatles' London* follows the footsteps of the Fab Four, while Peter Ackroyd's *London: A Biography* digs deep into the past while keeping a foothold in today.

That noted, there are books galore on the various facets of the city. *The Art and Architecture of London* by Ann Saunders is fairly comprehensive. *Inside London: Discovering the Classic Interiors of London,* by Joe Friedman and Peter Aprahamian, has magnificent color photographs of hidden and overlooked shops, clubs, and town houses. For a wonderful take on the golden age of the city's regal mansions, see Christopher Simon Sykes's *Private Palaces: Life in the Great London Houses.* For various other aspects of the city, consult Mervyn Blatch's helpful *A Guide to London's Churches,* Andrew Crowe's *The Parks and Woodlands of London,* Sheila Fairfield's *The Streets of London,* Ann Saunders' *Regent's Park,* Ian Norrie's *Hampstead, Highgate Village, and Kenwood,* and Suzanne Ebel's *A Guide to London's Riverside: Hampton Court to Greenwich.* For the last word on just about every subject, see *The London Encyclopaedia,* edited by Ben Weinreb and Christopher Hibbert.

Of course, the history and spirit of the city are also to be found in celebrations of great authors, British heroes, and architects. Peter Ackroyd's massive *Dickens* elucidates how the great author shaped today's view of the city; Martin Gilbert's magisterial, multivolume *Churchill* traces the city through some of its greatest trials; J. Mansbridge's *John Nash* details the London buildings of this great architect.

Nineteenth-century London—the city of Queen Victoria, Tennyson, and Dickens—comes alive through *Mayhew's London,* a massive study of the London poor, and Gustave Doré's *London,* an unforgettable series of engravings of the city (often reprinted in modern editions) that detail its horrifying slums and grand avenues. When it comes to fiction, of course, Dickens's immortal works top the list. Stay-at-home detectives have long walked the streets of London, thanks to great mysteries with London settings by Sir Arthur Conan Doyle, Dorothy L. Sayers, Agatha Christie, Ngaio Marsh, and Antonia Fraser. For a little-known fictional account of London's most deadly villain, Jack the Ripper, read Marie Belloc-Lowndes's *The Lodger.*

There are any number of films—from *Waterloo Bridge* and *Georgy Girl* to *Secrets and Lies* and *Notting Hill*— that have used London as their setting. But always near the top of anyone's list are four films that rank among the greatest musicals of all time: Walt Disney's *Mary Poppins,* George Cukor's *My Fair Lady,* Sir Carol Reed's *Oliver!,* and the Beatles' *A Hard Day's Night.*

LONDON AT A GLANCE

This date table parallels events in London's history with events in the world at large, especially in the Americas, to give a sense of perspective to the chronology of London. The dates of British kings and queens are those of their reigns, not of their lives.

ca. 400 BC Early Iron Age hamlet built at Heathrow (now London airport)

54 BC Julius Caesar arrives with short-lived expedition

AD 43 Romans conquer Britain, led by the emperor Claudius

AD 60 Boudicca, queen of the Iceni, razes the first Roman Londinium

ca. 100 The Romans make Londinium center of their British activities, though not the capital

856 Alfred the Great (871–99), king of the West Saxons, "restored London and made it habitable"

1042 Edward the Confessor (1042–66) moves his court to Westminster and begins the reconstruction of the abbey and its monastic buildings

1066 William the Conqueror (1066–87), Duke of Normandy, wins the Battle of Hastings

1067 William grants London a charter confirming its rights and privileges

1078 The Tower of London begins with the building of the White Tower

1136 Fire destroys London Bridge (new one built 1176–1209)

1185 The Knights Templar build the New Temple by the Thames

1191 First mayor of London elected

1265 First Parliament held in Westminster Abbey Chapter House

1314 Old St. Paul's Cathedral completed

1327 Incorporation of first trade guilds (which govern the City for centuries)

1348–58 The Black Death strikes London; one-third of the population dies

1382 The Peasants' Revolt destroys part of the city

1411 The Guildhall (already centuries on the same site) rebuilt

1476 William Caxton (1422–91) introduces printing to England in Westminster

1529 Hampton Court given by Cardinal Wolsey to Henry VIII; it becomes a favorite royal residence

1568 Royal Exchange founded

1588 Preparations at Tilbury to repel the Spanish invasion; the Armada defeated in the Channel

1599 Shakespeare's Globe Theatre built on the South Bank

1603 Population of London more than 200,000

1605 Unsuccessful Gunpowder Plot to blow up the Houses of Parliament

1649 Charles I (1625–49) beheaded outside the Banqueting House on Whitehall

1658 Oliver Cromwell (Lord Protector) dies

1660 Charles II (1649–85) restored to the throne (the Restoration) after exile in Europe

1665 The Great Plague; deaths probably reach 100,000 (official figure for one week alone was 8,297)

1666 The Great Fire burns for three days; 89 churches and 13,200 houses destroyed over an area of 400 streets

1675 Sir Christopher Wren (1632–1723) begins work on the new St. Paul's Cathedral

1694 The Bank of England founded

1698 Whitehall Palace destroyed by fire

1732 No. 10 Downing Street becomes the prime minister's official residence

1739–53 Mansion House built

1755 Trooping the Colour first performed for George II

1762 George III (1760–1820) makes Buckingham Palace the royal residence

1802 First gaslights on London streets

1817 First Waterloo Bridge built

1827 Marble Arch erected (in 1851 moved to the northeast corner of Hyde Park)

1829–41 Trafalgar Square laid out

1834 The Houses of Parliament gutted by fire (the present Westminster Palace built 1840–52)

1837 Victoria (1837–1901) assumes the throne

1838 National Gallery opens in Trafalgar Square

1845 British Museum completed

1851 The Great Exhibition, Prince Albert's brainchild, held in the Crystal Palace, Hyde Park

1863 Arrival of the Underground (the tube), first train on the Metropolitan Line

1869 Albert Embankment completed, first stage in containing the Thames's floodwaters

1897 Queen Victoria celebrates her Diamond Jubilee

1901 Victoria dies, marking the end of an era; London's population reaches about 4,500,000

1914–18 World War I—London bombed (1915) by German zeppelins (355 incendiaries, 567 explosives; 670 killed, 1,962 injured)

1939–45 World War II—in air raids between September 1940 and July 1941, 45,000–50,000 bombs (including incendiaries) are dropped on London; 1944 Flying Bomb (Doodlebug) raids; 1945 V2 raids. Total casualties for the whole war, about 30,000 killed, more than 50,000 injured

1946 Heathrow Airport opens

1951 The Festival of Britain spurs postwar uplift

1953 Coronation of Queen Elizabeth II (born 1926)

1956 Clean Air Act abolishes open fires and makes London's mists and fogs a romantic memory

1965 Sir Winston Churchill's funeral, a great public pageant

1974 Covent Garden fruit-and-vegetable market moves across the Thames; the original area is remodeled

1976 Royal National Theatre opens on the South Bank

1977 Queen Elizabeth celebrates her Silver Jubilee

1981 National Westminster Tower, Britain's tallest building, opens in the City; Prince Charles marries Lady Diana Spencer in St. Paul's Cathedral

1983 The first woman lord mayor takes office

1984 The Thames Barrier, designed to prevent flooding in central London, is inaugurated

1986 The Greater London Council (the city's centralized municipal government) is abolished by Parliament; London's population now stands at approximately 6,696,000

1991 Cesar Pelli's Tower—1 Canada Square—opens at Canary Wharf and becomes Britain's tallest building

1994 The Channel Tunnel opens a direct rail link between Britain and Europe

1996 The Prince and Princess of Wales receive a precedent-breaking divorce

1997 Diana, Princess of Wales, dies at 36 in a car crash in Paris on August 31. The world mourns at her Westminster Abbey funeral, televised around the globe to almost 800 million viewers. She is buried at Althorp, the Spencer family estate in Northamptonshire

2000 London welcomes in the new century with the Millennium Dome

2001 The Millennium Dome closes, its future uncertain

2002 Queen Elizabeth celebrates her Golden Jubilee

London Postal Districts

SMART TRAVEL TIPS A TO Z

ADDRESSES

Central London and its surrounding districts are divided into 32 boroughs—33, counting the City of London. More useful for finding your way around, however, are the subdivisions of London into postal districts. Throughout the guide we've given the full postal code for most listings. The first one or two letters give the location: N means north, NW means northwest, etc. Don't expect the numbering to be logical, however. You won't, for example, find W2 next to W3. The general rule is that the lower numbers, such as W1 or SW1, are closest to the city center.

AIR TRAVEL TO AND FROM LONDON

BOOKING

When you book, **look for nonstop flights** and **remember that "direct" flights stop at least once.** Try to avoid connecting flights, which require a change of plane. For more booking tips and to check prices and make on-line flight reservations, log on to www.fodors.com.

CARRIERS

British Airways is the national flag carrier and offers mostly nonstop flights from 18 U.S. cities to Heathrow and Gatwick airports, along with flights to Manchester, Birmingham, and Glasgow. As the leading British carrier, it has a vast program of discount airfare-hotel packages.

➤ MAJOR AIRLINES: **American Airlines** (☎ 800/433–7300; 020/8572–5555 in London) to Heathrow, Gatwick. **British Airways** (☎ 800/247–9297; 0845/7222–1111 in London) to Heathrow, Gatwick. **Continental** (☎ 800/231–0856; 0800/776464 in London) to Gatwick. **Delta** (☎ 800/241–4141; 0800/414767 in London) to Gatwick. **Northwest Airlines**

(☎ 800/447–4747; 0870/507–4074 in London) to Gatwick. **United** (☎ 800/241–6522; 0845/844–4777 in London) to Heathrow. **TWA** (☎ 800/892–4141; 0345/333333 in London) to Gatwick. **Virgin Atlantic** (☎ 800/862–8621; 01293/747747 in London) to Heathrow, Gatwick.

CHECK-IN & BOARDING

Assuming that not everyone with a ticket will show up, airlines routinely overbook planes. When everyone does, airlines ask for volunteers to give up their seats. In return, these volunteers usually get a certificate for a free flight and are rebooked on the next flight out. If there are not enough volunteers, the airline must choose who will be denied boarding. The first to get bumped are passengers who checked in late and those flying on discounted tickets, so **get to the gate and check in as early as possible,** especially during peak periods. Allow time to get to the departure gate, particularly at Heathrow, where it can be a five-minute walk.

Always **bring a government-issued photo I.D. to the airport;** a passport is best. You may be asked to show it before you are allowed to check in.

CUTTING COSTS

The least expensive airfares to London must usually be purchased in advance and are non-refundable. It's smart to **call a number of airlines, and when you are quoted a good price, book it on the spot**—the same fare may not be available the next day. Always **check different routings** and look into using different airports. Travel agents, especially low-fare specialists (☞ Discounts & Deals, *below*), are helpful.

Consolidators are another good source. They buy tickets for scheduled international flights at reduced rates from the airlines, then sell them at prices that beat the best fare available directly from the airlines, usually without restrictions. Sometimes you can even get your money back if you need to return the ticket. Carefully read the fine print detailing penalties for changes and cancellations, and **confirm your consolidator reservation with the airline.**

➤ CONSOLIDATORS: **Cheap Tickets** (☎ 800/377–1000). **Discount Airline Ticket Service** (☎ 800/576–1600). **Unitravel** (☎ 800/325–2222). **Up & Away Travel** (☎ 212/889–2345). **World Travel Network** (☎ 800/409–6753).

ENJOYING THE FLIGHT

For more legroom, **request an emergency-aisle seat.** Don't sit in the row in front of the emergency aisle or in front of a bulkhead, where seats may not recline. If you have dietary concerns, **ask for special meals when booking.** On long flights, try to maintain a normal routine, to help fight jet lag. At night, **get some sleep.** By day, **eat light meals, drink water** (not alcohol), and **move around the cabin** to stretch your legs. For additional jet-lag tips consult *Fodor's FYI: Travel Fit & Healthy* (available at bookstores everywhere).

FLYING TIMES

Flying time to London is about 6½ hours from New York, 7½ hours from Chicago, 11 hours from San Francisco, and 21½ hours from Sydney.

HOW TO COMPLAIN

If your baggage goes astray or your flight goes awry, complain right away. Most carriers require that you **file a claim immediately.**

➤ AIRLINE COMPLAINTS: U.S. Department of Transportation **Aviation Consumer Protection Division** (✉ C-75, Room 4107, Washington, DC 20590, ☎ 202/366–2220, WEB www.dot.gov/airconsumer). **Federal Aviation Administration Consumer Hotline** (☎ 800/322–7873).

AIRPORTS & TRANSFERS

International flights to London arrive at either Heathrow Airport (LHR), 15 mi west of London, or at Gatwick Airport (LGW), 27 mi south of the capital. Most flights from the United States go to Heathrow, which is the busiest and is divided into four terminals, with Terminals 3 and 4 handling transatlantic flights (British Airways uses Terminal 4). Gatwick is London's second gateway. It has grown from a European airport into an airport that serves 21 scheduled U.S. destinations. A third, state-of-the-art airport, Stansted (STN), is 35 mi east of the city. It handles mainly European and domestic traffic, although there is also scheduled service from New York. The cost of hotels and car rentals varies little between Heathrow and Gatwick.

➤ AIRPORT INFORMATION: **Heathrow Airport** (☎ 0870/000–0123). **Gatwick Airport** (☎ 01293/535353). **Stansted Airport** (☎ 0870/000–0303).

AIRPORT TRANSFERS

London has excellent bus and train connections between its airports and downtown. If you're arriving at Heathrow, you can pick up a map and fare schedule at a London Transport (LT) Information Centre (in Terminals 1 and 2). Train service is direct and there are multistop train routes; the downside to this mode of transport is having to move around on escalators and connecting subways with luggage. Airport link buses may ease the luggage factor and drop you closer to central hotels, but they are subject to London traffic, which can be horrendous. Taxis can be more convenient, but beware that prices can go through the roof. Airport Travel Line has transfer information and takes advance booking for transfers between airports and into London.

Heathrow by Bus: Airbus A2 takes one hour and costs £7 one-way and £10 round-trip. It leaves for King's Cross and Euston, with stops at Marble Arch and Russell Square, every 30 minutes 6 AM–9:30 PM, but there are around 14 stops along the route, so it can be tedious. For the same price, National Express buses leave every 30 minutes to Victoria Coach Station direct from 5:40 AM–9:30 PM.

Heathrow by Train: the cheap, direct route into London is via the Piccadilly line of the Underground (London's extensive subway system, or "tube"). Trains run every four to eight minutes from all four terminals from early morning until just before midnight; the 50-minute trip costs £3.50 one-way and connects with other central tube lines. The Heathrow Express provides more comfort and speeds into London Paddington in 15 minutes, but is more expensive. Standard one-way tickets cost £12 (£22 round-trip) and £20 for first class (more space and TV screens). Service is daily, from 5:10 AM to 11:40 PM, with departures every 15 minutes.

Gatwick by Bus: You can make the 90-minute journey on Jetlink 777 from Gatwick South Terminal Coach Station to Victoria Coach Station (hourly, 4:15 AM–9:15 PM, £7 one-way, £10 round-trip), with stops at Marble Arch, Hyde Park Corner, Baker Street, Finchley Road, and Hendon Central.

Gatwick by Train: Fast, nonstop Gatwick Express leaves for Victoria Station every 15 minutes 5:20 AM–12 AM, then hourly 1:35 AM–5:20 AM. The 30-minute trip costs £10.20 one-way, £20.40 round-trip. A frequent local train also runs all night.

Stansted by Bus: Hourly bus service on Jetlink 777 (12:30 AM–11:30 PM) to Victoria Coach Station costs £8 one-way, £10 round-trip and takes about 1 hour and 40 minutes.

Stansted by Train: The Stansted Skytrain to Liverpool Street Station runs every half hour and costs £12 one-way, £22 round-trip.

Heathrow and Gatwick by Taxi: Taxis can get caught in traffic; the trip from Heathrow, for example, can take more than an hour and costs £30–£40. From Gatwick, the taxi fare is at least £50. Add a tip of 10 to 15% to the basic fare.

➤ TAXIS & SHUTTLES: **Airbus A2** (☎ 0870/574–7777). **Gatwick Express** (☎ 0870/530–1530). **Heathrow Express** (☎ 0845/600–1515). **Jetlink 777** (☎ 0870/574–7777). **National Express** (☎ 0870/580–8080). **Stansted Skytrain** (☎ 0845/748–4950).

➤ TRANSFER INFORMATION: **Airport Travel Line** (☎ 0870/574–7777).

DUTY-FREE SHOPPING

Heathrow, Gatwick, and Stansted have an overwhelming selection of duty-free shops, but the tax-free advantages are for travelers departing the United Kingdom for a country outside the European Union. For travel outside these countries, duty-free shopping is business as usual. For allowances, *see* Customs & Duties, *below*.

BUS TRAVEL TO AND FROM LONDON

National Express is the largest British coach operator and the nearest equivalent to Greyhound. It is fast (particularly its Rapide services, which do not detour to make pick-ups and have steward service for refreshments) and comfortable (all coaches have washroom facilities on board). Services depart mainly from Victoria Coach Station, a well-signposted short walk behind Victoria mainline rail station. The departures and main information point is situated on the corner of Buckingham Palace Road, while the arrivals point is opposite at Elizabeth Bridge. It's wise to arrive at least 30 minutes before departure so as to locate the correct exit gate (it's an extremely busy place at peak holiday and weekends). Smoking is not permitted on board.

Green Line serves the counties surrounding London, as well as airports. Bus stops (there is no garage) are on Buckingham Palace Road, between Victoria mainline station and Victoria Coach Station.

FARES & SCHEDULES

Tickets can be bought from the Victoria, Heathrow, or Gatwick coach stations by phone with a credit card, via the National Express Web Site, or from travel agencies. Apex tickets save money on standard fares, and traveling midweek is cheaper than over weekends and at holiday periods. Tourist Trail Passes, sold by British Travel International, make great savings if you plan to tour Britain, and they can be bought in advance. Prices run from £49 for two days of unlimited travel to £187 for 14 days of unlimited travel. The Discount Coachcard for students costs £8 and qualifies you for 20 to 30% off many standard fares over a one-year period.

➤ BUS INFORMATION: **British Travel International** (☎ 540/298–1395). **Green Line** (☎ 020/8668–7261). **National Express** (☎ 0870/580–8080, WEB gobycoach.com). **Victoria Coach Station** (✉ Buckingham Palace Rd., SW1).

BUS TRAVEL AROUND
LONDON

The red London Transport (LT) buses, which travel all over town, have been joined by the bright colors of other private bus companies that cover the suburbs. Bus stops are clearly indicated; the main stops have a red LT symbol on a plain white background. When the word "Request" is written across the sign, you must flag the bus down. Each numbered route is listed on the main stop, and buses have a large number on the front with their end destination. Not all buses run the full route at all times; check with the driver or conductor. If you want to decipher the numbers, pick up a free bus guide at an LT Travel Information Centre (at Euston, Hammersmith, King's Cross, Oxford Circus, Piccadilly Circus, St. James's Park, Victoria tube stations, and at Heathrow). Buses are a good way of seeing the town, particularly if you plan to hop on and off to cover many sights, but **don't take a bus if you are in a hurry.** To get off, pull the cord running above the windows on old buses, or press the button by the exit. Expect to get a little squashed during rush hours, from 8 AM to 9:30 AM and 4:30 PM to 6:30 PM.

Night Buses, denoted by the prefix "N" to their route numbers, run from 11 PM to 5 AM on a more restricted route than day buses. Fares are slightly higher, and Travelcard passes are not accepted. Avoid sitting alone on the top deck of a Night Bus; it gives a mugger an ideal opportunity.

FARES & SCHEDULES

All journeys within the central zone are £1, and all others outside are 70p. Travel from the outer to the central zone costs £1. If you plan to make a number of journeys in one day, con-

sider buying a discount pass (☞ Underground Tube Travel, *below*) good for both tube and bus travel. Traveling without a valid ticket makes you liable for a fine (£10 at press time). Buses are supposed to swing by every five or six minutes, but, in reality, you may wait 15 minutes or more.

➤ BUS INFORMATION: **LT Travel Information** (☎ 020/7222–1234).

PAYING

Payment is made to the driver as you enter (exact change is best so as to avoid incurring the driver's wrath). On some of the old buses, a conductor issues you a ticket from a grinder-like contraption strapped to his or her front.

SMOKING

There is a no-smoking policy on all buses.

BUSINESS HOURS

Generally, businesses are closed on Sundays and national (bank) holidays (☞ Holidays, *below*). New Year's Day is a national holiday, but many major stores are open for the annual sales reductions. Many restaurants are closed over the Christmas period.

BANKS & OFFICES

Banks are open weekdays 9:30–4:30; offices, 9:30–5:30.

GAS STATIONS

Most gas stations in central London are open seven days, 24 hours. As you get farther out of town, and off trunk/major roads, hours vary considerably depending on the gas company, but are usually 8 AM–8 PM.

MUSEUMS & SIGHTS

The major national museums and galleries are open daily, with shorter hours on weekends than weekdays. But there is a trend towards longer hours, such as one late-night opening a week.

PHARMACIES

Pharmacies are called chemists and are open, for the most part, Monday–Saturday 9:30 AM–5:30 PM. The leading chain drugstore, Boots, is open until 6 PM (the Oxford Street and Piccadilly Circus branches are also open Sunday and until 8 PM Thursday).

SHOPS

Shops and offices in central London tend to keep longer hours than those in the surrounding districts. Usual business hours are Monday–Saturday 9 AM–5:30 PM. In the main shopping streets of Oxford Street, Kensington High Street, and Knightsbridge, hours are 9:30 AM–6 PM, with late-night opening in Oxford Street on Thursday until 7:30–8 PM, and in the latter areas, on Wednesday. Many small general stores and newsagents stay open on Sunday; some chain and fashion stores in the tourist areas of Oxford Street and Piccadilly (and out-of-town shopping malls) also remain open.

CAMERAS & PHOTOGRAPHY

Don't be surprised if you are asked not to take pictures during theater, ballet, or opera productions, and in galleries, museums, and stately homes. Locals are generally happy to feature in your photos, but it's polite to ask if they mind before fixing the lens. There are many must-take sights in London, but guards on horseback in Whitehall and Big Ben are top of the list. The *Kodak Guide to Shooting Great Travel Pictures* (available at bookstores everywhere) is loaded with tips.

➤ PHOTO HELP: **Kodak Information Center** (☎ 800/242–2424).

EQUIPMENT PRECAUTIONS

Don't pack film and equipment in checked luggage, where it is much more susceptible to damage. X-ray machines used to view checked luggage are becoming much more powerful and therefore are much more likely to ruin your film. Always **keep film and tape out of the sun.** Carry an extra supply of batteries, and **be prepared to turn on your camera or camcorder** to prove to security personnel that the device is real. Always **ask for hand inspection of film,** which becomes clouded after repeated exposure to airport X-ray machines, and **keep videotapes away from metal detectors.**

FILM & DEVELOPING

Film is available from pharmacies, newsagents, and supermarkets, as well as photographic stores. Kodak and Agfa are the most common brands, and prices range from £2–£4 for a roll of 36-exposure color print film. Larger drugstore branches and photographic stores stock the Advantix line. These stores provide 24-hour film developing services.

VIDEOS

Videos from the U.S. are not compatible with British and European models. If you're bringing your own video-camcorder, bring a supply of cassettes as well.

CAR RENTAL

Rental rates in London vary widely and are expensive, beginning at £50 ($80) a day and £200 ($320) a week for a small economy car (such as a sub-compact General Motors Vauxhall, Corsa, or Renault Clio), usually with manual transmission. Air-conditioning and unlimited mileage generally come with the larger-size automatic cars.

➤ MAJOR AGENCIES: **Alamo** (☎ 800/522–9696; 020/8759–6200 in the U.K.). **Avis** (☎ 800/331–1084; 800/879–2847 in Canada; 02/9353–9000 in Australia; 09/525–1982 in New Zealand; 0870/606–0100 in the U.K.). **Budget** (☎ 800/527–0700; 0870/607–5000 in the U.K., through affiliate Europcar). **Dollar** (☎ 800/800–6000; 0124/622–0111 in the U.K., through affiliate Sixt Kenning; 02/9223–1444 in Australia). **Hertz** (☎ 800/654–3001; 800/263–0600 in Canada; 020/8897–2072 in the U.K.; 02/9669–2444 in Australia; 09/256–8690 in New Zealand) **National Car Rental** (☎ 800/227–7368; 020/8680–4800 in the U.K., where it is known as National Europe).

➤ LOCAL AGENCIES: **Dimple Car Hire** (✉ Poplar Pl., London W2 4AS, ☎ 020/7243–4400). **Enterprise** (✉ 466–480 Edgware Rd., London W2 1EL, ☎ 020/7723–4800). **Europcar** (✉ 30 Woburn Pl., London WC1H 0JR, ☎ 020/7255–2339).

CUTTING COSTS

To get the best deal, **book through a travel agent who will shop around.**

Do **look into wholesalers,** companies that do not own fleets but rent in bulk from those that do and often offer better rates than traditional car-rental operations. It's far cheaper to **arrange for car rental from the U.S. before you arrive,** or an inclusive fly-drive package. Payment must be made before you leave home.

➤ WHOLESALERS: **Auto Europe** (☎ 207/842–2000 or 800/223–5555, FAX 800/235–6321, WEB www. autoeurope.com). **Europe by Car** (☎ 212/581–3040 or 800/223–1516, FAX 212/246–1458, WEB www. europebycar.com). **DER Travel Services** (✉ 9501 W. Devon Ave., Rosemont, IL 60018, ☎ 800/782–2424, FAX 800/282–7474 for information; 800/860–9944 for brochures, WEB www.dertravel.com). **Kemwel Holiday Autos** (☎ 800/678–0678, FAX 914/825–3160, WEB www.kemwel.com).

INSURANCE

When driving a rented car you are generally responsible for any damage to or loss of the vehicle. Before you rent, see what coverage your personal auto-insurance policy and credit cards provide—you may already be covered. Note that collision policies sold by car-rental companies for European rentals usually do not include stolen-vehicle coverage.

REQUIREMENTS & RESTRICTIONS

In London your own driver's license is acceptable (as long as you are over 23 years old, with no endorsements or driving convictions). An International Driver's Permit is a good idea; it's available from the American or Canadian Automobile Association and, in the United Kingdom, from the Automobile Association or Royal Automobile Club. International permits are universally recognized, and having one may save you a problem with the local authorities.

SURCHARGES

Before you pick up a car in one city and leave it in another, **ask about drop-off charges or one-way service fees,** which can be substantial. Note,

too, that some rental agencies charge extra if you return the car before the time specified in your contract. To avoid a hefty refueling fee, **fill the tank just before you turn in the car,** but be aware that gas stations near the rental outlet may overcharge.

CAR TRAVEL

The best advice on driving in London is: don't. London's streets are a winding mass of chaos, aggravated by one-way streets. Parking is also restrictive and expensive, and traffic is tediously slow at most times of the day; during rush hours—from 8 AM to 9:30 AM and 4:30 PM to 6:30 PM—it often grinds to a standstill, particularly on Friday, when everyone wants to leave town. The center shopping areas are to be avoided, including the roads feeding Oxford Street, Kensington, and Knightsbridge. Other main roads into the city center are also busy, such as King's Cross and Euston in the north. Watch out also for cyclists and motorcycle couriers who weave between cars and pedestrians and seem to come out of nowhere.

Remember that Britain drives on the left, and the rest of Europe on the right. Therefore, you may want to leave your rented car in Britain and pick up a left-side drive if you cross the Channel (☞ The Channel Tunnel, *below*).

EMERGENCY SERVICES

The general procedure for a breakdown is the following: position the red hazard triangle (which should be in the trunk of the car) a few paces away from the rear of the car. Leave the hazard warning lights on. If you are on a highway (motorway), emergency roadside telephone booths are positioned at intervals within walking distance. Contact the car rental company, or an auto club. The main automobile help groups in the U.K. are the Automobile Association (A.A.) and the Royal Automobile Club (R.A.C.) If you are a member of the American Automobile Association (A.A.A.) check your membership details before you depart for Britain as, under a reciprocal agreement, roadside assistance in the U.K. should cost you nothing. You can join and receive roadside assistance from the A.A. on the spot, but the charge is higher—around £75—than a simple membership fee.

► CONTACTS: **American Automobile Association** (☎ 800/564–6222). **Australian Automobile Association** (☎ 02/6247–7311). **Automobile Association** (☎ 0870/550–0600 or ☎ 0800/887766 for emergency roadside assistance). **Canadian Automobile Association** (☎ 613/247–0117). **New Zealand Automobile Association** (☎ 09/377–4660). **Royal Automobile Club** (☎ 0870/572–2722).

GASOLINE

Gasoline (petrol) is sold in liters and is increasingly expensive (85p per liter at press time). Unleaded petrol is predominant, denoted by green pump lines. Premium and Super Premium are the two varieties, and most cars run on regular premium. Supermarket pumps usually offer the best value, although they are often on the edge of the central city. You won't find too many service stations in the center of town; these are generally on main, multi-carriageway trunk roads out of the center. Service is self-serve, except in small villages, and these gas stations are likely to be closed on Sundays and late evening. Most accept major credit cards.

PARKING

During the day—and probably at all times—it is safest to believe that you can park nowhere except at a meter, in a garage, or where you are sure there are no lines or signs; otherwise, you run the risk of a towing cost of about £100 or a wheel clamp, which costs about the same, since you pay to have the clamp removed plus the cost of the one or two tickets you'll have earned first. Restrictions are indicated by the NO WAITING parking signpost on the sidewalk (these restrictions vary from street to street), and restricted areas include single yellow lines or double yellow lines. Parking at a bus stop or in a red-lined bus lane is also restricted. It is illegal to park on the sidewalk, across entrances, or on white zigzag lines approaching a pedestrian crossing.

Meters have an insatiable hunger in the inner city—a 20p piece buys just six minutes—and some will only permit a two-hour stay, with no return to top up. Meters take 10p, 20p, 50p, and £1 coins. In the evening, after restrictions end, meter bays are free. Daytime, take advantage of the many N.C.P. parking lots in the center of town, which are often better value (about £2.50–£3 per hour, up to 8 hours). A London street map should have the parking lots marked. The *London Parking Guide* (£4.99, Two Heads Publishing) provides indispensable advice.

RULES OF THE ROAD

If you must risk life and limb and drive in London, note that the speed limit is 30 mph in the royal parks, as well as in all streets—unless you see the large 40 mph signs (and small repeater signs attached to lampposts) found only in the suburbs. Other basic rules: pedestrians have right-of-way on "zebra" crossings (black and white stripes that stretch across the street between two Belisha beacons—orange-flashing globe lights on posts) and it is illegal to pass another vehicle at a zebra crossing. At other crossings pedestrians must yield to traffic, but they do have right-of-way over traffic turning left at controlled crossings—if they have the nerve.

Traffic lights sometimes have arrows directing left or right turns; try to catch a glimpse of the road markings in time, and don't get into the turn lane if you mean to go straight ahead. A right turn is not permitted on a red light. On designated bus lanes a sign at the beginning and end gives the time restrictions for use—usually during peak hours—if you are caught, you could be fined. The use of horns is prohibited between 11:30 PM and 7 AM. Seat belts are to be worn by law in the front and the back seats. Drunk-driving laws are strictly enforced and it is far safer to avoid alcohol altogether. The legal limit is 80 milligrams of alcohol, which roughly translated means two units of alcohol—two glasses of wine, one pint of beer, or one glass of whiskey.

THE CHANNEL TUNNEL

Short of flying, the "Chunnel" is the fastest way to cross the English Channel: 35 minutes from Folkestone to Calais, 60 minutes from motorway to motorway, or 3 hours from London's Waterloo Station to Paris's Gare du Nord.

➤ CAR TRANSPORT: **Le Shuttle** (☎ 0870/535–3535 in the U.K.).

➤ PASSENGER SERVICE: In the U.K.: **Eurostar** (☎ 0870/518–6186), **Inter-City Europe** (☎ 0870/584–8848 for credit-card bookings). In the U.S.: **BritRail Travel** (☎ 800/677–8585), **Rail Europe** (☎ 800/942–4866).

CHILDREN IN LONDON

There is a kaleidoscope of activity for children to enjoy in London, and museums and major attractions have made great strides in special interactive features and trails (particularly during summer and Christmas holidays). At many museums children now enjoy free admission, and between the great establishments there are masses of green spaces in the London parks. During the school holiday time, bookstores run story times; cinemas, concert halls, and theaters have plenty of programs to watch—and join in on. When packing, include things to keep children busy en route. If you are renting a car, don't forget to **arrange for a car seat** when you reserve. For general advice about traveling with children, consult *Fodor's FYI: Travel with Your Baby* (available in bookstores everywhere).

Up-to-date information is available in *Kids Out!* magazine, available monthly at better newsstands (£2.25) from the *Time Out* weekly listings stable. *Fodor's Around London with Kids* (available in bookstores everywhere) can help you plan your days together.

➤ LOCAL INFORMATION: *Kids Out!* (☎ 020/7813–6018). **Visitorcall** ("What's on for Children," ☎ 09064/123404 or "Places for Children to Go," ☎ 09064/123424).

BABY-SITTING

➤ AGENCIES: **Childminders** (☎ 020/7935–3000). **Nanny Connection** (✉ Collier House, 163–169 Brompton Rd., London SW3 1PY, ☎ 020/7591–4488). **The Nanny Service** (✉ 6 Nottingham St., London W1M 3RB, ☎ 020/7935–3515). **Universal Aunts**

(✉ Box 304, London SW4 0NN, ☎ 020/7738–8937).

FLYING TO LONDON

If your children are two or older, **ask about children's airfares.** As a general rule, infants under two not occupying a seat fly at greatly reduced fares or even for free. When booking, **confirm carry-on allowances** if you're traveling with infants. In general, for babies charged 10% of the adult fare you are allowed one carry-on bag and a collapsible stroller; if the flight is full, the stroller may have to be checked or you may be limited to less.

Experts agree that it's a good idea to use safety seats aloft for children weighing less than 40 pounds. Airlines set their own policies: U.S. carriers usually require that the child be ticketed, even if he or she is young enough to ride free, since the seats must be strapped into regular seats. Do **check your airline's policy about using safety seats during takeoff and landing.** And since safety seats are not allowed everywhere in the plane, get your seat assignments early.

When reserving, **request children's meals or a freestanding bassinet** if you need them. But note that bulk-head seats, where you must sit to use the bassinet, may lack an overhead bin or storage space on the floor.

FOOD

Chinatown is welcoming to children—as well as a colorful and interesting experience—and the many Italian restaurants and pasta and pizza places are practical. The key is to avoid the high-class establishments unless your children behave impeccably; you won't find a children's menu there, anyway. The Pizza Express chain is family-friendly. At Smollensky's Balloon and Sweeny Todd's, clowns and magicians provide entertainment on the weekends. Hard Rock Cafe and Capital Radio Café have lively, musical atmospheres. The Rainforest Café has waterfalls and thundering jungle fun. Babe Ruth is sporty with screens showing baseball coverage.

➤ BEST CHOICES: **Babe Ruth** (✉ O2 Centre, Finchley Rd., NW3, ☎ 020/

7433–3388). **Capital Radio Café** (✉ Leicester Sq., WC2, ☎ 020/7484–8888). **Hard Rock Cafe** (✉ 150 Old Park La., W1, ☎ 020/7629–0382). **Rainforest Café** (✉ 20 Shaftesbury Ave., W1, ☎ 020/7434–3111). **Smollensky's Balloon** (✉ 1 Dover St., W1, ☎ 020/7491–1199). **Sweeny Todd's** (✉ 3–5 Tooley St., SE1, ☎ 020/7407–5267).

LODGING

Most hotels in London allow children under a certain age to stay in their parents' room at no extra charge, but others charge for them as extra adults; be sure to **find out the cutoff age for children's discounts.**

The following hotels offer family rooms and/or cots, babysitting service, and children's portions and high chairs in the restaurant.

➤ BEST CHOICES: **Basil Street Hotel** (✉ Basil St., Knightsbridge, SW3 1AH, ☎ 020/7581–3311). **Edward Lear** (✉ 30 Seymour St., Bayswater, W1H 5WD, ☎ 020/7402–5401).**Elizabeth Hotel** (✉ 37 Eccleston Sq., Victoria, SW1V 1PB, ☎ 020/7828–6814). **Forte Hotels** (☎ 0345/404040 central reservations). **Forte Posthouse Kensington** (✉ Wrights La., W8 5SP, ☎ 020/7937–8170). **66 Camden Square** (✉ Camden, NW1 9XD, ☎ 020/7485–4622).

SIGHTS & ATTRACTIONS

The Tower of London, Tower Bridge Experience, London Dungeon, Madame Tussaud's, the Natural History Museum, and Pollock's Toy Museum are just a handful of sights to excite children. Places that are especially appealing to children are indicated by a rubber-duckie icon (🦆) in the margin.

TRANSPORTATION

On trains and buses, children pay half or reduced fares; children under five go for free. Car rental companies may have child seats available. By law, where there are seat belts in front and back, children must use them, but it is the responsibility of the driver to ensure that they do. Children do not need a child seat if they are over age five and are 1.5 m in height, but they must wear an adult seat belt. Children must be three to sit in the front seat, and if under 1.5 m in height will need a child seat or adult strap, whichever is available.

COMPUTERS ON THE ROAD

If you're traveling with a laptop, carry a spare battery and adapter: new batteries and replacement adapters are expensive, although if you do need to replace them head to Tottenham Court Road (W1), which is lined with computer specialists. John Lewis department store and Selfridges, on Oxford Street (W1), also carry a limited range. Never plug your computer into any socket before asking about surge protection. Some hotels do not have built-in current stabilizers, and extreme electrical fluctuations and surges can short your adapter or even destroy your computer. IBM sells an invaluable pen-size modem tester that plugs into a telephone jack to check if the line is safe to use.

CONCIERGES

Concierges, found in many hotels, can help you with theater tickets and dinner reservations: a good one with connections may be able to get you seats for a hot show or a table at the restaurant of the moment. You can also turn to your hotel's concierge for help with travel arrangements, sightseeing plans, services ranging from aromatherapy to zipper repair, and emergencies. Always, **always tip** a concierge who has been of assistance (☞ Tipping, *below*).

CONSUMER PROTECTION

Whenever shopping or buying travel services in London, **pay with a major credit card,** if possible, so you can cancel payment or get reimbursed if there's a problem. If you're doing business with a particular company for the first time, **contact your local Better Business Bureau and the attorney general's offices** in your state and (for U.S. businesses) the company's home state as well. Have any complaints been filed? Finally, if you're buying a package or tour, always **consider travel insurance** that includes default coverage (☞ Insurance, *below*).

➤ BBBs: **Council of Better Business Bureaus** (✉ 4200 Wilson Blvd., Suite 800, Arlington, VA 22203, ☎ 703/

276–0100, FAX 703/525–8277, WEB www.bbb.org).

CUSTOMS & DUTIES

When shopping, **keep receipts** for all purchases. Upon reentering the country, **be ready to show customs officials what you've bought.** If you feel a duty is incorrect or object to the way your clearance was handled, note the inspector's badge number and ask to see a supervisor. If the problem isn't resolved, write to the appropriate authorities, beginning with the port director at your point of entry.

IN AUSTRALIA

Australian residents who are 18 or older may bring home $A400 worth of souvenirs and gifts (including jewelry), 250 cigarettes or 250 grams of tobacco, and 1,125 ml of alcohol (including wine, beer, and spirits). Residents under 18 may bring back $A200 worth of goods. Prohibited items include meat products. Seeds, plants, and fruits need to be declared upon arrival.

➤ INFORMATION: **Australian Customs Service** (Regional Director, ✉ Box 8, Sydney, NSW 2001, Australia, ☎ 02/9213–2000, FAX 02/9213–4000, WEB www.customs.gov.au).

IN CANADA

Canadian residents who have been out of Canada for at least seven days may bring home C$500 worth of goods duty-free. If you've been away fewer than seven days but more than 48 hours, the duty-free allowance drops to C$200; if your trip lasts 24–48 hours, the allowance is C$50. You may not pool allowances with family members. Goods claimed under the C$500 exemption may follow you by mail; those claimed under the lesser exemptions must accompany you. Alcohol and tobacco products may be included in the seven-day and 48-hour exemptions but not in the 24-hour exemption. If you meet the age requirements of the province or territory through which you reenter Canada, you may bring in, duty-free, 1.14 liters (40 imperial ounces) of wine or liquor or 24 12-ounce cans or bottles of beer or ale. If you are 16 or older you may bring in, duty-free,

200 cigarettes and 50 cigars. Check ahead of time with Revenue Canada or the Department of Agriculture for policies regarding meat products, seeds, plants, and fruits.

You may send an unlimited number of gifts worth up to C$60 each duty-free to Canada. Label the package UNSOLICITED GIFT—VALUE UNDER $60. Alcohol and tobacco are excluded.

➤ INFORMATION: **Revenue Canada** (✉ 2265 St. Laurent Blvd. S, Ottawa, Ontario K1G 4K3, Canada, ☎ 613/993–0534; 800/461–9999 in Canada, FAX 613/991–4126, WEB www.ccra-adrc.gc.ca).

IN NEW ZEALAND

Homeward-bound residents 17 or older may bring back $700 worth of souvenirs and gifts. Your duty-free allowance also includes 4.5 liters of wine or beer; one 1,125-ml bottle of spirits; and either 200 cigarettes, 250 grams of tobacco, 50 cigars, or a combination of the three up to 250 grams. Prohibited items include meat products, seeds, plants, and fruits.

➤ INFORMATION: **New Zealand Customs** (Custom House, ✉ 50 Anzac Ave., Box 29, Auckland, New Zealand, ☎ 09/300–5399, FAX 09/359–6730, WEB www.customs.govt.nz).

IN THE U.K.

There are two levels of duty-free allowance for entering Britain: one for goods bought outside the European Union (E.U.) and the other for goods bought within the E.U. (Austria, Belgium, Denmark, Finland, France, Germany, Greece, the Irish Republic, Italy, Luxembourg, the Netherlands, Portugal, Spain, and Sweden).

Of goods bought outside the E.U. you may import duty-free: 200 cigarettes or 100 cigarillos or 50 cigars or 250 grams of tobacco; 2 liters of table wine and, in addition, (a) 1 liter of alcohol over 22% by volume (most spirits), (b) 2 liters of alcohol under 22% by volume (fortified or sparkling wine or liqueurs), or (c) 2 more liters of table wine; 60 milliliters of perfume; ¼ liter (250 ml) of toilet water; and other goods up to a value of

£145, but not more than 50 liters of beer or 25 cigarette lighters.

Of goods bought within the E.U., you should not exceed (unless you can prove they are for personal use): 800 cigarettes, 400 cigarillos, 200 cigars, and 1 kilogram of tobacco, plus 10 liters of spirits, 20 liters of fortified wine, 90 liters of wine, and 110 liters of beer.

No animals or pets of any kind can be brought in without a lengthy quarantine. The penalties are severe and are strictly enforced. Similarly, fresh meats, plants and vegetables, controlled drugs, and firearms and ammunition may not be brought into the U.K.

➤ INFORMATION: **HM Customs and Excise** (Customer Helpline, ☎ 0345/442236).

IN THE U.S.

U.S. residents who have been out of the country for at least 48 hours (and who have not used the $400 allowance or any part of it in the past 30 days) may bring home $400 worth of foreign goods duty-free.

U.S. residents 21 and older may bring back 1 liter of alcohol duty-free. In addition, regardless of your age, you are allowed 200 cigarettes and 100 non-Cuban cigars. Antiques, which the U.S. Customs Service defines as objects more than 100 years old, enter duty-free, as do original works of art done entirely by hand, including paintings, drawings, and sculptures.

You may also mail or ship packages home duty-free: up to $200 worth of goods for personal use, with a limit of one parcel per addressee per day (except alcohol or tobacco products or perfume worth more than $5); label the package PERSONAL USE and attach a list of its contents and their retail value. Do not label the package UNSOLICITED GIFT or your duty-free exemption will drop to $100. Mailed items do not affect your duty-free allowance on your return.

➤ INFORMATION: **U.S. Customs Service** (✉ 1300 Pennsylvania Ave. NW, Washington, DC 20229, inquiries ☎ 202/354–1000, WEB www.

customs.gov; complaints c/o ✉ 1300 Pennsylvania Ave. NW, Room 5.4D, Washington, DC 20229; registration of equipment c/o ✉ Resource Management, ☎ 202/927–0540).

DINING

The restaurants we list are the cream of the crop in each price category. Restaurants are indicated in the text by ✕.

CATEGORY	COST*
££££	over £22
£££	£16–£22
££	£9–£15
£	under £9

per person for a main course at dinner, excluding drinks, service, and VAT

MEALS & SPECIALTIES

In London, local could mean any global flavor, but for pure Britishness, roast beef probably tops the list. If you want the best-value traditional Sunday lunch, go to a pub. The traditional accompaniment of Yorkshire pudding is a savory batter baked in the oven until crisp, served with a rich dark gravy. More tummy liners include: shepherd's pie, made with stewed minced lamb and a mashed potato topping, baked until lightly browned on top. Steak and kidney pie is chunks of beef and pigs' kidneys braised in a thick gravy and topped with a light puff-pastry crust. Sweet bread-and-butter pudding is served hot, the layers of bread and dried fruit baked in a creamy custard until lightly crisp. The fish in fish-and-chips is usually cod or haddock, served with thick chips. A ploughman's lunch in a pub is crusty bread, English cheese (strong flavored with bite—cheddar, blue Stilton, crumbly white Cheshire, smooth red Leicester), and pickles with a side salad garnish. English cream tea consists of scones served with jam and thick cream and sandwiches made with wafer-thin slices of cucumber—and of course plenty of tea.

MEALTIMES

In London, you could find breakfast all day, and perhaps all night, but it is generally served between 7:30 and 10. Workmen's cafés and sandwich bars for office workers are sometimes open from 7:30, smarter cafés from 9–

10:30. Lunch is between noon and 2 and restaurant sittings will be booked within that time. Tea—often a meal in itself—is taken between 4 and 5:30, dinner or supper between 7:30 and 9:30, sometimes earlier. In London's theaterland, 6–6:30 is the time for pre-theater suppers, and 10 onwards for post-theater meals. Many ethnic restaurants, especially Indian, serve food until midnight. Sunday is proper lunch day, and some restaurants will open for lunch only. Unless otherwise noted, the restaurants listed in this guide are open daily for lunch and dinner, but some restaurants do not open on Sundays (or Mondays—a fish-and-chip shop worth its salt will not be open on Monday) at all.

PAYING

American Express, Diner's Club, MasterCard, and Visa are accepted almost everywhere, but a pub, small café, or ethnic restaurant (such as Indian or Chinese) might not take credit cards.

RESERVATIONS & DRESS

Reservations are always a good idea: we mention them only when they're essential or not accepted. Book as far ahead as you can, and reconfirm as soon as you arrive. We mention dress only when men are required to wear a jacket or a jacket and tie.

WINE, BEER & SPIRITS

The cheapest and best range of alcohol is in the supermarkets, but in the middle of town, go to an informative, friendly wine merchant, or off-license shop, such as Oddbin's, which sells wine from around the world, and beer, too. For beer, bitters, or ale, go to a pub.

DISABILITIES & ACCESSIBILITY

Compared to New York City, London has a way to go in helping people with disabilities, but it is moving toward making the city more accessible. Many of the tourist attractions and hotels are updating facilities, although traveling around is a problem. Here are organizations to help and advise.

➤ LOCAL RESOURCES: **Artsline** (☎ 020/7388–2227). **Holiday Care Service** (✉ Imperial Building, Victoria Rd., Horley, Surrey RH6 7PZ, ☎ 01293/774535). **London Transport's Unit for Disabled Passengers** (✉ 172 Buckingham Palace Rd., London SW1W 9TN, ☎ 020/7918–3312). **Royal Association for Disability and Rehabilitation** (RADAR, ✉ 12 City Forum, 250 City Rd., London EC1, ☎ 020/7250–3222). **Tripscope** (☎ 020/8580–7021).

LODGING

If you book directly through Holiday Care (☞ *above*), rates at some hotels with special facilities can be discounted.

➤ BEST CHOICES: **Copthorne Tara Hotel** (✉ Scarsdale Pl., Kensington, W8, ☎ 020/7937–7211). **Thistle Marble Arch** (✉ Bryanston St., W1, ☎ 020/7629–8040).

RESERVATIONS

When discussing accessibility with an operator or reservations agent, **ask hard questions.** Are there any stairs, inside *or* out? Are there grab bars next to the toilet *and* in the shower/tub? How wide is the doorway to the room? To the bathroom? For the most extensive facilities meeting the latest legal specifications, **opt for newer accommodations.**

SIGHTS & ATTRACTIONS

Tour Guides Ltd. can tailor a tour for you. The London Tourist Board has details of more easily accessible attractions. Suggested sights might include: London Planetarium, London Transport Museum, London Zoo, National Portrait Gallery, and Natural History Museum.

➤ CONTACTS: **Tour Guides Ltd.** (☎ 020/7495–5504).

TRANSPORTATION

London cabs have spacious interiors for wheelchair users. For other information, *see* Local Resources, *above*.

➤ COMPLAINTS: **Aviation Consumer Protection Division** (☞ Air Travel to and from London, *above*). **Civil Rights Office** (✉ U.S. Department of Transportation, Departmental Office of Civil Rights, S-30, 400 7th St. SW, Room 10215, Washington, DC 20590, ☎ 202/366–4648, FAX 202/366–9371, WEB www.dot.gov/ost/docr/

index.htm) for problems with surface transportation. **Disability Rights Section** (✉ U.S. Department of Justice, Civil Rights Division, Box 66738, Washington, DC 20035-6738, ☎ 202/514–0301 or 800/514–0301; 202/514–0383 TTY; 800/514–0383 TTY, FAX 202/307–1198, WEB www.usdoj.gov/crt/ada/adahom1.htm) for general complaints.

TRAVEL AGENCIES

In the United States, the Americans with Disabilities Act requires that travel firms serve the needs of all travelers. Some agencies specialize in working with people with disabilities.

➤ TRAVELERS WITH MOBILITY PROBLEMS: **Access Adventures** (✉ 206 Chestnut Ridge Rd., Scottsville, NY 14624, ☎ 716/889–9096, dltravel@prodigy.net), run by a former physical-rehabilitation counselor. **CareVacations** (✉ 5-5110 50th Ave., Leduc, Alberta T9E 6V4, Canada, ☎ 780/986–6404 or 877/478–7827, FAX 780/986–8332, WEB www.carevacations.com), for group tours and cruise vacations. **Flying Wheels Travel** (✉ 143 W. Bridge St., Box 382, Owatonna, MN 55060, ☎ 507/451–5005 or 800/535–6790, FAX 507/451–1685, WEB www.flyingwheelstravel.com).

➤ TRAVELERS WITH DEVELOPMENTAL DISABILITIES: **New Directions** (✉ 5276 Hollister Ave., Suite 207, Santa Barbara, CA 93111, ☎ 805/967–2841 or 888/967–2841, FAX 805/964–7344, WEB www.newdirectionstravel.com).

DISCOUNTS & DEALS

Be a smart shopper and **compare all your options** before making decisions. A plane ticket bought with a promotional coupon from travel clubs, coupon books, and direct-mail offers or on the Internet may not be cheaper than the least expensive fare from a discount ticket agency. And always keep in mind that what you get is just as important as what you save.

DISCOUNT RESERVATIONS

To save money, **look into discount reservations services** with toll-free numbers, which use their buying power to get a better price on hotels, airline tickets, even car rentals. When booking a room, always **call the hotel's local toll-free number** (if one is available) rather than the central reservations number—you'll often get a better price. Always ask about special packages or corporate rates.

When shopping for the best deal on hotels and car rentals, **look for guaranteed exchange rates,** which protect you against a falling dollar. With your rate locked in, you won't pay more, even if the price goes up in the local currency.

➤ AIRLINE TICKETS: ☎ **800/FLY-ASAP.**

➤ HOTEL ROOMS: **Hotel Reservations Network** (☎ 800/964–6835, WEB www.hoteldiscount.com). **International Marketing & Travel Concepts** (☎ 800/790–4682, imtc@mindspring.com). **Players Express Vacations** (☎ 800/458–6161, WEB www.playersexpress.com). **Steigenberger Reservation Service** (☎ 800/223–5652, WEB www.srs-worldhotels.com). **Travel Interlink** (☎ 800/888–5898, WEB www.travelinterlink.com). **Turbotrip.com** (☎ 800/473–7829, WEB www.turbotrip.com).

PACKAGE DEALS

Don't confuse packages and guided tours. When you buy a package, you travel on your own, just as though you had planned the trip yourself. Fly/drive packages, which combine airfare and car rental, are often a good deal. Discount passes, such as London Pass, are available from the Britain Visitor Centre and Tourist Information Centre branches; many offer local transportation, entrance to museums, movie theaters, and galleries, and tours at considerable savings.

If you **buy a rail/drive pass,** you may save on train tickets and car rentals. All Eurail- and Europass holders get a discount on Eurostar fares through the Channel Tunnel.

ELECTRICITY

To use electric-powered equipment purchased in the U.S. or Canada, **bring a converter and adapter.** The electrical current in London is 220/240 volts (coming into line with the rest of Europe at 230 volts), 50 cycles alternating current (AC); wall outlets take three-pin plugs, and shaver sockets take two round, oversize prongs.

If your appliances are dual-voltage, you'll need only an adapter. Don't use 110-volt outlets marked FOR SHAVERS ONLY for high-wattage appliances such as blow-dryers. Most laptops operate equally well on 110 and 220 volts and so require only an adapter. For converters, adapters, and advice, contact the British Airways Travel Shop.

➤ CONTACTS: **British Airways Travel Shop** (✉ 156 Regent St., W1, ☎ 020/ 7434–4725).

EMBASSIES

➤ AUSTRALIA: **Australia House** (✉ Strand, WC2, ☎ 020/7379–4334).

➤ CANADA: **MacDonald House** (✉ 1 Grosvenor Sq., W1, ☎ 020/7258– 6600).

➤ NEW ZEALAND: **New Zealand House** (✉ 80 Haymarket, SW1, ☎ 020/7930–8422).

➤ UNITED STATES: **U.S. Embassy** (✉ 24 Grosvenor Sq., W1, ☎ 020/7499– 9000); for passports, go to the **U.S. Passport Unit** (✉ 55 Upper Brook St., W1, ☎ 020/7499–9000).

EMERGENCIES

If you need to report a theft or an attack (London is a relatively safe city) go to the nearest police station (listed in the Yellow Pages or the local directory). For severe emergencies, dial 999 for police, fire, or ambulance (be prepared to give the telephone number you're calling from). National Health Service hospitals give free, 24-hour treatment in Accident and Emergency sections, where delays can be an hour or more. Prescriptions are valid only if made out by doctors registered in the U.K.

➤ DOCTORS & DENTISTS: **Dental Emergency Care Service** (☎ 020/ 7955–2186). **Doctor's Call** (☎ 020/ 8900–1000). **Eastman Dental Hospital** (✉ 256 Gray's Inn Rd., WC1, ☎ 020/7915–1000). **Medical Express** (✉ 117A Harley St., W1, ☎ 020/ 7499–1991).

➤ HOSPITALS: **Charing Cross Hospital** (✉ Fulham Palace Rd., W6, ☎ 020/

8846–1234). **Royal Free Hospital** (✉ Pond St., Hampstead NW3, ☎ 020/7794–0500). **St. Thomas' Hospital** (✉ Lambeth Palace Rd., SE1, ☎ 020/7928–9292). **University College Hospital** (✉ Grafton Way, WC1, ☎ 020/7387–9300).

➤ HOT LINES: **Samaritans** (☎ 020/ 7734–2800). **Victim Support** (☎ 020/ 7735–9166; 020/7582–5712 after office hours).

➤ LATE-NIGHT PHARMACIES: **Bliss the Chemist** (✉ 5 Marble Arch, W1, ☎ 020/7723–6116).

ETIQUETTE & BEHAVIOR

The British stiff upper lip is more relaxed, but on social occasions the rule is to observe and then go with the flow. If you're visiting a family home, a gift of flowers is welcome. If it's for a meal, then take a bottle of wine perhaps, and maybe some candy for the children—but not necessarily all three. Kissing on greeting is still too forward and Continental for most Brits. A warm handshake is just fine. For goodbyes, if the atmosphere warrants, a quick one-cheek kiss is appropriate. The British can never say please, thank you, or sorry too often; to thank your host, a phone call or thank-you card does nicely.

BUSINESS ETIQUETTE

In business, punctuality is of prime importance, so if you anticipate a late arrival, call ahead. On dinners: it is not assumed that spouses will attend unless pre-arranged, and if you proffered the invitation it is usually assumed that you will pick up the tab. If you are the visitor, however, it's good form for the host to do the taking. Alternatively, play it safe and offer to split the check.

GAY & LESBIAN TRAVEL

The main gay communities are in the center of London (Soho, Old Compton St., and west to Kensington and Earls Court). There is a thriving social scene of clubs and cafes, and the best notice board for gay life and services is Gay's the Word. The *Pink Paper,* available at libraries, large bookstores, and gay cafes, and *Time Out* have comprehensive listings. Hotel front desks should serve any couples with courtesy, but using the travel agents listed below should send you to the right direction.

➤ CONTACTS IN LONDON: **Gay's the Word** (✉ 66 Marchmont St., WC1, ☎ 020/7278–7654).

➤ GAY- & LESBIAN-FRIENDLY TRAVEL AGENCIES: **Different Roads Travel** (✉ 8383 Wilshire Blvd., Suite 902, Beverly Hills, CA 90211, ☎ 323/651–5557 or 800/429–8747, FAX 323/651–3678, lgernert@tzell.com). **Kennedy Travel** (✉ 314 Jericho Turnpike, Floral Park, NY 11001, ☎ 516/352–4888 or 800/237–7433, FAX 516/354–8849, WEB www.kennedytravel.com). **Now Voyager** (✉ 4406 18th St., San Francisco, CA 94114, ☎ 415/626–1169 or 800/255–6951, FAX 415/626–8626, WEB www.nowvoyager.com). **Skylink Travel and Tour** (✉ 1006 Mendocino Ave., Santa Rosa, CA 95401, ☎ 707/546–9888 or 800/225–5759, FAX 707/546–9891, WEB www.skylinktravel.com), serving lesbian travelers.

GUIDEBOOKS

Plan well and you won't be sorry. You may want to check out *Fodor's Exploring London* and *Fodor's Exploring Britain* (both full-color); *Fodor's upCLOSE London* and *Fodor's upCLOSE Great Britain* (budget travel); and the pocket-size *Citypack London* available at on-line retailers and bookstores everywhere.

HEALTH

Great Britain has been plagued in recent years by concern about Bovine Spongiform Encephalopathy (BSE), commonly known as "mad cow" disease. Humans may contract the disease by eating meat from infected cattle. Although the chance of catching the disease is extremely small, you may wish to avoid eating beef or choose beef or beef products, such as solid pieces of muscle meat (as opposed to burgers or sausages), that might have a reduced opportunity for contamination with tissues that might harbor the BSE agent. For the latest information, contact the Centers for Disease Control and Prevention.

In spring 2001, Great Britain was hit by another crisis, foot-and-mouth

disease, which affects animals. Although it had a catastrophic effect on the British economy—animals, even those suspected of being infected, were slaughtered immediately to control mass infection—the disease is very rare in humans and is harmless to them. Some tourist sights and attractions in the countryside have been closed to limit the spread of the disease by humans; however, sights and attractions in London have not been affected.

➤ CONTACTS: **Centers for Disease Control and Prevention** (☎ 877/394–8747, WEB www.cdc.gov).

HOLIDAYS

June 3rd and June 4th of 2002 are public holidays for celebrating the Queen's Golden Jubilee. Standard holidays include: New Year's Day, Good Friday, Easter Monday, May Day (first Monday in May), spring and summer bank holidays (last Monday in May and August, respectively), Christmas, and Boxing Day (day after Christmas). On Christmas Eve and New Year's Eve some shops, restaurants, and businesses close early. Some museums and tourist attractions are also closed then. If you want to book a hotel room during this period, make sure you do it well in advance, and check to see whether the hotel restaurant will be open.

INSURANCE

The most useful travel-insurance plan is a comprehensive policy that includes coverage for trip cancellation and interruption, default, trip delay, and medical expenses (with a waiver for pre-existing conditions).

Without insurance you will lose all or most of your money if you cancel your trip, regardless of the reason. Default insurance covers you if your tour operator, airline, or cruise line goes out of business. Trip-delay covers expenses that arise because of bad weather or mechanical delays. Study the fine print when comparing policies.

If you're traveling internationally, a key component of travel insurance is coverage for medical bills incurred if you get sick on the road. Such ex-

penses are not generally covered by Medicare or private policies. U.K. residents can buy a travel-insurance policy valid for most vacations taken during the year in which it's purchased (but check pre-existing-condition coverage). Australian citizens need extra medical coverage when traveling abroad.

Always **buy travel policies directly from the insurance company**; if you buy them from a cruise line, airline, or tour operator that goes out of business you probably will not be covered for the agency or operator's default, a major risk. Before making any purchase, **review your existing health and home-owner's policies** to find what they cover away from home.

➤ TRAVEL INSURERS: In the U.S.: **Access America** (⊠ 6600 W. Broad St., Richmond, VA 23230, ☎ 804/285–3300 or 800/284–8300, FAX 804/673–1586, WEB www.previewtravel.com), **Travel Guard International** (⊠ 1145 Clark St., Stevens Point, WI 54481, ☎ 715/345–0505 or 800/826–1300, FAX 800/955–8785, WEB www.noelgroup.com).

➤ INSURANCE INFORMATION: In Australia: **Insurance Council of Australia** (⊠ Level 3, 56 Pitt St., Sydney NSW 2000, ☎ 03/9614–1077, FAX 03/9614–7924). In Canada: **Voyager Insurance** (⊠ 44 Peel Center Dr., Brampton, Ontario L6T 4M8, Canada, ☎ 905/791–8700, 800/668–4342 in Canada). In New Zealand: **Insurance Council of New Zealand** (⊠ Box 474, Wellington, New Zealand, ☎ 04/472–5230, FAX 04/473–3011, WEB www.icnz.org.nz). In the U.K.: **Association of British Insurers** (⊠ 51–55 Gresham St., London EC2V 7HQ, U.K., ☎ 020/7600–3333, FAX 020/7696–8999, WEB www.abi.org.uk).

LODGING

London now ranks as one of the world's most expensive hotel capitals. Finding budget accommodations—especially during July and August—can be difficult; you should try to book well ahead if you are visiting during these months. Many London hotels offer special off-season (October–March) rates, however. The lodgings we list are the cream of the

crop in each price category. We always list the facilities that are available—but we don't specify whether they cost extra: when pricing accommodations, always ask what's included and what costs extra. Hotels are indicated in the text by 🛏 .

CATEGORY	COST*
££££	over £230
£££	£160–£230
££	£100–£160
£	under £100

*All prices are for a double room, VAT included.

Assume that hotels operate on the **European Plan** (EP, with no meals) unless we specify that they use the **Continental Plan** (CP, with a Continental breakfast), **Modified American Plan** (MAP, with breakfast and dinner), or the **Full American Plan** (FAP, with all meals).

APARTMENT RENTALS

If you want a home base that's roomy enough for a family and comes with cooking facilities, **consider a furnished rental.** These can save you money, especially if you're traveling with a group. Home-exchange directories sometimes list rentals as well as exchanges. In Britain, apartments are called flats. If you want to deal directly with local agents in Britain, get a personal recommendation from someone who has used the company, as, unlike hotels, there is no accredited system for standards. The London Tourist Board also has accommodation lists.

➤ INTERNATIONAL AGENTS: **At Home Abroad** (⊠ 405 E. 56th St., Suite 6H, New York, NY 10022, ☎ 212/421–9165, FAX 212/752–1591, WEB member.aol.com/athomabrod/index.html). **Hideaways International** (⊠ 767 Islington St., Portsmouth, NH 03801, ☎ 603/430–4433 or 800/843–4433, FAX 603/430–4444, WEB www.hideaways.com; membership $129). **Hometours International** (⊠ Box 11503, Knoxville, TN 37939, ☎ 865/690–8484 or 800/367–4668, WEB http://thor.he.net/~hometour/). **Interhome** (⊠ 1990 N.E. 163rd St., Suite 110, N. Miami Beach, FL 33162, ☎ 305/940–2299 or 800/882–6864, FAX 305/940–2911, WEB www.

interhome.com). **Vacation Home Rentals Worldwide** (⊠ 235 Kensington Ave., Norwood, NJ 07648, ☎ 201/767–9393 or 800/633–3284, FAX 201/767–5510, WEB www.vhrww. com). **Villanet** (⊠ 11556 First Ave. NW, Seattle, WA 98177, ☎ 206/417–3444 or 800/964–1891, FAX 206/417–1832, WEB www.rentavilla.com). **Villas and Apartments Abroad** (⊠ 1270 Avenue of the Americas, 15th floor, New York, NY 10020, ☎ 212/897–5045 or 800/433–3020, FAX 212/897–5039, WEB www.vaanyc.com). **Villas International** (⊠ 950 Northgate Dr., Suite 206, San Rafael, CA 94903, ☎ 415/499–9490 or 800/221–2260, FAX 415/499–9491, WEB www.villasintl. com).

➤ LOCAL AGENTS: **John D. Wood** (⊠ 2 Jubilee Pl., SW3, ☎ 020/7349–5453, WEB www.shortlet@jdw.co.uk). **The Landmark Trust** (☎ 01628/825925). **The Short Let Company** (⊠ 20 Montpelier St., SW7, ☎ 020/7589–2429, WEB www.shortletco. com).

B&BS

B&Bs are often large, attractive family homes that are almost like small hotels. These aren't corporate facilities, so you should be prepared to accept some charming quirks. Choose carefully from accredited agencies, as some so-called B&Bs could be simply unfortunate hostels for refugees and homeless.

HOME EXCHANGES

If you would like to exchange your home for someone else's, **join a home-exchange organization,** which will send you its updated listings of available exchanges for a year and will include your own listing in at least one of them. It's up to you to make specific arrangements.

➤ EXCHANGE CLUBS: **HomeLink International** (⊠ Box 47747, Tampa, FL 33647, ☎ 813/975–9825 or 800/638–3841, FAX 813/910–8144, WEB www.homelink.org; $98 per year). **Intervac U.S.** (⊠ Box 590504, San Francisco, CA 94159, ☎ 800/756–4663, FAX 415/435–7440, WEB intervacus.com; $93 yearly fee includes one catalogue and on-line access).

HOSTELS

No matter what your age, you can **save on lodging costs by staying at hostels.** In some 5,000 locations in more than 70 countries around the world, Hostelling International (HI), the umbrella group for a number of national youth-hostel associations, offers single-sex, dorm-style beds and, at many hostels, rooms for couples and family accommodations. Membership in any HI national hostel association, open to travelers of all ages, allows you to stay in HI-affiliated hostels at member rates; one-year membership is about $25 for adults (C$26.75 in Canada, £9.30 in the U.K., $30 in Australia, and $30 in New Zealand); hostels run about $10–$25 per night. Members have priority if the hostel is full; they're also eligible for discounts around the world, even on rail and bus travel in some countries.

➤ ORGANIZATIONS: **Hostelling International—American Youth Hostels** (⊠ 733 15th St. NW, Suite 840, Washington, DC 20005, ☎ 202/783–6161, FAX 202/783–6171, WEB www. hiayh.org). **Hostelling International—Canada** (⊠ 400–205 Catherine St., Ottawa, Ontario K2P 1C3, Canada, ☎ 613/237–7884, FAX 613/237–7868, WEB www.hostellingintl.ca). **Youth Hostel Association of England and Wales** (⊠ Trevelyan House, 8 St. Stephen's Hill, St. Albans, Hertfordshire AL1 2DY, U.K., ☎ 0870/8708808, FAX 01727/844126, WEB www.yha.org.uk). **Australian Youth Hostel Association** (⊠ 10 Mallett St., Camperdown, NSW 2050, Australia, ☎ 02/9565–1699, FAX 02/9565–1325, WEB www.yha.com.au). **Youth Hostels Association of New Zealand** (⊠ Box 436, Christchurch, New Zealand, ☎ 03/379–9970, FAX 03/365–4476, WEB www.yha.org.nz).

HOTELS

There are several systems that grade hotels in Britain. The English Tourist Board (ETB) presently uses crowns, while the AA and RAC motoring organizations award stars. Some are awarded more for service than individual room facilities. For a good standard of comfort, look at three stars and above. Modern hotels usually have air-conditioning, and if you wish to have a double bed, you should specify. All hotels listed have private bath unless otherwise noted.

➤ TOLL-FREE NUMBERS: **Best Western** (☎ 800/528–1234, WEB www. bestwestern.com). **Choice** (☎ 800/221–2222, WEB www.hotelchoice. com). **Clarion** (☎ 800/252–7466, WEB www.hotelchoice.com). **Comfort** (☎ 800/228–5150, WEB www. comfortinn.com). **Days Inn** (☎ 800/325–2525, WEB www.daysinn.com). **Forte** (☎ 800/225–5843, WEB www. forte-hotels.com). **Four Seasons** (☎ 800/332–3442, WEB www.fourseasons. com). **Hilton** (☎ 800/445–8667, WEB www.hilton.com). **Holiday Inn** (☎ 800/465–4329, WEB www.basshotels. com). **Howard Johnson** (☎ 800/654–4656, WEB www.hojo.com). **Hyatt Hotels & Resorts** (☎ 800/233–1234, WEB www.hyatt.com). **Inter-Continental** (☎ 800/327–0200, WEB www. interconti.com). **Marriott** (☎ 800/228–9290, WEB www.marriott.com). **Le Meridien** (☎ 800/543–4300, WEB www.lemeridien-hotels.com). **Nikko Hotels International** (☎ 800/645–5687, WEB www.nikkohotels.com). **Quality Inn** (☎ 800/228–5151, WEB www.qualityinn.com). **Radisson** (☎ 800/333–3333, WEB www. radisson.com). **Renaissance Hotels & Resorts** (☎ 800/468–3571, WEB www. renaissancehotels.com). **Sheraton** (☎ 800/325–3535, WEB www.star-wood.com). **Wyndham Hotels & Resorts** (☎ 800/822–4200, WEB www. wyndham.com).

MAIL & SHIPPING

Stamps may be bought from post offices (open weekdays 9–5:30, Saturday 9–noon), from stamp machines outside post offices, and from newsagents' stores and newsstands. Mailboxes are known as post or letter boxes and are painted bright red; large tubular ones are set on the edge of sidewalks, while smaller boxes are set into post-office walls. Allow seven days for a letter to reach the United States. Check the Yellow Pages for a complete list of branches.

➤ POST OFFICES: ⊠ 17 Euston Rd., NW1. ⊠ 125–131 Westminster Bridge Rd., SW1. ⊠ 110 Victoria St., SW1. ⊠ 15 Broadwick St., W1. ⊠ 54 Great Portland St., W1. ⊠ 43 Sey-

mour St., Marble Arch, W1. ⊠ The Science Museum, SW7. ⊠ 24 William IV St., Trafalgar Sq., WC2.

OVERNIGHT SERVICES

➤ MAJOR SERVICES: DHL (☎ 0845/710–0300). **Federal Express** (☎ 0800/123800). **Parcelforce** (☎ 0800/224466).

POSTAL RATES

Airmail letters up to 10 grams to North America, Australia, and New Zealand cost 45p; postcards, 40p. Letters within Britain are 27p for first-class, 19p for second-class (these rates are subject to change).

RECEIVING MAIL

If you're uncertain where you'll be staying, you can have mail sent to you at the London Main Post Office, c/o Poste Restante. The post office will hold international mail for one month. You can also collect letters at American Express.

➤ CONTACTS: **American Express** (⊠ 6 Haymarket, SW1Y 4BS, ☎ 020/7930–4411). **London Main Post Office** (⊠ 24–28 William IV St., WC2N 4DL).

SHIPPING PARCELS

Most department stores and retail outlets can ship your goods home. You should check your insurance for coverage of possible damage.

MEDIA

NEWSPAPERS & MAGAZINES

For the latest information about shops, restaurants, and art events, peruse Britain's glossy monthly magazines—*Tatler, Harpers & Queen, Vogue, Wallpaper, House & Garden, The Face,* and *Time Out.* The *London Times,* the *Evening Standard,* the *Independent,* and the *Guardian* have comprehensive Arts sections including reviews and advance news of future events. In addition, these newspapers have Web sites of their own, full of tips on what's hot and happening.

RADIO & TELEVISION

The main channels are BBC1 and BBC2 from the British Broadcasting Corporation. BBC2 is considered the more eclectic and artsy, with a higher proportion of alternative humor, drama, and documentaries. The independent channels are ITV (Independent Television), which is split into regional companies across the country: Carlton is the station for London and the southeast region. There are big-budget highbrow productions occasionally, but there are more mainstream soaps, both homegrown—*Brookside* and *Coronation Street* (which the Queen is rumored to watch)—and international (the Australian *Neighbors* and some U.S. daytime shows such as *Jerry Springer*). There are general-interest shows as well. Channel 4 is a mixture of mainstream and off-the-wall, while Channel 5 has a higher proportion of sports and films. Satellite and cable channels (many of which are beamed into hotel rooms) have increased the daily diet now available round the clock.

Radio has seen a similar explosion, from 24-hour classics on Classic FM (100–102MHz), and rock on Virgin (105.8MHz), or nostalgic on Heart (106.2MHz), or talk-talk on Talk Radio (MW1053 kHZ)—and that is just a sample of the independents. The BBC's Radio 1 (FM97.6) is for the young and hip; 2 (FM88) for middle-of-the-roadsters; 3 (FM90.2) for classics, jazz, and arts; 4 (FM92.4) for news, current affairs, drama, and documentary; and 5 Live (MW693 kHz) for sports and news with phone-ins.

MONEY MATTERS

A movie in the West End costs £6–£9.50 (at some cinemas less on Monday and at matinees); a theater seat, from £8.50 to about £35, more for hit shows; admission to a museum or gallery, around £5 (though some are free and others request a "voluntary contribution"); coffee, £1–£2; a pint of light (lager) beer in a pub, £2 and more; whiskey, gin, vodka, and so forth, by the glass in a pub, £2.50 and up (the measure is smaller than in the United States); house wine by the glass in a pub or wine bar, around £2, in a restaurant £3.50 or more; a Coke, around £1; a ham sandwich from a sandwich bar in the West End, £2; a 1-mi taxi ride, £4; an average Underground or bus ride, £1.60, a longer one £2.50. For standby theater tickets, many at half-price, go the SOLT (Society of London Theaters) booth in Leicester Square for that day's shows; it is open Monday–Saturday, 2:30–6:30, from noon on matinee days. There is a service charge of £2 or £1.25 on tickets under £12.50.

Prices throughout this guide are given for adults. Reduced fees—generally referred to as "concessions" throughout Great Britain—are usually available for children, students, and senior citizens. For information on taxes, *see* Taxes, *below.*

ATMS

Credit cards or debit cards (also known as check cards) will get you cash advances at ATMs worldwide if your card is properly programmed with your personal identification number. For use in London, your PIN must have no more than four digits.

CREDIT CARDS

Throughout this guide, the following abbreviations are used: **AE**, American Express; **DC**, Diner's Club; **MC**, MasterCard; and **V**, Visa.

➤ REPORTING LOST CARDS: **American Express**(☎ 01273/696933). **Diner's Club** (☎ 0800/460800). **MasterCard** (☎ 0800/964767). **Visa** (☎ 0800/895082).

CURRENCY

The units of currency in Great Britain are the pound sterling (£) and pence (p): £50, £20, £10, and £5 bills (called notes); £2, £1 (100p), 50p, 20p, 10p, 5p, 2p, and 1p coins. At press time, the exchange rate was about Australian $2.82, Canadian $2.25, New Zealand $3.53, and U.S. $1.44 to the pound (also known as quid).

CURRENCY EXCHANGE

For the most favorable rates, **change money through banks.** Although ATM transaction fees may be higher abroad than at home, ATM rates are excellent because they are based on wholesale rates offered only by major banks. You won't do as well at exchange booths in airports or rail and bus stations, in hotels, in restaurants, or in stores. To avoid lines at airport exchange booths, **get a bit of local currency before you leave home.**

➤ EXCHANGE SERVICES: **International Currency Express** (☎ 888/278–6628 for orders, WEB www.foreignmoney. com). **Thomas Cook Currency Services** (☎ 800/287–7362 for telephone orders and retail locations, WEB www. us.thomascook.com).

TRAVELER'S CHECKS

Do you need traveler's checks? It depends on where you're headed. If you're going to rural areas and small towns, go with cash; traveler's checks are best used in cities. Lost or stolen checks can usually be replaced within 24 hours. To ensure a speedy refund, buy your own traveler's checks— don't let someone else pay for them: irregularities like this can cause delays. The person who bought the checks should make the call to request a refund.

PACKING

London can be cool, damp, and overcast, even in summer. You'll need a heavy coat for winter and a lightweight coat or warm jacket for summer. **Always bring an umbrella and, if possible, a raincoat.** Pack as you would for an American city: jackets and ties for expensive restaurants and nightspots, casual clothes elsewhere. Jeans are popular in London and are perfectly acceptable for sightseeing and informal dining. Blazers and sport jackets are popular here with men. For women, ordinary street dress is acceptable everywhere. If you plan to stay in budget hotels, take your own soap.

In your carry-on luggage, **pack an extra pair of eyeglasses or contact lenses** and **enough of any medication you take** to last the entire trip. You may also ask your doctor to write a spare prescription using the drug's generic name, since brand names may vary from country to country. In luggage to be checked, **never pack prescription drugs or valuables.** To avoid customs delays, carry medications in their original packaging. And don't forget to carry with you the addresses of offices that handle refunds of lost traveler's checks. Check *Fodor's How to Pack* (available in bookstores everywhere) for more tips.

CHECKING LUGGAGE

How many carry-on bags you can bring with you is up to the airline. Most allow two, but not always, so make sure that everything you carry aboard will fit under your seat or in the overhead bin, and get to the gate early. Note that if you have a seat at the back of the plane, you'll probably board first, while the overhead bins are still empty.

If you are flying internationally, note that baggage allowances may be determined not by piece but by weight—generally 88 pounds (40 kilograms) in first class, 66 pounds (30 kilograms) in business class, and 44 pounds (20 kilograms) in economy.

Airline liability for baggage is limited to $1,250 per person on flights within the United States. On international flights it amounts to $9.07 per pound or $20 per kilogram for checked baggage (roughly $640 per 70-pound bag) and $400 per passenger for unchecked baggage. You can buy additional coverage at check-in for about $10 per $1,000 of coverage, but it excludes a rather extensive list of items, shown on your airline ticket.

Before departure, **itemize your bags' contents** and their worth, and label the bags with your name, address, and phone number. (If you use your home address, cover it so potential thieves can't see it readily.) Inside each bag, **pack a copy of your itinerary.** At check-in, **make sure that each bag is correctly tagged** with the destination airport's three-letter code. If your bags arrive damaged or fail to arrive at all, file a written report with the airline before leaving the airport.

PASSPORTS & VISAS

When traveling internationally, **carry your passport** even if you don't need one (it's always the best form of I.D.) and **make two photocopies of the data page** (one for someone at home and another for you, carried separately from your passport). If you lose your passport, promptly call the nearest embassy or consulate and the local police.

ENTERING GREAT BRITAIN

U.S. and Canadian citizens need only a valid passport to enter Great Britain for stays of up to 90 days.

PASSPORT OFFICES

The best time to apply for a passport or to renew is in fall and winter. Before any trip, check your passport's expiration date, and, if necessary, renew it as soon as possible.

➤ AUSTRALIAN CITIZENS: **Australian Passport Office** (☎ 131–232, WEB www.dfat.gov.au/passports).

➤ CANADIAN CITIZENS: **Passport Office** (☎ 819/994–3500; 800/567–6868 in Canada, WEB www.dfait-maeci.gc.ca/passport).

➤ NEW ZEALAND CITIZENS: **New Zealand Passport Office** (☎ 04/494–0700, WEB www.passports.govt.nz).

➤ U.S. CITIZENS: **National Passport Information Center** (☎ 900/225–5674; calls are 35¢ per minute for automated service, $1.05 per minute for operator service; WEB www.travel.state.gov/npicinfo.html).

SENIOR-CITIZEN TRAVEL

To qualify for age-related discounts, **mention your senior-citizen status up front** when booking hotel reservations (not when checking out) and before you're seated in restaurants (not when paying the bill). When renting a car, ask about promotional car-rental discounts, which can be cheaper than senior-citizen rates.

➤ EDUCATIONAL PROGRAMS: **Elderhostel** (✉ 11 Ave. de Lafayette, Boston, MA 02111-1746, ☎ 877/426–8056, FAX 877/426–2166, WEB www.elderhostel.org). **Interhostel** (✉ University of New Hampshire, 6 Garrison Ave., Durham, NH 03824, ☎ 603/862–1147 or 800/733–9753, FAX 603/862–1113, WEB www.learn.unh.edu).

SIGHTSEEING TOURS

BUS TOURS

Guided sightseeing tours from the top of a double-decker bus, which are open-topped in summer, are a good introduction to the city, as they cover all the main central sights. There is a choice of companies, each providing daily tours departing (between 8:30 and 9 AM) from central points. You may board or alight at any of the numerous stops to view the sights, and re-board on the next bus. Tickets are bought from the driver and are good all day. Prices vary according to the type of tour, although £12 is the benchmark.

➤ TOUR OPERATORS: **Big Bus Company** (☎ 020/8944–7810). **Black Taxi Tour of London** (☎ 020/7289–4371). **Evan Evans** (☎ 020/8332–2222). **Frames Rickards** (☎ 020/7837–3111). **London Bicycle Tour** (☎ 020/7928–6838). **London Pride** (☎ 020/7520–2050). **Original London Sightseeing Tour** (☎ 020/8877–1722).

BY CANAL

The tranquil side of London is to be found on narrow boats that cruise London's two canals, the Grand Union and Regent's Canal; most vessels operate on the latter, which runs between Little Venice in the west (nearest tube: Warwick Avenue on the Bakerloo Line) and Camden Lock (about 200 yards north of Camden Town tube station). Fares are about £5 for 1½-hour cruises.

➤ CRUISE OPERATORS: **Canal Cruises** (☎ 020/7485–4433). **Jason's Trip** (☎ 020/7286–3428). **London Waterbus Company** (☎ 020/7482–2660).

ON FOOT

One of the best ways to get to know London is on foot, and there are many guided and themed walking tours from which to choose. If you wish to tailor your own tour, you might consider hiring a Blue Badge accredited guide.

➤ TOUR OPERATORS: **Blue Badge** (☎ 020/7495–5504). **Citisights** (☎ 020/8806–4325). **Historical Walks** (☎ 020/8668–4019). **Jack the Ripper Mystery Walks** (☎ 020/8558–9446). **Original London Walks** (☎ 020/7624–3978).

BY RIVER

All year round, but more frequently from April to October, boats cruise the Thames, offering a different view of the London skyline. Most leave from Westminster Pier, Charing Cross Pier, and Tower Pier. Downstream routes go to the Tower of London, Greenwich, and the Thames Barrier via Canary Wharf. Upstream destinations include Kew, Richmond, and Hampton Court (mainly in summer). Most of the launches seat between 100 and 250 passengers, have a public-address system, and provide a running commentary on passing points of interest. Depending upon the destination, river trips may last from one to four hours.

A Sail and Rail ticket combines the modern wonders of Canary Wharf by Docklands Light Railway with a trip on the river. Tickets are available year-round from Westminster Pier or DLR stations; ticket holders also get discounted tickets to the London Aquarium in Westminster and the National Maritime Museum in Greenwich.

Details on all river cruise operators are available from London River Services.

➤ RIVER CRUISE OPERATORS: **Catamaran Cruisers** (☎ 020/7839–3572). **London River Services** (☎ 020/7941–2400). **Sail and Rail** (☎ 020/7363–9700). **Thames Cruises** (☎ 020/7930–3373). **Westminster Passenger Boat Services** (☎ 020/7930–4097).

EXCURSIONS

London Regional Transport, Green Line, Evan Evans, National Express, and Frames Rickards all offer day excursions by bus to places within easy reach of London, such as Hampton Court, Oxford, Stratford, and Bath.

STUDENTS IN LONDON

➤ I.D.S & SERVICES: **Council Travel** (CIEE; ✉ 205 E. 42nd St., 15th floor, New York, NY 10017, ☎ 212/822–2700 or 888/268–6245, FAX 212/822–2699, WEB www.councilexchanges. org) for mail orders only, in the U.S. **Travel Cuts** (✉ 187 College St., Toronto, Ontario M5T 1P7, Canada, ☎ 416/979–2406 or 800/667–2887 in Canada, FAX 416/979–8167, WEB www.travelcuts.com).

TAXES

An airport departure tax of £20 (£10 for within U.K. and other EU countries) per person is payable and may be subject to more government tax increases, although it is included in the price of your ticket.

VALUE-ADDED TAX

The British sales tax (VAT, Value Added Tax) is 17½%. The tax is almost always included in quoted prices in shops, hotels, and restaurants.

Most travelers can **get a VAT refund** by either the Retail Export or the more cumbersome Direct Export method. Many large stores provide these services, but only if you request them; they will handle the paperwork. For the Retail Export method, you must ask the store for Form VAT 407 (you must have identification—passports are best), to be given to customs at your last port of departure. (Lines at major airports can be long, so allow plenty of time.) The refund will be forwarded to you in about eight weeks, minus a small service charge, either in the form of a credit to your charge card or as a British check, which American banks usually charge you to convert. With the Direct Export method, the goods go directly to your home; you must have a Form VAT 407 certified by customs, police, or a notary public when you get home and then sent back to the store, which will refund your money. For inquiries, call the local Customs & Excise office listed in the London telephone directory.

Global Refund is a V.A.T. refund service that makes getting your money back hassle-free. The service is available Europe-wide at 130,000 affiliated stores. In participating stores, **ask for the Global Refund refund form** (called a Shopping Cheque). Have it stamped like any customs form by customs officials when you leave the European Union (be ready to show customs officials what you've bought). Then take the form to one of the more than 700 Global Refund counters—conveniently located at every major airport and border crossing—and your money will be refunded on the spot in the form of cash, check, or a refund to your credit-card account (minus a small percentage for processing).

➤ V.A.T. REFUNDS: **Global Refund** (✉ 99 Main St., Ste. 307, Nyack, NY 10960, ☎ 800/566–9828, 𝐅𝐀𝐗 845/ 348–1549, 𝐖𝐄𝐁 www.globalrefund. com).

TAXIS

Those big black taxicabs are as much a part of the London streetscape as the red double-decker buses, yet many have been replaced by the new boxy, sharp-edged model, and the beauty of others is marred by the advertising they carry on their sides. Hotels and main tourist areas have cab stands (just take the first in line), but you can also flag one down from the roadside. If the yellow FOR HIRE sign on the top is lit, the taxi is available. Cab drivers often cruise at night with their signs unlit so that they can choose their passengers and avoid those they think might cause trouble. If you see an unlit, passengerless cab, hail it: you might be lucky.

Fares start at £1.40 and increase by units of 20p per 281 yards or 55.5 seconds until the fare exceeds £8.60. After that, it's 20p for each 188 yards or 37 seconds. A 60p surcharge is added on weekday nights 8–midnight and until 8 PM on Saturday. Over Christmas and on New Year's Eve, it rises to £2—and there's 40p extra for each additional passenger. Tips are extra, usually 10%–15% per ride.

TELEPHONES

AREA & COUNTRY CODES

The country code for Great Britain is 44. The former London area codes of 0171 and 0181 have been merged into one code—020—with the previous 7 or 8 denomination being added before the first digit of the old phone number, making an eight digit number. For example, 0171/222–3333 is now 020/7222–3333. The existing 0800 numbers have not changed; national information numbers of 0345 are now 0845. Details are on the Internet at www.numberchange. org. There is help available, within England, at 0800/731–0202; from the U.S., at 020/7634–8700.

When dialing Great Britain from abroad, drop the initial 0 from these local area codes. The country code is 1 for the U.S. and Canada, 61 for Australia, 64 for New Zealand, and 44 for the U.K.

DIRECTORY & OPERATOR ASSISTANCE

For information anywhere in Britain, dial 192. For the operator, dial 100. For assistance with international calls, dial 155.

INTERNATIONAL CALLS

When calling from overseas to access a London telephone number, drop the 0 from the prefix and dial only 20 (or any other British area code) and then the eight-digit phone number. To give one example: Let's say you're calling Buckingham Palace—020/7839–1377 (or, in the old system, 0171/839–1377)—from the U.S. to inquire about tours and hours. First, dial 011 (the international access code), then 44 (Great Britain's country code), then 20 (London's center city code), then the remainder of the telephone number, 7839–1377.

LOCAL CALLS

You don't have to dial London's central area code (020) if you are calling inside London itself—just the new eight-digit telephone number.

LONG-DISTANCE CALLS

For long-distance calls within Britain, dial the area code (which begins with 01) followed by the number. The area-code prefix is only used when you are dialing from outside the city. In provincial areas, the dialing codes for nearby towns are often posted in the booth.

LONG-DISTANCE SERVICES

AT&T, MCI, and Sprint access codes make calling long distance relatively convenient, but you may find the local access number blocked in many hotel rooms. First ask the hotel operator to connect you. If the hotel operator balks, ask for an international operator, or dial the international operator yourself. One way to improve your odds of getting connected to your long-distance carrier is to travel with more than one company's calling card (a hotel may block Sprint, for example, but not MCI). If all else fails, call from a pay phone.

You can also pick up one of the many instant international phonecards from newsstands, which can be used from residential, hotel, and public pay phones. With these, you can call the United States for as little as 5p per minute.

➤ ACCESS CODES: **AT&T Direct** (In the U.K., there are AT&T access numbers to dial the U.S. using three different phone types—Cable & Wireless: ☎ 0500/890011; British Telecom: ☎ 0800/890011; and AT&T: ☎ 0800/0130011; ☎ 800/435–0812 for other areas). **MCI WorldPhone** (In the U.K., dial ☎ 0800/890222 for the U.S via MCI; 800/444–4141 for other areas). **Sprint International Access** (In the U.K., there are Sprint access numbers to dial the U.S. using two different phone types—Cable & Wireless: ☎ 0500/890877; and British Telecom: ☎ 0800/890877; 800/877–4646 for other areas).

PHONE CARDS

Public card phones operate with special cards that you can buy from post offices or newsstands. They are ideal for longer calls; are composed of units of 10p; and come in values of £3, £5, £10, and more. To use a card phone, lift the receiver, insert your card, and dial the number. An indicator panel shows the number of units used. At the end of your call, the card will be returned. Where credit cards are taken, slide the card through, as indicated.

PUBLIC PHONES

There are three types of phones: those that accept (a) only coins, (b) only British Telecom (BT) phone cards, or (c) BT phone cards and credit cards.

The coin-operated phones are of the push-button variety; the workings of coin-operated telephones vary, but there are usually instructions on each unit. Most take 10p, 20p, 50p, and £1 coins. Insert the coins *before* dialing (minimum charge is 10p). If you hear a repeated single tone after dialing, the line is busy; a continual tone means the number is unobtainable (or that you have dialed the wrong—or no—prefix). The indicator panel shows you how much money is left; add more whenever you like. If there is no answer, replace the receiver and your money will be returned.

All calls are charged according to the time of day. Standard rate is weekdays 8 AM–6 PM; cheap rate is weekdays 6 PM–8 AM and all day on weekends, when it's even cheaper. A local call before 6 PM costs 15p for three minutes; this doubles to 30p for the same from a pay phone. A daytime call to the United States will cost 24p a minute on a regular phone (weekends are cheaper), 80p on a pay phone.

TIME

London is five hours ahead of New York City. In other words, when it is 3 PM in New York (or 12 noon in Los Angeles) it is 8 PM in London. Note that London and most European countries also move their clocks ahead for the one-hour differential when daylight saving time goes into effect (although they make the changeover several days after the U.S.).

TIPPING

Many restaurants and large hotels (particularly those belonging to chains) will automatically add a 10%–15% service charge to your bill, so **always check if tipping is necessary** before you hand out any extra money.

Do not tip movie or theater ushers, elevator operators, or bar staff in pubs—although you can always offer to buy them a drink. Washroom attendants may display a saucer, in which it's reasonable to leave 20p or so.

Here's a guide for other tipping situations. Restaurants: 10%–20% of the check for full meals if service is not already included (if paying by credit card, check that tip has not already been included before you fill in the total on your credit slip), a small token if you're just having coffee or tea. Taxis: 10%–15%, or perhaps a little more for a short ride. Porters: 50p–£1 per bag. Doormen: £1 for hailing taxis or for carrying bags to check-in desk. Bellhops: £1 for carrying bags, £1 for room service. Hairdressers: 10%–15% of the bill, plus £1–£2 for the hair-washer.

TOURS & PACKAGES

Because everything is prearranged on a prepackaged tour or independent vacation, you spend less time planning—and often get it all at a good price.

BOOKING WITH AN AGENT

Travel agents are excellent resources. But it's a good idea to collect brochures from several agencies as some agents' suggestions may be influenced by relationships with tour and package firms that reward them for volume sales. If you have a special interest, **find an agent with expertise in that area**; ASTA (☞ Travel Agencies, *below*) has a database of specialists worldwide.

Make sure your travel agent knows the accommodations and other services of the place they're recommending. Ask about the hotel's location, room size, beds, and whether it has a pool, room service, or programs for children, if you care about these. Has your agent been there in person or sent others whom you can contact?

Do some homework on your own, too: local tourism boards can provide information about lesser-known and small-niche operators, some of which may sell only direct.

BUYER BEWARE

Each year consumers are stranded or lose their money when tour operators—even large ones with excellent reputations—go out of business. So **check out the operator.** Ask several travel agents about its reputation, and try to **book with a company that has a consumer-protection program.** (Look for information in the company's brochure.) In the United States, members of the National Tour Association and the United States Tour Operators Association are required to set aside funds to cover your payments and travel arrangements in the event that the company defaults. It's also a good idea to choose a company that participates in the American Society of Travel Agents' Tour Operator Program (TOP); ASTA will act as mediator in any disputes between you and your tour operator.

Remember that the more your package or tour includes the better you can predict the ultimate cost of your vacation. Make sure you know exactly what is covered, and **beware of hidden costs.** Are taxes, tips, and transfers included? Entertainment and excursions? These can add up.

➤ TOUR-OPERATOR RECOMMENDATIONS: **American Society of Travel Agents** (☞ Travel Agencies, *below*). **National Tour Association** (NTA; ✉ 546 E. Main St., Lexington, KY 40508, ☎ 859/226–4444 or 800/682–8886, WEB www.ntaonline.com). **United States Tour Operators Association** (USTOA; ✉ 342 Madison Ave., Suite 1522, New York, NY 10173, ☎ 212/599–6599 or 800/468–7862, FAX 212/599–6744, WEB www.ustoa.com).

TRAIN TRAVEL TO AND FROM LONDON

London has eight major train stations that serve as arteries to the rest of the country (and to Europe). All are served by the Underground. As a general rule of thumb, the stations' location in the city matches the part of the country they serve. Charing Cross serves southeast England, including Canterbury and Dover/Folkestone for Europe. Euston serves the Midlands, north Wales, northwest England, and western Scotland. King's Cross marks the end of the Great Northern Line, serving northeast England and Scotland. Liverpool Street serves East Anglia, including Cambridge and Norwich. Paddington mainly serves south Wales and the West Country, as well as Reading, Oxford, and Bristol. St. Pancras serves Leicester, Nottingham, and Sheffield in south Yorkshire. Victoria serves southern England, including Brighton, Dover/Folkestone, and the south coast. Waterloo serves southeastern destinations, including Portsmouth and Southampton. The Eurostar service to France and Belgium departs from Waterloo International, within Waterloo station.

Some trains have refreshment carriages, called buffet cars. Smoking is forbidden in rail carriages.

CLASSES

Some trains have first-class and reserved seats (for which there is a small charge, depending on the rail company). Check with National Rail Enquiries for details.

CUTTING COSTS

To save money, **look into rail passes.** But be aware that if you don't plan to cover many miles you may come out ahead by buying individual tickets.

Apex tickets, bought seven days in advance, provide savings. Many discount passes are also available, such as the Young Person's Railcard (for which you must be under 26 and provide two passport-size photos) and the Family Travelcard, which can be bought from most mainline stations. But if you intend to make several long-distance rail journeys, it is far better to invest in a BritRail Pass (if you're leaving from the U.S.).

FARES & SCHEDULES

Delays are often a national joking matter, particularly since a renovation of rails and rolling stock. National Rail Enquiries provides an up-to-date state-of-the-railways schedule. Rail travel is expensive: for instance, a round-trip ticket to Bath can cost around £60 per person at peak times. The fee reduces to around £30 at other times, so it's best to travel before or after the frantic business commuter rush (before 4:30 PM and after 9:30 AM). Credit cards are accepted for train fares paid both in person and by phone.

➤ TRAIN INFORMATION: **BritRail Travel** (in the U.S., ☎ 800/677–8585). **Eurostar** (☎ 0990/186186). **National Rail Enquiries** (☎ 0845/748–4950; outside the U.K. ☎ 0161/236–3522). **Rail Europe** (☎ 0870/584–8848).

TRANSPORTATION AROUND LONDON

By far the easiest and most practical way to get around is on the Underground or "tube." This subway system runs daily from early morning to night and provides a comprehensive service throughout the center with lines out to the suburbs. Tube fares can work out to be higher than bus fares, but if you are traveling a lot around town, then you should investigate buying a Travelcard pass, which gives you discounted flexible travel on the tube, plus bus and some overground rail travel (☞ Underground Tube Travel, *below*).

The overground rail system is a network that connects outlying districts and suburbs to the center. Prices are comparable to the Underground, and you can easily transfer between the Underground and other connecting rail lines at many tube stations. Some passes are good for both the Underground and the rail system, so check at the point of purchase.

If you want to see the city, buses crisscross all over town. Their routes are more complicated than the tube, but by reading the route posted on the main bus stop and watching the route on the front of the bus, you won't go far wrong. Bus travel prices are cheaper than the tube the farther you travel, but be prepared to get stuck in traffic, even though designated lanes for buses and taxis should speed up the journey. Services are frequent, but if you become frustrated and flag down a taxi, the fare can clock up to three times the price of a similar bus fare for the same distance. If you're traveling with several people, however, riding in a taxi is relatively inexpensive and is more comfortable and convenient.

TRAVEL AGENCIES

A good travel agent puts your needs first. Look for an agency that has been in business at least five years, emphasizes customer service, and has someone on staff who specializes in your destination. In addition, **make sure the agency belongs to a professional trade organization.** The American Society of Travel Agents (ASTA), with 27,000 agents in some 170 countries, is the largest and most influential in the field. Operating under the motto "Integrity in Travel," it maintains and enforces a strict code of ethics and will step in to help mediate any agent-client disputes if necessary. ASTA also maintains a Web site that includes a directory of agents. (If a travel agency is also acting as your tour operator, *see* Buyer Beware *in* Tours & Packages, *above*.)

➤ LOCAL AGENT REFERRALS: **American Society of Travel Agents** (ASTA; ☎ 800/965–2782 24-hr hot line, FAX 703/739–7642, WEB www.astanet. com). **Association of British Travel Agents** (✉ 68–71 Newman St., London W1T 3AH, U.K., ☎ 020/7637–2444, FAX 020/7637–0713, WEB www. abtanet.com). **Association of Canadian Travel Agents** (✉ 130 Albert St., Ste. 1705, Ottawa, Ontario K1P 5G4, Canada, ☎ 613/237–3657, FAX 613/237–7502, WEB www.acta.net). **Australian Federation of Travel Agents** (✉ Level 3, 309 Pitt St., Sydney NSW 2000, Australia, ☎ 02/9264–3299, FAX 02/9264–1085, WEB www.afta. com.au). **Travel Agents' Association of New Zealand** (✉ Box 1888, Wellington 10033, New Zealand, ☎ 04/499–0104, FAX 04/499–0827, WEB www.taanz.org.nz).

UNDERGROUND TUBE TRAVEL

London's extensive Underground system has color-coded routes, clear signage, and extensive connections. Trains run out into the suburbs, and all stations are marked with the London Underground circular symbol. (In Britain, the word "subway" means "pedestrian underpass.") Trains are all one class; smoking is *not* allowed on board or in the stations.

Some lines have branches (Central, District, Northern, Metropolitan, and Piccadilly), so **be sure to note which branch is needed for your particular destination.** Electronic platform signs tell you the final stop and route of the next train and how many minutes you'll have to wait for the train to arrive. There are two recent developments: Jubilee Line has a state-of-the-art extension, opened on the eve of the millennium, connecting Canary Wharf to the Millennium Dome. The zippy Docklands Light Railway runs through the modern Docklands with a new extension to the *Cutty Sark* and maritime Greenwich.

FARES & SCHEDULES

London is divided into six concentric zones (ask at Underground ticket booths for a map and booklet, which give details of the ticket options), so make sure to buy a ticket for the correct zone or you may be liable for an on-the-spot fine (£10 at press time).

You can buy a single or return ticket, the equivalent of a one-way and a round-trip, for travel anytime on the day of issue. Singles vary in price from £1.40 to £3.40. If you are planning several trips in one day then consider a Travelcard, which is good for unrestricted travel on both tube and bus and some overground railways; these are valid weekdays after 9:30 AM, weekends, and on all public holidays, but cannot be used on airbuses, Night Buses, or for certain special services. Other options are: One Day Travelcard (£3.80–£4.50); Weekend Travelcards, for the two days of the weekend and on any two consecutive days during public holidays (£5.70–£6.70); Family Travelcards, which are one-day tickets for one or two adults with one to four children (£3–£3.60 with one child, additional children cost 60p each); or the Carnet, a book of 10 single tickets valid for central Zone 1 (£10) to use anytime over a year. The Visitor's Travelcard may be bought in the United States and Canada for three, four, and seven days' travel; it is the same as the LT (London Transport) Card and has a booklet of discount vouchers to London attractions. In the United States, the Visitor's Travelcard costs $25, $32, and $49, respectively; in Canada, C$29, C$36, and C$55, respectively. Apply to travel agents or, in the United States, to BritRail Travel International.

Trains begin running just after 5 AM Monday–Saturday; the last services leave central London between midnight and 12:30 AM. On Sunday, trains start two hours later and finish about an hour earlier. Frequency of trains depends on the route and the time of day, but normally you should not have to wait more than 10 minutes in central areas.

There are LT Travel Information Centres at the following tube stations:

Euston, Hammersmith, King's Cross, Liverpool Street, Oxford Circus, Piccadilly Circus, St. James's Park, and Victoria, open 7:15 AM–10 PM; and at Heathrow (in Terminals 1, 2 and 4), open 6 AM–3 PM. For travelers with disabilities, get the free leaflet, "Access to the Underground."

➤ UNDERGROUND INFORMATION: "Access to the Underground" (☎ 020/7918–3312). **BritRail Travel International** (✉ 1500 Broadway, New York, NY 10036, ☎ 212/382–3737). **London Transport** (☎ 020/7222–1234, WEB www.londontransport.co.uk).

VISITOR INFORMATION

When you arrive in London, you can go in person to the London Tourist Information Centre at Victoria Station Forecourt for general information (Easter–Oct., daily 8–7; Nov.–Easter, Mon.–Sat. 8–6, Sun. 8:30–4) or to the Britain Visitor Centre for travel, hotel, and entertainment information (July–Sept., weekdays 9–6:30, weekends 10–4; May–Sept., Mon.–Sat. 9–5).

The London Tourist Board's Visitorcall phone guide to London gives information about events, theater, museums, transport, shopping, and restaurants. There is a separate phone number for regular updates on what's happening this week. There is also a faxback service, enabling you to have the major events calendar faxed to you. Just dial the number and press start/receive after the tone; after a short pause the pages will process through. Visitorcall charges start at 60p per minute at all times, plus any hotel/pay-phone surcharge. Note that this service is accessible only in the U.K.

The official Web site of the British Tourist Authority is www.visitbritain.com. Its new "gateway" Web site, www.usagateway.visitbritain.com, provides information most helpful to Britain-bound U.S. travelers.

➤ IN THE U.S.: **British Tourist Authority** (BTA; ✉ 551 5th Ave., 7th floor, New York, NY 10176, ☎ 212/986–2200 or 800/462–2748; 625 N. Michigan Ave., Suite 1510, Chicago, IL 60611, ☎ 800/462–2748 [personal callers only]).

➤ IN CANADA: **British Tourist Authority** (✉ 5915 Airport Rd., Suite 120, Mississauga, Ontario L4V 1T1, ☎ 905/405–1840 or 800/847–4885).

➤ IN THE U.K.: **British Tourist Authority** (✉ Thames Tower, Black's Rd., London W6 9EL, ☎ 020/8846–9000).

➤ IN LONDON: **Britain Visitor Centre** (✉ 1 Regent St., Piccadilly Circus, SW1Y 4NX). Visitorcall (☎ 09068/663344; events for the week ☎ 09068/123400; faxback service ☎ 09068/353715).

➤ U.S. GOVERNMENT ADVISORIES: **U.S. Department of State** (✉ Overseas Citizens Services Office, Room 4811 N.S., 2201 C St. NW, Washington, DC 20520; enclose a self-addressed, stamped, business-size envelope. ☎ 202/647–5225 for interactive hot line, WEB http://travel.state.gov/travel/html).

WEB SITES

Do check out the World Wide Web when planning your trip. You'll find everything from weather forecasts to virtual tours of famous cities. Be sure to **visit fodors.com** (www.fodors.com), a complete travel-planning site. You can research prices and book plane tickets, hotel rooms, rental cars, vacation packages, and more. In addition, you can post your pressing questions in the Travel Talk section and, in the site's Rants & Raves section, read comments about some of the restaurants and hotels in this book—and chime in yourself. Other planning tools include a currency converter and weather reports, and there are loads of links to travel resources.

For more information specifically on London, visit one of the following:

The official London web site is www.londontown.com, which supplies helpful links to other Web sites, including Evening Standard Online (www.thisislondon.com), London Transport, The Palace, No. 10 Downing Street, UK Weather, and the BBC. For travel around the U.K. by bus, check out gobycoach.com.

For London events and news months in advance, visit the following culture and entertainment Web sites: www.timeout.co.uk, www.officiallondontheatre.co.uk, and www.ukcalling.co.uk.royal-albert. For the hotel scene in London, visit www.demon.co.uk/hotel-uk. For the full array of walking tours offered by the excellent Original London Walks, try www.walks.com. For walks in and around the city, with maps to download, head to www.londonwalking.com.

WHEN TO GO

The heaviest tourist season in Britain runs mid-April–mid-October, with another peak around Christmas—though the tide never really ebbs. Spring is the time to see the countryside and the royal London parks and gardens at their freshest; early summer to catch the roses and full garden splendor; fall to enjoy near-ideal exploring conditions. The British take their vacations mainly in July and August, and the resorts are crowded. London in summer, however, though full of visitors, is also full of interesting things to see and do. But be warned: air-conditioning is rarely found in places other than department stores, modern restaurants, hotels, and cinemas in London, and in a hot summer you'll swelter. Winter can be rather dismal and is frequently wet and usually cold, but all the theaters, concerts, and exhibitions go full speed.

CLIMATE

London's weather has always been contrary, and in recent years it has proved red-hot and cool by turns. It is virtually impossible to forecast what the pattern might be, but you can be fairly certain that it will not be what you expect. The main feature of the British weather is that it is generally mild—with some savage exceptions, especially in summer. It is also fairly damp—though even that has been changing in recent years, with the odd bout of drought. The following list includes the average daily maximum and minimum temperatures for London.

➤ FORECASTS: **Weather Channel Connection** (☎ 900/932–8437), 95¢ per minute from a Touch-Tone phone.

London

Jan.	43F	6C	May	62F	17C	Sept.	65F	19C
	36	2		47	8		52	11
Feb.	44F	7C	June	69F	20C	Oct.	58F	14C
	36	2		53	12		46	8
Mar.	50F	10C	July	71F	22C	Nov.	50F	10C
	38	3		56	14		42	5
Apr.	56F	13C	Aug.	71F	21C	Dec.	45F	7C
	42	6		56	13		38	4

FESTIVALS AND SEASONAL EVENTS

Top seasonal events in and around London include the Chelsea Flower Show in May, Derby Day at Epsom Racecourse, Wimbledon Lawn Tennis Championships and Henley Regatta in June, and the London Arts Season, which combines many events in theater, art, and music with good deals on hotels and meals out. In 2002, there will be extra events in honor of the Queen's Golden Jubilee year, with Jubilee Week starting on Monday, June 3 (and a special Thanksgiving service at St. Paul's Cathedral on June 4). Check with the London Tourist Board for specific information on where to watch the pageantry.

There is a complete list of ticket agencies in *Britain Events,* available in person only from the Britain Visitor Centre. When in London, check the weekly magazine *Time Out,* available at newsstands, for an ongoing calendar of special events. Or, for

60p per minute, call London Tourist Board's Visitorcall service, which offers the latest on events throughout the city.

➤ MID-DEC.: The **Olympia International Show Jumping Championships** (☏ 020/7370–8209), an international equestrian competition, takes place in Olympia's Grand Hall.

➤ DEC. 31: **New Year's Eve at Trafalgar Square** is a huge, freezing, sometimes drunken slosh through the fountains to celebrate the new year. Unorganized by any official body, it is held in the ceremonial heart of London under an enormous Christmas tree, which is a gift from the people of Norway and set up from early December to early January. Unlike Americans, however, most Brits celebrate New Year's Eve at home.

➤ JAN. 1: The **London Parade** is a good ole U.S.-style extravaganza complete with cheerleaders, floats, and marching bands, led by the Lord Mayor of London. It starts on the south side of Westminster Bridge at 12:30, passing Parliament Square, Whitehall, Trafalgar Square, Lower Regent Street, Piccadilly, and finishing in Berkeley Square around 3 PM. No tickets are required.

➤ JAN. 31: **Charles I Commemoration** is held on the anniversary of the monarch's execution and brings out Londoners dressed in 17th-century garb for a march tracing his last walk from St. James's Palace to the Banqueting House in Whitehall.

➤ MAR. 17–28 AND SEPT. 15–24: The **Chelsea Antiques Fair** is a twice-yearly fair with wide range of pre-1830 pieces for sale. ✉ *Old Town Hall, King's Rd., Chelsea, SW3 4PW*, ☏ *01444/482514*.

➤ END-MAR.: **Head of the River Boat Race** offers the spectacle of 420 eight-man crews from Oxford and Cambridge universities dipping their 6,720 oars in the Thames as they race from Mortlake to Putney. The best view is from Surrey Bank above Chiswick Bridge (tube to Chiswick); check *Time Out* for the starting time, which depends on the tide. The **Oxford versus Cambridge University Boat Race** takes place often the week after,

over the same 4½ mi course, carrying on a tradition going back to around 1829. In 1912 both boats sank spectacularly.

➤ EARLY APR.: **Chaucer Festival** (☏ 01227/470379) allows Londoners to don medieval garb and parade from Southwark Cathedral to the Tower of London, where jugglers and strolling minstrels party the day away.

➤ MID-APR.: **London Marathon** is a New York–style marathon through London's streets. Runners from 68 countries start in Greenwich and Blackheath at 9–9:30 AM, then run via Docklands and Canary Wharf, the Tower of London and Parliament Square to finish in the Mall.

➤ END-MAR.: **British Antique Dealers' Association Fair,** the newest of the major fairs, is large and prestigious, with many affordable pieces. ✉ *Duke of York's Headquarters, King's Rd., Chelsea SW3*, ☏ *020/ 7589–6108*.

➤ APR. 21: **Queen's Birthday** earns a showy 41-gun salute at Hyde Park. In June (☞ *below*), Elizabeth II's ceremonial b-day is celebrated by Trooping the Colour.

➤ MID-MAY: **Punch and Judy Festival** is held on the second Sunday in May and offers a May Fayre Procession in the morning, services at St. Paul's Church, then puppet shows until dusk. A lovely event for children of all ages. ✉ *Covent Garden Piazza, London, WC2*, ☏ *020/7375–0441*.

➤ MID-MAY: **Royal Windsor Horse Show** (☏ 01753/860633) is a major show-jumping event attended by some members of the Royal Family.

➤ MAY 23–26: **Chelsea Flower Show,** Britain's most prestigious flower show, is always graced by the Royals and covers 22 acres. ✉ *Royal Hospital Rd., Chelsea, SW3*, ☏ *020/7630–7422*.

➤ LATE MAY–LATE AUG.: **Glyndebourne Festival Opera** is a unique opportunity to see international stars in a bucolic setting. Tickets go fast and early booking starts on May 2nd. ✉ *Glyndebourne Festival Opera, Lewes, Sussex BN8 5UU*, ☏ *01273/ 815000*.

➤ LATE MAY–LATE AUG.: **Shakespeare Under the Stars** gives you the chance to see the Bard's plays performed at Regent's Park Open Air Theatre. Performances are usually Monday–Saturday at 8 PM, with matinees on Wednesday, Thursday, and Saturday. ✉ *Inner Circle, London, NW1,* ☎ *020/7486–2431.*

➤ EARLY JUNE: **Beating Retreat by the Guards Massed Bands** is when more than 500 musicians parade at Horse Guards, Whitehall. *Tickets from Household Division Fund,* ✉ *Horse Guards, London SW1A 2AX,* ☎ *020/ 7414–2271.*

➤ EARLY JUNE: **Derby Day** is the best-known event on the horse-racing calendar. *Information from United Racecourses Ltd.,* ✉ *Epsom Downs Racecourse, Epsom, Surrey KT18 5LQ,* ☎ *013727/26311.*

➤ EARLY JUNE: **The Queen's Golden Jubilee Celebrations** include a Jubilee Week beginning June 3rd. A special Service of Thanksgiving is to be held on June 4th. To catch a glimpse of the fabulous gilded Coronation Coach on its procession to St. Paul's Cathedral from Buckingham Palace, prepare to stake your place on the route at the crack of dawn. ✉ *London Tourist Board,* ☎ *09068/353715 (calls 60p per minute).*

➤ MID-JUNE: The **Grosvenor House Antiques Fair** is one of the most prestigious antiques fairs in Britain. ✉ *Grosvenor House Hotel, Park La., London W1A 3AA,* ☎ *020/7399– 8100.*

➤ MID-JUNE: **Royal Meeting at Ascot** brings the horsey set and their enormous hats out in force during the third week in June (Tuesday–Friday; Thursday is the high-fashion Ladies Day). General admission is available but reserve months in advance; for tickets to the Royal Enclosure (you must be sponsored), write to ✉ Protocol Office, American Embassy, 24 Grosvenor Sq., London W1Λ 1AE. General admission: ✉ *Ascot Racecourse, Ascot, Berkshire SL5 7JN,* ☎ *01344/876876.*

➤ MID-JUNE: **Trooping the Colour,** Queen Elizabeth's colorful official birthday parade, is held at Horse Guards, Whitehall, usually on the second or third Saturday of June. Write for tickets *only* between January 1 and February 28, enclosing a self-addressed stamped envelope. ✉ *Ticket Office, Headquarters, Household Division, Horse Guards, London SW1A 2AX,* ☎ *020/7414–2479.*

➤ MID JUNE–EARLY SEPT.: **Kenwood Lakeside Concerts** offers fireworks and classical concerts under the stars in the park of London's regal stately house. ✉ *Kenwood House, Hampstead La., London, NW3,* ☎ *020/ 7973–3427.*

➤ LATE JUNE–EARLY JULY: **Henley Royal Regatta** (☎ *01491/572153*), an international rowing event and top social occasion, takes place at Henley-upon-Thames, Oxfordshire.

➤ LATE JUNE–EARLY JULY: **The Wimbledon Lawn Tennis Championships,** held at the All England Lawn Tennis and Croquet Club in Wimbledon. Write early to enter the lottery for tickets for Centre and Number One courts; tickets for outside courts are available daily at the gate. ✉ *Church Rd., Wimbledon, London SW19 5AE,* ☎ *020/8946–2244.*

➤ EARLY JULY: **Hampton Court Palace Flower Show** is a five-day event that nearly rivals the Chelsea Flower Show for glamour. ✉ *East Molesey,* ☎ *020/ 7834–4333; 0870/906–3791 ticket agency.*

➤ MID-JULY–MID-SEPT.: **Henry Wood Promenade Concerts** is a marvelous series of concerts at the Royal Albert Hall. ✉ *Box Office, Royal Albert Hall, Kensington Gore, London, SW7 2AP,* ☎ *020/7589–8212.*

➤ LATE AUG.: **Notting Hill Carnival** (☎ *020/8964–0544*) is one of the liveliest street festivals in England. Caribbean foods, reggae music, and street parades are part of the swirling event, usually held on the last Sunday and Monday in August.

➤ SEPT.: **Open House** (☎ *020/7267– 7697*) is a rare one-day chance to view historic London interiors of buildings usually closed to the public, organized by Architectural Dialogue.

➤ EARLY OCT.: **Pearly Harvest Festival Service** draws a crowd of costermongers to the Church of St. Martin-in-the-Fields on the first Sunday in October. The Pearly Kings and Queens strut their famous costumes. ✉ *Trafalgar Square, London, WC2,* ☎ *020/7930–0089.*

➤ EARLY NOV.: **London to Brighton Veteran Car Run** (☎ 01753/681736) is a run from Hyde Park in London to Brighton in East Sussex.

➤ EARLY NOV.: **Lord Mayor's Procession and Show** (☎ 020/7332–1456) is a procession, for the lord mayor's inauguration, that takes place from the Guildhall in the City to the Royal Courts of Justice.

➤ NOV. 5: **Guy Fawkes Day** celebrates a foiled 1605 attempt to blow up Parliament. Fireworks are presented throughout London, but the place to be is the bonfire festivity on Primrose Hill near Camden Town.

INDEX

Icons and Symbols

★ Our special recommen-
dations

✕ Restaurant

⌗ Lodging establishment

✕⌗ Lodging establishment
whose restaurant war-
rants a special trip

☺ Good for kids (rubber
duck)

☞ Sends you to another
section of the guide for
more information

⊠ Address

☎ Telephone number

⊙ Opening and closing
times

▥ Admission prices

Numbers in white and black
circles ③ ❸ that appear on
the maps, in the margins, and
within the tours correspond
to one another.

A

Abbey Court ⌗, 217
Abbey House Hotel ⌗, 209
Abbey Museum, 56–57
Abbey Road Studios, 138,
139, 140
Academy Town House ⌗,
219
Accessorize (shop), 254,
269–270
Addresses, 308
Adelphi, 69, 71
Admiralty Arch, 39, 41
Aerobics, 244
Agnès B (shop), 270
Ain't Nothin' but Blues (jazz
club), 231
Air travel, 308–310
Alastair Little ✕, 167
The Albert (pub), 190
Albert Memorial, 125, 127
Alfie's Antique Market, 260
Alhambra Hotel ⌗, 219
All Souls Church, 64
Allounak ✕, 181–182
American Bar, 225
Andrew Edmunds ✕, 168
Anne Hathaway's Cottage,
293
Antiquarius (shop), 260
Antiques, 253–254, 260–
262
Apartment agencies, 221–
222
Apartment rentals, 323–324

Apsley House (Wellington
Museum), 58, 59, 61
Aquascutum (shop), 265
Armoury of St. James's
(shop), 277
Arnold Circus, 101, 103
Arosfa Hotel ⌗, 220
Arts, 234–242
Ashmolean Museum, 291–
292
Asia de Cuba ✕, 172
Asprey & Garrard (shop),
253, 279
Assembly Rooms, 286
Astoria (rock club), 232
Atelier (gay club), 233
Athenaeum (club), 67
Athenaeum ⌗, 195, 199
Atlantic Bar and Grill, 225
ATMs, 326
Aubergine ✕, 179
Auction Houses, 262
Avenue ✕, 164

B

Bagley's Studio (nightclub),
228
Ballet, 234, 236
Balliol College, 291
Banana Cabaret, 226
Bank ✕, 171
Bank of England, 86, 88
Bankside Gallery, 109, 110
Banqueting House, 39, 41
Bar Gansa ✕, 139
Bar Italia ✕, 168
Bar Rumba (nightclub), 228
Barbican Centre (arts
complex), 86, 88, 236,
238
Barfly Club (rock club), 232
Bars, 225–226
Baseball, 244
Basil Street ⌗, 212
Bath, 285–286
Bath Abbey, 285
Bayswater, 215–218
BBC Experience, 59, 61, 64
Beach Blanket Babylon (bar),
225
Beating Retreat by the
Guards Massed Bands, 338
Beatles, 139, 140
Beauchamp Tower, 99
Beaufort ⌗, 209–210
Bed-and-breakfast agencies,
221–222, 324
Beigel Bake (shop), 104
Belgo Centraal ✕, 170
Belgrave Place, 121, 122
Belgravia, 119–123, 209–
215, 298–299
Bell & Crown ✕, 151
Bell, Book and Radmall
(shop), 263

Belvedere ✕, 180
Berkeley ⌗, 210
Berkeley Square, 61
Bermondsey (street market),
281
Bertorelli's ✕, 172
Berwick Street (street
market), 281
Bethnal Green Museum of
Childhood, 101, 103
BFI London IMAX Cinema,
109, 110
Bibendum ✕, 174
Bicycling, 244–245
Big Ben, 45–46
Bill Bentley's ✕, 186
Black Eagle Brewery, 101,
103
Black Friar (pub), 190
Black Market (shop), 264
Black Swan ✕, 294
Blakes ⌗, 207
Blazer (shop), 268–269
Blind Beggar (pub), 101,
103–104
Bloody Tower, 97–98
Bloomsbury, 75–84, 218–
220, 299
Bloomsbury Square, 76, 78
Blue Anchor ✕, 151
Bluebird ✕, 178
Boat tours, 146
Boating, 245, 247
Bodleian Library, 291
Bond Street, 59, 61–62
Bonhams (shop), 262
Books and videos about
London, 303
Books for Cooks (shop), 263
Bookshops, 262–264
Borderline (nightclub), 230
Borders (shop), 262
Bow Street Magistrates'
Court, 69, 71
Box (gay bar), 233
Box Tree Restaurant ✕, 294
Brasserie ✕, 49
Brasserie St. Quentin ✕, 177
Brass-rubbing centers, 52
Brick Lane, 100, 104, 281
Brick Lane Music Hall, 103
Bridgewater (shop), 265
Brighton, 286–288
Brighton Museum and Art
Gallery, 287
Brighton Pier, 287
British Airways London Eye
(Ferris wheel), 109, 110
British Antique Dealers'
Association Fair, 337
British Library, 77, 78
British Museum, 76, 78, 79
gift shop, 276
restaurant and café in, 80

NOTES

NOTES

FODOR'S LONDON 2002

EDITOR: Lauren A. Myers

Editorial Contributors: Stephanie Adler, Catherine Belonogoff, Jacqueline Brown, Roland Chambers, Julius Honnor, Tim Perry, Alex Wijeratna

Editorial Production: Linda K. Schmidt

Maps: David Lindroth Inc., *cartographer*; Rebecca Baer and Bob Blake, *map editors*

Design: Fabrizio La Rocca, *creative director*; Guido Caroti, *art director*; Jolie Novak, *photo editor*; Melanie Marin, *photo researcher*

Cover Design: Pentagram

Production/Manufacturing: Colleen Ziemba

COPYRIGHT

ISBN 0–679–00853–5

ISSN 0149–631X

SPECIAL SALES

Fodor's Travel Publications are available at special discounts for bulk purchases for sales promotions or premiums. Special editions, including personalized covers, excerpts of existing guides, and corporate imprints, can be created in large quantities for special needs. For more information, contact your local bookseller or write to Special Markets, Fodor's Travel Publications, 280 Park Avenue, New York, NY 10017. Inquiries from Canada should be directed to your local Canadian bookseller or sent to Random House of Canada, Ltd., Marketing Department, 2775 Matheson Boulevard East, Mississauga, Ontario L4W 4P7. Inquiries from the United Kingdom should be sent to Fodor's Travel Publications, 20 Vauxhall Bridge Road, London SW1V 2SA, England.

PRINTED IN THE UNITED STATES OF AMERICA

10 9 8 7 6 5 4 3 2 1

IMPORTANT TIP

Although all prices, opening times, and other details in this book are based on information supplied to us at press time, changes occur all the time in the travel world, and Fodor's cannot accept responsibility for facts that become outdated or for inadvertent errors or omissions. So always confirm information when it matters, especially if you're making a detour to visit a specific place.

PHOTOGRAPHY

Adina Toby/Photo 20-20, *cover (Royal Guards)*.

Axiom: Alberto Arzoz, *10B, 11E.* Ian Cumming, *11D, 20C.* James Morris, *12C.*

Bibendum, *10A.*

British Museum, *26B, 30J.*

The British Tourist Authority, *3 bottom left, 19D.*

Corbis, *1, 9E, 21F, 26A, 27C, 28D, 30H.*

Crown Copyright Historic Royal Palaces, *2 top left, 8B, 29E.*

Discover Islington, *2 bottom center, 2 bottom right.*

Firmdale Hotels, *30I.*

Floris, *13F.*

The Garden Picture Library: John McCarthy, *18B, 21D.*

Chris Gascoigne & Lifschutz Davidson, *2 top right.*

© Her Majesty Queen Elizabeth II, *3 top left, 8C.*

The Image Bank: Chris Close, *4-5.* Cralle, *32.* Lisl Dennis, *8A.* Tom Owen Edmunds, *30D.* John Hill, *6B.* Romilly Lockyer, *6A.* Michael Pasdzior, *18A.* Andrea Pistolesi, *9F, 20A.* Leonard Rhodes, *22B.* Marc Romanelli, *7D.* Antonio Rosario, *13D.* Guido Alberto Rossi, *7E, 12A, 23C.* Paul Trummer, *30C.* Alvis Upitis, *16F, 30G.* Matthew Weinreb, *18C.* Frank Whitney, *9D, 25C.*

Kelly/Mooney, *6C, 11F, 13E, 15C, 15D, 15E, 17G, 17I, 19E, 20B, 21E, 22A.*

La Tante Claire: Anthony Blake, *30E.*

James Lemass, *24A.*

Liberty, *3 bottom right.*

The National Gallery, *3 top right, 2 bottom left, 14B, 30B.*

Plum, *12B, 14A, 19F, 23E.*

Regent's Park Open-Air Theater, *25B.*

The Savoy Group, *30A, 30F.*

The Sound Republic, *25D.*

The Sugar Club, *10C.*

Three Greyhounds, *23D.*

The Victoria & Albert Museum, *17H.*

ABOUT OUR WRITERS

The more you know before you go, the better your trip will be. London's most fascinating small museum or its most delightful pub could be just around the corner from your hotel, but if you don't know it's there, it might as well be on the other side of the globe. That's where this book comes in. It's a great step toward making sure your next trip lives up to your expectations. As you plan, check out the Web as well. Guidebooks have been helping smart travelers find the special places for years; the Web is one more tool. Whatever reference you consult, be savvy about what you read, and always consider the source. Images and language can be massaged to make places appear better than they are. And one traveler's quaint is another's grimy. Here at Fodor's, and at our on-line arm, Fodors.com, our focus is on providing you with information that's not only useful but accurate and on target. Every day Fodor's editors put enormous effort into getting things right, beginning with the search for the right contributors—people who have objective judgment, broad travel experience, and the writing ability to put their insights into words. There's no substitute for advice from a like-minded friend who has just come back from where you're going, but our writers, having seen all corners of London, are the next best thing. They're the kind of people you'd poll for tips yourself if you knew them.

Stephanie Adler worked for three years as an editor at Fodor's before moving to London in spring 2000. She enjoys escaping the city on weekends, which made updating the Side Trips chapter all the more pleasurable.

Born and raised in San Francisco, **Catherine Belonogoff** started doing travel writing during her university days. In summer 2000 she and her husband moved to lovely London town. Although she is a resident of Islington in north London, Catherine was happy to venture south of the Thames to update part of the London Exploring chapter.

Being a settler in London, says writer and editor **Jacqueline Brown,** is mainly different from being a true native in that one really tries to get the most out of what the city has to offer. A London resident for 20 years, Jacqueline recently wrote *Fodor's Around London with Kids,* and she updated the Exploring, Shopping, and Smart Travel Tips sections of this book .

Roland Chambers received a degree in English literature from Edinburgh University. Currently living in Hackney Marshes, London, he writes and illustrates children's books and investigates hotels for this guide.

Julius Honnor, our Outdoor Activities and Sports updater, has traveled widely but now lives in London. He currently works for a company that makes tailored travel books. He enjoys playing sports in his free time and is a keen viewer of all things sports-related.

Since moving to London several years ago, travel writer **Tim Perry** has become increasingly nocturnal. Tim applied his knowledge of the city to the Nightlife and the Arts chapter, which includes hangouts he visits as a music critic for the *Independent* daily newspaper.

Londoner born and bred **Alex Wijeratna** is an old-school stalwart of fashionable Notting Hill. With his English/Sri Lankan roots, Alex is well aware that the real flavor of London is found in its ethnic diversity. He has written mainly for newspapers, including the *Times.* For this edition, he updated the Dining chapter.

Don't Forget to Write

Your experiences—positive and negative—matter to us. If we have missed or misstated something, we want to hear about it. We follow up on all suggestions. Contact the London editor at editors@fodors.com or c/o Fodor's, 280 Park Avenue, New York, NY 10017. Have a fabulous trip!

Karen Cure
Editorial Director